FROMMER'S

BUDGET TRAVEL GUIDE

AUSTRALIA '95-'96 ON $45 A DAY

by John Godwin

"Beaut"

MACMILLAN • USA

MACMILLAN TRAVEL
A Simon & Schuster Macmillan Company
1633 Broadway
New York, NY 10019

ISBN 0-671-88475-1
ISSN 8755-5425

Design by Robert Bull Design
Maps by Ortelius Design

Special Sales

Bulk purchases (10 + copies) of Frommer's Travel Guides are available to corporations at special discounts. The Special Sales Department can produce custom editions to be used as premiums and/or for sales promotion to suit individual needs. Existing editions can be produced with custom cover imprints such as a corporate logo. For more information write to: Special Sales, Macmillan Travel, 1633 Broadway, New York, NY 10019.

Manufactured in the United States of America

CONTENTS

1 GETTING TO KNOW AUSTRALIA 1

1. Geography & Wildlife 2
2. History & Government 8
3. Famous Australians 17
4. Art, Architecture & Literature 18
5. Myth & Folklore 20
6. Cultural & Social Life 20
7. Performing Arts & Evening Entertainment 24
8. Sports & Recreation 26
9. Food & Drink 28
10. Recommended Books & Films 31

SPECIAL FEATURES
- *Did You Know . . . ? 2*
- *Dateline 8*

2 PLANNING A TRIP TO AUSTRALIA 34

1. Information, Entry Requirements & Money 34
2. When to Go—Climate, Holidays & Events 38
3. Health & Insurance 42
4. What to Pack 43
5. Tips for the Disabled, Seniors, Families, Students & Singles 44
6. Alternative/Adventure Travel 45
7. Getting There 46
8. Getting Around 49
9. Enjoying Australia on a Budget 61

SPECIAL FEATURES
- *What Things Cost in Sydney 37*
- *Australia Calendar of Events 39*
- *Sydney Calendar of Events 41*
- *Frommer's Smart Traveler: Airfares 48*
- *Suggested Itineraries 59*
- *Fast Facts: Australia 68*

3 SYDNEY 72

1. From a Budget Traveler's Point of View 73
2. Orientation 74
3. Getting Around 77
4. Where to Stay 84
5. Where to Eat 94
6. Attractions 104
7. Sports & Recreation 122
8. Savvy Shopping 124
9. Evening Entertainment 126
10. Networks & Resources 132
11. Easy Excursions: New South Wales 133

SPECIAL FEATURES

- *What's Special About Sydney 73*
- *Neighborhoods in Brief 76*
- *Fast Facts: Sydney 82*
- *Frommer's Smart Traveler: Hotels 89*
- *Frommer's Cool for Kids: Hotels 91*
- *Frommer's Smart Traveler: Restaurants 100*
- *Frommer's Cool for Kids: Restaurants 103*
- *Did You Know . . . ? 107*
- *Frommer's Favorite Sydney Experiences 111*
- *Walking Tour I—The Rocks 115*
- *Walking Tour 2—Downtown Sydney 118*

4 MELBOURNE 137

1. From a Budget Traveler's Point of View 139
2. Orientation 139
3. Getting Around 141
4. Where to Stay 144
5. Where to Eat 150
6. Attractions 158
7. Sports & Recreation 166
8. Savvy Shopping 167
9. Evening Entertainment 170
10. Easy Excursions: Victoria 174

SPECIAL FEATURES

- *What's Special About Melbourne 138*
- *Neighborhoods in Brief 141*
- *Fast Facts: Melbourne 143*
- *Frommer's Cool for Kids: Restaurants 157*
- *Did You Know . . . ? 158*
- *Frommer's Favorite Melbourne Experiences 163*

5 ADELAIDE 179

1. From a Budget Traveler's Point of View 180
2. Orientation 181
3. Getting Around 182
4. Where to Stay 184
5. Where to Eat 189
6. Attractions 193
7. Sports & Recreation 198
8. Evening Entertainment 199
9. Excursions in South Australia 201

SPECIAL FEATURES

- *What's Special About Adelaide 180*
- *Neighborhoods in Brief 181*
- *Fast Facts: Adelaide 183*
- *Did You Know . . . ? 193*
- *Frommer's Favorite Adelaide Experiences 199*

6 BRISBANE & THE GOLD & SUNSHINE COASTS 207

1. From a Budget Traveler's Point of View 209
2. Orientation 209
3. Getting Around 211
4. Where to Stay 214
5. Where to Eat 220
6. Attractions 224
7. Sports & Recreation 229
8. Evening Entertainment 229
9. Gold Coast 231
10. Sunshine Coast 245

SPECIAL FEATURES

- *What's Special About Brisbane & the Gold & Sunshine Coasts 208*
- *Neighborhoods in Brief 210*
- *Fast Facts: Brisbane 211*
- *Frommer's Cool for Kids: Hotels 218*
- *Frommer's Cool for Kids: Restaurants 225*
- *Did You Know . . . ? 226*
- *Frommer's Favorite Brisbane & Gold Coast Experiences 227*

7 THE CAIRNS AREA & THE GREAT BARRIER REEF 252

1. Cairns 252
2. Kuranda, Port Douglas & Cooktown 269
3. Great Barrier Reef 272

SPECIAL FEATURES

- *What's Special About the Cairns Area & the Great Barrier Reef 253*
- *Fast Facts: Cairns 257*
- *Frommer's Cool for Kids: Restaurants 266*

8 PERTH & THE FAR WEST 279

1. Orientation 281
2. Getting Around 282
3. Where to Stay 283
4. Where to Eat 289
5. Attractions 292
6. Savvy Shopping 298
7. Sports & Recreation 299
8. Evening Entertainment 300
9. Easy Excursions: Western Australia 303

SPECIAL FEATURES

- *What's Special About Perth & the Far West 280*
- *Fast Facts: Perth 283*
- *Frommer's Smart Traveler: Hotels 286*
- *Frommer's Smart Traveler: Restaurants 291*
- *Frommer's Cool for Kids: Restaurants 293*
- *Did You Know . . . ? 295*

9 CANBERRA—AUSTRALIA'S CAPITAL 307

1. Orientation 309
2. Getting Around 310
3. Where to Stay 311
4. Where to Eat 315
5. Attractions 318
6. Savvy Shopping 324
7. Sports & Recreation 324
8. Evening Entertainment 325
9. Easy Excursions to Snowy Mountains Hydroelectric Scheme & Cooma 326

SPECIAL FEATURES

- *What's Special About Canberra 308*
- *Frommer's Cool for Kids: Hotels 312*
- *Frommer's Cool for Kids: Restaurants 317*
- *Did You Know . . .? 319*

10 ALICE SPRINGS—THE "RED HEART" 328

1. Orientation 330
2. Getting Around 331
3. Where to Stay 331
4. Where to Eat 335
5. Attractions 338
6. Savvy Shopping 342
7. Evening Entertainment 343
8. Excursions Around the Red Centre 344
9. Other Excursions in Northern Territory 348

SPECIAL FEATURES

- *What's Special About Alice Springs & Northern Territory 329*
- *Frommer's Cool for Kids: Hotels 335*
- *Frommer's Cool for Kids: Restaurants 337*
- *Did You Know . . .? 339*

11 TASMANIA—THE ISLAND STATE 353

1. Launceston 357
2. Hobart 364
3. Devonport 376

SPECIAL FEATURE

- *What's Special About Tasmania 354*

INDEX 379

LIST OF MAPS

Australia 4–5
Australia's Main Air Routes 51
Australia's Main Train Routes 53

TRANSIT MAPS

Sydney Transportation Systems: TNT Harbourlink Monorail, City Circle Line & Explorer Bus Routes 78–79
Sydney Ferries 81
Brisbane City Train Network 213

CITY MAPS

Sydney Accommodations 86–87
Sydney Dining 96–97
Sydney Attractions 108–109
Melbourne Accommodations 147
Melbourne Dining 153
Melbourne Attractions 159
Adelaide Accommodations 185
Adelaide Attractions 195
Brisbane Accommodations & Attractions 216–217
Cairns 255
Perth Accommodations, Dining & Attractions 285
Canberra Accommodations, Dining & Attractions 313
Alice Springs 333
Launceston 359
Hobart 365

SYDNEY WALKING TOURS

The Rocks 117
Downtown Sydney 119

REGIONAL MAPS

Victoria 175
South Australia 203
Gold Coast 233
Queensland 271
Great Barrier Reef 273
Western Australia 305
Red Centre 345
Northern Territory 349
Tasmania 355

INVITATION TO THE READERS

In researching this book, I have come across many fine establishments, the best of which I have included here. I am sure that many of you will also come across appealing hotels, inns, restaurants, guest houses, shops, and attractions. Please don't keep them to yourself. Share your experiences, especially if you want to comment on places that have been included in this edition that have changed for the worse. You can address your letters to:

John Godwin
Frommer's Australia on $45 a Day '95–'96
Macmillan Travel
15 Columbus Circle
New York, NY 10023

A DISCLAIMER

Readers are advised that prices fluctuate in the course of time and travel information changes under the impact of the varied and volatile factors that affect the travel industry. Neither the author nor the publisher can be held responsible for the experiences of readers while traveling. Readers are invited to write to the publisher with ideas, comments, and suggestions for future editions.

SAFETY ADVISORY

Whenever you're traveling in an unfamiliar city or country, stay alert. Be aware of your immediate surroundings. Wear a money belt and keep a close eye on your possessions. Be particularly careful with cameras, purses, and wallets, all favorite targets of thieves and pickpockets.

CHAPTER 1

GETTING TO KNOW AUSTRALIA

- DID YOU KNOW . . . ?
1. GEOGRAPHY & WILDLIFE
2. HISTORY & GOVERNMENT
- DATELINE
3. FAMOUS AUSTRALIANS
4. ART, ARCHITECTURE & LITERATURE
5. MYTH & FOLKLORE
6. CULTURAL & SOCIAL LIFE
7. PERFORMING ARTS & EVENING ENTERTAINMENT
8. SPORTS & RECREATION
9. FOOD & DRINK
10. RECOMMENDED BOOKS & FILMS

The distinguished British author James Cameron wrote, "One doesn't come to Australia by chance. When one arrives it means that one most definitely has meant to come."

This puts the tourist's angle in a nutshell. Australia isn't a transit point to anywhere else, and no one tours it as part of a package containing half a dozen other attractions. Australia is, decidedly, a destination in itself.

Why should it be yours? The prime reason, perhaps, is uniqueness. Australia is the only country that also happens to be a continent. It contains the only society that ever developed from a penal colony—and developed into one of the freest, happiest, and most progressive on earth. It is a place where plants and animals are primeval, unchanged since the time—millions of years ago—when the continent drifted loose from Asia, cutting off the flora and fauna from the processes of evolution.

For most of its brief recorded human history, Australia was the remotest of inhabited islands, virtually exiled from world affairs by what Geoffrey Blainey called "the tyranny of distance." By windjammer the 10,000-mile journey from England took eight months and considerable luck. In the days of the steamship, the trip required six weeks. The jet age has shrunk the traveling time to a matter of hours, but the *feeling* of remoteness remains.

Most Americans and Europeans tend to lump Australia together with New Zealand simply because they share the same hemisphere. However, the two countries are separated by 1,300 miles of turbulent ocean and are so different in character and appearance that virtually their only similarities consist of the English language and membership in the British Commonwealth. Few foreigners can name the capital of Australia or more than one of its large cities, nor do they have any idea of its size—roughly that of the United States minus Alaska. Australia, to most people, is a land of immense deserts, scores of tennis champions, a couple of great sopranos, and the Sydney Opera House.

The gigantic interior deserts are there all right, but so are snowcapped mountains with ski lifts and alpine huts. The tennis champions do proliferate—but so do symphony orchestras, a superb national ballet, avant-garde artists, and a remarkable film industry that is now gaining worldwide recognition. And this is precisely the reason why you should go there, for Australia is a vast surprise package.

The great, stark "Australian loneliness" nonetheless exists. This is a land where, through the "School of the Air," teachers and students stay in touch with the world by

DID YOU KNOW . . . ?

- Australian women received the right to vote in 1901—many years before American and British women.
- Australian Prime Minister Harold Holt disappeared in 1967—without a trace—while swimming.
- Carpet snakes, a small species of python, are employed in Australian warehouses as rat catchers.
- The "Long Straight," the railway line linking the Pacific Ocean port of Adelaide with the Indian Ocean port of Perth (1,316 miles away), is the longest straight railroad track on earth.
- Sir Sidney Kidman, Australia's undisputed "cattle king," controlled property measuring 126,000 square kilometers (78,120 square miles)—three times the size of Switzerland.
- Australia has the oldest airline in the English-speaking world. Founded in 1920 with one biplane, it's known today as Qantas, an acronym for "Queensland and Northern Territory Aerial Services."
- Australia has real buffalo—America has only bison. On the other hand, Australia has the Alligator River but no alligators—only crocodiles.
- Voting in Australia is compulsory for all citizens, to prevent a government being elected by default.
- The famous Surf Lifesavers were originally formed as a protest against the prosecution of a young clergyman for "surfing while insufficiently dressed"—that is, not wearing a neck-to-knee costume—in 1906.
- Capt. James Cook, the official discoverer of Australia, was killed—and possibly eaten—by natives of the Sandwich Islands, today's Hawaii.
- The father of the Australian wine industry was not a vintner but a schoolteacher, James Busby, who planted vines in the Hunter River Valley.

two-way radio, covering nearly a million square miles; where cattle ranches, worked by a few dozen people, are as large as entire nations in Europe; where the "Flying Doctor" makes house calls by aircraft; and where only 10 years ago explorers came on Aboriginal tribesmen who had never seen a wheel, a pair of shoes, or white skin.

But it is also a land of huge teeming cities: Sydney is bigger than Los Angeles; Melbourne has more people than Philadelphia; Brisbane more than Baltimore. The ratio of automobiles per person is as high as that in the United States. Canberra is one of the few *totally* planned national capitals in the world and could serve as a blueprint for urban development. There are traffic jams and skyscrapers, giant department stores and trendy little boutiques, experimental theaters, gourmet restaurants, earsplitting discos, suburban cocktail parties, and McDonald's hamburger chains. But there's also the world's largest monolith, Ayers Rock, glowing scarlet at sunrise and dusk in the midst of barren emptiness that looks like the surface of the moon.

Because the place is so vast and varied, it's important for prospective tourists to do their homework—you should know where you want to go and what you want to see—which is probably why you're reading this book.

1. GEOGRAPHY & WILDLIFE

GEOGRAPHY

On the map the Australian continent is a huge land mass of three million square miles washed by the Pacific Ocean on three sides and by the Indian Ocean on the west. Just off the southern tip hangs the island state of Tasmania. To the north the continent's closest neighbor is New Guinea, to the northeast it's New Caledonia, and to the southeast it's New Zealand. Due south lies the empty iciness of Antarctica.

These compass points are important in understanding Australia's upside-down climate—the farther north you go, the hotter it gets; the farther south, the cooler.

Most of Australia (but not Tasmania) is flat, broken here and there by surprisingly rugged mountain ranges. The Great Dividing Range runs parallel to the eastern seaboard all the way from Cape York to Victoria. At the southern end, straddling the border between New South Wales and Victoria, rise the highest peaks on the continent: the Snowy Mountains. (Remember the *Man from Snowy River*?) This is the nation's winter playground and prime skiing territory, as well as the site of its major technological achievement: the giant Snowy Mountains Hydroelectric Scheme.

The continent's most fertile regions stretch inland along the eastern and part of the southern coastal belt. This is also the area where all the great cities—except Perth—are located. Western Australia is cut off from the rest by a chain of deserts that proved almost insurmountable obstacles to early explorers. Even today "Westralia" has an aura of separateness, and Perth, its capital, is the only large city that faces the Indian Ocean instead of the Pacific.

The interior of the continent, mostly arid desert, is wildly spectacular in parts. The landscape around Ayers Rock, in the very center of Australia, looks like the surface of the moon. The reason for this aridity is Australia's lack of rivers bisecting the continent. Its only great river system—the Murray, Darling, and Murrumbidgee rivers—flows in the southeastern corner.

Above the Tropic of Capricorn stretch Australia's tropical regions, with Rockhampton, in eastern Queensland, as a major gateway. Offshore runs the Great Barrier Reef, one of the natural wonders of the world. Along the coastlines sprawl mangrove swamps and vast patches of rain forest and jungle. This is sugarcane and crocodile country; the interior boasts cattle ranches (called stations) as large as entire European countries.

The far North—Cape York and Arnhem Land—is the wildest and most desolate part of the continent, home of nomadic tribes that still hunt for a living. West of Arnhem Land, toward Darwin, lies the Kakadu National Park, a protected reserve of jungle splendors where the most dramatic scenes of *Crocodile Dundee* were filmed.

From the cool mountain forests of Tasmania to the broiling wilderness of Cape York, Australia has it all . . . but with immense distances in between.

REGIONS IN BRIEF

Disregarding such political divisions as states and territories, which are artificial, Australia consists of a few distinctive regions that transcend the boundaries you see marked on a map. Each of these regions has variations of its own, some quite drastic, but in broad outline the profile of the continent looks like this:

Southeastern Region Imagine a line drawn from Brisbane in the east to Adelaide in the south. This is the area that has the longest rivers, the highest mountains, the most fertile farmland, nearly all the industry, all but one of the big cities, and about nine-tenths of the population of Australia. It accounts for the startling lopsidedness of the country's demography, since the region comprises less than one-fifth of its size.

Northeastern Region Starting above Brisbane and stretching to the tip of the barren Cape York Peninsula in the far north, this region contains the green tropical coastline along the Great Barrier Reef as well as vast rock deserts. Its economy thrives on tourism, sugarcane, and pineapples, in that order.

Central Region An immense strip down the middle of the continent, with Alice Springs at the exact center and much of it known as the outback, this region is mostly desert, interspersed with grazing lands belonging to huge cattle stations that form the backbone of Australia's beef industry. Around Darwin, at the northern tip, you'll find some of the wildest, most fascinating jungle country extant. It is sparsely populated and barely explored.

Far West Falling roughly within the state borders of Western Australia, this is a gigantic expanse of a million square miles. The region contains some of the largest and most desolate deserts on the continent, but it also boasts the delightful metropolis of Perth, which has the balmiest of Mediterranean climates. Isolated from the mainstream, the Far West is a world of its own, frequently following the beat of a different drummer. The West had to be coaxed into the Australian Commonwealth—and it very nearly didn't join.

Tasmania Hanging like a pendant off the southern tip of the continent, this little island state is unique. The climate is almost European, the scenery resembles that of the Scottish Highlands, and the towns are small and picturesque. Yet the western

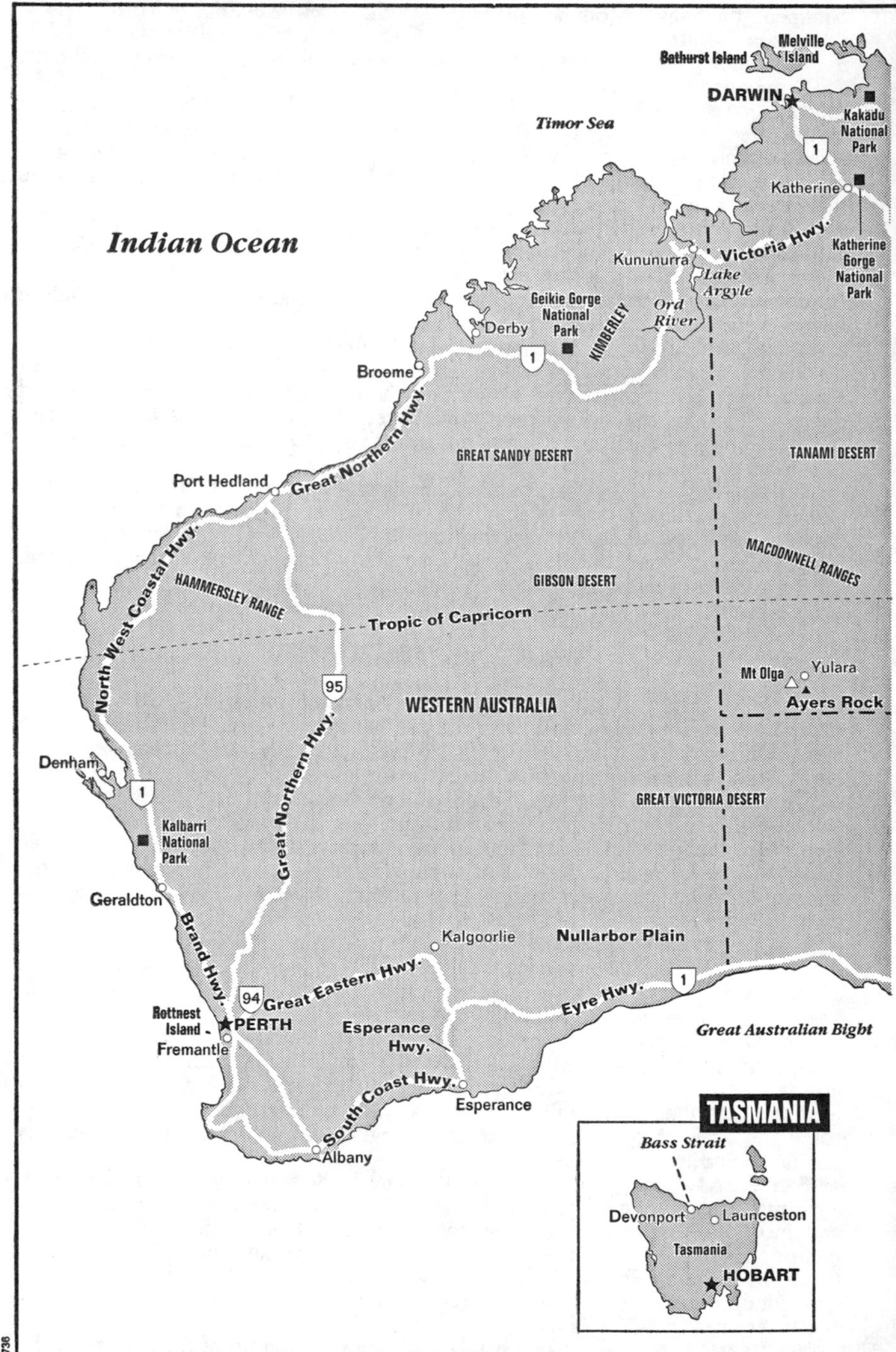

N
0
500 km
310 mi
Melville Island
Bathurst Island
DARWIN
Kakadu National Park
Timor Sea
1
Katherine
Katherine Gorge National Park
Indian Ocean
Victoria Hwy.
Kununurra
Lake Argyle
Geikie Gorge National Park
Ord River
KIMBERLEY
Derby
1
Broome
Great Northern Hwy.
GREAT SANDY DESERT
TANAMI DESERT
Port Hedland
North West Coastal Hwy.
MACDONNELL RANGES
HAMMERSLEY RANGE
GIBSON DESERT
Tropic of Capricorn
95
Mt Olga
Yulara
Ayers Rock
WESTERN AUSTRALIA
Denham
1
GREAT VICTORIA DESERT
Kalbarri National Park
Great Northern Hwy.
Geraldton
Brand Hwy.
Kalgoorlie
Nullarbor Plain
Great Eastern Hwy.
1
94
Eyre Hwy.
Rottnest Island
PERTH
Fremantle
Esperance Hwy.
Great Australian Bight
South Coast Hwy.
Esperance
TASMANIA
Bass Strait
Albany
Devonport
Launceston
Tasmania
HOBART
6736

AUSTRALIA

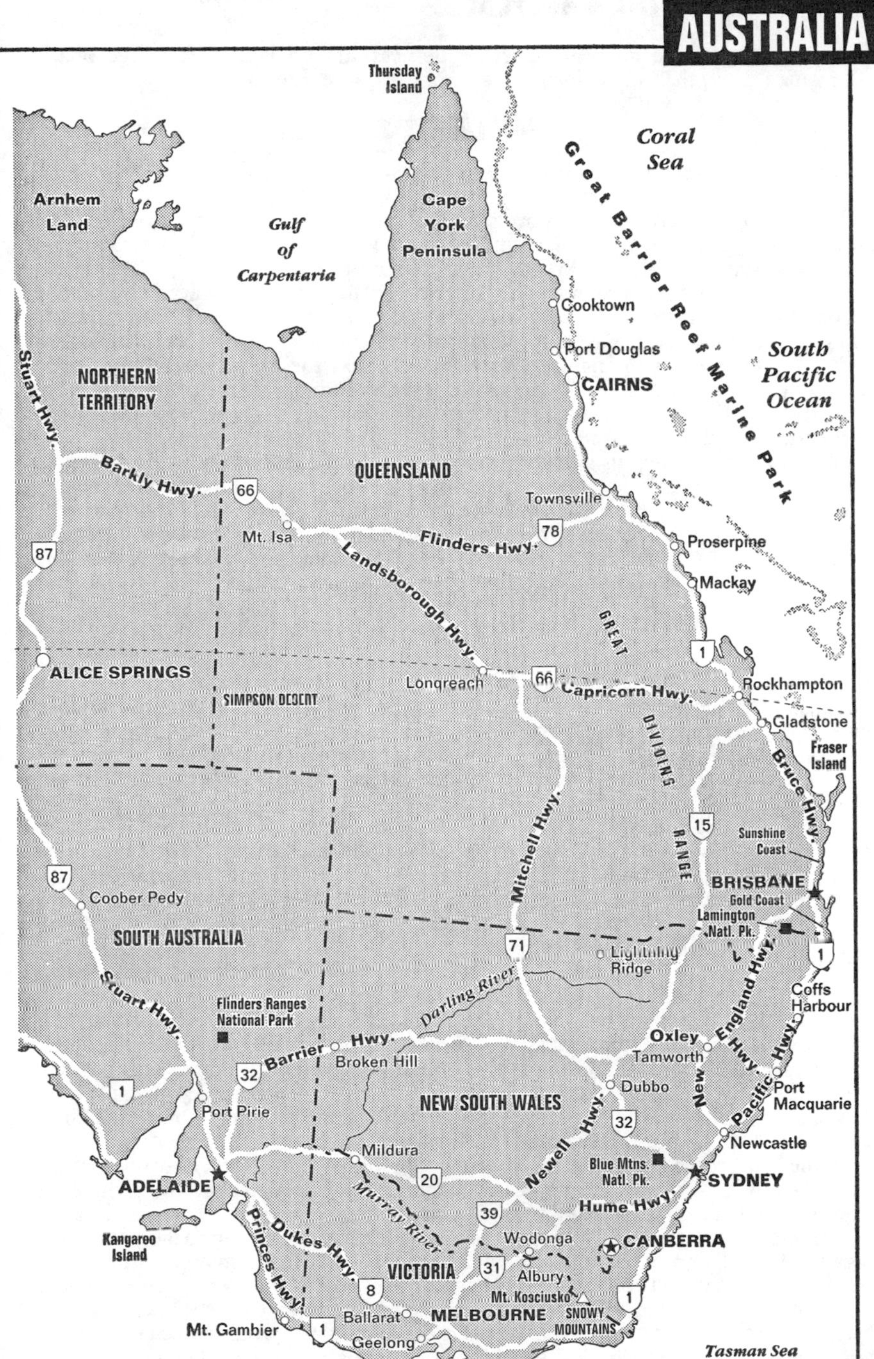
Thursday Island
Coral Sea
Great Barrier Reef Marine Park
Arnhem Land
Gulf of Carpentaria
Cape York Peninsula
Cooktown
Port Douglas
CAIRNS
South Pacific Ocean
NORTHERN TERRITORY
Stuart Hwy.
QUEENSLAND
Barkly Hwy.
66
Townsville
Mt. Isa
78
Flinders Hwy.
87
Landsborough Hwy.
Proserpine
Mackay
GREAT
DIVIDING
RANGE
1
ALICE SPRINGS
Longreach
66
Capricorn Hwy.
Rockhampton
SIMPSON DESERT
Gladstone
Fraser Island
Bruce Hwy.
15
Sunshine Coast
Mitchell Hwy.
87
Coober Pedy
BRISBANE
Gold Coast
Lamington Natl. Pk.
SOUTH AUSTRALIA
71
Lightning Ridge
1
Stuart Hwy.
Darling River
Coffs Harbour
Flinders Ranges National Park
New England Hwy.
Oxley Hwy.
Tamworth
Barrier Hwy.
Broken Hill
32
1
Dubbo
Port Macquarie
Pacific Hwy.
NEW SOUTH WALES
Port Pirie
32
Newell Hwy.
Newcastle
Mildura
Blue Mtns. Natl. Pk.
ADELAIDE
20
SYDNEY
Murray River
Hume Hwy.
39
Kangaroo Island
Dukes Hwy.
Princes Hwy.
Wodonga
CANBERRA
VICTORIA
31
Albury
8
Mt. Kosciusko
SNOWY MOUNTAINS
1
Ballarat
MELBOURNE
Mt. Gambier
1
Geelong
Tasman Sea
Apollo Bay
SEE INSET

portions remain a virtually unspoiled wilderness and offer the last refuge of the Tasmanian devil, the only marsupial carnivore still in existence.

WILDLIFE

FLORA

What the Aussies term "bush" covers a fabulous variety of scenery, from tropical hothouse jungles glowing with orchids to gently rolling grassland and mountain meadows carpeted with wildflowers. It's all "bush" to the locals.

Their continent harbors hundreds of native plants found nowhere else on the globe. Western Australia alone grows some 6,000 species of wildflowers, many unique. But the two plants that symbolize the country are the **acacia** (called "wattle"), featured in the national coat of arms, and the **eucalyptus gum.** The eucalyptus is as Australian as the kangaroo. It grows throughout the country, in more than 700 varieties, some reaching heights of 300 feet, their pungent blossoms shining white, deep scarlet, and coral pink.

For eons the eucalyptus gums were isolated from the rest of the world's flora by immense oceans, but today they are probably the most transplanted trees anywhere. They have been exported to California, Arizona, Japan, Canada, South Africa, and the Middle East, chiefly because they make ideal and astonishingly hardy windbreaks. And their unmistakable sharp, medicinal scent is guaranteed to make any Aussie homesick the moment he or she catches that characteristic whiff.

FAUNA

Foreigners may not recognize the singularity of much of Australia's flora, but there's no mistaking the uniqueness of the animal life. Australia is a gigantic outdoor museum for furred, feathered, and scaled phenomena that developed on no other portion of our earth. However, there is a curious lopsidedness about this development—nature went rampant in the marsupial department but left out virtually every other branch.

Marsupials are animals that carry their young in pouches. Their prime representatives are the **kangaroos** and their close cousins the **wallabies.** They come in an amazing assortment of sizes, from the tiny rat kangaroo to the hulking Great Grey, six feet tall when upright and strong enough to knock over a pony. There are also tree-climbing kangaroos and rock kangaroos, nest dwellers, swamp inhabitants, and those that stick to the wide-open plains.

All of them share the habit of tucking their babies back into their pouches when danger threatens and fleeing with fantastic leaps. Jumps of 25 feet are routine stuff: When pressed, they have been known to sail 40 feet in one leap. Kangaroos are a delight to watch, but unfortunately their hides can be turned into excellent leather, their tails into gourmet soup. And human greed being what it is, thousands of these gentle creatures are slaughtered yearly by professional hunters. So if you want to do Australia—and the world—a favor, *don't* buy kangaroo leather souvenirs. Otherwise, your only chance of seeing a live kangaroo may soon be in a zoo.

If the kangaroo is appealing, the **koala** is adorable. Although it closely resembles a teddy bear with fluffy ears, it's no bear but another marsupial. Slow moving and even slower thinking, koalas live in trees, dreamily munching gum leaves and rarely descending to the ground. When the young emerge from their pouches, they ride piggyback on their mothers until old enough to start munching on their own. Koalas need no water; they get enough moisture from their leaf diet to stay aloft permanently.

Another bearlike marsupial, equally cuddly but somewhat tougher, is the **wombat.** About the size of fox terriers, wombats dig holes in the ground at amazing speed and emerge from them at night to search for roots and shrubs. They make gentle, affectionate house pets and never bite. But don't underestimate them. Wombats have been known to weigh 80 pounds, and their backs are strong enough to crush any dog foolish enough to pursue them into their burrows.

Most marsupials are harmless vegetarians, but the family includes a few pretty fierce carnivores. The **native "cats,"** for instance, aren't feline at all, but remarkably catlike pouch animals. And the **Tasmanian devil** must rate as one of the most aggressive critters extant. They aren't very big—about as large as cocker spaniels—with disproportionately powerful forequarters and massive teeth. The devils eat anything that won't eat them—dead or alive. They're remarkably noisy for predators, snarling and screaming like demons when angered. Today they are found only in the remotest parts of Tasmania, although they're in no danger of becoming extinct.

The most common predator in Australia, the **dingo,** remains something of a mystery. The dingo is no marsupial but a genuine wild dog with every canine characteristic except the bark. Dingoes can only howl. Nobody knows for certain just how dingoes came to Australia. They were already there, although in small numbers, when white men arrived. Most zoologists now assume that they entered the continent with the migrating Aborigines, about 30,000 years ago. The dingoes multiplied rapidly when the colonists obligingly imported rabbits and sheep, and today these silent, tawny yellow outlaws are the scourge of sheep farmers and cattle ranchers alike. Fast, strong, tough, and highly intelligent, the dingoes are holding their own against every attempt to exterminate them, which includes aerial, chemical, and bacteriological warfare.

If the dingo is a mystery, the **platypus** is a living conundrum. When the first platypus skins reached Europe in the 18th century, zoologists flatly refused to believe they belonged to a genuine animal. You can't altogether blame them. How do you classify a creature that has a duck's bill, a mole's fur, a beaver's tail, webbed feet, and one poisonous claw and that lays eggs and then suckles its young?

The platypus is a very shy little aquatic animal living in quiet rivers and lakes, where it eats nearly its own weight of prawns and worms each night. Although it hunts in the water, it sleeps on land, building long underground tunnels with entrances just above the waterline. At one time the platypus was killed extensively for its fine fur, but now it is heavily protected and off the endangered species list.

Yet another phenomenon in Australia's menagerie is the Queensland **lungfish.** This is a prehistoric "fossil," survivor of a primitive marine species that thrived during the Triassic period—some 35 million years ago! The lungfish has a singular breathing apparatus that enables it to live out of the water—in dry mud—for entire summers.

Reptiles abound in Australia, including giant saltwater **crocodiles,** huge **pythons** (whose smaller relatives are frequently employed as rat catchers in fruit warehouses), and one of the world's deadliest snakes. This is the—luckily very rare—**taipan,** a rather drab brownish serpent that can inject more venom than a cobra. The various lizards are all harmless, even the **goannas** that grow up to eight feet in length and can run like greased lightning. Despite their dragonlike appearance they make very fancy eating—if you'd care to try.

The **emu** has the distinction of sharing his country's coat of arms with the kangaroo. This is the most Australian of birds, although not exactly popular with farmers. Closely resembling an ostrich, the emu is incapable of flying, but it hits running speeds of over 30 mph and has a kick that could stun a mule. Emus travel in flocks, and when they descend on crop fields it's good-bye to the harvest. Farmers have gone to great expense in stringing emu-proof fences around their land, but the birds seem to have a genius for finding weak spots in the barriers.

The **kookaburra,** on the other hand, is the most beloved bird in the Commonwealth, chiefly because it's a snake killer that can handle the most dangerous reptiles, scooping them up and dropping them from great heights or cracking them like a whip against a tree. The kookaburra—also known as the laughing jackass—has a sense of humor as well. It literally shrieks with laughter in the bush—and often seems to time its hilarity to when someone below has fallen flat on his or her face. They're completely fearless and will dive-bomb people or cats who come too near their nests. But they are also easily tamed, and once they learn that you'll feed them they'll form a cackling, giggling reception committee at your doorstep.

There is a strangely mystical quality about the bird known as the **brolga.** A member of the crane family, this handsome, graceful four footer figures largely in

Aboriginal legends. Brolgas perform amazingly stately and intricate dances, tossing their heads back and stepping high like chorus-line dancers while keeping rhythm in their hoarse trumpet voices. The brolga dances form the basis of Aboriginal corroborees and more recently have inspired modern ballet choreographers.

Perhaps the most startling aspect of Australia's fauna is the role played by imported animals. The country grew rich through imported sheep and cattle—but it nearly ruined itself by importing **rabbits.** The half dozen or so originals multiplied—well, like rabbits. They grew into hundreds of millions of bunnies that gobbled up the grass meant for livestock and required ruthless germ warfare to keep them under some kind of control.

Throughout the more rugged northern portions of the continent you'll come on wild **buffalo, camels,** and **donkeys.** None of these creatures were indigenous; all were imported for domestic purposes, but they ran wild, multiplied, and frequently became pests. Buffalo hunting is still a prime sport in the Northern Territory, but you'd better be sure of your marksmanship before joining the hunt. A wounded buff can be one of the most lethal customers you're likely to encounter.

The camels date back to the prerailroad era. They were brought in, together with Afghan drivers, to carry goods through desert country. The bearded, turbaned Afghans vanished when tracks replaced hooves. But the camels stayed and multiplied and are still there in the hundreds of thousands.

About 60 years ago, however, Australians imported their worst current plague. A group of Queensland sugarcane growers brought over a few hundred **cane toads** from Hawaii. The idea was that the toads would gobble up the grayback beetles that were decimating the sugar crop. The strategy suffered from one vital flaw: the beetles lived on top of the cane stalks and could fly. The toads, being earth bound, had no chance of getting their intended prey.

Having no natural enemies, the toads began proliferating at a fantastic rate—a single female produces over 30,000 young a year. The bug-eyed, hopping invaders have overrun nearly half of Queensland and are now spreading into other states. The glands on their backs can squirt a lethal poison that kills dogs, cats, predatory birds, and even snakes. They can survive spear and bullet wounds, scramble off after being clubbed, and swallow poison pellets with impunity. Nothing, it seems, can halt the victory march of *bufo marinus.*

At the moment Queensland's Toad Advisory Service is trying to conjure up some scientific defense against these ravenous imports. But the best advice they could offer their compatriots would be to stop upsetting the ecological balance of the continent.

2. HISTORY & GOVERNMENT

HISTORY

Dream time . . . that's the past. The way, way back shrouded past, half lost, half remembered, when anything could happen and nothing was recorded except by a faint imprint in the recesses of the human subconscious.

The original Australians have no chronicled history—only the Dreaming: the misty spectral memories of a time before the coming of the white man, when the world was young, the land was infinite, and life was beautiful and free. It could have been a thousand years ago, or a million, or even a hundred million—who knows? But they dream that once the earth was flat and featureless and roaming across it at will were the ancestors, the heroes, the Creative Beings.

DATELINE

- **1616** Dutch seafarers Jan Houtman and Dirk Hartog discover the southwestern coast of Australia, calling it New Holland.
- **1642** Dutch explorer Abel Tasman discovers Tasmania, naming it Van Diemen's Land, after the governor of the Dutch East Indies.
- **1688** Erstwhile English pirate Wil-

(continues)

As they wandered they created the country's topography: here a mountain range, there a forest, yonder a gigantic pebble—Ayers Rock.

Deep in the cavernous heart of the Rock lived the Rainbow Serpent, hundreds of yards long, fanged and bearded, with scaly skin reflecting all the colors of the rainbow. As the Serpent crawled along, it furrowed the riverbeds, which still wind and twist like the snake's body.

That's how they dream it in central Australia. They dream it differently in the south and in still other ways in the north and west. The original Australians were too isolated from one another to conceive a universal Genesis, but all their dreams contain the image of endless space and unfenced horizons, of a world where time and distance didn't matter.

The dream ended, abruptly, with the arrival of people who trapped the unmeasured space with instruments and carried time in their pockets.

THE UNKNOWN LAND In the second century A.D., the learned Ptolemy of Egypt designed a map of the then-known world. Into the southern region of what we now call the Indian Ocean he placed a huge misshapen blob and labeled it *Terra Incognita*—Unknown Land. And during the next 1,500 years information about this particular *terra* hardly advanced beyond Ptolemy's. It remained solidly *incognita.*

The reason was distance. For the transportation methods of our ancestors, the antipodes were nearly as remote as another planet. Marco Polo's journey to China and Columbus's cruise to America were mere hops compared to the traveling time required to cross the uncharted immensities of the Indian and Pacific oceans.

You can argue ad infinitum about who "discovered" Australia. The Spaniards and Portuguese traced the northern coastlines; the Dutch landed on the west coast in 1616 and promptly christened the inhospitable wilderness New Holland—a name it carried for 150 years. The first Englishman set foot there in 1688. He was the buccaneer (a polite word for pirate) William Dampier. But Dampier saw only the barren northwestern shores and decided that the country wasn't worth plundering or exploring.

Thus it was left to Capt. James Cook, one of the greatest navigators of all time, to become the new continent's founder. His Australian landfall was simply another stop along the road of his historic cruise of discovery that opened up the last unknown area of the globe.

On April 29, 1770, Cook's *Endeavour* sailed into Botany Bay, and four months later the captain formally claimed the entire eastern seaboard of the continent for King George III. Dream time was over. The men with watches, measuring rods, and muskets had arrived.

CONVICTS ARRIVE Australia owed its initial settlement to the success of the American Revolution. At first the British government had been totally uninterested in its acquisition of Australia. Only after the American colonies broke away did the Crown think of a use for the continent—as an alternative dumping ground for convicts!

DATELINE

liam Dampier lands on the northwestern coast.

- **1770** Australia's unofficial birth year. Capt. James Cook sails HMS *Endeavour* into Botany Bay, hoists the British flag, and names the region New South Wales.
- **1788** Capt. Arthur Phillip, first governor of New South Wales, arrives along with the first batch of 736 male and female convicts, establishing Sydney in honor of Viscount Sydney, Britain's Home Secretary.
- **1804** First (and worst) penal settlements founded in Van Diemen's Land (Tasmania).
- **1824** A new penal settlement (for "incorrigibles") founded at Moreton Bay and later named after Governor Brisbane.
- **1829** Western Australia becomes the first "free"—as distinct from "convict"—colony.
- **1835** John Batman declares Port Phillip "a place for a village" and originates Melbourne.
- **1836** Col. William Light designs Adelaide, Australia's first completely planned community.
- **1851** Gold discovered in New South Wales and Victoria. The gold

(continues)

DATELINE

rush draws 400,000 free settlers who transform the country.

- **1854** Fight between gold diggers and troops at the Eureka Stockade near Ballarat in Victoria. The only battle fought on Australian soil.
- **1868** The last batch of convicts arrives in Australia.
- **1873** William Gosse discovers Ayers Rock, named by him after the governor of South Australia.
- **1880** Ned Kelly, legendary bushranger, captured after gun battle at Glenrowan, Victoria, then taken to Melbourne and hanged. He lived on in three movies and countless ballads.
- **1901** The Australian colonies unite as a Commonwealth and self-governing dominion, with Melbourne as temporary capital.
- **1911** Work starts on the permanent Federal Capital of Canberra, designed by American Walter Burley Griffin.
- **1915** World War I. The Australian and New Zealand Army Corps (ANZAC) lands at Gallipoli, Turkey, a military catastrophe resulting in terrible casualty figures.

(continues)

Deportation for life was considered a "humane" sentence for such desperate lawbreakers as poachers, pickpockets, Irish rebels, trade-union organizers, prostitutes, and cardsharps. Murderers, coiners, and highwaymen were still publicly hanged. Thus the fleet of 11 ships that brought the first governor of New South Wales, Capt. Arthur Phillip, also carried 1,500 people—half of them convicts. In January 1788, they founded a settlement at Port Jackson, today the site of Sydney.

A second and a third fleet arrived within three years, and soon there were 4,000 whites in the colony commonly called Botany Bay. In England that name became synonymous with hell—and for good reasons. The settlement was supposed to be self-supporting, which was tantamount to starvation, scurvy, or death in the bush. How could the "settlers" wrest a living from the soil in a country where the seasons were turned upside down, where most of their imported seeds wouldn't grow, where they couldn't predict the rainfall, and where they didn't know what lay behind the next chain of hills? And, worst of all, half of them had to work in chains under the constant threat of the whip, which was used with incredible savagery on the most trifling pretexts.

The early years of Botany Bay were an unending agony of hunger, disease, floggings, and killings, made barely endurable by bouts of drunkenness. The only commodity that was in reasonable supply was rum—the universal balm, the precious relief from pain and homesickness, the real currency of Botany Bay.

Captain Bligh, of the *Bounty* mutiny fame, was to discover that precious cargo when he became governor of the colony in 1805. The brilliant but heavy-handed captain tried to suppress the illicit liquor traffic in his realm and promptly sparked yet another mutiny, the "Rum Rebellion," among his own officers, who threw the governor out of office and ignominiously shipped him back to England.

When convict transportations finally ended in 1853, more than 100,000 convicts had been dumped into the country. By then the prisoners were already outnumbered by free settlers, and the struggle for survival in the new environment won. But the convict pioneers left an indelible imprint on the Australian national character. They bequeathed a heritage of strong antiauthoritarian sentiments; a fierce egalitarianism that made every Jack and Jill as good as their master; and a peculiarly sardonic, self-mocking brand of humor, expressed by the jingle that was something like the early colony's unofficial motto:

> True patriots all, let this be understood,
> We left our country for our country's good.

But while the convicts had a strong influence on Australian history, the original inhabitants had none. Unlike New Zealand's past, interwoven with Maori wars and peace treaties, the role of the Australian Aborigines was simply that of victims. They were brushed aside, excluded from the mainstream, either ignored or massacred, never taken seriously as part of the nation. Australia's history is the chronicle of its white usurpers.

EXPLORATION The new continent began without a name or a definite shape. Nobody could even be sure it *was* a continent, not just a cluster of large islands. It was a vague amorphous outline, variously known as New Holland, New South Wales, or Botany Bay. Not until 1803 did Capt. Matthew Flinders circumnavigate the entire landmass, establishing that it was indeed a continent—three million square miles of it, roughly the size of today's mainland United States. Flinders was also the first to adopt the name Australia, meaning "Southland," for his discovery.

Although the settlements that later became state capitals were springing up along the coast, they lay in complete isolation. Between them stretched thousands of miles of unknown wilderness, and their only means of contact was by sea. Small parties of explorers set out to scout links between the townships. As long as these men hugged the shoreline their progress was hard but bearable. Once they struck inland, however, it became nightmarish. For the farther away they marched from the coast, the more barren the countryside grew, until at last it changed to absolute desert. By then many of the explorers were out of supplies and couldn't make it back. They perished in droves—of hunger, thirst, sheer exhaustion, snakebites, bushfires, fever, and occasionally, the spears of hostile Aborigines.

Edward Eyre, who pushed through the broiling waterless Nullarbor to the West Coast in 1841, made it but was practically reduced to a walking skeleton. German naturalist Ludwig Leichhardt, who tried to cross the continent from east to west seven years later, did not. Not a trace of his party was ever found. Also unsuccessful was the heroic trio of Burke, Wills, and Gray, who attempted to reach the far north Gulf of Carpentaria overland from Melbourne in 1861. All three died en route. One of the finest books written about Australia's past, Alan Moorehead's *Cooper's Creek,* describes their tragedy.

The exploration of the continent continues. Even today certain portions of Arnhem Land in the Northern Territory remain *Terra Incognita.*

DATELINE

- **1927** First session of Parliament in the new capital of Canberra.
- **1942** World War II. Japanese aircraft bomb Darwin; Japanese midget subs shell Sydney.
- **1950** Australian troops join the Korean War.
- **1956** Olympic Games held in Melbourne.
- **1973** Queen Elizabeth opens the Sydney Opera House.
- **1974** Darwin virtually wiped out by Cyclone Tracy.
- **1988** Australia celebrates its Bicentennial.
- **1993** Labor Party leader Paul Keating reelected prime minister.

GOLD Australia was peopled by a series of frantic rushes. The first was the mass transportation of convicts from Britain. The second was the discovery of fabulously rich goldfields at Ballarat and Bendigo in 1853. The timing was perfect—just at the stage when the great gold rush in California was petering out, thousands of American miners were lured to try their luck Down Under. Some came to dig for gold, others to help miners get rid of whatever they found. Miners came from every corner of the globe in every conceivable vessel. Within 10 years the population of the country jumped from 400,000 to 1,400,000, and the newcomers nearly wrecked the country in the process of populating it.

The colony of Victoria, where the goldfields were located, was both materially and psychologically unprepared for the rush. The administration of Governor Hotham, still accustomed to dealing with helpless convicts, applied somewhat similar methods to the newcomers. They levied a crushing license tax on each claim and proceeded to collect taxes by means of the whip, bayonet, and musket butt. Mounted troopers indulged in "Digger hunts" through the goldfields, trampling down prospectors in front of their comrades, who watched with clenched fists.

But there were rifles in many of those fists, and the Diggers were a fighting breed. (The term *Digger,* in fact, became the generic label for all Australian soldiers.) A clash was inevitable. It turned out to be the only battle fought on Australian soil to date.

The Diggers issued a ringing proclamation of "Right and Justice" and elected a

IMPRESSIONS

To a philosophic mind, this is a land of wonder and delight. To him it is a new creation; the beasts, the fish, the birds, the reptiles, the trees are all new—so beautiful and grotesque that no naturalist would believe even the most faithful drawings. . . .

—T. F. PALMER, 1793

---

fiery young Irishman named Peter Lalor as their commander. The famous Eureka Stockade—a rough barricade of logs and rifle pits—went up at Ballarat, manned by an ill-armed but determined bunch of Irish, English, Italian, German, American, and Australian defenders. Some had rifles, others had pikes, pistols, or pitchforks; above them floated a brand-new banner showing the Southern Cross on a blue field—the rebel flag that has since become the country's national emblem.

Governor Hotham's reply was to send a regiment of foot soldiers and squadrons of mounted police to crush the uprising. On the morning of December 3, 1854, the troops charged the Eureka Stockade. The battle was brief and bloody. The Diggers stood no chance against the precision-drilled redcoat regulars who advanced and fired, advanced and fired, like rows of robots. The log palisade went down under the bayonet charge, and the blue banner fell, riddled with bullets. Some 34 men were killed, and hundreds were wounded. Peter Lalor escaped, wounded and with a price on his head, and went into hiding. The cause of the Diggers seemed lost.

But the British authorities had learned quite a lot since the American Revolution. They had learned, above all, to recognize a dangerous situation when it confronted them. Instead of making a martyr of Lalor, they pardoned him. Less than a year after being outlawed, Lalor was elected to the Victorian Parliament, and most of the demands he had fought for were granted.

Mark Twain wrote this about the Eureka battle: "It was the Barons and John, over again; it was Hampden and Ship-Money; it was Lexington and Concord; small beginnings, all of them, but all of them great in political results, all of them epoch-making. It is another instance of a victory won by a lost battle."

Australians gained more than a flag, a hero, and recognition of some basic rights from the gold rush. They gained a wholesome infusion of cosmopolitan blood for their population base, including thousands of Chinese, many of whom came as camp cooks for the diggings. When the golden stream dwindled, some of them opened restaurants instead—the country's first relief from the dismal Anglo-Irish cuisine.

BUSHRANGERS Banditry was an inevitable by-product in a colonial frontier society. Australia very quickly developed its own special brand, which closely resembled the outlaws of the American West. At first they were mainly escaped convicts who robbed in order to survive in the bush. But soon they acquired professional flair together with fast horses, good weapons, and an organized intelligence service that was often far superior to that of the authorities. These bushrangers, as they were called, plundered gold transports, homesteads, banks, railroads, and the Cobb & Co. stagecoaches that were Australia's equivalent of Wells Fargo.

For a time the bushrangers multiplied at a frightening rate. There were white, black, and yellow bushrangers; "gentlemen" bushrangers; and half-demented maniacs. There was even a Jewish bushranger, Edward Davis, whose gang terrorized the Hunter River region.

Law enforcers were badly handicapped by the absence of a regular police force in the colonies. The towns had army garrisons (almost useless in the bush), but the immense wilderness was patrolled by a handful of mounted troopers who hadn't a hope of controlling their colossal territory. When situations became serious, police work had to be done by posses of armed civilians—and they invariably included men whose sympathies lay with the bandits. The law suffered from a pretty poor profile in the early days of the colonies. This was aptly expressed by the popular folksong "The Wild Colonial Boy," whose rollicking refrain runs:

> So come, all my hearties, we'll roam the mountains high,
> Together we will plunder, together we will die.
> We'll wander over valleys, and gallop over plains,
> We'll scorn to live in slavery, bound down with iron chains.

Bushrangerdom reached its peak with the Kelly Gang—the brothers Ned and Dan Kelly and two friends—whose exploits became as legendary as those of Frank and Jesse James in America. Ned Kelly possessed a certain rough chivalry, a wonderful flair for dramatics, and some genuine grudges against the authorities, including the alleged assault of his sister Kate by a trooper. He achieved a Robin Hood aura that still lingers. Even today you can buy into a fight in certain country pubs by making derogatory remarks about Ned, and "Game as Kelly" remains the highest tribute to a man's bravery in the Australian vocabulary.

The Kellys graduated from horse stealing to bank robbery and holding up entire country towns, where Ned made to his literally captive audiences speeches redolent with Irish patriotism, Australian republicanism, and sentimental pathos. The locals loved it. For five years the Kelly gang ran the authorities ragged. Then, in June 1880, they overreached themselves. The four outlaws raided the town of Glenrowan, herding most of the population into Glenrowan Inn, where they wined and dined them liberally—at the management's expense.

Told that a trainload of troopers was heading up from Melbourne, the Kellys sabotaged the railroad track, hoping to wreck the police train. But the scheme failed, and the troopers swarmed into town. The gang barricaded Glenrowan Inn for their last stand. Three of them died in the gunfire—Ned came out fighting. He appeared, his head encased in a crude iron helmet, his chest armored with beaten plowshares. For a while he seemed invulnerable—the hail of police bullets bounced screeching off his armor. Then the troopers aimed lower—at his unprotected legs—and Ned Kelly went down.

He was taken to Melbourne, sentenced to death, and duly hanged the following November—despite nationwide public petitions appealing for mercy on his behalf. His mother, a Ma Barker type, admonished her 25-year-old son, "Now mind that you die like a Kelly!" He did. Ned Kelly's plowshare armor, pockmarked with bullet dents, is still on display in Melbourne.

ON THE SHEEP'S BACK The bushranger plague faded out with the Kellys, leaving Australia one of the most law-abiding countries on earth. The reason for this was not so much improved police work as the coming of prosperity, accompanied by an astonishing rise in the standard of living.

The substance behind the good life was wool. Australia rode to prosperity "on the sheep's back." Poor sheep—an animal few people love and even fewer find interesting. They were nevertheless the factor that transformed a cluster of struggling colonies into one of the wealthiest nations in the world. Cattle, and later minerals, played their parts, but the initial miracle was wrought by wool.

Some 428 rams and ewes came to Australia with the first convict fleets; they were a miserable, runty lot, purchased partly in England, partly in the African Cape Province. Both their numbers and their wool clip were laughable by today's standards. The Commonwealth now boasts around 165,000,000 sheep; whereas their forebears yielded an average of less than three pounds of wool per head, the current clip is over nine pounds.

In 1801 a Capt. John Macarthur began to experiment with the breeding of fine-wool sheep, using Spanish merinos and English animals. In the meat-hungry colonies it took tremendous determination and foresight to breed for wool rather than mutton chops, but the effort paid off royally. By skillful husbandry Macarthur and his successors eventually succeeded in developing a kind of supersheep—the Australian merino—a walking mountain of wool of a quality no breed in Europe or America could match. Such was the demand for Australian wool overseas that the exporters could take the huge shipping costs in their stride and still beat all competitors in the international wool market.

Sheep raising was—and still is—a risky business. A single one of the devastating Australian droughts can ruin a middling sheep farmer. Only immense flocks and enormous grazing lands offered some security. In the early days land ownership was established simply by "squatting." The big pastoralists were known as squatters, and as they grew bigger and richer the term *squattocracy* came into use for these sheep and cattle barons who, until industrialists and mine owners caught up with them, formed the country's financial and social elite.

COLONY TO COMMONWEALTH For 80 years the British government followed an eminently sensible policy of granting limited home rule—including elected parliaments—to the Australian colonies. As the population increased, new colonies were carved out of the original ones and also granted constitutions. Thus by the end of the 19th century, Australia consisted of six separate colonies, each with its own constitution and legislature.

This pattern worked nicely from the viewpoint of the London Colonial Office, but not as well for Australia. Among other drawbacks it saddled the young country with three different railroad gauges—which took several generations to standardize. It also fostered a psychology of separatism that might have been fatal to any form of concerted national effort.

The demand for unity and continental self-government became overwhelming with the approach of the 20th century. Federation was the watchword in every colony except Western Australia, which—isolated from the rest—had no desire to federate with anyone but found itself forced to join by migrant gold miners.

The stage was set for Queen Victoria's proclamation issued on September 17, 1900. It established the Commonwealth of Australia as a united dominion of the British Empire, a self-governing nation in every respect, but owing a largely traditional allegiance to the Crown as represented by the governor-general. The Commonwealth Constitution, worked out by a special convention, did a splendid job of picking the raisins from various pies. It adopted the best of British parliamentary procedure, large helpings of American Federalism, and a few snippets of French democracy. Added to this mélange were some progressive touches that made it the most advanced political document of its time.

Women, for instance, received equal voting rights with men—20 years ahead of Britain and America! Voting was not only universal and secret, but compulsory (anyone who did not vote was fined), thereby eliminating any party's ballot victory through the lethargy of the public. And to prevent the rival cities of Sydney and Melbourne from battling for the honor of being the nation's capital, it provided that a new city—roughly halfway between them—should be built for the express purpose of housing the federal government. Founded 13 years later, this city, Canberra, was superbly designed by the American architect Walter Burley Griffin. Canberra had a stroke of luck in the final choice of its name: Among the ghastly labels suggested by politicians were Wheatwoolgold, Democratia, and—so help me—Marsupalia.

WAR The infant Dominion entered World War I simultaneously with its emancipation—and with the same naive enthusiasm as Great Britain. But unlike Britain, Australia never had to introduce conscription. Its problem was to find room for the avalanche of volunteers flooding the recruiting stations. Not even the gruesome casualty rate—the highest among all the Empire forces—did much to dampen the fervor. The Diggers were bigger, healthier, and more aggressive—although less well disciplined—than the Tommies (British soldiers), which made them ideal assault troops. They suffered accordingly.

On April 25, 1915, the Anzacs (from the initials of Australian and New Zealand Army Corps) landed at Gallipoli in Turkey. The date, commemorated as Anzac Day, is now an Australian (and New Zealand) national holiday, but the actual event was a tragedy. For eight months the Anzacs held the barren, shell- and fever-ridden peninsula in the face of crack Turkish infantry supported by German artillery before they were finally evacuated.

The Australian Light Horse Brigade spearheaded the British conquest of Palestine, and there were two Anzac corps fighting on the Western Front in France. Among their claims to fame is the (still-disputed) bagging of Manfred von Richthofen, the legendary "Red Baron," the war's number-one fighter ace. It is still debatable whether Richthofen was downed by a Canadian Sopwith pilot in the air or by Anzac machine guns from the ground. But when the celebrated red Fokker triplane—with its dead pilot—crash-landed in the Allied lines, an Aussie gunner peered at the German's face and yelled, "Cripes, we got the bloody baron!"

World War II, for Australia, opened very much like the first. Again the Dominion enlisted a large enthusiastic volunteer force and again it sailed to the Middle East, leaving an apparently safe homeland behind. But then Japan struck at Pearl Harbor, and with one blow the entire situation changed—fearfully.

Australia lay bare, wide open, and virtually undefended as the Japanese proceeded to swoop down through Southeast Asia. Most of the country's trained troops were fighting Rommel in Libya, 7,000 miles away. The remainder were lost when "impregnable" Singapore fell in February 1942. In July the Japanese landed in New Guinea, the huge island straddling Australia's northern doorstep. Japanese bombers wrecked Darwin, capital of the Northern Territory. Submarines shelled Sydney Harbour. The lights blacked out from coast to coast, and citizens grimly dug air-raid shelters in the backyards of their little suburban homes. War, at last, had reached the "Lucky Country."

What followed was a trauma that shook Australia out of its complacent isolation, its smug feeling of invulnerability. For the first time the country had to draft manpower—and womanpower as well. Australia learned what it was like to try and defend its immense coastline with barely 7,000,000 inhabitants. Conscription was enforced drastically. The motto was, "Don't check their eyes, count them!" By literally scraping the bottom of the barrel, Australia placed 800,000 men and women in the armed forces, a call-up ratio surpassed only by Israel.

In the dense mountain jungle of New Guinea's Owen Stanley Range, half-trained, badly armed militiamen tried to stem the Japanese advance toward Port Moresby, the springboard for an invasion of the Australian mainland. In the air Aussie pilots in light Wirraway trainers battled the Japanese Zeros. The Australians had to retreat, but they fought every step of the way along the muddy hell of the Kokoda Trail. And by the skin of their teeth they managed to slow the enemy long enough for help to arrive.

Help meant the seasoned veterans from the Middle East and the Americans. Over Churchill's violent protests, Australia's wartime prime minister, John Curtin, ordered his troops back home. When they arrived—and U.S. reinforcements began to pour in—the tide in New Guinea turned. Australia was saved. But it had been, as the duke of Wellington said about Waterloo, "a damned close run thing." Too close for any future complacency.

THE LUCKY COUNTRY This label was coined by Australian writer Donald Horne but with a somewhat different connotation than foreigners assumed. It meant fool's luck, luck by geographical and historical fluke, the kind of luck liable to run out any day unless backed by something more solid. And in the postwar decades Australia set out to create that backing.

Above anything, the continent needed people. The slogan "Populate or Perish" had been bandied about for half a century without resulting in action. The birthrate was—and still is—low. And on top of producing few natural citizens, Australia also had severely restrictive immigration rules designed to keep "lesser breeds" at a distance.

This changed drastically after 1945. Australia launched an assisted immigration scheme, with the government paying fares for overseas newcomers and their families, regardless of whether they spoke English. Now began the third great influx in the country's history, and this was by far the greatest. More than three million immigrants came and settled. Within 30 years the population topped 13½ million—almost double the prewar figure. Today about 40% of all Australians either were born overseas or have foreign-born parents.

At the same time Australia managed to avoid the minority ghetto enclaves that proved such a curse to America. The newcomers were not left to sink or swim on their own. They were given accommodation (of sorts), language tuition, health care, and considerable vocational guidance. Sternly enforced working standards prevented the "sweating" of migrant labor. Over the years a process of fusion occurred between old and "New Australians" and—equally important—among the newcomers themselves. The majority of them hailed from Britain, but over a million originated in countries habitually hostile to one another: Greece, Italy, Poland, Germany, the Netherlands, Austria, and Yugoslavia. It says much for the balm of their new environment that they quickly buried their feuds—their children are hardly aware of them.

Simultaneously the continent's economy was radically altered. Until the late 1940s Australia's prosperity depended on the land. Today it is still the world's leading wool producer and a major supplier of wheat, meat, sugar, butter, and fruit. But agriculture has now dropped to 7% of the total production, its place taken up by manufacturing (particularly iron and steel) and a boom in mining that quadrupled the value of the mine output within a decade.

Something else altered as well—the average Australian's self-image. Australia is actually the most urban nation on earth, with 61% of the population living in large cities (compared to 48% in the United States). If you consider that Sydney and Melbourne alone account for some 6½ million people between them, the other state capitals for around 3 million more, this leaves mighty few country folks. Yet until recently most Aussies believed themselves to be spiritually a rural nation, almost as if the teeming cities were mere aberations hiding the "real" Australia—in the outback—where only a handful lived. Now, at last, they have accepted the facts of their demography and shed the illusion of a Down Under Ruralia.

AUSTRALIA TODAY Australia today is a young and prosperous country, facing the future with a less nonchalant but more rational optimism than before. Its material living standard is enviable: 75% of all houses are owned by their occupants, there are two motor vehicles registered for every five people, its citizens' life expectancy is among the highest, and its infant mortality is among the lowest in the world. Because its a semiwelfare state, its people enjoy national health benefits (including the famed Flying Doctor Service of the outback), guaranteed minimum wages and holidays, old-age pensions, child endowments, and maternity benefits. Although not as comprehensive as the welfare schemes of Sweden or New Zealand, these benefits are well in advance of those in, say, America or Canada.

But there was a price tag attached to this plethora of social welfare, and currently Australia is paying it. Handicapped by high production costs, restrictive union rules, a bloated bureaucracy, and a small internal market, the nation suffers from the economic phenomenon known as "stagflation": the unemployment rate hovering around 6%, inflation topping 9%, and overseas debts swallowing up a large portion of income derived from exports.

In consequence, tourism has achieved a uniquely important place in the Australian economy—about 530,000 Japanese and some 272,000 Americans came in 1991. For the tourist, Australia now puts out the largest welcome mat in the international cupboard. It reads, "Welcome to the World Down Under; Welcome to the least-known, most explorable continent; Welcome to the Lucky Country."

GOVERNMENT

Australia is governed under a constitution that came into force on January 1, 1901. The country is divided into six states (New South Wales, Queensland, South Australia, Tasmania, Victoria, Western Australia) and three territories (Australian Capital Territory, Jervis Bay Territory, Northern Territory). The head of state of Australia is the British monarch, represented by a governor-general, who has very little real power. Effective executive power is vested in the Australian prime minister, who is responsible to the House of Representatives, made up of 148 members elected to terms of up to three years. The Senate of 76 elected members has little say in government. Each of the states, which retain considerable authority over internal affairs in the Australian federal system, is governed by a premier, who is responsible to the lower house of the state parliament. The territories as a rule enjoy less autonomy than the states. The country's principal political parties are the Australian Labor Party (ALP), the Liberal Party of Australia, the National Party of Australia, and the Australian Democrats Party. In elections in March 1993, Paul J. Keating, leader of the ALP, was returned as prime minister, despite Australia's economic troubles since he had taken office in 1991. During the election campaign Keating promised to hold a national referendum on whether the British monarch should remain as Australia's head of state.

3. FAMOUS AUSTRALIANS

John Batman (1801–39). A blacksmith, cattle farmer, and pioneer who led a boat expedition up the Yarra River and selected "the site for a village"—Melbourne.

Sir Thomas Blamey (1884–1951). The only Australian soldier ever to attain the rank of field marshal, he commanded the Allied Land Forces in the Pacific region (under the Supreme Command of Gen. Douglas MacArthur) during World War II.

Neville Thomas Bonner (b. 1922). Once a cane cutter, mounted stockman, and dairy-farm manager, Bonner became the first Aboriginal to win a seat in the Federal Parliament in 1971.

Sir John Brabham (b. 1926). Known as "Jack" Brabham, he was a three-time world motor-racing champion and twice named "Driver of the Year." He designs and races his own speed cars.

Sir Donald Bradman (b. 1908). Australia's most celebrated cricketer and a legend as a batsman in his own time.

Robert Burke (1821–61). Member of the tragic Burke and Wills expedition. Both partners perished while attempting to cross the continent from south to north. Their fate is masterfully described in the book *Cooper's Creek.*

Evonne Fay Cawley (b. 1951). Famous under her maiden name of Goolagong, she was the first Aboriginal to represent her country in world-class tennis. She won the Wimbledon singles, the French singles, and the Australian doubles and ranked as the world's number-one player.

Joseph Chifley (1885–1951). Former locomotive driver who became prime minister in 1945 and became the chief architect of the Australian welfare system.

John Curtin (1885–1945). Prime minister during most of World War II, his nation's most perilous period, Curtin rallied the country for defense and defied Winston Churchill by bringing Australian troops home from battle in North Africa against Rommel.

Sir William Dobell (1899–1970). Originally an architect, Dobell developed into Australia's most outstanding portrait painter. His portrait of Prime Minister Menzies appeared on the cover of *Time* magazine.

Sir Russell Drysdale (1912–81). Born in England, Drysdale became the most celebrated painter of Australian bush scenes, with a harsh and haunting flavor uniquely his own.

John Flynn (1880–1951). Presbyterian clergyman who achieved fame as "Flynn of the Inland." He founded and ran the ingenious Flying Doctor Service, bringing medical care to lone outback settlements.

Dawn Fraser (b. 1937). This Sydney woman was the world's only swimmer of either sex to win a gold medal at each of three successive Olympic Games, also setting 27 individual world records.

Dame Mary Gilmore (1865–1962). Poet and dedicated journalist, Gilmore was the grande dame of Australian letters, fighting for the rights of women as well as Aboriginals, long before she officially became a dame in 1937.

Francis Greenway (1777–1837). Convicted of forgery in England and transported to Sydney in 1814, he was employed by Governor Macquarie as the penal colony's first architect. Greenway designed some of the finest period buildings in Sydney. Eventually, however, he quarreled with the governor over fees and was fired from his post.

Germaine Greer (b. 1939). Controversial author and lecturer, Greer gained international fame (or notoriety) with her book *The Female Eunuch,* published in 1970.

Sir Robert Helpmann (1909–86). A dancer, an actor, and a superb choreographer, Helpmann was the founder of Australian ballet, many of which he wrote, directed, and performed. He had separate careers as a Shakespearean stage actor and in the film industry.

Thomas Keneally (b. 1935). First studying for the priesthood, then teaching school, Keneally turned to writing and acting and produced prize-winning documentary novels such as *The Chant of Jimmie Blacksmith* and *Schindler's Ark* (from which the noted film *Schindler's List* [1993] was derived).

Sir Charles Kingsford Smith (1897–1935). A Queenslander and his country's top aviator, "Smithy" achieved the first flight across the Pacific Ocean—California to Queensland—in 1928. He and his plane vanished during a flight from England to Australia. Sydney's International Airport is named after him.

Peter Lalor (1827–89). Leader of the rebel gold diggers at the Eureka Stockade battle in 1854, he was hunted as an outlaw. Later he was pardoned and became a member of the Victorian Legislative Assembly.

Henry Lawson (1867–1922). Australia's most beloved bard, bush poet, and prose writer, Lawson acquired national fame but very little income in his lifetime.

Dame Nellie Melba (1861–1931). The first Australian soprano to gain international fame. Although her real name was Mitchell, she called herself Melba after her hometown of Melbourne. The dessert peach Melba was in turn named after her.

Sir Robert Gordon Menzies (1894–1978). Australia's longest-serving prime minister, he held office for 16 years between 1949 and 1966.

Albert Namatjira (1902–59). An Arunda born on a mission station, Namatjira became an internationally acclaimed landscape painter, the pioneer of a school of Aboriginal artists.

Dame Joan Sutherland (b. 1926). Once a shorthand typist, she conquered the world operatic stage as a soprano, earning the title of "La Stupenda" after her appearance at La Scala in Milan.

Patrick White (1912–90). The first Australian to win the Nobel Prize for literature. Characteristic of this highly unorthodox genius, he used the entire prize money to finance an award to be bestowed on other distinguished but struggling authors.

Judith Wright (b. 1915). Celebrated poet and novelist, Wright was in the forefront of the nature-preservation movement long before it became a fashionable cause.

4. ART, ARCHITECTURE & LITERATURE

ART Australian artists did not come into their own until the advent of the so-called Antipodean School of Painting. Very roughly speaking, these were painters in revolt against standard academic forms. They set out to depict a national identity, to show their world as seen through *Australian* eyes, and they achieved an ambience quite unlike any other in the field.

Their work gained recognition in the late 1950s with the astonishing creations of Russell Drysdale, Arthur Boyd, and Sidney Nolan. Drysdale painted outback scenes of haunting loneliness and stark decay, while Nolan imparted an atmosphere of dreamlike surrealism to his figures of soldiers, bushrangers, and forlorn women.

Simultaneously, however, the Aboriginal painters and sculptors were gaining renown. They didn't represent any trend but expressed a cultural tradition more than 50,000 years old. Their pathfinder was Albert Namatjira, who lived on a mission station and whose "primitive" landscapes—blazing with the colors of the desert—first attracted international attention. Today Aboriginal settlements like Ngukurr and Papunya have become art colonies; their products—bark paintings, carvings, sculptures, and designs—look like, but aren't, highly contemporary abstracts. For Aborigines these are representational images of daily life. But viewed from either angle, they fetch top prices on overseas markets. The works of Clifford Possum and Billy Stockman regularly sell for $50,000 or more each.

ARCHITECTURE Australian architecture made a curious debut with Francis Greenway, an English convict deported for forgery in 1814 and lucky to escape hanging. But Greenway was also an architect of genius who designed Sydney's most beautiful colonial buildings (such as St. James's Church) and eventually received a pardon as reward.

Australia's modern architectural showpieces (all described in the appropriate sections of this book) include, first and foremost, the Sydney Opera House, a national landmark designed by the competition winner, Danish Joern Utzon. Also, in the very heart of the city rises the 1,000-foot Sydney Tower, a steel-cabled extravaganza that is the tallest structure in the South Pacific.

Melbourne's pride rests in the starkly impressive Performing Arts Centre, topped by a webbed, spidery tower creation and housing three absolutely magnificent theaters. One of them, the State Theatre, designed by John Truscott, has a ceiling decorated with 75,000 miniature brass domes. The Centre's Art Gallery is the only one in the world that you enter through a human-made waterfall. Another not-to-be-missed structure is Adelaide's Arts Centre. Built on the banks of the Torrens River, the Centre has an outdoor amphitheater and three huge auditoriums, the layout forming a perfect artistic whole that symbolizes Adelaide's title—the Festival City.

Generally, Australian architecture has been more dominated by overseas talent than any other art form. Even one of the country's leading architects, Harry Seidler, was born in Austria and trained in America. In addition, the nation's new Parliament building in Canberra was designed by the New York firm of Mitchell, Guirgola & Thorp.

LITERATURE Down Under literature has its beginnings with a group of "bush balladists" who expressed themselves in both poetry and prose. Their names—Adam Lindsay Gordon, Henry Lawson, and "Banjo" Paterson—are household words in Australia. They were not great lyricists but tremendously evocative writers, and reading their works today will give you the flavor of a young and thrusting society more sharply than a dozen history books.

Modern Australian literature, by contrast, is mainly an urban creation, reflecting the country's shifting self-image. There are exceptions: One of them was Patrick White, Australia's first winner of the Nobel Prize for literature. But White's vision of the outback was Homeric rather than rustic, his characters bizarre instead of matey. For accurate portrayals of Australian life in the early 20th century, one can turn to Henry Handel Richardson, notably her trilogy *The Fortunes of Richard Mahoney* (1930).

The keynote of contemporary Australian writing is a kind of ironic existentialism flavored with a strong dash of muckraking. You will find both these themes in the novels, short stories, and poetry of authors like Thomas Keneally, Judith Wright, Martin Boyd, Peter Mathers, and Thea Astley, herself the winner of the prestigious Patrick White Award. For undiluted muckraking, pure and simplistic, you can turn to Frank Hardy's *Power Without Glory*, one of the most scathing portraits of a country's shady politics and high finance ever penned. In the documentary field the outstanding name is Alan Moorehead, author of *The White Nile*, whose *Cooper's Creek* gives an unforgettable account of the tragedy that overtook three of Australia's early explorers.

Australian literature is still very much in the tentatively groping and searching stage, still not quite sure of its identity and place in the world of letters. But it is this very uncertainty that gives it such an intriguing ambience of its own.

5. MYTH & FOLKLORE

Australian mythology is a mélange concocted partly from Aboriginal tales and partly from immigrant and convict lore, with additions manufactured at home. Occasionally the three strands intertwine so that no one can pinpoint the origins of a particular myth. An example is the Bunyip, the Down Under version of the Loch Ness Monster or Abominable Snowman. The Bunyip is definitely a mythical creature but appears in so many shapes—some harmless, some dangerous—that you can't tell which guise sprang from where.

The Banksia Man, on the other hand—a kind of bush bogey man—is certainly of Aboriginal origin but has found his way into scores of scary tales for white children.

The Aussies have a distinct talent for spinning fables around real historical characters, particularly when they had antiestablishment leanings. Folklore has turned two of the most notorious bushrangers—Ned Kelly and Captain Thunderbolt—into veritable Robin Hoods, robbing the rich and lavishing alms on the poor. Both men did, in fact, possess a streak of rough chivalry and were generous hosts, but this didn't prevent them from leaving trails of bodies in their wake.

Another enduring legend concerns Australia's most famous racehorse, Phar Lap, which now stands stuffed in a Melbourne museum. Phar Lap died in the United States, and the tale—passed from generation to generation—has it that the great chestnut was treacherously poisoned because no American horse could win against it.

6. CULTURAL & SOCIAL LIFE

THE ABORIGINES It is a sadly significant fact that the original Australians are the only people in the world without a name. Racially they form a special category of humankind, the Australoids, but ethnically they are simply called Aborigines—natives. This namelessness remains symbolic of their tragedy: They were the people nobody recognized.

The Aborigines are believed to have migrated to Australia at least 30,000 years ago, perhaps by a land bridge that once linked the continent to Southeast Asia and was later submerged by the ocean. When the Aborigines arrived they were Stone Age hunters and food collectors—as were all *Homo sapiens* then. But while the rest of humanity developed into shepherds and peasants, the Aborigines—cut off from the mainstream—stayed nomadic hunters.

The reasons for this lay in their environment. Australia had no indigenous animals suitable for domestication and no grain food that could be cultivated. It was a harsh, largely arid wilderness that forced its inhabitants to keep wandering in search of game and water, thus preventing them from establishing permanent villages. Their isolation was so complete that they had no opportunities to copy the methods of other societies.

There were an estimated 300,000 Aborigines before the coming of white men, scattered throughout the gigantic continent in tiny groups that spoke 300 or more different languages. Unlike the New Zealand Maori and the Native Americans, the Aborigines were not organized for war and had no concept of warfare in our sense of the word. This was their particular misfortune, because it prevented them from offering large-scale resistance to the invaders.

White explorers saw nothing except the Aborigines' backwardness and noticed only the things they did *not* have, such as agriculture, pottery, woven cloth, seagoing vessels, and a military establishment. The explorers were blind to this culture's very real accomplishments, which are only now receiving some of the appreciation they deserve.

The Aborigines had invented aerodynamic marvels in the boomerang and the woomera—a kind of wooden extension of the throwing arm that imparts a bulletlike spin to a spear, vastly increasing its range, hitting power, and accuracy. They had perfected an amazingly sophisticated sign language—"finger talk"—that overcame tribal language barriers and acted as a universal lingua franca that such continents as Europe never possessed. They were the world's greatest trackers and hunters, capable of trailing a snake across bare, solid rock and of telling the age, sex, weight, height, and tribe of a person by a couple of footprints. Although they couldn't read or write, they communicated by message sticks that related intricate details by means of a few carved grooves.

They had a highly developed sense of artistry and worked wonders with primitive paint mixtures. Above all, they had established an ecological life pattern that most civilized nations would envy. They kept their birthrate at acceptable levels through a complex system of marriage taboos that avoided indiscriminate breeding among the tribes. Another set of taboos forbade certain members to eat or hunt certain animals—thereby assuring the survival of all animal species and their own survival as well.

But the entire delicate balance of Aboriginal existence was destroyed by the conquering white settlers. The Europeans either killed Aborigines outright or condemned them to death by starvation, imported diseases, and rotgut liquor. Periodically there were outbursts of mass slaughter, such as the systematic drive that exterminated the entire native population of Tasmania.

When you read about the historical martyrdom of the "nameless people," it will seem almost a miracle that any of them survived. Only about 50,000 full-blooded Aborigines are left today, although the total number of people with Aboriginal strains is around 150,000. And since their condition began to improve, their numbers once again have begun increasing.

A small minority—a few thousand at best—still live the nomadic life of their forebears in the remotest regions of Queensland and the Northern Territory. About 10 times that many are settled in mission stations and government-sponsored outback communities. Thousands more work as stockmen (cowboys) in the huge northern cattle stations, many of which couldn't operate without their specialized skill. Small groups also live in and around the capital cities, mostly in slum conditions.

But although the plight of most Aborigines is still bleak, a new and brighter era is dawning for them. The change began in the 1950s, when white Australia discovered some of the extraordinary artistry of the Aboriginal heritage. The superb ballet *Corroboree* thrilled capacity audiences who had never before realized the wild, magical beauty of this ceremonial dance form. The Aboriginal painter Albert Namatjira achieved world fame with his dazzling bush landscapes and opened a ready market for an entire generation of black artists. Aboriginal poets, authors, tennis stars, educators, and politicians have presented an entirely new image of their people to the white majority.

In 1972 the first Aboriginal knight was created by the queen. Sir Douglas Nicholls, a champion athlete as well as a leading churchman and tireless fighter for the advancement of his people, symbolized a huge step forward for the entire Australoid race.

A new spirit of pride and self-awareness is stirring among the original Australians.

IMPRESSIONS

I leave your shores with more hope for mankind than I had when I came among you.

—BERTRAND RUSSELL, 1950

For the first time since the discovery of the continent, Aboriginal voices and demands are being heard, and they are finding a sympathetic echo among thousands of whites who had hitherto hardly been aware of their existence. In January 1972, a group of militant young blacks pitched a tent on the lawn in front of Canberra's Parliament House and declared themselves the "Aboriginal Embassy." It was a dramatic move designed to catch the attention of politicians and the public alike—and it turned out to be one of the most successful public-relations gestures in the country's history. The "invisible people" had suddenly become very visible indeed. Since then, Aboriginal rights have gained due attention. In 1983, Ayers Rock was given back to the Aborigines. They in turn leased their venerated site to the government for all to enjoy.

Most Aborigines undoubtedly desire complete assimilation—on equal terms—into white society. But this goal may entail the sacrifice of their unique heritage, the oblivion of their special culture. Materially such a sacrifice might seem worthwhile, yet anyone who has had a glimpse of Australoid traditions would be saddened by their extinction. As Kath Walker, Australia's leading black poet, versed it,

> Pour your pitcher of wine into the wide river
> And where is your wine? There is only the river.
> Must the genius of an old race die
> That the race might live?

MEETING THE AUSSIES Few people in the world are quite as "meetable" as Australians. They will strike up acquaintances anywhere, anytime, needing no more than an introductory "How's it going?" If they perceive you as a visitor, the second question will invariably be "How do you like Australia?" And this is *not* the right moment for an in-depth discourse on the virtues and drawbacks of the Commonwealth. All you have to answer is "Beaut," and you've made a mate—for that moment at least.

It has been noted that the proverbial Aussie amiability is a somewhat shallow characteristic that may not extend further than a couple of shared beers. Nevertheless, it's a very agreeable fact of life. You see fewer arguments and less backbiting here than in most countries (except New Zealand), and the general pleasantness covers behavior in long post office waiting lines and at motor accidents as well. It's a rare Australian who won't take time off to exchange a few cheerful clichés with a stranger.

They also have a spirit of genuine helpfulness that can be heartwarming. For example, I had a flat tire but no jack with which to change the wheel. On top of that it was pouring rain. I stopped a passing cab and asked the driver to lend me his jack. He climbed out, viewed the damage, got his jack, and—without another word—proceeded to change the wheel for me. When he was finished, soaked to the skin, I offered him the fare he would have collected had he taken me to a garage. He said, "Aw, forget it, sport," and drove off.

Most visitors will experience incidents of this sort and treasure them. But some will notice that while Australians are quick to "shout" you drinks and do you favors, they take their time about inviting you to their homes. They don't have the spontaneous hospitality of, for instance, the Irish, who quite casually ask you home "to meet the missus" after an hour's conversation in a pub. For one thing the Australian's home is apt to be way out in the suburbs, and for another he'll want to know you a little better first.

This caution, however, vanishes if you have *any* kind of connection, no matter how remote. Knowing a friend of a friend of his second cousin in Baltimore or Birmingham is quite sufficient. Calling any phone number you've obtained overseas from someone who knows someone in Sydney will get you an instant invitation to "tea"—meaning dinner. And from that little "in" you'll be able to build a whole chain of acquaintances that may carry you right across the country. Don't forget this, though: Australians assume that you'll do exactly the same for any of *their* remote friends should they visit your hometown.

Australia's people have subtle magnetism based on their curious mixture of traditional heritage and uniqueness. The language is English, but of a kind you very likely haven't heard before. Their country is "Orstylia," a newspaper is a "piper," the Victorian capital is "Melbrn," Sydney is "Sinny," and anything unpleasant is "bloody." The soft, slightly twangy timbre with retracted vowel sounds takes a bit of getting used to, as does the general habit of using the feminine gender to describe situations as well as places, conditions, and persons. Remarks such as "She's beaut" and "She's bloody crook" can refer to the speaker's wife, his hometown, the weather, or the outcome of an election.

Strictly speaking, the country is a monarchy, with a degree of sentimental attachment to the British Crown. Titles such as Sir and Dame are still bestowed by the queen, and large numbers of parks, gardens, and public buildings are deemed "Royal." Yet simultaneously it is one of the most democratic societies extant, imbued with a fierce egalitarianism that falls heavily on anyone who may doubt that Jack is as good as his master.

On the other hand, Australia is strongly Americanized but in patches rather than universally. Sydney is deceptively American in spirit as well as appearance and might lead you to think that the entire country is likewise. But the moment you arrive in Melbourne or Adelaide you'll note the unmistakably British heritage. And so it goes: a bit of this and a bit of that, throughout the continent. While Australians now deal in dollars and cents, they still drive on the left. And even though Christmas falls during the hot antipodean summer, they faithfully eat plum pudding with brandy sauce for the occasion.

LANGUAGE Volumes could be—and have been—written about the Down Under derivation of the English language. An absolute *must* for those interested is Afferbeck Lauder's *Let Stalk Strine*—the title being the phonetic transliteration of how an Australian would enunciate "Let us talk Australian." (The author's nom de plume is the "Strine" equivalent of "in alphabetical order.")

There are no regional variations in the Australian accent, the only distinction being that urbanites talk faster than their rural counterparts. All Australians tend to speak nasally, shortening words of more than two syllables and then adding a vowel at the end of each. Thus "compensation" becomes "compo" and a member of the Salvation Army a "Salvo." They also employ diminutives whenever possible, turning surfers into "surfies," mosquitoes into "mozzies," and vegetables into "veggies." They use the word "like" in exactly the same meaningless manner in which Americans employ "you know"—simply to elongate sentences.

All this, however, is still not actual Australian slang, which has a vocabulary all its own. In "Strine" a *sheila* is a girl; a *chook* is a chicken; *back o' Bourke* is the bush or outback; *daks* are trousers; a *dill, ning-nong,* or *drongo* is an idiot; *dinkum* is honest or real; a *galah* is a loudmouth; a *pom* is an English person; a *poofter* is a gay person; a *ratbag* is any manner of villain; *tucker* is food; *crook tucker* is bad food; and so on, ad almost infinitum. Unfortunately the most widely known slang terms have become completely archaic. Nobody these days calls anyone *cobber* or a *fair dinkum Aussie* unless they mean it sarcastically. The term most commonly used is *ocker*—but with a distinctly derogative flavor. Being an ocker means being an urban redneck. Australia itself is known as *Oz*—as in "The Wizard of."

A study of Aussie slang may be entertaining but isn't essential for American visitors. A few nonslang terms, however, do need translating since they fall into daily tourist usage:

IMPRESSIONS

Australians enthuse about the bush, but they live in cities. . . . So the continent holds two world records: first, in cramming nearly everybody into the towns; second, in providing them with such lavish amounts of living space per head that the towns keep bursting at the seams and spilling their contents further and further into the blue yonder.

—ARTHUR KOESTLER, *THE FACELESS CONTINENT*, 1969

Strine	American
bonnet (car)	hood
boot (car)	trunk
bumpers (car)	fenders
crook (adj.)	ill, bad
cut lunch	sandwiches
duco	car paint
fireplug	hydrant
flake	shark meat
flog	sell
good on yer	term of approval (sometimes ironic)
grog	liquor
knock	criticize
lay-by	buying on deposit
loo	toilet (in Sydney, also *Woolloomooloo*)
lollies	candy
lift	elevator
middy	small glass of beer
pot	large beer mug
power	electrical outlet
schooner	large beer glass
shout	to treat (buy for) someone
smoke-o	tea or coffee break
stone weight	14 pounds
stubby	small beer bottle
tram	streetcar
ute	pickup truck (for utility)
wowser	killjoy, puritan

7. PERFORMING ARTS & EVENING ENTERTAINMENT

PERFORMING ARTS

Australian theater has come a long way since 1789, when 12 convicts performed a comedy called *The Recruiting Officer* in a theater lit by candles stuck into mud walls and tickets were purchased with rum, tobacco, and even turnips. Today Australia is home to some of the most beautiful and accoustically perfect theaters in the world, the most famous of which is the Sydney Opera House, drawing performers of world renown—many of them Australian.

Apart from standard professional theater, Australia boasts a thriving "little theater" movement. By "thriving" I don't mean in the financial sense but in terms of spirit, talent, enthusiasm, and the dogged determination not to succumb to bankruptcy. Several of them, like Sydney's Nimrod Theatre and Melbourne's La Mama, often present far more original and innovative productions than most of the well-known stages. And very often these are the only showcases open to young unknown Australian talent, either in acting, directing, or writing. They're also vastly cheaper than the professional houses, with tickets selling in the $A10 to $A15 range.

The Australian film industry rates a chapter to itself, but suffice it to say that the international acclaim of such film stars as Mel Gibson and comedian-actor Paul Hogan narrowly overshadows that of the brilliant filmmaking talent fast emerging within Australia itself (see "Recommended Books & Films," in this chapter). In dance, the Sydney Dance Company has also earned its place in the spotlight.

In music (reaching further back into the past), Australia's most famous soprano was Dame Nellie Melba, who made her European debut in 1887 and sang in virtually every opera house in the world. (In 1893 French chef Auguste Escoffier created a dessert in her honor and named it peach Melba.) Equally famous was the illustrious Dame Joan Sutherland, who gave her final performance in 1990. Australia's popular musicians—the Bee Gees, Olivia Newton-John, Men at Work, and INXS among many—have continued to attract worldwide attention for nearly three decades and are the third-largest contributers to the pop-music scene after the United States and Britain.

EVENING ENTERTAINMENT

Australians are essentially outdoors daytime people, as indicated by their early dinner hour—on the average around six o'clock. Nightlife, therefore, is a fairly neglected field. But let me hasten to add, that this is not true everywhere. Sydney, that wonderful scarlet sibling among municipalities, hums at night. Melbourne, too, has a goodly number of nightspots, scattered and overdiscreet though they may be. But as for Adelaide, Brisbane, and others, it's meager pickings. The locals will tell you that this is due to their being "small towns"—which is rather surprising since they're larger than, say, San Francisco. I suspect the temperament of the inhabitants has more to do with it than size: They simply prefer daylight action to the other kind.

NIGHTCLUBS All the cities have regular nightclubs, many of them both expensive and rather dreary. In the cheaper brackets I've done my level best to pick the raisins out of the pie on your behalf. Don't blame me if the result isn't exactly overwhelming. Think of how much cash and energy you'll save for other purposes.

PUBS Much of the after-dark action centers on pubs. Now that the Down Under publicans actually have to *compete* for customers (and they're still crying about that injustice), they've blossomed out in a variety of ways. You get rows of rock pubs, jazz pubs, and folk pubs, and their offerings are listed in the weekend editions of the local papers. Some have $A3 to $A5 admission charges; most do not.

DISCOS Every city also boasts its share of discos, but these are so youth oriented that you're virtually disqualified if you *look* 30. There are, however, plenty of dance halls that cater to the tango-and-foxtrot, as well as the rock, crowd. You'll see them listed in the entertainment columns, duly divided into "modern," "old time," and "50-50." The majority are very staid—in contrast to the discos, which pride themselves on their decibel levels.

THEATER RESTAURANTS Of recent vintage, but tremendously popular, are the theater restaurants. These are places where you eat, drink, and watch a show on a regular stage, a specialty of Victorian England now experiencing a worldwide revival. At their best they're magnificent, such as the Last Laugh Theatre Restaurant and Zoo in Melbourne. But even the second-raters can be a lot of fun, frequently on the raunchy side. The stage offerings vary, with old-time melodramas or vaudeville or parodies thereof being the hot favorites. Some theater restaurants insist on an all-inclusive price, while others allow you to eat elsewhere and merely turn up for the show, in which case you won't pay more than $A15.

COFFEE LOUNGES Every city also has coffee lounges, a few of which display immunity to the great Australian vice of early closing. They serve only soft drinks, snacks, and sweets; frequently feature some kind of musical entertainment; and may remain open until one or two in the morning.

GAMBLING Since the first edition of this book appeared, there has been a major upheaval in the realm of Down Under gambling. State governments discovered the wonderful tax revenue to be garnered from casinos and have encouraged their growth to the point where Australia is now one of the most casino-studded countries on earth. At the moment there are eight, with a couple more under way. And this does not include the scores of "service clubs" that live and thrive on the profits of their poker machines. I deal with them in the appropriate chapters.

I must warn you: The national game of *two-up, though universally played, is illegal outside casino premises* and can get you caught in a police raid—if the organizers have neglected to grease the correct palms.

SAFETY One final comment on Australia's after-dark scene—it's safe. Muggings are still rare enough to make newspaper front pages. And despite media complaints about a "rising crime wave," the degree of criminal violence is minuscule by American standards. You don't have to worry about entering parking lots at night, strolling through parks, or taking shortcuts through dark alleys. Australians don't have the furtive over-the-shoulder look that has become typical of the U.S. urbanite after nightfall. And in the suburbs they still leave their front-door keys under their mats.

8. SPORTS & RECREATION

Australia is a nation obsessed with sport. You have to be there to realize just how far this obsession goes. Some sociologists believe that this is due to a combination of an ideal sporting climate, a strong competitive instinct, and a passion for gambling. Whatever the causes, Australians live in a sporting atmosphere that permeates every nook and cranny of their consciousness. Television, a pretty reliable gauge of public taste, devotes around 26 hours of viewing time per week to sporting coverage.

Although the Aussies are known mainly as tennis players, tennis is an also-ran when it comes to drawing crowds. The great spectator sports are horseracing, cricket, and (in Victoria) Australian Rules football.

Horseracing, of course, is the major gambling sport and has a natural appeal to the world's greatest gambling nation. You can bet with licensed bookies at the racetracks or at official off track betting bureaus called **TABs.** On Saturday it's virtually impossible to escape the sound effects of horseracing—they come from thousands of transistor radios, car radios, and pub radios. And it's wondrous to hear the usually relaxed radio commentators break out in shrieking hysteria because Fufflebum is streaking half a length ahead of Nincompoop.

I'll give you a brief discourse on **Australian Rules football** in the appropriate place—see "Melbourne," Chapter 4. But it's quite impossible to describe the intricate subtleties of **cricket** and its rules in the space available. Cricket has certain similarities with baseball, and Australians take the "Ashes" (playoffs) even more seriously than Americans do the World Series. The closest Australia ever came to leaving the Commonwealth was during the historic "bodyline" cricket row of the 1930s. Oddly enough, cricket is a rather slow game, eminently suitable for filling long and leisurely summer afternoons. For anyone not familiar with the fine technical nuances, it can be an experience akin to a tone-deaf person's attending a symphony.

The Aussies are passionate sports participants as well as spectators. As the wife of former U.S. ambassador Ed Clark wrote, "Living in Australia is like living in a gymnasium—there's always somebody practicing something."

Usually it's **tennis.** Australian urbanites have more public and private courts at their disposal than any other race of city dwellers. Boys and girls start playing tennis in school and stay more or less wedded to their rackets thereafter. If you fly over Sydney at night you'll notice hundreds of little illuminated rectangles below you. These are night tennis courts on which the locals are lobbing balls long after darkness has fallen. Wherever you are, you'll have no difficulty renting a court and a racket. Winning a game may prove a bit more troublesome. Courts rent at around $A8 per weekday morning.

Surfing and **swimming** are the other great passions, which is not surprising, since virtually every large city has miles of superb beaches at its doorstep. (Sydney has 34 ocean beaches within the city limits.) A bit of advice to those unaccustomed to ocean swimming: Those warning notices aren't placed for fun. When they say "Bathe Between the Flags," ignoring them means risking your life. Even shallow water can have a terrific undertow and—well, I hate to lose readers.

This is where one of the greatest Australian institutions comes in: the **lifesavers.**

Basically they are a body of highly trained volunteers who patrol the beaches, keep a lookout for sharks, and rescue swimmers in distress. Actually they're far more than that—they represent a kind of civil elite force, a mystique based on unpaid service for the joy of it. Although they are unpaid in money (Australians consider the practice of *hiring* professional lifeguards as vaguely indecent), the lifesavers' payment comes in the shape of glory, admiration, and vast numbers of bathing beauties—which aren't bad either. They do a magnificent job, including tasks that in America would have to be tackled by cops. Whenever there is an outbreak of rowdiness on Australian beaches, the lifesavers put a very fast stop to it.

Every summer weekend throughout the country, the lifesavers stage **Surf Carnivals,** which are an absolute must for visitors. The competing clubs parade in multicolored bathing suits, using a curious form of goose step that enables them to march in soft sand. The competitions that follow are uniquely exciting: rescue drills executed with parade-ground precision; surfboat racing, in which the rowing crews maneuver their specially built craft over the breakers, frequently getting tossed high into the air. Phone the local Surf Life Saving Association to find out on which beach the carnival is being held and make sure to see at least one.

Yachting is very nearly as popular as surfing. In Australia, during any one weekend the number of yachts out on the water has been estimated at about 200,000. The Sunday-afternoon sailing races provide a wonderful—and free—spectacle. If you're lucky enough to be in Sydney on December 26, don't miss the start of the **Sydney-Hobart Yacht Race,** the greatest marine event of the season. The sight of this yachting armada streaming out through The Heads—en route for Tasmania—is one you'll never forget.

Australia's greatest canvas triumph occurred in 1983 with its capture of the America's Cup. The Cup, prime trophy of the yachting world, was originally English and known as the One Hundred Guinea Trophy. Won by an American schooner in 1881, it remained in New York despite all attempts at recapture. The Aussies attempted the feat seven times until the *Australia II,* skippered by John Bertrand, finally succeeded. You'll find more about the Cup in Chapter 8 on Perth.

REGIONAL SPORTS

Sporting opportunities are pretty near universal in Australia, but each region has specialties of its own. Herewith is a very brief rundown of their outstanding sporting attractions:

Adelaide Safe, calm-water swimming and sailing. Farther afield, the Southern Ocean ports of Port Lincoln and Kangaroo Island offer some of the best game fishing in Australia—including great white sharks of *Jaws* fame.

Brisbane and the Gold Coast Surfing, swimming, and skindiving in tropical waters. International motor racing.

Great Barrier Reef Skindiving, swimming, big-game fishing with world-record catches of black marlin.

Melbourne The finest golf courses and handsomest racecourses in the country. Australian Rules football with fanatical fans. Close to skiing grounds in the Australian Alps, with the season running from June through September.

Perth Surfing, swimming, and sailing. Harness racing (trotting) is exceptionally popular, with Gloucester Park the best trotting course in the Commonwealth.

Sydney Surfing, yachting, skindiving, powerboating. Offshore game fishing for marlin, sailfish, tuna, and sharks. Within easy reach of skiing grounds.

IMPRESSIONS

People come to Australia for a variety of reasons, some to get warm, some to make a new life (very many of these), some to wait for a scandal to blow over and some, like one old gentleman bringing with him a chauffeur, a white Rolls Royce and some cases of superb Cognac, to play in a croquet tournament.

—Clive Turnbull, *Aspects of Australia,* 1971

Tasmania The best trout fishing in the land. Also some of the best sea fishing, sailing, and mountain climbing.

Another "warning"—if you want to call it that. Australian beaches are topless, though the custom is entirely optional. But if the sight of bare suntanned bosoms offends you, don't go near the water.

9. FOOD & DRINK

FOOD

Australia has excellent food, but even its greatest admirers admit that the country has no such thing as a national cuisine. What passes as native cooking is an adaptation of English and Irish styles—bland, blah, and deathly dull, overcooked and underspiced, the tasteless vegetables barely balanced by the generally superb quality of the meat. The current excellence of the gastronomy is entirely due to the influx of non-English, non-Irish foreigners who not only cook wonderfully themselves but have taught large numbers of Aussies their art. In my listing of good and cheap eateries, the foreign establishments outnumber the native kind by about five to one—a ratio you will appreciate.

But Australia does have a small array of native dishes, ranging from great to gruesome. You should try at least some of them. Kangaroo-tail soup, by the way, is now difficult to obtain here. Kangaroos are a protected species in some states, and what little soup is still being produced gets canned for export, mostly to Japan.

But before we get down to specifics, this may be a good place to explain some Australian menu terms that might cause bafflement. "Entrée" does *not* mean a main course but exactly what the word implies: a dish with which to *start* a meal, an appetizer. "Sweets" is the final course; the term "dessert" is rarely used and frequently unknown. Occasionally you'll see "pudding" instead. This is old-fashioned English terminology and has a certain snob appeal for folks with a Dickensian bend.

NATIONAL SPECIALTIES The Down Under equivalents of hamburgers are meat pies, which Aussies devour at the rate of 680 million a year! This is an amazing concoction: The outer crust consists of soggy pastry, the filling of anonymous meat, and the whole thing is drenched in tomato sauce before consumption. They're sandwich size, weigh six ounces, and seem to weigh as many pounds after you've got them down. Everybody eats them, from members of Parliament to factory workers. A Melbourne football crowd gobbled 40,000 of them on a single memorable Saturday afternoon. Together with chips (french fries) they could be said to form the basic diet of a large segment of the population. To some people (like yours truly) these pies are the closest thing to culinary perdition. But they have found some unexpected champions. When Michel Guerard, one of the world's leading French chefs, tasted a sample, he chewed thoughtfully and then pronounced it *"formidable!"*

Other national specialties include damper, a kind of bush bread originally meant to be baked in the ashes of a campfire. Dampers are made of unleavened wheat flour mixed with water and kneaded into flat cakes three inches thick and up to two feet in diameter. They taste pretty good, providing you put lots of butter and jam on them. And they certainly beat the standard American sliced bread, which seems to consist of equal amounts of cotton wool and blotting paper. But, meat pies aside, the great Australian addiction is to a dark and strong-smelling yeast spread called Vegemite. Addiction is the only word for the fanaticism with which Aussies will drag the stuff with them wherever they go, including Antarctica. Australians abroad have been described as jars of Vegemite closely followed by tourists. Much to their sorrow, this elixir of life is rarely obtainable anywhere beyond Down Under. And, well, it tastes no worse than peanut butter.

FINE DINING But now we come to a batch of Australian specialties I would wager against any delicacy devised in other countries. One of them is roast spring lamb in mint sauce. Others are rabbit pie; carpetbagger steak (beef tenderloin stuffed with oysters); and that simple but wonderful local combination, steak and eggs: a plate-size steak with two fried eggs on top, which *some* farming folks eat for breakfast. Also, there's a selection of seafood that sets me dreaming: the small, sweet Sydney rock oysters; Queensland snapper; the delightfully subtle-tasting barramundi; Moreton Bay bugs, an outrageously misnamed miniature crustacean; Tasmanian scallops; grilled John Dory, an absolutely delicious fish unique to Australian waters; and Victorian yabbies—a small type of lobster—and their larger relative, the crayfish.

FOREIGN CUISINES In general, Australia's cuisine owes its current quality to the dishes served by thousands of small, family-run foreign restaurants that have sprung up during the past few decades—to Greek moussaka, Hungarian goulash, Austrian schnitzel, German Sauerbraten, Czech meat dumplings, Polish sausages, Italian lasagne, Yugoslav razmici, Indian curry, French coq au vin, Middle Eastern felafel, and so on, ad infinitum, usually cooked by Mom and served by Pop and the sons and daughters. It is this influence that has raised the standard of Down Under pub lunches to their present heights as well. Although the pubs are overwhelmingly Anglo-Irish, the chefs aren't.

You'll find a splendid lunchtime alternative in the delicatessen stores, which are among the best, cheapest, and most cosmopolitan I've seen anywhere. In Sydney and Melbourne today, you'll get far better salami, mortadella, rollmops, ham, liptauer, potato salad, camembert, and suchlike than in New York or Chicago, and for considerably less money. The same goes for sandwiches, which are less elaborate but far tastier than their U.S. counterparts. A first-rate meat, fish, or vegetarian sandwich costs between $A1.50 and $A2.50. (Stay away from the baked beans or spaghetti fillings. They're straight out of cans and taste accordingly.) You can follow the example of millions of Australian office workers, who eat their delicatessen lunches while stretched out on the lawn of the nearest park. There's always a park within walking range and usually enough sun to give you a tan while munching.

BUSH TUCKER In recent years Australians have developed a somewhat belated interest in their original native cuisine—the traditional food of the Aborigines. Ignored and despised for centuries, "bush tucker" has suddenly achieved status along with a small but devoted clientele. A TV series on the subject proved extremely popular, giving rise to books, lectures, cooking classes, and at least one commercial processing enterprise.

If you know where, you can now buy bunya nut soup, roasted witchety grubs, crocodile steaks, wild ginger, hairy litchi, grilled ants, sautéed mangrove worms (they taste similar to shrimp), or ground wattle seeds. These and hundreds of other delicacies grow wild in the bushland and were the staple diet of nomadic tribes before white men swept them into oblivion with canned bully beef.

Ironically, you can now get a fairly wide range of "bush tucker" neatly canned and packaged in certain stores. Even more ironically, you can order bush tucker in only a very few, highly select restaurants, all of which are way out of our budget range—and that of most Aborigines, too.

DRINK

BEER & WINE Although I have strong reservations about Australia's national dishes, there's only one word to describe its beers and wines: *magnifique!*

First a word on beer. This is the national drink Down Under, and although in recent years the Aussies have learned to appreciate their wines, beer is still the native nectar. Statistically they down 30 gallons of beer per throat annually—a figure that becomes even more impressive when you remember that this national consumption total counts children and teetotalers. This rate of consumption puts them slightly below the Belgians and Bavarians—but only slightly. On the other hand, Australian beer is so much stronger than the continental, British, or American brews that their intake should count about 20 points more. Be warned: You can get awfully drunk on Australian beer awfully quickly, as many unwary visitors have discovered to their astonishment.

The quality is among the world's highest, particularly in the Tasmanian, Victorian, and Western Australian brands. (Every state has its own breweries.) The only way you can decide for yourself which is best is to taste them, a very pleasant experience. Beer sells in medium-size "middies" or large "schooners," with a middy costing $A1.10 to $A1.50, depending on what part of town and what manner of pub you're in. If you're drinking in company, tradition demands that you "shout" in turn—meaning that every *male* member of the group pays for a round in sequence. But *never* out of sequence. Australians take a dim view of anyone ramming largesse down their gullets—unless he's just backed a winner at the races.

I could wax poetic about Australian wines, but I'll spare you the embarrassment. The Australian wine industry is almost exactly as old as the Californian, and the grapes grow in a very similar climate. There is a striking similarity in both the virtues and the drawbacks of Australian and Californian wines: Both produce great light table wines, not-so-good heavy varieties, and fair champagnes. The Australian surprise is the outstanding quality of the vermouth, dry or sweet, and the Riesling and chardonnay. Australian sherry is fine, by and large, the port less so. The burgundy, Moselle, Chablis, and sauterne are a joy and cheap to boot—as long as you buy them over the counter. Once a restaurant markup goes on top it's a different story. Thus a bottle of good Riesling, which may cost you $A6 in a store, becomes $A8 or more the moment it's served by a waiter.

We have an organized tour of Australia's prime wine region, the Barossa Valley, in Chapter 5 on Adelaide. Meanwhile, if you'd like to know more about the noble Aussie grape, contact the **Australian Wine Export Council,** Box 622, Magill SA 5072 (tel. 08/364-1388).

Australian Liquor Laws Before we leave the subject, let me enlighten you about Australia's liquor laws. The darkness fell during World War I, when the government introduced 6pm closing of hotel bars as a "wartime emergency measure." This "temporary" measure, it turned out, was still in force 40 years and another world war later and looked like it would last for all eternity. Why? Mainly because publicans had discovered the delightful advantages of the "five o'clock swill." During the hour between people getting off from work and the closing of the bars they consumed about as much liquor as they ordinarily would have in a leisurely evening's imbibing. The fact that they did so in conditions resembling a 1-hour cattle stampede didn't interest the grog dispensers in the slightest. They were saving staff wages, electric costs, and all the money they would otherwise have had to spend on making their joints attractive. So why should they have cared if between five and six you needed two hand grenades and a shoehorn to get to the bar?

Consequently the liquor interests linked up with the wowser lobby in preventing any change of the drinking times. Not until the mid-1950s, after several state referendums and an enormous amount of media agitation, was the government persuaded to rescind the hours. Today Australians will proudly point to their "liberalized" drinking spans, which are about as "liberal" as those of 19th-century Boston. (Before you start feeling superior, remember that Americans put up with the "noble experiment" of Prohibition for 15 years and that a whole bunch of countries still do to this day.)

In most places, pubs now stay open from 10am to 11pm: That is, they close at exactly the time when (if you're 18 or older) you're beginning to enjoy yourself. You then have a choice of either trotting off to bed or going to a restaurant with a license that permits selling drinks until midnight or later. The catch is that they're allowed to do so only if they sell you a meal as well. You don't have to eat it, but you must pay for it. Alternatively, some of the large hotels have cocktail bars where they serve liquor to their guests. If you amble in you can get drinks there as well—nobody will ask for your room number. But you'll pay double prices for the privilege, and this will be one of the few occasions when you'll be expected to tip the bartender as well—for letting you pass as a guest.

The only region in Australia unaffected by this legislative idiocy is Canberra, the federal capital. There the politicians have really liberalized the laws: Hostelries serve drinks as long as they please.

COFFEE Finally some comments on coffee. Traditionally the Aussies were a nation of tea drinkers, and tea is still one of their best concoctions. But the triumphant invasion of espresso and cappuccino machines now means that when you order coffee you'll almost automatically get cappuccino. If you don't care for either the froth or the sprinkling of chocolate, make sure to ask for a "flat white." In the cheaper hotels and in small towns it's still safer to stick to tea. The price is the same, between $A1.50 and $A2.50 per cup.

Hotels providing cooking facilities will hardly ever include a coffee percolator among the utensils (but always a teapot). So here is the recipe for French-style open pan or "camp coffee"—in case you feel the way I do and regard instant coffee as a dirty word:

All you need is good-quality coarsely ground coffee. You put the required number of cups of cold water into a saucepan and measure out 1 tablespoon of coffee per cup, plus 2 extra "for the pot." Stir well and heat until the first bubbles form—but *don't* let it boil. Turn down the heat until the brew just barely simmers and let it stand for 8 minutes. Stir it again and pour into a cup through a tea strainer to catch the grounds. The whole trick lies in exact measurement and in not letting it boil. *Voilà*—French coffee!

10. RECOMMENDED BOOKS & FILMS

BOOKS

HISTORY & GEOGRAPHY

Australian Dreaming by Jennifer Isaacs (Lansdowne Press, 1980). Aboriginal history, handed down by oral tradition.

The Australian People by Donald Horne (Angus and Robertson, 1972). The biography of a nation, warts and all.

A Short History of Australia by Charles Manning Clark (Macmillan, 1981). Concise, yet crammed with detail and excellently written.

Ned Kelly in Popular Tradition by Graham Seal (Hyland House, 1980). How a bushranger became a legend.

Under the Iron Rainbow by Osmar White (Heinemann, 1969). The rugged northwest described by a top-ranking journalist.

Australia, by Hammond Innes and Clive Turnbull (Andre Deutsch, 1971). An anthology covering 18 different aspects of the continent.

A Land Half Won by Geoffrey Blainey (Macmillan, 1980). The geographic and economic opening of the country.

FICTION & DICTION

Australian Folklore by W. Fearn-Wannan (Lansdowne Press 1970). A wonderful grab bag of fact and fable, encyclopedic in scope.

The Sentimental Bloke by C. J. Dennis (Angus and Robertson, 1965). The classic verse tale of a city roughneck with a soft core.

The Unspeakable Adams by Phillip Adams (Thomas Nelson, 1979). Selected arrows from the bow of Australia's wittiest columnist.

IMPRESSIONS

In the ocean cities Australians can live the life of the Mediterranean or the South Seas. To some they seem lazy. They are not really lazy, but they don't always take their jobs seriously. They work hard at their leisure.

—DONALD HORNE, *THE LUCKY COUNTRY*, 1964

Hunting the Wild Pineapple by Thea Astley (Putnam's, 1991). An outstanding selection of contemporary short stories.

The Chant of Jimmie Blacksmith by Thomas Keneally (Penguin, 1977). A masterly, searing indictment of racism in Australia.

They're a Weird Mob by Nino Culotta (Angus and Robertson, 1955). Purports to be the saga—often hilarious—of an Italian immigrant in Sydney.

Clancy of the Overflow by "Banjo" Paterson (Angus and Robertson, 1989). Classic Australian poem, splendidly illustrated by Evert Ploeg.

Let Stalk Strine by Afferbeck Lauder (Lansdowne Press, 1982). The definitive textbook on Down Under idiom. The title is the phonetic transliteration of how a native would enunciate "Let us talk Australian."

ART & ARCHITECTURE

The Rocks Sydney by Unk White and Olaf Ruhen (Rigby, 1966). Superb sketches and narrative illustrating the oldest parts of Sydney.

Great Houses of Australia by Douglass and Wilson Baglin (Lansdowne Press, 1984). Beautiful descriptions of some of the finest structures on the continent.

FILMS

The Australian film industry rates a chapter to itself—if I had one to spare. A usually acid-penned U.S. movie critic recently stated, "There seems to be no such thing as a bad Australian film." Which, while not quite accurate, summarizes the reputation Down Under filmmakers have won over the last few years.

The renaissance of the Australian cinema is a wonder to behold. Originally due to enlightened government assistance, it developed into a kind of soul-searching venture: the process of a young nation establishing an identity through the camera. Until around 1970 Australia produced very few and middling dismal movies. Some of its screen artists—Peter Finch, Errol Flynn, Diane Cilento, Leon Errol, Margaret Wilson—achieved international fame, but its films were mostly mediocre copies of English and American movies, lacking any vestige of originality.

The first overseas success was *Walkabout,* followed by *Stormboy,* which won the Best Foreign Entry award at the Moscow Film Festival of 1977. Then, as if the floodgates had opened, came a whole series of cinematic gems, every one bearing an unmistakably national stamp sharply defined as an artist's signature. The age of imitations was over.

The filmic self-portraits were by no means prettified—they showed all the warts. *The Chant of Jimmie Blacksmith* ranks among the most searing indictments of racism ever screened; *Breaker Morant* featured a war crime committed by Australian soldiers; *Gallipoli*'s theme was a total military fiasco; *Winter of Our Dreams* cast a bleak eye at the seamiest side of Sydney. All of them breathed an almost ruthless artistic honesty, a dedicated determination to come to grips with what might be called the collective soul of a country.

Simultaneously the Australian cinema developed its own strain of humor, a mixture of iconoclasm, farce, and sentimentality that looms very large in the national character. Two shining examples of this genre were *Crocodile Dundee,* which overseas audiences took quite seriously but Australians accepted as a joke, and *Malcolm,* the story of a misfit genius containing one of the zaniest episodes in motion-picture history: a bank holdup staged by radio-operated garbage cans on wheels.

The cinematic new wave also offered glimpses of delicate sensitivity few people would have expected from an otherwise pretty brash nation. *The Year My Voice Broke* and *Travelling North* dealt—unforgettably—with the two eternal crises of the human condition: puberty and aging. Most amazing, perhaps, considering the macho tenor of Down Under society, were the films in which the scenario was feminine as well as feminist. *Angel at My Table, Sweetie, The Piano,* and a marvelous collection of short films all directed by Jane Campion, as well as *My Brilliant Career, The Getting of Wisdom,* and *Careful, He Might Hear You* are women's films in the best sense of the word.

Nobody knows how long the current standard of quality will last. Meanwhile make the best of it by seeing Australian movies that may never reach your hometown. The only trouble lies in tracking them down among the piles of imported stuff that make up the routine fare of most Australian movie houses. Cinema prices, incidentally, are about the same as those in the United States, though a few small rerun houses charge as little as $A4.

CHAPTER 2

PLANNING A TRIP TO AUSTRALIA

1. INFORMATION, ENTRY REQUIREMENTS & MONEY
• WHAT THINGS COST IN SYDNEY
2. WHEN TO GO—CLIMATE, HOLIDAYS & EVENTS
• AUSTRALIA CALENDAR OF EVENTS
• SYDNEY CALENDAR OF EVENTS
3. HEALTH & INSURANCE
4. WHAT TO PACK
5. TIPS FOR THE DISABLED, SENIORS, FAMILIES, STUDENTS & SINGLES
6. ALTERNATIVE/ ADVENTURE TRAVEL
7. GETTING THERE
• FROMMER'S SMART TRAVELER: AIRFARES
8. GETTING AROUND
• SUGGESTED ITINERARIES
9. ENJOYING AUSTRALIA ON A BUDGET
• FAST FACTS: AUSTRALIA

This chapter may be the most useful one in the entire book. It tells you when to go, what documents you'll need to get in, what to pack, where to go and stay, where to make inquiries, what to eat and drink, as well as a few things to avoid.

Above all, it tells you how to enjoy the best Australia has to offer at the lowest possible cost. This doesn't mean that you should slavishly follow all the tips listed below. Most are merely money- and aggravation-saving guidelines, leaving plenty of leeway in all directions. The best travelers are always the creative ones—those who use guidebooks like compasses to indicate a general target, who travel at their own pace and according to their own tastes and wallets.

1. INFORMATION, ENTRY REQUIREMENTS & MONEY

SOURCES OF INFORMATION

The **Australian Tourist Commission** is possibly the most helpful, patient, sympathetic, and painstaking outfit ever created by a government. You can approach them with just about any question related to travel, and if they don't know the answer they're almost sure to put you in touch with someone who does. You'll find the addresses of the state (as distinct from federal) tourist bureaus in the appropriate chapters.

The tourist commission also has overseas offices you can consult before starting your trip. You'll find them in **Los Angeles** at 2121 Ave. of the Stars, Suite 1200, Los Angeles, CA 90067 (tel. 310/552-1988); in **New York** at 489 Fifth Ave., 31st Floor, New York, NY 10017 (tel. 212/687-6300); in **London** at Gemini House, 10–18 Putney Hill, Putney, London SW15 (tel. 081/780-2227); and in **Auckland** at Level 13, 44–48 Emily Place, Auckland (tel. 09/379-9594).

ENTRY REQUIREMENTS

DOCUMENTS You need a passport and a visa to enter Australia, unless you happen to be a New Zealander or a citizen of another Commonwealth country with permission to reside in either New Zealand or Australia. Australian visas are free and valid for a stay of up to three months. For a fee of U.S. $25, you can apply for a visa valid for a stay of up to six months or for a visa valid for up to four years, if you expect to make repeat visits. Applications for visa extensions have to be made at an office of the Department of Immigration in Australia and cost $A200. Visitors must also produce a return ticket and "sufficient funds"—whatever that means. Visas can be obtained from Australian or British government offices in major cities. Children up to 18 years may either be included on a parent's passport or have one of their own.

If you are British, Canadian, or Irish and between 18 and 30, you *may* be eligible for a working holiday visa. This entitles you to stay a maximum of three years and take employment during that period. Applications for this visa can be made only in your home country.

CUSTOMS

There are no customs charges on personal belongings that you intend to use in the country and take home again. In addition, you may import duty free 250 cigarettes, or 250 grams of cigars or tobacco, and one liter of alcoholic liquor, plus dutiable goods up to the value of $A400 for your own use or as presents.

QUARANTINE Australia has some of the strictest quarantine laws in the world. You can't bring in fresh or packaged food, fruit, vegetables, seeds, cultures, animals, or plants. If you have plenty of time you *could* bring in a pet, but quarantine laws are so stringent that this is quite impractical for tourists. There are strict laws regarding the import of drugs, firearms, and weapons.

DIPLOMATIC REPRESENTATION

For further information, contact the Australian embassy, consulate, or high commission nearest you:

United States

Australian Embassy, 1601 Massachusetts Ave. NW, **Washington,** DC 20036. (tel. 202/797-3000).

Australian Consulate-General, 1000 Bishop St., Penthouse Suite, **Honolulu,** HI 96813 (tel. 808/524-5050).

Australian Consulate-General, 1990 Post Oak Blvd., Suite 800, **Houston,** TX 77056 (tel. 713/629-9131).

Australian Consulate-General, 611 N. Larchmont Blvd., **Los Angeles,** CA 90004 (tel. 213/469-4300).

Australian Consulate-General, 636 Fifth Ave., 4th Floor, **New York,** NY 10111 (tel. 212/245-4000).

Australian Consulate-General, 1 Bush St., **San Francisco,** CA 94104 (tel. 415/362-6160).

Canada

Australian High Commission, 50 O'Connor St., #710, **Ottawa,** ON K1P 6L2 (tel. 613/236-0841).

Australian Consulate-General, 175 Bloor St. E., #314, **Toronto,** ON M4W 3R8 (tel. 416/323-1155).

Australian Consulate-General, World Trade Centre, 999 Canada Place, #602, **Vancouver,** BC V6C 3E1 (tel. 604/684-1177).

England

Australian High Commission, Australia House, The Strand, **London** WC2B 4LA (tel. 071/379-4334).

New Zealand

Australian High Commission, 72 Hobson St., Thorndon, **Wellington** (tel. 04/473-6411).

MONEY

Australia, you'll be glad to know, reckons in dollars and cents. A dollar is a buck, there as here, but forget about terms like nickels, dimes, and quarters. The Australian dollar ($A) tends to float several points *below* the U.S. buck, but these points vary from month to month. For simplicity's sake assume that all prices mentioned in this book are 40% lower in their American equivalent.

Coins come in 1¢ and 2¢ copper pieces (rarely seen); 5¢, 10¢, 20¢, and 50¢ in silver; and $1 and $2 in brass. Notes (*not* bills) are $5, $10, $20, $50, and $100.

There is no limit on the amount of money you may bring into the country. You may take out any unused foreign or Australian currency in the form of traveler's checks, but no more than $A250 in cash.

NOTE: The prices in this book are in Australian dollars unless indicated otherwise.

Traveler's Checks and Credit Cards

When you look for a bank to cash traveler's checks, keep in mind that service charges not only vary widely but change all the time. Not being a banker, I haven't the faintest idea why this should be so. I suspect it's one of the games cooked up by the gray gnomes of Zürich. The National Australia Bank charges $A5 to cash a foreign-currency traveler's check. The Commonwealth Bank charges $A3 or more for the same service, but most ANZ and Westpac banks charge nothing.

If you run out of traveler's checks, you can buy more at any **American Express** office provided you are one of their cardmembers and have remembered to bring a personal check on your home account. The headquarters of American Express in Australia is 388 George St., Sydney, NSW 2000 (tel. 02/239-0666).

It can be awkward to purchase items at a shop or pay for meals with foreign-currency traveler's checks because the personnel involved will probably not know the value of your check in Australian dollars. During banking hours this dilemma is easily solved, but after hours it can be a real problem. The simplest way to buy things and pay the tab in restaurants and hotels is to use a credit card.

Another alternative is to buy Aussie-dollar traveler's checks. You could get a cash advance against your MasterCard or VISA and use the money to buy traveler's checks in the local currency. Then you'd have the convenience of cash and the security of traveler's checks.

THE AUSTRALIAN DOLLAR, THE U.S. DOLLAR & THE BRITISH POUND

At this writing, U.S. $1 = about $A1.40 and U.K.£1 = about $A2.10. These rates fluctuate and may not be the same when you travel in Australia. Therefore, the accompanying table should be used only as a guide. Also remember that you usually receive a less-favorable exchange rate when you buy Aussie bucks in America or Great Britain or cash traveler's checks at Australian airports or currency exchanges or hotels. The best rates are usually those offered by banks.

$A	U.S.$	U.K.£	$A	U.S.$	U.K.£
0.25	0.18	0.12	6.00	4.29	2.86
0.50	0.36	0.24	7.00	5.00	3.33
0.75	0.54	0.36	8.00	5.71	3.81
1.00	0.71	0.48	9.00	6.43	4.29
1.50	1.07	0.71	10.00	7.14	4.76
2.00	1.43	0.95	12.00	8.57	5.71
2.50	1.79	1.19	14.00	10.00	6.67
3.00	2.14	1.43	16.00	11.43	7.62
3.50	2.50	1.67	18.00	12.86	8.57
4.00	2.86	1.90	20.00	14.29	9.52
4.50	3.21	2.14	30.00	21.43	14.29
5.00	3.57	2.38	50.00	35.71	23.81

American Express, Bankcard, Diners Club, MasterCard, and VISA are widely accepted at hotels, restaurants, and stores throughout Australia. Carte Blanche can also be used in some places. Since some establishments take one card and not another, I suggest that you carry two.

You can obtain a cash advance with a credit card at banks in Australia. If you carry VISA, the ANZ Bank should be able to help you. With MasterCard, head for a Westpac Bank.

WHAT THINGS COST IN SYDNEY

	$A
Taxi from Kingsford Smith Airport to City	18.00
Bus from Airport to City	6.00
Local telephone call	0.30
Double room at The Medina (expensive)	125.00
Double room at Barclay Hotel (moderate)	50.00–60.00
Double room at Springfield Lodge (budget)	44.00
Dinner for one, without wine, at Kings Cross Steak House (moderate)	18.00
Dinner for one, without wine, at No Names (budget)	11.00
Can of local beer	1.60
Cup of coffee	1.60
Haircut (either sex)	16.00
Admission to Museum of Contemporary Art	6.00

2. WHEN TO GO — CLIMATE, HOLIDAYS & EVENTS

CLIMATE

Keep in mind that Australia is a continent as well as a country, so the climate varies accordingly. The variations are not as great as those in America but sharp enough to make you regret wearing the wrong clothes during certain seasons. The seasons are the reverse of those in the northern hemisphere: September to November is spring, December to February summer, March to May fall, and June to August winter.

The climate regions are upside down as well. The tropics lie north, the temperate zones south. Tasmania, the island state off the southeastern tip of the continent, is the coolest, while north of Brisbane temperatures stay pretty hot most of the year. As a general rule you can assume that from November to March it's warm to broiling everywhere. In the far north—around Darwin—this is the monsoon season and definitely a time to stay away unless you enjoy getting drenched in lukewarm rainwater. But the northern winter offers close to ideal traveling weather—days of crystal-clear sunshine, strong enough to tan, and nights crisp enough for you to appreciate a fireplace. In the south, winter tends to be chilly, with plenty of snow and excellent skiing in the mountain ranges. But even in Melbourne, the most southerly of the mainland capitals, the mercury rarely hits the freezing point. Tasmania, however, has an almost—but not quite—European winter. All around, Australia can be said to have superb tourist weather, particularly in the capital cities that lie outside the extreme hot and cold belts.

Australia's Average Monthly Temperatures [°F] and Rainy Days*

	Winter			Spring			Summer			Fall		
	June	July	Aug	Sept	Oct	Nov	Dec	Jan	Feb	Mar	Apr	May
Adelaide												
Max. Temp.	61	59	62	66	73	79	83	86	86	81	73	66
Min. Temp.	47	45	46	48	51	55	59	61	62	59	55	50
Rainy Days	8	8	8	6	5	3	3	3	3	9	9	10
Alice Springs												
Max. Temp.	67	67	73	81	88	93	96	97	95	90	81	73
Min. Temp.	41	39	43	49	58	64	68	70	69	63	54	46
Rainy Days	3	2	2	1	2	4	4	5	4	9	8	8
Brisbane												
Max. Temp.	69	68	71	76	80	82	85	85	85	82	79	74
Min. Temp.	51	49	50	55	60	64	67	69	68	66	61	56
Rainy Days	7	7	6	5	7	10	11	12	12	13	11	12
Cairns												
Max. Temp.	79	78	80	83	86	88	90	90	89	87	85	81
Min. Temp.	64	61	62	64	68	70	73	74	74	73	70	66
Rainy Days	10	9	8	8	9	10	13	19	18	20	16	12

	Winter			Spring			Summer			Fall		
	June	July	Aug	Sept	Oct	Nov	Dec	Jan	Feb	Mar	Apr	May
Canberra												
Max. Temp.	53	52	55	61	68	75	80	82	82	76	67	60
Min. Temp.	34	33	35	38	43	48	53	55	55	51	44	37
Rainy Days	7	6	7	5	6	5	5	5	5	10	9	9
Darwin												
Max. Temp.	86	87	89	91	93	94	92	90	90	91	92	91
Min. Temp.	69	67	70	74	77	78	78	77	77	77	76	73
Rainy Days	2	1	2	1	6	11	15	18	17	16	11	8
Hobart												
Max. Temp.	53	52	55	59	63	66	69	71	71	68	63	58
Min. Temp.	41	40	41	43	46	48	51	53	53	51	48	44
Rainy Days	7	7	6	6	7	7	6	5	4	9	10	9
Melbourne												
Max. Temp.	57	56	59	63	67	71	75	78	78	75	68	62
Min. Temp.	44	42	43	46	48	51	54	57	57	55	51	47
Rainy Days	7	6	6	7	7	7	6	5	5	10	10	10
Perth												
Max. Temp.	64	63	67	70	76	81	73	85	85	81	76	69
Min. Temp.	50	48	48	50	53	57	61	63	63	61	57	53
Rainy Days	14	13	12	9	8	2	2	2	2	8	9	12
Sydney												
Max. Temp.	61	60	63	67	71	74	77	78	78	76	71	66
Min. Temp.	48	46	48	51	56	60	63	65	65	63	58	52
Rainy Days	11	11	8	8	8	8	7	8	9	12	13	12

*Source: Australian Tourist Commission, *Destination Australia (1993–1994)*.

HOLIDAYS

Australians celebrate plenty of national holidays, many on Monday to prolong the cherished weekend. All banks, post offices, government agencies, and private offices close, as do most shops. On top of these, all states—and some cities—have local holidays, such as the celebrated Cup Day in Melbourne in early November. **National holidays** in Australia are New Year's Day (January 1), Australia Day (January 26), Good Friday through Easter Monday, Anzac Day (April 25), Queen's Official Birthday (early June), Christmas Day (December 25), and Boxing Day (December 26).

These holidays affect hotel bookings and transport reservations, and most resort hostelries raise their prices on these dates. A similar situation arises during school holidays. These occur from mid-December until early February and in May, August, and September. Traffic, as well as bookings, is then at its peak in vacation areas.

AUSTRALIA CALENDAR OF EVENTS

JANUARY

☐ **Australia Day,** various cities. A Fourth of July of sorts, celebrating the landing of the first settlers. January 26.

FEBRUARY–MARCH

✪ ***Adelaide Festival of the Arts.*** *By far the most important cultural event in Australia, it features nearly all genres of theater, dance, and music by worldwide performers, as well as Aboriginal ceremonies, parades, films, and other events.*

Where: *Adelaide.* ***When:*** *Late February to early March.* ***How:*** *For more information, write to the General Manager, Adelaide Festival Centre, GPO Box 1269, Adelaide, SA 5001, or call 08/213-4788 (inquiries) or 08/213-4777 (reservations).*

- ☐ **Canberra Festival,** Canberra. The city celebrates with 10 days of sporting and performing-arts events, culminating in early March.
- ☐ **Moomba Festival,** Melbourne. Ten days of 175 events and highly versatile festivities, including concerts, parades, and exhibitions. Early March.

APRIL

- ☐ **Barossa Valley Vintage Festival,** Germanic folk dancing and joyous oompah music accompany this celebration featuring vintage-car parades, sheep shearing contests, and, of course, a plethora of wine tastings. First week of April.

MAY

- ☐ **Bangtail Muster,** Alice Springs. Named after the old practice of cutting the tails of horses before shipment, this rodeo also features a comic float parade lampooning current events and public figures. First Monday in May.
- ☐ **Camel Cup,** Alice Springs. That's right, camel races—which you may or may not want to view within spitting distance. Early May.

JUNE

- ☐ **Bougainvillea Festival,** Darwin. The highlight of this celebration of the start of the dry season is the Beer Can Regatta, in which all competing craft are constructed of used beer cans. Early June.
- ☐ **Western Australia Festival,** Perth and throughout the state. Open-air concerts, exhibitions, and parades are featured. June 3 to June 9.
- ☐ **Queensland Day,** Brisbane and throughout the state. Dates vary.
- ☐ **Melbourne Film Festival,** Melbourne. New films make their debut here and in Sydney. First three weeks of June.

JULY

- ☐ **Royal Darwin Show,** Darwin. The city displays the wealth, sporting spirit, and artistry of the Northern Territory.

AUGUST

- ☐ **Alice Springs Rodeo,** Alice Springs. August 20.
- ☐ **Festival of the Pearl,** Broome. This celebration recalls the era when Broome was the continent's pearling capital and naked divers risked their lives bringing up the beauties from shark-infested waters.
- ☐ **Apex Rodeo.** Top contenders from all over the continent compete in roughriding, bull riding, calf roping, and bareback riding, often on brumbies—freshly lassoed wild horses. August 20 to August 21.

SEPTEMBER–OCTOBER

- ☐ **Warana Festival,** Brisbane. Taken from the Aboriginal word meaning "blue skies," this annual carnival-like festival includes a huge street procession with floats and clowns, dancing in the squares, a riverside Mardi Gras, beauty competitions, pop-and-symphony concerts, and art exhibitions. Late September to early October.

OCTOBER

- ☐ **Henley-On-Todd,** Alice Springs. Bottomless boats propelled by foot compete on the dry riverbed of the Todd, with the ever-present danger of being capsized by a gust of wind. Early October.
- ☐ **Fun in the Sun Festival,** Cairns. The city marks the official start of summer with flowers everywhere. Also included are float processions, public dancing, and water-sport competitions. October 12.

NOVEMBER

- ☐ **Melbourne Cup Day,** Melbourne. This horseracing event at Flemington Racecourse is the largest in the southern hemisphere and is equally a fashion parade and society event. First Tuesday in November.
- ☐ **Australian Formula One Grand Prix,** Adelaide. The last and most crucial event on the Formula One calendar, this event makes a motor-racing circuit out of the city streets.

DECEMBER

- ☐ **Carols by Candlelight,** various cities. This balmy summer-evening event signals the approach of Christmas Down Under.
- ☐ **Salamanca Arts Festival,** Hobart. A week-long arts and theatrical event staged in the Salamanca Arts Centre on the city's historic waterfront. Begins December 28.

SYDNEY CALENDAR OF EVENTS

JANUARY

- ☐ **Festival of Sydney.** The Australian new year begins with a pleasantly chaotic mixture of artistic, theatrical, and sporting events: art exhibitions, open-air concerts, Mardi Gras parades, strolling minstrels, and capering clowns. The grand finale is the Harbour Ferrython, an armada review of harbor ferries, followed by a ferry race. On Australia Day, January 26, the living descendents of the First Fleet (1788) don the costumes of their forebears who landed on these shores and became the continent's first settlers—involuntary settlers, perhaps, but still the first. All January.

FEBRUARY

- ☐ **Chinese New Year,** Sydney and various cities. Sydney's Chinatown (the Haymarket area) is the focal point of the festivities, dragons and all. Dates vary.
- ☐ **Gay and Lesbian Mardi Gras Parade.** Featuring some of the most fantastic costuming you're ever likely to behold, the parade rolls right through the downtown streets and features theatrical events. Date varies.

APRIL

- ✪ ***Royal Easter Agricultural Show.*** *The cream of Australia's livestock and agricultural products compete for coveted awards and share the spotlight with home arts, farming equipment, parades, circus acts, and musical entertainment.*

Where: *Moore Park Showground.* ***When:*** *Twelve days before Easter.* ***How:*** *Write to the Royal Agricultural Society of NSW, GPO Box 4317. Sydney, NSW 2001 (tel. 02/331-9111).*

- ☐ **Sydney Cup.** Although it is not as glamorous as the Melbourne Cup, some of Australia's finest horses and top society turn out for this event. Mid-April.

JUNE

- ☐ **Sydney Film Festival.** Held in various theaters (check the newspapers), the festival brings out the newest and most innovative Australian films (some great, some woeful), along with an array of international imports—for which the same adjectives apply. Dates vary.

AUGUST

- ☐ **Around Australia Yacht Race.** Beginning in Sydney Harbour, this is the second-biggest sailing event in the country. Late August.

SEPTEMBER

- ☐ **Rugby League Grand Final.** At the Aussie equivalent of the Super Bowl, some 40,000 fans ("barrackers") crowd into the football stadium in Moore Park to munch meat pies and yell their lungs out, accompanied by large contingents of police and a first-aid staff. Date varies.
- ☐ **Open Day.** The famous Sydney Opera sponsors an operatic pageant. Date varies.

DECEMBER

- ☐ **Sydney-Hobart Yacht Race.** Colorful billowing spinnakers offer a magnificent spectacle in *the* canvas classic Down Under. If you can't find room on the harbor, the next-best vantage point is Lady Macquarie's Chair in the Botanic Gardens. December 26 to December 29.

3. HEALTH & INSURANCE

HEALTH PREPARATIONS

You'll encounter very few health hazards Down Under. The water is safe to drink and health care is first rate. You need vaccination certificates against smallpox and yellow fever *only* if you've visited a country infected with these diseases within 14 days of visiting Australia. You may take 4 weeks' supply of prescribed medication into the country, and more with a doctor's prescription. It's a good idea to bring along a copy of your written prescription using the generic name for the medication in case a question arises, although local pharmacies (chemists) can fill prescriptions written by Australian doctors only. Pack all medication in your carry-on luggage, so you will still have it with you even if your checked suitcase is lost.

Be sure to use sunscreen, sunglasses, and a visor or hat: Don't underestimate the strength of the Australian sun. It's no coincidence that Aussies have the highest rate of skin cancer in the world.

INSURANCE

Before purchasing any additional insurance, check your homeowner, automobile, and medical insurance policies. Also check the membership contracts issued by automobile and travel clubs and by credit-card companies. If, after close examination, you feel you still need insurance, consider the following.

HEALTH/ACCIDENT Many credit-card companies insure their users in case o travel accident, provided a ticket was purchased with their card. Sometimes fraternal organizations have policies that protect members in case of sickness or accidents abroad.

The best policies provide advances in cash or transferrals of funds so that you won't have to dip into your travel funds to settle any medical bills you might incur while away from home. To submit a claim, you'll need documentation from a medical authority that you did suffer the illness for which you are seeking compensation.

Another insurance option is **Travel Assistance International,** 1133 15th St. NW, Suite 400, Washington, DC 20005 (tel. toll free 800/821-2828), which offers travel coverage up to $A5,000 for urgent hospital care and medical evacuation back to the United States if necessary. For an additional fee you can be covered for trip cancellation, lost baggage, and accidental death and dismemberment. The fee depends on how long you plan to stay. Fees begin at $A40 per person ($A60 for family) for a 1- to 8-day trip. You can call a 24-hour "hotline" number (tel. 202/347-7113 in Washington; toll free 800/368-7878 in the United States and Canada) that will put you in touch with agents all over Europe.

LOSS/THEFT Many homeowner insurance policies cover theft of luggage during foreign travel and loss of documents—your passport or your airline ticket, for instance. Coverage is usually limited to about U.S. $500. To submit a claim on your insurance, you'll need police reports that you did in fact suffer the loss for which you are seeking compensation. Such claims can be filed only when you return from your journey.

CANCELLATION If you've booked a charter fare, you will probably have to pay a cancellation fee if you cancel a trip suddenly, even if it is due to an unforeseen crisis. It's possible to get insurance against such a possibility. Some travel agencies provide this coverage, and often flight insurance against a canceled trip is written into tickets paid for by credit cards from such companies as VISA and American Express. Many tour operators or insurance agents provide this type of insurance.

INSURERS Among the companies offering such health, loss, and cancellation policies are: **Travel Guard Internationale,** 1145 Clark St., Stevens Point, WI 54481 (tel. toll free 800/826-1300 in Wisconsin, 800/826-1300 outside Wisconsin), which offers a comprehensive 7-day policy that covers basically everything.

4. WHAT TO PACK

Two words on packing in general—*travel light.* Never bring more luggage than you yourself can carry without assistance. Porters aren't always available at air terminals and rail stations, and those handy little luggage carts have a knack of disappearing just when you need them. The ideal tourist baggage consists of one suitcase and a shoulder bag. In that respect those who follow this book are more fortunate than I, who wrote it. They don't have to lug a typewriter.

CLOTHING The wearables you should pack naturally depend on what time of the year you come and what you want to do (consult the section on climate in "When to Go," above).

Leave at home tropical whites for men, which spot hideously. Anyway, in torrid zones Australian males wear khaki. Include at least one warm sweater or jacket, even if you come in summer. You get occasional cold snaps everywhere except in the tropical north. A man should also bring a tie (an ascot will do), since there are still a few restaurants and hotel dining rooms around that won't serve you without one. Otherwise Australians are very casual dressers, although women tend to wear more skirts and fewer pants than Americans. But ladies' pantsuits are now universally accepted even as formal wear.

stralian warm-weather outfit for men is both smart and eminently practical: rts, high socks, shoes, and a short-sleeved shirt with or without a tie. They the office and almost everywhere else. The shorts are tighter in the butt merican versions, usually khaki or some other solid color, and *never* lowered. The whole ensemble looks faintly military and very neat.

Women needn't bother to stock up on pantyhose. They're sold everywhere—and cheaply—in Australia.

If you come in winter, the handiest item either sex can bring is an all-weather coat with a detachable lining. That, combined with a scarf, gloves, and a small travel umbrella, should see you through whatever the Down Under winter has in store.

OTHER ITEMS There are a few items you should bring under all circumstances, regardless of seasons and intentions. One is a washcloth in a plastic case; very few Aussie hotels supply them to their guests. A travel alarm clock makes you independent of hotel wake-up calls, which are pretty unreliable. Other items include sunglasses; a very small screwdriver (in 15 years of globe-trotting I've found that to be one of the handiest gadgets extant); a cigarette lighter (matches don't come free of charge anywhere outside America, and the standard Australian wood matches cost A30¢ a box); one pair of light plastic shoe trees; a magnifying glass to read the tiny print on maps; and stationery and envelopes, since these items are much more expensive in Australia than in the United States (the same goes for film).

Leave at home any kind of electrical gadgetry, unless you bring along a 220 to 240V, flat three-pin plug converter/adapter.

You should beware of taking any cosmetic liquid in glass bottles; stick to unbreakable plastic. International brand names of cosmetics are sold throughout Australia, and the local products are excellent and usually much cheaper.

5. TIPS FOR THE DISABLED, SENIORS, FAMILIES, STUDENTS & SINGLES

FOR THE DISABLED Australia takes great care to provide facilities for disabled visitors, in both transportation and accommodation. However, a good many of the older (and cheaper) establishments lack wheelchair access and may have steep stairs and no elevators. For a list of travel agents and tour operators specializing in travel for people with disabilities, contact **ACROD,** 33 Thesiger Court, Deakin, ACT 2605 (tel. 06/282-4333).

NICAN is an Australian database of details of organizations offering sport, recreation, tourism, and art information for the disabled. They also have access to the Australian Automobile Association's database of accommodations rated as either "fully wheelchair accessible" or "wheelchair accessible with assistance." Contact the Information Officer, **NICAN,** P.O. Box 407, Curtin, ACT 2605 (tel. 06/285-3713).

FOR SENIORS Unfortunately, few of the discounts available to Australian seniors apply to tourists, since you have to show an Australian Pensioner's Card to get them. However, several U.S. groups have programs for independent senior travelers Down Under (providing you are a member). These programs include motor travel, hotel, rail, airfare, and bus discounts and apartment bookings. The biggest group is the **American Association of Retired Persons (AARP),** 1909 K St. NW, Washington, DC 20049 (tel. 202/662-4850).

FOR FAMILIES All international airlines provide discounts for children, as do Australian internal air, bus, and rail lines (see the appropriate chapters). Infants not occupying separate seats usually fly at a fractional rate.

If you're traveling with infants, you'll be invited to board the aircraft before other passengers. Since strollers can be taken only as far as the aircraft door (they're stored in the hold for the flight) a "papoose"-type baby carrier comes in handy at transit stops. You can get free Baby Travel Packs on board the aircraft. These contain panty diapers, bib, table mat, cotton balls, washcloth, towels, and change lotion.

For older children cabin crews will supply coloring books, finger puppets, books, magic slates, and playing cards. But it's even better if you equip each kid with a little carry bag containing whatever items will keep them amused.

Special children's "Mini Meals" are available on aircraft, but you have to order them at the time of reservation. The same applies to special dishes needed if your child has food allergies.

Juvenile rates in Aussie hotels vary considerably. Some provide free roll-away beds, others charge for them. Some allow children up to certain ages to share a room with their parent(s) free, others charge heavily discounted rates. (See each chapter's "Where to Stay" section for individual hotels.) But very few budget establishments offer special facilities for children. Playrooms and day-care centers are pretty much a preserve of the deluxe bracket.

FOR STUDENTS Every major city in this book has a segment entitled "Campus Accommodations" listing the quarters Australian universities make available to outside visitors. These facilities are among the best (though not the cheapest) listed here. Conditions and rates differ considerably from college to college, as do the periods when they are available.

You should also get an International Student Identity Card, one of the handiest documents extant. It entitles you to special transport rates as well as discount tickets to sporting events, museums, exhibitions, and some theaters. Apply to the **Council on International Educational Exchange,** 205 E. 42nd St., New York, NY 10017 (tel. 212/661-1414).

FOR SINGLES Lone female tourists are rarely hassled in Australia, except in certain districts (like Sydney's Kings Cross, where propositioning passes as a conversation opener). However, the pub scene is still pretty much a male stamping ground, particularly in suburbia. Women will get some heavily inquisitive stares if they enter on their own. In pairs or groups they are readily accepted. In discos and other nightspots, the macho element does not apply and women frequently form the majority.

There is very little segregated accommodation available. Most of the Ys have long abandoned their sex distinctions, and—to the best of my knowledge—only one "Girls Hostel" survives (see Chapter 7 on Cairns). A few hostels have separate floors for females; most simply separate the dorms and bathrooms. But while this entails a certain lack of privacy, it seldom results in unwelcome attention. Both management and hostel dwellers deal very quickly with overzealous Casanovas.

The real drawback in solo travel is economical. A hotel may charge a single guest $A30 per night. For two persons in the same room the rate would be around $A40—meaning $A20 per occupant. The advantage of teaming up with someone becomes even greater when you rent serviced apartments with kitchens, the best of all accommodation deals and mostly unaffordable for singles. The same applies to rental cars, which can be the cheapest transport when used by three or four travelers.

This is the reason why the notice boards in hostels usually display hand-scrawled ads like "Looking for Companion" or "Third to make a Trio." A follow-up can work out to everyone's advantage. But before committing yourself to any such venture make sure of two vital points: the *kind* of travel and accommodations your colleagues have in mind and that *all* expenses (including, say, gas) are to be shared equally.

A U.S.-based group called **Travelin' Singles** (tel. 213/920-9009 or 818/902-9945) occasionally offers trips to Australia.

6. ALTERNATIVE/ADVENTURE TRAVEL

FARMHOUSE HOLIDAYS These are great ideas, providing you really enjoy country life and can do without the "bright lights" and whatever goes with them. A number of farms (stations) throughout Australia offer accommodations for paying guests, usually no more than five to eight at a time. The host farms change frequently, so it's best to get a current list of choices from the state government tourist bureau, which also tells you conditions, facilities, and prices and will arrange bookings. It can be a fascinatingly "different" experience, particularly if you have a modicum of interest in agriculture.

Accommodations vary considerably—as do the tariffs. Some homesteads offer independent cottages on their properties. Others put up guests in their houses, which means that you take all your meals with the host families and, in some cases, share their bathrooms. Still others provide completely independent guest wings with all private facilities. On some places you may—but don't have to—join in the farm activities. But all of them offer you the run of the place. You're free to fish in the creeks, ride the horses, and swim in the waterholes (or the family pool). The hospitality is invariably warm: You're treated as a member of the family. And the meals are country style—meaning enormous. Rates depend on the standard of accommodations and on whether you take bed-and-breakfast only or dinner as well. The range hovers between $A30 and $A50 per person a day.

BACKPACKING Every chapter of this book has a list of establishments catering to backpackers. Their rates are usually a bit above those charged by youth hostels but well below those of the Ys. You should try to get hold of a very handy bimonthly publication, *Aussie Backpacker,* which floats around wherever the packers gather. Write to ***Aussie Backpacker,*** P.O. Box 1264, Townsville, Queensland 4810, Australia.

There is also a **Backpackers Travel Centre,** Imperial Arcade, Pitt St., Mall Level, Sydney, 2000 NSW, Australia (tel. 02/232-5166), where you can purchase a $A10 VIP card that gets you discounts in hostels and on most (not all) bus lines.

BICYCLING Bicycles, known as "pushbikes" Down Under, don't eat up much of the continent's vast distances but are great for short jaunts. This applies particularly to Tasmania, the little island state. Every city has bike-rental outlets (mentioned in individual chapters) and you can, if you wish, join a cycling organization that arranges group tours. These come in all price ranges, but a sample would be a $A100 weekend excursion, camping gear included. Bike rentals depend on the type of bike and the length of time, starting at around $A5 per hour. Keep in mind, though, that Northern Queensland is tropical, so the cycling season there is only from April to October.

Cycling organizations include **Tasmanian Expeditions,** 59 Brisbane St., Launceston, TAS 7250 (tel. 003/34-3477), and a number of groups posted in youth hostels.

CANOEING Canoeing in Australia can mean anything from a gentle paddle along green banks to a white-water shoot or a jungle river cruise—depending on where you go. The craft can be hired at every town by a river at rates of around $A10 per hour, fishing gear extra. But if you pick one of the finest fishing rivers in the country, the Daly River in the Northern Territory, you'd better keep an eye peeled for crocodiles.

HOME EXCHANGES Trading your own home for someone else's in Australia for the duration can be ideal, providing that you know exactly *where* the home is located (check the maps and descriptions in this book), and you retain some freedom of movement—that is, you aren't expected to be there all the time. Several organizations publish lists of available homes and will assist you with arrangements, including **Vacation Exchange Club,** 12006 Young Town, AZ 85363 (tel. 602/972-2186); and **Loan-a-Home,** 2 Park Lane, GE Mt. Vernon, NY 10552 (tel. 914/664-7640).

7. GETTING THERE

The major item in any Australian travel budget is the cost of getting there. Time—which was once the top consideration—has become almost insignificant: You can now fly from San Francisco or Los Angeles to Sydney in just 14 hours and 40 minutes. And you can, by careful planning, minimize the price of that very big initial hop.

BY PLANE

Although Australia is still served by shipping lines and cruise companies, the vast majority of visitors prefer air travel. More than 20 international airlines will take you to Australia, but many of them take the long way around—via London, Frankfurt, or Tokyo.

Some advice for your flight: Let's face it, 14½ hours in the air is a *long* haul, more than most Americans have traveled before in one shot. During those hours you zip through four time zones, pass through the tropics, and arrive in a climate that is seasonally opposite from the one you left. What's more, the calendar gets slightly scrambled in the process. When you cross the international date line in mid-Pacific, you lose a day. So, when departing on Monday, you arrive on Wednesday. On the return journey you get it back; that is, you depart Australia on Friday and arrive in the United States on Friday.

Human bodies react to this kind of rapid transit with a curious 20th-century malaise called jet lag. In extreme cases, it can ruin the first couple of days after your arrival if you don't plan your activities well. Here are a few tips for avoiding jet lag:

Go easy on food and liquor, especially liquor, even though there's no charge on board. Good airlines tend to overfeed you at a time when your body gets no exercise. Once in a while take a walk around the aircraft or stand in the aisle for a while. Have a drink of water or a soft drink every four hours.

The best idea, if possible, is to stretch out across the seats and get as much sleep as possible. But if you can't sleep and fly, make sure you catch up on your slumber after arrival. Don't push yourself at first.

From North America

All the international carriers flying to Australia are good. On a hike like that they couldn't neglect your comfort and hope to stay in business for long. Carriers include **Air New Zealand** (tel. toll free 800/262-1234), **Canadian Airlines** (tel. toll free 800/426-7000), **Qantas** (tel. toll free 800/227-4500, and **United Airlines** (tel. toll free 800/631-1500).

Qantas offers the most flights, some 47 per week from the United States and Canada, 10 of them nonstop. It is also the only carrier that gives you a choice of afternoon or late-evening departures. The afternoon departure is a blessing for folks who suffer from jet lag. The flight arrives in Sydney just at bedtime, so you can catch a good night's sleep and wake up bright eyed next morning.

The Qantas ticket offices in Los Angeles and San Francisco can also issue Australian visas to travelers. This means that Qantas ticket holders can complete their travel formalities at the same time they make their airline bookings. All flights from North America leave from San Francisco, Los Angeles, or Vancouver. To reach your point of departure you can utilize the special add-on fares. These are very low fares from U.S. cities to the departure points. As their name suggests, add-on fares are added to your international ticket when you purchase it and cannot be bought separately. Qantas operates a partnership service with American Airlines from New York, Chicago, Boston, and Washington, D.C.

Best-for-the-Budget Fares

The key factor in determining airfares is *when* you travel. All airlines have different price ranges for low season, shoulder season, and high season. These seasons correspond roughly to winter, spring, and summer Down Under; although this doesn't apply to the tropical regions, which have seasons all their own. (See chapters on Queensland and Northern Territory.) Remember that Australian seasons are the reverse of yours—that is, winter is summer Down Under, so that the highest rates apply when it's coldest here and hottest there. If you choose to travel in high season you're likely to depart from, say, a subzero New York and land in a sweltering Sydney.

Qantas has three seasons: basic (April to August); shoulder (March and September to November); and peak (December to February). The normal price on an economy round-trip ticket from Los Angeles or San Francisco to Sydney, Melbourne, Brisbane, or Cairns is U.S. $2,008 basic, U.S. $2,108 shoulder, U.S. $2,308 peak.

In addition, most airlines offer promotional bargain fares hedged with stringent requirements, such as minimum and maximum stays, advance bookings, and cancellation penalties. The most common of these deals is the APEX (Advance Purchase Excursion). Details vary with every carrier and tend to change rapidly, so I would advise you to do some comparison shopping.

SUPER-APEX This is one of the best bargains Qantas offers. You can fly economy from San Francisco or Los Angeles during midweek in basic season for U.S. $948 round-trip, shoulder season U.S. $1,048, peak U.S. $1,248. These are point-to-point fares; no stopovers permitted. You must purchase your ticket at least 21 days before departure and stay in Australia at least 7 days, but not longer than 1 month.

CUSTOM-APEX This allows you one free stopover in addition to your point of turnaround. The ticket to Sydney, Melbourne, Brisbane, or Cairns costs U.S. $1,098 for midweek departure in basic season, U.S. $1,198 shoulder, U.S. $1,398 in peak season. For an additional U.S. $150 you can buy unlimited stopovers in Australia, New Zealand, Tahiti, and Fiji.

EXCURSION South Pacific Excursion fares have no advance purchase requirements, but stipulate a minimum 7-day, maximum 6 months stay. You get a maximum of six stops plus point of turnaround on your journey, letting you visit Australia, New Zealand, Fiji, and Tahiti. Round-trip fare in basic season is U.S. $2,008, shoulder U.S. $2,108, peak U.S. $2,308.

GROUP FARES These can mean substantial savings for any club, association, or impromptu group traveling together. However, every airline seems to have a different policy regarding group bookings. Your best bet is to contact several airline sales offices and see what kind of deal they're offering. It will depend on the season and the size of your group.

COURIER TRAVEL Air couriers are employed by companies that fly important documents or special pieces of equipment around the globe and want someone to accompany these items. About 35,000 Americans fly each year as air couriers, but it is a popular fallacy that they travel free. They don't—but they do fly at a fraction of the regular fare. The usual rate is about 50% less, though it can go as low as 15%, depending on the cargo and the urgency of the trip. On one memorable occasion a

FROMMER'S SMART TRAVELER: AIRFARES

1. Fly on a weekday. Weekend airfares are frequently higher.
2. Make use of the special discount fares offered to overseas visitors flying *inside* Australia.
3. Shop *all* airlines flying to Australia. New, competitive outfits may have entered the market.
4. Ask about fly-drive package deals but stay clear of those that include hotels, which are almost invariably in the deluxe range.
5. Ask about frequent-flyer programs that will give you bonus points.
6. If you're told that no cheap seats are available, call again—and again—closer to your departure date. Low-cost seats often materialize at the last moment.
7. Find out about the cheapest transportation from airport to city before you actually land.

courier was employed to fly the toupee of a famous movie actor from California to a film location in Scotland within 12 hours.

Courier flights have some drawbacks. Usually couriers get no baggage space and can take only carry-on luggage. And their length of stay is as a rule fixed at 7, 14 or 21 days. Otherwise the rules are casual. You should be reasonably neatly dressed and should not drink liquor in flight. It's a great plus if you're familiar with the airport you're flying from and to. Occasionally you'll have to fly at a moment's notice, though in most cases you get several days to prepare.

Competition for courier jobs is hot and heavy. The best way to get a start is to join the **International Association of Air Travel Couriers,** 8 S."J" St., P.O. Box 1349, Lake Worth, FL 33460 (tel. 407/582-8320). For a U.S. $35 annual fee they will send you a regular newsletter and bulletins informing you of available courier jobs.

STANDBYS At present there are no standby fares to Australia, but that situation could change at any time.

For discounts on travel within Australia, see "Getting Around," below.

8. GETTING AROUND

Keep in mind that Australia is a very large country (nearly three million square miles) with a relatively small population (about 17.3 million). Furthermore, most of the people live bunched together in five state capitals, leaving precious few for the immense hinterland. From the traveler's point of view, this means vast distances to cover between population centers.

DISTANCES FROM SYDNEY Since Sydney represents the entry point for most tourists, here is a table of air distances and traveling times between that city and some of the others described in this book:

To Alice Springs: 1,257 miles, 2⅗ hours by jet, 64½ hours by rail, 56 hours by bus.

To Adelaide: 725 miles, 1⅖ hours by jet, 25¼ hours by rail, 24 hours by bus.

To Brisbane: 464 miles, 1¼ hours by jet, 15 hours by rail, 17 hours by bus.

To Canberra: 147 miles, 40 minutes by jet, 4½ hours by rail, 4¼ hours by bus.

To Hobart: 646 miles, 1½ hours by jet, 12½ hours by rail, 14½ hours by bus.

To Melbourne: 440 miles, 1⅙ hours by jet, 12½ hours by rail, 14½ hours by bus.

To Perth: 2,041 miles, 4 hours by jet, 65 hours by rail, 72¼ hours by bus.

BY PLANE

With such great distances between cities, it is not surprising that Australians became "air minded" very early on. Their airlines, large and small, acquired outstanding safety records, due partly to stringently enforced government regulations but mainly to generally ideal flying conditions.

Until 1993 air traffic was handled by Australian Airlines and Ansett and their various subsidiaries, as well as 5 regional and 25 small commuter airlines connecting some 270 centers throughout the country. But in that year Qantas and Australian Airlines merged, forming an aviation giant that operates domestic as well as overseas routes. From then on the battle for domestic air passengers between Qantas and Ansett has been going hot and heavy, with each company trying to underbid the other. And *you,* the budget traveler, are reaping the benefits.

For that reason the standard airfares quoted below are merely guidelines. In practice virtually every fare listed can be replaced by a much lower one at any given moment. To name only one example: Officially, the one-way economy class fare from Sydney to Melbourne is $A239. But on the very day I wrote this the airlines announced a discount fare of $A149. For how long, nobody knows. Your best method, therefore, is to check the newspapers *and* call the airlines a day before your flight and ask for the *lowest* current ticket price.

Standard airfares on some of the most heavily used routes (one-way, economy class) are as follows.

Sydney-Melbourne	$A239
Sydney-Perth	$A601
Melbourne-Adelaide	$A225
Melbourne-Canberra	$A193
Adelaide–Alice Springs	$A360
Brisbane-Sydney	$A254
Perth-Adelaide	$A482
Canberra-Sydney	$A143
Sydney-Cairns	$A491
Sydney–Gold Coast	$A254

Saving Money

Both Ansett and Qantas offer standby fares, which save you 20% of the normal rate. There are no reservations—you buy your ticket at the airport and fly when there's a seat available. If you don't get on the first flight, you may wait for the next one. If you decide against this, your fare money is refunded.

Standby flying is a pretty good deal on heavily used routes with several flights a day between points. On routes with only one daily flight they're a serious time risk, since you stand a chance of losing an entire day waiting for the next connection. But the savings are considerable.

QANTAS BARGAIN FARES Two of Qantas's discount fares are specially tailored for overseas visitors. The first is the **Discover Australia** fare, available in connection with international travel tickets. It may be purchased after arrival in Australia at any Qantas office and lops hefty amounts off standard fares. On the Sydney–Gold Coast run, for instance, it can save you $A102 of the economy fare.

The **Australia Explorer Pass,** the second money saver, is based on nonspecific destinations over long hauls. The pass consists of coupons with a basic cost of $A150 each. The initial purchase must be made overseas, but up to eight additional coupons can be bought after arrival in Australia.

Both options take a bit of planning ahead and checking of detailed conditions. Book them either through a travel agent or at a Qantas office. For further information contact **Qantas,** 70 Hunter St., Sydney, NSW 2000 (tel., international, 02/951-4599; domestic, 02/951-4210).

Resort Packages Qantas owns a string of island-and-beach resorts along the Great Barrier Reef in tropical Queensland—places like Dunk Island, Brampton Island, Bedarra, Lizard, and Brampton. Facilities on these little coral havens range from ultradeluxe to near economy, but all of them come in some form of airline package deal. For instance five nights on Great Keppel Island can be had for $A685, including the return airfare from Sydney. You'll find the resorts and some of the package deals described in Chapter 7, "The Cairns Area & the Great Barrier Reef."

ANSETT Ansett is Qantas's domestic competitor and, as stated before, the competition is razor keen between them. Ansett offers some very advantageous deals, both for local passengers and overseas visitors. For international travelers it offers **See Australia,** which shaves roughly 25% off the full economy fare for travel on Ansett, Ansett Express, and Ansett WA. This fare can be purchased overseas or within 30 days of arrival in Australia at Ansett offices only. Travel must be completed within 60 days of arrival and proof of overseas residence is required when ticketing.

AUSTRALIA'S MAIN AIR ROUTES

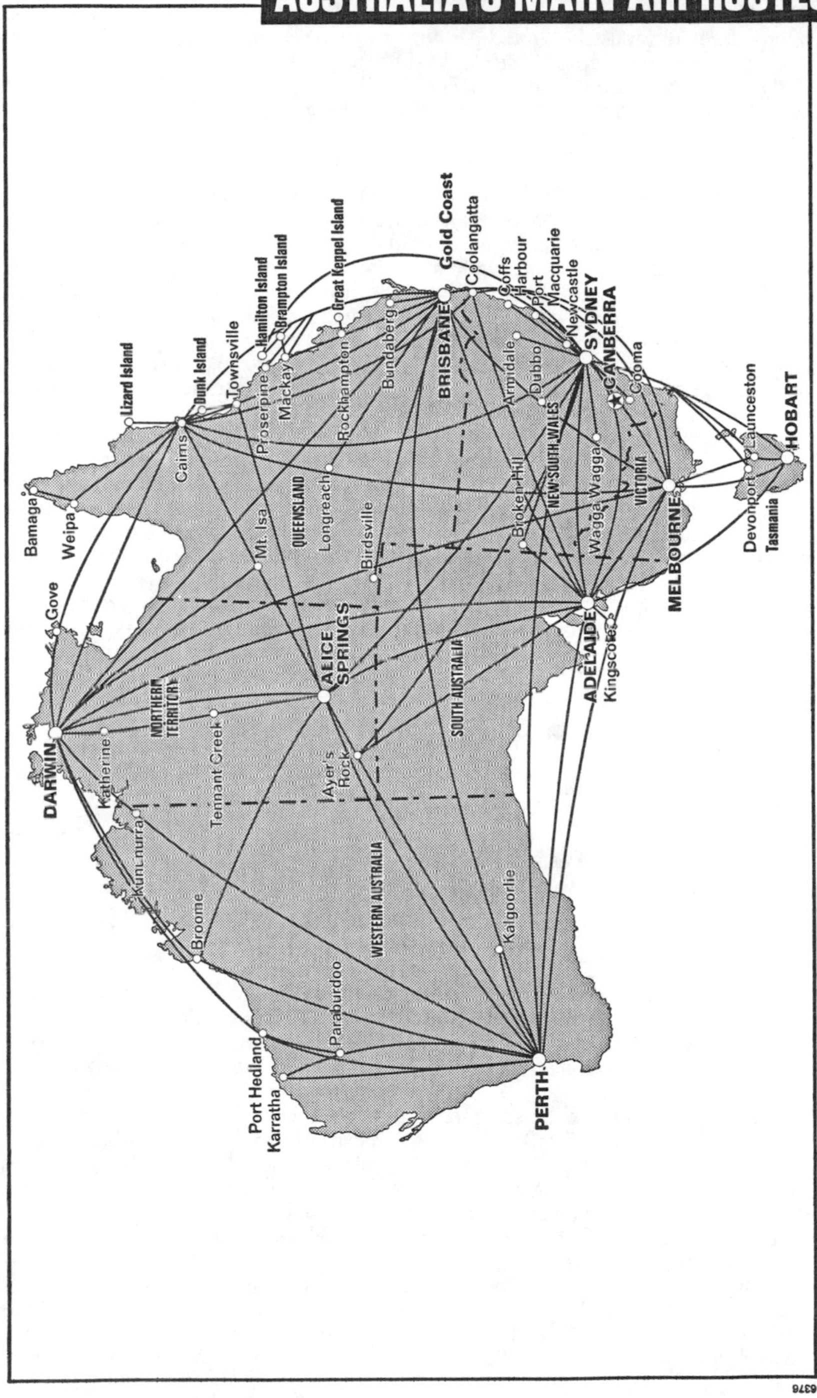

6376

The **Rock Bottom Return** is available to all, and can cut 45% off the regular economy fare. You must book and pay for your trip at least 14 days in advance and stay away at least one Saturday night. As the label indicates, these are return tickets and therefore entail doubling back. For details on these and other fares contact **Ansett,** 501 Swanston St., Melbourne, VIC 3000 (tel. 03/668-1211).

BY TRAIN

Australian railroads represent the cheapest form of travel available—except for your thumb. There are five distinct railway systems, four operated by state governments and one by the federal government, which eliminates even mild competition. As a result you get a few crack trains, comfortable but slow, and the rest, which are merely slow (the anthem of the Queensland state railroads is allegedly "I'll Walk Beside You"). The elite trains boast sleepers, parlor cars, bar service, good (although costly) dining-car meals, and attendants who bring early morning cups of tea or coffee to your berth. But even they run on tracks frequently resembling corrugated iron, suffer from fabulous delays, and are plagued by wildcat strikes that can leave you stranded at the flick of a union eyebrow.

Most of the iron horse's woes can be traced to amazing bungling in the colonial days. Australia, before federation and independence, consisted of six separate colonies. When the rails were laid, the featherbrains in charge managed things so that not one colony got the same rail gauge as a neighboring one! The system never quite recovered from that birth defect. It took 69 years after federation before the entire network was standardized and the celebrated Indian-Pacific run between Sydney and Perth could start operating.

With all their ailments, however, the railroads do offer bargain transportation, and some of their special economy deals are godsends for budget travelers. The table below, showing all single economy-class fares, will give you an idea of the typical price structure:

Sydney-Melbourne	$A49
Sydney-Adelaide	$A105
Melbourne-Canberra	$A45
Melbourne-Adelaide	$A45
Cairns-Brisbane	$A123
Perth-Adelaide	$A170
Alice Springs–Adelaide	$A139

Saving Money

Australian railways have introduced several types of discount fares that can cut the cost of traveling interstate by up to 30%. One is the **Caper Fare,** which simply stipulates that you book and pay for your seat at least seven days in advance. The only catch is that each train has a limited number of Caper seats and that the early bookers get most of them.

Some rail trips can also be spectacular in a way no air journey can match. The trans-Australian run, which links the Pacific Ocean port of Adelaide with the Indian Ocean port of Perth (Fremantle) spans 1,316 miles, taking 38 hours. Most of it goes through the Nullarbor Plain, a colossal scrub desert, flat as a tabletop and with not a tree in sight. The only structures en route are a few shacks and bungalows inhabited by railway workers, and they seem lost—engulfed—by the immense featureless solitude that stretches to the horizon day after day. This is the "Long Straight," the longest stretch of straight railway line in the world, where nothing exists except reddish brown scrub, pale-blue sky, and telegraph poles. Once you've crossed the Nullarbor, you'll know just how vast and empty this continent is. The trip, incidentally, is both comfortable and convivial; the busy bar in the club car takes care of that.

AUSTRALIA'S MAIN TRAIN ROUTES

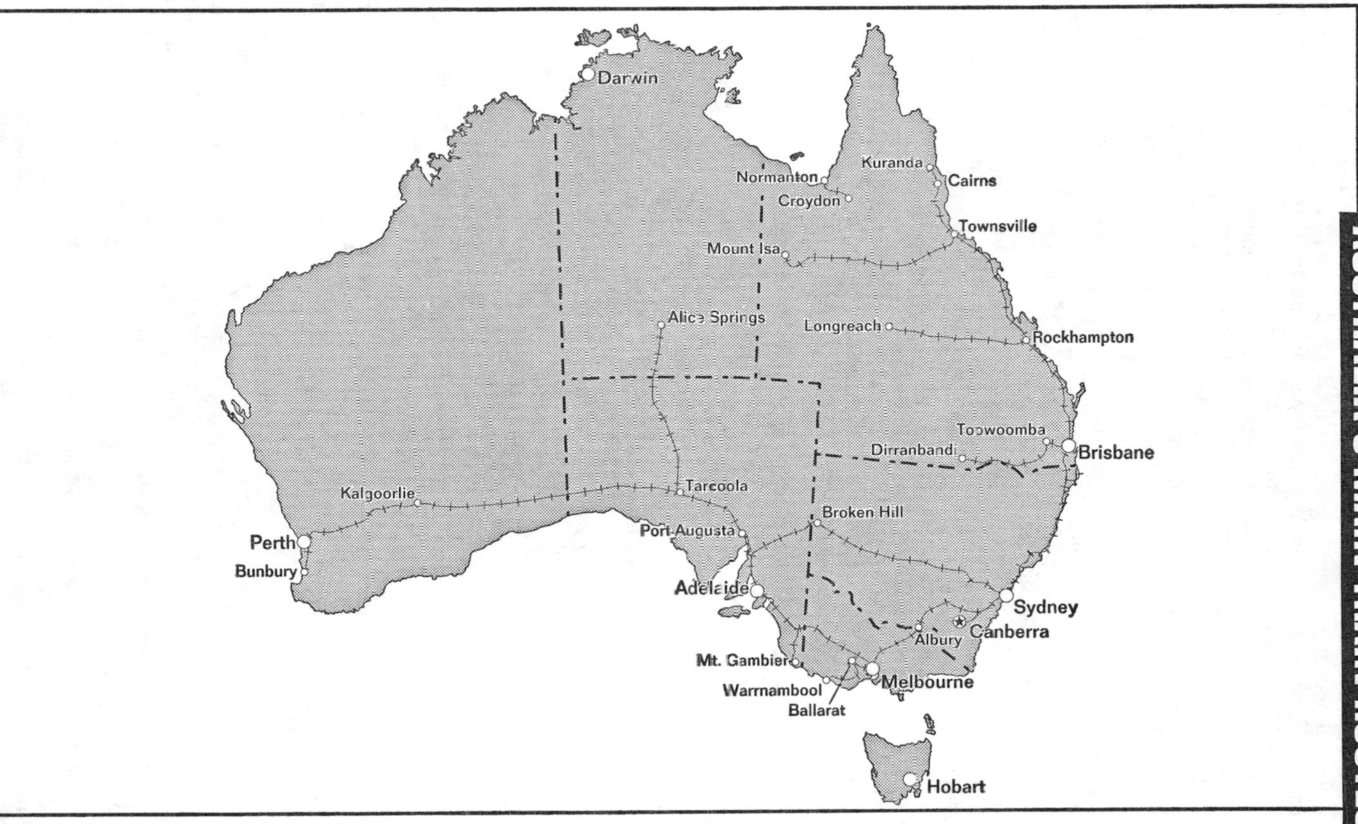

The best railroad bargain available is the **Austrailpass.** You must buy one *before* you leave home at any travel agency in the United States, Canada, Britain, South Africa, or New Zealand. The pass gives you unlimited rail travel in first class or economy for periods ranging from 14 to 90 consecutive days. You can travel anywhere, anytime, on the rail systems of Australia, including metropolitan trains. The only extra (optional) charges are meals and sleeping berths. For 14 days the passes cost $A725 first class, $A435 budget; for 21 days, $A829 first class, $A565 budget.

The **Kangaroo Road 'n' Rail Pass** is a two-pronged bargain deal. It allows unlimited travel anywhere on the country's rail network plus road travel on selected routes with Australian Coachlines. (Check whether the routes correspond with your travel agenda.) The pass is available for durations of 14, 21, and 28 consecutive days. Fourteen days cost $A1,040 first class, $A655 economy; 21 days, $A1,250 first class, $A900 economy; 28 days, $A1,530 first class, $A1,150 economy.

For details call **Rail Australia** at 02/217-8812.

The State Rail Authority of several states also operates combination tours by train, coach, launch, and ferry that can be great money savers. The New South Wales SRA, Transport House, 11 York St., Sydney NSW 2000 (tel. 02/29-7614), offers **DAYaWAY Tours,** combining every form of transportation the authority employs. As a sample, there's the **Canberra Luncheon Cruise.** Available Monday through Saturday, these 15-hour jaunts start with the air-conditioned Canberra-Monary express train. In Canberra you transfer to a launch for a cruise on Lake Burley Griffin, then to a coach for an afternoon's sightseeing through the capital, then back to the train for the return to Sydney.

In Victoria, the Public Transport Corporation (V/Line), 589 Collins St., Melbourne, VIC 3000 (tel. 03/619-5000), offers an outstanding bargain in the form of a 5-day jaunt to the fruit-and-wine center of Mildura. This includes a visit to the Pioneer Settlement at Swan Hill; visits to a zoo, nature reserves, museums, and wineries; plus a paddle-steamer cruise on the Murray River. The package, including meals, picnic lunches, and hotel accommodation, is $A446 (shared accommodations). For other tour bargains in Victoria, see Chapter 4, "Melbourne."

Still other states offer similar bargains—with the exception of Tasmania, which scrapped its last iron horse 10 years ago, to the dismay of local rail buffs. I'll mention these deals when we come to the states concerned.

BY BUS

This is almost—but not quite—as cheap as rail travel. Here I must add that Australian bus terminals are considerably cleaner, more cheerful, and less dangerous than their American counterparts. The Aussies turf out the drug addicts, winos, panhandlers, and pimps who often frequent these places elsewhere.

All major cities are linked by express bus services. The coaches have air conditioning and adjustable seats, and all overnight buses come with washrooms and toilets. Three private companies operate interstate services and their prices aren't always identical.

I have fond memories of my bus trip from Sydney to Canberra, a 4¼-hour jaunt costing $A26. For a start the Pioneer terminal in Sydney's Oxford Square was spacious, modern, spotless, and every inch as comfortable as an airport lounge. The station adjoins the lobby of the Oxford Koala, which places it handy to half a dozen shops in the hotel. The trip went through a gently rolling countryside, slowly rising in altitude. And the sights included some of Australia's oldest homesteads, churches, pubs, green fields, lush orchards, and small prosperous townships. Quite a change from the Nullarbor.

The driver, who had the kind of amiable gravel voice usually reserved for flight captains, was obviously enjoying his captive audience—and vice versa. He offered a running commentary on the landscape, sprinkled with historical, geographical, architectural, and political tidbits and little "in" jokes that invariably sparked a busload of guffaws. Once he referred to an extremely unpopular politician who had just lost his cabinet post: "Oh, yeah, him," drawled the driver. "I hear he's been appointed ambassador to the Bermuda Triangle."

But I digress.

As mentioned above, bus prices vary slightly, but this table will give you the idea:

Sydney-Melbourne	$A58
Sydney-Adelaide	$A89
Melbourne-Brisbane	$A115
Melbourne-Adelaide	$A42
Adelaide–Alice Springs	$A168
Brisbane-Cairns	$A125

To get complete price lists contact **Greyhound** and **Pioneer** (tel. in the U.S., toll free 800/828-1985; in Canada, 416/863-0799) or **Bus Australia** (tel. in the U.S., toll free 800/635-5488).

Saving Money

The three major road carriers, Greyhound, Bus Australia, and Pioneer, offer discount deals under the umbrella tag of **Australian Coachlines** (tel. 07/840-9300). Which means that the passes mentioned here apply to all three of them. To avoid confusion, keep in mind that Australian Coachlines is *not* another company.

Aussie Pass entitles you to unlimited, unrestricted travel on the coach network, anywhere in Australia, for periods ranging from 7 to 90 consecutive days. This pass allows maximum flexibility—you don't have to book your entire trip ahead but can change your itinerary as often as you like within the paid period. For 7 travel days adults pay $A343, children $A275; for 10 days it's $A490 adults, $A392 children; and so on for 21, 60, and 90 days.

Kangaroo Road 'n' Rail Pass is for those who might want a change of pace from bus travel. You can add an unlimited railroad pass (first class or economy) to your coach pass and ride the rails anywhere for periods of 14, 21, and 28 consecutive days. A 14-day economy class rail pass costs $A655; 21 days, $A900.

There are several other kinds of money-saving coach passes, including the special **Tassie Pass,** valid only on Tasmanian Redline Coaches; see Chapter 11, "Tasmania."

Bus pass holders can also choose from a number of package tours at prices roughly 35% below regular fares. One of them is the **Yulara Pass;** a set of three tours through the most dramatic landscapes of Australia's "Red Centre" (see Chapter 10, "Alice Springs"). You can select an early morning climb of Ayers Rock (bring sturdy shoes); a breathtaking sunset viewing of the Rock; or a walk through the prehistoric chasms of the Olgas. The Yulara Pass costs $A50, and the tours are available separately and in any order.

BY CAR

A word about driving conditions in general. Australian roads are not as good as those in the United States, Canada, Great Britain, or New Zealand. In the outback they can be incredibly bad. Don't, for instance, attempt to drive from Adelaide to Alice Springs. In Northern Territory you get road hazards you may not have bargained for—such as flash floods, wild buffalo, and equally wild camels. As mentioned earlier, distances between towns can be enormous, and you'll find far fewer service stations in between. The large metropolitan centers boast excellent freeway systems, but the network does not cover the country. Also, because some of these freeways are brand spanking new they may not be marked on city maps issued a few years before. This was a handicap I experienced in Brisbane and Perth, and it did gruesome things to my blood pressure, especially because my city map was innocent of the pattern of one-way streets that had been instituted since it was printed. Cab drivers finally showed me the way.

Traffic conditions vary from city to city. In Canberra they're ideal—the national capital was designed for motorists. Cairns and Alice Springs are easy: wide streets and not enough cars to congest them. Melbourne and Adelaide have heavy but highly disciplined traffic: stick to the rules or else. Sydney is fast and furious, the drivers displaying an almost Parisian aggressiveness. Brisbane is chaotic, with traffic snarled in a maze of ill-planned one-way streets, badly marked freeways, and lousy signposting. Hobart, although a small town, is surprisingly difficult. Streets in the downtown area are narrow, thronged, and desperately short of parking spots. They are also marked with that small-town haphazardness that fails to account for someone *not* knowing which street they're on.

Australian drivers, although not maniacal, tend to be cavalier. Bush motorists, in particular, have a deplorable habit of charging full speed from little dirt roads onto main highways. And they bother with signals only if there's a police car in the vicinity. By and large, Australians are not as amiable behind a steering wheel as they are on foot, a metamorphosis that affects many other nationalities as well.

Outside the city areas you must also beware of highway monsters in the shape of timber trucks, oil tankers, and road trains. The last are the size of battleships and behave like such. They ignore speed laws with regal nonchalance and think nothing of blasting you into a ditch if you don't move over fast enough. But meet their drivers after they've stopped for a cup of tea and they're once again souls of benevolence.

Car Rentals

Australia has three big nationwide car-rental companies and scores of small local ones. The Big Three are Hertz, Avis, and Thrifty, and you'll find their airport desks and downtown offices in virtually every major town. The small outfits are a bit cheaper, but they have definite drawbacks. They don't give you the service and trimmings of the big companies and—being local—they usually can't let you pick up a car in one state and return it in another.

The most economical of the three is Thrifty, and they have promised to give special consideration to customers who arrive clutching a copy of this book in their hot little hands.

Thrifty rents 12 categories of automobile, ranging from little economy cars to luxury limos and group-size 8- and 12-seat minibuses. Their cheapest vehicle currently is the manual-shift Mitsubishi Lancer two-door coupe, not reservable in advance and costing—when available—$A40 per day. One step up is the Lancer with A/C, renting at $A54 per day. All metropolitan rates include unlimited kilometers, but you must buy some type of insurance, the cost of which varies according to the amount of coverage.

There are also several special discounts that can save you quite a considerable amount of cash. Weekend specials mean one free driving day—pick up a car on Friday and return it on Monday: Drive for three days and get charged for only two. Thrifty's Australian headquarters is at 73 William St., East Sydney, NSW 2011 (tel. 02/360-4055). Certain branches of the company also rent special vehicles like camper vans, motorhomes, and "topless" runabouts. See specific chapters for details. For Thrifty car reservations from the United States, call toll free 800/367-2277. For **Avis,** call 800/331-2112; for **Hertz,** 800/654-3001; and for **Budget,** 800/472-3325.

It's important to remember that *all* rental companies, including the local outfits, charge higher rates in the Northern Territory and other remote areas where driving conditions are apt to be rougher. Thrifty's additional country rates come to $A5 per day or $A30 per week. You may also have to pay extra during certain holiday periods in certain resort regions. In compensation, Thrifty's Sydney, Gold Coast, and Perth offices give you booklets of 25 discount vouchers good for that number of local restaurants and attractions.

Also please note—for the sake of my reputation for accuracy—that rental-car rates in Australia, as elsewhere, are in a near-chaotic state of flux. All figures and conditions mentioned apply only to the time of writing and serve as guidelines rather than measuring rods. In the car-for-hire business practically every month brings a new ball game. Among the more enervating variables are peak-season rates that occur at different times of the year, depending on locale.

You may want to hire a **campmobile.** They come in several makes and are fitted with trailer hookups. The Volkswagen vans take up to five persons. Contact **Pound Motors,** 116 Leicester St., Carlton, Melbourne, VIC (tel. 03/347-6822); **Westland Travel,** 708 Canning Highway, Applecross, WA (tel. 09/364-5529); or **Mobile Camper Van Hire Service,** 459 N. East Rd., Hillcrest, SA (tel. 08/261-9732).

Saving Money

Buying a car can be a blissful buck saver providing that there are more than one of you traveling and that you start and finish your trip in Sydney.

The following deal is offered by Frank McCorquodale, director of **Mach 1,** 495 New Canterbury Rd., Dulwich Hill, Sydney, NSW 2203 (tel. 02/569-3374): He will sell you a budget-priced used car or station wagon, registration fees and third-party insurance not included in the price. Included is a *guarantee* to buy the vehicle back at the conclusion of your trip at a previously agreed sum—about half of whatever you paid for it. Assuming the original sale price was $A2,000 (some go for up to $A5,500), you'll get roughly $A1,000 when you sell it back, within two months, unless you wreck it en route. Split between, say, three persons, this works out to be $A333 in transport costs per head. And complete freedom of movement to boot. By the time you read this, other dealers may have come up with similar propositions, but at the moment Mach 1 is on its own. (Take bus no. 426 or 428 to Dulwich Hill Shopping Centre or take a train to Dulwich Hill Station, and the dealer will pick you up.)

Gasoline

It is called petrol here (gas is only what you cook with), and prices vary considerably—the farther outback you go, the higher they get. In Sydney it's around A65¢ per liter (about 3½ liters make a gallon).

Driving Rules

Before operating an automobile in Australia, there are a few things you should know. Traffic drives on the left-hand side of the road, and most cars therefore have right-hand steering wheels. Apart from that, the most important points to remember are to give right-of-way to all cars at T intersections if you're approaching on the stem of the T, and to give right-of-way to cars coming from the right at intersections, unless there are traffic lights or stop signs. Also, the wearing of seat belts is *compulsory,* and failure to do so can earn you a $A75 fine.

Overseas driver's licenses are valid throughout Australia but overseas insurance is *not.* Compulsory third-party insurance is automatically added to all car-rental charges, but more comprehensive coverage is an extra. You must be 21 years or older to rent a car, and you may be asked for a reference if you're under 25.

Breakdowns & Road Maps

Members of overseas organizations affiliated with the Alliance Internationale de Tourisme or Fédération Internationale de l'Automobile are entitled to all services provided by the Australian Automobile Associations on presentation of a current membership card. These outfits have different names in various states (see below). It's a good idea to get the brochures on state road rules from any of them. Don't forget to bring along your AAA (American Automobile Association) membership card. The membership card also entitles you to reciprocal rights with the affiliated automobile clubs in Australia. This means emergency breakdown service, free road maps, accommodation and camping directories, and touring information.

Adelaide Royal Automobile Association, 41 Hindmarsh Sq., Adelaide, SA 5000 (tel. 08/223-4555).

Brisbane Royal Automobile Club of Queensland, 300 St. Pauls Terrace, Fortitude Valley, Brisbane, QLD 4006 (tel. 07/361-2444).

Canberra National Roads & Motorists Association, 92 Northbourne Ave., Canberra, ACT 2601 (tel. 06/243-8826).

Hobart Royal Automobile Club of Tasmania, corner of Patrick and Murray streets, Hobart, TAS 7001 (tel. 002/32-6300).

Melbourne Royal Automobile Club of Victoria, 550 Princes Hwy., Noble Park, VIC 3174 (tel. 03/790-2627).

Perth Royal Automobile Club of Western Australia, 228 Adelaide Terrace, Perth, WA 6000 (tel. 09/421-4444).

Sydney National Roads & Motorists Association, 151 Clarence St., Sydney, NSW 2000 (tel. 02/260-9222).

BY FERRY

There was a time when you could take a comfortable leisurely sea journey from one Australian port to the next, and a lot of people did. But the coastal shipping services went the way of the mastodon, at least as far as passenger traffic is concerned. The one remaining maritime link is the ferry operating between the mainland and Tasmania.

The term "ferry" conveys a wrong impression. The *Spirit of Tasmania* is a full-fledged oceanliner of 31,356 gross tons, handsomely appointed and equipped with a restaurant, bar, cafeteria, gymnasium, and swimming pool. It takes 1,194 passengers, plus cars, motorcycles, and bicycles. The ship leaves Melbourne on Monday, Wednesday, and Friday at 6pm, and the 14-hour crossing to Devonport can be fairly rough. You have a choice of four-berth, three-berth, two-berth, or single cabins. Transport from the terminals to the railway stations at each end is available.

For bookings and inquiries, contact **TT Line,** Station Pier, Port Melbourne, VIC (tel. toll free 008/030-344).

SAVING MONEY The cheapest fare, a twin-share berth, in low season comes to $A85 per person (in high season, $A110). Cars up to 13 feet in length are $A90, whereas bicycles (Tasmania is ideal cycling country) cost $A14.

BY HITCHHIKING

Although perfectly legal, travel by thumb is frowned on by the minions of the law. But if you're determined to locomote in that fashion, don't let the frowns disturb you—it's a legitimate practice. The only thing they can book you for is "hampering traffic," which means don't stand out in the road.

Since I've been handing you advice about every other form of transport, I might as well pass the good word on this type as well. The following tips come from "reliable sources," people who've traversed the country by thumb propulsion. So treat them with the respect we owe to practical experience.

Have your national flag sewn prominently on your pack, particularly if you're American, Canadian, or Kiwi. It brings out the native instinct for hospitality. Two people are the ideal hitching number, preferably one male, one female. Two males may find it more difficult, two females take a degree of risk. And although hitching in Australia is a pretty safe custom, it is decidedly *not* recommended for solo women. The best place to get rides is on the outskirts of a town, at a junction where vehicles travel slowly and can stop easily.

Don't carry much luggage, and nothing that looks breakable. And wear a clean outfit. Shabbiness is fine—even helpful—but dirt is taboo. After all, your friendly chauffeur is going to spend some hours cooped up with you in a confined space. Displaying your destination also helps; it makes you look like a reliable veteran at the game.

If your numbers and appearance are right, you'll find hitching remarkably easy. Australians are a gregarious lot and not prone to fear of strangers. You'll be able to pick and choose rides to a certain extent. Don't hesitate to turn down short lifts. It pays to wait for a long haul to come along.

SUGGESTED ITINERARIES

The following itineraries are merely suggestions. They're here to give you an idea of how much sightseeing and traveling you can do comfortably in a given space of time. All of them use Sydney as your starting point (as it is for the vast majority of visitors). They would, of course, read quite differently if you first landed in Melbourne or Cairns.

Do yourself a favor and don't stick closely to the itineraries. They're go-go-go programs with one eye on the clock and another on transport schedules. You can cover a lot of territory in that fashion but at the expense of a great deal of enjoyment. Knowledgable hedonists will consider three days in Sydney, two days in Melbourne, and one day on the Great Barrier Reef as downright ridiculous. And the agenda necessarily has to ignore such interesting places as Darwin in the Northern Territory, Phillip Island off the coast of Victoria, the Sunshine Coast of Queensland, Coober Pedy in South Australia, Lightning Ridge in New South Wales, and so on.

These itineraries also have to ignore climatic contrasts, which you shouldn't. Sydney's climate is very much like Los Angeles's, but Melbourne tends to be cooler, and Tasmania is cool even in summer. You can expect blazing sunshine in Perth, dry desert heat in Alice Springs, and moist tropical warmth in Cairns and Brisbane . . . all at the same time of year.

IF YOU HAVE 1 WEEK

Days 1–3 Give yourself at least three days to explore Sydney. This should include a tour of the Sydney Opera House; a ride across the Harbour Bridge; a trip to the top of Sydney Tower for the view; a stroll through The Rocks; an afternoon at a surfing beach (Bondi is the closest); a ferry ride to Manly; a visit to Darling Harbour, Taronga Zoo, and the fabulous Queen Victoria shopping complex (right downtown); a look at the boutiques and art galleries of Paddington and at Pier One (underneath the Harbour Bridge); and an evening at Kings Cross.

Day 4 Take a train from Sydney's Central Station to Katoomba, in the Blue Mountains, which actually are a deep azure blue. The region has scores of attractions, among them the Jenolan Caves and the reputedly steepest Scenic Railway in the world.

Days 5–6 Fly to Canberra or take the much cheaper 4-hour bus trip. In the federal capital you should take a tour through the New Parliament House and a cruise on Lake Burley Griffin; visit the Australian War Memorial, the Mint, and the National Gallery; and take a ride to the top of Black Mountain for a view from the Telecom Tower.

Day 7 Take a tour bus to the Snowy Mountains Hydroelectric Scheme, Australia's prime technological achievement and stunning to behold. The gateway to the Scheme is Cooma, and from there the tours lead you to an underground power station, a huge artificial lake, displays and video shows, plus lunch at Thredbo, the highest township on the continent. (See "Canberra—Australia's Capital," Chapter 9, for details). You can then either catch a bus back to Sydney or continue on to Melbourne.

IF YOU HAVE 2 WEEKS

Days 1–3 After the minimal three days in Sydney (see the itinerary above), either fly to Melbourne (one hour) or take the overnight express train from Sydney's Central Station.

Days 4–5 You can see the major attractions of Melbourne in two fairly hectic days. This means going through the Victorian Arts Centre, the Old Melbourne Gaol, the Museum of Victoria, and Captain Cook's Cottage; window shopping along elegant Collins Street; sampling the cafés of Carlton; riding a tram (trolley) down St. Kilda Road, Australia's foremost boulevard; viewing the stately colonial mansion of Como (in South Yarra); and admiring the Royal Botanic Gardens.

Days 6–11 Fly to Tasmania (about one hour) or take the sea route. The *Abel Tasman* operates three times a week from Melbourne and takes a night for the crossing—which can be pretty rough. Once on the little island state, rent a car if you can swing it. If not, make use of Redline Coaches and buy a Tassie Pass that gives you unlimited bus travel for a week. The idea is to make a complete 5-day loop of the island, leaving out the rugged and sparsely populated southwestern portion.

Start in Launceston, the second-largest city of the island. It boasts an unusual attraction in shape of the Penny Royal World, a combination of cannon foundry, fort, artificial lake, and a naval sloop firing broadsides.

Head east to the coast at St. Helens, then south to Bicheno. Once a whaling station, this is now a pretty seaside resort with a Sea Life Centre, combining a fish zoo with a seafood restaurant.

From Bicheno, travel along the coast to Swansea, then on to the Tasman Peninsula. This is the grim cradle of Tasmania's history, and you should take one of the organized tours to Port Arthur, the strongbox at the southern tip—Australia's Alcatraz. Today this is a haunted semi–ghost town, but once it housed 12,500 of the colony's toughest convicts under unspeakable conditions.

From the peninsula, travel 68 miles northwest to the island capital of Hobart. An old and charming town of 164,000 people. Hobart has Australia's original *legal* gambling casino at Wrest Point; wonderfully atmospheric Salamanca Place with a market; the Tasmanian and Van Diemen's Land museums; a model Tudor village with 2-inch-high populace; Anglesea Barracks (built in 1811 and still garrisoned); and Constitution Dock, a colorful marina for ocean going yachts.

From there the main road strikes inland to New Norfolk on the Derwent River. (You might take a ride on the Devil Jets, running from beneath the Derwent River Bridge.) Then head west to Queenstown, formerly a rip-roaring mining town. Next, head due north, through wildly magnificent hills, until you reach the coast again at Burnie. The town is an industrial port with a scenic mountain backdrop. On the Civic Centre Plaza you'll find a fragment of the past in the shape of the Pioneer Village Museum.

Head east along the coastline to Devonport, the finishing point of your loop. Visit the Maritime Museum, afloat with an armada of ship's models. Tiagarra, at Mersey Bluff, is a cultural showcase of Tasmanian Aboriginals, a race now entirely extinct.

Day 12 From Devonport you can fly (or ferry) back to Melbourne and from there head to Adelaide, a flight of about an hour. The Festival City's prime sight is the Festival Centre Complex on the banks of the Torrens River. One block away, on North Terrace, stand the Art Gallery of South Australia and the South Australian Museum, with some of the finest paintings and Aboriginal artifact collections in the country. The Old Parliament House, also on North Terrace, is a surprise package showing laser-disc audiovisuals about the state's history.

Day 13 The Barossa Valley, Australia's greatest wine region, lies 40 miles northeast of Adelaide. Take a bus tour of the wineries (you can do more tasting if someone else is doing the driving).

Day 14 Just off the coast southwest of Adelaide lies Kangaroo Island, a wildlife paradise. There's a daily ferry connection from Port Adelaide for the 6½-hour crossing. By air it's a 40-minute flight. The island teems with semitame 'roos, emus, goannas, seals, and penguins, but it is also a famed tourist resort with accommodations from luxury to budget—a great place to spend your final day.

IF YOU HAVE 3 WEEKS

Days 1–14 Follow the 2-week itinerary above. With an additional week before you and Adelaide as your last stop, you face a problem: Perth is eminently worth a trip, but it *is* a long one—four flying hours westward from Adelaide, and two days driving by bus or car.

Days 15–16 Perth, on the Indian Ocean, is a sun-drenched fun city of a million people. The adjoining harbor of Fremantle is a mecca for yachtspeople and was the scene of the 1987 America's Cup races. The Hay Street Pedestrian Mall ranks as a tourist sight, and the Perth Cultural Centre is one of the newest and most architecturally striking complexes in the country. Burwood Casino, in suburban Riverdale, gambles round-the-clock, and the Fremantle Museum, whose courtyard becomes a theater on summer nights, is a treasure trove of relics relating to Westralia's past.

Days 17–18 From Perth you have another long flight to Alice Springs, in the very center of Australia. "The Alice" is a desert oasis, but it boasts all the modern conveniences, including a shopping mall and a casino. It is also the springboard for a multitude of tours going to Uluru National Park and Ayers Rock, some 280 road miles southwest. The Rock is one of the great natural wonders of the world, a truly titanic edifice twice the size of central London. You can climb up, providing you're reasonably fit.

Day 19 From the dry desert vastness of Central Australia you can fly directly to the tropical lushness of Cairns, in Northern Queensland. This is a gateway to the Great Barrier Reef, another of the continent's wonders. The reef is the world's largest coral creation and stretches 1,250 miles along the coast. You could spend a month exploring it, but the closest excursion point from Cairns is Green Island. A launch will whisk you over in 90 minutes. Green Island has the Underwater Coral Observatory, the famous Marineland Melanesia, as well as glass-bottomed boats to study the denizens of the reef.

Day 20 From Cairns it's 2¼ hours to the Queensland capital of Brisbane by air. You're back in a big city now, subtropical and boasting an impressive Cultural Centre, a Wilderness Walk (right downtown at the corner of Creek and Adelaide Streets), and the Science Centre. At Fig Tree Pocket, 15 driving minutes west, lies Lone Pine Sanctuary, the first koala colony established in Australia. The nicest way to get there is by river ferry, a tour taking 2¼ hours.

Day 21 From Brisbane you can take a bus 50 miles south to Australia's number-one beach playground—the Gold Coast. This is a 20-mile chain of resorts, crammed with fun parks, hotels, nightspots, and tourists, that you will either adore or abhor. The long string of surf resorts ends at Coolangatta, on the border of New South Wales. The advantage of the jaunt is that you don't have to retrace your route: You can catch a direct flight and arrive back in Sydney in half an hour.

9. ENJOYING AUSTRALIA ON A BUDGET

THE U.S. $45-A-DAY BUDGET

The first reaction of every Australian who heard the title of this book was, "Sounds great—but can you do it?"

The answer is *yes,* absolutely, within the terms laid down for this entire long-standing series of budget guides. These terms stipulate that the U.S. $45 a day cover only your basic expenses of a clean bed and three solid meals. All other outlays count as extras. Here my job was to collect the information that will enable you to get the most for your money as far as all those extras are concerned. This also applies to the "splurge" opportunities I've included in each chapter. They may be above our budget bracket but are economical in terms of the value offered for the price.

The $45 in the title is U.S. currency. Just about all other amounts mentioned in the book are in Australian money—and here you're in for a very happy surprise. For currently the American dollar fetches around $1.40 in Aussie money, or 40% more for easier calculation, which means that your basic U.S. $45 actually amounts to $A63. A nightly hotel charge of $A42 (for a double) comes to only about U.S. $30 (U.S. $15 per person).

Budget travelers Down Under also enjoy another big advantage over tourists in Europe and America: They can disregard "hidden costs." Every price displayed anywhere is exactly what you pay. There are no additional taxes or tips to reckon with, additions that elsewhere may increase your bills by 25% or more. This goes not only for services but also for store purchases, and it makes a mighty difference in the long run.

I personally have checked out every establishment mentioned, and a large number of possible candidates were dropped by the wayside for a variety of reasons, sometimes merely because the vibes were bad. So what you're getting is a selection—not a listing. Wherever I have included a place solely because it was ultraeconomical, I say so plainly in the text. The purpose for including such places is to give you a downward margin, just as the splurge spots provide you with an upward one.

All prices are accurate—for the time at which they were gathered. Unfortunately they won't stay that way. We're caught in an age of some inflation, a constant edging up of living costs that operates Down Under as it does everywhere else. However, since all the establishments in the book are essentially budget oriented, they will still offer you, relatively speaking, the best deals available.

Money value is a basic consideration of the book, but not the only one. Australia has things that cannot be assessed in dollars: dramatic beauty, a sense of newness and adventure, the fascinating dynamics of a young and free society shaping its future, and a wonderful spirit of "mateship" that enfolds natives and visitors alike. I hope that by helping you extract the most from your money I can enable you to take a close look at an exciting human experiment in a part of the globe that has long been veiled by the "tyranny of distance."

SAVING MONEY ON ACCOMMODATIONS

Australia offers an immense range of accommodations, from super deluxe to rock-bottom economy. However, during holiday periods (see "When to Go," in this chapter) you'll be competing for beds with half of the country's population. The choice, particularly in the budget line, can then become pretty meager. Also, most places in resort areas and some in the big cities charge higher rates during holidays. So, if possible, arrange your travels outside the public holidays. You can always get accommodations of some kind through the various state tourist bureaus (you'll find addresses listed in specific chapters), but they may not be in the area and price range you want. Every chapter also contains my personal selection of budget hostelries, with a few higher-bracket places thrown in for good measure. But in the event that you do find yourself on your own when selecting accommodations, keep the following in mind.

LIQUOR & LODGINGS There is a certain degree of desperate confusion in the Australian terminology for hostelries, entirely due to the country's somewhat antiquated liquor laws. The laws were so ludicrous that restaurateurs could be—and were—prosecuted for serving sherry trifle dessert with real sherry while not possessing a liquor license. Rum-filled chocolates were likewise taboo; candy stores don't have liquor licenses either. Even today, while the wowsers' grip has been loosened, enough irritating restrictions remain to demonstrate that the black-shrouded bluenose brigade is still very much around.

And what has all this to do with accommodations? The laws stipulated that in order to qualify for a liquor license, a "public house" had to be a hotel, meaning that it had to sleep guests and serve food as well as liquid refreshments. But for most hotels only the bar trade brought in profit; they hated the idea of houseguests. Therefore a great many of them operated as hotels in name only—they maintained a few rooms but kept them permanently empty by informing would-be guests that they were occupied.

The trouble is that a lot of these hotels are still functioning in the same fashion. The word "hotel," therefore, can mean either a genuine accommodation place or simply a drinking establishment. You have no way of telling until you ask to sleep there. And to add to the confusion, both types of hostelries are known as "pubs." Only in the past few years have the powers that be grudgingly issued a few tavern licenses—permission to operate honest-to-goodness bars clearly distinguishable from hotels.

The term "hotel," in Australia, still means an establishment that runs a bar and may—*or may not*—accommodate guests. A private hotel takes guests but does not have a license to sell liquor and might not serve meals. A guest house also does not have a liquor license but always serves at least breakfast. In my listings I make a point of informing you whether meals are available in a particular hostelry.

HOTEL LANGUAGE Some of the terms used in Australian hotels may also need explanation. Here is a glossary:

B&B: Bed-and-breakfast. This means that the tariff includes breakfast of some kind (See the distinctions below.)

Casual: This refers to guests paying by the night or week, as distinct from permanent or monthly residents.

Continental breakfast: This bears little resemblance to the European coffee-and-rolls ensemble. Here it means juice or fruit, cold cereal, toast with butter and jam, and coffee or tea.

Cooked or full breakfast: This is the works: juice; hot cereal; eggs, bacon, sausages, or (sometimes) steak; plus tea or coffee. Where a **menu breakfast** is offered it means additional choices of fish, lamb chops, or spaghetti or beans on toast.

Fans: This indicates that the place is not air-conditioned. Few establishments in the budget bracket are. Some don't provide fans either.

Guest kitchen: Communal kitchen shared by the houseguests.

H&C: Short for "hot and cold," denoting that the room has a sink with hot-and-cold water.

Jug: Same as an electric kettle but breakable. Provides boiling water for making tea or instant coffee and works within moments.

Morning tea: The curse of late nighters like myself, it means that no later than 7am some excessively cheerful sadist comes charging in, bearing a cup of tea plus two biscuits (cookies) on a plate. Where offered, you must make absolutely clear that you don't want it—unless, of course, you do.

Private facilities: This means a private bathroom with shower and/or tub. Very often it stands for just a shower and toilet.

Surcharge: This is the extra fee frequently charged for holiday periods and/or room service.

Tea- and coffee-making facilities: These are almost universal features in Australian hostelries and one of their best points. The facilities consist of an electric jug (see above), cups, saucers, spoons, a teapot, sugar, and mostly—but not invariably—free tea bags or sachets of instant coffee.

Tray service: Room service.

BEST BUDGET BETS

YOUTH HOSTELS The **Australian Youth Hostel Association (AYHA)** is affiliated with the International Youth Hostel Federation and honors international membership cards. The 152 YHA hostels can be found in every Australian state and territory. They range from modern, specially designed hostels to a convict-built church in New South Wales, from a former tollhouse in Tasmania to a defunct railroad station in Western Australia. Comfortwise they range from cozy to primitive.

Overnight charges vary from $A9 to $A14, depending on the location and the facilities provided. All hostels require that you use regulation sleeping sheets. You can either make one yourself or buy one from the YHA for around $A12. The hostels have no age limit, but all of them bar alcohol and most (but not all) impose a curfew on their guests. All provide cooking facilities of some kind, and most have hot showers and laundry facilities. The YHA's Australian head office is at 10 Mallett St., Camperdown, Sydney NSW 2050 (tel. 02/565-1325). The AYHA puts out an excellent annual brochure, the "Australian Youth Hostels Handbook," listing every hostel in the country—with its prices, rules, and facilities—together with a map showing you how to get there. Membership cards can be obtained in the United States through **Hostelling International, American Youth Hostels,** National Offices, P.O. Box 37613, Washington, DC 20013-7613. They cost U.S. $10 for juniors (under 18), U.S. $25 for adults, and U.S. $15 for those 55 or over. Some Australian hostels also charge lower rates for juniors.

BACKPACKERS A new accommodation concept is proliferating at a rate impossible to keep up with. There are now several hundred of these hybrid creations around Australia, and their label has lost virtually all of its original meaning: You don't have to carry a pack to get into any of them. Nor do you have to belong to any group or association.

Backpackers lodgings fall somewhere between the Ys and the youth hostels: They're cheaper than the former and less regulated than the latter. In terms of creature comfort they range from near scruffy to near luxurious—some boasting air conditioning and swimming pools, with others resembling overpopulated gopher holes. Rates range from $A9 to $A19 per night, depending on where and how. All of them share a very laid-back ambience as well as a tendency to burst at the seams. Several are operated by the patrons themselves. Guests may stay a few nights, work as staff members for a few weeks, then drift on to be replaced by the next shift. You will find a number of them listed in every chapter but, as indicated, they are not tailored for folks who like strictly enforced hostelry rules.

THE Y'S Both the YMCA and the YWCA have hostels/hotels scattered throughout Australia. But in certain cities one or the other has become defunct, with the result being that most YMs now also take women and most YWs also accommodate men. Several—although by no means all—are real bargains at about $A19 per night. You'll find a description of the Ys among my accommodation listings in the various city chapters.

COLLEGES Both students and nonstudents can stay at certain university colleges during vacations, although bona fide students usually get priority. These dorms are mostly comfortable, congenial, and wonderfully relaxed as well as cheap. You'll find a selection of them listed in the city chapters.

CAMPING & R.V. PARKS Many caravan (R.V.) camps hire out on-site vans (house trailers) at very reasonable rates. The trouble is that the majority of these camps are located way out of town, sometimes with poor public transport. They are universally practical only when you have your own wheels. Get a list of campsites from the relevant state tourist bureau or state motoring association and pinpoint them on a map before you inquire about rental vans. If you're motorized or if the camp is near a bus stop to the city, this is the most economical group or pair accommodation you'll find. Rates start at around $A13 per night but go up according to the time of year.

Campsites have been accused of catering only to the caravan (R.V.) folks, caring little or nothing for the genuine tent campers. This is probably true, but most of them still let you pitch your canvas and provide you with access to hot showers, electricity, drinking water, sewerage, and laundry facilities for $A7 to $A10 per night.

MOTELS These are a relatively recent innovation in Australia, which means that most of them are modern, well equipped, and comfortable in their own plastic fashion. They also go under titles like "motor inn" and "motor lodge," but I've not been able to discern any difference. As in America, they run the gamut from little five-unit establishments to luxury high-rises with Olympic-size swimming pools and saunas. Unlike their American counterparts, however, they have no real budget bracket. The basic cut-price category is missing. I have listed some of the cheaper ones, but there just aren't very many around. If an establishment is called a "hotel-motel," it usually means an older hotel with a newer motel patched on. And you can bet that the hotel portion will be less expensive.

Most motels provide tea- and coffee-making facilities and refrigerators for their guests. Breakfast, usually served on trays brought to each unit, may be included in the tariff. The majority offer family units with room for up to six people and will give discount rates for children.

BED & BREAKFASTS This lodging concept, the mainstay of budget travelers in Britain, Ireland, and Europe, is less clearly defined in Australia. As a general rule, you may assume that all higher-priced hostelries will charge you extra for breakfast, while in some economy-class places it's included in the price. Thus a bed-and-breakfast place can be anything from an elderly guest house to a brand-new hotel, although mostly it's the former. In my listings I have separated the bed-and-breakfast establishments from the rest to make your selection easier (note the specialized outfit called **Bed & Breakfast Australia** in Chapter 3, "Sydney") and also tell you what *kind* of breakfast they serve, since the difference may be between a three-course meal and a morning snack.

SERVICED APARTMENTS For couples, groups, or families these are the greatest money savers of them all. Such apartments (flats in local parlance) consist of one to three rooms, plus bathrooms and kitchens. They come fully equipped with cooking-and-eating utensils and appliances and enable you to set up house for days, weeks, or months. Your food bills go down fabulously when you cook for yourself.

Australia is not as well supplied with these establishments as, for instance, New Zealand, but there are proportionally far more of them than in America. In the resort and tourist areas they can make the difference between an economy vacation and a purse-breaking one. Serviced flats can be located in buildings containing nothing else, in motels, and occasionally in hotels. Sometimes the management also supplies breakfast (as an extra), but usually the only meals available on the premises are those you make. Tariffs are given either as a daily rate for one or two people or as a weekly rental for the whole apartment.

Motel flats are usually more expensive than the other kinds, because they almost invariably include television, telephone, and laundry facilities. The other kinds *may* have these trimmings; mostly they don't. All of them have maid service, but while the maids will clean the rooms, they will *not* wash your dishes. Furnishings range from the bare basics to the near sumptuous, but they always include bed linen, towels, blankets, and the amount of dishes and cutlery required by the maximum number of tenants. See my listings in the city chapters for tariffs, locations, and quality.

COUNTRY PUBS These can be real money savers, providing you don't mind lodging well away from the bright lights. The "bush pub" is a famous Australian institution: subject of a hundred ballads, butt of a thousand jokes. And in a land where highway motels tend to be scarce and expensive, they can be lifesavers.

A few country pubs look idyllic, but the majority have a weathered, frontier appearance. Beauty is not their strong point; hospitality and cleanliness are. A few boast "all mod cons" (all modern conveniences)—and charge accordingly. The majority make do with shared bathrooms, ceiling fans, and bedrooms furnished with the "basics." All have a lively bar trade and serve excellent cold beer. Meals, as a rule, are simple, ample country fare. Prices range from $A30 upward per night (sometimes for two people) and usually include breakfast. You can get lists of country pubs at the tourist bureaus of the various state capitals; advance reservations are rarely necessary.

Australian Pubstays is an organization of pubs throughout the country. Their rates run from $A40 to $A70 per night for double occupancy and include a hearty breakfast. In the United States you can get lists and information about Pubstays by calling Australia Naturally at 213/552-6352.

OTHER MONEY-SAVING STRATEGIES

Take advantage of the special weekend discount rates offered by some hotels. If you're a traveling trio, the third person may be able to share a double room at a minimal rate. As I've noted in the listings, a number of establishments give discounts to readers of this book—therefore show it.

Meals

Lunch menus in Australia are almost universally shorter and cheaper than those for dinner. This applies particularly to pubs, which try to lure lunchtime patrons. It is therefore wise to make lunch your main meal of the day—you'll be eating 25% to 30% cheaper. Alternatively, frequent the delis and sandwich shops. Australian sandwiches are considerably cheaper (and less elaborate) than the U.S. versions, the contents frequently better. And you'll always find an al fresco spot (outdoor tables or a park) if you don't like crowded interiors.

One of the best bets is to follow the student, hostel, or backpacker crowds to their feeding stations. These folks have an uncanny homing beam for good, inexpensive restaurants—most of which you'll find listed here anyway.

If there's more than one of you, consider renting a service apartment with kitchen facilities. The rate may be somewhat above budget level, but the money you save by doing your own cooking will more than make up for it.

Sightseeing & Entertainment

A great many of Australia's "sights" are free, and this includes a large number of museums, exhibitions, galleries, and historical landmarks. Some ask for "donations": purely voluntary and of any size. But even those institutions that charge admission will often have a particular gratis day or half-price day. Many such bargains are listed in this book, but since they frequently change it's best to peruse the notices outside before you enter.

When taking organized tours, you'll find that admission prices are often included in the ticket, but make sure of that. Otherwise, it can raise the cost mightily. Wherever possible, I have stated this in my tour descriptions, but companies have a habit of changing their policies overnight. Most large cities operate some kind of gratis sightseeing transportation, with or without commentary. You'll find these mentioned in every city chapter. Make sure you use them; they'll save you both shoe leather and money.

Australia provides heaps of free outdoor entertainment, mostly connected with some festival or other—concerts, parades, beach carnivals, dance performances, even street theater (though actors frequently pass around the hat afterward). You'll see them announced in the local newspapers.

Indoor entertainment rarely comes gratis. But here as elsewhere, matinee performances are cheaper than evening shows. Sydney and several other cities also have Halftix outlets, where seats (not the best) go for half price. You have to buy tickets at the booth and pay cash, and you can get them only on the afternoon of the performance.

Shopping

Australia is not a happy-bargain-hunter's playground. Most men's and women's clothing costs more than it does in the United States, and the same goes for toys, books, and gadgetry. Here are some best buys.

Souvenirs In the souvenir field, it's a question of sifting through veritable mountains of junk to select some worthwhile objects. Every shopping street has stores crammed with stuffed koalas, plastic boomerangs, mulga wood maps of Australia, kangaroo-hide wallets, and sheepskin coats, plus millions of color postcards of the "Having a Great Time in . . ." type, which is fine if you like that manner of stuff—only you'd better watch out for hidden "Made in Japan" labels.

Australiana If it's genuine Australiana you're after, look over some of the **Aboriginal arts-and-crafts outlets** I mention throughout the book. Aboriginal artifacts are unique, a blending of forms and colors that seem to reflect the immense, haunting bushland that inspired them. They were primitive in the same way Haitian paintings can be called that, with an artistry that conveys moods and impressions rather than details. Their abstract ornamentation has a strikingly "modern" look—almost as if our contemporary taste had just caught up with their traditions.

Other good—although not necessarily cheap—buys are **Digger hats,** perhaps the most attractive military headgear ever devised and equally so on men and women. As for **Australian art** and travel posters and prints, try to get hold of reproductions of some works by Russell Drysdale and Sir Sidney Nolan; no one has captured the *essence* of the "wide brown land" and its people like these two artists. Also, **Australian folk records** can be remarkably good. You might even discover one with the *original* version of "Waltzing Matilda" instead of the hackneyed derivation that's been thumped to death.

Opals These are Australia's national gemstones, and nearly all the world's supply comes from here. They're on sale in special gem stores in every city, and their variety is endless—from the famous iridescent black opal to the flashing fire opal with a light-greenish base. Most opals are found at Lightning Ridge in New South Wales and at Coober Pedy and Andamooka in South Australia, scorched and arid regions that seem to guard their treasures. I tell you how to get there in Chapter 5, "Adelaide," and you can even try a bit of fossicking (or "noodling") yourself—good luck, mate. Meanwhile, the stores offer opals in every imaginable setting or as rough, unset specimens you can polish yourself. There are also mounted stones called **doublets** or **triplets,** which possess some of the richness of the full gems but are considerably less expensive. Visitors pay no duty or purchase tax on opals destined for export.

Wool Products Australia, as they say, rode to prosperity "on the sheep's back"—meaning its wool clip. Sheep, the men who herd and shear them, and their amazingly skilled dogs occupy a large niche in Down Under folklore, with hundreds of songs and poems romanticizing their joys and hardships. Australian wool fabrics are probably the world's best, but they're not particularly cheap. At the top of the range, a Merino Gold sweater, made from fiber finer than cashmere, retails for about $A200. You can, of course, get far less expensive items, but none that could be described as a bargain.

When you buy them, however, make sure they come with the Woolmark ticket: A logo guaranteeing that this is a genuine Australian product, not an imported proxy. The tag shows a sheepishly smiling lamb, under a deep-blue sky and with the Southern Cross in the background, plus an explanatory text in English, German, and Japanese. The ticket, incidentally, makes a handy bookmark.

Note: You can utilize your tourist status by buying at **duty-free shops** at international airports and in the larger cities. You can get some real bargains there (providing you take time to look around), but can use the items only after you leave the country.

Services & Other Transactions

TIPPING Australians have an international reputation for being woeful tippers, but they also have a good excuse: They haven't been brainwashed into accepting this form of legal blackmail. Down Under a tip is still what it was originally—a reward for exceptionally good service. Neither hotels nor restaurants add service charges to their bills. Only in the plushest eateries, where the service *is* outstanding, are you expected to tip about 10% of your check; also, it is customary to leave some change for bar service. Hotel porters usually get $A1 if they've helped you with your luggage. Taxi drivers and porters at air-and-rail terminals have set scales of charges.

MONEY CHANGING You'll have no trouble cashing overseas **traveler's checks,** though some banks ask to see your passport. Australian states impose a stamp duty of about A10¢ per check, so it's cheaper to stick to higher denominations. It is also better to cash your checks at a bank rather than a hotel—the hotel exchange rate is nearly always several points below the bank rate. But here's the rub: Most banks charge a fee for the transaction, and the fees vary (greatly), as do the rates at those banks that do the job gratis. Therefore ask about the fee before you cash your checks and, if possible, shop around.

TELEPHONE CALLS Local calls from a public booth cost A30¢ for an unlimited amount of time, although hotels will charge you up to A60¢. Long-distance (STD) calls can be made from gray green STD phones on which you dial direct and only pay for the time actually used.

OTHER SERVICES Prices vary greatly for hairstyling. Typical Sydney charges are $A16 for women's or men's haircuts, $A14 to $A20 for a shampoo and set.

Medical care is first class by any standard and far more patient oriented than that in America. Doctors actually make house calls. However, visitors are not covered by the Medibank national health insurance plan. For more information on health insurance, see "Health & Insurance," in this chapter.

AUSTRALIA

When traveling in a foreign country, you tend to get stumped by the kind of basic details you don't even think about at home. This (very) basic alphabetical listing is designed to reduce some of the aggravations that stem from unfamiliarity—such as what kind of razor plug to use, how to send a telegram, and how much it costs to mail a letter. Consider this merely an opener. You'll find more information in specific chapters.

American Express Amex offices are located throughout Australia, but the main office is at 92 Pitt St., Sydney, NSW 2000 (tel. 02/239-0666). Hours for business and mail distribution (clients only): Monday to Friday 8:30am to 5:30pm, Saturday 9am to noon.

Business Hours In general, **business hours** are Monday to Friday 9am to 5pm. **Banking hours** are Monday to Thursday 10am to 4pm, Friday until 5pm. In central Sydney, some banks keep extended hours daily. **Pub hours** vary in some states, but generally are daily 10am to 10pm. General **shopping hours** for most stores are Monday to Friday 9am to 5:30pm, Saturday until noon. In Tasmania most shops are closed Saturday. There's late shopping (until 9pm) on Friday in Melbourne and on Thursday in Sydney and Canberra. Luckily not all stores stick to this schedule. Family-run food stores in certain resort and nightlife areas are open every day and stay open until around midnight. So do some downtown bookshops, milk bars, souvenir stores, and tobacconists. Every large city has several chemist shops (drugstores) offering daily round-the-clock service.

Cameras/Film See "Photographic Needs," below.

Cigarettes Cigarettes cost around $A3.55 for a pack of 20. But most large cities have cut-price tobacconists selling single packs for A5¢ to A10¢ less, bigger cuts for cartons. Watch for the signs announcing these reductions.

Climate See "When to Go," in this chapter.

Crime See "Safety," below.

Currency See "Information, Entry Requirements & Money," in this chapter.

Customs See "Information, Entry Requirements & Money," in this chapter.

Documents Required See "Information, Entry Requirements & Money," in this chapter.

Driving Rules See "Getting Around," in this chapter.

Drug Laws Laws against illegal drugs are very strictly enforced throughout the country. Although you won't get hanged for dope possession (as you would in Malaysia), you *will* go to jail for a lengthy stretch.

Drugstores Known as chemists Down Under, they concentrate chiefly on medications and cosmetics and carry nothing like the range of goods in U.S. drugstores. Every city has several all-night chemists, which you'll find listed in each chapter.

Electricity Voltage is 220 to 240V, and plugs are flat three-pin affairs. The more expensive hostelries have wall plugs that fit U.S. razors; the cheaper ones usually don't. You'll need a converter/adapter to make your gadget work.

Embassies/Consulates All foreign embassies and their Commonwealth equivalents, the High Commissions, are located in Canberra in the Australian Capital Territory; many are in the centrally located Yarralumla district. Some countries also maintain consulates in Sydney. **United States Embassy,** State Circle, Yarralumla, ACT 2600 (tel. 06/270-5000); **Canadian High Commission,** Commonwealth Avenue, Yarralumla, ACT 2600 (tel. 06/273-3844); **British High Commission,** Commonwealth Avenue, Yarralumla, ACT 2600 (tel. 06/270-6666); **New Zealand High Commission,** Commonwealth Avenue, Yarralumla, ACT 2600 (tel. 06/270-4211).

Emergencies To alert police, the fire department, or call an ambulance, dial **000** anywhere in the country at no charge.

Etiquette This differs little from the American pattern, except that Aussies handle knives and forks British style. Bar etiquette, however, demands that if someone "shouts" (buys) you a drink, you must shout one in return. In groups everybody shouts a round, but you must wait your turn to do so.

Hitchhiking See "Getting Around," in this chapter.

Holidays See "When to Go," in this chapter.

Homosexuality Tasmania is the only Australian state where male homosexuality is illegal. Lesbian sex has never been outlawed in Australia.

Information See "Information, Entry Requirements & Money," in this chapter, and also specific city chapters for local information offices.

Language See "Cultural & Social Life," Chapter 1.

Laundry Public laundries are located in all major cities, and some hotels and motels have facilities for guest use. Most are open daily, some round-the-clock. A load of wash costs $A1; dryers cost A20¢ for 5 to 10 minutes.

Liquor Laws Pub (bar) hours vary but usually run Monday through Saturday 10am to 11pm; some places are closed Sunday, and those that are open don't get started until noon and close by 10pm. The drinking age throughout the country is 18. And remember that Aussie laws are very strict about drinking and driving, so don't.

Mail Definitely the feeblest of Australia's public services, it manages to be expensive, slow, *and* unreliable in one breath. Mail delivery comes once a day, five days a week, usually late—unless there's no delivery at all because of strikes or holidays. The only good thing to be said about the post office is that the personnel are wonderfully helpful and go to great trouble trying to find the letters they so frequently lose. Standard letters within Australia cost A36¢; overseas aerograms A65¢; air letters to the United States A90¢; postcards to the United States A70¢.

Letters can be sent to you in care of General Delivery (poste restante) at any post office in Australia. For example: (your name), c/o General Delivery, GPO, Sydney, Australia.

You can also receive mail in care of the local American Express office if you are a cardmember or carry their brand of traveler's checks.

Maps Apart from the maps in this book, you can get special excursion and transportation maps at the state tourist offices in capital cities. Road-and-highway maps (some marked with special scenic routes) are also available at the various state motoring association offices. See "Getting Around," in this chapter.

Newspapers/Magazines Every large Australian city has morning and afternoon newspapers, plus one-edition Sunday papers. There is, aside from the *Financial Review,* one national daily, *the Australian,* which covers the country as a whole and carries more overseas news. All state capitals have at least one shop that stocks overseas papers. Certain American periodicals also publish Pacific editions, which are sold at all regular newsstands. These editions, however, are revamped to fit the interests of local readers, so U.S. news figures less prominently.

Passports See "Information, Entry Requirements & Money," in this chapter.

Pets Importation of pets is strictly controlled; the animals may be subject to lengthy quarantines.

Photographic Needs Most major brands and types of film are obtainable in the larger cities and at roughly the same prices as those in the United States. Developing and processing, on the other hand, cost more and frequently take longer. While traveling you should avoid packing undeveloped film in your check-in luggage because baggage X rays will ruin your pictures. Carry unprocessed film with you through security checks and have them inspected by hand.

Police Dial **000** anywhere in Australia to reach the police.

Radio/TV Australia boasts four major and one minor TV networks. ABN2 is the government-run station, equivalent to Britain's BBC, and carries no commercials. The other three networks, ATN 7, TCN9, and TEN10, are stridently commercial. The mixture of soaps, sports, comedies, thrillers, and current affairs they show will be all too familiar to you. The small channel, SBS TV, is a government multicultural station, presenting programs in various languages with English subtitles. Very often you can catch excellent foreign-language films on it.

Radio follows a similar pattern but with some different angles. Some of the FM stations, such as Radio National are hot on current news, while 2PB is entirely devoted to parliamentary broadcasts—a revelation if you're interested in the rough side of Aussie politics.

Restrooms As in U.S. cities, restaurants and pubs prefer you to purchase something if you'd like to use the restroom.

Safety Despite what I've said earlier about Australian cities in general, you should always be prepared: Whenever you're traveling in an unfamiliar city or country, stay alert. Be aware of your immediate surroundings. Wear a money belt and don't sling your camera or purse over your shoulder. This will minimize the possibility of your becoming a victim of crime. Every society has its criminals. It's your responsibility to be aware and alert even in the most heavily touristed areas. See specific chapters for more information.

Taxes The only one that concerns you is a $A25 airport tax, payable *in Australian dollars only* when leaving the country. Otherwise, there are no sales or hotel taxes of any kind.

Telephone/Telex/Fax You'll find coin-operated public phones at all the usual places. "Silver phones," which take credit cards, are rarer. Local calls cost A30¢ for an unlimited time. Call booths take A10¢, A20¢, and A50¢ pieces. Long-distance calls within Australia (STD) have an area code (02 for Sydney, 03 for Melbourne, etc.) which you dial first. Overseas calls (ISD) can be made directly by first dialing 0011, then the country code, the area code (minus the zero), and the number. Charges depend on distance and the time of call. You'll find area codes and prices in the A–K White Pages of the phone book. But if you call from your hotel room, remember that hotels add a hefty surcharge.

Telex and electronic mail services can be sent from the General Post Office of any city. You can send telegrams from the post office or by phoning 015. Many of the larger hotels, even in the budget bracket, now have fax facilities.

Time The Australian continent has three time zones: Eastern Standard Time, 10 hours ahead of Greenwich Mean Time; Central Australian Time, 9½ hours ahead; and Western Time, 8 hours ahead. During the summer months all states introduce daylight savings, putting clocks 1 hour ahead.

Not taking daylight savings into consideration, international times are staggered as follows:

When it's noon in Sydney and Melbourne, it's

11:30am in Adelaide/Darwin
11am in Tokyo/Seoul
10am in Hong Kong/Manila/Singapore/Perth
9am in Jakarta/Bangkok
7:30am in Delhi/Calcutta
3am in Paris/Rome/Frankfurt/Amsterdam
2am in London/Lisbon
11pm yesterday in Buenos Aires
9pm yesterday in New York/Washington
8pm yesterday in Mexico City/Chicago
6pm yesterday in San Francisco/Los Angeles
4pm yesterday in Honolulu

Tipping See "Other Money-Saving Strategies," in this chapter.

Tourist Offices See "Information, Entry Requirements & Money," in this chapter, and also specific city chapters.

Visas See "Information, Entry Requirements & Money," in this chapter.

Water Tapwater is perfectly drinkable throughout the country. In fact, it generally tastes considerably better (because it's less chemicalized) than in America.

Yellow Pages Located in the phone book, they serve the same function as in the United States—listing every (well, almost every) business enterprise in town.

CHAPTER 3

SYDNEY

- WHAT'S SPECIAL ABOUT SYDNEY
1. FROM A BUDGET TRAVELER'S POINT OF VIEW
2. ORIENTATION
- NEIGHBORHOODS IN BRIEF
3. GETTING AROUND
- FAST FACTS: SYDNEY
4. WHERE TO STAY
- FROMMER'S SMART TRAVELER: HOTELS
- FROMMER'S COOL FOR KIDS: HOTELS
5. WHERE TO EAT
- FROMMER'S SMART TRAVELER: RESTAURANTS
- FROMMER'S COOL FOR KIDS: RESTAURANTS
6. ATTRACTIONS
- DID YOU KNOW . . . ?
- FROMMER'S FAVORITE SYDNEY EXPERIENCES
- WALKING TOUR 1—THE ROCKS
- WALKING TOUR 2—DOWNTOWN SYDNEY
7. SPORTS & RECREATION
8. SAVVY SHOPPING
9. EVENING ENTERTAINMENT
10. NETWORKS & RESOURCES
11. EASY EXCURSIONS: NEW SOUTH WALES

For any overseas visitor landing here for the first time, Sydney comes as a double surprise: The city is unexpectedly huge and astonishingly beautiful—a very rare combination. The bigness is a matter of statistics: Greater Sydney has 3.7 million people and sprawls over some 670 square miles, making it considerably larger than, say, Rome or Los Angeles.

But the beauty is a kind of indestructible miracle, a gift of nature that has survived any amount of shoddy boom building, bad planning, and mindless wrecking. Nothing, it seems—not even real-estate sharks and boneheaded bureaucrats—can mar that gemlike harbor setting. The blue Pacific Ocean protects the city against any disfigurement that human greed and myopia can devise: You could turn half the city area into cement parking lots and it would *still* remain a pearl.

Sydney Harbour is more than a harbor. It is immense enough to reduce any clutter of cranes, derricks, and dumps to insignificance—in Governor Phillip's words, "a thousand sail of the line may ride in the most perfect security here." Its configurations splinter the coast into hundreds of coves, bays, and inlets, creating a foreshore of 150 miles and putting much of the city within sight or walking distance of the sea. And since Sydney is hilly, the harbor gesticulates at you from the most unexpected places, providing an endless kaleidoscope of surprise views. With ruffles of white surf fringing golden beaches, with thousands of multicolored sails slicing through sparkling water, with deep-green foliage marking the shores, the harbor casts a spell of almost magic loveliness over the entire metropolis.

The natural magic has proved stronger than human creations, which were frequently awful. The Harbour Bridge is a clumsy slab of steel and mortar. Most of Sydney's downtown streets are ill-designed warrens clogged with chaotic traffic. Portions of its suburbia could win booby prizes for drabness. Even now, building speculators and freeway fanatics are trying to demolish the last of the little 19th-century terrace houses whose ornate wrought-iron balconies provide the only touch of charm in some areas.

Yet somehow the magic triumphed. The city remains irresistibly attractive, imbued with an appeal that makes you forget all its shortcomings. The spectacle of a white oceanliner berthed next to the gleaming wings of the Opera House, framed against the green water and the dazzling blue sky, blots out all the industrial wastelands that stretch beyond.

WHAT'S SPECIAL ABOUT SYDNEY

Beaches

- ☐ Thirty-four ocean beaches within city limits.
- ☐ Bondi Beach, the world's most famous surfing beach.

Architectural Highlights

- ☐ Sydney Opera House, truly one of a kind.
- ☐ Sydney Tower, a giant silver needle soaring 1,000 feet skyward.
- ☐ St. James's Church, designed by convict-architect Francis Greenway.
- ☐ State Library, a beautiful building next to the State Parliament.
- ☐ Hyde Park Barracks, another Georgian-style gem by Greenway.
- ☐ Elizabeth Bay House, a classic colonial mansion built in 1838.

Museums

- ☐ Powerhouse Museum, a showcase of science and technology.
- ☐ Australian Museum, the largest natural history museum on the continent.
- ☐ Art Gallery of New South Wales, with paintings by some of the finest Australian artists.

Shopping

- ☐ Queen Victoria Building (QVB), a marvel of interior design.
- ☐ Centrepoint, a giant complex topped by Sydney Tower.
- ☐ Pitt Street Mall, a pedestrian walk crammed with shops.

Streets/Neighborhoods

- ☐ Chinatown, a bustling, noisy quarter chock a block with restaurants.
- ☐ Paddington, a hunting ground for art gallery fans.
- ☐ Double Bay, an exclusive beach suburb with an elegant shopping mall.

Ace Attractions

- ☐ Sydney Harbour, best admired on a harbor cruise.
- ☐ Darling Harbour, a former backwater turned into a giant fun complex.

After Dark

- ☐ Some 27 live theaters, plus myriad discos, clubs, cabarets, and entertainment pubs.
- ☐ Kings Cross, where the red lights blink until dawn.

Sydney is the largest, oldest, and liveliest city in Australia—with a scarlet past and a tempestuous present. In 1800 it had a population of just 5,000—41% of them convicts and most of the females "transported" prostitutes. But even this unpromising start turned to its advantage: Convict mementos are now among its best tourist attractions, and convict labor created some of its finest buildings. And perhaps Sydney owes some facets of its hell-raising, hard-driving, slightly rakish, and tremendously convivial personality to those rough forebears who founded it against their will.

This, then, is the gateway to Australia, the first and often the final glimpse visitors get of this amazing continent. No place on earth could wish for a more fascinating welcome mat.

1. FROM A BUDGET TRAVELER'S POINT OF VIEW

Among Australians, Sydney is known as a very expensive place. And so it is—for those who buy houses, rent apartments, or drive cars there. But for visitors the city is no costlier than other spots on the continent; in some respects it is even less so. Cabs, for instance, are cheaper in Sydney than elsewhere, and restaurant competition is so fierce that you can easily find meals as economical (and considerably better) than those dished up in country towns. Only in the deluxe bracket of accommodations and eateries do Sydney prices hit the sky. And this book, luckily, doesn't deal with the three-star echelons.

To keep down your transportation costs, read the segment on "Getting Around" carefully and utilize all the discount passes and gratis rides mentioned there. However, using a bicycle for city travel can be risky. Sydney traffic is fast and chaotic, and the motorists are inconsiderate of anything on two wheels.

For inexpensive eating stick to the *small* ethnic restaurants (particularly the Asian ones). Make lunch your main meal of the day, paying particular attention to pub lunches (shorter menus, lower prices). Alternatively, try the excellent (mostly European) delis and sandwich shops, the majority of which unfortunately close at night.

A number of hotels (but not hostels) offer special weekend rates. Ask about them. If you're traveling in a trio, the third person sharing a double room always pays a very low rate. The cheapest accommodation periods are those without a festival or major sporting event—try to pick those in-between times. Unlike the resort areas, Sydney hotels don't generally lower their rates during winter. But they smartly *raise* them for festivities.

Serviced apartments have rates well above the budget bracket, but they can be bargains if there's more than one of you. They offer kitchen facilities that can cut your eating bills in half.

Sydney is awash with free entertainment, chiefly outdoor concerts, exhibitions, and dance performances. But several of the museums and galleries are likewise free (or have certain gratis days).

Occasionally, though, a little splurge helps the morale, so I've included the worthwhile splurges in every segment of this book. They run from somewhat costlier hotels and restaurants to special treats, like taking the speedy hydrofoil—instead of the slow ferry—over to Manly, or having panoramic cocktails at the Bennelong, alongside the Opera House.

2. ORIENTATION

ARRIVING

BY PLANE Chances are that Sydney will be your first touch-down point in Australia. Located in Mascot, about five miles from the city center, **Kingsford Smith Airport** is the biggest air terminal in the country and one of the busiest in the world (with more daily flights than Paris's Charles de Gaulle Airport). Built on the shores of—and partly *into*—Botany Bay, the airport consists of an international and a domestic portion. Intransit passengers transfer from one part to the other by domestic airline coach for $A3. Kingsford Smith has every conceivable facility for travelers: currency exchange, showers, round-the-clock cafeterias, restaurants and bars, shops, bookstalls, boutiques, hotel information, and car-rental desks (Avis, Budget, Hertz, Thrifty), all run with what *Newsweek* magazine termed "Aussie-friendly" efficiency. The airport may be huge, but it has less of the sausage-machine spirit that makes others so nerve grinding.

You can travel to the city center either on the **Kingsford Smith Airport Coach** or on the **Airport Express** operated by State Transit. Both cost about $A6 one way for adults, half price for children under 12, and leave the airport every 20 minutes for the half-hour trip into town. The buses start running at 6am and serve both the international and the domestic terminals.

The Kingsford Smith bus drops its passengers at the doors of their hotels or motels; the Airport Express delivers people to one of nine predetermined points in the city, from which they must walk or take a taxi. A **taxi** to Sydney from the airport costs about $A18.

Departing passengers can arrange for the Kingsford Smith Airport Coach to pick them up at their hotel if they call at least an hour in advance (tel. 667-3221).

BY TRAIN Sydney's hulking **Central Station** is right downtown at the end of Pitt Street. There is a cab rank at the entrance (wait in line) and a bus stop outside on Pitt Street.

BY BUS The terminal for **Greyhound, Bus Australia,** and **Pioneer Express** is on the ground floor of the Greetings Oxford Koala Hotel, at the corner of Oxford and Riley streets in Darlinghurst. This is about a mile east of the city center, less from Kings Cross. Local buses stop near the entrance. Cabs are usually standing outside the hotel.

BY CAR Your entrance into the city depends on where you come from. If it's from the north (Brisbane or the Gold Coast), you'll be on the **Pacific Highway,** which winds through the northern suburbs until it feeds into the Harbour Bridge. Drive across and you'll be downtown. Approaching from the south (Melbourne), you'll be taking the **Princes Highway,** running through Sylvania, Rockdale, and Newtown, until it leads into King Street and into the City. The Princes Highway is part of a 670-mile road system called Australia One, which skirts the Pacific Ocean most of the way. The **Great Western Highway** and the **Hume Highway** enter Sydney from the west.

TOURIST INFORMATION

A plethora of information is available to Sydney's visitors. The **Travellers' Information Service** at the international airport terminal is open 365 days a year from 6am until the last flight arrives. These folks are helpful with hotel reservations and can sometimes arrange favorable rates for those who did not reserve lodgings in advance. They can also arrange cruises and coach tours. A free telephone information service is in operation daily from 5am to 6pm (tel. 669-1583 or 669-5111).

In the city center, information is available at the **New South Wales Travel Centre,** 19 Castlereagh St. near Martin Place (tel. 231-4444). This well-stocked office is open Monday to Friday from 9am to 5pm, and the staff is ready and willing to answer questions and make reservations for you. The **Sydney Visitors Information Booth** (shared with Halftix), in Martin Place between Castlereagh and Elizabeth streets (tel. 235-2424), is also a good place to get information—Monday to Friday from 9am to 5pm.

Seven days a week, the people at **The Rocks Visitor Centre,** 104 George St. (tel. 255-1788), answer questions about their part of town. They also offer films and a museum of local history (open daily 9am to 5pm).

You can get good tourist information at the **National Roads and Motorists' Association (NRMA),** 151 Clarence St. (tel. 260-9222), if you are a member of an affiliated club. They're open Monday to Friday from 8:30am to 5pm and Saturday from 8:30 to 11:30am.

For information about the seaside suburb of Manly, contact **Manly Tourist Promotions,** South Steyne Street, Manly (tel. 977-1088). They're open daily from 10am to 4pm and are closed public holidays.

The **Travellers' Aid Society** at the Central Station offers help to distraught travelers, including a lounge and a daybed weekdays from 7am to 5pm and Saturday until noon.

CITY LAYOUT

Sydney, capital of the state of New South Wales (a singularly misnamed state that bears not the faintest resemblance to its original), is divided into two major (and many minor) portions by the undulations of its harbor. The main divisions are **Sydney**

proper and **North Sydney,** linked by the gigantic traffic-jammed **Sydney Harbour Bridge.** Some of the most glamorous suburbs and beauty spots lie north of the bridge, but nearly all the tourist attractions—except Taronga Park Zoo and Manly—are in the southern part.

The focal point of the city is the pedestrian plaza on **Martin Place.** If you stand with your back to the pillared General Post Office, you'll be facing due north. That is the direction for Circular Quay—terminal for all ferry services—the Harbour Bridge and, at the tip of Bennelong Point, the Sydney Opera House. Northeast and east stretch the Royal Botanic Gardens and their southward extension, the Domain. Southeast of you lies Hyde Park, from which point William Street runs straight uphill to **Kings Cross.**

South of you, at the end of Pitt Street, stands **Central Station,** the country-and-interstate rail terminal. Due west extends **Darling Harbour,** Sydney's main cargo reception point. Two streets away from you to the northwest is Wynyard Station, the terminal for the city's train-and-bus transport. And going either through or by Martin Place are all of the city's main shopping streets: George Street, Pitt Street, Castlereagh Street, and Elizabeth Street.

NEIGHBORHOODS IN BRIEF

Sydney has hundreds of neighborhoods—it would take several chapters to list them all. The selections below are merely those visitors are most likely to see:

Chinatown Also known as Haymarket; it borders on Darling Harbour and the Entertainment Centre and is a colorful mix of restaurants and specialty stores.

Kings Cross An adjunct to the City, this is the area where Darlinghurst, Potts Point, and Elizabeth Bay meet. It is like Times Square and Montmartre rolled into one, but it's interspersed with first-class hotels, excellent restaurants, and charming cafés.

Woolloomooloo Known as "The Loo," this erstwhile slum at the dockside adjoining the Domain has undergone intense gentrification and now boasts some of the best entertainment pubs and most lovingly refurbished houses in town.

Darling Point Separated from Kings Cross by Rushcutters Bay Park, it is studded with posh homes and contains luxury marinas and the Cruising Yacht Club.

Double Bay Closest of the fashionable eastern suburbs, which stretch all the way to the Watsons Bay peninsula, Double Bay borders Darling Point and contains the svelte Cosmopolitan Centre shopping hub—*not* for bargain hunting—nicknamed "Double Pay."

Bondi Pronounced bon-DIE, this very lively, though not particularly charming, area lives on its celebrated surfing beach, the closest to the city.

Paddington "Paddo," as it's known to the locals, stretches north of Oxford Street, a winding, hilly region centered by Five Ways. It's famous for antiques shops, private art galleries, yuppy-bohemians, and trendy interior decorating.

Surry Hills Gentrification is in progress in this area east of Central Station. Once a stronghold of (largely Irish) blue-collar workers, it now contains the Belvoir Street Theatre, the pick of the avant-garde stages, plus several excellent restaurants and scores of chic homes and studios.

Oxford Street Sydney's longest and most varied, but not very fashionable, shopping drag runs from Bondi Junction all the way to Hyde Park, changing complexion several times en route. Around Taylor Square in Darlinghurst it becomes decidedly gay as well as crammed with restaurants, cafés, and ambling humanity.

Glebe and **Camperdown** The two districts adjoining the vast campus of Sydney University are thronged with students of every race and persuasion, and likewise with inexpensive eateries.

Kirribilli On the North Shore just across Sydney Harbour Bridge, this hilly and rather elegant area boasts panoramic views and high-rent apartment blocks.

Hunters Hill Just across the "other" bridge—the Gladesville—this peninsula juts out of the North Shore and is allegedly Sydney's snootiest enclave. Legend has it that its inhabitants never set foot downtown. It is sprinkled with charming old colonial houses, some made of stone hand hewn by convicts.

Manly Thirty-five minutes by ferry from Circular Quay, Manly is Sydney's vacation world, with four ocean beaches, a giant aquarium, fun parks, promenades, and 700-or-so diverse attractions.

Parramatta Now a western suburb 18 miles from the city, this was once a separate town and the intended capital of the colony. It has a dozen historic buildings dating from the early colonial period and an individual small-town flavor all its own.

Street Maps You can obtain maps of Sydney and the surrounding area from the **New South Wales Travel Centre,** 19 Castlereagh St. (tel. 231-4444), or, if you're a member of an affiliated auto club, contact NRMA, 151 Clarence St. (tel. 260-9222).

3. GETTING AROUND

BY PUBLIC TRANSPORTATION

Sydney is serviced by electric trains (surface and underground), double- and single-decker buses, and ferries. You will use the last only for harbor cruises and fairly leisurely trips to the North Shore.

You can save quite a bit of money by purchasing a **Sydney Pass.** Costing $A50 for adults, $A40 for children, this ticket gives you three days of unlimited travel on all buses (including the Sydney Explorer and Airport Express), all ferries, hydrofoils, and Jetcats, and it takes you on three different harbor cruises. Passes can be bought at the airport, the NSW Travel Centre, Circular Quay, The Rocks, and the Queen Victoria Building.

Sydney also has two gratis bus services: Bus no. 666 takes you to the State Art Gallery in the Domain; bus no. 777 does a circuit of the city and runs a shuttle service for shoppers every 10 minutes until 4pm.

SUBWAY [CITY RAIL] The quickest way to get around is by the underground rail system, which connects the city with the suburbs and operates daily from 4:30am to midnight. Travel is priced by sections, starting at $A1.20, half price for children under 16. There are eight route systems, each with its identifying color code on which you can check your route. A money saver here is the **CityHopper,** costing $A2.10. This entitles you to unlimited train travel for one day, after 9am weekdays and anytime weekends. For information contact Metrotrips (tel. 954-4422).

State Rail operates CityRail service and Countrylink trains, which carry passengers farther afield. For Countrylink reservations, call 132-232 between 6:30am and 10pm or stop in at the Countrylink Travel Centre, 11–31 York St. (tel. 224-4744), Monday to Friday between 8:30am and 5:30pm.

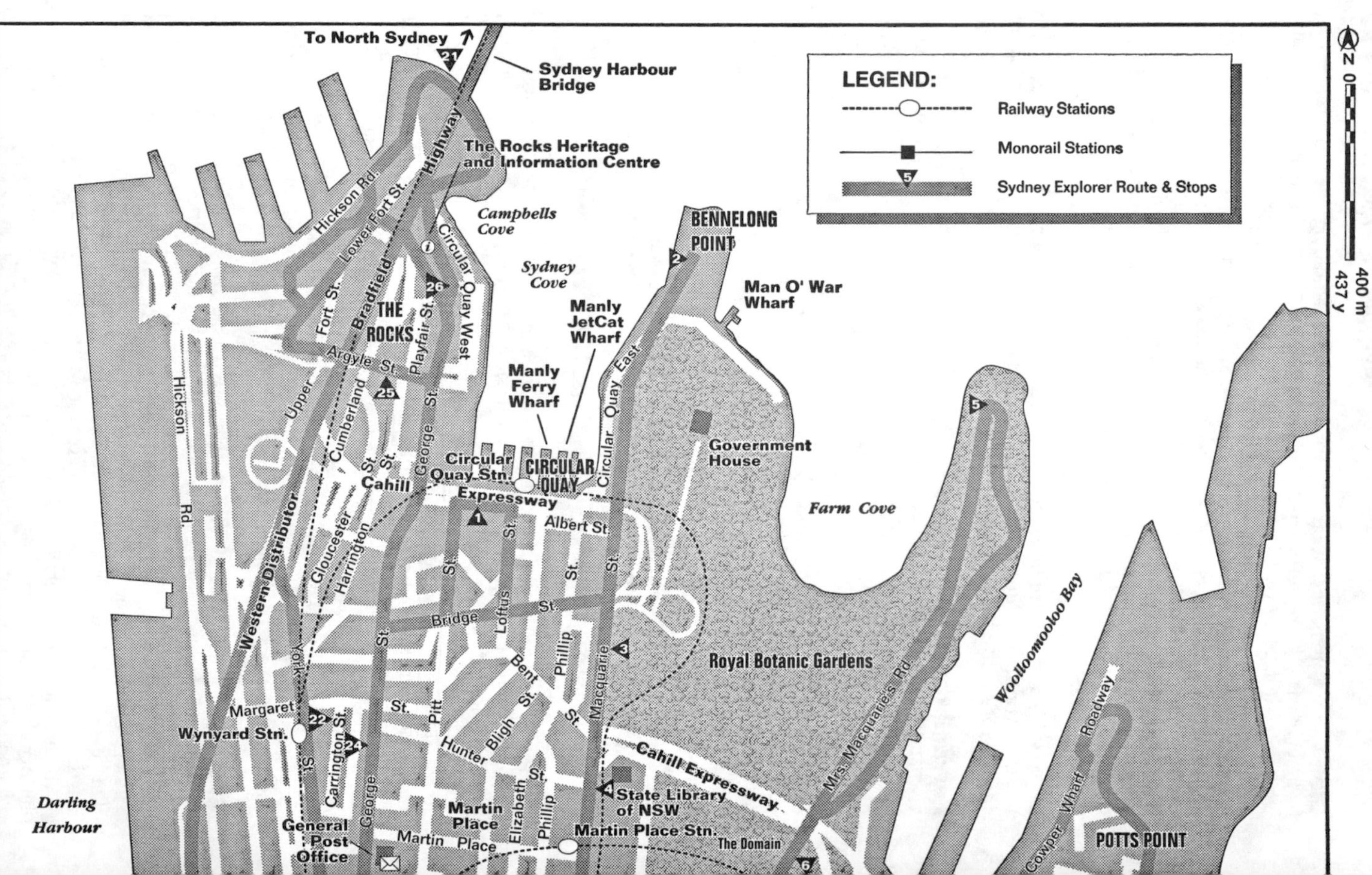
N
0
400 m
437 y
LEGEND:
Railway Stations
Monorail Stations
Sydney Explorer Route & Stops
To North Sydney
Sydney Harbour Bridge
The Rocks Heritage and Information Centre
Campbells Cove
Sydney Cove
BENNELONG POINT
Man O' War Wharf
Manly JetCat Wharf
Manly Ferry Wharf
Circular Quay Stn.
CIRCULAR QUAY
Circular Quay West
Circular Quay East
Government House
Farm Cove
THE ROCKS
Hickson Rd.
Lower Fort St.
Fort St.
Bradfield Highway
Playfair St.
Argyle St.
Upper
Cumberland St.
George St.
Cahill Expressway
Albert St.
Gloucester
Harrington
Western Distributor
Loftus
Bridge St.
Phillip St.
Macquarie St.
Bent St.
Bligh St.
Hunter St.
Pitt St.
York St.
Margaret St.
Wynyard Stn.
Carrington St.
Martin Place
Elizabeth
Phillip
State Library of NSW
Martin Place Stn.
The Domain
General Post Office
Royal Botanic Gardens
Mrs. Macquarie's Rd.
Woolloomooloo Bay
Cowper Wharf Roadway
POTTS POINT
Darling Harbour

SYDNEY TRANSPORTATION SYSTEMS:
TNT HARBOURLINK MONORAIL, CITY CIRCLE LINE & EXPLORER BUS ROUTES

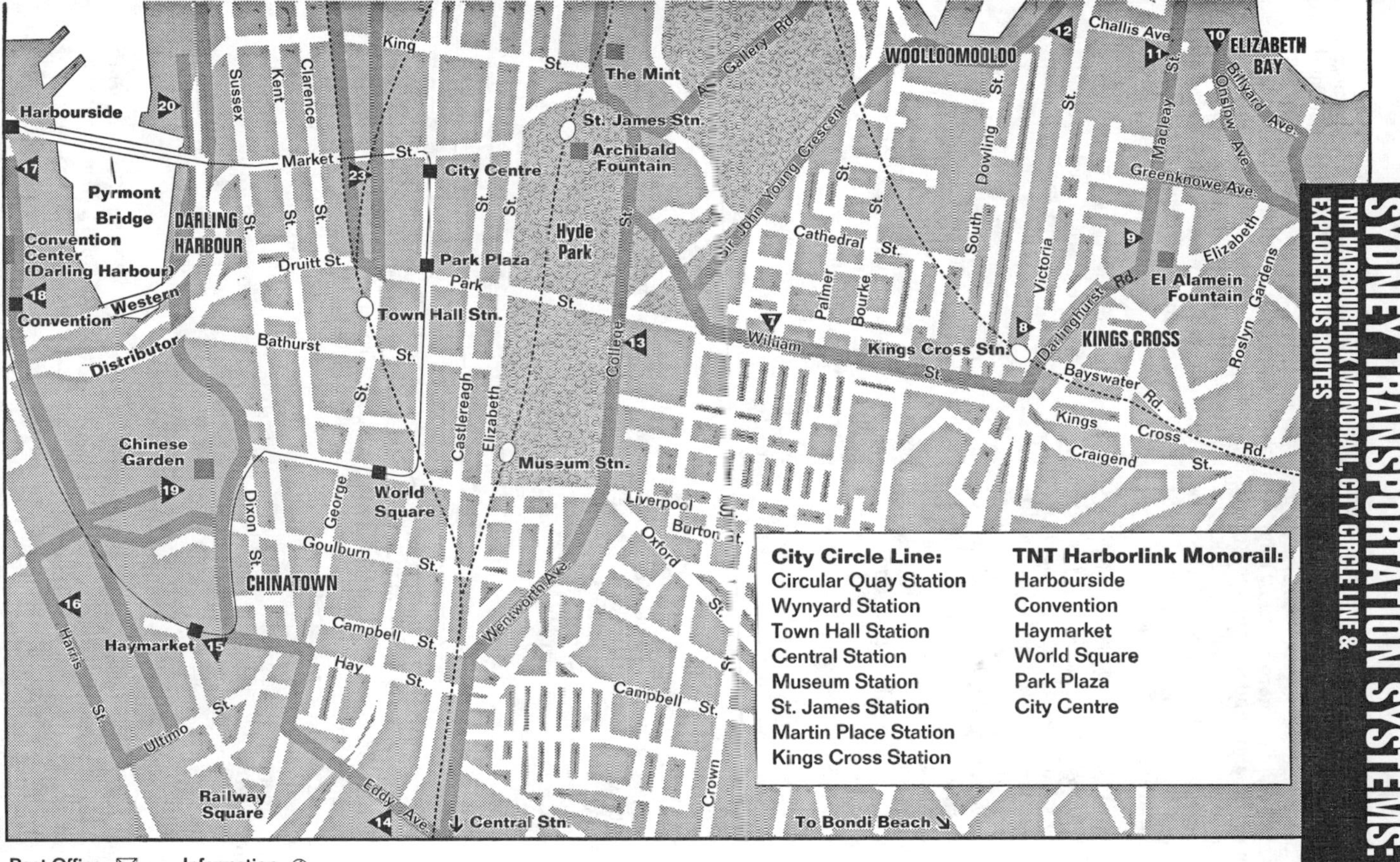

City Circle Line:
Circular Quay Station
Wynyard Station
Town Hall Station
Central Station
Museum Station
St. James Station
Martin Place Station
Kings Cross Station

TNT Harborlink Monorail:
Harbourside
Convention
Haymarket
World Square
Park Plaza
City Centre

Post Office ✉ Information ⓘ

MONORAIL Like the underground train, the speedy monorail connecting the central business district to Darling Harbour doesn't compete with vehicular traffic. Instead, Sydney's sleek, state-of-the-art system glides over the heads of pedestrians and above congested streets. The system usually operates Monday to Wednesday from 7am to 10pm, Thursday and Friday from 7am to midnight, Saturday from 9am to midnight, and Sunday from 9am to 8pm, but it's a good idea to check the hours on signs posted in the stations. The city center/Darling Harbour round-trip takes approximately 12 minutes. Tickets cost $A2.50; children under 5 ride free. The monorail connects with trains at Town Hall Station. For more information call TNT Harbourlink (tel. 552-2288).

BUS Like the subway fares, bus tickets are priced by sections. The minimum fare is $A1.20 for a 4-kilometer (2½-mile) section. Tickets are purchased directly from the driver, and exact change is not needed. (See the introduction to this section for information on discount passes and free buses.)

For sightseeing, you can use one of the fleet of distinctive red Mercedes buses called **Sydney Explorers** (tel. 399-0681), which run a continuous shuttle service between 20 of the most popular visitor's attractions. For $A20 per adult, $A45 per family, you can spend any day of the week from 9:30am to 5pm on these buses, getting on and off as often as you like. The buses stop at each location every half hour, so you can hang around as long as you please, then catch the next Explorer to the next highlight. These include Circular Quay, the Opera House, Parliament House, Kings Cross, Chinatown, The Rocks, and Pier One; you can buy your ticket as you board.

Suburban buses leave from Circular Quay for eastern suburbs and beaches, from Carrington and York streets at Wynyard Park for northern suburbs and beaches. **Interstate buses** leave from the bus terminal at the corner of Riley and Oxford streets.

TAXI Taxis are more numerous in Sydney than anywhere else in the country, and the locals use them as casually as New Yorkers. The flag-drop rate is $A1.65, and each additional kilometer costs A85¢. Phone bookings add an extra A60¢ to the meter, and crossing the Harbour Bridge costs an additional A20¢. Some of the main cab companies are **Legion Cabs** (tel. 289-9000), **Taxis Combined** (tel. 332-8888), and **RSL Cabs** (tel. 699-0144), all of which accept American Express and Diners Club credit cards.

BY CAR

For car rentals there are (among many others) **Budget,** 93 William St. (tel. 361-3366); **Dollar,** 80 William St. (tel. 332-1033); **Hertz,** corner of William and Riley streets (tel. 360-6621); and **Thrifty,** 73 William St., Kings Cross (tel. 360-4055 or 669-6677 at Kingsford Smith Airport). For rates see "Getting Around" in Chapter 2. And don't forget those special weekend deals.

Cars are great for excursions or the shorter distances between cities, but I don't recommend them for sightseeing in downtown Sydney. Unless you're thoroughly familiar with the city layout, you'll be so busy watching street signs that you won't see anything. And the parking situation ranges from difficult to impossible.

BY BICYCLE

One of the places where bicycles (pushbikes) can be rented: **All Bike Hire,** corner of Canterbury Road and Gibson Avenue, Bankstown (tel. 707-1691). When possible, however, confine your riding to designated bike trails. City traffic is ruthless, the streets are narrow and jammed, and motorists' driving habits are lethal. Like New York, Paris, and London, central Sydney is *not* a biking city.

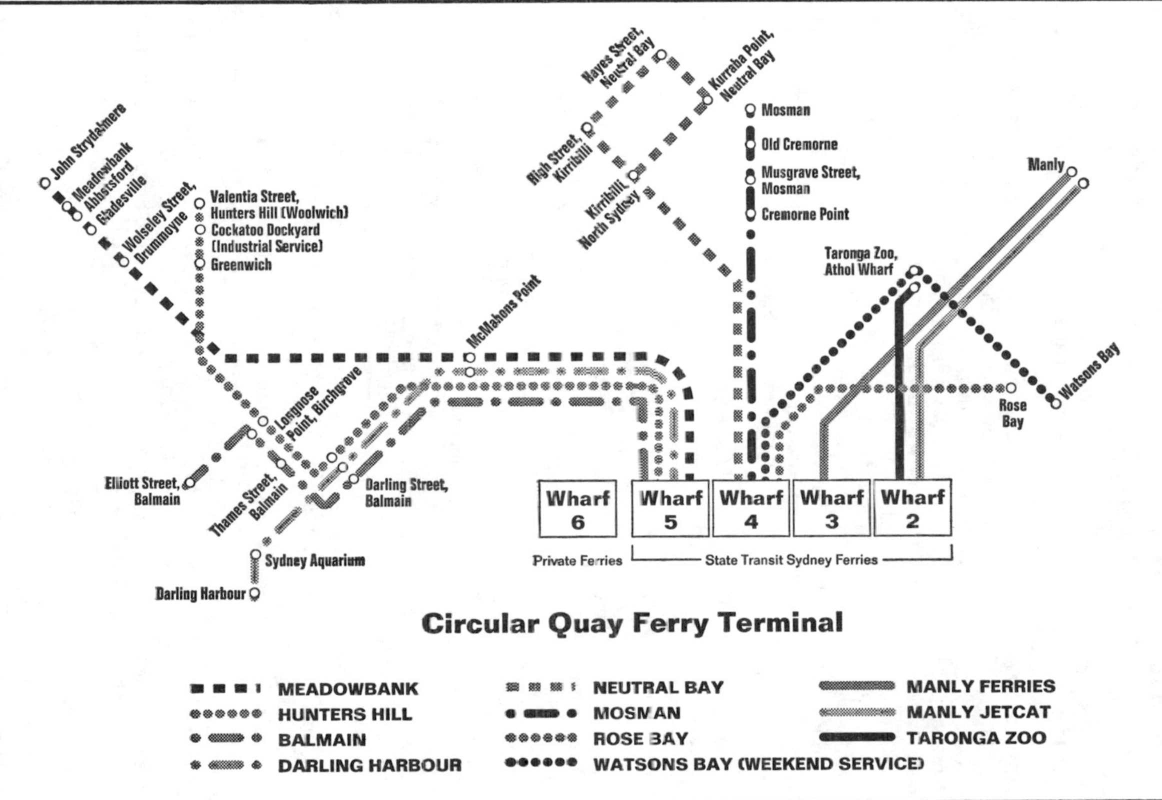
John Strydalmere
Meadowbank
Abbotsford
Gladesville
Wolseley Street,
Drummoyne
Valentia Street,
Hunters Hill (Woolwich)
Cockatoo Dockyard
(Industrial Service)
Greenwich
McMahons Point
Longnose Point, Birchgrove
Elliott Street,
Balmain
Thames Street,
Balmain
Darling Street,
Balmain
Sydney Aquarium
Darling Harbour
Hayes Street,
Neutral Bay
High Street,
Kirribilli
Kirribilli,
North Sydney
Kurraba Point,
Neutral Bay
Mosman
Old Cremorne
Musgrave Street,
Mosman
Cremorne Point
Taronga Zoo,
Athol Wharf
Manly
Watsons Bay
Rose
Bay
Wharf
6
Wharf
5
Wharf
4
Wharf
3
Wharf
2
Private Ferries
State Transit Sydney Ferries
Circular Quay Ferry Terminal
MEADOWBANK
HUNTERS HILL
BALMAIN
DARLING HARBOUR
NEUTRAL BAY
MOSMAN
ROSE BAY
WATSONS BAY (WEEKEND SERVICE)
MANLY FERRIES
MANLY JETCAT
TARONGA ZOO

6379

SYDNEY

American Express The office in Sydney is at 92 Pitt St. (tel. 02/239-0666), open Monday to Friday 8:30am to 5:30pm and Saturday 9am to noon.

Area Code The telephone area code is **02.**

Babysitters The Sydney City Council operates the **Hyde Park Family Centre** on the corner of Park and Elizabeth streets (tel. 265-9411). Child minding, up to six hours per week, costs $A2.50 for one hour. Hours are Monday to Friday 7:30am to 6pm. The **All Sydney Baby Sitting Service** (tel. 521-3333) comes to your hotel and charges about $A6 per hour plus traveling costs.

Bookstores **Dymocks** (pronounced DIM-icks) **Book Arcade,** 426 George St. (tel. 235-0155), just north of Market Street, is open daily: Monday to Tuesday and Friday 8:30am to 5:30pm, Wednesday 9am to 5:30pm, Thursday 8:30am to 9pm, Saturday 9am to 5pm, and Sunday 10am to 5pm.

Angus & Robertson Bookstore, in the Imperial Arcade, 168 Pitt St. (tel. 235-1188), is open Monday to Wednesday and Friday 8:30am to 6pm, Thursday 8:30am to 9pm, Saturday 9am to 5:30pm, and Sunday 10:30am to 5pm.

Business Hours Most **banks** are open Monday to Thursday 9:30am to 4pm and Friday 9:30am to 5pm. **Stores** are generally open Monday to Friday 9am to 5:30pm (Thursday until 9pm) and Saturday 9am to 5pm. Some shops stay open later on Friday, and some are open only until noon on Saturday.

Car Rentals See "Getting Around," in this chapter.

Climate See "When to Go," Chapter 2.

Crime See "Safety," below.

Currency See "Information, Entry Requirements & Money," Chapter 2.

Currency Exchange In addition to the office of American Express, traveler's checks can be cashed at **Thomas Cook,** Kingsgate Shopping Centre, Kings Cross (tel. 356-2211), open Monday to Friday 8:45am to 5:30pm and Saturday to Sunday 8:45am to 1pm. The **Interforex Money Exchange** at no. 6 jetty, Circular Quay (tel. 247-2082), is open Monday to Friday 8am to 9pm, Saturday 8am to 8pm, and Sunday 9am to 6pm; it has several other offices as well.

While there are many **Westpac** banks in Sydney, one of the most convenient for tourists is located at 47 George St., The Rocks (tel. 226-2388); it's open during regular bank hours (see "Business Hours," above).

Dentist For dental problems, contact the **Dental Emergency Information Service,** an official service of the Australian Dental Association (tel. 267-5919). For emergency dental services on Sunday and public holidays, phone 332-3092.

Doctor See "Hospitals," below.

Drugstores All-night chemists (drugstores) are located at 197 Oxford St., Darlinghurst, and 28 Darlinghurst Rd., Kings Cross. For emergency prescriptions, call 438-3333 (24 hours).

Embassies/Consulates All embassies are in Canberra, the capital. Sydney is home to the following consulates. **Canada:** 50 Bridge St. (tel. 231-6522). **New Zealand:** 25th floor, State Bank Building, 52 Martin Place (tel. 233-8388). **United Kingdom:** Level 16 Gateway, 1 Macquarie Place (tel. 247-7521). **United States:** Level 59, MLC Centre, 19 Martin Place (tel. 373-9200).

Emergencies The emergency number for police, fire brigade, or ambulance is a delightfully simple **000.**

Eyeglasses For optical repair or prescriptions see the **OPSM** branches at 183 Macquarie St. (tel. 217-1948) or 73 King St. (tel. 217-1885).

Hairdressers/Barbers Try **Eddie Azzi,** Sky Garden, Castlereagh Street, Suite 106A (tel. 232-1116).

Handicapped Persons Contact **Consumer Information for the Disabled,** 58 Oxford St., Darlinghurst (tel. 331-2606).

Holidays See "When to Go," Chapter 2.

Hospitals For emergency medical attention contact **Sydney Hospital,**

Macquarie Street (tel. 228-2111), or **Royal Prince Alfred Hospital,** Missenden Road, Camperdown (tel. 516-6111).

Hotlines **Poison Information Centre:** 519-0466; **Rape Crisis Centre:** 819-6565; **Life Line:** 264-2222; **Youth Line:** 264-1177; **Gay and Lesbian Hotline:** 319-2799; **AIDS Hotline:** 332-4000.

Information See "Tourist Information," in this chapter. Information on other states of Australia is available in Sydney by contacting **Canberra Tourist Bureau,** 14 Martin Place (tel. 233-3666); **Northern Territory Tourist Bureau,** 345 George St. (tel. 262-3744); **Queensland Government Travel Centre,** 75 Castlereagh St. (tel. 232-1788); **South Australian Government Travel Centre,** 143 King St. (tel. 232-8388); **Tasmanian Government Tourist Bureau,** 149 King St. (tel. 233-2500); **Victorian Tourism Commission,** 61 Market St. (tel. 233-5499); and **Western Australian Tourist Centre,** 92 Pitt St. (tel. 233-4400).

Laundry/Dry Cleaning **Wash on the Rocks,** 9 Argyle Place, The Rocks (tel. 247-4917), is open Monday to Friday 7am to 6pm and Saturday 8am to 3pm. If they do the laundry for you the cost is $A15 for two loads.

One-hour dry-cleaning service is available at **Lawrence Dry Cleaners,** Wynyard Station (tel. 262-1583), and Maurice Dry Cleaners, 11 AMP Centre (tel. 231-2498).

Library The State Library of New South Wales (Mitchell Library) is on Macquarie Street (tel. 230-1414).

Lost Property **Airport:** go to the Federal Airport Corporation's administration office, second floor, International Terminal (tel. 667-9583). In taxis: Phone the office of the taxi company. **Ferries:** Phone 256-4655 or 256-4656. **Trains:** Go to 470 and 490 Pitt St. near the Central Station (tel. 219-4757 or 211-1176). **Buses:** Each bus depot has its own lost property office. There is no general lost property bureau in Sydney. Other than the above suggestions, go to the police station closest to where you lost the item.

Luggage Storage/Lockers There are baggage lockers at the Kingsford Smith Airport: $A1 for the first 24 hours, $A2 per day thereafter. The lockers in Central Station cost $A1.10 per day.

Newspapers The *Sydney Morning Herald* is the major metropolitan paper. The *Australian,* distributed across the country, is also widely read. *OutRage* is Australia's leading monthly magazine for gay men. The *Sydney Star Observer* is a free newspaper for gays.

For overseas publications try **Alison's,** 83 Clarence St.; **Newsagency,** Australia Square; **Aroney's,** 238 Pitt St.; or **Brimar,** 167 Kent St.

Photographic Needs For camera equipment and repairs try **Paxton's,** 285 George St. (tel. 299-2999) or **Fletcher's,** 317 Pitt St.

Police See "Emergencies," above.

Post Office The **General Post Office (GPO)** is on Martin Place, between George and Pitt streets (tel. 230-7033), open Monday to Friday 8:15am to 5:30pm, Saturday 8:30am to noon.

Radio For contemporary or classical music try 873 AM, 702 AM, 1170 AM, 92.9 FM; for rock, 104.9 FM. For current affairs and news, try 576 FM, 702 AM, 87 AM, or 954 AM; for continuous parliamentary broadcasts, 630 AM. Radio is also known by its British designation—*wireless.*

Religious Services Sydney is well supplied with places of worship. **Anglican:** St. Andrew's Cathedral, Sydney Square (tel. 269-0642 or 264-8834). **Baptist:** North Sydney (tel. 929-8643). **Christian Scientist:** Liverpool Street and Forbes Street, Darlinghurst (tel. 357-5721). **Greek Orthodox:** 242 Cleveland St., Redfern (tel. 699-5811). **Jewish:** Elizabeth Street (tel. 267-2477 or 358-3726). **Lutheran:** St. Paul's Church, 3 Stanley St. (tel. 419-6586). **Muslim:** 13 John St., Erksineville. **Presbyterian:** Scots Church, at York and Margaret streets (tel. 29-1804 or 92-1259). **Roman Catholic:** St. Mary's Cathedral, College Street (tel. 232-3788). **Seventh-Day Adventist:** 219 Edgecliffe Rd., Wollahra (tel. 858-4061). **Unitarian:** 15

Francis St. (tel. 33-4863). **Uniting Church:** St. Stephen's, 197 Macquarie St. (tel. 221-1688).

Restrooms In the central business district, you can avail yourself of the facilities in the Queen Victoria Building, any department store, or outside of business hours, any hotel. In Darling Harbour, there are nice restrooms in the Harbourside Marketplace. In addition, the **Hyde Park Family Centre,** at the corner of Park and Elizabeth streets, provides facilities for mothers of infants and small children to change and breast-feed them, heat bottles, and so on.

Safety A matter of relativity. By Australian standards Sydney is crime ridden; by American standards it's not. There are relatively few muggings, but a lot of hotel burglaries, purse snatchings, and auto thefts. Wear a money belt and don't sling your purse or camera over your shoulder; wear the strap diagonally across your body. Even scarlet Kings Cross is quite safe in the wee hours, because the streets are thronged with people. But it's best not to wander through little dark alleys or parks and gardens at night.

Shoe Repairs Two of the downtown repairers are **Brice's,** P60 Imperial Arcade, Pitt Street; and **Sullivan's,** Wynyard Ramp, York Street.

Taxes There are no sales or hotel taxes of any kind.

Taxis See "Getting Around," in this chapter.

Telegrams/Telex/Fax Send them from any post office or through your hotel switchboard by dialing **015.** Telex and electronic mail services can be sent from the General Post Office, Martin Place. Phone 232-6071 for information. But even some hotels in the budget bracket now boast fax facilities.

Television Sydney has two government-run networks (no commercials), ABC 2 and SBS 1. The latter is a multicultural station broadcasting foreign-language programs with English subtitles, plus some first-rate foreign movies. The three commercial stations—ATN 7, TCN 9, and TEN 10—present the customary mélange of game shows, soaps, sitcoms, and thrillers, but with a very strong accent on sports.

Transit Info For information on times, connections, and fares for all bus, rail, and ferry services within the Greater Sydney area, call **Metrotrips** at 954-4422, daily 6am to 10pm.

Useful Telephone Numbers Stage-and-screen attractions: tel. 11681; telephone directory assistance: tel. 013; time: tel. 1194; news: tel. 1199; Student Travel Association: tel. 516-9866; NRMS road report: tel. 11571; Travel Centre of NSW: tel. 221-2659.

Weather Sydney's winter temperatures rarely drop below 8°C (44°F), but in summer you can get several days in a row climbing to the 34.7°C (a scorching 100°F) mark. Call 1196 for weather forecasts, which are about as reliable as those you get at home. But temperatures are quoted in degrees Celsius, quite different from the Fahrenheit degrees you are accustomed to. A special boating weather forecast is given when you call 11541.

Youth Hostel Association The New South Wales head office is at 422 Kent St., City. Tel: 02/261-1111.

4. WHERE TO STAY

The majority of Sydney's good budget establishments are clustered in two distinct areas: Kings Cross, one mile from downtown and the city's entertainment district; and Bondi, the most popular (although not particularly pretty) beach suburb, 15 minutes by bus from downtown. If you're stuck for accommodations turn trustingly to the **Travel Centre of NSW,** 19 Castlereagh St. (tel. 231-4444). They'll find you something, but not necessarily in the bargain basement. The listings below are my own selections, organized *not* in order of preference but according to location.

DOUBLES FOR LESS THAN $A42

KINGS CROSS & VICINITY

CHALLIS LODGE, 21 Challis Ave., Potts Point, NSW 2011. Tel. 02/358-5422. Fax 02/3574742. 62 rms (36 with shower and toilet). TV TEL **Subway:** Kings Cross.

$ Rates: $A26–$A36 single, $A34–$A54 double. BC, MC, V.

Challis Lodge consists of twin peach-and-white Victorian terrace buildings, nicely restored with charming period touches. (The bathrooms boast cathedral-like stained-glass windows, depicting knights and saints.) The interior has a maze of nicely carpeted but confusing corridors and stairways (no elevator), but also high ceilings that make for airiness. More than half the bedrooms have private showers and toilets; the others have hot- and cold-water basins. Light fixtures and hanging space are ample throughout, and the wood flooring is polished to a high sheen, though you don't get any ornamental trimmings. Some rooms have private balconies, and refrigerators. No meals are served, but the restaurants of Kings Cross are within ambling distance. Ask about the special weekly rates.

MONTPELIER, 39A Elizabeth Bay Rd., Kings Cross, NSW 2011. Tel. and fax 02/358-6960. 37 rms (none with bath). TV **Subway:** Kings Cross.

$ Rates: From $A25 single per night, from $A130 single per week; from $A30 double per night, from $A150 double per week. No credit cards.

The Montpelier, on a quiet street, is basic but clean and well managed, specializing in budget-and-backpacker accommodations. The rooms are rather small and the furniture is simple, but all rooms have refrigerators and hand basins. Wardrobe space is fair. The hotel offers a fully equipped communal kitchen as well as on-premises laundry facilities. The airport bus stops at the door.

PARK HOTEL, 20 Yurong St., East Sydney, NSW 2010. Tel. 02/380-5537. 106 rms (none with bath).

$ Rates: $A20 per person. No credit cards.

The Park Hotel is one of the cheapest places around and should be viewed in that light. A basic budget hostelry, it doesn't offer much by way of service and facilities but is very clean and efficiently managed. Most of the rooms are singles. There are no elevator, cooking facilities, or meals served, but the eight bathrooms are nicely kept. Bedrooms are small, with the basic fittings: Each has hot-and-cold water and a mirror above the sink, a small curtained wardrobe, fluorescent lights on the ceiling, and individual bedside lamps as well as wall-to-wall carpeting.

SPRINGFIELD LODGE, 9 Springfield Ave., Kings Cross, NSW 2011. Tel. 02/358-3222. Fax 612/357-4742. 72 rms (46 with bath). TV TEL **Subway:** Kings Cross.

$ Rates: $A28–$A30 single without bath, $A42 single with bath; $A36 double without bath, $A44 double with bath. Special weekly deal: Stay 7 nights, pay for only 5. MC, V.

There's a distinct private-mansion air about this establishment, a pillared white frontage behind an outdoor terrace with tables and chairs overlooking a fairly sedate sidestreet of the Cross. Its charming lobby is lit by small chandeliers, and there are beautifully maintained corridors. The bedrooms are quite well furnished, most of good size and airy, with ample lighting and wardrobe space.

DOWNTOWN

C. B. HOTEL, 417 Pitt St., Sydney, NSW 2000. Tel. 02/211-5115. Fax 02/281-9605. 215 rms (none with bath).

$ Rates: $A25 single, $A40 double, $A50 triple. AE, MC, V.

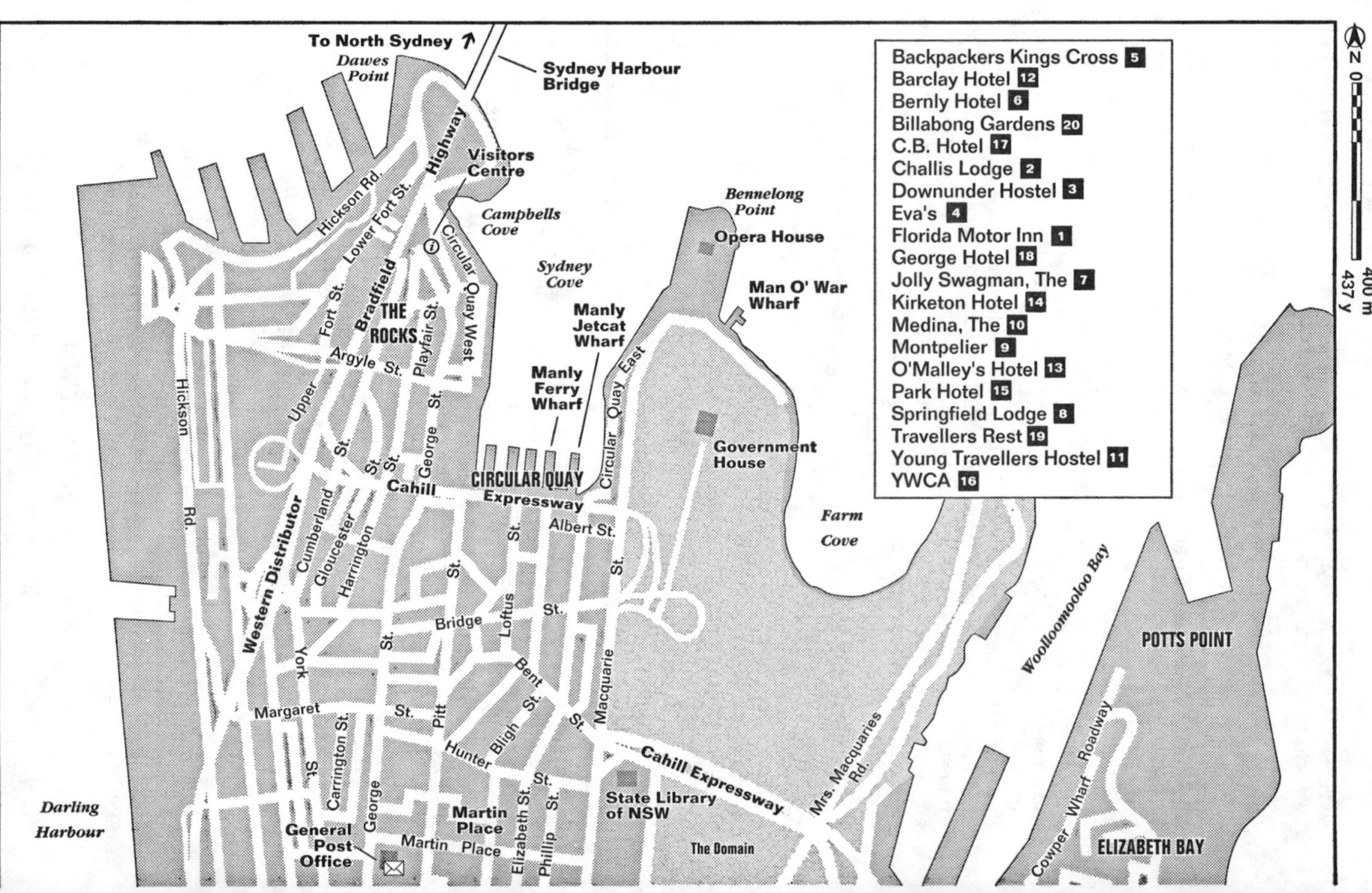

Backpackers Kings Cross 5
Barclay Hotel 12
Bernly Hotel 6
Billabong Gardens 20
C.B. Hotel 17
Challis Lodge 2
Downunder Hostel 3
Eva's 4
Florida Motor Inn 1
George Hotel 18
Jolly Swagman, The 7
Kirketon Hotel 14
Medina, The 10
Montpelier 9
O'Malley's Hotel 13
Park Hotel 15
Springfield Lodge 8
Travellers Rest 19
Young Travellers Hostel 11
YWCA 16
N
0
400 m
437 y
To North Sydney
Dawes Point
Sydney Harbour Bridge
Visitors Centre
Campbells Cove
Sydney Cove
Bennelong Point
Opera House
Man O' War Wharf
Manly Jetcat Wharf
Manly Ferry Wharf
CIRCULAR QUAY
Government House
Farm Cove
Woolloomooloo Bay
POTTS POINT
ELIZABETH BAY
Cowper Wharf Roadway
Mrs. Macquaries Rd.
Cahill Expressway
State Library of NSW
The Domain
Hickson Rd.
Lower Fort St.
Bradfield Highway
THE ROCKS
Fort St.
Circular Quay West
Playfair St.
Argyle St.
Upper Fort St.
George St.
Circular Quay East
Cahill Expressway
Western Distributor
Cumberland St.
Gloucester St.
Harrington St.
Albert St.
Bridge St.
Loftus St.
Macquarie St.
Bent St.
Bligh St.
York St.
Margaret St.
Pitt St.
Hunter St.
Carrington St.
Martin Place
Elizabeth St.
Phillip St.
General Post Office
Darling Harbour

SYDNEY ACCOMMODATIONS

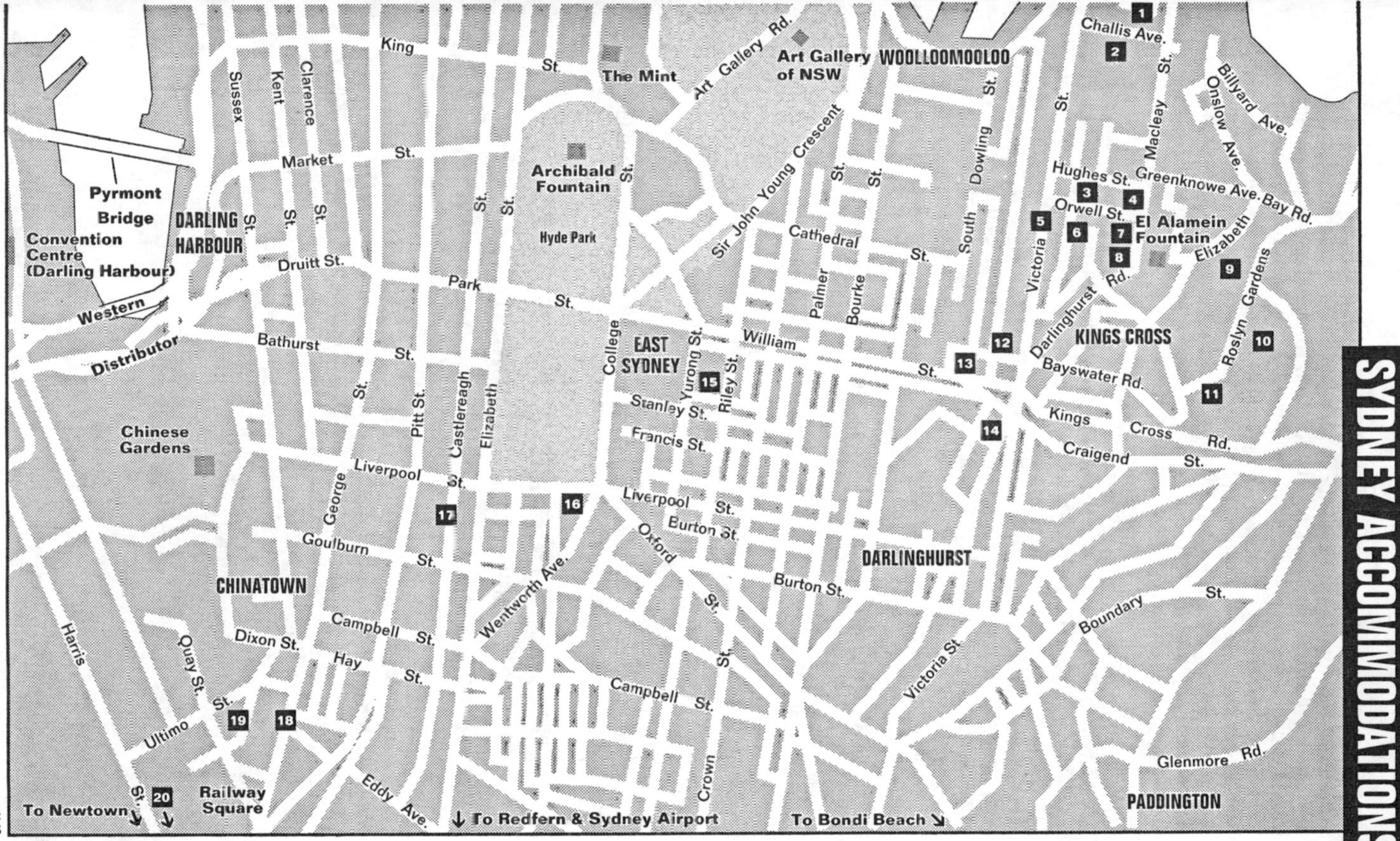

Post Office ⊠ Information ⓘ

6741

The C. B. Hotel has no ban on liquor, although it doesn't sell any. Nor, for that matter, does it sell food. A large, ancient structure close to Central Station, the recently renovated hotel has a brightly lit lobby with vending machines, piped-in music, and a public phone. There is a TV lounge upstairs and in-house movies for guests. The 215 rooms are impeccably clean and airy, equipped with essential furnishings only. None has a hand basin, radio, or bedside lamp; the only razor plugs are in the communal bathrooms (four per floor). There are, however, a guest laundry and an exceptionally friendly staff.

BONDI BEACH

THELELLEN BEACH INN, 2 Campbell Parade, Bondi Beach, NSW 2026. Tel. 02/30-5333. Fax 02/365-6427. 71 rms (none with bath). TV TEL **Bus:** No. 380.

$ Rates: $A30 single, $A39–$A42 double. AE, BC, MC, V.

This inn, close to the famous surfing beach, has good-sized rooms, all nicely carpeted and quite attractively furnished, each equipped with a refrigerator and a fan. The four-story hotel (no elevator) boasts a panoramic sun deck, TV lounge, and games room. Only a light breakfast is served, but you'll find an Italian restaurant in the same building.

THELELLEN LODGE, 11A Consett Ave., Bondi Beach, NSW 2026. Tel. 02/30-1521. 14 rms (none with bath). A/C TV **Bus:** No. 380.

$ Rates: $A30 single, $A39 double. AE, BC, MC, V.

The Thelellen Lodge stands on a quiet residential street, just one block from the beach. A smallish white stucco structure, fronted by a small lawn and palm trees, this place combines a high level of comfort with remarkably low rates. Each room has a hot- and cold-water basin, air-conditioning in summer and heat in winter, a radio, a toaster, tea-making facilities, and a refrigerator. Add wall-to-wall carpeting, lights over the beds, pastel-colored walls, bright bedspreads, and leafy potted plants, and you get the picture of this homey, restful place. Light breakfast ($A4.50 extra) is served in your room, and there is also a guest kitchen. A pay phone and washing machine are available to guests, and the morning paper is delivered on request.

DOUBLES FOR LESS THAN $A75

KINGS CROSS & VICINITY

BARCLAY HOTEL, 17 Bayswater Rd., Kings Cross, NSW 2011. Tel. 02/358-6133. Fax 02/358-4363. 40 rms (30 with shower). A/C TV TEL **Subway:** Kings Cross.

$ Rates: $A40–$A50 single, $A50–$A60 double. AE, BC, MC, V.

The Barclay is an elderly five-story building that has undergone a thorough facelift and rejuvenation process, rendering the interior comfortably modern though not exactly streamlined. It has an excellent position, with a bus stop at the front door and the airport express around the corner. The rooms are simply furnished but come with facilities like refrigerators, air-conditioning, big wardrobes, bedside-and-wall lamps, and ample drawer space. A restaurant, café, and guest laundry are on the premises. Bayswater Road is busy and noisy, but the sounds don't penetrate the sleeping quarters.

BERNLY HOTEL, 15 Springfield Ave., Kings Cross, NSW 2011. Tel. 02/358-3122. Fax 02/356-4405. 83 rms (22 with shower). TV **Subway:** Kings Cross.

$ Rates: $A40–$A45 single, from $A50–$A55 double. AE, V.

The Bernly Hotel, tucked away in a calm corner, is an example of what competent, conscientious management can do for an establishment. While by no means luxurious, it's well maintained and comfortable. The rooms are on the small side, with modern furnishings, wall-to-wall carpeting, dressing tables, *good* mirrors, bedside lamps, refrigerators, and hot and cold water; 22 rooms have private showers

FROMMER'S SMART TRAVELER: HOTELS

1. Budget hotel rates in Sydney depend mainly on whether or not you want a private bathroom, not on the hotel's location. So keep in mind that shared bathrooms are almost invariably spotless and in excellent condition and can save you $A20 or more per day.
2. Virtually all hotels in Australia provide gratis coffee/tea-making implements in their rooms. You can almost take it for granted. What you can't take for granted is decent lighting. Budget hotels are the prime consumers of 20-watt bulbs, so check the light fixtures before renting a room. Supplies of soap and towels are mostly good, but washcloths are as scarce as the proverbial hens' teeth. Ergo, bring your own.
3. Many hotels offer sharply reduced rates for weekends or weekly stays, especially from June through September. Make a point of inquiring about them. And while Sydney gets no snow, it can turn pretty wet and chilly during those months, so make sure your room has some form of heating before you lodge there.

but no toilets. The hotel has several family rooms plus two penthouses with fabulous views and a sun deck. There's no food service, but there are scores of restaurants all around.

DOWNTOWN

THE GEORGE, 700A George St., Sydney, NSW 2000. Tel. 02/211-1800. Fax 02/211-1800. 60 rms (10 with bath). TV

$ Rates: From $A30 single, $A45–$A60 double. Overseas students receive 10% discount. BC, MC, V.

The George, close to Central Station and Chinatown, is an elderly city building newly refurbished by its proud owners. The hotel has rooms on three floors (no elevators) and a reception lobby one flight up from the street. Apart from a central location, it offers such amenities as a guest laundry, some rooms with baths, 12 good shared bathrooms, a lounge area on each floor, an airport bus stop at the door, and large family accommodations—altogether a budget find. Corridors are quiet and spotless; room furnishings are basic: large wardrobes, ceiling lights only, bedside tables, and in *some* rooms, hot- and cold-water basins.

HAYMARKET & DARLING HARBOUR

TRAVELLERS REST HOTEL, 37 Ultimo Rd., Haymarket, NSW 2000. Tel. 02/281-5555. Fax 02/281-2666. 96 rms (70 with bath). TV **Subway:** Central Station.

$ Rates: $A64–$A75 single, $A74–$A86 double, $A29 quad. AE, BC, MC, V.

A remarkably versatile private hotel (no bar) within walking distance of Darling Harbour, Chinatown, and Central Station, this pleasant three-story building offers the entire accommodation spectrum from budget quadruples to family rooms with or without private baths. The entire place (including the shared bathrooms) is absolutely spotless; the lobby is quite spacious and equipped with drink-and-snack machines and a lounge. Also on the premises are a restaurant, laundry, and a dry-cleaning shop. Room furnishings are fair, there is sufficient clothes-hanging space, and the beds are well sprung.

WOOL BROKERS ARMS, 22 Allen St., Pyrmont, NSW 2009. Tel. 02/552-4773. Fax 02/552-4771. 30 rms (none with bath). TV TEL **Monorail:** Convention Station.

$ Rates: $A55 single, $A75 double. AE, MC, V.

A hotel for nonsmokers only, this restored and refurbished Victorian heritage building stands adjacent to the Darling Harbour Project. The Victorian bedrooms have the high ceilings of the period and come equipped with refrigerators, color TVs, and intercom connections with the front desk. The establishment has a guest laundry on each floor as well as a public phone. The pleasant dining room serves breakfast and light evening meals and the place is thoughtfully and efficiently managed.

BONDI BEACH

HOTEL BONDI, 178 Campbell Parade, Bondi Beach, NSW 2026. Tel. 02/30-3271. Fax 02/30-7974. TV TEL **Bus:** No. 380.

$ Rates: $A25 single, $A30–$A60 double. AE, BC, MC, V.

This vast, rambling white structure is built in a style that might be described as "beachfront Gothic"—you'll find this breed along the shores of the entire Anglo-Saxon world. If it's action you're after, this is your abode. The Bondi pulsates with the beach crowd: Legions of golden-tanned lads and lasses populate the four bars, beer garden, disco, bistro, billiard room, and barbecue—all are fairly humming throughout the surfing season. Among the big attractions here is the "grill your own" barbecue, open to nonguests as well. Rooms are very comfortable and attractively decorated. (Rates depend on whether you want a room with or minus bathroom or private balcony.)

BED & BREAKFASTS

Bed & Breakfast Australia, P.O. Box 408, Gordon, NSW 2072 (tel. 02/498-5344, fax 02/498-6438), is a remarkable enterprise aimed at letting you stay with Australian families while touring the country. It fulfills the dual purpose of letting you meet the Aussies and enjoy budget accommodations. Actually you get far more than the terms promise. As a "paying guest" you get the use of the living room, plus a lot of home hospitality not mentioned in the brochures. And the homes listed are carefully vetted beforehand.

The places listed are divided into homestays and farmstays (about 400 host families altogether), the former in various cities, the latter in country areas throughout four states. Farmstays usually entail full board (in lavish country style) instead of just bed-and-breakfast. All homes fall into one of three categories: economy, quality, and superior.

Economy homestays run from $A45 for singles, from $A37 per person for double accommodation. A hearty breakfast is included. Farmstays start at $A112 per person for full board.

BROOKLYN, 25 Railway St., Petersham, NSW 2049. Tel. 02/564-2312. Fax 02/797-0725. 5 rms (none with bath). **Train:** Petersham.

$ Rates: $A45 single, $A65 double. No credit cards.

A stately Victorian residence about five miles from downtown, the Brooklyn was featured as the setting of an Australian TV serial and looks the part. Lacy ironwork balconies and stained-glass windows give the place a dreamy period air, reinforced by the spaciousness of the rooms. Located in a quiet residential area, this bed-and-breakfast provides fresh fruit and bathrobes for houseguests, along with high-quality breakfasts served either in the dining room or garden. Most of the bedrooms have balconies and there is a separate guest lounge for TV viewing.

THE KIRKETON HOTEL, 229 Darlinghurst Rd., Kings Cross, NSW 2010. Tel. 02/360-4333. 63 rms (20 with bath). TV TEL **Subway:** Kings Cross.

$ Rates (including continental breakfast): $A38.50 single without bath, $A51.50 single with bath; $A58 double without bath, $A68 double with bath. AE, DC, MC, V.

This is an exceptionally well-equipped and well-run budget house. The lobby is small and rather cluttered and the decor nondescript, but the range of facilities is impressive and the management first rate. The Kirketon has an Indian restaurant on the premises, and its bedrooms are equipped with telephones, radios, TV, refrigerators, and smoke alarms. Ask about special 3-day packages.

FROMMER'S COOL FOR KIDS: HOTELS

Hotel Bondi *(see p. 90)* Located right on the beachfront, with the surfside play area at its doorstep, the Hotel Bondi also has a barbecue in the rear and a billiard room for those youngsters big enough to handle a cue.

Florida Motor Inn *(see p. 94)* Priding itself on catering to family groups, the inn has an excellent palm-fringed swimming pool, an adjoining open-air netball court and Ping-Pong table, and barbecue facilities.

O'MALLEY'S HOTEL, 228 William St., Kings Cross, NSW 2011. Tel. 02/357-2211. Fax 02/357-2656. 15 rms (10 with bath). A/C TV TEL **Subway:** Kings Cross.

$ Rates: $A50 single, $A60 double.

A landmark building dating from 1907, O'Malley's is a haven of Irish hospitality set among pretty lively surroundings. The decor is cozily old-fashioned (no elevator), but the facilities make the place extremely comfortable. Even the five technically bathless rooms actually have their own—just across the hall and used by nobody except the room occupants. The reception is one flight up—you must ring a buzzer—and the hotel quarters are strictly separated from the action-packed bar regions below. The bedrooms come with electric hair dryers, bedside-and-ceiling lights, and tall wardrobes with generous hanging space. Bathrooms are compact, equipped with large mirrors, and the management counts among the most amiable in town. The pub at street level has nightly entertainment: bands ranging from great to god-awful and occasionally excellent comedians.

PENSION ALBERGO, 5 Day St., Leichhardt, NSW 2040. Tel. 02/560-0179. 3 rms (none with bath). **Bus:** No. 440 or 438 to Leichhardt Town Hall.

$ Rates: $A38 single, $A60 double. No credit cards.

In the inner suburb of Leichhardt, a pleasantly cosmopolitan casserole of a region flavored with Italian, Latino, and Asian ingredients, is the Pension Albergo. This small tree-fronted Victorian home offers comfortable guest rooms and winning hospitality, as well as a tranquil garden and a charming dining room that becomes a TV lounge after breakfast. "Brecky" here is a real day starter, with *fresh* in-season fruit salad, crackling croissants, hot Italian rolls, and percolated coffee. The place rates tops for congeniality.

A COTTAGE

THE COTTAGE, HERBERT & RENATE FILLA, 213 Ryde Rd., West Pymble, NSW 2073. Tel. 02/498-7148. TV TEL

$ Rates: $A53 double per night for 3 nights minimum, $A42 double per night for 7 nights. No credit cards.

A separate cottage apartment in the garden of the private home of Herbert and Renate Filla, the Cottage is located in a handsome suburb about 20 minutes by train from downtown. The Filla cottage nestles behind loaded fruit trees and overlooks a swimming pool. It is completely self-contained with a bath and kitchen, and the surrounding garden is a joy. The Fillas are both agreeable and highly knowledgeable hosts. This place does not use an answering machine. Give at least eight rings.

HOSTELS

Hostels in Sydney have proliferated so wildly that in certain areas they're jostling each other cheek by jowl. Competition for patrons is fierce, and it pays to shop around a bit to discover the best possible accommodations for your money. There is, however, a sharp difference between official youth hostels, which are run according to pretty strict rules, and the backpackers' hostels, which can be somewhat chaotic.

The backpackers' abodes, whose numbers are legion, are growing by the month . . . maybe by the week. They cluster mostly in two areas: Kings Cross and Glebe, both very lively and brimming with international restaurants. You can reach Glebe by taking bus no. 431 or no. 433 from George Street and Railway Square.

KINGS CROSS & VICINITY

BACKPACKERS KINGS CROSS, 162 Victoria St., Kings Cross, NSW 2011. Tel. 02/356-3232. Fax 02/368-1435.

$ Rates: From $A10 dorm, $A15 per person double room, $A12 per person flat. AE, MC, V.

The Backpackers Hostel caters to many folks besides backpackers. A small, old building on a charming tree-shaded street, the place has double rooms, dormitory accommodations, and flats that can house two to five people. The double rooms come with hot- and cold-water basins; there are shared bathrooms and cooking facilities, plus a TV room. Space is a little cramped, but the location couldn't be more convenient—almost adjacent to the Kings Cross subway and within a few hundred feet of the bright lights. The management hands out maps gratis, and a very thoughtful notice outside tells you when the next vacancy is due—other hostels, please take note!

DOWNUNDER HOSTEL, 25 Hughes St., Kings Cross, NSW 2011. Tel. 02/358-1143. Fax 02/357-4675. 35 rms (none with bath). **Subway:** Kings Cross.

$ Rates: $A14 dorm, $A32 single or double. MC, V.

This hostel gets a bit crowded occasionally, but it's a warm, friendly, well-run place. The reception office is stacked with backpacks, the notice board brimming with budget tips, job offers, and items for sale. It has a capacity of 105 people, one, two, or three per room. There are a communal kitchen and a rooftop TV lounge. Most rooms have hot- and cold-water basins; all have bunk beds, fluorescent lighting, and a new sprinkler system.

EVA'S, 6 Orwell St., Kings Cross, NSW 2011. Tel. 02/358-2185. Fax 02/358-3259. 7 dorms, 26 rms (5 with bath).

$ Rates: $A15 dorm, $A16 single, $A34 double.

Sporting a multi-colored frontage, this mixture of a hotel and a hostel puts on gratis tea and coffee all day. There are a rooftop barbecue, guest laundry, and a kitchen. Guests must bring their own soap.

THE JOLLY SWAGMAN, 14 Springfield Mall, Kings Cross, NSW 2011. Tel. 02/358-3330. 53 rms (none with bath).

$ Rates: From $A20 single, from $A24 double, from $A10 per person triple. MC, V.

The Jolly Swagman is one of three such establishments in this area, and it is exceptionally strong on creature comforts. The two-bunk rooms have fluorescent lights, hot- and cold-water basins, refrigerators, hot plates, and carpeting. The house boasts a TV lounge, a roof garden, and eight modern bathrooms.

GLEBE & SUBURBAN SYDNEY

BILLABONG GARDENS, 5–11 Egan St., Newtown, NSW 2042. Tel. 02/550-3236. Fax 02/550-4352. Rms and dorms.

$ Rates: $A12–$A14 per person dorms, $A50 single or double, $A60 triple. No credit cards. **Bus:** 422, 423, 426, or 428. Also airport bus.

Part hostel, part private hotel, this remarkably versatile budget find stands in an inner suburb that is fast becoming "in." Alongside dormitories, the Billabong has cool, brick-walled bedrooms with private baths. Furnishings are simple, with open hanging spaces, fair lighting, and good beds. Swimming pool, spa, barbecue facilities, guest kitchen, laundry, and TV lounge are on the premises, as well as a leafy courtyard ideal for socializing. Located close to Newtown's main drag, King Street, which brims with cafés, pubs, restaurants, clubs, cut-rate clothing stores, and music outlets. The Billabong operates a courtesy bus service 9am to 9pm.

GLEBE POINT VILLAGE, 256 Glebe Point Rd., Glebe, NSW 2037. Tel. 02/660-8133. Fax 02/552-3707. TV **Bus:** No. 431 or 433.

$ Rates: $A40 double (no singles available), dorm (4–8) $A15 per person. MC, V.

Glebe Point Village has near-village dimensions, with five adjoining buildings. Accommodations range from double rooms to four-bunk dorms. Facilities include bed linen, a fax machine, guest kitchen, and a coffee shop.

Glebe Point Road is Sydney's university street, thronged with a cosmopolitan student crowd that populates the equally cosmopolitan cafés, restaurants, and nightspots. Only the cracked and bumpy pavements remind you that gentrification here is a fairly recent development.

GLEBE POINT YHA, 262 Glebe Point Rd., Glebe, NSW 2037. Tel. 02/692-8418. Fax 02/660-0431. 150 beds. **Bus:** No. 431 or 433.

$ Rates: $A20 per person double (no singles available), $A16 per person dorm (quad). MC, V.

The hostel has a guest kitchen, a TV lounge, a sun deck, a guest laundry, and barbecue facilities. The area abounds with restaurants, and many local restaurants and shops offer discounts to YHA members.

HEREFORD LODGE, 51 Hereford St., Glebe, NSW 2037. Tel. 02/660-5577. Fax 02/552-1771. 250 beds. **Bus:** No. 431 or 433.

$ Rates: $A15–$A22 senior (over 18), juniors half price. BC, MC, V.

The Youth Hostel Association (YHA) operates only two establishments in central Sydney. The largest and most modern is the Hereford Lodge, with a rooftop pool, sauna, and bistro. This is one of the best hostels in Australia, with covered parking and nearby tennis courts.

WATTLE HOUSE, 44 Hereford St., Glebe, NSW 2037. Tel. 02/552-4997. Fax 02/337-5640. 9 rms (none with bath).

$ Rates: $A15 per person. Discount of $A1 per night for 7 nights to owners of this book. (Show it!) No credit cards. **Bus:** No. 431, 433, or 434; pick-up shuttle bus from airport.

Wattle House is attractive, friendly, and newly expanded. Located about 1½ miles from the city center, it provides a guest kitchen, laundry facilities, a TV lounge, and a garden with an outdoor barbecue. The bathrooms are bright and sparkling, and the amenities of the University of Sydney lie within walking distance.

A Y FOR MEN & WOMEN

YWCA, 5–11 Wentworth Ave., Darlinghurst, NSW 2010. Tel. 02/264-2451. Fax 02/283-2485. **Subway:** Museum.

$ Rates: $A18 per person dorm; $A42 single without bath, $A60 single with bath; $A60 double without bath, $A85 double with bath. AE, BC, DC, MC, V.

The Sydney YMCA no longer offers accommodations, but the YWCA has new premises and now offers rooms to all people.

The place is easy to miss because it looks like an office building. Two floors are in fact offices; the other six comprise the Y. Centrally situated, this new establishment has a large cafeteria, TV lounges, laundry facilities, and excellent public bathrooms. Smoking is not permitted in the building. The bedrooms are of fair size and functional; well carpeted; and fitted with large wardrobes and mirrors, fluorescent ceiling lights, and bedside lamps. Some have hot- and cold-water basins. There is also a room equipped for disabled travelers.

CAMPUS ACCOMMODATIONS

Rooms are available on the two city campuses during university vacations (mid-January through mid-February and June through July). The first is at the **Interna-**

tional House of the University of Sydney, on the campus at 96 City Rd., Chippendale, NSW 2008 (tel. 02/692-2040). Full board costs $A40 per day. The **International House of the University of South Wales,** High Street, Kensington (tel. 02/663-0418) charges $A35 per day, full board, for students, $A45 for nonstudents. In both cases, expect facilities to be campus casual. And in both cases it's best to book ahead. No credit cards are accepted.

WORTH THE EXTRA MONEY

MOTEL APARTMENTS

Sydney has many self-contained motel suites (called flats in Australia), mostly too expensive for single budget travelers, but they can be ideal for couples or families; the kitchens allow you to cut food bills by nearly half. Following are a few motel apartments that offer outstanding value for the money charged.

FLORIDA MOTOR INN, 1 McDonald St., Kings Cross, NSW 2011. Tel. 02/358-6811 or toll free 800/782-8738 from the U.S. Fax (61) (2) 358-5951. Telex 21128 Florida. 89 rms (all with bath). A/C MINIBAR TV TEL **Subway:** Kings Cross.

$ Rates: $A95 single or double; $A170 2-bedroom apartment for up to 6. 15% discount to owners of this book. (Show it!) AE, MC, V.

This inn, one of the Best Western chain, stands tucked away at the end of a quietly elegant street, just outside the city's nightlife center. A modern brown-and-white nine-story building (with elevator), the Florida surrounds a palm-fringed lawn with a large swimming pool, a Ping-Pong table, a sauna, and barbecue facilities. The units range from singles to six-person accommodations, all spacious, bright, and exceptionally well equipped. Each unit has a kitchen with electric appliances and utensils (even egg cups). Rooms are carpeted and furnished with wide beds, built-in wardrobes, day couches, and armchairs. Amenities include radios, electric heaters, and in some rooms, air conditioners. The inn also serves breakfast (if desired); arranges babysitting services, car rentals, and same-day dry cleaning; and has on-premises washing machines.

THE MEDINA, 70 Roslyn Gardens, Elizabeth Bay, NSW 2011. Tel. 02/356-7400 or toll free 008/25-1122. Fax 02/357-2505. 58 apts (all with bath). A/C TV TEL **Subway:** Kings Cross.

$ Rates: $A110 single, $A125 double. 15% discount for owners of this book. (Show it!) AE, MC, V.

The Medina is a converted apartment block in the fashionable waterfront suburb adjoining Kings Cross. A modern, gleaming-white six-story structure, the building is fronted by a small rock garden with a miniature waterfall. Guests use a private entrance, apart from the reception lobby, and the units are grouped around an inner courtyard. Elevator (lift) service is fast, room decor tasteful, and furnishings complete. The well-lit, air-conditioned units have built-in wardrobes with silent sliding doors, new beds and couches in inviting pastel colors, and bathrooms with ventilators that turn on with the lights. The large kitchens are streamlined and fully stocked with appliances, utensils, cookware, and dinnerware, including wine glasses. The accent here is on privacy—the feeling of living in your own apartment. You can have your morning milk delivered along with the newspaper.

5. WHERE TO EAT

Sydney is one of the world's great restaurant towns, and this applies not only to the quality but also to the quantity and variety of its eateries. Thanks to the influx of "New Australians," Sydney now boasts a quite astonishingly cosmopolitan culinary scene.

The most pleasing feature about the immense proliferation of international restaurants is their authenticity. Sydney establishments are run by first-generation immigrants who haven't modified their cooking yet. So enjoy the New Australian gastronomy—while it lasts.

Because of the superabundance of small, inexpensive restaurants all over town, hotel counter lunches play a far less important role here than in most of Australia. Their standard, however, is high, and their prices are usually very reasonable. In the "Where to Stay" section of this chapter I mentioned the toothsome barbecue buffet spreads put on by the **Hotel Bondi,** 178 Campbell Parade in Bondi, which are served from noon to 10pm. Downtown, the main business streets are lined with pubs offering similar fare for similar prices. The norm is a choice of steak, mixed grill, or ham steak, with as much salad as you can eat, for around $A6 to $A7.

The most remarkable selection of fine-quality, well-priced restaurants in all Australia is found in **Darlinghurst,** just south of Kings Cross. Take bus no. 399 from Circular Quay to Taylor Square. Get off and stroll up Oxford Street toward Darlinghurst Road, savoring the posted menus as you go. Most of these places invite you to BYO (Bring Your Own—bottle, that is), and there are plenty of good wine shops nearby.

The **Kings Cross** region has by far the densest concentration of restaurants in Sydney, and they span the spectrum from deluxe to rock-bottom economy—sometimes side by side. But it's the cafés that give Kings Cross its special character. Here they proliferate indoors and out, spilling onto the pavements in best Parisian style. Their stock in trade is, of course, coffee and people watching, but some of them double very nicely as restaurants, especially in the wee hours.

BYO means "bring your own" alcoholic drinks—usually because the restaurant is not licensed to sell such beverages.

MEALS FOR LESS THAN $A11

KINGS CROSS & VICINITY

THE ASTORIA, 7 Darlinghurst Rd., Kings Cross. Tel. 358-6327.
Cuisine: AUSTRALIAN. **Reservations:** Not necessary.
$ Prices: Main courses $A4.50–$A7.50. No credit cards.
Open: Mon–Sat 11am–2:30pm, 4pm–8:30pm.

The Astoria is *the* bargain dinery of the district and one of the very few Australian cuisine establishments around. Small and narrow, with two rows of booths and a large standing fan as sole decoration, this establishment serves plain, well-cooked Anglo meals, devoid of spices, at unequivocal budget prices: barley broth for A75¢, Irish stew or lamb cutlets for $A6.50, roast pork and apple sauce for $A7.50, and desserts for under $A2.

CAFE PRALINKA, 4B Roslyn St., Kings Cross. Tel. 358-1553.
Cuisine: CZECH. **Reservations:** Not necessary.
$ Prices: Main courses $A6.90–$A7.90. No credit cards.
Open: Tues–Sat 11am–9pm.

This café is an early closer in an all-night neighborhood. A colorful miniature eatery, very Czech in flavor, including pictures of the "Good Soldier Schwejk" along the walls, the Pralinka boasts only five tables in toto. All available wall space is covered with pictures, posters, and memorabilia, and in the window table (the best in the house) potted plants tickle your neck. Helpings are huge; the fare is first rate; and the prices are as minuscule as the premises—nothing over $A7. Choices run between beef goulash, stuffed cabbage, roast beef with salad, and chicken paprika with rice—depending on what's chalked on the blackboard that day.

GEOFFREY CAFE, 18 Roslyn St., Kings Cross. Tel. 357-1205.
Cuisine: INTERNATIONAL. **Reservations:** Not necessary.

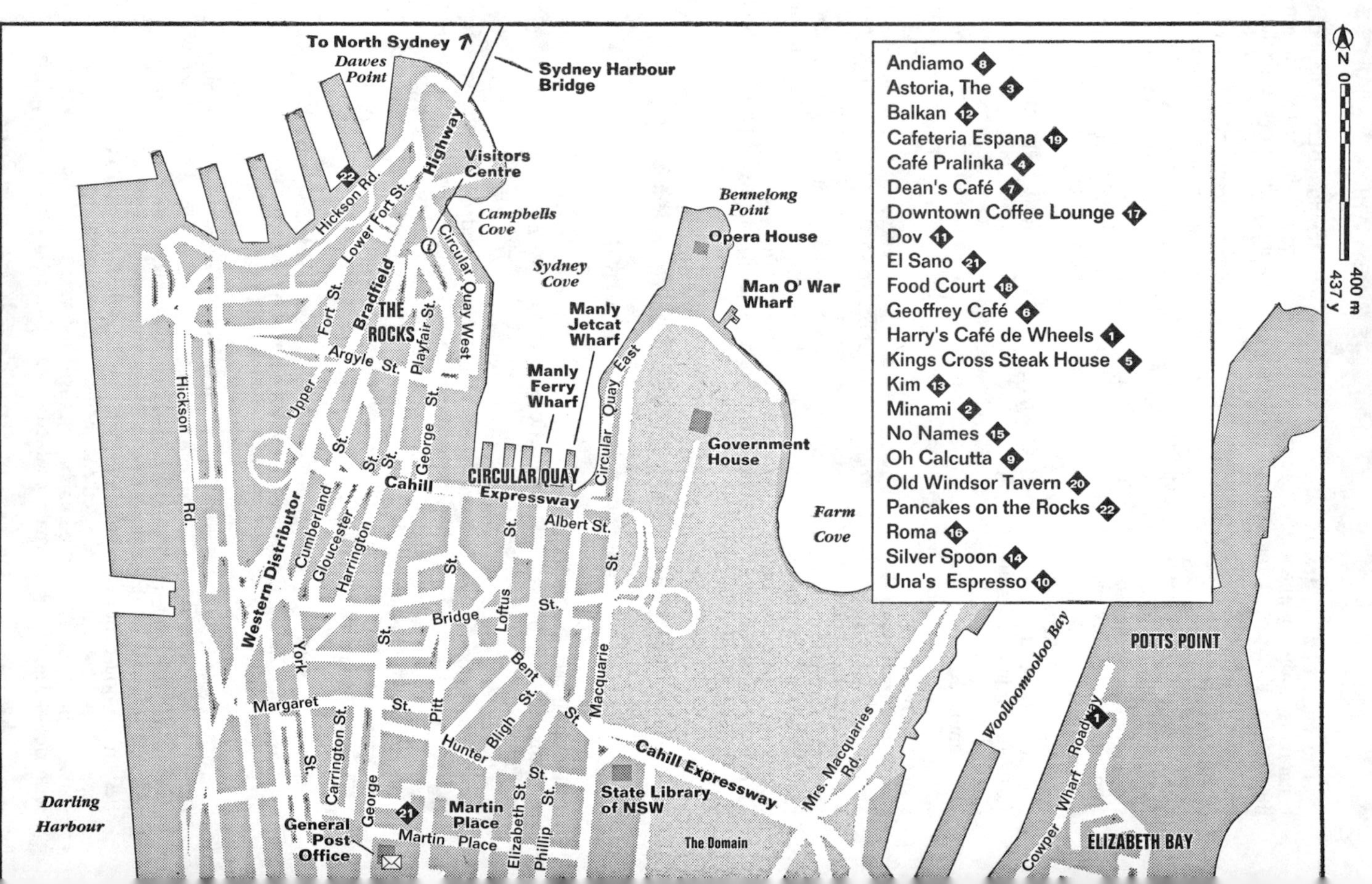
Andiamo 8
Astoria, The 3
Balkan 12
Cafeteria Espana 19
Café Pralinka 4
Dean's Café 7
Downtown Coffee Lounge 17
Dov 11
El Sano 21
Food Court 18
Geoffrey Café 6
Harry's Café de Wheels 1
Kings Cross Steak House 5
Kim 13
Minami 2
No Names 15
Oh Calcutta 9
Old Windsor Tavern 20
Pancakes on the Rocks 22
Roma 16
Silver Spoon 14
Una's Espresso 10
N
0
400 m
437 y
To North Sydney
Dawes Point
Sydney Harbour Bridge
Visitors Centre
Campbells Cove
Sydney Cove
Bennelong Point
Opera House
Man O' War Wharf
Manly Jetcat Wharf
Manly Ferry Wharf
CIRCULAR QUAY
Government House
Farm Cove
THE ROCKS
Hickson Rd.
Lower Fort St.
Highway
Bradfield
Fort St.
Playfair St.
Argyle St.
Circular Quay West
Circular Quay East
Upper
George St.
Cahill Expressway
Western Distributor
Cumberland
Gloucester
Harrington
Albert St.
Bridge
Loftus
Macquarie
Bent St.
York
Margaret
Carrington St.
Pitt
Hunter
Bligh St.
Elizabeth St.
Phillip St.
Martin Place
General Post Office
State Library of NSW
The Domain
Mrs. Macquaries Rd.
Woolloomooloo Bay
Cowper Wharf Roadway
POTTS POINT
ELIZABETH BAY
Darling Harbour

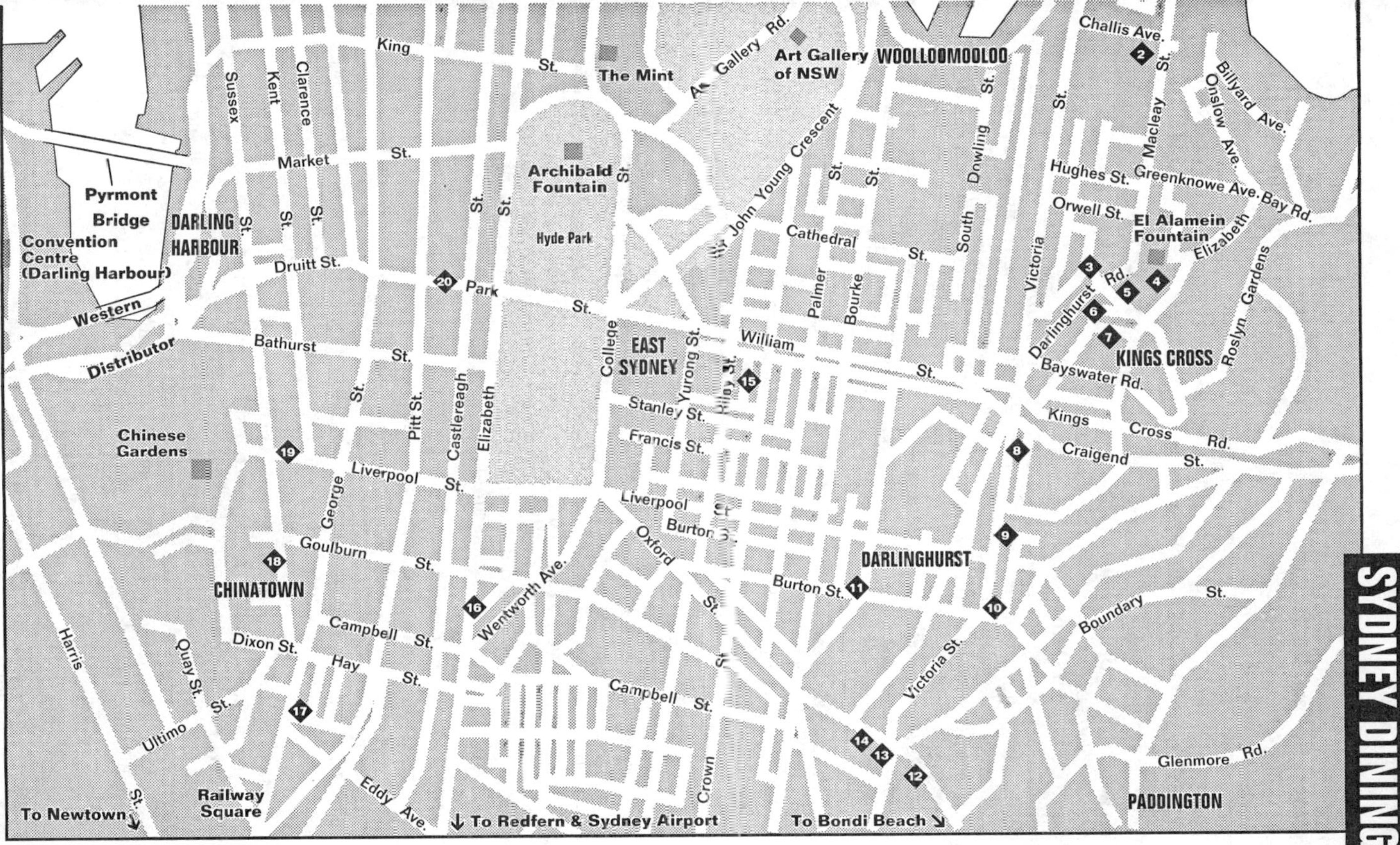

WOOLLOOMOOLOO
Art Gallery of NSW
The Mint
Art Gallery Rd.
King St.
Challis Ave.
Macleay St.
Billyard Ave.
Onslow Ave.
Hughes St.
Greenknowe Ave.
Bay Rd.
Orwell St.
El Alamein Fountain
Elizabeth
Roslyn Gardens
Darlinghurst Rd.
KINGS CROSS
Bayswater Rd.
Kings Cross Rd.
Craigend St.
Victoria
South Dowling St.
Cathedral St.
Palmer St.
Bourke St.
Sir John Young Crescent
William St.
Archibald Fountain
Hyde Park
Sussex St.
Kent St.
Clarence St.
Market St.
Pyrmont Bridge
DARLING HARBOUR
Convention Centre (Darling Harbour)
Druitt St.
Park St.
Western Distributor
Bathurst St.
College St.
EAST SYDNEY
Yurong St.
Riley St.
Stanley St.
Francis St.
Liverpool St.
Burton St.
Oxford St.
DARLINGHURST
Boundary St.
Victoria St.
Glenmore Rd.
PADDINGTON
Chinese Gardens
Pitt St.
Castlereagh
Elizabeth
George
Goulburn St.
CHINATOWN
Wentworth Ave.
Campbell St.
Dixon St.
Hay St.
Harris
Quay St.
Ultimo St.
Railway Square
Eddy Ave.
Crown
To Newtown
To Redfern & Sydney Airport
To Bondi Beach
1
2
3
4
5
6
7
8
9
10
11
12
13
14
15
16
17
18
19
20
6742
Post Office
Information

$ **Prices:** Appetizers $A3.50–$A4, main courses $A7.50–$A10.90. No credit cards.
Open: Daily 7am–2am.

Geoffrey Café is tiny, but the tables out on the pavement partly shaded by trees are excellent for people watching. This is a delightful spot late on a warm night or early in the morning to dine while watching the strolling, standing, and occasionally rambunctious passing parade. Coffee—good and strong—goes for $A2; main dishes such as chicken with schnitzel go for $A7.50.

MINAMI, 87C Macleay St., Kings Cross. Tel. 357-2481.
Cuisine: JAPANESE. **Reservations:** Not necessary.
$ **Prices:** Main courses $A6–$A9.50. No credit cards.
Open: Daily noon–1am.

This minuscule noodle dispensary has a tremendous following of knowledgeable Japanese tourists who keep it permanently crammed. Lacking even a hint of decor, the place consists of a U-shaped plastic counter just wide enough for one slender waitress to squeeze inside, straight metal chairs, and gray walls, all bathed in merciless neon light. The noodle dishes are huge, tangy, and delivered with lightning speed. You can get *yakisoba,* fried noodles with pork and vegetables, for $A6; *hiyashi ramen,* chilled noodles with sesame sauce, cucumber, and roast pork, for $A8; or an immense bowl of soy soup noodles with pork, bamboo shoots, and bean sprouts for $A9.50.

MOHR FISH, 202 Devonshire St., Surry Hills. Tel. 318-1326.
Cuisine: SEAFOOD. **Reservations:** Not accepted.
$ **Prices:** Main courses $A8.50–$A11.50. No credit cards.
Open: Daily 7am–10pm.

No, this isn't a misprint but the proprietor's name: Hans Mohr, a Breton Frenchman who serves what may be the freshest, tastiest fish in Sydney. At minimum prices and in a modicum of comfort. His restaurant is tiny, seating is mainly along a counter, but the patrons literally storm it like the Bastille. The fare makes you forget all inconvenience, from the huge steaming bowls of bouillabaisse to grilled sardines, tuna, or flathead (whatever is freshest on the market that morning) to subtle little fruit tarts and powerful espresso. And everything under $A12. There is always a crowd waiting for a vacant slot, most of them at the bar of the Shakespeare Hotel opposite. When seats become empty one of the busy waitresses skips over and calls out the names of the next in line. It's BYO and no corkage, so you can take your drinks along.

NO NAMES, 2 Chapel St., East Sydney. Tel. 360-4711.
Cuisine: ITALIAN. **Reservations:** Not necessary.
$ **Prices:** Appetizers $A5, main courses $A5.50–$A7.50. No credit cards.
Open: Daily 11am–3pm, 6–9pm.

There are actually two places called thus—neither has a name—but one is known to regulars as Caesar's. Anyway, they are among the best budget eateries in town. You'll find the second in Glebe, where it occupies premises at the Friend in Hand Hotel. The East Sydney and Glebe establishments frequently require you to wait in line, share a table, and pay without getting a bill, but all three serve rich, tasty victuals at rock-bottom prices. The East Sydney establishment is BYO, the other licensed. Their crispy fresh bread comes heaped in baskets. You can get single courses for between $A5.50 and $A7.50 or two-course meals for $A10, including salad. Pasta entrées are huge and meaty, and the veal stew, roast, and fish are of superb quality.

The establishment in Glebe, 58 Cowper St. (tel. 660-2326), is closed on Sunday.

DOWNTOWN

CAFETERIA ESPANA, 79 Liverpool St. No phone.
Cuisine: SPANISH. **Reservations:** Not necessary.
$ **Prices:** Appetizers $A4, main courses $A8–$A10. No credit cards.

Open: Mon–Sat 8am–10pm.

This downtown restaurant is an exact replica of a Barcelona or Madrid fast-food dispensary: high bar stools along tall counters, an equally high sound level, and richly filling bean soup with bread for $A4. Most of the main dishes go for $A9, and the Spanish churros and the tripe are exceptional.

DOWNTOWN COFFEE LOUNGE, 701 George St. Tel. 211-5562.

Cuisine: INTERNATIONAL. **Reservations:** Accepted.

$ Prices: Appetizers $A3–$A7, main courses $A8–$A10. No credit cards.

Open: Mon–Sat 9am–8pm.

Located near Central Station, this eatery is a surprise package in comfort and cuisine. Air conditioned, comfortable, and decorated with touches of elegance and deft patches of greenery, the place offers both tables and intimate dining booths. The cakes and pastries are fresh and authentically European; the range of chicken dishes alone is cosmopolitan: chicken Cordon Bleu, chicken Mexicana, chicken with schnitzel, chicken shashlik, or chicken filets with mushrooms for $A8.

EL SANO, Shop 2, 14 Martin Place, Tel. 232-1304.

Cuisine: VEGETARIAN. **Reservations:** Not necessary.

$ Prices: Main courses $A5.20–$A6.70. AE.

Open: Mon–Fri 8:30am–5pm.

El Sano serves vegetarian fare counter-service style with an intriguingly "different" Latin flavor—soybean casseroles, cabbage roles (minus meat), vegetable pies, and good rich soups. For dessert, your choice of cakes includes aniseed and persimmon.

OLD WINDSOR TAVERN, 185 Castlereagh St. Tel. 267-6650.

Cuisine: ENGLISH. **Reservations:** Accepted.

$ Prices: Appetizers $A4–$A6, main courses $A8–$A10. AE, MC, V.

Open: Mon–Sat 11am–8pm.

The venerable Old Windsor Tavern is a rather posh pub, decorated with rakish Hogarthian murals depicting the naughtier aspects of Georgian England. The place features live music every night, but the main attractions here are the roast meals: lamb, chicken, pork, beef, steak—plus a free and sumptuous salad bar.

P AND S CAFE, 410 Pitt St. Tel. 212-1241.

Cuisine: ENGLISH. **Reservations:** Not necessary.

$ Prices: Appetizers $A4–$A5, main courses $A5.50–$A9.80. No credit cards.

Open: Mon–Fri 6:30am–7pm, Sat until 1pm.

This is a real old-fashioned Anglo-Aussie "fish caf" that's been going strong for over 80 years, and it has the vintage Sydney photographs on the walls to prove it. When you taste the fish here you'll know the reason for its longevity. Although the menu is short and the fare simple, the fish is delivered fresh daily, and you get mountains of the indispensible french fries (chips) with each dish. Seafood—including nicely barbecued prawns—also reigns supreme here. The hamburgers, grills, and sausages are mere sidelines.

DARLINGHURST

ANDIAMO, 292 Victoria St., Darlinghurst. Tel. 360-4890.

Cuisine: ITALIAN. **Reservations:** Not accepted.

$ Prices: Appetizers $A2.50–$A6.50, main courses $A8.50. No credit cards.

Open: Mon–Sat 6:30am–midnight.

Andiamo greets you with a pleasant front veranda under a blue awning. The tables, sheltered beneath a vine-covered roof, are open to the street. One of the most popular of the row of Italian cafés here, it's a place to meet as well as to eat. Amid lively conversation, attractive patrons, and the spectacle of the passing parade, you get flavorful focaccias and pizzettas for $A9 or one of the four main dishes, each costing $A9.80. Most patrons come for the excellent coffee and desserts.

FROMMER'S SMART TRAVELER: RESTAURANTS

1. As a general (but not universal) rule, lunch prices are cheaper than those at dinner, so it's a good idea to make lunch your main meal of the day.
2. Leave out the appetizers, which sometimes cost nearly as much as main courses. Australian helpings are very solid.
3. Although some BYO eateries charge corkage fees, your tab will still be less than if you'd bought wine at the restaurant.
4. Thai and Vietnamese places are usually cheaper than Chinese or Japanese, French are usually the most expensive, and Italian and German restaurants run the entire gamut from top-dollar to rock-bottom prices.
5. Tips are expected only in very fancy establishments, but if you're dining in a group and have given your server a lot of work, it's a nice gesture to leave a couple of extra bucks.
6. One important linguistic point: If a server asks, "Are you all right?", it's not an inquiry about your health. It means "Have you ordered yet?"
7. Sydney teems with budget eateries, and the following thoroughfares offer a plethora of additional choices: Oxford Street in Darlinghurst and Paddington, Victoria Street in Kings Cross and Darlinghurst, Glebe Point Road in Glebe, and Campbell Parade in Bondi Beach.

KIM, 235 Oxford St., Darlinghurst. Tel. 357-5429.
Cuisine: VIETNAMESE. **Reservations:** Accepted.
$ **Prices:** Appetizers $A4.50, main courses $A8.20–$A10. BC, MC, V.
Open: Wed–Mon 6–10:30pm.

This little Vietnamese BYO qualifies as possibly the best of its breed in Australia, employing some of the most charming French-accented Vietnamese servers around. The decor of wood-paneled walls and softly gleaming lanterns beneath a beamed ceiling produces a subtle ambience. The menu—printed in Vietnamese with English translations—offers specialties that are slightly spicier and considerably more startling than their Chinese counterparts, but this is a place for a little culinary courage—the reward being an outstanding meal at a very gentle price. Try the pineapple soup with fish, the braised chicken with ginger, or the wondrously subtle pork satay; don't forget the savory rice cakes. Kim has only 19 tables and gets very crowded on weekends, not surprisingly.

SILVER SPOON, 203 Oxford St., Darlinghurst. Tel. 360-4669.
Cuisine: THAI. **Reservations:** Accepted.
$ **Prices:** Appetizers $A4.50–$A7, main courses $A9.90–$A12.90. AE, BC, MC, V. 10% discount for cash.
Open: Daily noon–3pm, 6–11pm.

Despite a veritable explosion of Thai eateries in Sydney, the Silver Spoon is so popular that you'd better make advance bookings. It's a delicate and exquisite BYO place that folds its paper napkins into gentle floral shapes. But the curries served here are truly robust, quite likely to scorch unseasoned palates. Choose from the minced-pork chili, the sliced squid in a bed of salad, or one of the half a dozen curry combinations. For starters I'd recommend a plate of the little curried vegetable puffs.

UNA'S ESPRESSO, 340 Victoria St., Darlinghurst. Tel. 360-6885.
Cuisine: AUSTRIAN. **Reservations:** Not necessary.
$ **Prices:** Appetizers $A3.50, main courses $A6–$A7.60. No credit cards.
Open: Daily 6:30am–11pm.

Una's Espresso bears a misleading name because this is actually an unconventional restaurant open for breakfast, lunch, and dinner. The espresso bit is more of a sideline. There are a very small coffee bar and a much larger dining room, with pictures on the walls, candles on the tables, and a general air of conviviality, as befits a real neighborhood eatery of 23 years standing. The menu features very good continental rissoles, wienerschnitzel, and a strong beef soup—and don't forget the homemade cakes.

SUBURBAN SYDNEY

FATIMA, 294 Cleveland St., Surry Hills. Tel. 698-4895.
Cuisine: MIDDLE EASTERN. **Reservations:** Accepted.
$ Prices: Platters $A5–$A9. AE, MC, V.
Open: Daily 5pm–"late."

This Lebanese BYO—old, established, and comfortable—specializes in mixed plates of Middle Eastern favorites at very basic prices. The platters come in small, medium, and large sizes, starting at $A5 and climbing to $A9. You can munch your way through the whole range of hummus, kofta, tabbouleh, garlic chicken, kebabs, and on and on, all served with olives and bread in pleasing quantities; you can finish with a range of desserts including semolina, Turkish delight, and baklava.

MEALS FOR LESS THAN $A20

KINGS CROSS & VICINITY

DOV, corner of Forbes and Burton Sts., East Sydney. Tel. 360-9594.
Cuisine: JEWISH-MEDITERRANEAN. **Reservations:** Not necessary.
$ Prices: Main courses $A6.50–$A11. No credit cards.
Open: Mon–Sat 6:30am–10pm.

This is probably *the* "in" café in town, with a clientele ranging from art students to youngish executives, all exceedingly laid-back. The vibes are friendly, and the fare is even more so. Most dishes cost $A7.50, including the splendid cold plates of chopped liver, herring, and Russian salad. Desserts are downright dreamy (try the hazelnut torte with whipped cream), and the coffee is outstanding, even in a town like Sydney, where competition for the best "cuppa" rages fiercely.

KINGS CROSS STEAK HOUSE, 2F Roslyn St., Kings Cross. Tel. 358-5639.
Cuisine: AUSTRALIAN. **Reservations:** Accepted.
$ Prices: Appetizers $A7.20–$A9.90, main courses $A9–$A12.50. AE, MC, V.
Open: Daily 6pm–2am.

Although the name doesn't reveal it, this BYO for beef lovers offers considerably more than steaks. The service is fast and friendly, the cuisine is hearty and cooked exactly as ordered, and the oysters that make up the appetizers are ocean fresh. Several pasta and seafood dishes are also on the menu. Bring a solid appetite.

DARLINGHURST

BALKAN RESTAURANT, 209 Oxford St., Darlinghurst. Tel. 360-4970.
Cuisine: YUGOSLAV. **Reservations:** Not necessary.
$ Prices: Appetizers $A6–$A14, main courses $A12–$A23.90. AE, MC, V.
Open: Tues–Sun 11am–11pm.

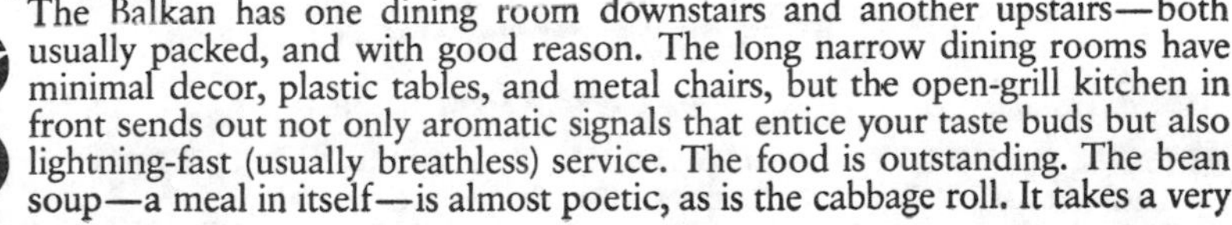

The Balkan has one dining room downstairs and another upstairs—both usually packed, and with good reason. The long narrow dining rooms have minimal decor, plastic tables, and metal chairs, but the open-grill kitchen in front sends out not only aromatic signals that entice your taste buds but also lightning-fast (usually breathless) service. The food is outstanding. The bean soup—a meal in itself—is almost poetic, as is the cabbage roll. It takes a very hearty appetite to manage more than one course in this place. Between mealtimes the restaurant doubles as an espresso café.

OH CALCUTTA, 251 Victoria St., Darlinghurst. Tel. 360-3650.
Cuisine: INDIAN. **Reservations:** Accepted.
$ Prices: Appetizers $A5.90–$A9.90, main courses $A8.90–$A15.90. AE, MC, V.
Open: Lunch, Thurs–Fri 12–3pm; dinner, daily 6–11pm.

The Calcutta is both dignified and trendy (a rare combination). Its decor is done in a black-and-turquoise color scheme with Indian-artifact-style ornamentation, but you won't hear one sitar in the background music. The fare is lavish tandoori, including the excellent bread, and vegetarians have at least half a dozen flavorful choices. I recommend the *gosht palak,* lamb cooked in cream and spinach, or the much hotter beef vindaloo (the mixed seafood platters are rather expensive). The star dessert—dumplings in hot syrup—is a filling finale. (This BYO charges for corkage.)

SUBURBAN SYDNEY

BUON GUSTO, 368 Abercrombie St., Chippendale. Tel. 319-4798.
Cuisine: ITALIAN. **Reservations:** Recommended Fri–Sat.
$ Prices: Appetizers $A6–$A7.20, main courses $A10.50–$A13.50. AE, MC, V.
Open: Lunch, Mon–Fri noon–3pm; dinner, Mon–Sat 6–11pm.

This restaurant has a low, straw-matted ceiling festooned with dangling Chianti bottles, bare tiled floors, and a general air of rustic conviviality—noisy, friendly, and usually packed. The accent is on seafood, but the homemade fettuccine is famous in its own right. Also highly recommended are the egg soup and the *alla diavola* (bacon in Neapolitan sauce), to be concluded with zabaglione, the empress of Italian desserts. You may bring your own bottle or buy one on the premises.

GERONIMO'S, 106 Curlewis St., Bondi. Tel. 30-2756.
Cuisine: INDIAN. **Reservations:** Accepted.
$ Prices: Appetizers $A4.90–$A7.90, main courses $A9.90–$A12.90. BC, V.
Open: Tues–Sun 5:30–10:30pm.

Despite the Apache label, this restaurant specializes in fare from the Indian subcontinent, including India, Pakistan, Afghanistan, and Bangladesh. The decor is cool, understated, and voguish, with lime-washed walls, raw timber, and some tasteful Indian artifacts. The menu displays all the standard Indian favorites as well as some provincial gourmet items you may never have encountered before. Servings are generous but the big drawing card is the "Eat till you're Beat" Thali banquet, served every evening between 5:30 to 7:30pm. Customers help themselves from traditional silver Thali platters, choosing from six dishes (three meat, three vegetarian) which come with rice, pickles, chutney, and pappadums. The whole treat costs $A12.90 per banqueter, $A6.50 for children. BYO with A50¢ corkage.

ROMA, 202 Elizabeth St., Surry Hills. Tel. 211-0439.
Cuisine: ITALIAN. **Reservations:** Not necessary.
$ Prices: Main courses $A7.50–$A13. No credit cards.
Open: Mon–Fri 8am–5:30pm, Sat until 3pm.

The Roma is a legend among Sydneysiders who have either a sweet or a savory tooth. Italian to the backbone, permanently packed, short on elbow space and high on quality, this wonderful little coffee shop serves sumptuous lasagne and cannelloni with spinach, plus superlative cakes and pastries for around $A2 to $A4.

SPECIALTY DINING

VEGETARIAN

SLOANE RANGERS, 312 Oxford St., Paddington. Tel. 331-6717.
Cuisine: VEGETARIAN. **Reservations:** Accepted.
$ Prices: Appetizers $A5.50–$A6, main courses $A7.90–$A9.80. No credit cards.

FROMMER'S COOL FOR KIDS: RESTAURANTS

Roma *(see p. 102)* With a distinct family atmosphere. Café Roma takes multitudes of youngsters in stride. The rows of hefty Italian desserts help nicely.

Food Court *(see below)* Kids love the noisy bustle, the competing vendors, and the immense variety of tidbits tempting them.

Harry's Café de Wheels *(see p. 104)* Although basically a nocturnal operation, the famous cart is a magnet for children. They'd live on the hot dogs it dispenses if allowed.

Pancakes on the Rocks *(see p. 104)* This is the top spot with the juniors, partly because of the fare but chiefly because of the zany decorations and games.

Open: Daily 7:30am–6pm.

A rather plain café with a charming green backyard portion, the Sloane dispenses hefty breakfasts and lunches plus dinners for very early diners. The fare is extremely varied and includes items like corn cakes with spinach, nachos, tabbouleh, hummus, plus the inevitable mushroom and tofu burgers. All at under $A10. Try the outstanding grilled tomatoes with herbal cheese sprinkles. BYO with a $A1 corkage charge.

FOOD COURTS

Sydney has nearly a dozen of these comestible market places, and more springing up all the time. One of the handsomest is the **Food Court in the MLC Centre,** Martin Place, a circular layout around an open-air atrium in the middle of the shopping center in the heart of the city. Walking clockwise you can eat your way through Singapore noodles in every form, European deli snacks, hot-and-cold seafood, Lebanese kebabs, and a vast array of focaccia and antipasto, with stops in between for fresh oysters, French pastries, and sizzling hamburgers. All the items are priced between $A3 to $A7, and the stalls are open Monday to Saturday 7am to 6:30pm.

The huge **Ⓢ Food Court,** 25 Dixon St., is located in the basement of Chinatown Centre. But Chinese fare here is only one note in a symphony of Asian vittles. The indoor court houses rows of little stalls offering Japanese, Korean, Chinese, Indonesian, Thai, Vietnamese, and Malaysian meals and snacks at very low prices. It's noisy, busy, and not very comfortable—you buy your food at a stall and your drinks at a bar, then retire to the nearest free table (if there is one)—but the cuisine is as tasty as any you get in elegant restaurants. And it costs about half the price. For about $A5 you can load up on barbecue beef; pork noodles; tempura; curry chicken; teriyaki; fish dumplings; spring rolls; heaps of steamed, fried, or pickled vegetables; and mounds of rice. The Food Court is in full action daily from 10:30am to 10pm. No credit cards are accepted.

LATE-NIGHT/24-HOUR

DEAN'S CAFE, 7 Kellett St., Kings Cross. Tel. 358-2174.

Cuisine: INTERNATIONAL SNACKS. **Reservations:** Not accepted.
$ Prices: $A5–$A12. AE, MC, V.
Open: Daily 9pm–4am or later.

This is one of four establishments in a row, all tailored for nightbirds and insomniacs. None of them even start to fill up before around 10pm, but then tend to become very populous indeed. The clientele is mostly young and upscale, the atmosphere intimate, service leisurely. Most of the action takes place in the charming outdoor patio facing the street; the interior is dim enough to render all guests incognito. You can order very light snackeries or a tangy chicken pie with salad for $A8.50 or a positively titanic bowl of nachos for $A11.50. BYO.

HARRY'S CAFE DE WHEELS, 1 Cowper Wharf Rd., Woolloomooloo. Tel. 357-3074.
Cuisine: FAST FOOD.
$ Prices: Most items $A2.50. No credit cards.
Open: Daily 7:30am–3am. Weekends 24 hrs.

In the 'Loo stands Harry's Café, which doesn't belong to anyone named Harry and isn't a café—but it is an institution. It started as a pie cart back in the wartime 1940s, when the customers were wharf laborers and Allied sailors of a dozen or so nationalities. The original cart is now a museum piece, but its successor still feeds the hungry in dawn's early light. Now patrons consist mostly of the night-owl set at the end of a spree—the BMW set as well as the T-shirt brigade. Harry's sells pie "floaters" (not recommended for sensitive palates), hot dogs (voted "best of breed"), and powerful coffee.

PANCAKES ON THE ROCKS, 10 Hickson Rd., The Rocks. Tel. 247-6371.
Cuisine: PANCAKES. **Reservations:** Accepted.
$ Prices: $A5–$A12. AE, MC, V.
Open: 24 hrs.

The historic area called The Rocks boasts a restaurant that provides fun along with comestibles. It features—among other amusements—games of chess, backgammon, and Trivial Pursuit. The breakfast menu here includes a "bottomless" cup of coffee. The savory "pancakes" include one offering called Tabriz; sweet Jewish blintzes with cheese, brandied sultanas, and sour cream; as well as a basic stack of three.

6. ATTRACTIONS

Sunlit Sydney is perfect for exploration. It's for delving into Australia's past, as carved by convicts into the stones of its first settlement, as read in the portraits of the founders at the Mitchell and Dixson Galleries. It's for enjoying the present—at the beaches and zoo; on the ferries; and in the museums, boutiques, and shops. It's for seeing those futuristic showcases—the Opera House, Australia Square, Centrepoint—and then resting in the Domain, within earshot of the town's self-appointed orators, to contemplate whence this society came and whither it goes. And at what pace!

All of this can be accomplished with remarkable ease, because the majority of Sydney's sights are clustered in the central city, and the balance can easily be reached by ferry from Circular Quay (which is not circular, just as Australia Square isn't square). As walking is the preferred propulsion to gain in-depth knowledge of any city, I've included the walking tours below, after the listings of the places to see.

SUGGESTED ITINERARIES

IF YOU HAVE 1 DAY Have breakfast at one of the outdoor cafés in Kings Cross, then take the bus downtown. Visit the magnificent Queen Victoria shopping complex; take a guided tour of the Opera House; then amble through The Rocks (see Walking Tour 1, below), having a quick pub lunch on the way. In the evening you'll have time for a cursory look around Darling Harbour before catching the 1½-hour Harbour Lights Cruise departing from Circular Quay. I guarantee you'll sleep well that night.

IF YOU HAVE 2 DAYS Your first morning and afternoon agenda could be much as above, but take a good three hours at Darling Harbour. Afterward, take the

Harbour Lights Cruise and have a late dinner at one of the Oxford Street restaurants in Darlinghurst (see "Where to Eat," in this chapter).

Devote your second morning to sightseeing, starting with the panoramic lookout from Sydney Tower, the Pylon Lookout at Harbour Bridge. Pier One, followed by the entertainment complex underneath the bridge, is also a good spot for an outdoor lunch. Move on to Circular Quay, where you can catch the speedy hydrofoil to Manly. There you can swim or surf, admire the giant Oceanarium, and saunter along the famous Corso. Later take the slow chugging ferry back to the city, viewing the immense expanse of the harbor en route. Take the bus to Kings Cross for dinner. After that . . . well, there's enough nightlife to keep you spinning for a week.

IF YOU HAVE 3 DAYS Your additional day might start with a grand-slam (window)-shopping tour. Take in the pedestrian malls in Martin Place and Pitt Street; nose through the intimate little boutiques of the Royal, Strand, and Imperial Arcades; and drop in (actually *up*) at the Opal Skymine in Australia Square to watch the gems being dug out and processed. Visit Chinatown for exotic displays and an inexpensive lunch.

In the afternoon take the Mosman ferry from Circular Quay over to Taronga Park Zoo. Take the bus up the hill so you'll have an easy walk downhill back to the wharf. You'll be back in the city in time to visit the Australian Museum or the Art Gallery of New South Wales or take a stroll through part of the Botanic Gardens. In the evening, the choices are endless: go to one of the 23 professional theaters or dozens of amateur shows currently in action; join the crowds at one of the music pubs; dance at a disco; sip drinks in a piano bar; sample the assorted comics at a comedy club; or try one of the Leagues Clubs for a bout with the poker machines. If you prefer a little of each, take the "Sydney After Dark" tour—not cheap, but fairly comprehensive and with narration thrown in.

IF YOU HAVE 4 DAYS OR MORE On your fourth morning "do" Oxford Street in Darlinghurst, watching its character change as it goes on and on. Walk from Darlinghurst to Paddington, visit the little art shops and pop-culture dispensaries, then have lunch at one of the cafés en route. Reserve the afternoon for Bondi Beach (don't pick a weekend) and rent a rubber surfboard. Join the beach crowds at one of the cafés along Campbell Parade for a drink, a snack, or a full meal. Alternatively, you could attend one of Sydney's "art"-movie houses to catch an Australian film that hasn't been exported or some resurrected cinema classic. Try the Chauvel Cinema in Paddington, the Village Cinema in Double Bay, or the Roma in downtown George Street.

On your fifth day you might leave the urban sprawl and take a train from Central Station to the Blue Mountains. Rising 50 miles west of Sydney, they actually *are* deep blue. They're also the city's playground—a National Park fringed by a string of resorts, each with its own bag of attractions. The largest of them is Katoomba, with spectacular panoramic vistas; the Skyway, an aerial cable car over a dizzying chasm; and the Scenic Railway, allegedly the steepest rail track in the world.

Return to Sydney for a farewell splurge (pocketbook permitting) at the Argyle Tavern. It's far from cheap but offers great fun, great food, and frequently the happiest memory visitors carry home from Oz. For more economical revelry, there's the Hard Rock Café in Kings Cross, which houses five floors of concentrated merriment, all high on the decibel scale but with varying admission prices.

You could fill a great many additional days in and around Sydney. Exploring the beaches—all the way out to Palm Beach—would take a week. Featherdale Wildlife Park, Waratah Park, Old Sydney Town, the Hunter Valley (wine country), New England, Thredbo, the Snowy Mountains, and Lightning Ridge are just a few of the many more attractions you might want to see.

THE TOP ATTRACTIONS

SYDNEY OPERA HOUSE, Bennelong Point. Tel. 250-7111 or 250-7777.

✪ In 1954 a group of noted Sydney citizens decided that the time had come in the city's maturity for a performing-arts center. They chose the present site and began an international competition for a suitable design. In 1957 Danish architect Joern Utzon won the $A10,000 prize for his unique sails-along-harbor design, a magnificent concept fraught with untried techniques. He also won the dubious right to direct construction on an estimated budget of $A7.2 million. By 1966, after battling governments, unions, and his own unworkable plans, Utzon rejected the privilege and scooted for home. The government stepped in, and the budget shot up to $A50 million. From there on, the project supported the building trades through work stoppages and labor disputes, through blunders and oversights, until the final cost, when Queen Elizabeth cut the blue ribbon on October 20, 1973, was a staggering $A102 million (U.S. $73 million). Not that milk was swiped from children to pay the tab. It was all financed by lottery, and with Australian gambling fever what it is, the entire building was paid off by 1975. (Suggestion: Let's let the Diggers handle the U.S. federal budget deficit.)

A common expression among locals, since the first derricks thrust their giraffe necks into the skyline, has been "It'll never fly." It nearly didn't. The builders forgot to put in dressing rooms, planned no parking facilities, and paved the promenade with slabs of pink granite, not realizing that heavy trucks delivering the final equipment would crack it all. Everything had to be rectified. The parking station didn't open until 1993.

And all this in full view of the verbal populace, spawning an avalanche of waggeries. The New South Whale, they called it, the Hunchback of Bennelong Point, the Operasaurus, a haystack with a tarpaulin, a pack of French nuns playing football, an opera house eight sheets to the wind. Then it was finished. The *London Times* said it was "the building of the century," and the Aussies shut up, looked again, and saw a pearl-pale sculpture glowing suspiciously like a national symbol on their waterfront. For the truth is, what man hath wrought in wrangling and union negotiations occasionally comes out right. The building is *exquisite*. From every angle. It has no contemporary peer.

Go along on a guided tour by day to view the remarkable workmanship of the interior, with its beautifully treated timber panels, its tinted glass merging into the sea beyond, its curtains woven in the bold hues of the Australian day and night. Then go back at night to sample the perfect acoustics and the first-class talent. In all, there are four performance halls (within a total of 980 rooms), one for concerts, one for opera and ballet, one for drama, and a smaller one for recitals. Pop groups and comedians as well as classical musicians make their appearances; the people throng to them all, and the mischievous sea monster 30 years in the hatching has been embraced and turned into a prince.

Admission: $A9 adults, $A6 children.
Open: Tours daily 9am–4pm.

MUSEUM OF CONTEMPORARY ART, 132 George St., Circular Quay. Tel. 241-5892.

Sydney's newest museum exhibits everything from oil portraits to garbage-heap collages, from the works of Aborigines to those of Andy Warhol and Roy Lichtenstein. Also featured are computer-based "art," modern design, sculptures, films, videos, and laser creations. The museum boasts a café that offers superb views across Circular Quay, along with contemporary Australian food.

Admission: $A6 adults, $A4 children.
Open: Daily 11am–6pm.

DARLING HARBOUR

✪ The greatest urban redevelopment project in Australian history covers the western dockside region, bordering Chinatown. Darling Harbour used to be Sydney's back door, but it fell into decrepitude with the advent of container shipping. Now the

DID YOU KNOW . . . ?

- One square yard of Sydney is officially French soil: the La Perouse monuments, dedicated to the Comte de la Perouse, who landed there in 1788—just a few weeks after Captain Cook.
- "Sydney lace" is not a textile but ornamental wrought iron used for colonial-style balconies.
- Paul Hogan, of *Crocodile Dundee* fame, worked as a rigger on the Harbour Bridge before becoming an international movie star.
- The guns on Fort Denison, in Sydney Harbour, were erected during the Crimean War to protect the town against a Russian invasion.
- An old incinerator, a former Presbyterian church, and a converted pumping station house three of Sydney's upper-bracket restaurants.
- The Harbour Bridge is so big that as soon as the paint crews finish at one end they have to go back and start painting afresh at the other.
- Convict-architect Francis Greenway is the only forger in history ever to have his portrait depicted on money—the old $10 bill.
- William Bligh, having survived one mutiny on his ship *Bounty*, encountered another in Sydney after becoming governor of New South Wales when he tried to stop his army officers' lucrative trade in black-market rum.
- Sydney's oldest pub, the Hero of Waterloo, was originally built as a jailhouse, and later it became a notorious dive from which drugged sailors were "shanghaied."
- One of the most popular tour companies in Sydney is Pat's Uninteresting Tours, which promises to show participants the dullest sights in town.
- The New South Wales Parliament House was originally a wing of the old Rum Hospital—often the source of sobriety jokes about state legislators.

area has been transformed into a gigantic entertainment-and-cultural complex, served by a monorail system that links it with the city center.

This monorail is a touchy subject with Sydneysiders: They either hate it or love it. The controversial apparatus glides silently above all traffic snarls but runs on unsightly support pillars. The trains run a complete loop over the project site and cost $A2.50 per ride. Some of the Darling Harbour attractions include the following.

POWERHOUSE MUSEUM, 500 Harris St., Ultimo. Tel. 217-0111.

Australia's largest museum is a wondrous mix of technology, sociology, history, and plain fun. It contains 25 exhibitions that include an old-time steam locomotive, a NASA space station, plasma balls, entire aircraft hung from the ceilings, computer games, engines, furniture, ball gowns, decorative arts spanning three centuries, and a working 1930s cinema. It's amazing what can be done with a once-defunct power station.

Admission: $A5 adults, $A2 children. Free on the first Sat of each month.

Open: Daily 10am–5pm.

SYDNEY AQUARIUM, Wheat Rd., Pier 26. Tel. 262-2300.

The largest aquarium in the southern hemisphere, it contains 5,000 aquatic animals in their natural environments. You actually walk beneath the "sea" through huge tunnels, coming face-to-face with giant rays, sharks, turtles, exotic lungfish, and saltwater crocodiles. There are a "touch tide pool" and robotic cameras that magnify tiny ocean denizens to 40 times their size.

Admission: $A13.90 adults, $A6.50 children.

Open: Daily 9:30am–9pm.

NATIONAL MARITIME MUSEUM. Tel. 552-7500.

This museum shows the realm of seafaring from primitive tribal canoes to early European explorations to sport sailing and racing. It also features regular shows and lectures, including songfests of sea chanties and whaling ballads. Some of the exhibits are on dry land inside, while others are afloat in the harbor.

Admission: $A7 adults, $A3.50 children.

Open: Daily 10am–5pm.

HARBOURSIDE, Festival Marketplace.

This huge day-and-night marketplace is roofed against rain. It contains some 200

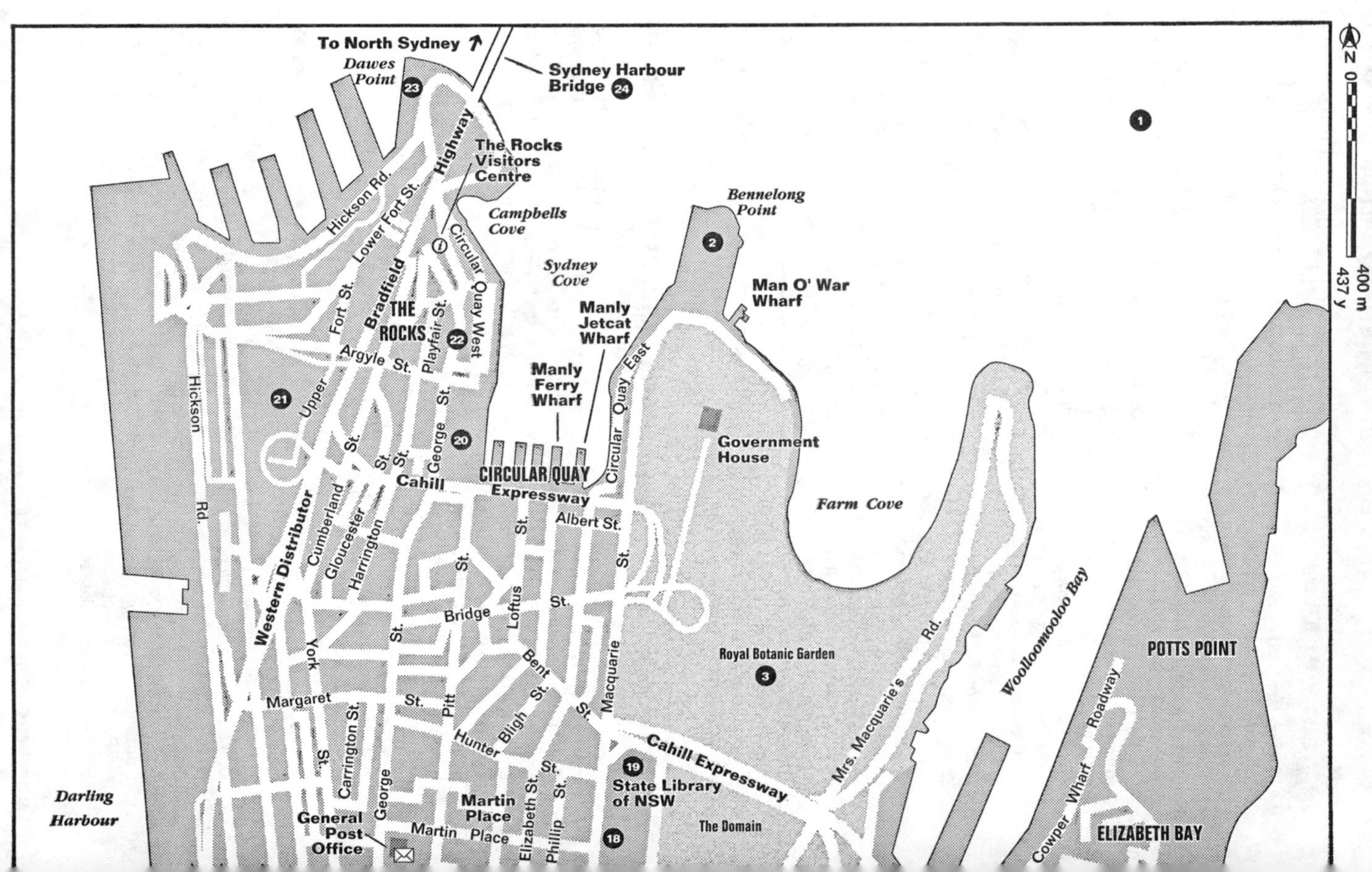

N
0
400 m
437 y
To North Sydney
Dawes Point
23
Sydney Harbour Bridge
24
1
The Rocks Visitors Centre
Highway
Hickson Rd.
Lower Fort St.
Campbells Cove
Bennelong Point
2
Circular Quay West
Sydney Cove
Man O' War Wharf
Fort St.
Bradfield
THE ROCKS
Playfair St.
22
Manly Jetcat Wharf
Argyle St.
Upper
Manly Ferry Wharf
Circular Quay East
Hickson Rd.
21
George St.
20
Government House
CIRCULAR QUAY
Cahill Expressway
Farm Cove
Albert St.
Western Distributor
Cumberland
Gloucester
Harrington
Loftus St.
Bridge St.
Macquarie St.
Woolloomooloo Bay
Mrs. Macquarie's Rd.
POTTS POINT
Royal Botanic Garden
3
York St.
Margaret St.
Pitt St.
Bent St.
Bligh St.
Hunter St.
Carrington St.
Cahill Expressway
19
State Library of NSW
Cowper Wharf Roadway
Darling Harbour
General Post Office
Martin Place
Martin Place
Elizabeth St.
Phillip St.
18
The Domain
ELIZABETH BAY

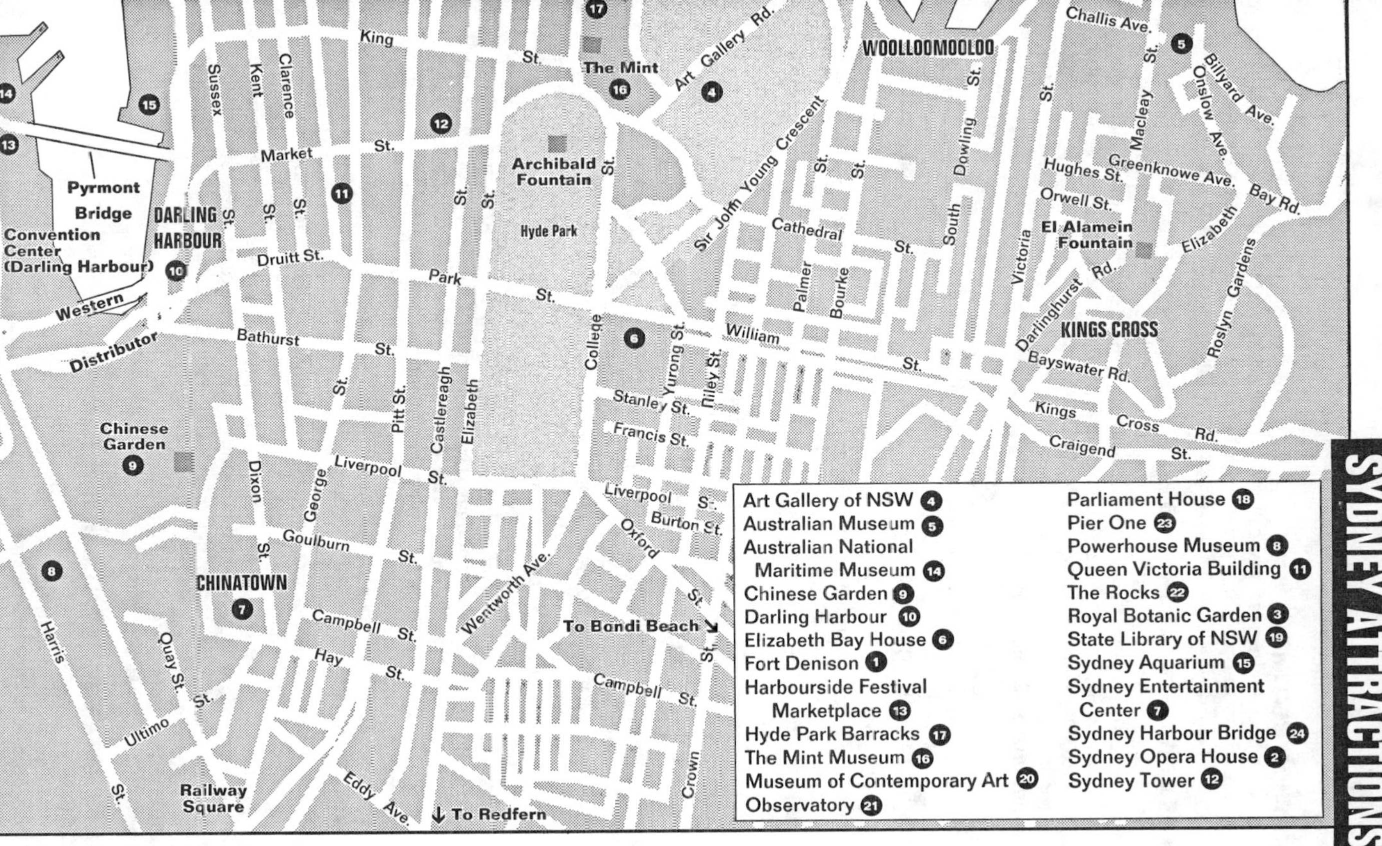
SYDNEY ATTRACTIONS
Art Gallery of NSW 4
Australian Museum 5
Australian National Maritime Museum 14
Chinese Garden 9
Darling Harbour 10
Elizabeth Bay House 6
Fort Denison 1
Harbourside Festival Marketplace 13
Hyde Park Barracks 17
The Mint Museum 16
Museum of Contemporary Art 20
Observatory 21
Parliament House 18
Pier One 23
Powerhouse Museum 8
Queen Victoria Building 11
The Rocks 22
Royal Botanic Garden 3
State Library of NSW 19
Sydney Aquarium 15
Sydney Entertainment Center 7
Sydney Harbour Bridge 24
Sydney Opera House 2
Sydney Tower 12
WOOLLOOMOOLOO
KINGS CROSS
CHINATOWN
DARLING HARBOUR
The Mint
Archibald Fountain
Hyde Park
El Alamein Fountain
Pyrmont Bridge
Convention Center (Darling Harbour)
Chinese Garden
Railway Square
To Bondi Beach
To Redfern
Western Distributor
King St.
Market St.
Druitt St.
Park St.
William St.
Bathurst St.
Liverpool St.
Goulburn St.
Campbell St.
Hay St.
Sussex St.
Kent St.
Clarence St.
George St.
Pitt St.
Castlereagh
Elizabeth
College
Oxford St.
Wentworth Ave.
Art Gallery Rd.
Sir John Young Crescent
Cathedral St.
Palmer St.
Bourke St.
Dowling St.
South
Victoria St.
Darlinghurst Rd.
Bayswater Rd.
Kings Cross Rd.
Craigend St.
Macleay St.
Challis Ave.
Billyard Ave.
Onslow Ave.
Greenknowe Ave.
Bay Rd.
Hughes St.
Orwell St.
Elizabeth
Roslyn Gardens
Stanley St.
Francis St.
Yurong St.
Riley St.
Burton St.
Crown St.
Dixon St.
Quay St.
Ultimo
Harris St.
Eddy Ave.
6743
Post Office
Information

specialty shops, four terrace cafés, and five large restaurants—all with spectacular views of the city skyline.

EXHIBITION CENTRE.

This vast edifice has a great roof canopy suspended from steel masts. Seven stories high, with an enormous column-free interior expanse, the center holds a banqueting hall designed for 3,500 simultaneous feasters or a buffet accommodating 5,000.

CHINESE GARDEN. Tel. 281-6863.

This is an exquisite piece of horticultural-and-architectural workmanship, designed by specialists from Guangdong Province—the largest and most elaborate outside China. In its center is a two-story pavilion surrounded by a system of interconnected little lakes and waterfalls, bridges, and crisscrossing secluded and tranquil walkways.

Admission: $A2 adults, A50¢ children.

TUMBALONG PARK.

Tumbalong Park is a collection of amusement and thrill rides, some of them mildly hair-raising. Because the area of Darling Harbour is vast, a People Mover train operates between the attractions, costing A50¢ for adults, $A1.50 for children.

PYRMONT BRIDGE.

At night the Pyrmont Bridge, linking the city with Darling Harbour, is illuminated, and the entire region turns into a fairyland of colored lights, flashes, and flickering wheels, reflected by the lights of the vessels in the harbor—sheer magic to behold.

MORE ATTRACTIONS

ARCHITECTURAL HIGHLIGHTS

QUEEN VICTORIA BUILDING, 660 George St. Tel. 264-1955.

Here you'll find the magnificent restoration/modernization of a grand edifice that had fallen on hard times. For several decades it housed the Municipal Library, the elevators of which were rumored to have been driven by fumes harnessed from the wine cellar below. Now the venerable QVB has been transformed into one of the most palatial shopping complexes on earth. With a cathedral-like stained-glass dome, a regal grand staircase, wrought-iron balustrades, and a Royal Clock (weighing a ton) that shows animated scenes from British history along with the time, the structure is air-conditioned and equipped with escalators. Housing 194 shops, cafés, restaurants, boutiques, and entertainment spots, the QVB displays Victorian memorabilia as well as a breathtaking range of sellable merchandise. Don't go looking for cheapos here—they don't thrive in this environment.

Open: 24 hours.

SYDNEY TOWER, at the corner of Market and Pitt Sts. Tel. 229-7444.

Sydney Tower is the tallest landmark in a town that fairly bristles with them. A giant sky needle stabbing 1,000 feet up from Centrepoint, the tower offers spectacular views that are aided by high-powered binoculars. Also featured are a weather station, a free audio tour, and two revolving restaurants—which make Sydney the world's revolving-restaurant capital.

Admission: $A6 adults, $A2.50 children.

Open: Daily 9:30am–9:30pm.

SYDNEY ENTERTAINMENT CENTRE, Harbour St., Haymarket. Tel. 211-2222.

Australia's largest auditorium, impressive though not particularly photogenic, resembles an oversized airport terminal. The building is a marvel of flexibility: Four different layouts allow the complex to be used for single star performers, theatrical productions, or giant sporting events. It can hold from 3,500 to 12,000 with nary a pillar to block anyone's view of the stage.

FROMMER'S FAVORITE SYDNEY EXPERIENCES

Wine Tasting on the Deck of *Phantom of the Opera* Boats and ferries skim the water and the harbor lights twinkle while you solemnly taste your way through 30 mouthfuls to decide which wine to have with dinner.

Sheepshearing at the Argyle Tavern The shearing proceeds to the exact rhythm of the song "Click Go the Shears," and the last curl drops with the last "click."

Attending a Sydney Surf Carnival Grand Finale As the bands play, all the competing Lifesavers Clubs march past cheering crowds in their colorful costumes, their flags flying, and move in the peculiar high-stepping gait that enables them to march in soft sand.

Listening to Tchaikovsky's *1812 Overture* under the Stars While the Sydney Symphony performs, the audience stretches out on the grass in Centennial Park, awaiting the climactic cannon salvos provided by the Royal Australian Artillery that make the earth shake.

Meeting Skippy the Bush Kangaroo Star of Australia's most popular TV series and a resident of Waratah Park, Skippy has a way with people. When we met, he gravely placed both his forepaws on my shoulders, then nibbled my ear.

Watching the Start of the Sydney–Hobart Yacht Race An armada of billowing white sails streams out of the harbor.

HISTORIC BUILDINGS & MONUMENTS

VICTORIA BARRACKS, Oxford St. Tel. 339-3445. Museum 339-3330.

This living history of Australia's military forces is located in Paddington. Built largely by convict labor and finished in 1848, the barracks were designed to house one regiment of British infantry. The British garrison troops were withdrawn in 1870, since there was no enemy imaginable who couldn't be handled by the Royal Navy. Since then Australia's own forces have occupied the barracks, which today are the hub and command post of the Commonwealth's field-and-supporting units. The place is a splendid example of late Georgian architecture, crammed with military memorabilia. Every Thursday at 10am (except December and January) there's a military band display. Following this the barracks are open to tours. The museum is also open on Sundays, 10am to 3:30pm.

Admission: Free.

FORT DENISON, Sydney Harbour. Tel. 364-9100.

You can't miss the little lump of rock with the round tower sticking out of Sydney Harbour. Officially named Fort Denison, the islet was known as Pinchgut to thousands of convicts sent there on starvation rations as a "mild" form of punishment. Built and armed to protect Sydney from invasion (which never came), Fort Denison today is a maritime tide observation station as well as a landmark. The massive Martello Tower still houses the huge cannon and balls earmarked for an enemy (Russian at that time) who failed to test them.

Tours: $A8 adults, $A5.50 children.

Departures: From Circular Quay, Pier G, Tues–Sun 3 times daily. Tours last 2 hours.

ELIZABETH BAY HOUSE, 7 Onslow Ave. Tel. 358-2344.

This enchanting period mansion was built for the colonial secretary of New South Wales in 1838. Laid out around a superb central staircase, its salon lit by an oval lantern from above, the white villa shows the tasteful splendor in which the colonial upper classes dwelled at a time when Australia's lower orders were somewhat less stylishly housed. The furnishings have the typical elegant simplicity of the Georgian era—soon thereafter obliterated by the overstuffed red-brick monstrosities of the Victorians, who spread their architectural ham-handedness all over the globe.

Admission: $A5 adults, $A3 children.

Open: Tues–Sun 10am–4:30pm.

SYDNEY HARBOUR BRIDGE, Sydney Harbour.

An immense structure linking the downtown business district with the North Shore, this is the second-longest single-span bridge in the world. Measuring 2¾ miles (2 feet shorter than San Francisco's Golden Gate Bridge), the Harbour Bridge weighs 52,800 tons and was *the* Sydney landmark until the coming of the Opera House. Too bulky to be called beautiful, the bridge is known affectionately as the "Old Coathanger" among the locals. The four massive stone pylons at the corners were unnecessary additions, since the bridge is supported solely by its span girders. But during World War II these pylons served as antiaircraft-gun positions. Today one of them is the **Pylon Lookout.** If you're willing to climb up some 200 steps, you'll have the whole expanse of the harbor at your feet. Admission is $A1, and the lookout is open daily from 10am to 5pm.

Pier One, underneath the Harbour Bridge, adjacent to The Rocks, is not stylish, but it is delightfully relaxed, inexpensive, and impressively cosmopolitan and has so many attractions that you'd have to list them alphabetically. Located in a row of converted warehouses are dodge-'em cars; a movie theater; merry-go-rounds; an excellent bookstore (John Cookson); market stalls; shops selling anything from jewelry to junk; a colonial village from the turn of the century; and an array of restaurants, cafés, and snack shops. You can gorge yourself on sashimi, pasta, tabbouleh, tacos, satay, baklava, samosas, hamburgers, or Sydney rock oysters while listening to strolling balladeers, brass bands, or jazz combos and watching jugglers, dancers, or the constantly changing harbor scene around you. The place also boasts an "astro analyst," a futuristic shooting gallery, and electronic games. Open daily until midnight.

MUSEUMS & GALLERIES

THE MINT, Queens Square, Macquarie St. Tel. 217-0122.

A gracious colonial building, the Mint houses a large collection of historic coins and stamps, as well as ceramics, antique furniture, and costumes.

Admission: Free.

Open: Thurs–Tues 10am–5pm, Wed noon–5pm.

ART GALLERY OF NEW SOUTH WALES, The Domain. Tel. 225-1744.

The two wings of the Art Gallery of New South Wales, one built at the turn of the century and the other in 1970, are admirably suited to their contrasting exhibits. The traditionally skylit, wine-walled galleries of the old wing contain European and Australian art dating from the Renaissance to the early 20th century. The new wing, all angled white walls and harbor-framing glass, houses impressionist and modern works, including some striking paintings by those most famed Australian artists, William Dobell, Russell Drysdale, and Sidney Nolan. Pick up a free guide to the collection in the bookshop to the left of the entrance.

Within the museum is a licensed café serving hot dishes, sandwiches, and snacks. Exit from the front door and follow the winding path halfway across the Domain to the circular building trimmed with window boxes, and you can purchase inexpensive teas, lunches, and sandwiches at the **Domain Restaurant** (unlicensed).

Admission: Free.

Open: Mon–Sat 10am–5pm, Sun noon–5pm. **Closed:** Good Friday and Christmas.

STATE LIBRARY OF NEW SOUTH WALES, Macquarie St. Tel. 230-1414.

Next door to Parliament is the State Library of New South Wales, where you should definitely clamber up the long stone steps to view the **Mitchell and Dixson Galleries.** A repository of papers, prints, paintings, and proclamations dealing with the settlement of Sydney, the galleries mount various showings of the trove. I immensely enjoyed one called "Our Origins—From Penal Camp to Parliament." It included over 300 fascinating items, but possibly the most telling was Governor Davey's Proclamation, circa 1828, a pictorial broadsheet explaining British justice to the Aborigines. The potentialities are graphically expressed. Black chief and white chief shake hands (warriors to rear). Black man spears white man, white warriors hang black man. White man shoots black man, white warriors hang white man. Ultimate potential: black and white man with arms around shoulders, black and white children holding hands, black woman cradling white baby, white woman cradling black baby. Everybody happy—in white fella clothes. The library is noted for its photographic exhibitions.

Admission: Free.

Open: Mon–Fri 9am–9pm, Sat–Sun 11am–5pm.

AUSTRALIAN MUSEUM, corner of William and College Sts. Tel. 339-8111.

The largest museum of natural history on the continent, and Australia's first, it also houses an impressive section on Aboriginal and Pacific Islands anthropology, including replicas of New Guinea villages. There are gigantic whale skeletons; models of sharks and other marine creatures; and hundreds of tribal weapons, artifacts, and ornaments.

Admission: $A4 adults, $A8 families.

Open: Daily 10am–5pm.

HOLDSWORTH GALLERIES, 86 Holdsworth St., Woollahra. Tel. 363-1364.

The largest *private* art gallery in the southern hemisphere, this is also one of the premier showcases for contemporary Australian artists, so beautifully designed and constructed that it could pass as an artwork itself. The exhibitions change—sometimes three shows are held simultaneously—but they invariably reflect the best efforts produced by local painters and sculptors. Works by artists like Sidney Nolan, Sali Herman, and Arthur Boyd are staples; new unknowns occasionally get their meteoric start here.

Admission: Free.

Open: Daily 10am–5pm, Sun noon–5pm.

SYDNEY JEWISH MUSEUM, 148 Darlinghurst Rd., Darlinghurst. Tel. 360-7999.

Opened in 1993, this museum is a showcase of Jewish history in Australia and simultaneously a spine-chilling memorial to the Holocaust in Europe. Presented in the form of a high-tech multitiered exhibition, it lets visitors meet the original Australian Jews—transported over as convicts on the First Fleet—one of whom, the remarkable Esther Abrahams, eventually became the First Lady of New South Wales. The gradual rise of the Jewish community Down Under stands in searing contrast to the destruction of the communities in Europe, shown here through deliberately understated exhibits that are hard to forget.

Admission: $A5.

Open: Mon–Thurs 10am–4pm, Sun noon–5pm.

ZOOLOGICAL GARDEN

TARONGA ZOO, Mosman. Tel. 969-2777.

Taronga Zoo has the most beautiful setting of any zoological garden in the world. Perched on a hillside 12 minutes by ferry from Circular Quay, it offers harbor panoramas together with the animals and 75 acres of bushland park. Take the ferry from wharf no. 2 ($A2.40 for adults, $A1.20 for children), then catch the waiting bus to the top of the hill and sightsee downhill all the way. There is also a cable car, the "Aerial Safari," from the wharf to the top of the zoo. See koalas at their own treetop level in their specially designed enclosure. Get your photo taken with a koala at the Encounter Exhibit. Check out the platypus house, the rain-forest aviary where you walk *into* the cage and have the birds fly above and around you, and the friendship farm where you can pet a lamb or a wombat. In the underground building, where special lights turn day into night, you can watch the nocturnal denizens of Australia and New Guinea at their busiest. Also in residence are the inevitable lions, tigers, chimps, elephants, and reptiles.

Admission: $A13.50 adults, $A6 children. A Zoopass that includes a ferry trip, a cable-car ride, and zoo admission costs $A17 for adults, $A8.70 for children.

Open: Daily 9am–5pm.

BEACH

MANLY BEACH, Manly.

If you only have one day to experience an Australian beach, then I'd say make it Manly. (If you have more time, see "Sports & Recreation," later in this chapter.) Speed the seven miles in 13 minutes via Jetcat from jetty no. 2, Circular Quay, for $A4.50. Coming back, surfeited with sun and saltwater, cruise in on the slow boat: Ferries commute between Manly and wharf no. 3, Circular Quay. It's a leisurely and wonderful 35-minute chug that costs $A3.30 for adults, $A1.60 for children.

Manly has four ocean beaches, two ocean swimming pools, and six calm harbor beaches. It also has a **Fun Pier,** with spinning wheels, dodge-'ems, and whirlers. Considerably more impressive is the **Oceanworld,** West Esplanade (tel. 949-2644), which has a 250,000-gallon tank viewable from above and from three depth levels. The pool is swarming with thousands of ocean critters, from tiny rainbow fish to enormous sea turtles, giant rays, groupers, and killer sharks. At feeding time (twice on weekdays, thrice on Saturday and Sunday), divers descend into the tank and actually hand-feed the inhabitants. How they manage not to get their hands bitten off is one of the permanent puzzles and special thrills of the place. Admission is $A11 for adults, $A5.50 for children. Open daily 10am to 5:30pm.

The **Manly Waterworks,** across the park from the ferry wharf, consists of four giant water slides that sluice you, twisting, turning, and yelling, from considerable heights into a gentle pool below. It feels nerve tingling but is absolutely safe, and you vary the speeds of the rides. In cool weather they thoughtfully heat the water. It's open daily, and the cost is $A6 for an hour's slithering.

If you're ready for a slower brand of locomotion, take the **Manly Horse Tram,** which dates from 1903 and is the only such vehicle surviving in Australia. Propelled by one four-legged horsepower, it costs $A2 for adults, $A1 for children. Open daily until 5pm.

COOL FOR KIDS

Three quarters of Sydney's attractions are decidedly cool for the youngsters. To start with, there are all of Darling Harbour and Pier One. There are also Taronga Zoo and virtually all of Manly. At the Pylon Lookout of the Harbour Bridge, kids find the 200-plus steps considerably easier than their elders. The view from Sydney Tower enthralls all generations. Old Sydney Town could have been built for kids' entertainment.

There are also the wildlife sanctuaries—Featherdale and Waratah Park—swarming with furry pettables. The Powerhouse Museum has hands-on moving gadgetry that could pass for toys. And then there are the beaches, all 34 of them, with rubber surfboards for hire and warm breakers to tumble in. For a finale, you can take them to the multidimensional *Story of Sydney,* on The Rocks, for a backward glimpse that resembles a ride in a time machine.

In between you can sprinkle the harbor cruises and ferry rides. The craft range from little chug-chuggers to huge streamlined luxury jobs. They may be called coffee cruises or harbor sight jaunts or history cruises, but all leave from Circular Quay, all show portions of the truly fabulous harbor setting, and all are great fun.

NEARBY ATTRACTIONS

WARATAH PARK, Terry Hills. Tel. 450-2377.

In this patch of bushland turned into an animal reserve, most of the fauna—wallabies, emus, koalas, wombats—roam around freely. Kangaroos and wombats are gentle critters, but emus—the ostrichlike flightless birds of Australia—can be ill-tempered at times, so be cautious about petting any. Other Oz natives, such as dingoes and Tasmanian devils, you can watch through wire mesh. Tasmanian devils, although only the size of terriers, are ferocious carnivores that will tackle and devour game three times their size. If you watch one feeding, you'll know how it got its name. Waratah is the home of one of Australia's top television stars, Skippy the Bush Kangaroo, who loves meeting his fans and has never been known to throw star tantrums.

Admission: $A11.60 adults, $A5.80 children.

Open: Daily 10am–5pm.

FEATHERDALE WILDLIFE PARK, Kildare Rd., Doonside. Tel. 622-1644.

About an hour's travel time west of the center city, this compact wildlife reserve harbors all the well-known—and some very obscure—Aussie animals. The less familiar ones include awesome-looking (but quite innocuous) frilled lizards, wonderfully multicolored parrots, the little spiny ant-eating echidnas, flying squirrels, strutting brolga birds, and miniature rat kangaroos. But the top attraction is the large walk-in koala enclosure, where you can roam around, photograph and cuddle the inhabitants, and generally discover what a koala is all about. They may resemble teddy bears but are actually marsupials, carrying their young in pouches like kangaroos. Koalas eat nothing but certain types of gum leaves, don't drink water, rarely come down from their trees, and have *very* placid dispositions. They smell strongly of eucalyptus, and while they are in no way vicious, they have been known to well—er—urinate on whomever is holding them (including, on one regal occasion, Queen Elizabeth).

The most illustrious citizen here is Sydney, the Qantas koala and star of prize-winning TV commercials. Sydney, as you may recall, *hates* Qantas for bringing all those pesky tourists to his home habitat.

Admission: $A9 adults, $A5 children.

Open: Daily 9am–5pm. **Directions:** Take the train to Blacktown, then take bus no. 725.

OLD SYDNEY TOWN, Pacific Hwy., Somersby. Tel. 043/401-104.

A major attraction for interstate-and-overseas visitors, this is a fairly faithful replica of colonial Sydney two centuries ago. Houses, workshops, taverns, barracks, churches, and government offices have been re-created as close to the originals as possible. And so have the events. You can hear a town crier bellowing out the news, watch a military drill, or witness a colonial magistrate's court in action. (The main historical deviation here is that all participants are stone-cold sober.) The spectators (including you) take part in the action—at least in the sound effects. You see the convicted culprit marched to a public triangle and given a flogging with a cat-o'-nine-tails (not for the squeamish). After that you can take a break by attending a colonial wedding.

Admission: $A14.50 adults, $A8.20 children.

Open: Wed–Sun 10am–4pm. **Directions:** Take the train to Gosford, then take the connecting bus to Old Sydney Town.

WALKING TOUR 1 — THE ROCKS

Start: Visitors Centre, at 104 George St.
Finish: Sailors Home, at 108 George St.

Time: Allow an hour or more.
Best Times: Any day.
Worst Times: At night when attractions are closed.

You could spend three hours or three days exploring this, the cradle of Sydney. To simplify matters, I've mapped out a walking tour for you that covers all the salient points. But before you start, picture the land along the peninsula as it was in 1788, when Captain Phillip ordered his motley cargo to pitch tents and hoist the Union Jack. Here it all began: with 800 bedraggled human beings and a few rows of wooden huts and leaking tents. The immense sprawl that is contemporary Sydney, over the hills behind you and along the coves in every direction as far as your eye can see, grew from this minute patch.

The Rocks today are part of a large-scale redevelopment scheme that has altered the face of the city while lovingly preserving its picturesque wrinkles. For a long time this area was the roughest, toughest scene in the southern hemisphere: a place for notorious taverns, prostitutes, and nightly knifeplay, where the infamous "Sydney Ducks" reigned supreme and the garrison soldiers collected a few lifeless bodies every morning.

The old buildings have been restored, and the thug element has vanished. Today The Rocks include one of Sydney's smartest hotels, the Parkroyal; trendy cafés; arts-and-crafts studios; and a steady stream of tourists. Enjoy your walk through history.

The Rocks are so honeycombed with cafés, bars, restaurants, tearooms, and snackeries—indoors and out—that you could "refresh" yourself every 50 yards or so.

Start at the:

1. **Visitors Centre,** 104 George St. (tel. 247-4972), where you can find maps, books, pamphlets, and brochures about Old Sydney and watch a free audiovisual show on the history of the area.

   Turn right from the centre and walk to Circular Quay West, where you'll see:
2. **Campbells Storehouse,** dating from 1839 and today crammed with restaurants instead of cargo goods. From there you can catch one of the most spectacular harbor views Sydney has to offer.

   Turn left and come to the:
3. **Earth Exchange,** 18 Hickson Rd. (tel. 251-2422), a museum about the ground we live on and its development throughout a billion years. Exhibits include gold; gems; minerals and opals; a simulated earthquake; and an impressive volcano eruption, complete with flowing lava and sulfur aroma. Adults $A7.50, children $A5.50.

   Turn right, climb up through the Metcalfe Stores, and then turn left on George Street. In a small side street you'll find the:
4. **Westpac Banking Museum,** 6 Playfair St. Westpac was once the Bank of New South Wales, the oldest such establishment on the continent, founded in 1817. The money exhibited includes the doughnutlike "holey dollars" of 1812; other features depict the bank's running fight against bushrangers, the gold-rush era, and a re-created (and fully working) bank branch of the 1890s.

   Return to George Street and bear left. You'll pass a row of small terrace houses known as Sergeant Majors Row, which was the original name of the entire street before King George got into it. Pass the Mercantile Hotel (a hallowed Irish pub), turn right, and walk under the mighty Sydney Harbour Bridge to:
5. **Dawes Point Park.** This was the first fortified position in Australia, and the guns are still standing there—waiting for the French fleet or czarist Russian raiders that never came. Today they are used chiefly as climbing trees by the local kids (quite a useful occupation for cannon).

   Go back under the bridge, turn left, and march past Foundation Park down to:
6. **The Argyle Cut,** one of the early colony's major engineering feats—a 300-foot

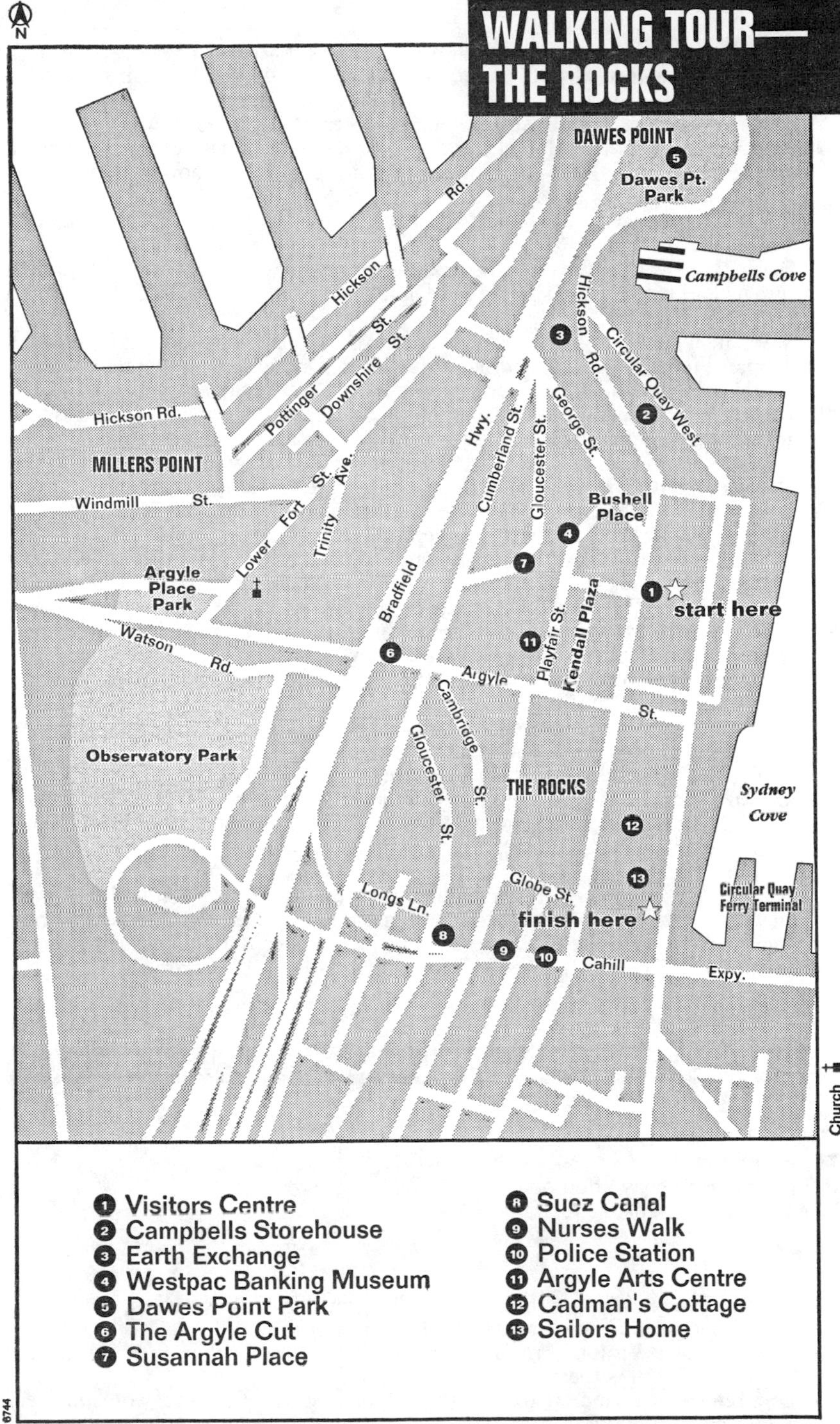
WALKING TOUR—
THE ROCKS
N
DAWES POINT
Dawes Pt. Park
Campbells Cove
Hickson Rd.
Hickson St.
Pottinger St.
Downshire St.
Hickson Rd.
Circular Quay West
George St.
Gloucester St.
Cumberland St.
Bradfield Hwy.
MILLERS POINT
Windmill St.
Lower Fort St.
Trinity Ave.
Bushell Place
Argyle Place Park
start here
Playfair St.
Kendall Plaza
Watson Rd.
Argyle St.
Cambridge St.
Gloucester St.
Observatory Park
THE ROCKS
Sydney Cove
Circular Quay Ferry Terminal
Globe St.
Longs Ln.
finish here
Cahill Expy.
Church
1 Visitors Centre
2 Campbells Storehouse
3 Earth Exchange
4 Westpac Banking Museum
5 Dawes Point Park
6 The Argyle Cut
7 Susannah Place
8 Suez Canal
9 Nurses Walk
10 Police Station
11 Argyle Arts Centre
12 Cadman's Cottage
13 Sailors Home
6744

tunnel hollowed out of the solid stone to give direct access to Millers Point from Circular Quay. It was begun with convict labor in 1843, and you can still see the prisoner's marks on the granite.

Cross Cumberland Street to Gloucester Street. At no. 58 stands:

7. **Susannah Place,** a colonial working-class terrace that has been preserved as a kind of museum house—possibly to give an idea of just how uncomfortably blue-collar urbanites once dwelled.

   Cross onto Harrington Street, where just by the Harbour Rocks Hotel there is a little alley called:

8. **Suez Canal.** This was once the riskiest passage in Sydney Town—after dark, a sure invitation to a knock on the head and an emptied pocket. Walk through and turn right into:

9. **Nurses Walk.** This stretch is dedicated to Australia's first working nurses—all deported female convicts without a nursing certificate among them.

   Take the next alley to George Street. At no. 127 is the erstwhile:

10. **Police Station,** still proudly marked by a stone lion's head with a nightstick in its jaws. Today the place is an interesting crafts gallery and workshop.

    Turn left on George Street, then left on Argyle Street, which brings you to the:

11. **Argyle Arts Centre.** Formerly a bond warehouse, the building is now a complex of galleries and shops selling art, crafts, gifts, and souvenirs—the objects ranging from delightful to deplorable.

    Walk over to Playfair Street, turn left past the sculpture called *First Impressions,* walk down the stairs to Mill Lane, and turn right onto cobbled Kendall Lane. Then walk to George Street. At no. 110 is:

12. **Cadman's Cottage.** Built in 1815, this is the oldest remaining dwelling in Sydney. John Cadman was a pardoned convict who became superintendent of the governor's boats. His former abode now serves as headquarters of the Parks and Wildlife Service.

    Overlooking the cottage is a statue of iron-browed Captain Bligh, arms folded, in his best "hang you from the masthead" pose.

    On the same side of George Street, at no. 108, stands the:

13. **Sailors Home.** This was built in 1864 in order to provide "clean, wholesome lodgings for seafarers," to lure them away from the temptations of brothels and rum taverns—with, sad to report, very limited success.

The above stroll covers only the highlights of the region. For a complete survey, conducted by knowledgable guides steeped in the lore of the place, you should take the official 1¼-hour **Rocks Walking Tour,** which is offered five times daily from 39 Argyle St. (tel. 247-6678). It costs $A7 for adults, $A4.50 for children.

WALKING TOUR 2 — DOWNTOWN SYDNEY

Start: Martin Place.
Finish: Martin Place.
Time: 2 hours.
Best Times: Sunday afternoon.
Worst Times: Weekday rush hours.

Start your tour at:

1. **Martin Place,** which is the center of downtown Sydney as well as a pedestrian mall. There you can pick up an excellent map at the:
2. **New South Wales Travel Centre.** The most striking feature of the flower-filled mall is the:
3. **Cenotaph,** a memorial to Australia's fallen servicemen and women. Every Thursday at 12:30pm the army stages a ceremony at the Cenotaph, then marches

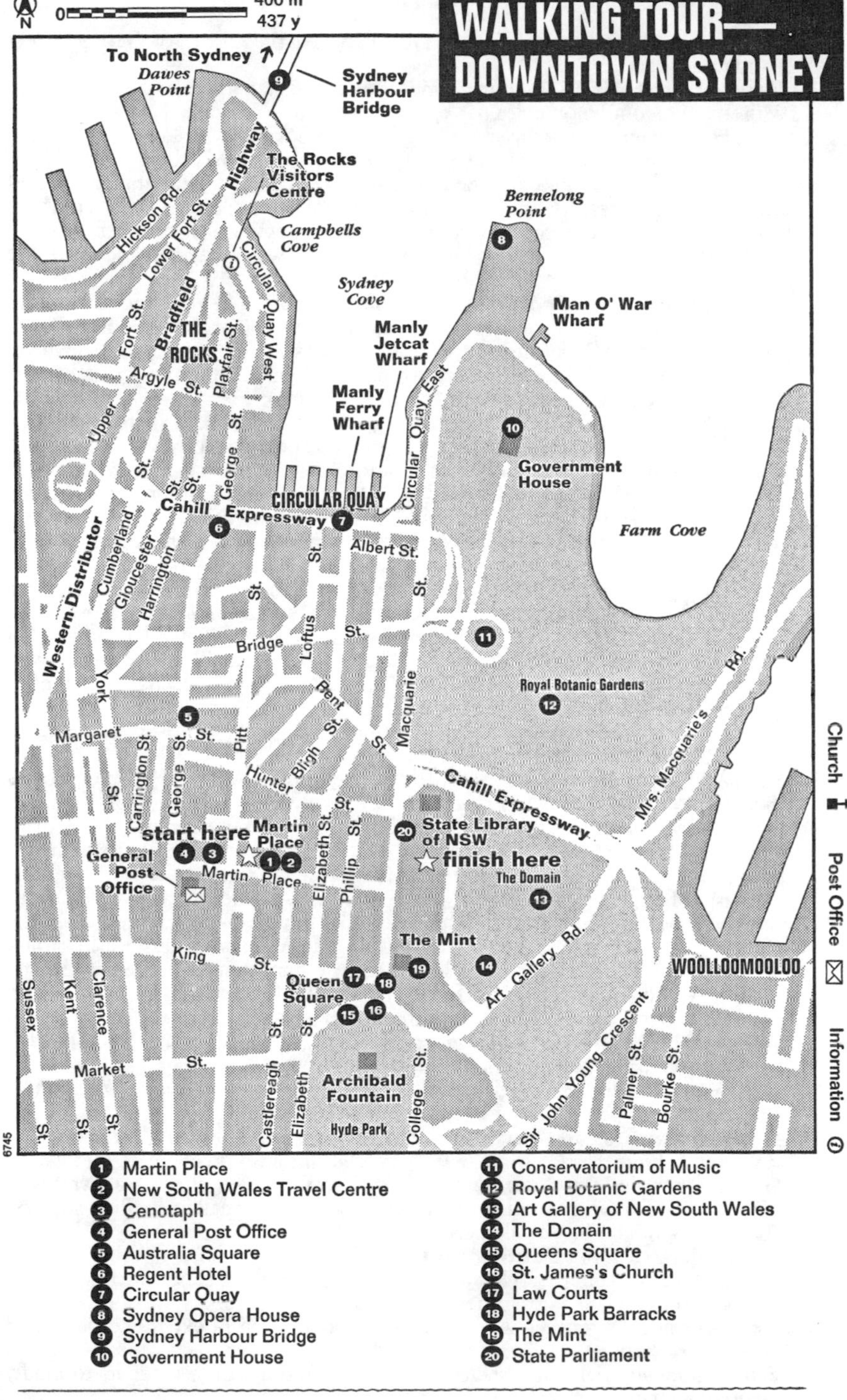
WALKING TOUR—DOWNTOWN SYDNEY
N
0
400 m
437 y
To North Sydney
Dawes Point
Sydney Harbour Bridge
Highway
The Rocks Visitors Centre
Campbells Cove
Bennelong Point
Hickson Rd.
Lower Fort St.
Circular Quay West
Sydney Cove
Man O' War Wharf
Manly Jetcat Wharf
Fort St.
Bradfield
THE ROCKS
Playfair St.
Argyle St.
Manly Ferry Wharf
Circular Quay East
Upper
George St.
St.
Government House
CIRCULAR QUAY
Cahill Expressway
Farm Cove
Western Distributor
Cumberland
Gloucester
Harrington
Albert St.
Bridge St.
Loftus
Macquarie St.
Royal Botanic Gardens
York
Margaret St.
Carrington St.
Pitt
Bent St.
Bligh St.
Mrs. Macquarie's Rd.
Hunter St.
Elizabeth St.
Phillip St.
Cahill Expressway
start here
Martin Place
State Library of NSW
finish here
General Post Office
Martin Place
The Domain
The Mint
King St.
Queen Square
Art Gallery Rd.
WOOLLOOMOOLOO
Sussex St.
Kent St.
Clarence St.
Market St.
Castlereagh St.
Elizabeth St.
Archibald Fountain
Hyde Park
College St.
Sir John Young Crescent
Palmer St.
Bourke St.
Church
Post Office
Information
6745
1 Martin Place
2 New South Wales Travel Centre
3 Cenotaph
4 General Post Office
5 Australia Square
6 Regent Hotel
7 Circular Quay
8 Sydney Opera House
9 Sydney Harbour Bridge
10 Government House
11 Conservatorium of Music
12 Royal Botanic Gardens
13 Art Gallery of New South Wales
14 The Domain
15 Queens Square
16 St. James's Church
17 Law Courts
18 Hyde Park Barracks
19 The Mint
20 State Parliament

to the Anzac Memorial in nearby Hyde Park. At the corner of George Street stands the huge:

4. General Post Office, built in a kind of ersatz Venetian Renaissance style, but with inviting cool colonnades.

Turn right on George Street and walk two blocks to:

5. Australia Square. Part of the Sydney skyline since 1967, the 50-floor (three below ground) **Australia Square Tower** is a circular cement, aluminum, and glass structure presently noted as the third-tallest building in the southern hemisphere. Take the fastest elevators in the southern hemisphere to the **Summit,** the largest revolving restaurant in the world, where prices are yet another Australia Square superlative.

Level 4, the **Shopping Circle,** is a colorful arcade of stores and services. In the main entrance, note the tapestries that were woven at Aubusson in France from designs by Le Corbusier and Vasarely. A massive Calder sculpture squats on the George Street plaza. (Modesty forbids me to print what the locals call it.) Continue on George Street, where you next come to:

6. Regent Hotel. A fluted 36-story tower (actually 35, because there is no 13th floor) behind a sloping beige stone front, the Regent is possibly Sydney's poshest hotel. An immense amount of movie footage has featured its polished marble foyer, with a central atrium warmed by diffused sunshine filtering through the skylight. You could take afternoon tea in this photogenic oasis, but I'd advise you to choose a somewhat more economical refreshment break farther on. Turn right and walk onto:

7. Circular Quay. Today the busy site of the ferry wharves and Overseas Passenger Shipping Terminal, this horseshoe-shaped quay embraces Sydney Cove, "the cradle of Australian history." It was here that Capt. Arthur Phillip landed in 1788 with his flock of 1,500 (700 convicts) to begin building a colony. It was he who "honoured" the cove—and, by extension, the city—with its name, after Viscount Sydney. Sydney past, present, and future converge on this quay.

Stand facing the harbor. To your right, jutting into the froth-tipped waves, is Australia's fabulous futuristic folly, the:

8. Sydney Opera House (see "The Top Attractions," above). To your left arches the:

9. Sydney Harbour Bridge, linking the business district to the northern suburbs. The bridge is too massive and fussy for beauty, but Sydneysiders are nevertheless prompt to point out that, while not the longest single span in the world, it's the heaviest! A full 52,800 tons of steel went into its 2¾-mile length. But the Harbour Bridge grows on you quickly. When viewed from the harbor entrance in the softening haze of dusk, framing the fragility of the Opera House in its stolid, protective curve, it's a sight to strike joy from the most sight-hardened breast.

From Circular Quay, pass the ferry wharves and food stands on your left and continue around the quay to Bennelong Point, past the gloriously controversial Sydney Opera House. Cross the forecourt and the lawns beyond and you'll reach the sandstone keep and turrets of:

10. Government House, residence of the governor of New South Wales. (Not open to the public.) Continue on and you come to the:

11. Conservatorium of Music, which, for reasons unknown, was built to resemble a Tudor castle. To your left stretches the lush greenery of the:

12. Royal Botanic Gardens, with rolled lawns, labeled shrubs, a pyramidal greenhouse filled with orchids and ferns, and a restaurant kiosk. Turn right on Art Gallery Road and you come to the:

13. Art Gallery of New South Wales (see "More Attractions," above). There's a second-floor restaurant serving afternoon tea and light meals, which makes an inexpensive refueling stop. Otherwise wander south across:

14. The Domain. During the week this is just a vast, pleasant expanse of lawn and trees, but on Sunday it becomes populated with self-appointed saviors—political and religious—proclaiming their creeds from the rungs of stepladders to mildly amused audiences.

Art Gallery Road becomes Prince Albert, facing:

15. Queens Square, the most architecturally impressive part of Sydney, with handsome colonial Georgian structures all around.

To your left on the square rises the graceful copper-sheathed spire of:

16. St. James's Church, elegantly designed by the convict-architect Francis Greenway and completed in 1819. On your right are the:

17. Law Courts, another Greenway design, and one that so delighted Governor Macquarie that he granted the convicted forger a full pardon.

Walk straight ahead onto Macquarie Street where, on the right, is the:

18. Hyde Park Barracks, also by Greenway. Built as a dormitory for male convicts, it was actually used to house the New South Wales Regiment. Today parts of the building are a museum, each room devoted to a different aspect of social life from the colonial period to the 1950s. Admission is free, and the museum open Wednesday to Monday from 10am to 5pm.

REFUELING STOP The **Hyde Park Barracks Café,** located in what used to be the officers mess, overlooks the parade ground. You can get a full meal as well as sandwich snacks here and can drink tea or something stronger (the place is licensed).

Duly refreshed, step out on Macquarie Street and walk a few steps to:

19. The Mint (see "More Attractions," above), which today houses a permanent collection of decorative arts, coins, flags, and stamps.

You now have a choice, probably depending on the state of your puppies, of either walking the length of Macquarie Street to the:

20. State Parliament, or turning left onto Martin Place, where you started.

ORGANIZED TOURS

AAT King's, Shop W1, Wharf 6, Circular Quay (tel. 252-2788), offers a wide range of city and state excursions. "Sydney in a Day," all day, every day, includes most of the sights of the city; a harbor cruise; visits Vaucluse House and Bondi Beach; and tours the famous surfing beaches of Dee Why, Curl Curl, and Manly. The tour departs daily at 9:15am from Circular Quay, George Street; returns at 5:30pm; and costs $A65 for adults, $A55 for children.

Australian Pacific Tours (tel. 252-2988) hosts "Sydney after Dark." This tour is made in a scarlet double-decker bus (try to get seats on top) and takes in a fair slice of Sydney's nocturnalia. You get panoramic night vistas, dinner and a show at the Argyle Tavern, a fling at the poker machines in a private club, and glimpses of Kings Cross after dark. It departs from various hotels Tuesday to Saturday at 7pm, and costs $A79 or $A95, depending on the night (adults only).

Sydney Hostel Tours are a unique arrangement for the exclusive benefit of hostel dwellers, run by a woman named Chris and her partner, Andy. Their tour is **Oz Trek Adventure,** P.O. Box 1328, Darlinghurst, NSW 2010 (tel. 360-3444), and they pick up people from their hostels and take them for drive/hike visits to the Blue Mountains. You can choose between Wednesday and Saturday outings, each costing $A28, departing at 8:15am and returning around 7pm. These are friendly excursions in a minibus; the hiking portions are not overstrenuous, and the company is cosmopolitan.

The ✪ **Riverboat Mail Run,** where you ride along with Australia's last river postman, delivering mail, groceries, and so forth to the population along the scenic Hawkesbury River, is bookable through the Hawkesbury River Ferries (tel. 985-7566). A tremendously popular 3-hour chug run Monday to Friday, it costs $A20 for adults, $A10 for children. Bookings advisable.

HARBOR CRUISES

No city in the world utilizes its harbor setting for pleasure jaunts to the extent that Sydney does. You can rent rides on virtually every kind of craft (including passenger sailing yachts) and with every kind of provisioning, including midnight champagne suppers. Below are some of the cheapest and most popular of a dozen similar water ventures.

Every Sunday a ferryboat leaves Pier 2, Circular Quay, at 1:45pm for a close-up view of the spectacular sailing races staged by the **NSW 18-Foot Sailing Club.** The fares are $A4 for adults, $A4 for children, and you can book by phoning 32-2995.

Captain Cook Cruises, jetty no. 6, Circular Quay (tel. 206-1111), offers a 1¼-hour minicruise of the harbor that takes in the major points of interest. Cruises are offered four times a day and cost $A15 for adults, $A10 for children. But if you can possibly spare the time, go on the **Coffee Cruise,** which really shows you what the celebrated harbor is all about. (The sights include a closeup of a nudist beach, but watching is not compulsory.) It departs daily at 10am and 2:15pm; takes 2½ hours; and has a running sociohistorical commentary on Sydney's past, present, and future by a knowledgeable tour guide. The price is $A26 for adults, $A16 for children, coffee refreshments included.

Ferry cruises are operated by **Sydney Ferries** (tel. 247-5151). There is a morning and an afternoon cruise, each taking 2½ hours, departing from Circular Quay at 10am weekdays and 1:30pm weekends. You get highly photogenic views of Fort Denison, Shark Island, Darling Harbour, and the Opera House, as well as some of Sydney's most exclusive (and expensive) waterfront homes, accompanied by a well-informed commentary. The cruise costs $A15 for adults, $A10 for children.

7. SPORTS & RECREATION

SPECTATOR SPORTS

AUSTRALIAN FOOTBALL A winter game, played from April to August, soccer is known as "footy" Down Under. Sydney's newest and costliest sports arena is the $A60-million Football Stadium, located next to the Cricket Ground in Moore Park and seating 40,000 spectators. Take the bus Clovelly, Coogee, or Maroubra from Circular Quay or Central Railway.

CRICKET A rather mysterious game for Americans, cricket is played with fanatical fervor during the summer months of October to March. For information about the games, call the New South Wales Cricket Association at 27-4053.

GOLF Although Sydney is well equipped with golf courses, the game here is nowhere near as popular as in the United States. The top golfing event is the New South Wales Open. For details contact the NSW Golf Association at 264-8433.

HORSERACING Australian's grand passion is horseracing, because it caters simultaneously to their love of gambling and their love of horses. You can bet with licensed bookies at the racetracks or at official offtrack bureaus called TAB. Sydney has four racecourses, open year-round. Admission to any of them is $A6 to $A8. The closest is Randwick, Allison Road (tel. 663-8400), only three miles from downtown and easily reached by the Special Randwick bus service going from Circular Quay and Central Railway.

TENNIS The major tournaments are held at White City in Rushcutters Bay and at the Entertainment Center in Darling Harbour. The top-class events are usually scheduled between October and February.

RECREATION

BOATING & SAILING The best opportunities for both (also for bush walking) can be found in Ku-ring-gai Chase National Park, 18 miles north of Sydney. Take the train from Central Station to Mount Ku-ring-gai, Berowra, or Cowan Station. Bait 'n Boats, 83 Brooklyn Rd., Brooklyn (tel. 455-1206), rents out small aluminium craft, plus fishing tackle, for around $A48 per day. For deluxe cruisers there is Skipper a Clipper, Coal and Candle Creek, Akuna Bay (tel. 450-1888), renting at between $A35 and $A100 per person per day. For sailboats contact Pittwater Yacht Charter, Lovett Bay (tel. 99-3047).

GOLF Sydney has 82 golf courses within the metropolitan area. The cost of playing a round of 18 holes varies sharply between $A7 and $A14, depending on where and when you play. Some of the closer public courses are Woollahra Golf Club, Woollahra Park, Rose Bay (tel. 327-5404); Bondi Golf Links, Military Road, North Bondi (tel. 30-1981); and Moore Park Golf Course, Anzac Parade, Moore Park (tel. 663-3960).

HORSEBACK RIDING Centennial Park has both the most popular biking and horseback riding trails. You can hire a live steed (around $A13 per hour) from Centennial Park Horse Hire, RAS Showground, Driver Avenue, Moore Park (tel. 332-2770).

SWIMMING & SURFING Thirty-four glorious ocean beaches exist within the city limits, stretching along a golden undulating path from Port Hacking, 20 miles south of Sydney Harbour, to Palm Beach, 20 miles north. When picking your patch of pine-shaded sand (only those born to it can bear the Sydney summer sun full strength), rest assured that all border a sea where the average annual temperature is 68°F. The primary variables are proximity, noise level, and crowdedness. Whatever you choose, be prepared for the fact that Sydneysiders *utilize* their beach hours longer than any people I know, and they enjoy their roaring surf in any number of reckless ways—in surfboats, in canoes, in inflated rubber rafts, on mere slips of surfboards, or by "body-shooting" with nothing but high spirits and skin for buoyancy.

The most popular beaches on summer weekends are Bondi, Manly, Coogee, Maroubra, and Cronulla—all easily reached by public transportation from downtown. Whale Beach, Avalon, and Bilgola have been characterized as "tranquil." To survey the northern beaches, you can catch bus no. 190 from Carrington Street behind Wynyard Station to Palm Beach, which skirts an approximately 26-mile-long shoreline.

I should add that all of the city's public beaches are netted and that there hasn't been a shark attack for over 30 years. Periodically, however, they are invaded by a type of jellyfish known as bluebottles, which can inflict very painful stings. Don't swim where you see a bluebottle warning posted.

Sydney beaches are patrolled by Lifesavers, whose instructions you should follow. (They don't give many.) This applies, above all, to the warning "Swim between the Flags," which denotes the risks of a strong undertow.

It's impossible to describe all of Sydney's 34 beaches in this space, so here's a rundown of a select few:

Bondi This is the closest, liveliest, and most crowded, where weekend parking spots are at a premium. There are rows of restaurants and cafés. Take bus no. 380 from Circular Quay.

Bronte Allegedly the roughest surfing beach, it is surrounded by shady pine trees and picnic areas. Take bus no. 378 from Central Station.

Coogee With calmer water than most beaches, this one is very popular. Take bus no. 373 from Circular Quay.

Camp Cove and Lady Jane Beach These are a pair of nonidentical twins: Camp Cove has rather calm water and a parking problem; Lady Jane—reached via Camp Cove—is a nudist beach, accessible only by climbing down a steep ladder from the cliff face. Take bus no. 324 from Circular Quay.

Manly See "Attractions," above.

Maroubra Surfing aficionados swear that this one has the best rollers in the region. Take bus no. 395 from Central Station.

Palm Beach The most fashionable and most northerly of Sydney beaches, it is vast, picturesque, and rarely crowded—but a l-o-n-g way off. Take bus no. 190 from Wynyard Station.

Collaroy Located on the North Shore, this is Sydney's largest beach—two miles long, running through two suburbs. It doesn't get crowded even on holiday weekends. Take bus no. 182 from Wynyard Station.

Try to watch at least one of the **Surf Carnivals** held on Sydney beaches during the summer. These are competitions between the various Lifesavers Clubs in which they show their skill at surfboat racing and rescue operations, concluded by a grand parade of the competing teams. It's a terrific free spectacle. For the major surfing tournaments, held at Bondi during December, get the dates from the NSW Surf Board Riders' Association (tel. 251-8852).

TEN-PIN BOWLING The cost per game is around $A5, and the closest center is Rushcutter Bowl, 110 Bayswater Rd., Rushcutters Bay (tel. 361-0558).

TENNIS Tennis is played almost universally throughout Australia and at a very high level. Sydney is studded with courts, most equipped for night tennis, but even so bookings can be difficult over weekends and during holidays. Some of the handy inner-suburb courts are Trumper Park, Quarry Street, Paddington (tel. 32-4055); Tennis Factory, Prince Alfred Park, Chalmers Street, Surry Hills (tel. 698-9451); Moore Park Tennis, Anzac Parade, Paddington (tel. 662-7002); and Lyne Park Tennis Centre, New South Head Road, Rose Bay (tel. 371-6048). Court rentals cost between $A7 and $A17 per hour, depending on where and when you want to play.

WINDSURFING You can rent windsurfers at the same place you learn to ride them. Fees range from $A12 to $A18 per hour. These places are open all week, weather permitting, but only in summer: Rose Bay Aquatic Hire, 1 Vickery Ave., Rose Bay (tel. 371-7036), and Milson's Marine, 2 The Esplanade, Balmoral Beach (tel. 969-6006).

8. SAVVY SHOPPING

Sydney is a shopping paradise but decidedly *not* a bargain basement. The general run of merchandise costs as much as in America, and any type of gadgetry is apt to be more expensive. The same applies to books, records, and toys. Beachwear is somewhat cheaper, but regular womens' and mens' clothing prices are considerably above U.S. levels. As in every metropolis, a great deal of what you pay depends on *where* you buy. I have already mentioned the **Queen Victoria Building** (see "Attractions," above) and **Double Bay** (see "Orientation," above) as the chicest, smartest, and costliest retail regions in town, but there are other hunting grounds.

SHOPPING AREAS

DEPARTMENT STORES Sydney has two huge department stores: **David Jones,** corner of Elizabeth and Market streets and corner of Castlereagh and Market streets (tel. 266-5544); and **Grace Bros.,** corner of George and Market streets (tel. 238-9111). Both sell what such emporiums sell the world over—virtually everything.

SHOPPING ARCADES For charm (not cheapness) you should look into the shopping arcades, where the boutiques huddle in clustered rows and tiers and designer labels run wild. **Royal Arcade,** beneath the towering Sydney Hilton, links Pitt and George streets and houses about 50 shops. **Strand Arcade** is the oldest in town and has the distinctly Victorian appearance of a refined railroad station. It contains 82 shops and runs between Pitt and George streets. **Imperial Arcade,** 83 Castlereagh St., has 114 shops concentrating on fashions—in the widest sense—for both sexes.

DUTY-FREE SHOPS Sydney is awash with them, and they can provide bargains for overseas visitors. Competition is fierce, so you'd do well to devote some time to comparison shopping. You must present your passport and return ticket at the time of purchase. And although you can buy at any time, you can collect your purchases only 48 hours ahead of departure. The goods are sealed in plastic, which must not be broken until you've cleared airport formalities. They must then be carried on board the plane as hand luggage.

A few of the dozens of duty-frees in the inner city include **Downtown Duty Free,** 84 Pitt St. (tel. 221-4444); **Hardy Brothers** 74 Castlereagh St. (tel. 235-0083); and **Le Classique,** 33 Bligh St. (tel. 233-1455).

STREET MARKETS It would be great if Sydney had a quarter as many street markets as it has souvenir stores. As it is, there are only three in the central region, with a fourth way out in Blacktown. At the following stalls you're likely to run across real bargains, providing you take your time, have a good nose for nuggets, and do much comparison shopping: **Paddy's Market,** held at Haymarket alongside Chinatown, with over 1,000 stalls, is open Saturday and Sunday from 9am to 4:30pm; **Paddington Street Market,** Oxford Street, Paddington, held Saturday and Sunday from 9am to 4:30pm; and **Flemington Markets,** Parramatta Road, Flemington (take the train to Flemington), held Friday from 11am to 4:30pm and Sunday from 9:30am to 4:30pm.

CREDIT CARDS, SHIPPING & SHOPPING HOURS

The most widely accepted credit cards are American Express, VISA, and MasterCard. Most shops show in their windows the credit cards they will take (as do a great many restaurants). There is no sales tax of any kind. Most shops listed here will also arrange for packaging and shipping purchases to the United States. However, always ask about this beforehand; some retailers will change their policy overnight.

General shopping hours for most stores are Monday to Friday from 9am to 5:30pm, until noon Saturday. Many stores stay open on Thursday until 9pm, but there are many exceptions. The Queen Victoria shopping complex, for example, hums 24 hours a day. And in Kings Cross scores of stores are open daily and don't close until midnight.

BEST BUYS

What you're probably after is Australiana—items that show that you've been to Oz. Here I'd like to issue a warning: There is an immense amount of sheer junk sold in the guise of souvenirs—anything from the Opera House in a glass bowl to Harbour Bridges cast in tin and Digger hats made of rubberized cardboard. Most of these horrors aren't even made in Australia but imported by the ton from Hong Kong and Taiwan. Listed below you'll find some of the "fair dinkum" stuff to buy . . . not exactly cheap, but guaranteed genuine.

ABORIGINAL ARTS & CRAFTS

ABORIGINAL AND OCEANIC ART GALLERY, 98 Oxford St., Paddington. Tel. 332-1544.

This is both an art gallery and a retail outlet for a vast range of Aboriginal and Melanesian artworks, ornaments, weaponry, tools, pictures, ceramics, basketry, and jewelry. One of the partners is an "urban tribal elder."

BOOKS

DYMOCKS BOOK DEPARTMENT STORE, 424 George St. Tel. 235-0155.

The largest bookstore in Australia and among the biggest anywhere, it has specialized sections on matters Australian as well as an outstanding map department.

BOOMERANGS

THE BOOMERANG SCHOOL, 200 William St., Kings Cross. Tel. 358-2370.

The school sells every type of boomerang for prices ranging from $A5 to $A50. Included in the purchase price are lessons in throwing, given every Sunday morning by expert teachers.

CLOTHING

MORRISONS, 105 George St., The Rocks. Tel. 27-1596.

This store specializes in Oz male attire: very smart bush hats, sheepskin coats, riding breeches, moleskins, hacking jackets, and so on.

GIFTS

WATTLE TREE, 294 Oxford St., Paddington. Tel. 331-3096.
Anything from Down Under greeting cards to goanna oil (for body massages), toys, and baby wear is for sale.

MUSIC

FOLKWAYS, 282 Oxford St., Paddington. Tel. 33-3980.
Beyond the mainstream records and tapes, this store places special emphasis on Australian sounds: Aboriginal chants, convict songs, bush ballads, musical scores of Australian films, jazz, and rock.

OPALS

COSTELLO'S, 280 George St. Tel. 232-1011.
Opals are Australia's unique native gemstones. At this cross between a museum and a retail store, you can watch continuous films of the stones being dug, sorted, cut, and polished before being displayed at the counters. Those on sale range from $A15 to $A50,000 and up. Costello's also offers South Sea pearl jewelry and stays open seven days a week.

PRINTS

STROKES, 308 Oxford St., Paddington. Tel. 360-4646.
The store offers an immense selection of limited-edition etchings, woodcuts, lithographs, silk screens, and prints by Australian artists, as well as wall posters worth taking home.

SHOES

PALM BEACH, 370 Oxford St., Paddington. Tel. 357-5092.
Here you'll find shoes, boots, and leather goods from punk to posh, both Australian and imported.

T-SHIRTS & TOWELS

SYDNEY HARBOUR SHOP, 123 George St., The Rocks. Tel. 27-2737.
Chances are that you'll recognize the work of Ken Done, even if you don't know his name. His explosively joyous creations are selling as fast overseas as here. This is his retail center, where you can buy his designs on anything from T-shirts and postcards to tapestries. The sweats go to around $A35, the tapestries to $A5,000.

9. EVENING ENTERTAINMENT

Lighthearted Sydney has no taste for early hours, and "what's happening" in Sydney nightlife is what's happening in most every other city in the world—a little less subtly than in Paris, less frantically than in New York, and fraught with fewer funky possibilities than in San Francisco.

Although wine bars and pubs close tight at 10pm—except in summer, when they close at 11pm—everybody and her brother belongs to a private club where the slot machines clang out until midnight or beyond seven days a week and where the brew is cold and cheap (tourist directions are in the text below). If you dine in a licensed restaurant, you can drink until the proprietor starts stacking the chairs. If you purchase your own bottle (before 10pm) and bring it to a nonlicensed eatery, you can do likewise. Finally, there are the discos, jazz joints, and nightclubs where you are required to order something trivial in the food line (often included in the admission charge) for the privilege of dancing and drinking to as late—or early—as 3am. And ultimately there's Kings Cross, where rows of liquor joints operate by some special dispensation until dawn's early light. A concentrated cluster of bright and/or red lights, King's Cross is the only such district in Australia and contains every conceivable brand of nocturnal action within one square mile: from svelte international eateries to strip joints, from roaring discos to intimate little back-lane cafés. It's a place for drifting around and dropping into whatever tickles your fancy and for doing so in *physical* safety. For while you're likely to get propositioned every few yards, you almost certainly won't get assaulted.

The odd thing about Kings Cross is that, technically, it doesn't exist. The area is merely a vague geographical definition, the region where Darlinghurst, Potts Point, and Elizabeth Bay meet and join hands in a bit of heel kicking before going their own businesslike ways. But to tens of thousands of GIs who flocked here on "R&R" from the hell of duty in Vietnam, the Cross was a patch of sulfurous paradise to be dreamt about when you were back among the rice paddies. The locals, who had added a third "R"—for Remuneration—deeply mourned the passing of this bonanza.

The two main thoroughfares are Darlinghurst Road and Macleay Street. At the arterial hub of the Cross, El Alamein Fountain shimmers in the floodlights like a giant thistledown, dispensing delicate beauty in all directions, free of charge.

Your best guide to after-dark activities is the daily newspaper, which lists the international artists and touring casts in town, plays, movies, concerts, and Opera House programs. The *Sydney Morning Herald* prints a comprehensive "Amusements" page: Dial the given numbers for ticket-and-price information.

THE PERFORMING ARTS

MAJOR PERFORMING ARTS COMPANIES

The best-known companies are the **Australian Chamber Orchestra, Sydney Philharmonia Choir, Sydney Symphony Orchestra, Australian Opera, Australian Ballet, Sydney Dance Company,** and **Sydney Theatre Company,** all of which perform at the **Opera House** (see below) but also headline at other venues.

Equally intriguing but less well known (and less expensive where tickets are concerned) are the following:

New Theatre, 542 King St., Newtown (tel. 519-3403), is not "new" at all; it started during the depression as a platform for social commentary and continues in that role today, although somewhat less earnestly. For 60 years the New Theatre has played in homes, on street corners, at meetings, and even down in a mine to striking miners, making dramatized comments on vital issues of the time. Success has mellowed the group, but only to a point. Its most famous production was Australia's first authentic musical, *Reedy River,* a lively if somewhat naive depiction of life in the outback of the 1890s, with a score woven around genuine and wonderfully catchy old bush ballads. If it's playing—it gets repeated at intervals—don't miss it. The actors are nonprofessional and perform on Friday, Saturday, and Sunday—sometimes beautifully. Tickets run about $A16.

The **Kent Street Theatre,** 420 Kent St. (tel. 267-6646), one of the longest established Sydney troupes, puts on anything from local talent to imported hits.

MAJOR CONCERT HALLS & ALL-PURPOSE AUDITORIUMS

SEYMOUR CENTRE, corner of City Rd. and Cleveland St. Tel. 692-3511.

The Seymour Centre combines three stages and usually offers comedy and drama. It often has visiting overseas companies, mostly excellent.

STATE THEATRE, 49 Market St. Tel. 264-2431.

A former "picture palace" in the architectural mode known as Sam Goldwyn Gothic, this is now chiefly devoted to grandiose musicals and visiting dance troupes, as well as solo celebrities.

SYDNEY OPERA HOUSE, Bennelong Point. Tel. 250-7111.

Actually an arts (and restaurant) complex of which the Opera House forms only a part, the famous "sail roof" also shelters a dance theater, a concert hall, a drama theater, and several more intimate auditoriums—all staging simultaneous productions, but starting at different times and charging different prices. On a given evening you may get the Grand Opera, the Sydney Dance Company, the Sydney Symphony Orchestra, chamber music, an avant-garde satirical comedy, and a one-woman show of cabaret tunes. Opera tickets are the costliest, between $A26 and $A122, but the others aren't exactly cheap.

THEATERS

Although Sydney lacks an actual theater district, standard "Broadway" theater is easy to locate through the newspapers and about as pricey Down Under as in America. A popular local alternative—and a window into Aussie life for foreigners—are the various theater/restaurants presenting topical revues, ribaldry, and political satire. They include dinner—mostly uninspired—in their ticket prices, as well as drinking privileges (see "The Club & Music Scene," below).

It may seem paradoxical to talk about off-Broadway productions in a town without Broadway, but that's the only way to describe the group of nonestablishment playhouses that give Sydney its theatrical dash of paprika.

There are many more where this selection came from. The best guide to what's currently playing is the "Metro" section in Friday's *Sydney Morning Herald*. You can buy theater tickets over the phone by credit card through **Ticketek** (tel. 266-4800) or by calling the individual theaters. Prices vary sharply, depending on who's performing what. This applies particularly to musical events, be they classical, pop, rock, jazz, or folk. Cheap tickets are available at the **Halftix** booth in Martin Place. They're not the best seats, and you have to buy them personally and pay cash.

BELVOIR STREET THEATRE, 25 Belvoir St., Surry Hills. Tel. 699-3273.

This is one of the best, most original, and most variegated show stages in Australia—or rather two stages, because there are an upstairs and a downstairs portion. It was originally bought by some 700 actors and supporters. Located in a distinctly drab part of town, with decor that badly needs a facelift, this theater puts on sparkling performances that feature local playwrights, directors, and actors at their unvarnished finest. Tickets cost around $A24.

CROSSROADS THEATRE, 159 Forbes St., Darlinghurst. Tel. 332-3649.

Small but enterprising, this stage often comes up with real surprise productions, featuring mostly local talent. Tickets cost $A18.50.

ENSEMBLE THEATRE, 78 McDougall St., Milsons Point. Tel. 929-0644.

Located just across the Sydney Harbour Bridge, it specializes in intimate productions. Tickets cost from $A21.

FOOTBRIDGE THEATRE, Parramatta Rd., Glebe. Tel. 692-9955.

Actually located behind a footbridge spanning the road in front, the theater is part of Sydney University and puts on excellent dramas and comedies. Ticket prices start at $A28.

HER MAJESTY'S, 107 Quay St. Tel. 212-3411.

Very mainstream, the theater favors lavish musicals with celebrity casts enjoying long runs. Tickets cost from $A26.

Q THEATRE, corner Railway and Belmore Sts., Penrith. Tel. 047/21-5735.

This used to be a lunchtime theater down by Circular Quay, but it has now graduated to being the only fully professional stage in the western area of Sydney. The ideal time to catch a play there is when you're on your way to or from the popular Blue Mountains region (see "Easy Excursions: New South Wales State," later in this chapter). Tickets cost around $A20, which is somewhat cheaper than in the city.

STABLES THEATRE, 10 Nimrod St., Kings Cross. Tel. 33-3817.

This is the only fully clothed live show in the area and therefore discreetly tucked away on a backstreet. It specializes in original Australian works, mostly serious and frequently excellent. Tickets cost around $A20.

SYDNEY ENTERTAINMENT CENTRE, Harbour St., Haymarket. Tel. 211-2222.

The showcase for all the big names in pop entertainment, the center holds 11,500 people and is regularly packed.

THEATRE ROYAL, MLC Centre, King St. Tel. 231-6111.

More blockbuster musicals are offered here, mostly overseas imports. Ticket prices fluctuate between $A35 to $A75 according to the fame of the productions.

THE CLUB & MUSIC SCENE

NIGHTCLUBS/CABARET

ARGYLE TAVERN, 18 Argyle St. Tel. 27-7782.

For a bit of communal jollity, decidedly tourist oriented but fun nonetheless, opt for a big-splurge evening of dinner, song, and dance at the Argyle Tavern. Occupying a basement room of the restored warehouse that contains the Argyle Arts Centre (see "Walking Tour 1—The Rocks," earlier in this chapter), the tavern exudes early Aussie atmosphere, complete to convict-hewn rock walls and long wooden tables lit by candles. Young women in calico gowns and white dust caps share the serving chores with young men in red sashes—and it's happy, willing service, if not overbrisk. They hand out souvenir menus printed under the masthead of the *Sydney Monitor* circa 1829 and tie around your neck paper bibs that you can flip up come sing-along time to read the words of "Click Go the Shears" and "Tie Me Kangaroo Down, Sport." Then they bring on your choices from the à la carte menu—generous servings of roast lamb, pork, crayfish, beef, chicken, or plump meat pies, possibly followed by blueberry pie or fresh strawberries with whipped cream to top it off. All items on the menu are fresh and reasonably traditional. Food comes first, so go no later than 8pm. At 9:30pm the band strikes up and leads the congregation in 30 minutes of stirring song, including the unofficial national anthem, "Waltzing Matilda," and such international old favorites as "My Bonnie Lies Over the Ocean." With the ice (if there was any) truly broken, the rest of the evening is dedicated to lively dancing to popular music and fueling up on the tavern's specialty, rum punch.

Prices: Dinner and show $A42.50.

HARBOURSIDE BRASSERIE, Pier One, Millers Point. Tel. 252-3000.

Built on a pier over the water, this elegant club mixes rock, jazz, blues, and reggae with imported solo acts. It has a 24-hour license, which means that some shows don't start until after 11pm.

Admission: $A10–$A20.

JULIANA'S, Hilton Hotel, 259 Pitt St. Tel. 265-6065.

One of the snazziest nightspots, this place features international celebrities for its executive-class clientele. The show, with dinner, costs $A80.

STUDEBAKERS, 33 Bayswater Rd., Kings Cross. Tel. 358-5656.

An American-oriented hangout with a Studebaker chassis as a shingle and a U.S. diner–style interior, Studebakers brings a blend of 1950s and 1960s rock and a staff that participates in the floor shows.

Admission: $A6–$A12.
Open: Tues–Sun.

COMEDY CLUBS

The following is a mélange of basement dives and pub theaters devoted—more or less—to comedy, in which bracket I also include male strippers. Charges range from a lowly $A5 to a steep $A26 (including supper), and the shows may feature amateurs or national celebrities.

A whispered warning here: The humor dispensed can be either extremely raunchy or very "in." In the first instance, you run the risk of being offended; in the second, of not understanding the jokes.

Below is merely a snap selection. There's about a dozen more where these came from.

THE COMEDY STORE, 278 Cleveland St., Surry Hills. Tel. 699-5731.

The Comedy Store, off Jamison Street in the city center, specializes in stand-up comics. On Wednesday, Thursday, and Friday, it holds women's night with male strippers. On Tuesday, you get amateurs.

Admission: $A5–$A10.

Open: Tues–Sat.

HAROLD PARK HOTEL, Wigram Rd., Glebe. Tel. 692-0564.

This is a modest pub that hides one of the best entertainment programs in Sydney. You get variations from entire staged comedy plays to one-comic recitals, group improvisations, and amateur stand-ups. Shows are at 8:30 and 10:30pm.

Admission: $A6–$A10.

KIRRIBILLI PUB, 42 Ainsworth St., Lilliefield. Tel. 560-5093.

This place is inexpensive and frequently hilarious. Some knowledge of Aussie idiom is an advantage for spectators.

Admission: $A5.

Open: Thurs–Sat.

LES GIRLS, 2 Roslyn St., Kings Cross. Tel. 358-2333.

This decidedly offbeat program features young and less-so female impersonators, highly talented and stunningly attired. They romp through a middling Rabelaisian variety show brimming with campy humor and awash in double entendres. All the singing is (superbly) mimed to pretaped voices, but the dancing and stripping is done in person. It has a sumptuous setting, done in scarlet and glitz, with velvet wherever you look. All slightly hysterical and deliberately overdone, it's a tremendous drawing card for visitors who've never witnessed such gyrations. Show times are 9:15 and 11:15pm Wednesday through Saturday.

Prices: Dinner and show $A40.

MUSIC PUBS

ROSE, SHAMROCK AND THISTLE, 193 Evans St., Rozelle. Tel. 555-7755.

The name refers to the English, Irish, and Scottish folk music offered here (local folks call it the Three Weeds). Originally an old pub, it's cozy, friendly, and inexpensive. The music ranges from folk and pop to reggae. Admission varies according to the band, $A4 to $A16.

WOOLLOOMOOLOO BAY HOTEL, 2 Bourke St. Tel. 357-1928.

A delightful old pub, once notorious but now dry cleaned and trendy, with a charming beer/wine garden in back, it features a mixed musical bag Wednesday through Sunday, including swing, jazz, and occasional classics.

DANCE CLUBS/DISCOS

These are so numerous they'll make your head spin and so frequently changing they can't be packed into separate segments: Pubs become discos one week, rock venues the next, and cabarets the one after. The term "club," in any case, has no meaning except that some contain legal poker machines and make you an honorary member at the door.

The best guides to this scene are two gratis publications, *OTS* and *Drum Media,* which you can pick up in pubs, hostels, and some news agencies. Both are extremely "in," churned out by fans for fans, and expect you to be familiar with bands, performers, and terminologies that you've probably never heard of.

THE CAULDRON, 207 Darlinghurst Rd., Darlinghurst. Tel. 331-1523.

Very smooth and aimed at the well-heeled over-30 crowd, this place has a disco playing dance classics and also puts on occasional solo celebrities, fashion parades, and art exhibitions.

Open: Daily until 3am.

COLOSSEUM, 54 Darlinghurst Rd., Kings Cross. Tel. 357-3800.

This disco with a very lively deejay has free entry Monday and Tuesday, Ladies Night Wednesday (free cocktails), and parties until dawn nightly.

HARD ROCK CAFE, 121 Crown St., Darlinghurst. Tel. 331-1116.

World famous and swarming with tourists, native and overseas, this is a museum of musical memorabilia, only louder.

ILLUSIONS, 17 Earl Place, Kings Cross. Tel. 358-3408.

There's no dress code here: Come as you are and dance your T-shirt off until 2 or 3am. The crowd is young, enthusiastic, and usually dense.

Admission: Free.

KINSELAS, 383 Bourke St., Darlinghurst. Tel. 331-6200.

This is an erstwhile funeral parlor transformed into a three-level entertainment den. The ground floor has pool tables and weekly jazz offerings; the top floor has a disco spinning Monday to Saturday until 3am.

Admission: $A5–$A7.

MARS, 169 Oxford St., Darlinghurst. Tel. 331-4001.

Mars is a dance club downstairs and a live-rock venue upstairs; both keep going about six nights a week (closed Sunday). The clientele is young, about half gay.

Admission: $A5.

METROPOLIS, 99 Walker St., North Sydney. Tel. 954-3599.

Very handsomely decorated, this club is divided into a restaurant and a disco, the latter hopping weekdays until midnight, Saturday until 5am. (Closed Sunday).

Admission: Free Mon and Wed, $A10 Tues and Thurs–Sat.

PLAYERS, 209 Oxford St., Bondi Junction. Tel. 389-5051.

This is a big operation with a restaurant on the bottom and a disco on top; the idea is to eat first and dance off the calories afterward.

Admission: $A5–$A10.

Open: Nightly until 1am.

ROGUES, 16 Oxford St., Darlinghurst. Tel. 332-1718.

A disco besides a restaurant, Rogues aims at the upmarket crowd and enforces a (not very strict) dress code. Relay teams of deejays spin the latest until 3am.

Admission: Free Tues–Wed, $A10 Thurs–Sun.

Open: Tues–Sun.

MORE ENTERTAINMENT

MOVIES

Sydney's mainstream movie houses charge an outrageous $A11.50 per seat, and for that you must also endure 10 endless minutes of screened commercials of the kind you doze by when they appear on TV. On Monday, however, admissions drop to $A5 to $A6. The fringe theaters, running either oldies or "art" films, charge around $A10.

The main movie houses are grouped in multiscreen blocks downtown, giving you a choice of four to six different features per complex. They include the following: **Greater Union,** Pitt Street Centre (tel. 264-1649); **Greater Union,** George Street (tel. 267-8666); **Hoyts,** George Street (tel. 267-9877); and **Village,** George Street (tel. 264-6701).

Some of the most popular alternative independent cinemas are **Dendy,** Martin

Place (tel. 238-8166); **Academy Twin,** Oxford Street, Darlinghurst (tel. 361-4453); **Valhalla,** Glebe Point Road, Glebe (tel. 660-8050); and **AFI,** Oxford Street, Paddington (tel. 361-5398).

THE LEAGUES CLUBS [GAMBLING]

Not too long ago, with the advent of the poker (slot) machine in New South Wales, the cry that arose from city publicans was, "Where have all the young men gone?" Where was obvious: to the private clubs. Why was equally obvious: Flush from their gambling gains, the clubs offered low-priced food and drink, the finest nightclub entertainment in the country at virtually no charge, longer drinking hours, luxurious surroundings, and that eternally seductive chance to hit the jackpot—an irresistible combination to the Aussie mind.

Although likewise appealing to the visitor, the word "private" has proved daunting. True, the clubs are open to members only on a day-to-day basis, but they also welcome tourists from overseas and out of state. Simply call the club and tell them where you are from and that you would like to see their show. Your name will be left with the doorman. Upon arrival, present your passport or out-of-state identification (driver's license, for example) and you will be smoothly admitted. For the rest of your Sydney stay, you will be an honorary member.

Clubs can be founded on almost any pretext (although legalized gambling is the common thread), but the largest and most lavish are the athletic associations, or Leagues Clubs, open to any and all over the age of 18, regardless of sporting affiliation. These are vast casinos featuring rows of slot machines in all configurations, elegant restaurants where dinner can be purchased for under $A8, bars where the beer sells for A90¢ per glass, and showrooms where the entertainers are international names. The admission ranges from low to free!

Most clubs are open Monday through Friday from 10am to midnight, Saturday and Sunday until 1am.

SOUTH SYDNEY JUNIOR RUGBY LEAGUE CLUB, 558 Anzac Parade, Kingsford. Tel. 349-7555.

This is Australia's largest club, with 52,000 members. Here the show is staged in a 1,000-seat auditorium, and the cast includes top-level entertainers—all gratis! Call for a current program or consult the "What's on in Your Club" column in the Sunday papers.

ST. GEORGE LEAGUES CLUB, 124 Princes Hwy. Tel. 587-1022.

The most lavish revues in the city are staged at this 36,000-member club, whose glittering suburban edifice is known as the "Taj Mahal." Name artists appear—call for program and reservations (required). Shows start at 8:30pm on Friday and Saturday night, with jazz on Sunday afternoon.

STRIPS & SUCH

The strip and "adult-entertainment" clubs jostle each other along Darlinghurst Road, Kellett Street, and parts of Baywater Road in Kings Cross. Most of them have "pink"-something in their names, sandpaper-voiced spielers outside, and "girls, girls, girls" inside. It's useless to recite their shingles because they change all the time, while the shows remain exactly the same. The stripping is total, no nonsense about G-strings for them.

10. NETWORKS & RESOURCES

The **Wayside Chapel,** 29 Hughes St., was built in 1964 with volunteer labor by a freewheeling Methodist minister named Ted Noffs. Open "to all faiths and none," the chapel has since married more people than any other church in Australia, and it has probably helped more desperate souls as well. Now run by Rev. Ray Richmond, it's where you go when you're in trouble (it functions as a 24-hour crisis center); if you want to locate any group or association in Sydney (straight, gay, or otherwise); if you need a crash pad or a solo bed for the night; or if you're sick in body or spirit, or pregnant, or suicidal, or lonely, or broke. You'll get whatever help human goodwill and know-how can bestow, and you'll get no hassles.

The chapel itself, welcoming behind plate-glass windows, is tiny. Instead of normal services, it holds "Celebrations" every Sunday, featuring jazz, folk, and rock music and Buddhist chants—whatever aids. Sunday evening is Question Time, when Mr. Noffs leads discussions on topics like drugs, racism, rape, and the relevance of religion. Upstairs is a coffee shop selling meals at way-down prices. In the theater behind the chapel, plays and films are shown—and not the "message" kind either—debates are held, and problems of the day are thrashed out. Phone the Wayside Chapel at 358-6577 to find out what's going on that evening. Or better still, drop in and deposit something in the donation box. It'll be your best-spent money in Australia.

11. EASY EXCURSIONS: NEW SOUTH WALES

New South Wales, as residents will be swift to inform you, is the "chief" state of the Commonwealth—meaning that it's the most populous and industrialized. But remember they're speaking in strictly Aussie terms: New South Wales has just over 5 million people and measures a full third of a million square miles. And when you realize that 3½ million people are bunched happily into metropolitan Sydney, you get some concept of how much space is left to the rest.

The state boasts a greater variety (if not number) of beauty spots and tourist attractions than any other portion of the continent. New South Wales has four distinct geographical regions, each with its own brand of splendor. First, there's the 1,000-mile coastal strip, offering some of the finest surfing-and-swimming beaches on the globe; second, the inland mountain ranges and plateaus, with snowy peaks sweeping up to over 7,000 feet; third, the gold green lushness of the western slopes, an area of warm lazy rivers and rich wheatfields, ideal for fishing and waterskiing; and finally, the western plains, the "woolbelt" of the state, with immense flocks of sheep and horizons that stretch into eternity.

BLUE MOUNTAINS

Just 50 miles west of Sydney, the **Blue Mountains** rise from the coastal plain and form a backdrop almost as spectacular as the harbor entry. These rolling cliff-toothed ranges really *are* of a deep dreamlike blue, a natural phenomenon produced by countless oil-bearing eucalyptus. The trees constantly release fine droplets of oil into the surrounding atmosphere, reflecting the blue light rays of the sun and wrapping the whole landscape in a vivid azure haze.

The Blue Mountains National Park is fringed with resort towns, ribboned with magnificent waterfalls, and crisscrossed by trails. Each of the mountain townships has its own bag of scenic delights. **Katoomba,** heart and capital of the region, operates the **Scenic Railway** and **Scenic Skyway:** the former reputedly the steepest in the world (at least that's what it feels like while you're riding), the latter an aerial cable car suspended above a fabulous chasm. **Leura** has eight unforgettable gardens (admission A50¢) landscaped into the mountain ruggedness. West of Katoomba lies **Explorers' Tree Birdland,** swarming with brightly colored tropical birds. **Springwood** features the **Norman Lindsay Gallery,** a collection of paintings and statues by Australia's artistic sensualist who shocked a generation of his compatriots and still startles a few. **Wentworth Falls Deer Park** (admission A60¢), laid out in a gentle valley, has tame deer, black swans, hundreds of other water birds, and vast picnic areas. **Jenolan Caves** are the most famous and awesome underground limestone caves in the state, while the largest single-drop waterfall in the region is **Govett's Leap** near **Blackheath.**

Trains for the Blue Mountains leave several times a day from Sydney's Central Railway Station. The round-trip fare is $A10.60.

Two companies offer full-day tours around the Blue Mountains. **AAT King's Tours,** Circular Quay (tel. 252-2788), has a coach leaving daily at 9am and returning at 5:30pm. This excursion includes an optional ride on the Scenic Railway and costs $A49.50 for adults, $A38 for children. **Australian Pacific Tours** (tel. 252-2988), takes in the Jenolan Caves as well as Katoomba, Blackheath, and Mount Victoria. The coach leaves from Circular Quay at 9am and returns at 7:30pm. Adults pay $A57, children $A46.

HUNTER VALLEY

About 125 miles northwest of Sydney stretches the oldest wine region on the continent. The Hunter Valley started harvesting grapes in 1828—long before California. Today the Hunter vintages are overshadowed by those of South Australia's Barossa Valley, but some of the finest table wines served in Sydney's gourmet restaurants are Hunter products.

The Hunter Valley leads a curious double life. Partly industrialized and a major coal-mining district, it is simultaneously a favorite touring-and-excursion region for multitudes of Sydneysiders with wine palates. It is, in fact, the only valley in the world where mineshafts and vineyards coexist, each discreetly hidden from the other.

The old and famous wineries here—Wyndham Estate, Saxonvale, Hermitage, Lindemans, Tuloch, and McWilliams, to name just a few of the 42—all have tasting rooms and sales counters. The wines are cheaper when bought in dozen lots, but approximate prices for single bottles would be $A12 to $A14 for chardonnay, $A6 to $A11 for Riesling, and $A8 to $A20 for port.

The gateway to the region is **Cessnock,** where you'll find the Hunter Valley Wine Society, 4 Wollombi Rd. (tel. 90-6699). They'll shower you with location maps of the vineyards, as well as brochures and pamphlets on the wines available (about 620 varieties the last time I counted).

From Cessnock the road goes on to **Pokolbin,** the self-proclaimed "Heart of the Hunter Valley"; then to **Dalwood** and **Branxton;** and then into the Upper Hunter region with the townships of **Jerrys Plain, Denman,** and **Wybong.** The vineyards are sprinkled over the area, with many offering conducted tours. It's entirely up to you how much sampling you do.

This is a prime goal for weekend crowds from Sydney, so you'd be wise to come during the week. And although you need a car for detailed exploration, it might be equally wise to let someone else do the driving. For an inexpensive and nicely balanced tour, take the "Hunter Valley Winetaster," operated by **AAT King's** (tel. 252-2788). These tour coaches leave Circular Quay, Sydney, three mornings a week, returning at 7:30pm. Call the company for touring dates, exact times, and prices.

NEW ENGLAND

North of Sydney, stretching up to the Queensland border, run a series of verdant ranges and plateaus known as New England. The countryside doesn't really resemble England very much, but it is cool, green, lush, and pleasant, with a special patrician-academic flavor of its own. This is a region of prosperous sheep-and-cattle holdings; of European elms, oaks, willows, and silver birch trees; of red-breasted robins, waterfalls, and an almost British-style university town.

The main town is **Armidale,** 352 miles north of Sydney on the New England Highway, and it radiates academic vibes over the entire region. Of Armidale's 17,000 people, over 2,000 are students and staff of the **University of New England,** and they go to remarkable lengths to live up to their reputation as a Down Under twin of Oxford. True, inside the campus park deer mingle with kangaroos in a most un-Oxonian fashion, but the collegians make up for it by having officials called Yeoman Bedells and talking in terms of "Town and Gown." The frequent fisticuffs between the two factions, which characterize the real Oxford, haven't happened in Armidale yet. But give them time.

The university has six established faculties and maintains very high standards. The town has a sprinkling of cathedrals with dreaming spires; excellent and numerous pubs; and the crispest, most multicolored autumn in the state. For visitors interested in educational facilities, there is also Australia's first country **Teacher's College.** It houses a remarkable art collection (including a Rembrandt etching) given to the college by a shipping tycoon who wound up being worth about $A50, because he spent all his fortune on pictures and gave them to galleries. There are daily trains from Sydney to Armidale.

SNOWY MOUNTAINS

Here are more peaks, but much higher this time, and (we hope) covered from June through September in superbly skiable snow. The Snowy Mountains start their climb 300 miles southwest of Sydney, and their tallest peak, Mount Kosciusko (7,314 feet), is the highest point in Australia. Mount Kozzie, as the natives know it, forms part of a vast winter playground that embraces all 2,100 square miles of the Kosciusko National Park and looks much like a patch of Switzerland transplanted to the southern hemisphere.

THREDBO

This is the skiing capital—a brand-new "all-mod.-cons." (meaning, all modern conveniences) resort village. The brainchild of former Czechoslovakian ski champion Tony Sponar, Thredbo Alpine Village was founded in 1957 and built in the image of the famous European winter sport resorts. In similar style, it offers outdoor-and-indoor fun in roughly equal portions but at less than European expense. You can share a room in an "economy" lodge or rent a holiday flat; all-inclusive, 6-day "snow holiday" packages start as low as $A500 to $A600. In season, the whole village merges into one big party, scattered between the thumping disco of the Keller and half a dozen more intimate, but just as swinging, restaurants, bars, and bistros. Maybe it's the marvelously bracing mountain air, but most of the swingers manage to stumble onto a 2,000-foot chair lift the next morning to zoom down the 25 miles of ski trails, jet-turning and paralleling as if they hadn't rocked through the night. Off-season, the attractions include glorious views—a 1½-mile chair lift operates year-round to the top of Mount Crackenback (6,350 feet)—and such relaxing diversions as fishing, swimming, hiking, barbecuing, campfire nights, and dinner dances. Prices relax, too, slipping even lower than winter levels.

You reach Thredbo by bus, or plane to Cooma, 56 miles away. Coaches take you into the ski fields. For information, contact **New South Wales Travel Centre,** 19 Castlereagh St., Sydney (tel. 231-4444).

LIGHTNING RIDGE

A destination of opposite appeal, here you have the real outback—hot, dry, flat—but with a distinction unique among tourist lures: You might leave far richer than you came. Lightning Ridge, 480 miles northwest of Sydney, is the only place in the world where the most beautiful and valuable type of opal is found: the "black" opal, which actually blazes in a rainbow of colors from raven black to molten green and which some connoisseurs consider the finest gem in the world. The first black opal was discovered in 1907; production peaked in 1914 and declined steadily thereafter. The current population of approximately 1,000 (plus 500 in the outlying opal fields) engages in sifting the old mullock, the rejected residue excavated by the pioneer miners, by means of a "puddler," a revolving colander type of metal sieve. "Puddlers" are for rent and visitors are invited to fossick on the heaps or dig in any "unoccupied" holes. Do they find anything? Many don't, but some garner enough rough opal pebbles (called "nobbies") to pay for their vacation. A few—a very few—strike it rich, such as the schoolboy who picked up a nobby worth $A3,000.

But even if you leave with no souvenir beyond the dirt under your fingernails, you will be richer for the experience. This is the frontier Australia so many of us come seeking: that taut, hot—broiling five months of the year—countryside where you can sip an ice-cold Fosters in a grand old pub called Diggers Rest beside men called Crank Joe, Shameless, and Spider Brown. For your (reasonable) comfort there is a caravan (R.V.) park with on-site vans for overnighting, plus several motels. Fresh bread and meat arrive four times weekly, and mail comes five times weekly; the road into town has recently been paved, and electricity has been installed throughout. A 24-hour artesian bore pool provides year-round warm swimming. Gemstones are on display, and the friendly townspeople are very willing to talk prospecting with other enthusiasts—and show their specimens. It is one of the few places left to "get away from it all" among people who have done just that.

You reach Lightning Ridge by flying the Airlines of New South Wales (tel. 268-1262) to Walgett (three flights weekly) or going by rail from Central Station. Between Walgett and the Ridge, 46 miles away, there is no public transport. Three taxis operate out of Walgett, and you may be able to hitch a ride on the mail truck. Organized coach tours and charter flights also go to the Ridge. It's best to discuss transportation with the carriers or tourist bureau.

CHAPTER 4

MELBOURNE

- **WHAT'S SPECIAL ABOUT MELBOURNE**
1. **FROM A BUDGET TRAVELER'S POINT OF VIEW**
2. **ORIENTATION**
- **NEIGHBORHOODS IN BRIEF**
3. **GETTING AROUND**
- **FAST FACTS: MELBOURNE**
4. **WHERE TO STAY**
5. **WHERE TO EAT**
- **FROMMER'S COOL FOR KIDS: RESTAURANTS**
- **DID YOU KNOW . . . ?**
6. **ATTRACTIONS**
- **FROMMER'S FAVORITE MELBOURNE EXPERIENCES**
7. **SPORTS & RECREATION**
8. **SAVVY SHOPPING**
9. **EVENING ENTERTAINMENT**
10. **EASY EXCURSIONS: VICTORIA**

Melbourne—like Chicago—is a Second City. Unlike Chicago, though, it has never resigned itself to that position. One reason Sydney moves so fast is undoubtedly because Melbourne is snapping at its heels and breathing down its neck, ready to take its place.

Melbourne looks and behaves like the senior city of the Commonwealth. No other town makes so much of its history or is so concerned about lineage and tradition. Yet Melbourne actually rates third on the seniority ladder, since it is outranked by Hobart as well. As a permanent settlement it's decidedly a latecomer, founded in 1835, and then only because its founding fathers had failed to obtain the required acreage in Tasmania and tried the mainland instead.

Be that as it may, Melbourne remains proudly aware that it was once the largest city in Australia and—for a brief, heady spell—the acting capital. Canberra, in fact, was dreamed up chiefly in order to stop the incessant supremacy struggle between Sydney and Melbourne.

Melbourne may have lost the population race (the greater city has about 3.1 million inhabitants) and the seat of parliamentary power, but it won hands down in other areas. It is Australia's financial and commercial hub; home of the most prestigious schools and colleges; the social arbiter; the art, fashion, and culinary capital; and, incidentally, the breeding ground of the nation's most influential politicians, right and left.

As the Victorian capital, it lacked the natural advantages of its rival. It had nothing like Sydney's breathtaking harbor, and its river, the Yarra, is a trickling brown apology. Melburnians therefore determined to create their own setting and succeeded so well that the inner core of Sydney appears tawdry by comparison. Melbourne was designed to *look* like the nation's number one, even though the whims of history deprived it of that place.

Nothing in Sydney can match the majestic sweep of St. Kilda Road—one of the grandest boulevards on earth—or the tree-lined elegance of Collins Street. Melbourne's wide, handsome thoroughfares, meticulously laid out in a grid pattern, pulsate with the best-regulated traffic in Australia. The 100-acre Royal Botanical Gardens is the most beautiful in the southern hemisphere; the main department store, Myer Emporium, is the largest in the country (second largest in the world); the little boutiques are the trendiest; and the theaters, orchestras, and restaurants are the best in the Commonwealth. And when Sydney flashed its vaunted Opera House, Melbourne

WHAT'S SPECIAL ABOUT MELBOURNE

Architectural Highlights

- ☐ Victorian Arts Centre, with its 400-foot white lacework tower.
- ☐ Menzies-Rialto Hotel, a blend of Victoriana and contemporary classic.
- ☐ Como House—colonial living at its most gracious.
- ☐ Shrine of Remembrance, a memorial with panoramic views.
- ☐ Collins Place, a study in tasteful opulence.
- ☐ Sidney Myer Music Bowl, an immense band shell that becomes an ice-skating rink in winter.

Beaches

- ☐ Albert Park, Middle Park, St. Kilda, and (the best) on Half Moon Bay—all excellent for sailing and windsurfing.

Museums

- ☐ National Gallery, with a magnificent Australian art section.
- ☐ Museum of Victoria, combined with a planetarium.
- ☐ Old Melbourne Gaol—grim, even gruesome, but quite unique.
- ☐ Museum of Performing Arts, an exhibition designed like a theater.
- ☐ Gallery of Sports, crammed with athletic memorabilia.

Events

- ☐ Australian Rules Football Grand Final, when the fans go wild in September.

For the Kids

- ☐ Attractions galore—the Melbourne Zoo, Healesville wildlife sanctuary, and Luna Park.

Shopping

- ☐ Bourke Street Mall, for shoppers and trams only.
- ☐ Block Arcade and Royal Arcade for Victorian elegance.
- ☐ Toorak Road in South Yarra for exclusive boutiques.
- ☐ Collins Place for modern deluxe comfort.
- ☐ Queen Victoria Market, an absolutely immense spread of products, plus other bargains.

Streets/Neighborhoods

- ☐ Lygon Street in Carlton, with everything Italian, especially food.
- ☐ Collins Street, with exclusive stores and tree-lined urban charm.
- ☐ St. Kilda, with European cafés and shops, beachfront fun, and some shady nightlife.
- ☐ St. Kilda Road, Australia's longest and most impressive boulevard.
- ☐ Chinatown, along Little Bourke Street, brimming with Asian eateries.
- ☐ Toorak, the crème de la crème of neighborhoods—in local estimation.

Parks

- ☐ Royal Botanic Gardens, which Sir Arthur Conan Doyle called "the most beautiful place I have ever seen."
- ☐ Fitzroy Gardens, which harbors a miniature Tudor village.
- ☐ Yarra Park, with the Melbourne Cricket Ground, the most celebrated sports arena on the continent.

After Dark

- ☐ The spectacular State Theatre, which heads some 20 other live stages.

replied with the superlatively designed Victorian Arts Centre, housing by far the finest exhibits on the continent.

All this was the result of much dedicated effort, and the strain shows a little. Melburnians have been accused of being snooty, stuffy, class conscious, and money worshipping, with a certain degree of justification. Nowhere else in Australia is it considered so important to attend the *right* schools, live in the *right* suburbs, and—in some circles—have the *right* ancestry. Melburnians are indeed a nuance more reserved than their compatriots and suffer from an inability to let their hair down—except at sporting events.

The climate has a certain influence there; Melbourne is cooler than most Australian state capitals and has a longer winter. But these characteristics were also instrumental in creating a city of three million people afflicted with fewer urban woes and blights than any place of similar size on the globe.

1. FROM A BUDGET TRAVELER'S POINT OF VIEW

BUDGET BESTS Melbourne's indoor attractions all charge admission fees, but there's a fair amount of gratis outdoor fun to be had. The city's wonderful parks and gardens are free, and on summer Sundays you can attend concerts at them—from pops to symphony—without paying a dime. Also free are the beaches, though those nearby can't compare to those of Sydney or Perth.

WORTH PAYING FOR Melbourne has some of the best jazz-and-rock pubs in Australia (see "Evening Entertainment," below), and the cost of listening ranges from a beer at bar price to a $A5 cover charge. Equally cheap is the pavement café scene on Lygon and Brunswick streets, where the cost of a cappuccino can give you a whole afternoon or evening's entertainment watching the exceedingly colorful passing parade. In the same areas are also some of the most outstanding budget meals served in town (see "Where to Eat").

2. ORIENTATION

ARRIVING

BY PLANE All overseas-and-interstate planes arrive at **Melbourne Airport** in Tullamarine, which is approximately 14 miles northwest of downtown. The main interstate carriers are **Ansett,** 465 Swanston St. (tel. 13-1300), and **Qantas** (tel. 13-1313), which offers Blue Roo Fares from Sydney, Brisbane, Adelaide, Perth, and Hobart. Call the airline for current rates. (For additional fare-and-discount information on interstate-and-international airlines, see "Getting There" in Chapter 2.)

Ground transportation is provided by **Sky Bus,** which offers daily service from the airport to downtown hotels for $A8. By **taxi,** transportation from the airport into the city costs around $A20. The major **rental-car companies** also have desks at the airport.

BY TRAIN Melbourne has direct rail connections with every mainland capital city except Canberra, to which you must take some combination of bus-and-train service. Interstate trains arrive downtown at **Spencer Street Station,** with a cab rank and bus-and-tram stops just outside (but baggage carts are in short supply). From Sydney and Adelaide the trip takes about 12½ hours and can be done either overnight or by daylight express. (See "Getting Around" in Chapter 2 for rail fares and discounts.)

BY BUS **Pioneer** and **Greyhound** coachlines operate daily and nightly services to Melbourne from other capitals. Buses arrive downtown at the **Franklin Street Terminal,** which has washrooms, lockers, and other facilities. Local transportation is available from Swanston Street, one block away. From Sydney the ride takes about 14½ hours, from Adelaide 9½ hours, and from Brisbane some 25 hours. (See "Getting Around" in Chapter 2 for fares and discounts.)

BY CAR From Sydney you can reach Melbourne by two major roads: the quicker Hume Highway, which runs inland, and the more scenic Princes Highway, which winds along the east coast. From Adelaide you can take the Great Ocean Road, and from Brisbane you can come either via Toowoomba or the resort ocean strip of the

Gold Coast. Driving from Perth is not recommended—the road is fair but crossing the Nullarbor Plain seems an endless journey over tabletop-flat scrub desert.

TOURIST INFORMATION

The handiest tourist publication is *This Week in Melbourne,* which can be picked up free in hotel lobbies and at the **RACV Travel Centre,** 230 Collins St. (tel. 650-1522).

CITY LAYOUT

The central portions of Melbourne are wonderfully easy to find your way around in. It's almost as if the city had been built for the benefit of mail carriers and foreigners. If you look down from the top of the **National Mutual Building** at 447 Collins St. (the view is gratis) you'll see why.

The city (as distinct from the suburbs) is laid out in a grid of vertical and horizontal main streets bisecting one another. Each of the horizontal main streets (but not the vertical ones) has a narrow "little" street running parallel and bearing the same name. Thus there is a **Collins Street** and Little Collins Street alongside, a **Bourke Street** and a Little Bourke Street, a **Flinders Street** and a Flinders Lane, and so on. There are no intruding squares or roundabouts, no freeways, and no railroad tracks to spoil the pattern. Some of these streets change their character several times along their way, but not their direction. You could lay a straight ruler down their entire lengths.

Stroll along and observe the way Collins Street changes character en route without ever losing its highly individualistic stylishness. At the western end, near Spencer Street Station, it's high-finance territory, boardroom land, flanked by the towering business edifices, banks, insurance companies, and brokerage houses that govern Australia's commercial ledgers. At the center—between the Queen Street/Swanston Street intersections—it becomes a hustle of hotels, restaurants, and smart retail stores. Above that starts the upper or "Paris"-like end of the street: tree lined and slightly subdued, sprinkled with small cafés, bistros, and petite boutiques competing with Toorak Road for the patronage of Melbourne's formidable suburban matrons in their British or German chariots.

To the south the city is bordered by the gently curving Yarra River. On the south side of Princess Bridge (beside the immense Flinders Street rail station) starts **St. Kilda Road,** which runs all the way to the beach suburb of St. Kilda. Flanking St. Kilda Road to the east are vast expanses of parklands bearing different names (Botanic Gardens among them) but actually forming one colossal green oasis on both banks of the Yarra. This contains, besides many other attractions, the 120,000-seat **Melbourne Cricket Ground** (home of Australian Rules football, Test Cricket, and the 1956 Olympic Games), the residence of Victoria's governor, and the **Shrine of Remembrance** to the fallen of two world wars.

The western fringe of the city consists of the maze of rail tracks emanating from Spencer Street Station. To the northwest are the two major airports, at Tullamarine and Essendon. Due north, across Victoria Street, starts the once-slummy but now passingly chic suburb of **Carlton.** To the east stretch Fitzroy Gardens and Treasury Gardens, parts of the aforementioned parklands. South of the parks lie the posh districts of **South Yarra** and **Toorak,** the "innest" of residential areas. Toorak Road counts as Melbourne's classiest shopping, dining, and dating strip although—true to local tradition—it is less showy than similar stretches elsewhere.

Australians use the English rather than the American concept of terms like "city" and "suburbs." To them the *urb*—or downtown—is merely the small patch at the very center, which is devoted to business and where hardly anybody lives. All the huge rest is suburbia; even though some of these "suburbs" border the city and would in America be considered part of downtown. In Melbourne this applies to areas like Carlton, Fitzroy, Parkville, North Melbourne, South Melbourne, East Melbourne, Richmond, and so on, distinguished from the city only by the fact that they have residential streets. The Victorian Arts Centre, for instance, stands in South Melbourne, yet every American would regard it as being in the city. I have tried to clarify matters by using the label "inner suburb" whenever possible.

Melbourne contains two pedestrian malls—**Bourke Street Mall** and **Swanston Street Walk,** which crosses it. The first contains the city's major department stores (see "Savvy Shopping," below) and also serves as an impromptu outdoor stage for street performers ranging from classical guitarists to mobile jazz combos. The second, inaugurated in 1993, has a sprinkling of pleasant pavement cafés. Trams run through both malls, but no other vehicles are permitted. If you're driving, look them up on our maps because they necessitate somewhat complicated detours.

NEIGHBORHOODS IN BRIEF

Chinatown At the eastern end of Little Bourke Street, Chinatown consists mainly of restaurants and souvenir stores—some very pricey.

Carlton At the northern edge of downtown, this predominantly Italian neighborhood is swarming with university students of every ethnic hue. It has some of the best economy (as well as some of the costliest) restaurants in town and the liveliest street fair in Australia.

Toorak The wealthiest homes, poshest clubs, and trendiest fashion salons lie a short distance southeast of the city. Toorak borders on its social twin, **South Yarra.** The two districts are connected by Toorak Road, Melbourne's most exclusive thoroughfare. It intersects South Yarra's Chapel Street, considered by many to be the finest shopping strip in Australia. These addresses mean a great deal more in Melbourne than can be conveyed in a brief summary.

St. Kilda A seaside suburb 15 minutes by tram from the city, it contains Luna Park (a popular oceanfront esplanade), great continental restaurants along Acland Street, and some rather unsavory night action around Fitzroy Street. It also has the densest concentration of budget hotels.

Port Melbourne Southwest of the city, this is Melbourne's working harbor. While nowhere near as impressive as Sydney's, it's a good place to watch the big freighters and cruise liners docking and departing.

Williamstown Some 15 minutes from the city, this is a region of lovely old colonial homes, yacht clubs, boat builders, and armadas of bobbing pleasure craft. The place has a dreamy atmosphere and no regrets over missing the urban rat race.

Richmond On the eastern edge of the city, Richmond has a curious mix of Greek and Vietnamese currents, with good eateries of both persuasions. The main drag, Bridge Road, known as Little Saigon, is lined with budget-priced Vietnamese restaurants.

Brunswick Just north of the city along Royal Parade, Brunswick has a distinct Turkish flavor, Sydney Road being the mecca for Turkish food.

Brunswick Street Oddly enough, this street runs through **Fitzroy,** the rather shabby eastern neighbor of Carlton. Brunswick Street is the home of alternative life-styles, a quirky and stimulating mix of Yoga, vegetarianism, feminism, New Age cultism, and old-fashioned bohemianism. One store, the Pigtale, sells everything porcine in shape. There are a boutique called the Misfit and a café that has walls crowded with grotesque handmade dolls. The annual gala event, held in September, is the Fringe Arts Festival.

3. GETTING AROUND

BY PUBLIC TRANSPORTATION

TRAM & TRAIN Melbourne's public transportation system is by far the best and most comprehensive in Australia. In part it owes this edge to its innate conservatism.

While other cities were scrapping their trams (streetcars and trolleys) as fast as they could manage and replacing them with buses, Melbourne not only stuck to its trams but even updated them with new models. As a result it now boasts a tram network with much greater carrying capacity than equivalent numbers of buses. What's more, the trams don't pollute the air, run on cheap electricity instead of expensive gasoline, and generally give more comfortable rides. You can actually ride them for fun—particularly no. 15, which rumbles down St. Kilda Road and stops at the beach, or no. 8, which takes you from the city to Toorak Road.

Melbourne also has a suburban electric train system, radiating from **Flinders Street Station,** a structure as unattractive as it is efficient. A row of clocks above the main entrance indicates departure times for the trains and constitutes the single most popular rendezvous spot in the country. "Meet you under the clocks" is probably the best-known assignation line in Australia.

One of Melbourne's trams is absolutely unique. This is the **Colonial Tramcar Restaurant,** a 1927 model converted into a rolling restaurant, fitted with stabilizers so effective that not even a wine glass trembles as you glide along. The interior looks like a dining car of the Orient Express in its heyday, and you partake of (very expensive) French cuisine as the city unfolds outside the curtained windows.

The beauty of the Met system is that you can change from tram to train to bus all on one ticket. The drawback is the fare structure, which has all the stark simplicity of a doctoral thesis. The city is divided into three zones, each with different fares for long-and-short trips, some valid for three hours, some for all day. The cheapest stretch costs $A1, the most expensive $A5.30. Your best bet is the **City Saver,** which entitles you to 10 trips and costs $A11.

You can also get the **Met Explorer Pass,** a complete sightseeing kit explaining everything about the system and where to go on it. This pass is sold at the **Met Shop,** 103 Elizabeth St., along with mountains of Met T-shirts, travel bags, jackets, and postcards. It's good for three days and costs $A13. For all Met inquiries, telephone 617-0900.

Melbourne's public transportation system suffers from one grave ailment: It curls up and dies around midnight. After the witching hour you have to depend on your legs, your thumb, or a taxi.

TAXI Melbourne's cabs are nowhere near as plentiful as Sydney's. In fact, they are notoriously elusive. Two of the major cab companies are **Silver Top Taxis** (tel. 345-3455) and **Embassy** (tel. 320-0320).

BY CAR

For rental cars there is **Thrifty,** with a desk at the airport and a city base at 390 Elizabeth St. (tel. 663-5200). For rentals of six days or more, they'll give you rates reduced by 20% to 25%. There's also a weekend deal, allowing you three days of driving for the price of two days.

With wide thoroughfares and a grid-pattern layout, Melbourne is an easy city to navigate in. Parking, however, presents problems, and all traffic regulations are enforced with quite un-Australian strictness. Being the only Oz city with a streetcar system, Melbourne also has some regulations all its own. The center of the road must be kept clear for trams (even if there aren't any in sight). This means that drivers turning left at intersections must give way to oncoming cars turning right across their path. When driving behind a tram, drivers must stop when the tram stops because passengers board and alight from the middle of the road. And although there are few one-way streets, turning onto certain main drags is banned during rush hours. I've had to traverse the entire length of the city before being allowed to turn onto Swanston Street during the evening rush.

BY BICYCLE

Bicycles—known as pushbikes—can be rented at the **Yarra Bank,** Princess Bridge (tel. 801-2156), for $A12 per day.

MELBOURNE

American Express The Amex office is located at 105 Elizabeth St. (tel. 602-4666).

Area Code The telephone area code is **03.**

Babysitters **Dial-an-Angel,** (tel. 525-9261).

Business Hours **Stores** are generally open Monday to Thursday 9am to 5pm, Friday and Saturday until 9pm. However, hours vary in St. Kilda and other areas. **Banks** generally are open Monday to Thursday 9:30am to 4pm, Friday until 5pm.

Car Rentals See "Getting Around," in this chapter.

Climate See "When to Go," Chapter 2.

Consulates The following countries maintain consulates in Melbourne. **Great Britain:** 90 Collins St. (tel. 650-4155). **Canada:** 1 Collins St. (tel. 654-1433). **New Zealand:** 60 Albert Rd., South Melbourne (tel. 696-0399). **United States:** 24 Albert Rd., South Melbourne (tel. 697-7900).

Crime See "Safety," below.

Currency See "Information, Entry Requirements & Money," Chapter 2.

Currency Exchange The exchange counter at the airport, banks, and the offices of **American Express** (see above) and **Thomas Cook** at 257 Collins St. all change money.

Dentist Call the **Royal Dental Hospital,** corner of Elizabeth Street and Flemington Road (tel. 347-4222).

Doctor See "Hospitals," below.

Drugstores Try **Henry Francis Chemist,** 286 Little Bourke St. (tel. 663-3915). Open seven days a week.

Emergencies For the police, fire department, or an ambulance, call 000.

Eyeglasses Try **Alfred Nott,** 135 Collins St. (tel. 654-5911).

Hairdressers/Barbers **Avant Garde** (for men and women) is located at 206 Bourke St. (tel. 663-1025). **Hairroom** (also for men and women) is at 112 Acland St., St. Kilda (tel. 537-1175). Both are open seven days a week.

Holidays See "When to Go," Chapter 2.

Hospitals For medical attention, go to **Prince Henry's Hospital,** St. Kilda Rd. (tel. 620-0621), or **Royal Melbourne Hospital,** Parkville (tel. 347-7111).

Hot lines Useful telephone numbers in crisis times (major or minor) are the **Citizens Advice Bureau** (tel. 650-1062) for general information; **Link-Up** (tel. 94-8281) for psychiatric, medical, drug, or welfare problems; **Travel Centre Holiday Hotline** (tel. 790-2121); **Rape Hotline** (tel. 344-2210); **Poison Information** (tel. 345-5678); and the 24-hour **Crisis Line** (tel. 329-0300).

Information See "Tourist Information," in this chapter.

Laundry/Dry Cleaning Try **Flinders,** 89 Flinders Lane (tel. 650-4088).

Libraries The **State Library** at 328 Swanston St. is open daily 10am to 6pm.

Lost Property Contact the police (tel. 667-1911) or Flinders Street and Spencer Street rail stations.

Luggage Storage/Lockers The airport, the Flinders Street and Spencer Street rail stations, and the Pioneer Bus Terminal have lockers available.

Newspapers/Magazines Melbourne's two daily newspapers are the *Age* and the *Herald Sun;* one appears in the morning, the other in the afternoon. Both are hometown oriented, but the *Age* has a fair amount of overseas coverage.

Photographic Needs Try **Mannie Bolton Pharmacy,** 55 Elizabeth St. (tel. 629-1248).

Police For nonemergencies, contact the police at 667-1911.

Post Office The **General Post Office** is located at the corner of Bourke and Elizabeth streets (tel. 321-8855); open Monday to Friday 8:15am to 5:30pm, Saturday 10am to 1pm. You can also call 660-1344 for postal information.

Religious Services Several denominations are represented in Melbourne. **Anglican:** St. Paul's Cathedral, corner of Swanston and Flinders streets (tel. 650-3791). **Lutheran:** St. John's Church, 47 City Rd., South Melbourne (tel.

629-4995). **Jewish:** Temple Beth Israel, 74 Alma Rd., St. Kilda (tel. 510-1488). **Presbyterian:** 621 Punt Rd., South Yarra (tel. 267-4637). **Roman Catholic:** St. Patrick's Cathedral, Albert Street, East Melbourne (tel. 662-2233). **Uniting:** Wesley Church, 148 Lonsdale St. (tel. 662-2355).

Restrooms You can find public restrooms in all department stores, shopping complexes, city parks, and airline-and-coach terminals.

Safety Avoid St. Kilda in the wee hours and parks and gardens after nightfall.

Shoe Repairs Try **Flinders Way,** 238 Flinders Lane (tel. 654-4148).

Taxes There are no taxes of any kind added to bills.

Taxis See "Getting Around," in this chapter.

Telegrams/Telex/Fax The General Post Office (see "Post Office," above) can provide you with all these services.

Transit Info Call **Met** at 617-0900.

Useful Telephone Numbers Traveller's Aid: 654-2600; Monash University Student Union: 565-4000; Melbourne University Student Union: 341-6973; Latrobe University Student Union: 347-2319; Student Services Australia: 348-1777; Student Counselling and Advice Bureau: 380-5253; the Also Foundation (for gay men and lesbians): 650-7711; Gay Advisory Service: 489-2059; Lesbian Lines: 416-0850; Women's Information and Referral Exchange: 645-6844.

Weather Call 669-4900.

4. WHERE TO STAY

Melbourne is well supplied with tourist lodgings (too well, according to some proprietors), but they are not arranged in convenient motel strips or guest-house squares. Accommodations tend to cluster in districts rather than on certain streets. The two areas most thickly sprinkled are the city and the beach suburb of St. Kilda, a 10-minute tram ride from downtown. If you're unable or unwilling to pick your own lodgings, the **RACV Travel Centre,** at 230 Collins St. (tel. 03/795-5511 for information, 03/790-2121 for Holiday Hotline bookings), will do it for you—providing, that is, you get there on a weekday before 5:15pm or on Saturday before noon. They won't, however, guarantee you a budget berth. The **Travellers Aid Society** keeps longer hours and caters especially to the economy bracket. Their City Centre is at 169 Swanston St., Floor 2 (tel. 654-2600), open Monday to Friday from 8am to 5pm and Saturday 10am to 4pm. They also have facilities at Spencer Street Railway Station (tel. 670-2873). These include lockers, showers, a baby-feeding room, an ironing room, toilets for the disabled, and an information desk.

All the places I have selected fall into the budget range, although in a few cases—when the value offered was particularly good—I've stretched the limits a little.

DOUBLES FOR LESS THAN $A60

DOWNTOWN

HOTEL ENTERPRIZE, 44 Spencer St., Melbourne, VIC 3000. Tel. 03/629-6991. Fax 03/614-7963. 154 rms (106 with bath). A/C TV TEL

$ Rates: $A39 single without bath, $A78 single with bath; $A49 double without bath, $A88 double with bath. AE, MC, V.

The Enterprize is an intriguing combination of the venerable and the modern—an Edwardian edifice partly refurbiched to three-star standards. Located opposite the huge Spencer Street Railway Station and facing a decidedly noisy thoroughfare, the hotel offers a quietly secluded courtyard, blue-lit at night; a restaurant; a pizza bar; and a guest laundry. The rooms that concern us here are the economy units: with shared bathrooms and no-frills furnishings but good beds and lighting and excellent maintenance. The self-service lobby snack bar stays open round-the-clock. I highly recommend the huge country-style breakfast, which, for $A7, will tide you over lunch.

KINGSGATE, 131 King St., Melbourne, VIC 3000. Tel. 03/629-4171. Fax 03/629-7110. 233 rms (90 with bath). AC TV TEL

$ Rates: $A34–$A58 single, $A58–$A80 double. AE, BC, MC, V.

The Kingsgate is an old building, extensively refurbished and with an exceptionally friendly staff. Some of the rooms here have private baths; others have hot- and cold-water basins, plus six bathrooms per floor. There are a restaurant on the premises, two TV lounges, pinball machines, and laundry facilities. The Kingsgate has a hospitable, well-carpeted lobby and a maze of corridors and passageways in which you can get lost with the greatest of ease. Bedroom furnishings in the budget rooms are rather Spartan, with narrow wardrobes and beds, but you get bedside as well as ceiling lights and a very central location. Rates vary according to whether you want a private bathroom and air-conditioning.

TOAD HALL GUESTHOUSE, 441 Elizabeth St., Melbourne, VIC 3000. Tel. 03/600-9010. 36 rms (2 with bath).

$ Rates: $A25–$A35 single, $A40–$A45 double, $A18 dorm (4 persons). AE, MC, V.

You can easily miss this guest house because the entrance is tucked inside a brick gateway. A small, recently renovated three-story building (no elevator), it has rooms with hot- and cold-water basins and refrigerators. The place is proudly maintained—the public bathrooms positively sparkle. There are a communal kitchen, a guest laundry, two TV lounges, and a garden with barbecue facilities on the premises. There is no restaurant, but several are in the vicinity. The facade and lobby are uninviting, but all rooms come with bedside lamps, open clothes-hanging space, and fair carpeting. The location is central, near the airline-and-bus terminals.

WEST MELBOURNE

MIAMI, 13 Hawke St., West Melbourne, VIC 3003. Tel. 03/329-8499. Fax 03/328-1820. 102 rms (1 with bath). **Tram:** 50 or 57 to Stop 12.

$ Rates (including breakfast): $A36 single, $A52 double. BC, MC, V.

The Miami is my favorite in this category, not so much for its facilities but for the tremendous pride its management and staff take in the place. An attractively sturdy red-brick corner building, minutes from the heart of downtown, the Miami has a welcoming reception area and even more welcoming rates. The bedrooms are small and compact, the furnishings not lavish, but the care bestowed on them is. All rooms have hot-and-cold water, double wardrobes offering ample hanging space, fluorescent bedside lights, and good carpeting. The hotel offers a TV guest lounge, drink machines, an air-conditioned dining room, a billiard table, public phones, and a well-equipped laundry.

You can choose between bed-and-breakfast and full board (meaning two meals), with the manager's guarantee that "nothing out of tins is served here." A three-course dinner is just $A10.

ST. KILDA

BAYSIDE ST. KILDA MOTEL, 63 Fitzroy St., St. Kilda, VIC 3182. Tel. 03/525-3833. Fax 03/534-8131. 40 rms (all with bath). TV TEL **Tram:** 15, 16, or 96.

$ Rates: $A42 single, $A48 double. $A18 per person in backpackers apartments. AE, BC, MC, V.

A modern three-story building set amid the bustle of St. Kilda's liveliest street, the

Bayside has a nondescript lobby but nicely maintained interior. Bedrooms are midsized with metal furnishings, but well carpeted and equipped with bedside clock radio, refrigerator, toaster, and generous wardrobe space. Front rooms have street views (and sounds), those in the rear view a parking lot, which is quiet. Bathrooms are compact and modern. No restaurant is on premises, but rows of eateries and snackeries, clubs, bars, and shops are all around. The beach lies a few hundred yards away. (Don't confuse this establishment with the Bayside Hotel in Elwood.)

CARLISLE LODGE, 32 Carlisle St., St. Kilda, VIC 3182. Tel. 03/534-0316. Fax 03/525-5048. 17 rms (all with bath). TV TEL **Tram:** No. 15 or 96.

$ Rates: $A50 single or double. AE, BC, MC, V.

The Carlisle Lodge is a cross between a motel and an apartment block, but it's a find either way. A solid two-story red-brick structure, 10 walking minutes from the beach, the Carlisle has units accommodating up to four and flats for up to eight. Each unit has a shower and a kitchenette; each flat has a bathroom with tub and a spacious kitchen. Carpeting is excellent throughout, and the motel-style furniture seems brand-spanking new. And don't forget how much money you save by doing your own cooking.

The management also operates the Florida Lodge.

ESQUIRE MOTEL, 65 Acland St., St. Kilda, VIC 3182. Tel. 03/525-4547. Fax 03/534-8131. 22 rms (most with bath). TV TEL. **Tram:** No. 15 or 96.

$ Rates: $A45 single or double, $A210 per week; $A10 per person for backpackers' apartments (2–3 persons). AE, BC, MC, V.

Standing on pillars in the urban-motel style, with the office one flight of stairs up, the Esquire offers comfortable, functionally furnished units. They come with kitchen facilities, modern bathrooms, refrigerators, TVs, and all the utensils you need. There is ample wardrobe space, although the lighting arrangements could be brighter. The Esquire has no restaurant, but there's a McDonald's next door.

FLORIDA LODGE, 37 Grey St. Reserve through the Carlisle Lodge (above). Tel. 03/525-5048.

$ Rates: $A55 double, $A350 per week double; $A65 4 people, $A350 per week 4 people. TV **Parking:** Free.

Under the same management as the Carlisle Lodge and booked through its office (see above), the Florida has large, self-contained apartments, suitable for four or six persons. They are newly-furnished and come with full-sized kitchens (gas ranges), refrigerators, all cooking-and-eating utensils, TVs, and radios. The fittings, while not lavish, are ample, including for each room a wardrobe, a dresser with mirror, a good-sized bathroom, and bedside as well as ceiling lights.

OLEMBIA, 96 Barkly St., St. Kilda, VIC 3182. Tel. 03/537-1412. 26 rms (none with bath). **Tram:** No. 3, 15, or 16.

$ Rates: $A13 dorm, from $A35 single, from $A48 double. BC, MC, V.

Described as a "European-style pension," Olembia is run along much more personalized lines than the average pension. It has, for instance, a display of topical news items, photo-and-magazine clippings, and an excellent private library. The TV lounge/sitting room is a 1920s period piece, complete with a fireplace and fringed lampshades. The bedrooms, while not lavish, are meticulously kept, as are the four shared bathrooms in the house. Most rooms have hot- and cold-water basins, and all feature razor plugs, good carpeting, and small closets. They range from smallish singles to good-size family rooms suitable for four persons. Breakfast is on a help-yourself basis and costs $A5. There's a shady courtyard, and the beach is within walking distance.

SOUTH YARRA

WEST END, 76 Toorak Rd. W., South Yarra, VIC 3141. Tel. 03/866-3135. 26 rms (none with bath). **Tram:** No. 8 to South Yarra.

$ Rates (including breakfast): $A30 single, $A48 double; $A10 for children under 12. AE, MC, V.

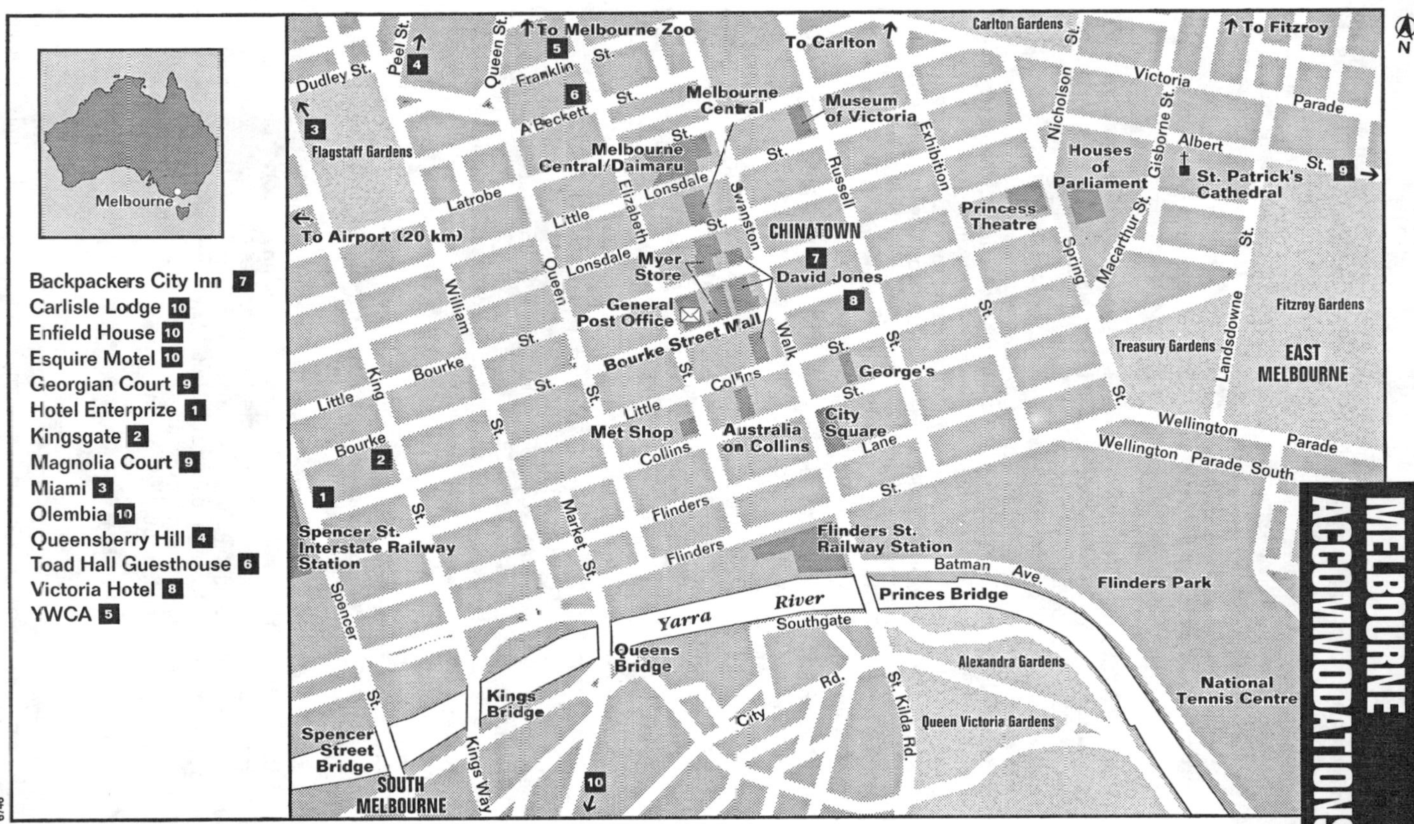

MELBOURNE ACCOMMODATIONS
Melbourne
Backpackers City Inn 7
Carlisle Lodge 10
Enfield House 10
Esquire Motel 10
Georgian Court 9
Hotel Enterprize 1
Kingsgate 2
Magnolia Court 9
Miami 3
Olembia 10
Queensberry Hill 4
Toad Hall Guesthouse 6
Victoria Hotel 8
YWCA 5
To Melbourne Zoo
To Carlton
To Fitzroy
To Airport (20 km)
Carlton Gardens
Flagstaff Gardens
Melbourne Central
Museum of Victoria
Melbourne Central/Daimaru
Houses of Parliament
St. Patrick's Cathedral
Princess Theatre
CHINATOWN
Myer Store
David Jones
General Post Office
Bourke Street Mall
Met Shop
Australia on Collins
City Square
Fitzroy Gardens
Treasury Gardens
EAST MELBOURNE
Spencer St. Interstate Railway Station
Flinders St. Railway Station
Flinders Park
Yarra River
Princes Bridge
Queens Bridge
Kings Bridge
Spencer Street Bridge
SOUTH MELBOURNE
Alexandra Gardens
Queen Victoria Gardens
National Tennis Centre
N
6746

This find is in Melbourne's geographically most desirable neighborhood—the last place to expect budget accommodations. The West End overlooks the palm-lined quiet end of Melbourne's poshest shopping street. It's a very attractive hostelry—with large, airy rooms, some with San Francisco–style bay windows; an elegant TV lounge; and a cozy dining room, where only breakfast is served. The rooms, mostly doubles, all have hot-and-cold water, plus dressing tables with big mirrors. The rooms are in deep-green color schemes, which makes for a soothing atmosphere. There's no charge for cots.

BED & BREAKFASTS

BAYSIDE HOTEL, 65 Ormond Esplanade, Elwood, VIC 3184. Tel. 03/531-9238. 50 rms (12 with shower). TV **Tram:** No. 15 or 16 to St. Kilda, then bus no. 600 to Elwood.

$ Rates (including full board): from $A35 single, from $A50 double. No credit cards.

In the seaside suburb of Elwood you'll find this handsome cream-colored three-story structure with large windows overlooking the esplanade and the ocean beyond. A newish and very well-kept establishment, the Bayside has medium-size bedrooms that are bright and airy; the furnishings are simple but attractive, and the fittings include wall-to-wall carpeting, hot- and cold-water basins in some rooms, generous closet space, and handy little refrigerators. Rates here are for *full board*—meaning a cooked breakfast and three-course dinner (on weekends, breakfast only) in the large downstairs dining room. Guest laundry on the premises.

COOK COTTAGE, 2 Cook St., Mornington, VIC 3931. Tel. 059/75-7568. 4 rms. **Transportation:** Airporter bus stops 2 blocks away.

$ Rates (including breakfast): $A45 double.

If you prefer lodgings in the tranquillity of outer suburbia, try this charming English-style cottage run by Daryll Johnson. A small operation with only four double bedrooms, the house is directly across from the Mornington beaches and close to a smart shopping and restaurant street. The building looks like a picture postcard, the bathrooms are good, and the inclusive breakfast is large enough to tide you over lunch.

GEORGIAN COURT, 21 George St., East Melbourne, VIC 3002. Tel. 03/419-6353. Fax 03/416-0895. 33 rms (5 with bath). TV

$ Rates (including breakfast): $A55 single, $A65–$A85 double. AE, BC, V. **Parking:** Available. **Tram:** 48 or 75.

The Georgian Court stands in a quiet, smart, tree-lined area within walking distance of downtown. The frontage is truly Georgian, with white pillars and large garden windows. Rooms are of fair size and range from single to family-size. The shared bathrooms have been completely modernized. All rooms come with color TVs and tea/coffee-making equipment. Laundry facilities and a comfortable TV lounge are on the premises, with newspapers and magazines provided. Breakfast here includes cereal, juice, fruit, fresh rolls, and jam.

JO & NOEL BURRISS, 22 Hargreaves St., Mornington, VIC 3931. Tel. 059/75-5663. 1 rm (with bath). TV **Transportation:** Airporter bus.

$ Rates (including breakfast): $A30 single, $A45 double. No credit cards.

A rather quaint early Australian home, this offers a large bedroom that takes up the entire top floor and can accommodate three adults. There are a private bathroom and balcony, a TV, and delightful views over the bay. Breakfast is hefty, and the beach just two minutes away. Suitable mainly for the motorized.

BACKPACKERS

Melbourne now approaches Sydney's range in this category, but only two are listed below. *Backpackers* has become a generic term in Australia, and those patrons actually carrying packs are a distinct minority. Today the label simply indicates economy quarters, slightly overcrowded in summer, for a youngish clientele that is in most cases laid-back, friendly, and cosmopolitan.

BACKPACKERS CITY INN, 197 Bourke St., Melbourne, VIC 3000. Tel. 03/650-2734. Fax 03/650-5474.

$ Rates: From $A10 per person. No credit cards.

The most centrally situated of hostels, but very inconspicuous, the Backpackers City Inn occupies the three top floors of the Carlton Hotel and has only a small sign at the entrance. Guests bunk in dormitory rooms holding three to four persons. Accommodation space is somewhat tight, but the inn has a pleasant rooftop garden, a communal kitchen, a TV room, a guest laundry, and Melbourne's main shopping street right at the doorstep.

ENFIELD HOUSE, 2 Enfield St., St. Kilda, VIC 3162. Tel. 03/534-6150. Fax 03/534-5579. 40 rms (none with bath). TV TEL **Tram:** No. 15 or 16 to Stop 30. Free pickup from train and bus stations and airport.

$ Rates: $A30 single, $A40 double. AE, MC, V.

This is a very handy hostel, although it's tucked away and hard to locate at the end of a little dead-end off Jackson Street. The inn is clean and very friendly and has a roof garden, cooking facilities, a laundry, and a guest lounge. There are acres of notices announcing car rides to Adelaide or wherever and proclaiming (inaccurately) the alleged "best" of whatever is going in town. Free city tours for guests. No chores are demanded, and the management has several buildings in the area to accommodate the overflow of residents.

A Y FOR MEN & WOMEN

The Melbourne **YMCA** offers no accommodations—worse luck. But the **YWCA** caters to both genders.

YWCA, 489 Elizabeth St., Melbourne, VIC 3000. Tel. 03/329-5188. Fax 03/328-2931. 58 rms (all with bath).

$ Rates: $A48 single, $A64 double. Bunk room (4 persons) $70. BC, MC, V.

The YWCA occupies a large downtown motel complex. The building resembles a concrete garage, but the interior is a pleasant surprise. Each unit has shower and toilet, comfortable furnishings, and wall-to-wall carpets. The building also contains a swimming pool, a fairly cozy TV lounge, laundry facilities, and a restaurant open seven days a week. The complex is two walking minutes away from the domestic airlines terminal.

YOUTH HOSTELS

CHAPMAN STREET, 76 Chapman St., North Melbourne, VIC 3051. Tel. 03/328-7863. Fax 03/329-7863. 100 beds. **Tram:** No. 50, 57, or 59 to Stop 19. Skybus from airport (request stop).

$ Rates: $A13–$A16 (most rooms twin share). BC, MC, V. **Parking:** Free.

A somewhat simpler establishment than the Queensberry Hill (see below), Chapman Street has a guest kitchen, laundry facilities, and a bicycle-hiring service.

QUEENSBERRY HILL, 78 Howard St., North Melbourne, VIC 3051. Tel. 03/329-8599. Fax 03/326-8427. 300 beds. TV **Tram:** No. 55 to Stop 14. On route of Airport Skybus.

$ Rates: $A13–$A16 dorm, $A54 room with bath. BC, MC, V.

A large, pleasantly modern building about a mile from the city center, the Queensberry Hill offers an unusual range of facilities: from six-bed dorms to rooms with private baths. Furnishings are new, and there are a licensed cafeteria, guest kitchen, several lounges, a rooftop garden with barbecue facilities, and a laundry. This place is decidedly superior.

CAMPUS ACCOMMODATIONS

Melbourne has a regular bonanza of good budget college accommodations—no fewer than 19 colleges to choose from. Most, however, are available during vacations only—that is, January, February, May, August, and December. The following is the *only* one available all year round.

INTERNATIONAL HOUSE, University of Melbourne, 241 Royal Parade, Parkville, VIC 3052. Tel. 03/347-6655. TV TEL **Tram:** No. 19 or 20 from Elizabeth St. to Stop 21.

$ Rates (including 3 meals per day): $A39–$A57 single, $A81–$A86 double.

Located about 2½ miles from downtown, International House has single rooms with shared bathrooms, some doubles with private bath, a TV room, a lounge, a billiard room, a laundry, and squash-and-tennis courts.

WORTH THE EXTRA MONEY

MAGNOLIA COURT, 101 Powlett St., East Melbourne, VIC 3002. Tel. 03/419-4222. Fax 03/416-0841. 25 rms (all with bath). A/C TV TEL

$ Rates: $A105 single, $A110 double. AE, MC, V.

This selection is in elegant East Melbourne, just on the edge of the city and near Fitzroy Gardens. It has a beautifully mellow colonial frontage and a completely refurbished and modernized interior. Calling itself a "boutique hotel," the Magnolia houses a garden-fronted breakfast room; a year-round heated spa/pool; and suites that manage to be stylish, tranquil, and comfortable in equal degrees. All rooms come with refrigerators and tea- and coffee-making facilities. There are also a communal laundry, a Victorian garden, and an exceptionally helpful management. Lighting and wardrobe space are ample, and the modernizers of the place knew just where to leave some old-fashioned touches that make for coziness. It's out of the budget range for singles, but it just might fit a double.

VICTORIA HOTEL, 215 Little Collins St., Melbourne, VIC 3000. Tel. 03/653-0441 or toll free 008/331-147. Fax 03/650-9678. 520 rms (all with bath except budget). A/C TV TEL

$ Rates: Standard, $A65 single, $A80 double; budget, $A38 single, $A50 double. Children under 14 free in parents' room. AE, MC, V. **Parking:** $A3 per day.

The Victoria is an old but completely refurbished establishment right in the city center, with an elegant restaurant, a quick-service coffee shop, a laundry, and a duty-free shop on the premises. It also has a very amiable staff, fast elevator service, and a permanently thronged cosmopolitan lobby. Of the 520 rooms, only the budget rooms lack their own showers and toilets, but they come with hot- and cold-water basins, tea/coffee makers, and telephones; public bathrooms are conveniently located on each floor. Despite the downtown location, rooms are quiet, though they tend to be dark. There are good lighting and wardrobe space and excellent hot-water service.

CARAVAN [R.V.] PARK

FOOTSCRAY CARAVAN PARK, 163 Somerville Rd., West Footscray, VIC 3012. Tel. 03/314-6646.

Located about 4½ miles from the city center by direct train service, this is one of Melbourne's most centrally situated caravan parks, so you don't need a car to get downtown, and there's a shopping center right near the gate. The park rents on-site caravans and park homes, at $A35 to $A40 for two persons per night, and it provides hot showers, washing machines, and refrigerators.

5. WHERE TO EAT

I have referred to Melbourne as Australia's culinary capital, based on some 3,200 eateries representing 70 national cuisines. Instead of its half a dozen or so world-class luxury restaurants, what establishes Melbourne's reputation is the quality of the local cuisine in the lower-price brackets. Sample any given counter lunch in Melbourne and then in, say, Brisbane, and you'll instantly notice the difference.

SAVING MONEY ON MEALS

Melbourne's gastronomic preeminence was achieved despite the city authorities, who for 50 years have passed many nitpicking ordinances that might well have hampered the restaurant business. Fortunately, the local entrepreneurs have managed to turn to advantage the liquor laws that make the granting of wine licenses to restaurants costly and difficult. Their solution was the BYO (the sacred initials meaning "bring your own"), which allows patrons to bring along their own liquor to drink with their meals. Those bottles are bought at over-the-counter prices, say for $A6 instead of the $A8 or $A9 a restaurant would charge. The result is a considerable savings in meal expenses, since few establishments have the temerity to charge for glasses or corkage. So watch for those initials. You may assume that any hostelry that boasts a license is automatically more expensive than a BYO. Some, however, are *both,* and their price bracket can be anywhere.

Melbourne's culinary reputation rests on the small mom-and-pop restaurants that are scattered all over town, mostly—although not always—foreign. And there are certain exceptions. By and large Chinese restaurants run below par, and those in Melbourne's miniature Chinatown, Little Bourke Street, are often overpriced as well. But the Asian newcomers there—Thai, Cambodian, Malay, and Vietnamese—must struggle hard to compete and therefore do their utmost for lower tabs.

Melbourne's pub grub is of an almost universally high standard, so all I can do here is give you a few pointers with the proviso that these are merely a handful out of a hundred. All are open until 10pm and are closed Sunday.

MEALS FOR LESS THAN $A14

DOWNTOWN

BYO PELLEGRINI'S, 66 Bourke St., Melbourne. Tel. 662-1885.
Cuisine: ITALIAN. **Reservations:** Not necessary.
$ Prices: Appetizers $A4, main courses $A6.50–$A7.50. No credit cards.
Open: Mon–Sat 8am–11:30pm.

BYO Pellegrini's is a contender for the honor of serving the best cappuccino in Melbourne, which is quite a contest. Neither elegant nor atmospheric, the place is nevertheless aflutter with good-looking people. The risotto primavera and pasta dishes are excellent, but don't miss having a slice of cheesecake along with the outstanding cappuccino, which comes in the correct style—in a glass.

FAST EDDY'S, 32 Bourke St., Melbourne. Tel. 662-3551.
Cuisine: AUSSIE-AMERICAN. **Reservations:** Not necessary.
$ Prices: Main courses $A5.95–$A11.95. No credit cards.
Open: 24 hrs.

Very large and white pillared outside, with picture windows fronting the street and decorated with antique framed advertisements inside, Eddy's sells T-shirts, sun visors, badges, and watches as well as food. This is no gourmet temple, but the fare is tasty, colorful, cheap, and served as fast as the name promises. Breakfast is available around-the-clock, in either modest or huge portions, and morning-and-afternoon teas are served at all times. Main meals range from hamburgers and pastas for around $A7 to marinated kebabs, grilled fish, chicken breasts, and fairly genuine American spareribs at around the $A9.50 mark. A glass of passable house wine costs $A1.80. This is one of the few spots dispensing American banana splits and chocolate sundaes. The menu reads like a funny paper, and you're encouraged to take it with you.

MAC'S HOTEL, 34 Franklin St., Melbourne. Tel. 663-6855.
Cuisine: AUSTRALIAN. **Reservations:** Not necessary.

$ **Prices:** Counter lunches $A3.50–$A6. No credit cards.
Open: Mon–Sat 11am–10pm.

Located near the Ansett offices, this is a beautiful old colonial building, with an upstairs veranda and a glass-encased bistro in the rear. The counter here is swarming with airline personnel, who know a good thing when they taste it.

TACO BILL, 142 Russell St., Melbourne. Tel. 654-3369.
Cuisine: MEXICAN. **Reservations:** Accepted.
$ **Prices:** Appetizers $A4, main courses $A9–$A13. AE, MC, V.
Open: Mon–Sat 5:30–10pm.

In the center city is the abode of one of Australia's pioneer Mexican restaurants: Taco Bill. Up a flight of stairs and usually thronged with youthful clients, this taco temple has a pretty authentic air and the aroma to go with it. For Mexican palates the spices are on the gentle side, though by Anglo standards they're red hot. A platter of nachos costs $A12.25, a burrito costs $A9.95.

YOUNG AND JACKSONS, corner of Flinders and Swanston Sts., Melbourne. Tel. 650-3884.
Cuisine: AUSTRALIAN. **Reservations:** Not necessary.
$ **Prices:** Main courses $A9–$A13.90. AE, MC, V.
Open: Mon–Thurs 11:30am–11pm, Fri–Sat until 2am.

Melbourne's most venerable pub is hallowed to the memories of departing soldiers since the Boer War. No thing of beauty from the outside, the hotel nevertheless houses Australia's best-known nude, who now glories in her very own parlor. *Chloe,* painted by French artist Jules Lefebvre in 1875, is a shapely and eternally young lady dressed in nothing but a fashionable pallor, an object of barfly desire for over a century. Take a look at her, then drift over to the formidable lunch counter serving from noon to 2:30pm, which includes braised steak and mushrooms or roast chicken for $A6.20 per serving.

CARLTON

UNIVERSITA BAR, 257 Lygon St., Carlton. Tel. 347-2142.
Cuisine: INTERNATIONAL. **Reservations:** Not necessary.
$ **Prices:** Appetizers $A5–$A7, main courses $A7–$A11.50. AE, BC, DC, MC, V.
Open: Daily 7am to around midnight.

Università Bar spells its shingle Italian style, but it draws a very cosmopolitan clientele who know good-and-cheap comestibles when they taste them. Plain, dark brown, and densely populated most of the time, the Università has shaded tables on the pavement outside (as well as a decidedly more upscale restaurant upstairs.) The sole decorations are colored wall posters and attractive clients. Entertainment comes in the form of highly animated debates going on simultaneously at half a dozen tables. The vibes are friendly, the decibel level is high, and the service is leisurely. Most menu items hover around $A8, though some specialties go up to $A11.50. Try the excellent prosciutto and melon, followed by the outstanding chocolate mousse. Italian coffee is served in a glass, as it should be.

ST. KILDA

THE GALLEON, 9 Carlisle St., St. Kilda. Tel. 534-8934.
Cuisine: ECLECTIC. **Reservations:** Not necessary.
$ **Prices:** Appetizers $A3.80, main courses $A4–$A8.50. No credit cards.
Open: Mon–Sat 9am–midnight, Sun from 10:30am.

This might possibly be the cheapest restaurant in town. A cross between a diner and a coffeehouse, the Galleon is festooned with lengthy notices announcing jobs, trips, merchandise, roommates wanted, and theater productions. They set the general tone of the establishment. Clientele and staff are equally young, laid-back, and amiable; the fare is simple but well prepared. You get chicken-and-leek pie for $A4, pumpkin soup for $A3.50, and a very respectable Bratwurst with sauerkraut for $A7. Drinks are strictly fruit juices.

MELBOURNE DINING

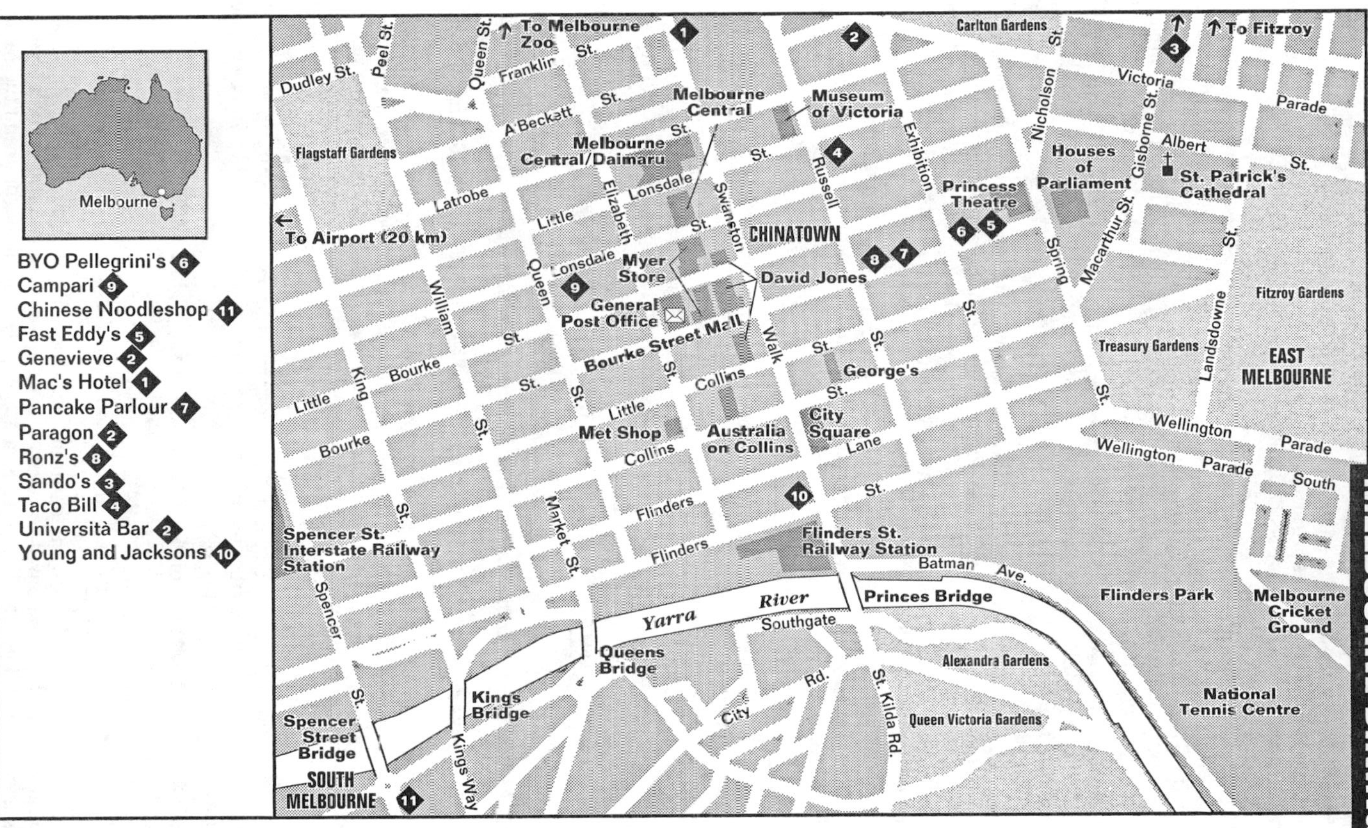

SOUTH YARRA

BAROLO, 74 Toorak Rd., South Yarra. Tel. 866-2744.
Cuisine: ITALIAN. **Reservations:** Accepted.
$ Prices: Appetizers $A5–$A9.50, main courses $A9.90–$A17.50. AE, MC, V.
Open: Daily 8:30am–12:30am.

The Barolo proves again that you can find inexpensive eateries in a deluxe shopping area. Very plain, with crude wooden tables and benches and brick-lined doorways to give it a Parisian Left Bank–cellar touch, the Barolo is a BYO decorated with Italian scenes on posters quite in keeping with its bistro air. The fare is, happily, gargantuan: gnocchi, cannelloni, roast veal, and chicken pizzaiola—all equally excellent.

PINOCCHIO'S PIZZA, 152 Toorak Rd., South Yarra. Tel. 867-2772.
Cuisine: ITALIAN. **Reservations:** Not necessary.
$ Prices: Pizzas $A7–$A11.50. AE.
Open: Daily 1–10pm.

Pinocchio's has a fanatical following that swears it produces the best pizza in town—a much-debated claim. Pinocchio's is considerably fancier than most of its clan, loaded with atmosphere and decorated with superb illustrations from its namesake children's classic—all with the original Italian texts. The famous pizzas come large and small.

TAMANI BISTRO, 156 Toorak Rd., South Yarra. Tel. 866-2575.
Cuisine: ITALIAN. **Reservations:** Accepted.
$ Prices: Appetizers $A4.50–$A7.90, main courses $A6.80–$A11. No credit cards.
Open: Daily 9am–10:30pm.

The Tamani Bistro features Italian cooking and a charming Australian proprietor —Margaret Benassi. Functionally modern yet remarkably cozy, the Tamani offers minestrone soup for $A4.50, lasagne for $A7, and an almost artistic salad bar where selections begin at $A4.50. This BYO bistro draws an intriguing cross section of customers, with senior executives clashing forks with junior road repairmen.

MEALS FOR LESS THAN $A18

DOWNTOWN

CAMPARI, 25 Hardware St., Melbourne. Tel. 670-3813.
Cuisine: ITALIAN. **Reservations:** Accepted.
$ Prices: Appetizers $A6–$A9.50, main courses $A10.80–$A14.80. AE, BC, MC, V.
Open: Mon–Fri 7am–8:30pm, Sat 9am–2pm.

Campari is considered by some to be the best Italian restaurant in the city. It's certainly genuine—you hear more Italian than English spoken, always a sign of ethnic authenticity. A large, handsomely decorated place, it has an upstairs and a downstairs portion, red-brick floors, and walls hung with gleaming copperware beneath shelves of olive-oil bottles, giving the establishment the air of a grandly stocked country kitchen. This is not an economy restaurant, but you can pick some excellent budget dishes from the extensive menu: cannelloni for $A10.50 or lasagne for $A8.80. Campari is licensed, but you can also BYO.

RONZ'S, 105 Little Bourke St., Melbourne. Tel. 663-1709.
Cuisine: MALAYSIAN. **Reservations:** Accepted.
$ Prices: Appetizers $A2.60–$A6.50, main courses $A6–$A10.50. AE, BC, DC, MC, V.
Open: Daily 6–11pm.

This is a Malaysian BYO with an astounding repertoire of great jazz tapes and jazz posters for wall decorations. The fare, however, is authentic and straight K. L. (which is how we global gourmets refer to Kuala Lumpur). I highly recommend the Malay sausages—actually bean-curd skins stuffed with minced pork and spiced vegetables. The intriguing-sounding ayam jazz (?) turned out to be fried chunks of chicken served with rice. The curry beef is cooked in coconut milk and so subtly blended with spices that the slight sweetness harmonizes perfectly with the meat. Main courses are around $A10.

SOUTH MELBOURNE

CHINESE NOODLESHOP, 331 Clarendon St., South Melbourne. Tel. 699-4150.

Cuisine: CHINESE. **Reservations:** Not necessary.

$ Prices: Appetizers $A2.60–$A5.80, main courses $A8.50–$A15. AE, MC, V.

Open: Daily 11:45am–3pm, 5–10pm.

As the name indicates, this place specializes in noodle dishes, either to take out or to eat there. Take your pick at the food counter lined with stools. The place is spotless and serves mighty portions. Its prices are some of the lowest in the business: roast pork noodles for $A9.60; soy-sauce noodles with beef for $A10.50; and the biggest bowl of the most variegated wonton soup around.

CARLTON

GENEVIEVE, 233 Faraday St., Carlton. Tel. 347-3052.

Cuisine: ITALIAN. **Reservations:** Not accepted.

$ Prices: Appetizers $A6–$A9.50, main courses $A9–$A14.90. BC, MC, V.

Open: Mon–Thurs, Sun 9am–midnight; Fri–Sat until 2:30am.

This popular rendezvous spot as well as restaurant looks like an ice-cream parlor decked out in bright orange and browns. It serves some of the finest economy meals in town: homemade lentil soup for $A4, tortellini alla panna for $A7.50, and a dreamy cassata and cream.

PARAGON, 651 Rathdowne St., Carlton. Tel. 347-7715.

Cuisine: MEDITERRANEAN-ASIAN. **Reservations:** Not necessary.

$ Prices: Appetizers $A4.80–$A5.80, main courses $A7–$A14. BC, MC, V.

Open: Daily 9am–11pm.

The Paragon is housed in a beautifully restored Victorian building, now air-conditioned and supplemented with outdoor tables set beneath the shelter of a lacy antique iron veranda. The menu matches the setting—an intriguing combination of Mediterranean, Asian, and vegetarian goodies: spinach cannelloni for $A8.80, lamb, olive, and feta burger for $A13, plus an imposing array of desserts made on the premises. You have a choice of food bar or table service (a rarity). It's *both* licensed and BYO, with the house wine going for $A2.80 per glass but a BYO corkage charge of $A2.50.

FITZROY

SANDO'S, 272 Brunswick St., Fitzroy. Tel. 419-8472.

Cuisine: INDIAN. **Reservations:** Accepted.

$ Prices: Appetizers $A6–$A8, main courses $A10–$A15. AE, BC, MC, V.

Open: Daily 5:30–11:30pm.

Sando's is one of Melbourne's most famed tandoori restaurants, though you wouldn't know it by the prices. The downstairs dining room has dignified elegance minus much ornamentation; the tandoor oven operates in full view of the patrons and makes interesting watching—like an aphrodisiac for the taste buds. The Indian cuisine served at this BYO gives you a fair choice between the mildly spicy tandoori chicken and the red-hot beef vindaloo. At various stages in between are the lamb chops marinated in rum-soaked spices and the curried lamb served with saffron rice, cucumber, and tomatoes.

NORTH FITZROY

THE LOADED DOG, 324 St. Georges Rd., North Fitzroy. Tel. 489-8222.

Cuisine: PUB FARE. **Reservations:** Accepted.
$ Prices: Main courses $A10–$A14. AE, MC, V.
Open: Mon–Sat 10am–9pm.

The Loaded Dog is a fun pub by day or night. It's named after a classic Australian bush story by Henry Lawson (you can read it on the dining-room wall). The pub not only brews its own beer on the premises but sells what is probably the largest beer selection on the continent—103 brands, including Papuan, Malaysian, and the establishment's own highly potent Thunder ale. Lunchtime vittles range from $A9 to $A12. If you're puzzled by the "chook burger," it's a chicken hamburger; the "loaded dog" is a hot-and-spicy sausage smothered in cheese sauce.

MARIOS, 303 Brunswick St., Fitzroy. Tel. 417-3343.
Cuisine: ITALIAN. **Reservations:** Accepted.
$ Prices: Appetizers $A5–$A7.50, main courses $A9.50–$A11. No credit cards.
Open: Sun–Wed 7am–midnight, Thurs–Sat 7am–1am.

This shiny modern bar-restaurant has a picture window to gaze at the street scene and prints and sketches displayed gallery style on the wall. There is a rack with free periodicals and brochures to peruse and a clientele that changes from business to funky according to the time of day. Marios serves an outstanding turkey shashlik with couscous and a memorable dessert in the form of hazelnut-and-frangelico ice cream with marinated figs and macaroons.

BRUNSWICK

ALASYA, 555 Sydney Rd., Brunswick. Tel. 387-2679.
Cuisine: TURKISH. **Reservations:** Accepted.
$ Prices: Set menus $A14 and $A19.50. AE, BC, DC, MC, V.
Open: Mon–Thurs 11:30am–1:30am, Fri–Sun noon–1am.

This BYO is a local institution, the first Turkish eatery in town to open its gates, and a place for gargantuan appetites. The decor is far from svelte, with laminated tables and an illuminated board showing color pictures of the restaurant specialties. In the background is a glowing red-brick oven churning out piles of fresh crackling Turkish bread. The range of dishes—over 100—makes the choice difficult, and portions are so huge that you can barely plow through the so-called "minimenu." Try the cabbage-and-carrot salad, stuffed vine leaves, the Turkish meat loaf, and the *vezir* kebab of lamb in a casserole.

SOUTH YARRA

DOWNSTAIRS AT ERICS, corner of Darling St. and Toorak Rd., South Yarra. Tel. 820-3804.
Cuisine: INTERNATIONAL. **Reservations:** Accepted.
$ Prices: Appetizers $A6–$A8, main courses $A12–$A15. AE, DC, MC, V.
Open: Mon–Fri noon–2:30pm, Mon–Sat 6pm–12:30am.

Deep in the heart of Melbourne's poshest dining region, Eric's is a delightful mélange of bistro/wine bar/jazz cellar, with an award-winning chef thrown in for good measure. The basement has an art deco ambience, with polished floorboards, multihued wall hangings, an immense bar, plus a grand piano. Illuminated by little green lamps, it looks like a setting for a cold war vintage Berlin spy thriller. The fare ranges from venison carpaccio and goat-cheese terrine to roast suckling pig, kangaroo filet, and glazed quail; gourmet comestibles, but none priced higher than $A15. Live jazz comes on Friday and Saturday around 10pm, and in between regular mealtimes you can breast the wine bar and quaff. Eric's has a unique arrangement with the nearby Longford Cinema. During September and October you can bring your movie tickets to the restaurant and get your meal at half price. The establishment also publishes a somewhat irregular but extremely amusing news sheet called "Off the Spike," in which the owners are accused of hideous crimes—such as murdering the original "Eric."

ST. KILDA & VICINITY

MADAME JOE JOE, 9 Fitzroy St., St. Kilda. Tel. 534-0000.
Cuisine: GREEK-ITALIAN. **Reservations:** Accepted.
$ Prices: Appetizers $A5.50–$A11, main courses $A12–$A17.50. AE, BC, DC, MC, V.
Open: Daily 7:30am–1am.

A new glitzy, sparkling, and exceedingly "in" place, this rendezvous for the fashionably laid-back serves Greek and Mediterranean fare with nouvelle innovations—none of your standard stomach liners. The menu is fastened to a clipboard, the wine list is longer than the food selection, and the rhythmic background music sets your adrenaline pumping. Try the chicken broth with sorrel dumplings and the confit rabbit and bay-leaf risotto with wild onions. And, if possible, capture one of the pavement tables outside.

SCHEHEREZADE, 99 Acland St., St. Kilda. Tel. 534-2722.
Cuisine: AUSTRO-HUNGARIAN. **Reservations:** Accepted.
$ Prices: Appetizers $A5.50–$A8, main courses $A11–$A15. AE, BC, DC, V.
Open: Daily 9am–midnight.

Despite its Arabian Nights name, Scheherezade is solidly middle-European—an irreplaceable survivor from the time when its clientele hailed from the same region. Today its devoted patrons come from anywhere, and they come for the fare alone because the place has no atmosphere whatever (the only ornaments are some excellent pencil sketches displayed on the wall). They come for the paprika chicken, the goulash, the Russian cutlets and fried calf's liver, and the Viennese tortes afterward; all served fast and in copious quantities. Bring a hearty appetite.

TRATTORIA TIBERIO, 133 Church St., Brighton. Tel. 592-1671.
Cuisine: ITALIAN. **Reservations:** Accepted.
$ Prices: Appetizers $A5, main courses $A10–$A14. AE, MC, V.
Open: Dinner daily from 5:30pm.

Located in a pleasant beachside suburb, Trattoria Tiberio has a very plain milk bar frontage and an absolutely genuine Italian family-style interior: plain, clean, inviting, and awash with friendly vibes. As a rule it's also crowded and fairly noisy. The patrons are for the most part regulars, which speaks volumes for Papa's Neapolitan cooking. The taped background music is as true to form as the chef. One of the finest items on the menu is the scampi, dressed in olive oil and lemon sauce, as light as it is tasty. The plateful of baby octopus is so fresh you can almost taste the ocean. Main courses cost between $A10 and $A14, but pasta dishes are correspondingly cheaper. Do, I implore you, cast calories to the wind and order the special house "torte"—filled with chocolate cream—along with your espresso.

FROMMER'S COOL FOR KIDS: RESTAURANTS

Fast Eddy's *(see p. 151)* Serving an irresistible array of burgers, hot dogs, pies, and sundaes, Fast Eddy's also sells T-shirts, badges, and sun visors.

Pinocchio's Pizza *(see p. 154)* Kids love the original Italian illustrations of the children's classic decorating the walls.

The Pancake Parlour *(see p. 158)* Kids love the fare as much as the Crazy House decor, and the menu includes such children's specials as Mad Hatter's Plates and Alice's Wonderland Surprise.

DID YOU KNOW . . . ?

- Melbourne used to be the biggest city as well as "temporary capital" (1901–27) of Australia.
- Samuel Clemens (aka Mark Twain) stoked the furnace of the fashionable Menzies Hotel. Twain, who was a guest, didn't ask for payment—he did it for exercise.
- The Daimaru shopping complex contains the antique brick tower of a shot factory under a glass cone 20 floors high.
- Just outside Melbourne, the Worm Museum displays live earthworms up to seven feet long.
- Sir Arthur Conan Doyle, creator of Sherlock Holmes, originally intended his famous detective to be killed in Melbourne but dropped the idea because "it would take Holmes too long to get there."
- Until 1940 Melbourne and San Francisco were the only two cities to use cable cars as public transport. Today only San Francisco uses them.
- The Performing Arts Museum drew record crowds by exhibiting a capsule of Elvis Presley's perspiration.
- Melbourne is the only place to have an official public holiday for a horse race—the Melbourne Cup, run on the first Tuesday of each November.

SPECIALTY DINING

LOCAL BUDGET BETS

An honorary citation must go to the **View Room** (tel. 417-2544), located among the superb flower beds in . . . the Botanical Gardens! You might call it a kiosk, but the place serves full meals at economy prices—around $A6 to $A7 for two generous courses. Open daily 9am to 5pm.

LATE-NIGHT/24-HOUR

Late-night eateries are scattered far and wide, but it's best to know where some of them can be found before night starvation sets in: **Waiter's Restaurant,** 20 Meyers Place (off Bourke Street), specializes in Italian budget food; **Ma's Hot Dog Stand,** outside Flinders Street Station, serves hot dogs, coffee, and the like until 4am; **Johnny's Green Room,** 194 Faraday St., Carlton, combines pool playing and food dispensing 24 hours a day (foreign visitors get a gratis cup of coffee here); and **Fast Eddy's,** 32 Bourke St., serves breakfast, lunch, and dinner around-the-clock.

The Pancake Parlour, 25 Market Lane, (tel. 663-7300), is the local representative of a national chain and sits opposite the Southern Cross Hotel. These parlors are distinguished by their inspired menus, which make excellent mealtime reading, plus the fact that they're open around-the-clock. The restaurant occupies five levels, including an "attic," and devotes as much attention to pulchritude as to pancakes. All the walls are covered with bosomy 1890s ladies tossing pancakes. Don't miss the huge *Police Gazette*-style mural depicting the "Great Colonial Pancake Tossing Race for Ladies," in which all contestants seem to be Victorian-brand *Playboy* bunnies. Ah, yes, the pancakes . . . they come in 33 varieties, from Canadian with bacon and eggs ($A9.20) to the brandied-apricot kind ($A7.80). The place also serves breakfast all day, offers a secluded bower for chess players, and waxes apologetic about every surcharge they have to make on weekends and public holidays.

6. ATTRACTIONS

Lacking Sydney's idyllic harbor setting, Melbourne had to create its own attractions. You will notice that all of them are human-made, including the city's glorious parks and gardens. Melbourne's natural charmers all lie outside the city limits and come under the heading of "Excursions." The really fine ocean beaches, for instance, are out on the Mornington Peninsula.

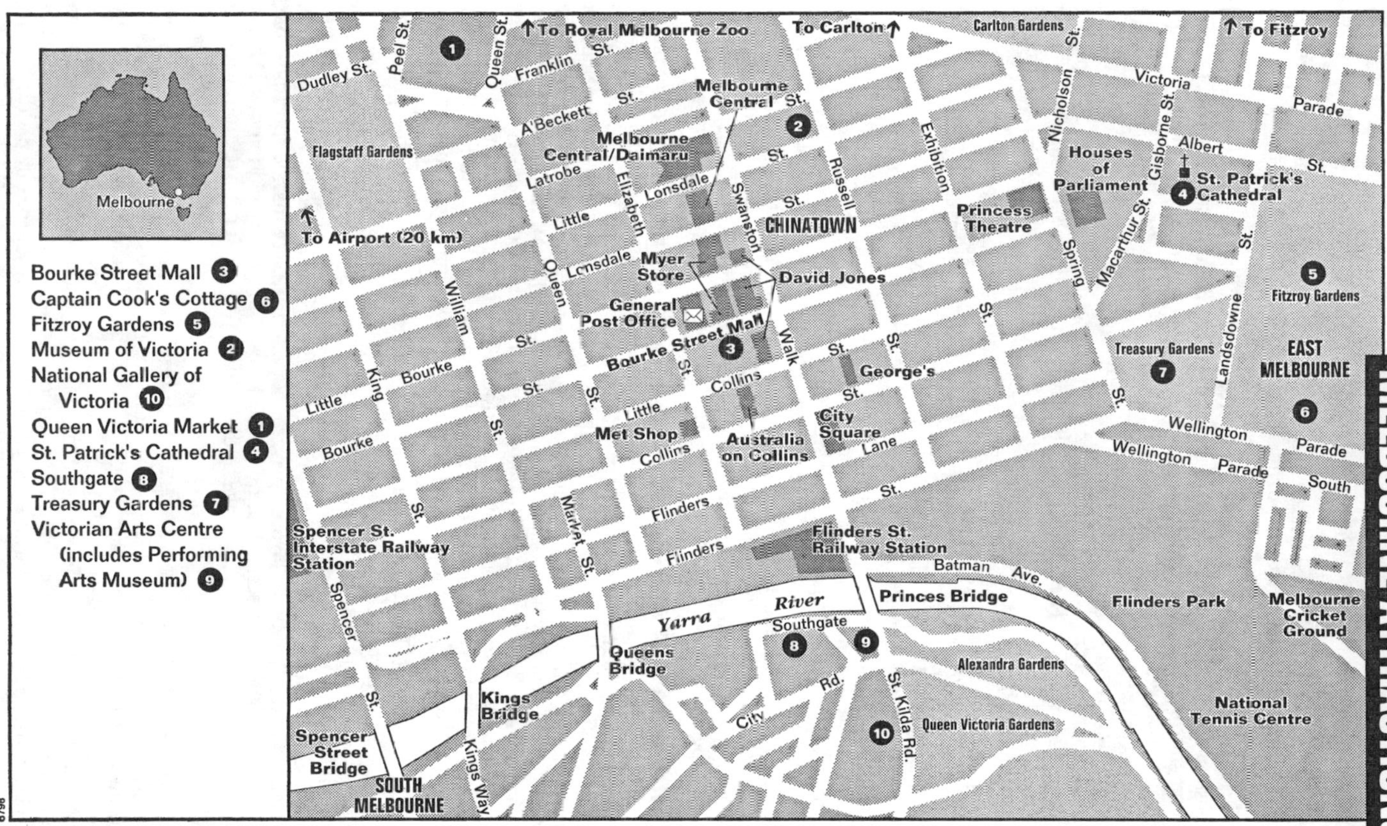
MELBOURNE ATTRACTIONS
N
Melbourne
Bourke Street Mall 3
Captain Cook's Cottage 6
Fitzroy Gardens 5
Museum of Victoria 2
National Gallery of Victoria 10
Queen Victoria Market 1
St. Patrick's Cathedral 4
Southgate 8
Treasury Gardens 7
Victorian Arts Centre (includes Performing Arts Museum) 9
To Royal Melbourne Zoo
To Carlton
To Fitzroy
To Airport (20 km)
Carlton Gardens
Flagstaff Gardens
Fitzroy Gardens
Treasury Gardens
Alexandra Gardens
Queen Victoria Gardens
Melbourne Central
Melbourne Central/Daimaru
Houses of Parliament
St. Patrick's Cathedral
Princess Theatre
CHINATOWN
Myer Store
David Jones
General Post Office
Bourke Street Mall
George's
City Square
Met Shop
Australia on Collins
Spencer St. Interstate Railway Station
Flinders St. Railway Station
Princes Bridge
Queens Bridge
Kings Bridge
Spencer Street Bridge
Yarra River
Southgate
Flinders Park
Melbourne Cricket Ground
National Tennis Centre
EAST MELBOURNE
SOUTH MELBOURNE
Dudley St.
Peel St.
Queen St.
Franklin St.
A'Beckett St.
Latrobe St.
Little Lonsdale St.
Lonsdale St.
Elizabeth St.
Swanston Walk
Russell St.
Exhibition St.
Spring St.
Nicholson St.
Victoria Parade
Gisborne St.
Albert St.
Macarthur St.
Lansdowne St.
Wellington Parade
Wellington Parade South
Little Bourke St.
Bourke St.
Collins St.
Little Collins St.
Flinders Lane
Flinders St.
King St.
William St.
Market St.
Spencer St.
Batman Ave.
City Rd.
St. Kilda Rd.
Kings Way
6798

But Melbourne has a wealth of sights, ranging from magnificent street vistas to lovingly preserved edifices. Don't be misled by the disappointing City Square at the geographical center in front of the Town Hall and St. Paul's Cathedral on Swanston Street. Decorated with waterfalls that remind you irresistibly of flushing toilets, its main function (currently) is to provide office workers with an al fresco haven at lunchtime.

Just around the corner, however, runs tree-lined Collins Street, one of the most stylish avenues on earth, terminating in the Treasury Building at the top. The next broad thoroughfare, Bourke Street, has a famous shopping mall at the center and stately Parliament House to complete the vista at the top end. These streets are the essence, the real heart, of Melbourne and—as every local will tell you—nothing in her old rival Sydney can match them.

Melbourne's attractions, apart from vistas, are a scattered lot. They don't come in clusters like Sydney's The Rocks or Darling Harbour. But public transport between them is excellent, or you can use the City Explorer tour (see "Organized Tours," below) to get from one to the next.

SUGGESTED ITINERARIES

IF YOU HAVE 1 DAY Have breakfast at one of the outdoor cafés on Lygon Street in Carlton, then either stroll down tree-lined Collins Street or window shop along Bourke Street. Catch a tram to St. Kilda Road and take in a tour of the Victorian Arts Centre. Have lunch at the café of the National Gallery there. Then stroll to the Princes Walk landing stage and take a cruise on the Yarra River, viewing Melbourne from the best vantage point. Have dinner at one of the downtown restaurants described in "Where to Eat," above, then, according to taste and inclination, either crash one of the discos along King Street or a pub offering musical entertainment or attend one of the little theater shows offered all over town (see "Evening Entertainment," below).

IF YOU HAVE 2 DAYS Since you have more time you can utilize the City Explorer (see "Organized Tours," below). This not only adds eight attractions to the above but offers you lower admission prices to several of them. You'll see the Old Melbourne Gaol, the Victorian Museum, the Performing Arts Museum, and the Victoria Markets in the city area, as well as the Royal Melbourne Zoo. Write off an entire day for the tour. On the next day take a tram to the seaside suburb of St. Kilda, which features Luna Park and European cafés, then take a bus to South Yarra to inspect Como, one of the stateliest colonial homes on the continent. Stay in the neighborhood and have dinner in one of the restaurants on Toorak Road listed in "Where to Eat," above. At night you might try your luck at the Tabaret (see "Evening Entertainment," below).

IF YOU HAVE 3 DAYS Use the third day for ventures out of town—perhaps to the beautiful beaches of the Mornington Peninsula; or to the Blue Dandenongs (see "Easy Excursions: Victoria," below), where you can ride a delightful little steam train called Puffing Billy; or to Healesville, a wildlife sanctuary some 40 miles northeast of Melbourne. Alternatively, visit Phillip Island, which is connected by a bridge to the mainland and is Victoria's favorite playground, offering every marine sport possible, as well as colonies of seals, mutton birds, koalas, and the world-famous Penguin Parade. Since the parade takes place in the evening you won't get back to town until rather late . . . and so to bed.

IF YOU HAVE 4 DAYS OR MORE Your best bet is to participate in some of the special tours arranged by V/Line, the state rail network (see "Organized Tours," below). They take you to Ballarat, the historic gold-rush town and scene of the only battle fought on Australian soil; to Swan Hill, where you can wander through a faithful replica of a pioneer township, complete with weatherboard bank and stagecoach office, that puts on a most unpioneerish Sound and Light spectacle at night; to the Murray River, where you can take a leisurely journey by paddle steamer and feel the 20th-century rat race seep out of your bones. Or take the bus to Lakes Entrance—a chain of beaches, coves, and inlets; lakes with swarms of black swans;

and islands harboring kangaroos. This region reputedly has the best bream fishing in the state, and you can rent the tackle required to see if the claim is true.

THE TOP ATTRACTIONS

VICTORIAN ARTS CENTRE, St. Kilda Rd. Tel. 684-8484.

This is Melbourne's answer to the Sydney Opera House, Victoria's top tourist attraction, and one of the great showpieces of the southern hemisphere. The vast complex embraces the National Gallery of Victoria, the Melbourne Concert Hall, an opera house, three theaters, plus bars, restaurants, an outdoor stage, and shops—the whole crowned with an abbreviated version of the Eiffel Tower transformed into a silvery beacon at night.

The **National Gallery,** which draws 750,000 visitors a year, looks like an immense granite slab from the outside, but the interior is a wonderfully sensitive blend of the severely monastic and the lighthearted artistic. Gray granite courtyards, green with shrubbery and sparkling with fountains; entrance windows with water flowing permanently between the thick panes; and unexpected shafts of sunlight all add to the happy mood of classical restraint and playfulness. The entire ground floor is devoted to Asian art, the second floor to Australian. There are a European section covering the period before 1800 and a European and American floor exhibiting pieces from 1800 to the present, including works by Manet, Degas, Pissarro, and Frank Gallo. The third floor houses photography in all its artistic phases. There are also changing exhibitions on loan from the United States, Japan, China, Austria, and Germany.

The **Melbourne Concert Hall** is a three-level acoustic marvel. The sound is honed by 24 perspex shells and 24 acoustic banners that can be altered for different sound requirements. The hall's Grand Concert Organ, built by Canadian Casavant Frères, has 4,189 pipes. The organist, invisible to the audience, communicates with the stage through closed-circuit TV. The decor is nothing short of magnificent: a mélange of paintings, sculptures, and harmonized color schemes that are a symphony for the eyes. The foyer blazes with the 100 frames of a mammoth creation by Sir Sidney Nolan titled *Paradise Garden,* depicting Australian flora from its organic beginnings, pushing through the earth, and following seasonal cycles. The hall seats 2,600 amid visual as well as audio splendor.

The centre also contains the huge **State Theatre,** designed for opera, ballet, and large-scale productions; the **Playhouse** for drama; and the intimate **George Fairfax Studio,** a multipurpose space for experimental shows, dance, and music. All mirror the architectural brilliance of the concert hall and contain some of the most advanced technical equipment in the world.

You can spend a wonderfully variegated day in this complex, visiting the gallery first, dining at one of the restaurants (which include a budget eatery), going on to a concert, and finishing off with a late-night show.

Admission: Art gallery, $A6 adults, $A3 children; free Mon. Concert Hall tours, $A6 adults, $A5 children.

Open: Museum, daily 10am–5pm. Concert Hall tours, Mon–Fri noon and 2:30pm.

MUSEUM OF VICTORIA, 328 Swanston St. Tel. 669-9997.

This museum concentrates on natural history, with sections on anthropology, zoology, geology, and so on. What makes the place a pilgrimage spot for turf addicts are the mounted remains of Phar Lap, Australia's greatest-ever racehorse, allegedly poisoned while running in America.

The **Planetarium** (tel. 669-9864), part of the museum, is a circular theater that holds 115 people. It has a 34-lense projector that beams the images of 5,000 stars onto a domed ceiling, creating the illusion of the night sky. Various planetary shows are performed with highly realistic effects.

Admission: Museum, $A5 adults, $A2.50 children. Planetarium, $A4 adults, $A2 children.

Open: Museum, daily 10am–5pm. Planetarium shows, Mon–Thurs 2pm; Fri 2 and 8pm; Sat and Sun 1, 2, and 3pm.

MARITIME MUSEUM, Phayer St., South Melbourne. Tel. 699-9760.

Originally launched in 1885 and used for deep-water commerce, the *Polly Woodside* is a restored square-rigged windjammer that now forms the centerpiece of the Maritime Museum and is surrounded by a vast collection of nautical memorabilia.

Admission: $A7 adults, $A4 children.

Open: Daily 10am–4pm. **Tram:** No. 10 or 12 from Collins St.

OLD MELBOURNE GAOL & PENAL MUSEUM, Russell St. Tel. 663-7228.

Appropriately situated opposite police headquarters, this is a bluestone prison built in 1841. It contains relics from the grimmest and wildest pages of Australia's history. The prize exhibit here is Ned Kelly's—the king of the bushrangers—bullet-dented armor made from plowshares (see Chapter 1) and the scaffold on which he was hanged and where he uttered the not very original words, "Such is life." The jail is carefully restored, and you can wander through the cells and see what conditions were like.

Admission: $A7 adults, $A3.50 children.

Open: Daily 9:30am–4:30pm.

CAPTAIN COOK'S COTTAGE, Fitzroy Gardens. Tel. 419-4677.

This is the parental home of one of the world's greatest explorers and the discoverer of Australia (see Chapter 1), brought over from England in pieces and reassembled here.

Admission: $A2.50 adults, $A1.25 children.

Open: Daily 9am–5pm.

LA TROBE COTTAGE, The Domain. Tel. 654-5528.

Near the Botanical Gardens, this was Victoria's first Government House. Quite small and simple on the outside (as befitted the power center of a colony with fewer than 6,000 settlers), it has a remarkably elegant interior. Governor La Trobe, who ran the colony until 1854, was as much a visionary as an administrator. He conceived, among other projects, the Melbourne Botanical Gardens, which now bloom in his memory.

Admission: $A2.

Open: Sat–Thurs 11am–4:30pm.

SHRINE OF REMEMBRANCE, St. Kilda Rd.

The Shrine of Remembrance, dedicated to Australia's war dead, has a great dome with an opening so contrived that precisely at 11am "Armistice Hour 1918" on November 11 each year, a single ray of light shines on the Stone of Remembrance below. The edifice has an observation deck that offers panoramic views of the entire city.

Admission: Free. Donations welcome.

Open: Daily 10am–5pm.

ROYAL MELBOURNE ZOO, Royal Park, Elliott Ave. Tel. 285-9300.

This beautifully landscaped setting holds over 350 species of animals in near-ideal environmental conditions. There is an astonishingly realistic Gorilla Rainforest; the Great Flight Aviary for 50 kinds of Australian birds; and bushland settings where you stroll among wombats, emus, and kangaroos. One of the top attractions is the Butterfly House, where visitors walk through a glassed-in tropical rain-forest habitat aflutter with about 1,000 Australian butterflies.

Admission: $A12 adults, $A6 children.

Open: Daily 9am–5pm. **Directions:** Take the City Explorer Bus or Tram no. 55 or 56 from William St.; Tram no. 68 from Elizabeth St. on Sun.

SOUTHGATE.

This remarkable strip of riverside development has been described as a marriage of art, food, and fashion—to which should be added "and fun." Opened in 1992, Southgate lies on the south bank of the Yarra River alongside the Victorian Arts Centre and is best reached over the pedestrian bridge across the river.

The landmark of the site is the superdeluxe multistar Sheraton Towers Hotel, but

FROMMER'S FAVORITE MELBOURNE EXPERIENCES

Melbourne Cup Race A parade of "haute couture" ladies and their top-hatted, frock-coated escorts marks the formal opening of the race.

Lygon Street Fiesta In the human chess game, two local chess champions match wits using chess piece–costumed members of the Ballet Company.

Dinner in the Colonial Tramcar The street scene outside constantly changes, but the streetcar glides along the tracks so smoothly that the wine waiters never spill a drop.

Armistice Day at the Shrine of Remembrance The rays of the morning sun fall precisely on the Memorial Stone in this moving ceremony.

Walking through the Butterfly House at the Melbourne Zoo A cloud of butterflies surround you in this hothouse rain-forest habitat.

Friday Night at Victoria Market A scene of joyful chaos—every stall promises a treasure and occasionally you even find one.

the magnet drawing millions of visitors is the three-level Arts and Leisure Precinct—a colorful, whirling, green-shrouded complex of shops, galleries, cafés, restaurants, wine bars, specialty stalls, exhibitions, and theaters. It's a joyful world of its own, catering to the rich as well as the barely heeled and doing so with style, elegance, and considerable ingenuity.

The precinct houses shops selling anything from handcrafted "whatnots" to Madonna posters, from quilted opera coats to stuffed koalas. There are 10 restaurants at various levels—French, Greek, Swedish, Italian, Chinese, and hamburger, all with views of the river. There is a small aquarium with sharks swimming at eye level, a photo studio, and a news agency that serves cappuccino along with the daily papers at riverside tables. You can buy flowers or Chagall prints or get your hair styled or your shoes repaired or sip a glass of wine on an open balcony.

The **Scenic River Cruise** departs from Southgate hourly for a 45-minute chug upstream and back with a commentary on the sights and landmarks en route. Adults pay $A8, children $A5.

On the ground floor of the precinct is a unique little theater, the **AustraliaGate** (tel. 690-9800.) This is the world's first multivision-multisensory movie house, and an astonishing experience it is. The 50-minute performance tells the history of Australia by means of huge visuals on a series of screens, using images, sound, and scent in a synchronized whole that has you hearing, seeing, and breathing the action. You smell the sweet scent of eucalypts and rain forests and the acrid stench of explosives when the guns bark at Eureka and Gallipoli. You see the visions of Aboriginal dream time, the convicts, the settlers, the animals, the cheering crowds at the Melbourne Olympics, the unfolding of the present, multicultural Australia.

Admission: $A6 adults, $A3.50 children.

Open: Daily, screenings once an hour, 11:30am–4:30pm.

MORE ATTRACTIONS

HISTORIC BUILDINGS

COMO, 16 Como Ave., South Yarra. Tel. 827-2500.

This century-old mansion is preserved by the National Trust. On view inside is the entire life-style of the Victorian rich—coaches and kitchen gear, furniture, drapes, and bathroom utensils. The house is enchanting, with wonderful white verandas and delicate wrought-iron railings, set among five acres of manicured lawns, flower gardens, and fountains.

Admission: $A7 adults, $A3.50 children.

Open: Daily 10am–5pm. **Tram:** No. 8 from Swanston St. to Stop 30.

RIPPON LEA, 192 Hotham St., Elsternwick. Tel. 523-6095.

More ornate than Como (above) but equally stylish is Rippon Lea, another Victorian mansion on 13 acres of gardens, with lakes populated by strutting peacocks.

Admission: $A5.50 adults, $A2.50 children.

Open: Daily 10am–5pm. **Train:** Rippon Lea Station.

MUSEUMS

PERFORMING ARTS MUSEUM, 100 St. Kilda Road. Tel. 684-8325.

This is a theatrical museum in the widest sense, displaying anything connected with showbiz, from the publicity angle to stage paraphernalia. The changing exhibitions have included costumes worn by celebrities, rare photos taken of them and by them, posters announcing them, and the stage sets erected for them. There's no telling what will be on view by the time you get there.

Admission: $A5 adults, $A3.50 children.

Open: Mon–Fri 11am–5pm, Sat and Sun noon–5pm.

JEWISH MUSEUM OF AUSTRALIA, corner Toorak Rd. and Arnold St., South Yarra. Tel. 866-1922.

Melbourne has the largest Jewish community on the continent. The exhibits change frequently but always have Jewish life as a central theme—ranging from historical photographs to modern designs by Australian artists.

Open: Wed and Thurs 11am–4pm, Sun 2–5pm.

PARKS & GARDENS

Melbourne has half a dozen great parks, and Melburnians utilize, cherish, and enjoy the "green lungs" of their city like few other urbanites. To help the enjoyment, several parks feature A10¢-operated gas jets for barbecue picnics—a unique innovation. Throughout the summer months the City Council sponsors free outdoor concerts—classical, jazz, folk, and rock—in various parks and squares.

ROYAL BOTANIC GARDENS, between Alexandra Ave. and Domain Rd. Tel. 655-2341.

The Royal Botanic Gardens are unreservedly the most beautiful in Australia and among the world's finest examples of classical landscaping. They comprise 3 lakes, some 43 acres of flower beds, and 35 acres of lawns. The **King's Domain,** between the Botanical Gardens and downtown, embraces several gardens and displays a flower clock containing 10,000 plants. It also contains the **Sidney Myer Music Bowl,** a huge but strangely graceful auditorium surrounded by a glorious park where free symphonic and modern concerts are performed from November to February. Check the newspapers for the programs.

Admission: Free.

Open: Daily dawn to dusk.

AN AMUSEMENT PARK

LUNA PARK, St. Kilda Lower Esplanade. Tel. 534-0654.

This is a handily compact amusement park, crammed with devices to shake, whirl, rattle, bump, swing, slide, and bounce for squealing patrons willing to pay money for these pleasures.

Admission (for one ride): $A3.50 adults, $A2.50 children.

Open: Hours change with season. In summer every weekend.

COOL FOR KIDS

Kids love watching the big ocean freighters being loaded at **Port Melbourne.** If they're lucky they can catch the docking of a sleek white cruise liner. At the Maritime Museum, there's the ***Polly Woodside,*** which may be the first full-sized windjammer your kids have ever seen.

When the kids are ready for a ride of their own, there's **Luna Park,** with every thrill-and-spill contraption imaginable. And don't forget the **trams**—although this is the most common form of public transportation in Melbourne, a streetcar ride is a unique experience for most children today.

Concerts and performances of various kinds are held every summer weekend at the **Royal Botanic Gardens.** For a behind-the-scenes theatrical visit, the stage equipment at the **Performing Arts Museum** enthralls some kids and leaves others . . . *cool,* while the **Planetarium** puts on "sky shows" that leave spectators of all ages awed.

For the tamest entertainment of all, there's the **Royal Melbourne Zoo,** which has a special section where youngsters can pet and feed wombats, echidnas, kangaroos, and other nonbiting, nonpecking Aussie fauna.

ORGANIZED TOURS

There are large numbers of organized tours available in and around Melbourne. The listings below merely give you an idea of the prices and areas visited.

BUS TOURS **Gray Line,** 181 Flinders St. (tel. 654-7700), offers several tours. The daily Melbourne sights tours (morning or afternoon) are arranged to complement one another and visit different places. Adults are charged $A30, children $A28. The Blue Dandenongs tour starts at 8:50am and returns at 12:30pm. Adults pay $A33, children $A31. Tours to Sovereign Hill, Ballarat (see "Easy Excursions: Victoria," later in this chapter), run from late September to May daily, leaving at 9am and returning at 5:30pm. Adults pay $A62, children $A57.50.

The **City Explorer** is a double-decker bus that starts a circular tour of Melbourne seven times a day at Flinders Street Station. Run by **Australian Pacific Tours** (tel. 650-1511), the bus stops at the main sightseeing attractions, giving you a chance to get off, sightsee, then catch the next round an hour later. One ticket covers the entire circuit and costs $A15 for adults, $A8 for children.

A relatively new venture are the **Autopia** tours, undertaken in a small bus and specially tailored for hostel dwellers. These jaunts go out of town and will pick up passengers at four specified hostels before departing from the Queensberry Hill Hostel at 78 Howard St. in North Melbourne. They take you to Phillip Island for $A40; to Port Campbell National Park for $A49; or to a picnic at Hanging Rock (remember the movie?) for $A30, including the picnic lunch. Book by calling 326-5536 or by going to any YHA hostel.

RAILROAD JOURNEYS Some of the best, most comfortable, and cheapest excursions are operated by **V/Line,** 589 Collins St. (tel. 132-232). This is the government rail authority covering Victoria outside the Melbourne metropolitan area. Because of Victoria's small size, it has the densest rail network of all the states, enabling you to take a train to almost anywhere. V/Line organized tours include Ballarat, the historic gold-rush town and scene of Australia's only battle within its borders—the Eureka Stockade. It departs daily from the Spencer Street Station and costs $A40 for adults, $A22 for children. You might even earn the fare if you try your hand at a spot of gold panning—the stuff is still there, allegedly.

If you prefer to explore on your own, V/Line offers the **Victoria Pass.** This entitles you to two weeks of unlimited first-class travel on Victoria's railroads for $A120, half price for children.

RIVER CRUISES River cruises are available on four spacious, comfortable motor vessels that cruise up and down the Yarra River, letting you view the city from the best possible vantage point. One trip heads down to Port Melbourne, the largest containerized port in the southern hemisphere. The other goes past the Botanical Gardens and Olympic Stadium for a glimpse of the stately (meaning very expensive) homes and gardens of South Yarra. The cruises depart thrice daily from the Princes Bridge at Flinders Street Terminal and cost $A11. For times contact **Melbourne River Tours,** Princes Walk (tel. 650-2054).

LIVING-HISTORY WALKS For the most original and amusing tour in all of Australia, contact **Historic Rambles,** 62 River St., Newport, VIC 3015 (tel. 391-0787). This is a very impromptu form of street theater in which a famous literary character named Archie—aka actress Wilma Farrow—conducts strolling groups through selected locales ranging from Chinese temples and colonial cottages to ghost-ridden theaters and legislative assemblies. Archie (he's the cobber of the notorious "Ginger Mick" in the classic Australian ballad "The Sentimental Bloke") changes his or her personality en route, becoming a high court judge, a Chinese porter, rebel leader Peter Lalor, or a Victorian maid as befits the occasion. The ramblers participate in the acts, and the tours last around two hours, costing $A10 per person—no fees are paid to the volunteer extras.

NIGHTLIFE TOURS The **Melbourne Nitelife Mystery Tour** lasts five hours and covers a round of nightclubs, pubs, bars, and bands you might never locate on your own. The rules demand that you be (or at least look) over 18 and turn up neatly dressed. The fee includes all admissions—$A29 covers the lot. Book by calling 563-7888.

7. SPORTS & RECREATION

Sporting events are just about the only occasions when Melburnians "let fly" en masse. And they do it with a vengeance, breaking out in positive orgies of inhibition shedding. There is a story about two Russian (or Chinese or German or Japanese) agents who allegedly visited the town in order to spy out invasion possibilities. They reported back that it would be better to drop the idea. Melburnians, they explained, were so bloodthirsty that they spent Saturday afternoons maiming each other for fun.

AUSTRALIAN RULES FOOTBALL What these mythical agents had witnessed was undoubtedly **Australian Rules football,** a remarkable mélange of rugby, soccer, Gaelic football, and guerrilla warfare. Players wear no protective gear, which accounts for the fabulous casualty rate. What's difficult to account for is why this native version of football became popular *only* in Victoria and why it became so to such a degree that it borders on religious frenzy. Begun in 1858, Australian football now has 14 clubs (the Australian Football League) battling for the annual premiership. Between April and September each year, the Melbourne media is saturated with football coverage (six matches are held each Saturday) climaxing with the six finals. Four of the finals take place at the Melbourne Cricket Ground and pack in more than 100,000 fans.

For comprehension of the rules, get the special free brochure published by the **AFL,** GPO Box 1449 N, Melbourne, VIC 3001. Free conducted tours of the colossal MCG (yes, they play cricket there, too) are held every Wednesday at 10am.

CANOEING If you want to paddle your own canoe, you can hire one at Albert Park Lake, Albert Park. For longer trips on the lower Yarra River, there's the Boathouse in Studley Park, Kew (tel. 861-8707), which rents out paddle craft for $A13 per hour.

GOLF Melbourne is Australia's undisputed golf capital, with by far the largest number of world-class courses in the country. Most of these, of course, are private, members-only links, but a lengthy list are open to the public. These include Albert Park, Queens Road (tel. 51-5588); Brighton Municipal, 230 Dendy St., Brighton (tel.

592-1388); Elsternwick Park, corner of New and Glenhuntly roads, Elwood (tel. 531-3200); Dorset Golf, Trawalla Road, Croydon (tel. 725-3777).

HORSERACING Melbourne's other great passion—horseracing—is shared by most of its compatriots. Horseracing may be called the "Sport of Kings," but in Australia it's very much a sport of the butchers and bakers and candlestick makers, with audience participation to the outer limits of lung power. It goes on year-round at Melbourne's metropolitan courses in Flemington, Caulfield, Moonee Valley, and Sandown.

On the first Tuesday in November, the entire nation grinds to a halt for the running of the **Melbourne Cup,** Australia's richest horserace. Traffic stops in the streets as a million radios pour out the race description in tones ranging from anguish to ecstasy.

The Melbourne Cup is also *the* fashion event of the season, and it's astonishing to behold thousands of exquisitely coiffed-and-frocked ladies abandoning their poise as the horses head into the homestretch.

SPORTS MUSEUM The **Gallery of Sport and Olympic Museum,** Melbourne Cricket Ground, Jolimont Terrace, East Melbourne (tel. 654-8922), displays a vast array of athletic memorabilia and shows sports films daily from 10am to 4pm. Adults pay $A3, children $A1.50.

TENNIS As in all Australian cities, public tennis courts abound. The trouble is that they tend to be booked solid over weekends, so you'd better arrange your sets on a weekday. (Weeknights are apt to be booked full as well.) Try Collingwood Tennis Centre (indoor), 100 Wellington St. (tel. 419-8911); or Fawkner Park Courts, Toorak Road, South Yarra (tel. 266-1953). Court rentals come to between $A10 and $A18 per hour, depending on which court and when.

8. SAVVY SHOPPING

As stated earlier, Melbourne is Australia's commercial capital and the country's shopping center par excellence. This applies to the entire retailing range from monumental department stores to plush little boutiques, from flea markets to budget emporiums. The two main shopping drags are **Bourke Street** and **Collins Street.** While Bourke is home to many of Melbourne's major department stores (see "Department Stores," below), Collins Street is more exclusive (ergo, more expensive) and has a legion of small, trendy specialty stores, from fashions and jewelry to chocolates and rare books.

All of Melbourne's downtown thoroughfares show the growth pattern of the city: 19th-century colonial brick next to the soaring glass-and-concrete cloudscrapers of the nuclear age. But, unlike those in Sydney, they somehow blend into an amazingly harmonious whole, their basic starkness relieved and hidden by tree-lined boulevards, unexpected patches of miniparks, and lighting effects.

SHOPPING AREAS

SHOPPING COMPLEXES **Collins Place** is Australia's costliest real-estate development to date. The place is actually a superdeluxe shopping center incorporating the Regent Hotel in upper Collins Street. It houses boulevard-style cafés and restaurants, galleries of swank little stores, and a transparent elevator to waft you from level to level. You can spend half a day there window shopping in almost sinful comfort.

Melbourne Central is a giant downtown shopping complex covering the entire block bordered by Elizabeth, Lonsdale, and Swanston streets. It contains 150 small retailers, but most of the space is taken up by **Daimaru** (tel. 660-6666), Melbourne's first international department store. Daimaru, which opened in 1991, is a branch of a Japanese store founded in Kyoto some 276 years ago. Stretching over six sumptuous shopping floors, it concentrates on marketing upscale fashions, food, and furnishings.

But the place also contains two exclusive restaurants, a sushi bar, a health-food bar, and four casual cafés.

There are also some architectural attention grabbers: a huge pocket watch that opens and has figures dancing to the strains of "Waltzing Matilda" and an ancient brick munitions tower, a local landmark, covered in glass and rising to the roof. (They weren't allowed to demolish the tower when building the complex, so they incorporated it.) Daimaru is open Monday to Wednesday from 9:30am to 6pm, Thursday and Friday until 9pm, Saturday until 5pm.

DEPARTMENT STORES Bourke is the site of most of the *big* stores: **Myer** (after Chicago's Marshall Field's, the world's largest department store); **David Jones,** its more traditional neighbor; and **G. J. Coles,** specializing in an enormous range of budget goods.

DUTY-FREE SHOPS For overseas visitors only, these special stores offer a substantial saving on retail prices. They offer jewelry, perfume, liquor, watches, and the like at what—for bona fide travelers from abroad—are bargain rates. (One tip for the unwary: There is no such thing as Australian jade. The stones so misnamed—and sold—are actually inferior gems that *look* like jade without being in the same class.) The stores include the **West End Duty Free,** 53 Queen St., and the **Downtown Duty Free,** 128 Exhibition St.

SHOPPING ARCADES & STREET MARKETS The shopping arcades should be explored individually. They vary from tawdry gimcrack to blazing elegance, but all contain surprising little stores that reveal the dazzling range of goods this town has to offer (see especially the **Royal Arcade** on Bourke Street, where Gog and Magog strike the time; the **Australia Arcade;** and **Block Court,** off Collins Street.)

Melbourne also has a host of street markets, where shopping is a matter of sharp eyes and good luck. The **Flea Market** on Drummond Street in Carlton opens Friday night and Saturday morning. **Victoria Market** on Victoria Street in North Melbourne is open Tuesday, Thursday, Friday, and Saturday morning. At **Prahran Market** on Commercial Road you'll find a vast array of European goods, edible and otherwise. There are about half a dozen more, including the **St. Kilda Art Banks** in Upper Esplanade, open on Sunday and featuring sidewalk displays of paintings, pottery, jewelry, and leather work that runs the gamut from masterful to terrible.

BEST BUYS

Australian specialties are probably what you're after. At every step you'll come across shops selling stuffed koalas, plastic boomerangs, sheepskin rugs, Aboriginal art, and kangaroo skins. Some of this is plain junk, homemade or imported from Japan and Hong Kong. You'll have to use your own taste and expertise when buying.

ARTS & HANDCRAFTS

ABORIGINAL HANDCRAFTS, Floor 9 in the Century Bldg., 125 Swanston St., Melbourne. Tel. 650-4717.

This is a small shop, operated by an auxiliary of the Uniting Church, that offers guaranteed-genuine Aboriginal art and artifacts. The goods are mostly bought directly from the craftspeople—with no middleman profits to push up prices. They include carvings and bark paintings, spears and boomerangs, baskets, woven mats, and ceremonial decorations; also sold is the strange musical drone pipes called didgeridoos, which produce a haunting, almost unearthly hum for those patient enough to learn to play them. They cost between $A60 to $A170, but you can also get smaller items for $A10. Open Monday to Thursday from 10am to 4:30pm, Friday from 10am to 5pm.

MEAT MARKET CRAFT CENTRE, 42 Courtney St., North Melbourne. Tel. 329-9966.

An erstwhile wholesale meat market building transformed into a tastefully fashionable showcase for Australian handcrafts, sculptures, ceramics, paintings, collages, and photographs, this splendidly laid out and subtly lit store is a tourist attraction as well as a retailer. There's a coffee shop on the premises, and the place is open daily from 10am to 5pm.

PHOTOGRAPHIC CENTRE, 384 Church St., Richmond.

For vintage-photo buffs, the Photographic Centre has a wonderful collection of antique Australian photographs, the kind you admire on restaurant-and-pub walls but can never get for yourself.

DIGGER HATS

MITCHELL'S, 134 Russell St. Tel. 654-5785.

For genuine Australian Digger hats (new), try Mitchell's, which specializes in military disposals. With the martial spears-and-bayonets emblem removed, this is possibly the only military headgear that flatters men and women alike.

FOOD

DAVID JONES FOOD BASEMENT, 299 Bourke Street Mall. Tel. 669-8200.

This may be the grandest collection of comestibles in the southern hemisphere and has been compared to London's Fortnum & Mason's. Its orgiastic array of gourmet items, from cans of caviar to jars of preserved ginger, from Hungarian salami to roast beef, look as if they belong in a jewelry-store window. It also has counters selling sandwiches and desserts at very reasonable prices, but in general this is *not* a noshing station for backpackers.

OPALS

ALTMANN & CHERNY, 120 Exhibition St. Tel. 650-9685.

Altmann & Cherny, as much a showplace as a store, is the place for buying Australian opals. Their prize exhibit is the *Olympic Australis*, the largest, costliest gem opal in the world, duly recorded in the *Guinness Book of World Records*. Found in the Olympic year of 1956 (hence the name) at the Coober Pedy field in South Australia by a prospecting old-timer, the stone weighs 17,700 carats, or 7 pounds; sparkles white, brown, silver, and amber; and is definitely *not* for sale. Other stones are. You can watch the entire process of sorting, cutting, and polishing the gems, and the products sell for anything from A10¢ per gram to $A100 per gram; opal pendants cost from $A20 upward, gold opal rings from $A60. Tourists get a 20% discount here.

LE SOUEF OPALS, 145 Russell St., 1st Floor. Tel. 654-4444.

An opal trove of a different hue is Nick Le Souëf's. Mr. Le Souëf is an opal miner, stuntman, and naturalist who combines expertise with gems with a fascination for poisonous critters. He once spent a couple of nights in a tank swarming with stingrays and appeared on the American TV show "That's Incredible" swimming in a pool with live piranhas. His mezzanine-level gem store and showroom is "guarded" by deadly funnel-web spiders, blue-ringed octopi, scorpions, and assorted tiger snakes—all safely behind glass, of course.

REGENT JEWELLERS, Collins Place, Regent Hotel, Melbourne. Tel. 650-4223.

This subsidiary of Altmann & Cherny has a dazzling exhibit: the world's most valuable black opal. The *Aurora Australia* hails from Lightning Ridge, weighs 180 carats, and is valued at $A1.5 million—a trifle beyond our budget bracket. You can ogle it gratis at Collins Place, however.

SOUVENIRS

TASMAN DISCOUNTS, 215 Little Collins St. Tel. 654-8845.

This is possibly the most economical Australian souvenir store in town. Bring your passport and airline ticket to get the lowest prices. They sell a huge range of Aussie gifts, T-shirts, stuffed animals, boomerangs, and so on. Open Monday to Friday until 7pm, Saturday and Sunday until 1pm.

9. EVENING ENTERTAINMENT

Sydneysiders are wont to sneer that "Melbourne shuts up with the shops," but—like most such sneers—this is basically untrue. Melbourne merely *seems* to curl up because it has no nightlife district. Its nearest facsimile thereof, St. Kilda, does such a dismal job that you're afraid to turn your head in case it flickers out behind your back, like an anemic candle. The fact is that Melbourne has a large array of nightspots—some quite gloriously boisterous—but they're scattered all over the map. Isolated and introverted, they bestow no glow on their surroundings and have to be pinpointed and targeted. You can't just stroll along and drop into something you fancy, because the Via Veneto this isn't.

To find out what and who is playing where, consult the "Entertainment" pages of the *Sun-Herald* on Thursday, the "Entertainment Guide" of the *Age* on Friday. Specializing in rock gigs and fringe entertainment are several free periodicals, such as *InPress,* which you can pick up in cafés, music stores, and a few hotel lobbies.

Half-price tickets to many shows are available at the **Halftix** booth in the Bourke Street Mall (tel. 639-420). These are cash only—no refunds—available on the day of the performance.

THE PERFORMING ARTS

Melbourne has the most active live stage in Australia. Ticket prices for theater cost between $A18 and $A35; for ballet and opera they go up to $A76.

MAJOR CONCERT HALLS & ALL-PURPOSE AUDITORIUMS

VICTORIAN ARTS CENTRE, 100 St. Kilda Rd., Melbourne. Tel. 617-8211.

This complex comprises the State Theatre, the Playhouse, the Fairfax Studio, and the Melbourne Concert Hall. It shows everything from grand opera and ballet to classical theater, intimate comedy, and cabaret.

PALAIS THEATRE, Lower Esplanade, St. Kilda.

A palatial erstwhile movie house, the Palais has been transformed into a live showcase for ballet-and-concert groups.

NATIONAL THEATRE, Carlisle St., St. Kilda. Tel. 525-4611.

A former cinema, the National now presents guest celebrities of every kind.

PRINCESS THEATRE, 163 Spring St., Melbourne. Tel. 663-3300.

The grande dame of Australian stages, this is a landmark building through which you can take guided tours when no shows are in progress.

HER MAJESTY'S, 219 Exhibition St., Melbourne. Tel. 663-3211.

Although another temple of tradition, Her Majesty's stages very contemporary material.

ATHENAEUM THEATRE, 188 Collins St., Melbourne. Tel. 650-1500.

The Atheaneum concentrates on musicals, such as a grand-slam revival of *Hair.* Tickets $A15 to $A45.

SMALL THEATERS

There are about a dozen of these in town, mostly of high professional quality. Ticket prices are lower than those in the big showcases, usually between $A10 and $A18.

THE C.U.B. MALTHOUSE, 117 Sturt St., South Melbourne. Tel. 685-5111.

This is an unusual setup consisting of two separate stages, a gallery, café, and bar. You can choose between two—often contrasting—performances on any evening. Tickets $A27 to $A32.

UNIVERSAL THEATRE, 19 Victoria St., North Fitzroy. Tel. 419-3777.
The Universal specializes in parodies, satires, and other characteristic "off-Broadway" material.

ANTHILL THEATRE, 21 Graham St., Albert Park. Tel. 699-3253.

A veteran among the smaller stages, it is consistently innovative and consistently good.

THEATREWORKS, 14 Acland St., St. Kilda. Tel. 534-4879.
This theater concentrates on works by Australian authors, including unknowns, whose scripts quite often turn out better than those of established scribes.

DINNER THEATER

There are about 15 dinner theaters in Melbourne, most good and all fairly expensive, since the price of a meal comes with the show.

DIRTY DICK'S, 23 Queens Rd., Melbourne. Tel. 867-4788.
Some of the raunchiest sing-alongs and bawdiest characters anywhere are here, with admission costing $A28 or $A35, depending on the night.

DRACULA'S, 98 Victoria St., Carlton. Tel. 347-3349.
This hilarious chamber of horrors has hunchbacked Igor playing host. The gimmick's are suitably blood curdling, the four-course dinner fine. You pay either $A32 or $A45 per head.

NAUGHTY 90s, 675 Glenferrie Rd., Hawthorn. Tel. 818-7567.
The theater puts on 2½ hours of comedy and music to go with your dining and wining. Naughtiness is served in moderation.

THE CLUB, PUB & MUSIC SCENE

COMEDY CLUBS

Melbourne has a number of comedy ventures, but the following are outstanding.

LAST LAUGH, 64 Smith St., Collingwood. Tel. 419-8600.
Highly original, regardless of whether the jokes are native or overseas imports, this mirth factory dates back to 1976 and still packs in the crowds. Shows Wednesday through Saturday, tickets $A12 to $A22.

LA MAMA, 205 Faraday St., Carlton. Tel. 347-6142.
A nice mix of comedians and short plays are presented to a passionately devoted audience here. Tickets $A11.

DANCE CLUBS & DISCOS

It is impossible to distinguish between the two, since the clubs aren't really clubs, and the discos, despite their label, often feature live bands. Equally impossible to pin down are their cover charges, which may be $A8 to $A10 or $A1, depending on the fame/notoriety of the current performers or deejays. In the city, most of the places cluster around King Street, but the majority are scattered throughout the inner suburbs.

THE PALACE, Lower Esplanade, St. Kilda. Tel. 534-0655.
Large, glittering, and versatile, this place stages a nice mix of international events, including sponsored talent competitions.

METRO, 20 Bourke St., Melbourne. Tel. 663-4288.
One of the top nightspots in town with corresponding prices, it features highly evolved computer-based audio-and-video effects.

CLUB CHEVRON, 519 St. Kilda Rd., Melbourne. Tel. 510-1281.

This large disco and video room flashes Monday through Saturday until breakfast time.

SILVERS, 443 Toorak Rd., Toorak. Tel. 827-8244.

A nightclub with a famous cocktail bar, Silvers has a rapidly changing lineup of bands.

THE EVELYN, 351 Brunswick St., Fitzroy. Tel. 417-3238.

The Evelyn has a roof garden and a successive cavalcade of bands, and it takes pride in charging no admission, regardless of who's performing.

DOWN UNDER ROCK CAFE, 186 Lygon St., Carlton. Tel. 663-6570.

Actually an entire entertainment complex, the Down Under spreads over two levels housing a band venue, a restaurant, several bars, a gaming room, and a liquor store. The term *café* is a complete misnomer, but the place does give you a wide choice of evening amusements.

KAZBAR, 481 Chapel St., South Yarra. Tel. 826-6442.

It's very hard to classify this one, except as an exceptionally pleasant hangout. A combination bar and restaurant with a combination deejay and master of ceremonies, Kazbar draws a hip crowd of mostly beautiful people.

THE ZIG ZAG FACTORY, 118 Elgin St., Carlton.

The unusual entertainment here includes screenings of wrestling matches as well as music videos. The fans yell loudest for the wrestling hulks.

CHASERS, 386 Chapel St., South Yarra. Tel. 827-6615.

A pleasing mixture of bands and trendies and funk and pop is offered by a pair of talented deejays and reinforced by various dance acts.

INFLATION, 60 King St., Melbourne. Tel. 614-6122.

One of the elaborately chic biggies, Inflation is divided into three levels: general disco, supper floor, and intimately dim dance area on the top.

PIANO BARS

OLD MELBOURNE HOTEL, 5 Flemington Rd., North Melbourne. Tel. 329-9344.

Located in a wonderful Victorian hotel crammed with genuine antiques glittering in candlelight, the piano bar (one of several bars) has a silver candelabra and the mellowest of keyboard sounds.

FAWKNER CLUB, 52 Toorak Rd. W., South Yarra. Tel. 820-1555.

A famed drinking establishment, the Fawkner features excellent piano mood music Friday and Saturday nights. On other nights it makes do with relays of visiting celebrities.

ROCK, JAZZ, FOLK & WESTERN

The vast majority of Melbourne bands perform in pubs. This is a unique feature of the Australian music scene and is based on the fact that it's much easier for a pub to get an entertainment license than for a music club to obtain a liquor permit. Whatever the cause, it works out well for audiences because pubs are the cheapest nightspots. Admissions range from gratis to a rare $A5 or so. Once inside, drinks go at bar prices—beer for around $A2 a glass. You have nearly 100 entertainment pubs to choose from. The only drawback is that most of them close near midnight. The better type enforce a dress rule of sorts, meaning no T-shirts or thongs. Shorts usually pass, and for the ladies no such rules apply.

EAST BRUNSWICK CLUB HOTEL, 280 Lygon St., Brunswick. Tel. 380-1206.

The Melbourne Folk Club is featured on Friday, rock groups on other nights.

BRIDGE HOTEL, 642 Bridge St., Richmond. Tel. 428-3852.

I heard the New Orleans Traditionals here, sounding as if they'd just escaped from Basin Street. Swing is offered in addition to jazz.

ESPLANADE HOTEL, 11 Upper Esplanade, St. Kilda. Tel. 534-0211.

This large, rambling place is usually packed for the rock groups and special guest vocalists.

TOK-H, 459 Toorak Rd., Toorak. Tel. 827-7481.

A somewhat mysteriously titled tavern and one of Melbourne's traditional watering holes, Tok-H presents a freewheeling cavalcade of rock, funk, rap, and swing groups; black freestyle dancers; and—believe it or not—fashion shows.

ROYAL ARTILLERY HOTEL, corner of Elizabeth and Queensberry Sts., Melbourne. Tel. 347-3917.

One of the few hotels licensed to stay open until 3am, it presents rock bands, Latin groups, and occasional talent contests—for which the invitation says "BYO—Bring Your Own Instruments."

PRINCE OF WALES HOTEL, Fitzroy St., St. Kilda. Tel. 534-8251.

Once a rather staid establishment, this is now the venue for some of the wildest lineups in town. Heavy metal predominates, but you also get every other variation of ear buster.

DICKENS ON COLLINS, 290 Collins St., Melbourne. Tel. 654-1821.

Downstairs in the Block Court, this pub has a strong English flavor underscored by the half a dozen British beers on tap. There's also a party of one sort or another going on seven nights a week.

CENTRAL HOTEL, 120 Church St., Brighton. Tel. 592-1535.

Constantly confused with two other "Centrals" in other parts of town, Central Hotel is a regular venue for rock groups and features a different band almost every night.

MORE ENTERTAINMENT

MOVIES

Most of Melbourne's mainstream city cinemas are packed into multitheater blocks: **Village,** 206 Bourke St. (tel. 667-6565); **Hoyts,** 140 Bourke St. (tel. 663-3303); and **Greater Union,** 131 Russell St. (tel. 654-8133). Both the films shown and the ticket prices are roughly the same as those in the United States. But on Tuesday night you can get into the Village or Hoyts for half the usual ticket price.

There is also a scattering of small independent outfits that will screen undubbed foreign movies, revived classics, and films aimed at the cognoscenti market: **Agora,** La Trobe University, Melbourne (tel. 478-3998); **Brighton Bay,** 294 Bay St., Brighton (tel. 596-3590); **Longford,** 59 Toorak Rd., South Yarra (tel. 867-2700); **Trak Cinema,** 445 Toorak Rd., Toorak (tel. 827-9333); **Croydon Cinema,** 3 Hewish Rd., Croydon (tel. 725-6544); and **Cinematheque,** 360 Swanston St., Melbourne (tel. 663-2916).

CASINOS

Until 1990 Melbourne was a capital city without any legal gambling facilities (though plenty of the other kind). But that year it unveiled a betting establishment that is unique in the world and actually is sponsored by the state government.

TABARET, in the basement of the Menzies-Rialto Hotel, 525 Collins St. Tel. 612-2900.

This avant-garde–style casino lets you place wagers on the results of computer games. The maximum bet is $A5, and players can choose among games of golf, horseraces, cricket, or soccer matches. None of them involves any degree of skill, and the payout odds are about the same as on a slot machine.

The action, however, is considerably more exciting. The computer terminal screen shows the game in graphics. Players can bet on the result of a golf stroke or the place of a horse in a race and listen to realistic sound effects and have their triumphant jackpot wins heralded by ringing bells. A bar on one side provides refreshments, though otherwise the atmosphere is redolent with all the pulsating glamour of a post office. The terminals blink away 16 hours a day, from 11am to 3am.

10. EASY EXCURSIONS: VICTORIA

Victoria is the smallest state on the mainland, but it's "small" only by Australian standards. Victoria could comfortably hold Kansas plus Connecticut, with some acreage to spare. The climate is what tourist brochures call "equable," meaning that it lacks the desert sizzlers you encounter farther north, although you can experience four seasons in one day along the coast.

Because of its relative compactness and the excellent transportation system radiating from Melbourne, Victoria is an ideal field for tourist exploration, offering colorful variety within an easily manageable area. Just 75 miles from Melbourne, for instance, bubble the mineral springs of the spa country around **Hepburn Springs,** where you imbibe mountain air and medicinal water along with resort fun. Or for a complete change of pace, try a trip by paddle steamer along the lazy **Murray River,** the most relaxing mode of travel since Huck Finn's raft. Or visit the **Grampians** in spring, when carpets of wildflowers turn the mountain slopes into painters' palettes.

THE DANDENONGS

Known as the Blue Dandenongs, this is a range of rolling hills and timbered valleys so close to Melbourne that they form a natural backdrop to the city. The hills are gray green with gum trees; ablaze with fields of tulips, daffodils, and gladiolus; and studded with panoramic lookout spots and wildlife preserves. The most popular point is **Mount Dandenong Lookout** (over 2,000 feet high), which presents a view of all of Melbourne and its suburbs.

Running bravely from nearby Belgrave to Menzies Creek is **Puffing Billy,** a delightful little narrow-gauge steam train that seems imbued with a personality of its own. Billy may be a relic, but he's the real thing, not a replica, and there's something very endearing about the way he huffs and blusters his way up and down the ranges, pulling the original wooden passenger cars packed with tourists. A round-trip costs $A12.50 for adults, $A8.30 for children. Suburban electric trains from Flinders Street can take you directly to Billy's station at Belgrave. For time tables, call 870-8411.

My personal favorite in the Dandenongs is the **William Ricketts Sanctuary** at Churinga. William Ricketts was a musician who turned to sculpture to express his overwhelming love for nature and the people closest to it—the Australian Aborigines. Ricketts purchased a tract of steep forest land and set about populating it with the Aboriginal theme—clay figures of men, women, and children that seem to grow among and out of the trees. The union between plants and people is so wonderfully demonstrated in these sculptures that you suddenly grasp the true meaning of Aboriginal mythology: its timelessness that doesn't divide eternity into human life spans but thinks in the endless growth cycles of evolution. In Rickett's carvings are innocence and knowingness, tremendous joy and inherent sadness. The only word that describes them is *unforgettable.*

Sherbrooke Forest, near Upper Ferntree Gully, is a nature preserve crisscrossed by some of the prettiest trail walks I've ever trodden. (It also has picnic facilities and a snack kiosk.) This is the home of the lyre bird, an amazing feathered mimic that imitates the sounds it hears with uncanny accuracy—including machinery noises. Your best chance of either seeing or hearing one is by taking a forest trail. You may also come across a waddling wombat or an echidna, the little spiky marsupial

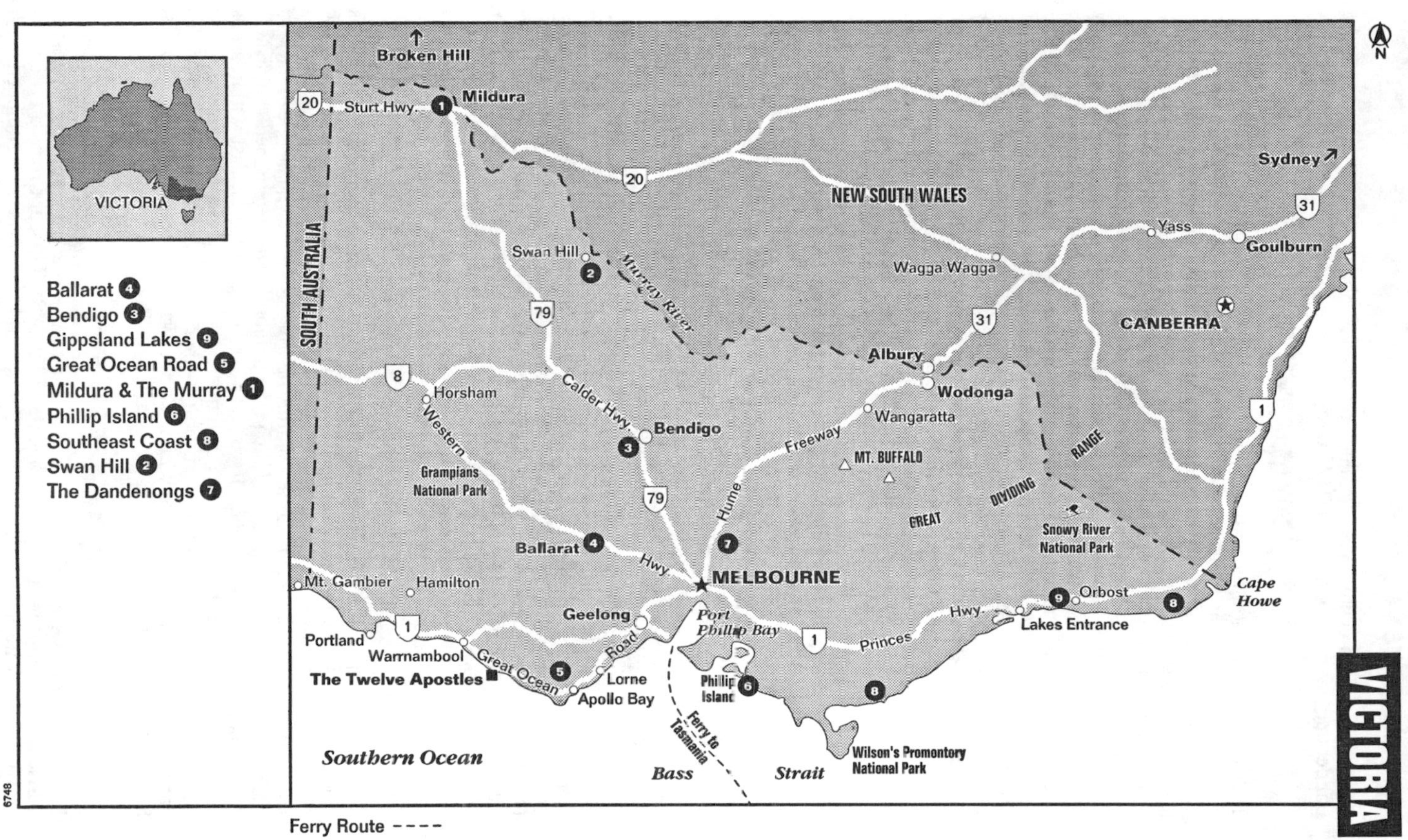

VICTORIA

N
VICTORIA
Ballarat 4
Bendigo 3
Gippsland Lakes 9
Great Ocean Road 5
Mildura & The Murray 1
Phillip Island 6
Southeast Coast 8
Swan Hill 2
The Dandenongs 7
Broken Hill
Mildura
Sturt Hwy.
20
SOUTH AUSTRALIA
NEW SOUTH WALES
Sydney
31
Yass
Goulburn
Wagga Wagga
Swan Hill
Murray River
79
CANBERRA
Albury
Wodonga
Wangaratta
1
8
Horsham
Western
Calder Hwy.
Bendigo
Freeway
MT. BUFFALO
RANGE
DIVIDING
GREAT
Grampians National Park
Hume
Snowy River National Park
Ballarat
Hwy
MELBOURNE
Mt. Gambier
Hamilton
Orbost
Cape Howe
Geelong
Port Phillip Bay
Hwy.
Lakes Entrance
Portland
Warrnambool
Great Ocean
Road
Princes
Lorne
Apollo Bay
The Twelve Apostles
Phillip Island
Ferry to Tasmania
Wilson's Promontory National Park
Southern Ocean
Bass
Strait
6748
Ferry Route - - - -

version of the porcupine. For detailed information about this region contact the Dandenong Tourist Council, tel. 03/752-5455.

HEALESVILLE

Tucked away beneath the mountains some 40 miles northeast of Melbourne, Healesville is an idyllic pleasure resort in the valley of the Watts River. In or around the town you'll find just about everything in the spectrum of holiday fun: smart hotels and budget guest houses, picnic and camping grounds, horseracing, horseback riding, golf, and nature unspoiled and carefully preserved.

Healesville's top attraction is the **Sir Colin Mackenzie Sanctuary,** Badger Creek Road (tel. 059/62-4022), internationally famous as a wildlife haven. Originally developed as a research station, the sanctuary is now open to the public every day. The green scrub and tall grass rustle with emu families; the trees harbor neon-colored parrots and leaf-munching koalas; clusters of kangaroos prick their ears at your approach and close in for a cuddle; and occasionally giant goanna lizards scuttle through the grass, black tongues flicking. The platypus, which remains practically invisible under normal circumstances, can be seen close up in glass-sided observation tanks. What it does, nearly all the time, is search for worms and yabbies along the rocky bottom. If there's one way to describe a platypus, it's an elongated piece of fur stretched over an appetite. Admission $A10 for adults, $A5 for children. Open daily 9am to 5pm.

PHILLIP ISLAND

Located at the entrance of Westernport Bay, Phillip Island is now connected to the mainland by a concrete bridge. You can get there by road, by sea (hydrofoil or ferry from Stony Point), or by air (twin-engine planes fly from Melbourne International in Tullamarine, from Essendon, or from Moorabbin airports). The island, about 90 miles southeast of Melbourne, is the finest wildlife preserve in Victoria, in addition to boasting its own fishing fleet; sheltered, safe, and sunny beaches; every marine sport in the book; plus a famous motor-racing circuit.

But the animals are the real draw. There's a colony of fur seals to be seen at close range at the Nobbies, where they bask in the sun with the total flipper-fanning abandon only seals and humans can muster. There are mutton birds, looking quite small while resting but demonstrating an enormous wing span once they take off. During November they seem to blacken the sky when they return from their astonishing migratory flights to Japan, Alaska, the American coast, and back to their island rookeries. The island is patterned in individual sanctuaries, one marked by a sign: "Travel Slowly—Watch for Children and Koalas." The koalas, incidentally, were in danger of becoming extinct. The islanders saved them by importing and planting manna gums—the only species of gum leaf (out of hundreds) the cuddly little blighters will eat.

Many tourists visit Phillip Island for just one sight: the **Penguin Parade.** This is held every evening of the year around dusk, with the starting time posted outside the fence of the motor-racing circuit. The performers are waves of fairy penguins splashing ashore at Summerland Beach after hunting fish all day. They head back to their burrows in the sand dunes, waddling ceremoniously and determinedly, oblivious of the spotlights turned on them. If you sit quietly they'll march past within arm's reach like so many portly little men in dinner jackets filing out of a banquet. The parade lasts from half an hour to an hour—there are more than 2,000 penguins participating, all with very full tummies. Parade watching costs $A6.50 for adults, $A2.50 for children.

WHERE TO STAY

For economical overnight stays on the island there's the **Boomerang Caravan Park,** 121 Thompson Ave., Cowes (tel. 059/52-2348). The park rents on-site four- and six-berth caravans (R.V.s) from $A29 to $A46. They come equipped with cooking facilities, refrigerators, water, electricity, color TVs, and foam-rubber mattresses. Also available are showers and toilets, gas barbecues, and washing machines. You have to supply your own linen, blankets, and pillows—or you can rent them. Alternatively there's **Rothsaye,** 2 Roy Court, Cowes, VIC 3922 (tel. 059/522-057), a bed-and-breakfast charmer where rooms start at $A65 for doubles and "brekky" includes the freshest eggs laid by free-range hens.

BALLARAT

Victoria owes its start to one of the wildest gold rushes in history. During the 1850s one-third of all the gold in the world was mined here! If you want to relive some of the excitement of those rip-roaring days, head for Ballarat. Seventy miles west of Melbourne by rail or road, this otherwise sedate city has re-created its gold and gunpowder past on **Sovereign Hill.** For the $A15 (half for children) admission you walk onto 36 acres of gold-rush ground, correct in every detail but with the violence removed.

Stroll along re-created Main Street and you'll be back in 1855. There's the Gold Office, where Diggers took their gleanings to be weighed and stored until the heavily armed Gold Escort transported the stuff to Melbourne—with one wary eye on the bush from which "Captain Moonlight" could pounce any moment. There's also the building for the *Ballarat Times,* whose editor was publicly horsewhipped by the fiery Lola Montez for writing that she "danced like a hussy." Also included are the Chinese Joss House, Johnny Alloo's famous restaurant, a blacksmith forge in full operation, livery stables, Diggers' huts, a gold museum, and a mine.

You can actually pan for gold in the creek; don't expect any nuggets, but you may get some yellow flakes if your pan "comes up smiling."

"Blood on the Southern Cross" is the title of the sound-and-light show staged nightly a short distance away on the site of Australia's one and only armed rebellion (see "History" in Chapter 1). Using ingenious illumination and sound effects, the spectacle re-creates the drama of that December night of 1854 when the young colony fought its Bunker Hill. Some 150 Diggers defended the Eureka Stockade against twice as many troops and police—and you hear and see the blaze of the Eureka Hotel, the thunder of the cavalry charge, the rattle of musketry, and the new flag of the Southern Cross waving over the shambles. Tickets cost $A17 for adults, $A8 children, and booking is essential. Call 053/33-5777. Ask about the special family passes that include dinner and the show.

SWAN HILL

At Horseshoe Bend on the Murray River, 214 miles northwest of Melbourne, lies Australia's finest theme park. **Pioneer Settlement** (tel. 050/32-1093) is a community enterprise of Swan Hill that originally grew from the idea of converting an old paddle steamer into a folk museum. The steamer is now the **Riverboat Restaurant,** a unique and delightful hostelry serving such culinary adventures as billabong platter, grilled yabbies and bacon, kangaroo tail soup, and witchetty grubs; it has hosted not only Queen Elizabeth and a couple of prime ministers but also every gourmet in the Commonwealth. Admission $A8.50 adults, $A4.50 for children. Open daily 9am to 5pm.

Around the lagoon-locked riverboat has grown the faithful replica of a pioneer community: a Cobb & Co. stagecoach office—the Down Under equivalent of Wells Fargo; a century-old weatherboard bank; a saddler's shop; a bush schoolhouse; a barbershop; a mud-brick kitchen; a pioneer log cabin; a fire station; and a printer's workshop, all equipped with the implements and crudely ingenious machinery of the period. On the streets and river you can see the vehicles of another age: firefighting contraptions, gigs, buggies, drays, log carts, horse omnibuses, steam-powered tractors, penny-farthing bicycles, and massive wool barges. One section is devoted to Aboriginal displays—hunting weapons, musical instruments, and carved canoe trees.

Four times a night Swan Hill puts on its own version of a **Sound and Light spectacle.** But this is a mobile performance, with visitors being guided through the area by special lighting effects linked dramatically by atmosphere music, narration, and authentic wildlife sounds.

You can reach Swan Hill by train or bus from Melbourne or zoom by Bizjet, a daily air service flying from Essendon Airport and taking less than an hour.

GIPPSLAND LAKES

"Two holidays for the price of one" could be the slogan of this resort region. The Gippsland Lakes, starting 100 miles or so east of Melbourne, form a connected chain running parallel to the ocean, some separated from the sea only by narrow strips of sand dune. So, in a manner of speaking, you can wade with one foot in saltwater and the other in fresh, enjoying ocean beaches and lakefronts simultaneously.

A lot of locals have discovered this, and around **Lakes Entrance** the area is awash with neon-glaring motels, caravan parks, and diners. But the lakes and beaches stretch on and on, offering scores of uncrowded coves, bays, and inlets that are hedged in green and flanked by blue, with nary a neon sign to mar the horizon. The scenery is lush, the picnicking great, and the fishing wonderful. (Just off the coast lie the happy hunting grounds of Australia's largest trawler fleet.)

You can chug or sail or paddle or zip from one lake to another in every conceivable type of watercraft, heading out into the Pacific when the weather is calm. Occasionally you run into schools of sleek, bubble-spouting dolphin, and if you throttle your motor way down they'll play games around your boat.

Thousands of black swans dot the lakes, and some of the lake islands have kangaroos and koalas. But most of the visitors come for the fishing. And if you make friends with the natives—which isn't hard—they'll give you the recipe for bream fried in beer batter.

BENDIGO

Some 92 miles north of Melbourne along the Calder Highway stands **"Golden Bendigo,"** the gold now a remnant of the past. By Australian—or Californian—standards this is a city "steeped in history." At the height of the early 1850s gold rush there were 20,000 Diggers (including 4,000 Chinese) working in the fields around the town and spending the yellow dust on women, dice, cards, and liquor considerably faster than they found it.

Today Bendigo is a prosperous and smugly respectable provincial center, but it's still sprinkled with reminders of its hectic youth. It has the **Chinese Joss House** at Emu Point, where the "Diggers in pigtails" used to pray for a rich strike. There is the **Central Deborah,** the last mine to cease production when the gold petered out. Today the mine has been restored as a museum. You can see the primitive shower rooms where miners were stripped and searched. Or you can sit in the engine driver's huge seat, from which the driver hauled the miners' cage up the 1,385-foot-deep shaft.

From the same era dates the 115-year-old **Bendigo Pottery,** Midland Highway (tel. 054/48-4404), the oldest in Australia, in Epsom. Unlike the gold-rush relics, this place is still in full production—you can watch the entire process, from the wet clay stage and firing in the kilns to the finished piece. Open daily 9am to 5pm. Admission is free, but guided tours cost $A3.50 for adults, $A2.50 for children.

CHAPTER 5
ADELAIDE

- WHAT'S SPECIAL ABOUT ADELAIDE
1. FROM A BUDGET TRAVELER'S POINT OF VIEW
2. ORIENTATION
- NEIGHBORHOODS IN BRIEF
3. GETTING AROUND
- FAST FACTS: ADELAIDE
4. WHERE TO STAY
5. WHERE TO EAT
- DID YOU KNOW . . . ?
6. ATTRACTIONS
7. SPORTS & RECREATION
- FROMMER'S FAVORITE ADELAIDE EXPERIENCES
8. EVENING ENTERTAINMENT
9. EXCURSIONS IN SOUTH AUSTRALIA

Once upon a time—15 or so years ago—Adelaide was known as **Wowserville,** or, a little more politely, as the "City of Churches." What both titles meant was that this was the metropolis the bluenoses and killjoys had built in their own image and ran accordingly. Everybody admitted that the place was beautiful, but it was a dead loss as far as even a modicum of *joie de vivre* went. Adelaide's reputation resembled that of Boston a few decades back: a locality where they rolled up the sidewalks after sunset.

But time has a knack for marching on. Today Adelaide is perhaps the most liberal and enlightened Australian city—having duly adopted most of Sydney's virtues and few of its vices. The churches are still there in dazzling profusion, but the wowsers no longer rule the roost.

There were various reasons behind this transformation: the immense cultural impact of the biennial Adelaide Festival of Arts, with its explosion of artistic creativity; a new generation of natives and the influx of overseas migrants; rapid growth (Adelaide now tops one million people); a change of government; and the influence of abundant local wine on people's life-styles. Amazingly, although Adelaide had been sitting atop one of the world's greatest wine barrels for a century, few locals drank the stuff. It took the example of the European newcomers to educate their palates.

Whatever the reason, Adelaide has changed almost beyond recognition. Perhaps the most telling proof of this metamorphosis was the fact that Adelaide opened the *first* nudist beach in Australia a few miles south. And it didn't even cause an earthquake!

Somehow Adelaide has managed to retain its leisurely charm and natural dignity and the air of tranquil calm that has always been its chief attraction. It didn't join the neon-lit rat race that makes Sydney both so stimulating and so frazzling. Adelaide is still a city of strollers and smilers, catering to pedestrians rather than motorists, to amblers rather than speedsters.

No other city boasts proportionately more parkland or pedestrian malls that make shopping (window or otherwise) such unhassled pleasure. And no other place goes to such pains to enhance these facilities. In Rymill Park (which harbors one of the world's greatest rose gardens), replicas of native birds perch in the trees. Press a button on the trunk and the birds sing! And in order to reduce the number of private cars clogging downtown, Adelaide launched Australia's first free bus service—the Beeline. The buses take you on a shopping circuit on the house, or rather on the municipality.

WHAT'S SPECIAL ABOUT ADELAIDE

Architectural Highlights
- ☐ Adelaide Festival Centre, a superb performance complex including an open-air amphitheater.
- ☐ Old Parliament House, constructed entirely of costly Kapunda marble.
- ☐ Ayers House, a magnificent 19th-century mansion.

Beach
- ☐ Glenelg, a popular, fun resort southwest of the city.

Museums
- ☐ South Australian Museum, with a world-famous collection of early Pacific artifacts.
- ☐ Migration Museum, showing the origins of the people who shaped the state.

Events/Festivals
- ☐ Adelaide Festival of Arts, the grandest of its kind in Australia. It's held in late February and early March of even-numbered years.
- ☐ Adelaide Grand Prix, a fantastic international motor race through the city streets.
- ☐ Barossa Valley Vintage Festival, celebrating the harvest of Australia's finest wines.

For the Kids
- ☐ Adelaide Zoo, with exotic, pettable animals—right in the middle of town.
- ☐ Maritime Museum, offering a realistic but stationary "voyage" on a windjammer.
- ☐ Aquatic Centre, a world of river rapids, cascades, bubble beaches, and gushing fountains.
- ☐ Dazzleland, a popular indoor amusement park, with an amazing roller coaster.

Streets/Neighborhoods
- ☐ Victoria Square, the precise center of Adelaide, around which the city was laid out.
- ☐ North Adelaide, a residential section interlaced with parklands and sports grounds.
- ☐ Port Adelaide, sprinkled with colonial-era marine structures and vessels, sail makers, and seamans' pubs.

Parks
- ☐ Botanic Gardens, dividing Adelaide city from North Adelaide and containing the zoo.
- ☐ Bonython Park, on the banks of the Torrens River, with the Picnic Gardens—ideal for al fresco snacks.

After Dark
- ☐ Fezbah, a svelte little retreat in the Adelaide Festival Centre.
- ☐ Adelaide Casino, the world's only gambling casino housed in a former railroad station.

1. FROM A BUDGET TRAVELER'S POINT OF VIEW

BUDGET BESTS Adelaide has several splendid beaches close to downtown. But if you're unwilling to take even a short bus ride, there are the Botanic and Cresswell gardens right in city center. For people watching—very easy on the purse—stroll through Hindley Street, which blossoms at night but is quite entertaining by daylight as well.

WORTH PAYING FOR Spend $A2.50 to ride the unique **O-Bahn Busway.** This not only gives you a thrilling trip on a futuristic means of transport, but also gets you to the upscale shopping complex of Tea Tree Plaza.

2. ORIENTATION

ARRIVING

BY PLANE **Adelaide Airport** lies about five miles to the west. It's a smallish, comfortable terminal, with showers, a cafeteria, and a bar, plus the inevitable car-rental desk. Most facilities close at 9:30pm. Watch for the illuminated display of the famous Vickers Vimy bomber that carried four men on the first-ever England-Australia flight (28 days) in 1919. The coach fare to the city is $A3.50. Cab fare is around $A9.

BY TRAIN Interstate trains arrive at the **Keswick Rail Passenger Terminal,** Keswick, southwest of the city. Bus fare to town is $A2.40. For bookings and information call Keswick at 132-232 and Adelaide Railway Station at 210-1000.

BY BUS **Greyhound** coaches arrive at the Central Bus Station at 111 Franklin St., (tel. 233-2700) right downtown. Country buses also arrive and depart from here.

BY CAR If you're coming from Melbourne, the closest capital city, you'll be approaching from the southeast. The Princes Highway from Murray Bridge leads into Glen Osmond Road. This runs into South Terrace. Turn right onto King William Road to reach the city center.

TOURIST INFORMATION

The **South Australian Tourism Commission,** centrally located at 1 King William St. (tel. 212-1505), is open Monday to Friday from 8:45am to 5pm, on Saturday and Sunday from 9am to 2pm. You can obtain free maps here and make bookings at no charge for tours and accommodations in South Australia. For information on current activities in town, consult *This Week in Adelaide,* free from the Travel Centre. The *Advertiser* gives a good roundup of nighttime doings.

CITY LAYOUT

Adelaide owes much of its pleasant layout to an army officer—Col. William Light—who designed the city in 1836 and happened to be a genius at town planning. He projected the central area inside one square mile, encircled it with parks, stipulated wide avenues bisecting at right angles, and made all five city squares into gardens. As a result you virtually can't get lost in the city and you walk beneath shady trees or awnings almost wherever you go.

The exact center of Adelaide is **Victoria Square,** not in the least Victorian but marked by a very handsome modernistic fountain. From there, incidentally, you can catch Adelaide's last remaining streetcar to the beach resort of Glenelg. The city proper forms an almost perfect square, bounded on four sides by North, East, South, and West Terrace thoroughfares. **North Adelaide,** an intriguing area of restored bluestone cottages, old hotels, and plush new restaurants, actually forms part of the city but lies three-quarters of a mile north. The two parts are separated by parklands and the **Torrens River,** connected by **King William Road.** Due west lies the seashore with 20 miles of beaches and a string of resort towns, as well as Adelaide Airport. To the east and south the suburbs stretch endlessly, right to the foot of the rolling Mount Lofty Ranges. To the north beckon the wineries of the Barossa Valley (see "Easy Excursions in South Australia," below). The entire city is separated from the suburbs by an unbroken green belt of parks and recreation areas—the lungs of Adelaide and the joy of visitors from less thoughtfully designed municipalities.

NEIGHBORHOODS IN BRIEF

Unlike Sydney and Melbourne, Adelaide has no ethnic areas. There are merely streets and districts with certain characteristics, some of which are outlined below.

King William Road Adelaide's prime thoroughfare runs right through the city and changes from fairly drab at the southern end to majestic stateliness at the northern end.

North Terrace This tree-lined boulevard is flanked by some of the town's most impressive buildings, among them Parliament House and the swank Adelaide Casino.

North Adelaide Separated from downtown by a green park belt, this is a garden-wreathed residential area with some of Adelaide's costliest homes.

Melbourne Street North Adelaide's shopping-and-entertainment strip has been known for smart boutiques and antiques stores, excellent restaurants, and a sprinkling of nightspots.

Port Adelaide This venerable seaport has a lighthouse, taverns, workshops, and storage sheds dating back nearly 150 years, as well as the very modern Maritime Museum.

Springfield A garden suburb about five miles south of downtown, Springfield nestles in gently sloping hills and contains some imposing English-style mansions with private art collections.

Glenelg This popular oceanside resort is filled with typical seaside fun devices and is the destination of Adelaide's one and only streetcar ride, departing from Victoria Square downtown.

Semaphore Once a signal station and fashionable excursion goal, this oceanside resort suburb west of Adelaide is now garnished with antiques shops and is the site of Fort Glanville, restored as a showpiece of 19th-century colonial military life.

Largs Bay Another of the resort suburbs west of Adelaide, Largs Bay has more antiques shops and historic landmarks along Jetty Road. The veteran post office of the township has been turned into a coffee shop.

3. GETTING AROUND

BY PUBLIC TRANSPORTATION

BUS Buses are run by the **State Transit Authority** (STA; tel. 210-1000). There is one free service, the **Beeline Bus,** which goes along King William Road Monday to Saturday morning (during the shopping periods).

Fares are keyed to sections and travel times. The lowest fare is $A1.10, but you can save 30% by buying a book of 10 tickets—you pay only for 7.

The pride of the city's transport system is the **O-Bahn Busway,** the longest and fastest guided bus line in the world. A ride on this amazing speed track is a *must.* You catch the sleek white Mercedes-Benz coaches at stops near the corners of Currie and King William streets, and at James Place and Grenfell Street. They go through a beautiful parkland and river setting to the suburb called Paradise, and from there to the shopping center of Tea Tree Plaza. The thrilling part comes when the bus rolls onto a concrete track and is steered automatically by guided wheels that engage the edges of the track. Then the vehicle zooms along at an absolutely smooth 80 m.p.h. without the driver touching the wheel. O-Bahn buses run every few minutes and cost the same as ordinary buses.

TAXI Taxi stands are located in the city center for direct hire, or you can call **Suburban Taxi Service** (tel. 211-8888) or **Yellow Cabs** (tel. 223-3111).

BY CAR

The main office of **Thrifty** is at 100 Franklin St. (tel. 211-8788). Other companies include **Avis,** 108 Burbridge Rd. (tel. 354-0444); **Hertz,** 233 Morphett St. (tel. 231-2856); and **Budget,** 274 North Terrace (tel. 223-1400).

Adelaide is one of the easiest motoring cities in the world. The layout is logical, the roadways are generally wide, and there are very few one-way streets. Traffic is well disciplined, and fellow drivers are exceptionally courteous.

BY BICYCLE

All of Adelaide is bordered by parklands, each with special bike trails, which makes it an ideal cycling city. You can rent the steeds at **Freewheelin,** 314 Gilles St. (tel. 232-6860), at the rate of $A5 per day.

ADELAIDE

American Express The Amex office is at 13 Grenfell St. (tel. 212-7099).

Area Code The telephone area code is **08.**

Babysitters Call **AAA** (tel. 212-7090).

Business Hours **Banks** are usually open Monday to Thursday 9:30am to 4pm, Friday until 5pm. **Stores** are usually open Monday to Thursday 8:45am to 5:30pm, Friday 9am to 9pm, Saturday 8:45am to 12:30pm.

Car Rentals See "Getting Around," in this chapter.

Climate See "When to Go," Chapter 2.

Currency See "Information, Entry Requirements & Money," Chapter 2.

Currency Exchange In addition to **American Express** (see above), currency can be exchanged at **Thomas Cook,** 45 Grenfell St. (tel. 212-7713), and at most major banks and hotels.

Dentist When toothache strikes, call the **Emergency Dental Service** (tel. 272-8111).

Doctor If you require medical attention, go to **Royal Adelaide Hospital,** North Terrace (tel. 223-0230).

Drugstores Try **Maddern's Chemist,** 118 King William St. (tel. 231-2460).

Emergencies Call **000** for fire, police, or an ambulance.

Eyeglasses Try **City Vision Care,** 96 Gawler Place (tel. 212-5377).

Hairdressers/Barbers **Cross Cut Shops,** 7–8 City Cross, Rundle Mall (tel. 212-4384), cuts both men's and women's hair.

Holidays See "When to Go," Chapter 2.

Hospitals See "Doctor," above.

Hotlines **Crisis Care Service:** tel. 272-1222; **Lifeline:** tel. 212-3444.

Information See "Tourist Information," in this chapter.

Laundry/Dry Cleaning Ninety-minute cleaning can be obtained at **Adelaide Valet Service,** 120 Hindley St., open Monday to Friday 8am to 5:30pm, Saturday 8am to noon. If you arrive at the beginning of a load cycle, you'll have your garment after 90 minutes, but if the load cycle has already started, you'll have to wait another 90 minutes after the cycle has finished. They also do quick alterations and repairs. There are no laundrys in the city center. However, there are two on Hutt Street and two on O'Connell Street in North Adelaide.

Libraries The **State Library** is on North Terrace (tel. 223-8911).

Lost Property The STA maintains a lost property office at Adelaide Railway Station, North Terrace (tel. 218-2552).

Luggage Storage/Lockers Lockers are available at the railway-and-bus stations.

Newspapers/Magazines The *Advertiser* is a daily newspaper, and the *Sunday Mail* comes out on Sunday.

Photographic Needs Try **James Place Cameras,** 8 James Place (tel. 231-2464).

Police Call 218-1212 for nonemergencies.

Post Office The **General Post Office** (GPO) is at 141 King William St. (tel. 216-2222). Open Monday to Friday 8am to 6pm. There is poste restante service open Monday to Friday 8am to 5pm.

Radio Tune in to ABC-FM for classical music, or search the dial if you want to try to find something else.

Religious Services You can attend services at the following locations. **Anglican:** St. Peter's Cathedral, Pennington Terrace, Lower North Adelaide (tel. 267-4551). **Baptist:** Flinders St. (tel. 223-4550). **Greek Orthodox:** 286 Franklin St. **Jewish:** Temple Shalom, 39 Hackney Rd., Hackney (tel. 362-8281). **Roman Catholic:** St. Francis Xavier's Cathedral, Wakefield Street (tel. 231-3551). **Uniting** (Congregational, Methodist, and Presbyterian): Scots Church, 237 North Terrace (tel. 223-1505).

Restrooms Facilities are located in all parks, department stores, shopping centers, and main squares.

Safety After dark, avoid the banks of the Torrens River and the sidestreets off Hindley Street.

Shoe Repairs Try **Arnold's,** 134 Wakefield St. (tel. 223-2974).

Taxes No taxes are added to purchases or hotel and restaurant bills.

Taxis See "Getting Around," in this chapter.

Telegrams/Telex/Fax The GPO and some hotels offer these services.

Television ABC (channel 2) is the Australian Broadcasting Commission (government) station. It offers quality dramas, documentaries, concerts, news, and so forth. SBS offers ethnic programming. Channels 7, 9, and 10 are the commercial stations and offer a variety of movies, soaps, news, and sports.

Useful Telephone Numbers SA Council on the Ageing: 212-2252; Citizens' Advice Bureau: 212-4070; Youth Enquiry Service: 211-8466; Rape Enquiry Unit: 218-1212; Women's Information Switchboard: 223-1244; Gay Line: 232-0794 (7 to 10pm); AIDS Line: 232-0022; Poisons Information: 267-4999; and Disabled Information: 223-7522.

4. WHERE TO STAY

Not so long ago Adelaide suffered from an acute shortage of downtown economy lodgings. This has been alleviated—and now it's suburbia's turn to run short of budget beds. (In some Australian cities the situation is reversed.)

Accommodations can be arranged through hotels or the **South Australian Tourism Commission,** 1 King William St., Adelaide, SA 5000 (tel. 08/212-1505)—open Monday to Friday from 8:45am to 5pm, Saturday and Sunday from 9am to 2pm.

DOUBLES FOR LESS THAN $A40

PLAZA HOTEL, 85 Hindley St., Adelaide, SA 5000. Tel. 08/231-6371.
64 rms (14 with bath).
$ Rates: $A25 single without bath, $A35 single with bath; $A35 double without bath, $A45 double with bath.

The Plaza Hotel, an older building with much charm and a youngish clientele, is maintained with a great deal of tender loving care. The interior balconies look down on a palm-studded courtyard that gives the place a distinctly New Orleans air. The rooms come with hot- and cold-water basins and innerspring mattresses. The shared bathrooms are excellent and colorful.

WEST'S PRIVATE HOTEL, 110B Hindley St., Adelaide, SA 5000. Tel. 08/231-7575. Fax 08/2314804. 31 rms (none with bath).
$ Rates: $A25 single, $A35 double. Extra person $A15. BC, MC, V.

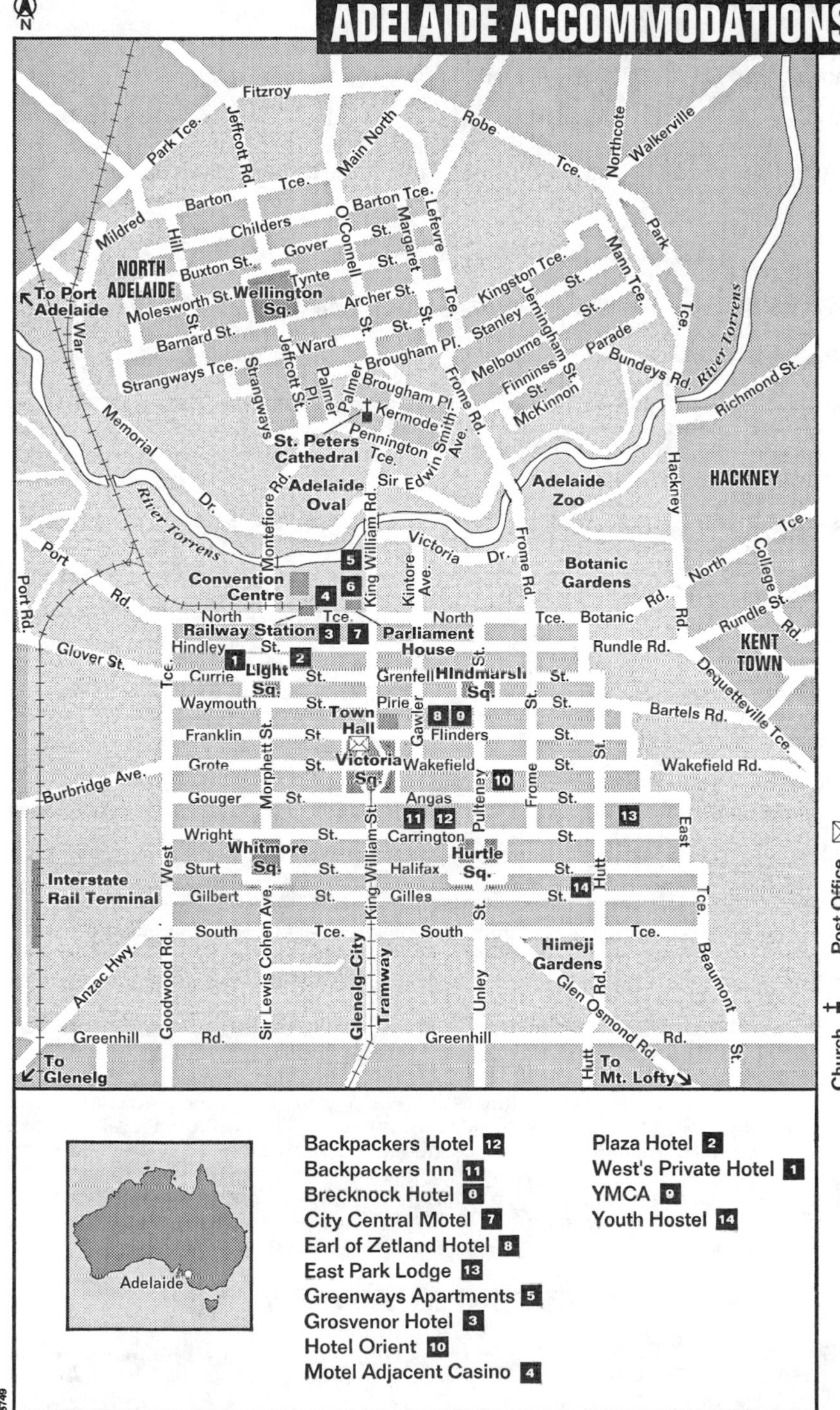
ADELAIDE ACCOMMODATIONS
N
Fitzroy
Park Tce.
Jeffcott Rd.
Main North
Robe
Tce.
Northcote
Walkerville
Barton
Tce.
Barton Tce.
Mildred
Hill
Childers
St.
Gover
St.
O'Connell
Margaret
Lefevre
Park
NORTH ADELAIDE
Buxton St.
Tynte
Wellington Sq.
Kingston Tce.
Mann Tce.
To Port Adelaide
Molesworth St.
Archer St.
St.
Tce.
Tce.
War
Barnard St.
Ward
St.
Stanley
Jerningham
River Torrens
Strangways Tce.
Jeffcott St.
Brougham Pl.
Melbourne
Parade
Bundeys Rd.
Richmond St.
Strangways
Palmer Pl.
Brougham Pl.
Frome Rd.
Finniss St.
Memorial
Kermode
Smith Ave.
McKinnon
St. Peters Cathedral
Pennington Tce.
Hackney
HACKNEY
Montefiore Rd.
Adelaide Oval
Sir Edwin
Adelaide Zoo
Dr.
River Torrens
King William Rd.
Victoria Dr.
Frome Rd.
Botanic Gardens
Port Rd.
Port
Convention Centre
Kintore Ave.
North
College
Tce.
Rd.
North Tce.
North Tce.
Tce.
Botanic
Rd.
Rundle St.
Railway Station
Parliament House
Rundle Rd.
KENT TOWN
Glover St.
Hindley St.
Light Sq.
Currie St.
Grenfell
Hindmarsh Sq.
St.
Dequetteville Tce.
Waymouth St.
Pirie
Town Hall
St.
Bartels Rd.
Franklin St.
Flinders
St.
Gawler
Grote St.
Victoria Sq.
Wakefield
St.
Wakefield Rd.
Burbridge Ave.
Gouger St.
Morphett St.
Angas
Pulteney
Frome
St.
East
Wright St.
Carrington
St.
Whitmore Sq.
Hurtle Sq.
Interstate Rail Terminal
West Tce.
Sturt St.
Halifax
St.
Hutt
Gilbert St.
Gilles
St.
South Tce.
South
Tce.
Tce.
Anzac Hwy.
Goodwood Rd.
Sir Lewis Cohen Ave.
Glenelg–City Tramway
Unley
Himeji Gardens
Glen Osmond Rd.
Beaumont
Greenhill Rd.
Greenhill
Rd.
St.
To Glenelg
Hutt
To Mt. Lofty
Post Office
Church
Adelaide
Backpackers Hotel 12
Backpackers Inn 11
Brecknock Hotel 6
City Central Motel 7
Earl of Zetland Hotel 8
East Park Lodge 13
Greenways Apartments 5
Grosvenor Hotel 3
Hotel Orient 10
Motel Adjacent Casino 4
Plaza Hotel 2
West's Private Hotel 1
YMCA 9
Youth Hostel 14

6749

This is an economy find with a very plain exterior but comfortable and excellently maintained sleeping quarters. Behind the glass doorway, the hall is bare and the stairs are rather steep; there's no elevator. The bedrooms share nine sparkling-clean bathrooms, and there is a guest laundry and a TV lounge on the premises. The rooms have no frills but all essentials: hot- and cold-water basins, ceiling fans, bedside lamps, decent-size wardrobes, and wall-to-wall carpeting. The hotel provides no meals, but there are plenty of restaurants nearby.

DOUBLES FOR LESS THAN $A70

CITY CENTRAL MOTEL, 23 Hindley St., Adelaide, SA 5000. Tel. 08/231-4049. Fax 08/231-4804. 12 rms (all with shower). A/C TV TEL

$ Rates: $A49 single, $A54 double. AE, MC, V.

This is not, technically, a motel, but it couldn't be any more central: right in the heart of the busiest shopping street. The reception desk is up one flight of steep stairs. The units are on the small side and devoid of decoration, but they are very well equipped—each with its own shower and toilet, refrigerator, radio, small wardrobe, ceiling light, and bedside lamp.

COLLEY MOTEL, 22 Colley Terrace, Glenelg, SA 5045. Tel. 08/295-7535. 9 rms (all with bath). A/C TV TEL **Tram:** Take the Glenelg tram (the only streetcar in town).

$ Rates: $A40–$A75, depending on the season. AE, MC, V.

The Colley Motel is located in Adelaide's most popular seaside suburb, about six miles from downtown. A red-brick building facing the oceanfront and amusement park, the Colley offers handsomely furnished and completely self-contained units. Each has a goodsize kitchen with a refrigerator, plus all utensils for housekeeping, and particularly well-sprung beds. (Rates vary sharply between normal and high season because this is a resort establishment.)

EARL OF ZETLAND HOTEL, corner of Gawler Place and Flinders St., Adelaide, SA 5000. Tel. 08/223-5500. Fax 08/223-5243. 31 rms (all with shower). A/C TV TEL

$ Rates: $A45–$A50 single, $A59 double. AE, MC, V.

Located in central Adelaide this small peach-colored building has a very busy location. The hotel is fully air-conditioned and has a main front bar and two more intimate—and comfortable—saloon bars, plus the salad bar restaurant. Rooms are nicely decorated and well furnished, all with tea- and coffee-making equipment and radios. It's a mite above our budget for singles, but the doubles make it nicely.

MOTEL ADJACENT CASINO, 25 Bank St., Adelaide, SA 5000. Tel. 08/231-8881. Fax 08/231-1021. 49 rms (all with bath). A/C TV TEL

$ Rates: $A50–$A60 single, $A70–$A79 double. AE, BC, DC, MC, V.

Located in the heart of Adelaide (the casino is across the road), the motel has a small unassuming lobby but a lot of facilities on the premises. The position is ideal—a small alley just off busy Hindley Street. Corridors are impeccably kept, the bedrooms pleasantly furnished, with vast wardrobes, good bedside lights, plenty of drawers, and big mirrors you can actually see all of yourself in. Some rooms come with full-cooking facilities. There is a restaurant in the building as well as a guest laundry, dry cleaner, tour-booking desk, and souvenir shop. Rates vary according to season.

SERVICED SUITES

GREENWAYS APARTMENTS, 41–45 King William Rd., North Adelaide, SA 5006. Tel. 08/267-5903. Fax 08/267-1790. 24 rms (all with bath). A/C TV TEL **Parking:** Off street.

$ Rates: 1-bedroom suite $A70 single, $A80 double; $A130 and up 3-bedroom suite for 7. Minimum stay of 3 days required. BC, MC, V.

Somewhat high on the price scale but also handy to town is the Greenways Apartments, an attractively modern three-story building so close to the center as to be almost in it. Its rooms are tastefully furnished as well as complete, with light-and-cheery color schemes and little extras such as electric blankets and clock radios. The units have separate, fully equipped kitchens, bathrooms, lounge-and-dining areas, ample wardrobe and drawer space, and intimate bedside lamps. There is also a guest laundry. It's an outstandingly well-managed place.

POWELL'S COURT MOTEL, 2 Glen Osmond Rd., Parkside, SA 5063. Tel. 08/271-7033. Fax 08/271-1511. 16 rms (12 with bath). A/C TV TEL **Parking:** Off street.

$ Rates: From $A45 single to $A48 double to $A55 triple to $A60 quad. Weekly rates available off-season. AE, MC, V.

This is a real find for budget travelers, particularly groups of three or more. Apartments here come in eight different layouts, so you can pick one that fits your exact requirements. All are surprisingly large and have spacious, fully equipped kitchens—*not* kitchenettes. The flats have separate sitting rooms and bedrooms, big refrigerators, and excellent beds fitted with allergy-free mattresses. The furnishings are not lavish, but there are ample wardrobe space, wall-to-wall carpeting, and bedside lamps. You can arrange daily fresh bread, newspaper, and milk deliveries. The white four-story building has an elevator and a fine view of the surrounding green hills.

BED & BREAKFASTS

Most bed-and-breakfast establishments in central Adelaide are large or small pubs, all with a busy bar trade.

BRECKNOCK HOTEL, 401 King William St., Adelaide, SA 5000. Tel. 08/231-5467. Fax 08/410-1968. 8 rms (none with bath). A/C

$ Rates (including breakfast): $A30 single, $A45 double. AE, MC, V.

A mellow white corner building with a round tower on top, the Brecknock is run by an enthusiastic Aussie-Canadian couple who have turned it into a budget showpiece. The lobby, stairs, and rooms are nicely carpeted; the hotel beer garden is charming, and the TV lounge spacious. The restaurant on the premises provides three meals six days a week—on Sunday, breakfast comes by way of room service (it's continental but ample). There are also three bars downstairs, plus a snooker room and a guest laundry. Despite the pub action below, the guest rooms are remarkably quiet and tranquil. Although not luxurious, rooms are well equipped, with hot- and cold-water basins, ceiling fans, electric blankets, large wardrobes, bedside mirrors, tea- and coffee-making equipment, and ceiling lights. The entire house is immaculately kept, and the management bends over backward to please.

HOTEL ORIENT, corner of Wakefield and Pulteney Sts., Adelaide, SA 5000. Tel. 08/223-3551. 10 rms (none with bath).

$ Rates (including breakfast): $A25 single, $A35 double. AE, MC, V.

The Hotel Orient calls itself "The Country Pub in the Middle of Town," and there is a certain rustic ambience about the simple two-story building. There are a busy bar downstairs and spick-and-span guest rooms above, plus a nicely appointed lounge. Guests share two bathrooms and a large kitchen, which has all the necessary utensils. Breakfast is a help-yourself affair. Most of the rooms are carpeted, have ceiling lights only, and provide ample wardrobe space, but otherwise furnishings are somewhat Spartan. The hotel dining room supplies lunch daily, for which you pay extra.

KING'S HEAD HOTEL, 357 King William St., Adelaide, SA 5000. Tel. 08/212-6657. Fax 08/231-2602. 9 rms (none with bath).

$ Rates (including breakfast): $A20 per person. AE, DC, MC, V.

This is one of the most economical bed-and-breakfasts: a lovely old colonial structure, stone fronted, with brass coach lanterns above the doorway and an overhanging balcony providing shelter from rain or sun. The place exudes 19th-century charm and has been in the same family for four generations, but it has very limited facilities for houseguests.

HOSTELS, Y's & DORMS

The **Youth Hostel** here is the most central of any—about a mile from the city. The YH, 290 Gilles St., Adelaide, SA 5000 (tel. 08/223-6007), is near a bus stop, post office, and several stores in adjacent Hutt Street. Overnight fees are $A11 for seniors, $A7.50 for juniors. Sheet bags are for rent for $A2. Only members may stay at the hostels, but it's possible to join at the door. Sleeping bags and smoking are not permitted.

Adelaide University, North Terrace, used to be a gold mine for either providing or finding student accommodations during the holidays. Alas, the situation has changed. Your chances of finding accommodations have become slimmer, but it's still worth a try. Call 223-4333, ext. 2915, Monday to Friday from 9am to 5pm.

Currently there are five centrally located backpackers in Adelaide—by the time you get there they'll probably have multiplied.

BACKPACKERS HOSTEL, 263 Gilles St., Adelaide, SA 5000. Tel. 08/223-5680.

$ Rates: $A12 per person. MC, V.

This hostel is located in a century-old colonial cottage with considerable period charm and is known for its excellent travel-information service. It is centrally located and has a garden and barbecue areas.

BACKPACKERS INN, 112 Carrington St., Adelaide, SA 5000. Tel. 08/223-6635. 52 beds (shared bath).

$ Rates: $A13 single, $A15 double. BC, MC, V.

This is a restored history-steeped former pub now fitted with double rooms and dormitory accommodations, a modern kitchen, plus showers and laundry. The inn also arranges tour bookings, and displays an invaluable notice board for lifts and local events.

EAST PARK LODGE, 341 Angas St., Adelaide, SA 5000. Tel. 08/223-1228. 50 rms (none with bath).

$ Rates: $A12 dorm, $A16 single, $A15 per person double. MC, V.

A charming three-story heritage building converted into a hostel, the East Park Lodge beckons you with a large front veranda in the best colonial tradition. The interior is surprisingly modern, with a large guest kitchen, a dining room that is equipped with an automatic "café bar," a TV lounge, and a rooftop sunbathing area. Rooms are small but bright and airy and furnished with the basics. The lodge stands in central Adelaide, handy to everything, and it arranges courtesy transport from the nearby bus terminal.

YMCA, 76 Flinders St., Adelaide, SA 5000. Tel. 08/223-1611. Fax 08/232-2920.

$ Rates: $A11 dorm bed per day; $A18 single per day, $A108 single per week; $A30 twin per day, $A180 twin per week. AE, MC, V.

Adelaide's centrally located YMCA, like so many institutions, has dropped its sex barriers and now caters to men, women, and family groups. It's a very modern building with glass walls overlooking a small rock garden. The rooms are bright and airy, nicely carpeted, and equipped with fair-size wardrobes, but lighting fixtures are not the best. The Y has vending machines dispensing hot-and-cold edibles and potables, a TV lounge, a reading room, and laundry facilities, as well as squash courts and a sauna. The rates do not include breakfast—which comes à la carte—but prices on the premises are among the lowest in town. You can get cereal and milk, poached eggs, buttered toast, and tea or coffee for $A4.30.

NEARBY ACCOMMODATIONS

These are bed-and-breakfast operations inspected by **Tourism South Australia.** They feature a wide choice of settings—historic cottages, farmhouses, guest rooms in private homes, and resort suites, most in country areas but some within an easy train or bus ride of Adelaide. It's a good way to see the state beyond the metropolitan area and the best way to meet the locals. Rates vary considerably, but the standard of comfort and meals is very good in all price ranges, and the hospitality is warm and personal. The establishments below were chosen for their proximity to Adelaide and for their modest tariffs, but there are dozens of others available. Bookings can be made either directly or through the **South Australian Tourism Commission,** 11 King William St., Adelaide, SA 5000 (tel. 08/212-1505).

ALDGATE LODGE, 27 Strathalbyn Rd., Aldgate, SA 5154. Tel. 08/370-9337. Fax 08/339-4899. 3 rms (all with shower). A/C TV TEL

$ Rates (including breakfast): $A45 single, $A65–$A120 double. BC, MC, V.

The lodge is set on part of a historic estate, surrounded by trees and shrubs and an herb garden. All rooms have private entrances, and the house has a communal lounge with a working fireplace. Furnishings are a mix of modern and cottage antique, and rooms are decorated with fresh flowers. Aldgate is near national flora-and-fauna parks and about 30 minutes by train from Adelaide.

CHIPPINGS, 32 Ludgate Hill Rd., Aldgate, SA 5154. Tel. 08/339-1008. 1 suite (with bath). A/C TV TEL **Transportation:** Bus to Stirling or train to Aldgate. **Parking:** Free.

$ Rates (including pick up at transportation terminals): $A65 single, $A80 double. No credit cards. Special discount for stays over 4 nights.

Located in the beautiful Adelaide hills, Chippings is a private cottage in a garden setting, close to a wildlife sanctuary. The cottage has antique furniture and a modern bathroom. A full breakfast is served, with bacon and eggs and all the trimmings—gratis.

CAMPING

Adelaide has about 20 caravan (R.V.) parks within a 15-mile radius of the city. Two of the closest with on-site caravans for rent (at around $A34 per night) are **Adelaide Caravan Park,** Bruton Street, Hackney (tel. 08/363-1566); and **West Beach Caravan Park,** Military Road, on the seafront (tel. 08/356-7654), for towed caravans or tenters.

WORTH THE EXTRA MONEY

GROSVENOR HOTEL, 125 North Terrace, Adelaide, SA 5000. Tel. 08/231-2961. Fax 08/231-0765. Telex AA 82634. 290 rms (all with bath). A/C MINIBAR TV TEL **Parking:** Free.

$ Rates: $A65 single; $A80 double. AE, BC, DC, MC, V.

The majestic Edwardian Grosvenor Hotel, directly opposite the railway station, would appear squarely in the luxury class. And so it is, except for its "budget sleepers," an arrangement other establishments should copy. These rooms are simpler—and very much cheaper—than the Grosvenor's standard accommodations. But their guests get all the trimmings of a deluxe hostelry—bars, restaurants, hall porters, and a very svelte atmosphere. The building is air-conditioned and has a guest laundry, a gymnasium, a suana, and one of the finest dining rooms in town. Breakfast here is an event: Apart from juices, coffee, cereals, toast, honey, and jams, it includes an absolutely sumptuous hot buffet guaranteed to tide you over lunch for $A15. Rates quoted are for the budget sleepers, *not* for the standard rooms, which hover around the $A120 mark.

5. WHERE TO EAT

Being a much smaller city than Sydney and Melbourne, Adelaide does not have the volume or variety of eateries found in those cities. But the local culinary standards are remarkably high, particularly in the realm of pub grub. You'll probably agree with this, providing that you don't start off by sampling the South Australian specialty—**floaters,** a meat pie floating on or in pea soup. It tastes nearly as gruesome as it reads.

In Adelaide the **hotel counter lunch** is still a flourishing institution. Stroll along Hindley Street and drop into any of the wayside pubs competing for the city crowds at noon. For a tab of $A6 to $A7, you can fill up on richly simple items like chicken Maryland, lamb cutlets, or steak and mushrooms, as long as you don't mind the throng of humanity doing likewise.

Apart from counter lunches, most of the good cheap establishments are non-Australian, which is pretty much the rule throughout the country. Because of pleasantly liberal licensing laws, Adelaide has few BYOs, which is nice on the one hand, because you can have the great local wines with almost every meal. On the other hand, this tends to cost you more because no restaurant sells liquor at store prices. Ah, well, you can't win them all.

MEALS FOR LESS THAN $A13

CEYLON HUT, 27 Bank St., Adelaide. Tel. 231-2034.

Cuisine: INDIAN. **Reservations:** Accepted.
$ Prices: Appetizers $A3.25–$A8.30, main courses $A10.30–$A15. AE, MC, V.
Open: Mon–Sat noon–10pm.

This is a richly carpeted (walls and all) Indian eatery, redolent with the aroma of curry and kindred spices. Curry dishes go from $A10.30 for beef, chicken, and pork to $A15 for the most expensive seafood curry. The restaurant also has an excellent range of South Australian wines.

THE COSY HOME COFFEE HOUSE, 116 Melbourne St., North Adelaide. Tel. 267-2469.

Cuisine: AUSTRIAN. **Reservations:** Not necessary.
$ Prices: Appetizers $A4.50–$A5.60, main courses $A4.50–$A10.80. AE, MC, V.
Open: Mon–Wed 11am–6pm, Thurs–Sat until 10pm, Sun noon–9pm.

The Cosy Home Coffee House doesn't look very much like either a cosy home or a coffeehouse. It's a delicatessen festooned with original landscape paintings. The white garden tables and chairs inside and out front, plus bare tile floors, don't make for much atmosphere. But the place serves some of the best and cheapest German-Austrian specialties anywhere, and the service is what you'd expect in a vastly more deluxe eatery. A copious quantity of goulash with noodles goes for $A6.20, Kasseler (smoked pork) with sauerkraut for $A7.20. Don't forget to leave room for a slice of the memorable Esterhazy torte. The background music—a delightful mélange of German folk and vintage jazz—keeps your meal happy.

EAT STREET CAFE, 138 Gawler Place, off Pirie St., Adelaide. Tel. 231-4778.

Cuisine: INTERNATIONAL. **Reservations:** Not necessary.
$ Prices: Main courses $A6. No credit cards.
Open: Mon–Fri 10am–6pm, Sat until 1pm.

The Eat Street Café is a bright, shiny, glassed-in eatery, with tables and chairs spilling out into the little yard—about as intimate as a goldfish bowl, but with fast-and-efficient service and ample breathing space. Any one hot meal with salad costs $A5.50; any two hot meals with rice go for $A6.50. Try the schnitzelburger or the roast chicken. Or, if you're on a tight budget, try the excellent hot roast-lamb roll for $A3.

FAST EDDY'S, Central Hindley St.

Cuisine: AUSSIE-AMERICAN. **Reservations:** Not accepted.
$ Prices: $A3.95–$A10.95. No credit cards.
Open: 24 hrs.

Another link in the chain that now girdles most Australian capitals, Fast Eddy's lives up to its title, but hurries only the service—not the eaters. You can get any breakfast combination here round-the-clock, even at midnight. There are also eight kinds of hamburger (including vegetarian), charcoal-grilled steak, pasta, pizza, "Fast Eduardo's nachos," pancakes, and American-style milk shakes. The menus are a scream (steal one), and good South Australian Riesling comes at $A1.65 a glass.

PASTA PALACE, 100 Hindley St., Adelaide. Tel. 231-9500.
Cuisine: ITALIAN. **Reservations:** Accepted.
$ Prices: Appetizers $A4–$A7.90, main courses $A9–$A12.90. AE, MC, V. Owners of this book get a 10% discount.
Open: Mon–Thurs 5:30pm until 9:45pm, Fri–Sat 5:30pm until "late," Sun until 9:30pm.

This place has high ceilings and joyous decorations in the form of banners, posters, abstract art, potted plants, and hanging ferns, as well as smartly polished wooden chairs and good elbow space between tables. A fine blended house wine is served for $A1.50 per glass, and this is one of the few places in Adelaide that offers good crusty Italian bread instead of the ubiquitous garlic bread that restaurateurs love because it enables them to use up all their stale loaves. The fresh homemade pasta dishes cost between $A9 and $A10; there's also a line of vegetarian selections. Try the truly superb *tartuffo* chocolate delight if you've left room for such a frivolity.

PENANG, 23 Gilbert Place. Tel. 231-2552.
Cuisine: MALAYSIAN. **Reservations:** Accepted.
$ Prices: Appetizers $A1.20–$A3; main courses $A4.50–$A6. No credit cards.
Open: Mon–Sat 11am–10pm. Closed Sun.

Penang is a plain little eatery with metal tables and chairs, the walls enlivened by colorful Malaysian posters. The windows overlook a picturesque alley and the service is smooth and fast. You get most of the standard Malay favorites, including a dozen kinds of rich noodle soup and the same number of spicy noodle dishes. You might try the combination *yee mee* with chicken, prawns, pork, and vegetables. Another hot highlight is the dried curry beef *rendang*. The place serves a very agreeable chardonnay house wine at $A2 per glass.

TUN SING, 147 Hindley St., Adelaide. Tel. 212-4967.
Cuisine: CHINESE. **Reservations:** Accepted.
$ Prices: Appetizers $A4, main courses $A8.50–$A10.50. AE, MC, V.
Open: Daily 6pm–2am.

This is a blessed late bird with a large, handsome dining room that has street windows through which to watch the passing parade, tasseled lanterns, and an un-Chinese chalked blackboard announcing the chef's specials. The menu is limited to the usual Cantonese favorites, but the helpings are larger than those elsewhere. Each dish amounts to a meal in itself. Most come to $A9.50, but certain specialties—like king prawns in *sartee*—cost $A11.80. Another first-rate item is the chicken in ginger sauce.

MEALS FOR LESS THAN $A18

ARKABA STEAK CELLAR, Gilbert Place, Adelaide. Tel. 211-2912.
Cuisine: AUSTRALIAN. **Reservations:** Not necessary.
$ Prices: Appetizers $A7.50, main courses $A10.50–$A13. AE, BC, MC, V.
Open: Mon–Sat noon–10pm.

Directly opposite Penang (see above) is the Arkaba Steak Cellar, a costlier establishment but a beautiful place. It looks exactly like a European cellar bistro, with heavy wooden tables, tiled floors, and wine cask ends set into the walls. A club or rump steak served with baked potato, coleslaw, and potato salad will set you back $A13.

KUBLAI KHAN, 3 St. Ann's Place, Parkside. Tel. 272-8688.
Cuisine: MONGOLIAN. **Reservations:** Not necessary.
$ Prices: All you can eat $A14.50. AE, BC, MC, V.
Open: Daily noon–10pm.

(S) This place does not have an ideal name, for the Great Khan allegedly ate horsemeat ridden tender under his saddle, but this excellent Mongolian establishment makes a theatrical event out of its repasts. You choose your delectables from a vast range of meats and vegetables, then watch the chef pick them up with gigantic chopsticks and cook them on the likewise gigantic barbecue. The rule here is *All You Can Eat for $A14.50!* So it's up to you to have a gigantic feast. Mongolian fare is about as fiery as Hunan cuisine, but the Kublai also puts on à la carte seafood. The restaurant is about five minutes away from downtown.

THE WELLINGTON, 2 Wellington Sq., North Adelaide. Tel. 267-1322.
Cuisine: AUSTRALIAN. **Reservations:** Accepted.
$ Prices: Appetizers $A7.50, main courses $A12–$A14. AE, DC, MC, V.
Open: Mon–Sat 6–9pm.

This is the dining room of the Wellington Hotel, a traditional Oz pub, and the fare is not to be confused with what's being served over the counter in the hotel's saloon bar. The dining area is a lovely garden room with open front windows overlooking big shade trees and adjoining rose gardens. The mixed salads here are outstanding and come in heaped platters with ingredients so fresh that they seem to have been picked that morning. And the french fries that accompany the main courses have the right crunchy crispness you so rarely get. As a main course I'd suggest either the char-grilled salmon or the fettuccine prepared with bacon and spinach.

ZAPATA'S, 42 Melbourne St., North Adelaide. Tel. 267-4653.
Cuisine: MEXICAN. **Reservations:** Recommended.
$ Prices: Appetizers $A3.90–$A7.90, main courses $A11.90–$A14.90. AE, BC, DC, MC, V.
Open: Mon–Sat from 6pm.

✪ You imbibe the spirit of Zapata the moment you enter, for authentic historical photos of the great revolutionary and his gun-toting contemporaries decorate the walls. They watch over you while you sample a plate of nachos and sip a frozen margarita. The menu is also authentic, but diverse enough to range from mildly flavorful to wildly spicy. The house specialty is fajitas, which come in sizzling steak, chicken, or vegetarian versions. Postprandial refreshments include an exotic tipple called "rattler bite." If you've never handled one before, manager Tony Spalding will be glad to give you instructions.

SPECIALTY DINING

LOCAL BUDGET BETS

FLOATERS This aforementioned South Australian specialty is the main draw of the two mobile pie carts that take up position each night and stay until early morning. One is adjacent to the General Post Office, the other is at the Railway Station. In a city not blessed with too many late-night eateries, they *are* a blessing. And luckily they also sell pies and pea soup separately. It's amazing how much better they taste apart. You can also get tea and coffee there—the former good and strong, the latter unmentionable.

INTERNATIONAL DINING COMPLEX The **Underground,** in the basement at the corner of Hindley and Bank streets, is dressed up (or down) like a London tube station, train signs and all. But the fare offered by the rows of food stalls along the walls is truly international. Choose from authentic Lebanese, Chinese, Italian, Thai, Singaporean, seafood, or vegetarian offerings. The range goes from breaded calamari to Penang curry to marinated chicken wings to a delicious mixture called *hey mee*, consisting of prawns, pork, noodles, and bean sprouts swimming in prawn soup. Main dishes cost from $A3.80 to $A5. There is a separate bar on the premises, and the place is open Monday to Saturday from 10am "until late."

COFFEE BREAKS & AFTERNOON TEA Adelaide has a number of delightful coffee-and-snack retreats, most of which also serve light meals, and two of which I consider absolutely outstanding. ✪ **The Coffee Pot,** 27 Rundle Mall, at James Place (tel. 212-1613), is a wonderfully aromatic coffee store and lounge selling every conceivable kind of coffee-making utensil, including the beans. Try the hot apricot pie

- International newspaper tycoon Rupert Murdoch, an Adelaide native, began his rise with one family paper, the *News*.
- The Adelaide Grand Prix is a motor race run through the downtown streets at speeds of up to 280 m.p.h.
- The world's largest rocking horse stands at the Gumeracha toy factory. It's 50 feet high and has an observation platform on its back.
- Adelaide's deluxe gambling casino is part of a railroad station.
- Australia's first nudist beach was solemnly opened at Maslins, outside Adelaide.
- Coober Pedy is an Aboriginal term meaning "white man's hole"—most of the 2,000 inhabitants of that opal-mining town live underground to escape the heat.
- Kangaroo Island, South Australia's popular wildlife resort, contains about three-quarters of the world's estimated 10,000 sea lions.

with whipped cream for $A2.95 or the cream and fruit-smothered Pavlova for $A2.50. Coffee costs $A2.15 per superb cup, but an extra cup is free—a rare gesture in Australia. Likewise free is the selection of newspapers and magazines. Open Monday to Saturday 8:30am to 6:30pm, **Café Boulevard,** on Hindley Street at Gilbert Place (tel. 231-5734), is rather elegantly European, with plushly upholstered seating to spoil your derriere and half-curtained windows to provide you with a view of the street life. There are Tiffany-style lamps over the window tables and, in the rear, a glass display case presenting tempting Italian-style desserts. (I recommend the apricot-and-custard slices and the napoleons.) Open daily until midnight.

At 36 Melbourne St., North Adelaide, and in a class of its own, is the **Olde Vic** (tel. 267-5115). An antiques shop combined with a very English tearoom, the Olde Vic caters simultaneously to your artistic, acquisitive, and culinary cravings. For good measure it has a charming back garden. The antiques for sale range from furniture to riding saddles, from oil lamps to oil paintings. After browsing, settle down to a scrumptuous Devonshire tea with home-baked scones, cream, and strawberry topping for $A5.70. Open Wednesday to Sunday from 10:30am to 5pm.

LATE-NIGHT/24-HOUR A late-night alternative to the floaters carts is the **Pancake Kitchen,** Gilbert Place (tel. 211-7912). The Pancake Kitchen hums in what was originally a small cottage; now it has been extended into five oddly shaped dining rooms. The management provides free magazines in case you like reading with your meals. The majority of the young and very lively clientele prefer talking or flirting, which they do enthusiastically in the booths set aside for that purpose—maybe. The menu offers much besides pancakes—Russian or Jewish blintzes, for instance—all in the $A5.60 to $A11.60 range. This is a haven for hungry wayfarers. You can make reservations if you wish and pay by credit card.

6. ATTRACTIONS

If you happen to hit Adelaide during the Festival of Arts (see "Australia Calendar of Events" in Chapter 2), you'll have a difficult time deciding which of the avalanche of attractions to watch. But even in off years the **Adelaide Festival Centre Complex** (see below) is the town's top tourist draw.

The Adelaide Festival, staged in March every second year, is Australia's premier cultural event. For three weeks the nation's top performers, reinforced by overseas celebrities, turn the city into the artistic hub of the continent. The festivities cover almost the entire range of artistic expression, from theater, music, and dance to cabaret, films, Aboriginal ceremonies, street parades, and experimental happenings difficult to categorize. For Australian performers an invitation to participate can be either a first step to fame or the high point of a career.

Along the gently winding **Torrens River,** between Adelaide and North Adelaide, you can hire one of the sailing, rowing, or pedaling craft that form the Popeye fleet, based on a jetty in beautiful **Cresswell Gardens.** If you're feeling a bit more energetic, you can climb Montefiore Hill (off Montefiore Road) to the splendid lookout called **Light's Vision,** stand under the statue of Col. William Light, and get a panoramic vista of the city he designed so well.

SUGGESTED ITINERARIES

IF YOU HAVE 1 DAY Fortunately, the main sights of Adelaide are concentrated in a relatively small area. Start with a tour of the Adelaide Festival Centre, an impressive theater-and-concert complex. It stands just behind the casino, an amazing structure with Adelaide Railway Station on the ground floor and the gambling facilities upstairs.

Step out onto North Terrace, Adelaide's famed "kilometre of culture." Turn left and walk past the marble splendor of Government House to the huge block containing Adelaide University, the Art Gallery of South Australia, and the South Australian Museum. Before you start touring them it might be a good idea to stop for refreshments at one of the university's very economical bistros.

North of North Terrace stretch the vast and beautiful parklands containing the Botanic Gardens and Adelaide Zoo, the most conveniently situated in Australia. When you're through admiring the inhabitants, catch the bus to Rundle Street, which parallels North Terrace. Rundle Mall is Adelaide's prime shopping region, a pedestrian haven of arcades and specialty stores.

Now it'll be dinnertime. Cross King William Road to Hindley Street, *the* food-and-entertainment strip. You'll find several restaurants there described under "Where to Eat" earlier in this chapter. Afterward, enjoy some of the nightspots within ambling distance on the street (see "Evening Entertainment," below).

IF YOU HAVE 2 DAYS Follow the itinerary above for your first day. Use the morning of your second day to tour the fascinating Migration Museum on Kintore Avenue, off North Terrace. Then head over to the Old Parliament House on North Terrace to see the state's history unfold in a laser-disk audiovisual.

For the afternoon and evening you face a difficult choice: it's either Port Adelaide or Glenelg. You can't manage both in the allotted time, so it depends what you're in the mood for. Port Adelaide means historic walks, historic ships, buildings, and taverns. Glenelg is sheer fun: the ocean beach, the amusement park, jet skis, a free museum of exotic seashells, and bevies of beachcombers.

Have dinner in one of the score of seafood restaurants, then catch the last tram back to town.

IF YOU HAVE 3 OR 4 DAYS Follow the itinerary above for your first two days. Your third day gives you a chance to venture out into Adelaide's outstandingly lovely surroundings or to visit Port Adelaide or Glenelg, whichever one you missed, then venture out on your fourth day. The Adelaide Hills fringe the city like a protective shield, and you can be among them in 50 minutes by taking bus no. 820 from the corner of Currie and Grenfell streets. The hills are dotted with picturesque villages and swarming with wildlife. This is the only place where you'll see koala ladders laid over concrete highways to help the little critters cross safely. There are three wildlife parks in the hills, including Warrawong, which runs a special platypus-breeding program.

The most intriguing village is Hahndorf, the oldest existing German settlement in Australia. The original inhabitants came from East Prussia in the 1840s to escape religious persecution. Today the population is mixed and tourist minded, but a whole cluster of German workshops, stores, and restaurants seem to have been transported directly from Europe.

IF YOU HAVE 5 DAYS One of Adelaide's greatest attractions, the wine-growing region of the Barossa Valley, gets a special tour under "Easy Excursions: South Australia State" at the end of this chapter. It takes an entire day, at the very least, to sample its charms.

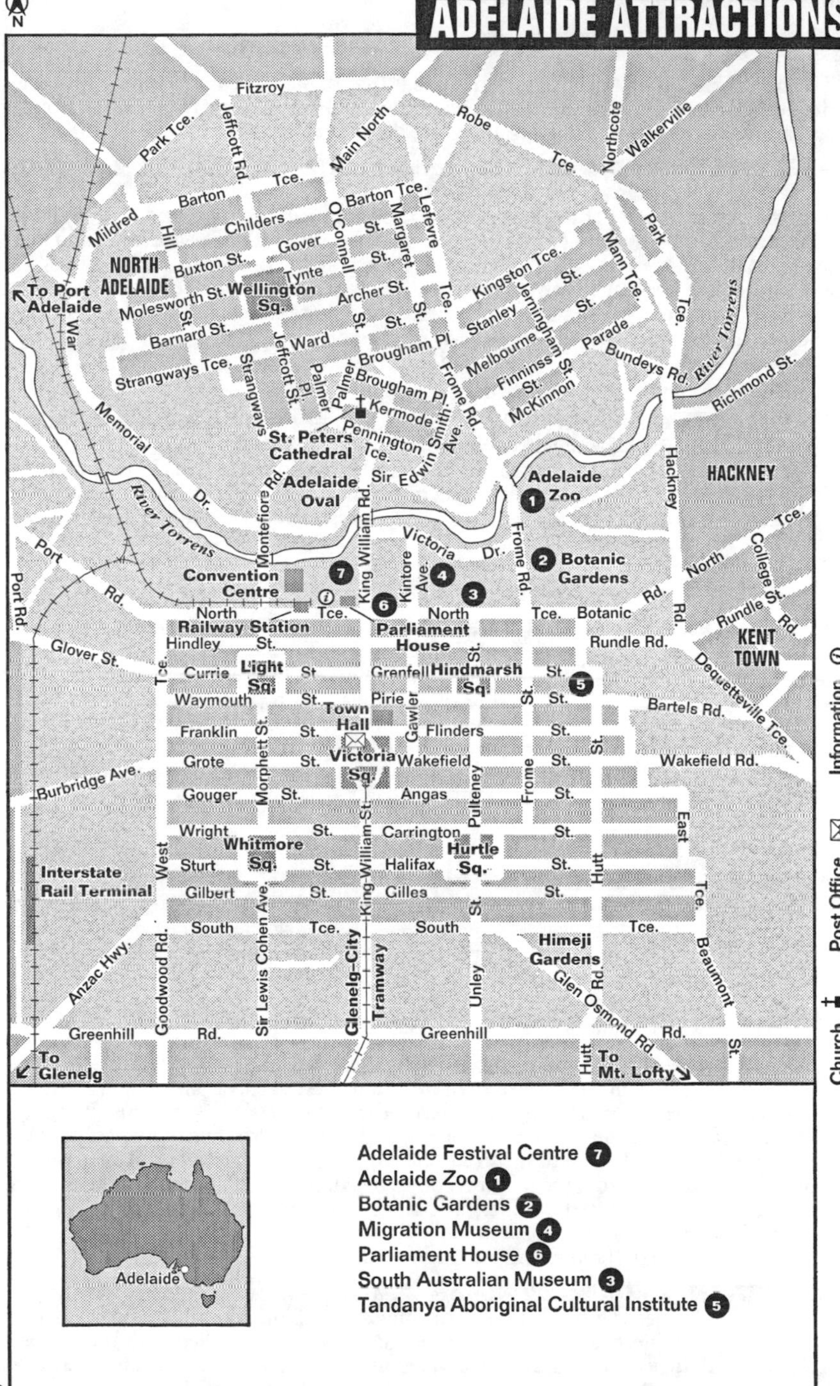

ADELAIDE ATTRACTIONS
N
NORTH ADELAIDE
HACKNEY
KENT TOWN
To Port Adelaide
To Glenelg
To Mt. Lofty
Wellington Sq.
St. Peters Cathedral
Adelaide Oval
Adelaide Zoo
Botanic Gardens
Convention Centre
Railway Station
Parliament House
Light Sq.
Hindmarsh Sq.
Town Hall
Victoria Sq.
Whitmore Sq.
Hurtle Sq.
Interstate Rail Terminal
Himeji Gardens
Glenelg–City Tramway
River Torrens
Fitzroy
Park Tce.
Jeffcott Rd.
Main North
Robe Tce.
Northcote
Walkerville
Barton Tce.
Mildred
Hill St.
Childers St.
O'Connell St.
Margaret St.
Lefevre Tce.
Gover St.
Buxton St.
Tynte St.
Molesworth St.
Archer St.
Kingston Tce.
Mann Tce.
Park Tce.
Barnard St.
Ward St.
Stanley St.
Jerningham St.
Strangways Tce.
Brougham Pl.
Melbourne St.
Parade
Bundeys Rd.
Richmond St.
Strangways
Jeffcott St.
Palmer Pl.
Frome Rd.
Finniss St.
McKinnon
Kermode
Pennington Tce.
Sir Edwin Smith Ave.
Memorial Dr.
War
Montefiore Rd.
King William Rd.
Victoria Dr.
Hackney Rd.
North Tce.
College Rd.
Port Rd.
Kintore Ave.
Botanic
Rundle St.
Rundle Rd.
Hindley St.
Glover St.
Currie St.
Grenfell St.
Dequetteville Tce.
Waymouth St.
Pirie St.
Bartels Rd.
Franklin St.
Flinders St.
Gawler
Grote St.
Wakefield St.
Wakefield Rd.
Burbridge Ave.
Gouger St.
Angas St.
Morphett St.
Wright St.
Carrington St.
East Tce.
West Tce.
Sturt St.
Halifax St.
Hutt St.
Gilbert St.
Gilles St.
Pulteney St.
South Tce.
Anzac Hwy.
Goodwood Rd.
Sir Lewis Cohen Ave.
King William St.
Unley Rd.
Glen Osmond Rd.
Beaumont St.
Greenhill Rd.
Hutt St.
Adelaide
Church
Post Office
Information
Adelaide Festival Centre 7
Adelaide Zoo 1
Botanic Gardens 2
Migration Museum 4
Parliament House 6
South Australian Museum 3
Tandanya Aboriginal Cultural Institute 5
6750

THE TOP ATTRACTIONS

The best thing about Adelaide's attractions is that they're so easy to get to. Although the city's population tops the million figure, the central area is so compact that most landmarks lie within walking distance of each other.

ADELAIDE FESTIVAL CENTRE, corner of King William Rd. and North Terrace, Adelaide. Tel. 216-8600.

Rising on the banks of the Torrens River, this dramatic yet wonderfully functional edifice to culture is the finest stage complex in Australia, both in its acoustics and in its facilities. Completed in 1973 (within three years) it contains a main 2,000-seat auditorium (the Festival Theatre); an astonishingly versatile smaller drama theater (the Playhouse); and a revolutionary experimental showcase (the Space Theatre); a tiered outdoor amphitheatre; an art collection; restaurants; and a bar.

Admission: Tours, $A3 adults, children free.

Open: Mon–Sat; call for hours.

SOUTH AUSTRALIAN MUSEUM, North Terrace between the Art Gallery and the State Library, Adelaide. Tel. 223-8911.

One block away from the Adelaide Festival Centre Complex (see above) stands the South Australian Museum. This building contains one of the largest and most varied collections of Aboriginal artifacts in the state, a fascinating Melanesian display, and a large array of New Guinea amphibia.

Admission: Free.

Open: Daily 10am–5pm.

ART GALLERY OF SOUTH AUSTRALIA, North Terrace, Adelaide. Tel. 207-7000.

This gallery, with its elegant neoclassical facade, houses (after Melbourne) the most comprehensive collection of Australian, European, and Asian art in the country. The Australian greats are represented by Sidney Nolan, Hans Heysen, Margaret Preston, Russell Drysdale, and Arthur Boyd. European masters include Claude Lorrain and Jacob van Ruisdael. Asian displays include Edo-period Japanese silk screens and a unique collection of Southeast Asian ceramics.

Admission: Free.

Open: Daily 10am–5pm.

AYERS HOUSE, 288 North Terrace, Adelaide. Tel. 223-1655.

Ayers House, opposite the Royal Adelaide Hospital, is an elegant bluestone home that was once the residence of a state premier. Today it provides an enchanting reminder of 19th-century colonial-style graciousness—a study in wealth coupled with taste. It also houses a very posh restaurant and a bistro.

Admission: $A2 adults, A50¢ children.

Open: Tues–Fri 10am–4pm, Sat and Sun 2pm–4pm.

OLD PARLIAMENT HOUSE, North Terrace. Tel. 207-1077.

The Old Parliament House may be the biggest surprise in town. This is the state's former legislature, now devoted to a variety of witty and intriguing displays about the assembly's volatile and sometimes scandalous past. But the real attraction is "The South Australia Story," a 20-minute laser-disk audiovisual marvel that takes you from the infant colony's beginnings in 1836 through the present. After seeing this you'll better understand the unique character of this state.

Admission: $A4 adults, $A2.50 children.

Open: Mon–Fri 10am–5pm, Sat and Sun 12–5pm.

MIGRATION MUSEUM, 82 Kintore Ave., Adelaide. Tel. 207-7580.

More knowledge can be gleaned at this mosaic of multiculturalism that's aided by realistic displays. Here is the epic of an immigrant society, starting with the English, Scottish, and Irish pioneers and widening into the stream of Italians, Germans, Greeks, Lebanese, Chinese, and others who shaped the state.

Admission: Free.

Open: Mon–Fri 10am–5pm, Sat and Sun 1–5pm.

TANDANYA ABORIGINAL CULTURAL INSTITUTE, 253 Grenfell St., Adelaide. Tel. 223-2467.

The Tandanya is a showplace for Aboriginal art and artifacts on a big scale. Paintings, carvings, and sculptures are beautifully displayed in what was formerly the city's power station. There is also a performing-arts space showing video programs on Aboriginal culture.

Admission: $A4 adults, $A3 children.

Open: Mon–Fri 10:30am–5pm, Sat and Sun 12–5pm.

POSTAL MUSEUM, 2 Franklin St., Adelaide.

This small, interesting museum shows the development of the mail service and lets you try your hand at Morse Code.

Admission: Free.

Open: Mon–Fri 11am–2pm.

MARITIME MUSEUM, 117 Lipson St., Port Adelaide. Tel. 240-0200.

This is the newest and largest museum of its kind in Australia. Located in Adelaide's harbor suburb, the museum spreads over seven sites and includes an authentic 1869 lighthouse you can climb up. There are historic sailing vessels, windjammer relics, and an amazing sound-and-light "voyage" in a replica windjammer that'll make you swear you're on the high seas.

Admission: $A7 adults, $A3 children.

Open: Tues–Sun 10am–5pm. **Directions:** Take the Outer Harbour train or bus no. 153 or 157 from North Terrace.

PORT DOCK STATION RAILWAY MUSEUM, Lipson St., Port Adelaide. Tel. 341-1690.

A feast for iron-horse buffs, this display features some 30 locomotives and passenger coaches—steam and diesel—as well as a small railroad theater and operating HO-gauge model trains hurdling over miniature landscapes.

Admission: $A6 adults, $A2.50 children.

Open: Sun–Fri 10am–5pm, from noon Sat.

ADELAIDE ZOO, Frome Rd. Tel. 267-3255.

Set in superbly landscaped surroundings, the zoo displays some 1,500 native and imported creatures and various habitats: the very rare and beautiful yellow-footed rock wallabies; red pandas—the smaller, livelier cousins of the famous giant pandas; a walk-through artificial rain forest; and a re-created seal colony. The children's zoo boasts an animal nursery and special areas to pet, stroke, and feed the tamer residents.

Admission: $A6 adults, $A3 children.

Open: Daily 9:30am–5pm.

BOTANIC GARDENS, North Terrace.

A patch of paradise planted right in the city, the gardens contain the largest conservatory in the southern hemisphere (over 4,000 plants) and a glass-enclosed tropical rain forest. There is also a fully licensed restaurant in the garden center.

Admission: Tours, free.

Open: 9am until dusk.

DAZZLELAND, Myer Centre, Rundle Mall. Tel. 231-8300.

In terms of numbers of patrons this is Adelaide's most popular attraction, it beats even the famous casino. Dazzleland is an indoor amusement theme park located on the two top floors of the huge Myer shopping center downtown. The "theme" is a bit hazy, the amusements unmissable. There is an amazing roller coaster, suspended in the atrium seven stories above ground; a replica of the Russian MIR Orbital Space Station; a Zone 3 laser tag game; half a dozen whirling and spinning fun rides; a vast video arcade with every breed of electronic skill game; and enough snack dispenseries to feed a summer camp. Although the park's appeal is mainly for the kids, parents become equally enthralled by the razzle of Dazzleland.

Admission: Free. Ride tokens start at $A1.

Open: During shopping hours.

THE INVESTIGATOR, Rose Terrace, Wayville. Tel. 410-1115.

A hands-on science and technology showcase aimed at kids from kindergarten to dotage. The fun exhibits include a laser tunnel of synchronized light and sound, five scientific-theme galleries, and a science theater. There are regular shows on such subjects as "fantastic fluids," "colorful chemistry," and "virtual reality." The Curiosity Shop sells scientific gizmos.

Open: Daily 10am–5pm. **Directions:** Take the Glenelg tram.

COOL FOR KIDS

For letting off steam, kids love the waterlogged fun at the **Aquatic Centre** in North Adelaide (see "Sports & Recreation," below); the maritime adventures aboard one of the water craft of the ***Popeye* fleet,** located at the jetty in Cresswell Gardens; the **Magic Mountain** (tel. 294-8199) amusement park in Colley Reserve, in Glenelg; and **Dazzleland,** a four-level, multiattraction children's world with dozens of rides, games, and exhibition stalls. Dazzleland is located in the Myer Centre, Rundle Mall (see "Dazzleland," above).

The Investigator's hands-on pavilion at the Wayville Showgrounds is the site of some (literally) hair-raising science, aimed specifically at kids.

For quiet times, visit **Story Book Cottage and Whacky Wood** in Tanunda in the Barossa Valley, or take the kids to the petting, feeding, and cuddling section of the **Adelaide Zoo.**

ORGANIZED TOURS

By far the best method of sightseeing is by the **Adelaide Explorer.** This is a tour bus disguised as a trolley that starts from the South Australian Tourism Commission, 11 King William St. (tel. 215-1505), three times daily on a 2-hour jaunt around the city's top attractions. You can join or leave the bus at any of the 12 stopping points and catch a following one as many times as you like for an entire day. Tickets cost $A18 for adults, $A12 for children.

The ***P.S. Mundoo,*** a two-story paddle steamer, chugs on scenic cruises along the Torrens River. They depart every Saturday at 9:30am and return at 5pm. Tickets are $A16 for adults, $A8 for children not including an optional lunch. For bookings and inquiries contact **Premier's Day Tours** at 415-5555.

7. SPORTS & RECREATION

AUSTRALIAN RULES FOOTBALL A much-quoted *mot* runs that "Melburnians regard football as a religion. But in South Australia we take it seriously." They do, indeed. Australian Rules football is far and away the most popular winter sport here. If you're interested, use a Saturday afternoon to watch the crowd frenzy at either the **Adelaide Oval** (at King William Street and War Memorial Drive) or **Football Park** (Turner Drive, in West Lakes) when the home team, the Adelaide Crows, is playing.

GOLF **City of Adelaide Golf Links,** War Memorial Drive, North Adelaide (tel. 231-2359), offers several short courses and a full championship course. Clubs can be rented at the pro shop, and green fees come to around $A6.

SKIING & SKATING It sounds unlikely in a region without snowfall, but Adelaide boasts the world's largest indoor frozen snowfield: Mt. Thebarton, 23 E. Terrace, Thebarton (tel. 352-7997). This roofed winterland has skating rinks and a 150-meter ski slope, with skates and skis for rent, a special rink for beginners, plus a bar/bistro where you can relax and watch others take their spills. Skiing costs $A10.50 (including ski rentals), skating $A6.70 (including skates). Open daily; call for hours.

FROMMER'S FAVORITE ADELAIDE EXPERIENCES

Seeing *La Traviata* performed by the Australian Opera Company. The free concert takes place beneath a star-spangled sky in Elder Park.

Dining Aboard the Replica Windjammer *Buffalo* After wandering through the maritime exhibits, go to Glenelg for an expensive seafood dinner.

Visiting the Plaster Fun House Kids (and their parents) run amok with borrowed paints and brushes at this melee in Brighton.

Cooling Off at Aquatic Center Run the artificial river rapids or float in the pool at this indoor oasis.

Attending a Houseboat Party on the Murray River Relays of guests periodically dive overboard to cool off.

Swinging at the Fezbah An eight-piece brass combo masterfully blows its way through the swingshift at the Adelaide Festival Centre's cabaret spot.

SURFING & SWIMMING All the beaches close to Adelaide have calm water, ideal for swimming and boating but useless for surfing. The surf turf starts at **Southport,** about 20 miles south of the city, and runs along the Mid Coast to Moana.

For pool swimming there's the **Adelaide Aquatic Centre,** Jeffcott Road, North Adelaide (tel. 344-4411). The center offers much more than its Olympic-size pool. It's a tropical indoor oasis, with simulated river rapids, fountains, bubble beaches, cascades, a gym, a spa, a sauna, and a restaurant. Open daily; call for hours and admission fees.

TENNIS The handiest public courts are at the **War Memorial Drive Tennis Club,** North Adelaide (tel. 231-4371). Call for available bookings and try to make it a week*day*. Weekends and evenings are in heavy demand.

8. EVENING ENTERTAINMENT

Adelaide has a nightlife strip of sorts in the shape of Hindley Street. There, interspersed with excellent restaurants and cafés, you'll find some rather rheumatic bare-skin establishments. Melbourne Street in North Adelaide has some more nocturnal action. Otherwise nightlife is scattered and has to be pinpointed before embarking on a crawl. A free periodical named *Ripit Up,* which you can grab in coffee-and-music shops, keeps you current on who is gigging where.

THE PERFORMING ARTS

ADELAIDE FESTIVAL CENTRE, corner of King William Rd. and North Terrace, Adelaide. Tel. 216-8600.

The center is a magnificent complex for staging everything in the performing arts, from drama and classical ballet to symphony and comedy, including outdoor productions. See the newspapers for what is being shown currently.

Tickets: $A25–$A79, the high end for celebrity appearances.

HER MAJESTY'S THEATRE, 58 Grote St., Adelaide. Tel. 212-6833.

This is a large traditional showcase for plays and big glittering musicals, mainly overseas imports.

Tickets: $A10–$A30.

THE CLUB, PUB & MUSIC SCENE

The majority of clubs and discos are lined along Hindley Street, interspersed with cafés and restaurants. Some enforce a pretty lenient dress code, and their charges vary wildly. The free weekly *Ripit Up* presents good coverage of the scene.

FEZBAH, in the Adelaide Festival Centre, King William Rd., Adelaide. Tel. 213-4788.

This is the most surprisingly versatile nightspot in town. A rather svelte and trendy little retreat, the bar features "mood music" by some of Adelaide's top piano talent. Every Friday it stages "The Late Show," which generates tremendous popularity. From 11pm until very late (or early) you can dance and party to the sounds of rock, country, soul, funk, jazz, and Afro-Caribbean bands and vocalists in unison with what seems half of Adelaide's younger set.

Admission: $A7.

KOKLUB, 171 Hindley St. W., Adelaide. Tel. 231-0677.

This disco, brimming with technological gadgetry and very popular deejays, sells $A1 drinks before midnight.

THE VENUE, 145 Hindley St., Adelaide. Tel. 231-3477.

A Hindley Street stalwart, famed as a rock-band showcase, the Venue features different groups and rock-video shows on successive nights. The action continues until 5am.

Admission: Sun–Thurs, free; Fri and Sat $A5–$A6.

BRECKNOCK HOTEL, 401 King William St., Adelaide. Tel. 231-5467.

This is Adelaide's Irish scene. Thursday to Saturday you get Irish and folk music and solo entertainers.

Admission: Free.

OLD LION HOTEL, 163 Melbourne St., North Adelaide. Tel. 267-3766.

An atmospheric colonial pub combined with an entire entertainment complex, plus a beer garden, the hotel's nightspots include the Piano Bar and the Underground, the latter a showcase for top-level rock groups that blast from 8am until "early am." The hotel originated with a small brewery that was founded in 1850 and is still brewing. You can watch the brewing-and-kegging process from the two levels of the Alehouse, then sample the finished products at the bar.

Admission: $A10.

HOTEL ENFIELD, 184 Hampstead Rd., Clearview. Tel. 262-3944.

Farther out, and usually higher in the price bracket, is the Hotel Enfield. This establishment contains two of Adelaide's top night entertainments under one roof. The first is the **Stardust Room,** featuring gaming machines and evening shows. The second is the **Baron of Beef,** an amusing mix of smorgasbord and cabaret acts—the former including seafood; the latter lashings of singing, dancing, and comedy until 11pm, then dancing by the guests until midnight. It costs $A32 per person on Friday and Saturday, $A44 including liquor.

MORE ENTERTAINMENT

ADELAIDE CASINO, North Terrace, Adelaide. Tel. 212-2811.

Adelaide is the only city in the world that has turned its railroad station into a gambling casino. The suburban trains still run in and out of the place, but where the administration offices used to be there is now a vast and very plush gaming palace. The casino features 100 gaming tables for roulette and blackjack, as well as a granite-floored ring for the traditional (and mostly illegal) Australian game of two-up. (For details on this fascinating obsession, see "Tasmania—the Island State," Chapter 11.) The casino also includes a superb wine bar, offering 300 brands of South Australian wines; and a suitably expensive restaurant, the Pullman, which has wandering minstrels competing with the resident band. (I did mention that the "City of Churches" has changed somewhat.)

Open: Mon–Thurs 10am–4am, Fri–Sun 24 hrs.

9. EXCURSIONS IN SOUTH AUSTRALIA

The huge state (about 1½ times the size of Texas) of South Australia occupies the central position on the map of Australia and has within its borders a portion of everything that makes up the continent—golden surfing beaches in the south and vast broiling deserts in the northwest; lush green wine-growing valleys and spectacularly rugged mountain ranges; rolling plains swarming with wild emus and kangaroos and carefully cultivated wheat lands; cattle stations, industrial complexes, and warm meandering rivers; and regions of densely profuse forests and regions where nothing grows at all. It's all there in South Australia, so take your pick.

For those who want to stay closer to Adelaide, the city's **beaches** are probably the safest in Australia. Stretching from Seacliff in the south to Outer Harbour in the north, they offer miles of dazzling white sand and the virtual absence of that fierce undertow characteristic of the more open surfing beaches. The most popular beach suburb is **Glenelg** (take the tram), with a roisterous amusement park and a first-rate shopping center. There's also **Shell Land,** at the corner of Mary and Melbourne streets, North Glenelg, displaying 1,800 seashells from around the world.

BAROSSA VALLEY

One of Adelaide's greatest attractions—and Australia's most celebrated wine region—lies 40 miles northeast of the city. The valley was named after a vaguely similar piece of terrain in Spain, but there the similarity ends. There is nothing Spanish whatever about the Barossa. The keynote is German, in both the brand names of the wines and the physical appearance of the villages. If you've traversed Central Europe you'll recognize those houses, churches, and barns immediately: solid stones and slender steeples, lovingly regimented hedges and wine gardens in the shade of old trees, with no trace of the colonial rawness and impermanence that marks so many Australian (and American) country towns. The first brick wall tells you that these people built things to last—not only for decades but for centuries.

The people who settled the valley during the 1840s were strict Lutherans from Prussia who had migrated in order to practice their religion without undue government interference. They knew little about wine but plenty about orcharding and agriculture. It was only when a geologist drew their attention to the wine-growing potential of the soil that they tilled for viticulture. The resulting combination of ideal earth and ideal climate, plus skill and hard work, produced a valley that looks like one vast garden. The place enraptures your eyes long before its wines delight your palate.

Although the people of Barossa are staunchly Australian, the German influence is still strong. You drive along a road called Wein Strasse and pass inns called Gasthaus, shops selling *Obst und Gemüse*, butchers displaying Mettwurst, and a juvenile fashion store advertising *Kinderkleider*.

The valley's cuisine is a happy hodgepodge of Teutonic and Down Under—the same establishments serving Sauerbraten, Eisbein, and Streuselkuchen offer hot meat pies and barramundi cheek by jowl. But the wines are truly native—the best the country produces. Here you'll find the essence of crisp Australian whites, full-bodied reds, smooth rosés, and party-spirited sparklers, as well as the more sedate ports and clarets (Bordeaux).

But here's a word of advice: Pace yourself carefully. The valley has some 35 wineries, ranging from primitive iron sheds to huge combines with palatial châteaux and replicas of Rhineland castles. And nearly all of them invite you to drop in and taste, and they pour generous measures. Unless you watch your intake you'll find yourself either incapable of driving or unable to enjoy the journey. The first eventuality would be dangerous, the second a pity. So sip with caution and travel proud.

This is particularly advisable if you're lucky enough to make your trip during the **Vintage Festival,** celebrated in odd-numbered years (in order not to clash with the Adelaide Festival of Arts), usually during the week after Easter—the Australian autumn. Well, the fountains don't gush wine, but half a million bottles do, and the valley goes into a whirl of parades, parties, dancing, feasting, and DRINKING, and to hell with the hangovers. Don't say you weren't warned.

The Barossa Valley proper (as distinct from the district) is a 20-mile strip running from Williamstown to the St. Kitts Hills, just north of Nuriootpa. Tanunda is the focal point of the area. Various companies run organized tours of the region. If you're doing your own driving, here's a suggested route that takes in most of the highlights.

LYNDOCH

Take the Main North Road from Adelaide, turn right onto Sturt Highway (Route 20) and follow it through Elizabeth and Gawler to Lyndoch. This is the gateway of the Barossa Valley, a pretty little hamlet about 130 years old. By local standards that's antique.

At the **Château Yaldara** you'll get an idea of the magnificence of some of the wine establishments in the area. The main hall and upper halls are downright palatial, like the reception rooms of minor European royalty. The mansion itself is a superb hewn-stone structure, crammed with art objects, lit by impressive chandeliers, and hung with Persian carpets and gold-framed oil canvases. The wine tasting is subtly regulated: starting with the driest and leading slowly to the sweeter table wines, thence to the liqueurs. It's free of charge—but they hope that you'll buy a bottle or two or ten. Tours are given five times a day on Monday to Friday. The cellars are open on Saturday and most holidays. There is also a picnic and barbecue area open to the public.

TANUNDA

Farther north along the Sturt Highway lies Tanunda, the unofficial capital of Barossa and a name so synonymous with wine that many Australians don't know whether this is a town or a bottle label. Quite apart from its grape glory, Tanunda is one of the most captivating villages in the southern hemisphere. The town gateway is flanked by green embankments. A decorated arch—crowned by a wine barrel—welcomes you, and you drive in among small white or weathered-gray houses half-hidden behind trees and hedges, with music in the air mingling with the aroma of wine and country cooking. At first glance the whole place seems to have been cut out of a children's picture book.

The town's old post office has been converted into the **Tanunda Museum,** 47 Murray St. (tel. 085/633-295). There you can see the tools, furnishings, and musical instruments used—and made—by the early German settlers in the days before mail-order service, as well as the religious memorabilia characteristic of the time when the Lutheran faith became deeply entrenched in the Barossa. Open daily from 10am to 5pm. Admission is $A2 for adults, A50¢ for *Kinder.*

Almost opposite the museum and designed for serious eating is **Bergman's,** 66 Murray St. (tel. 085/63-2788). It's a genuine cellar restaurant, cool and dim, with massive ridgum ceiling beams, oil-lamp lighting, and whitewashed-brick walls interlaced with wooden crossbars. On sunny afternoons or warm nights you can eat and drink in the vine-ranked courtyard in the shade of old trees. Main courses cost around $A16, but you can also get excellent open sandwiches for $A3.50 to $A7.50.

Tanunda takes special pride in the **Langmeil Church,** which houses the burial ground and monument of Pastor Kavel—the man who immigrated here from Berlin in 1838, took his entire congregation with him, and founded the Evangelical Lutheran church in Australia.

The **Story Book Cottage** and **Whacky Wood,** Oak Street, are twin

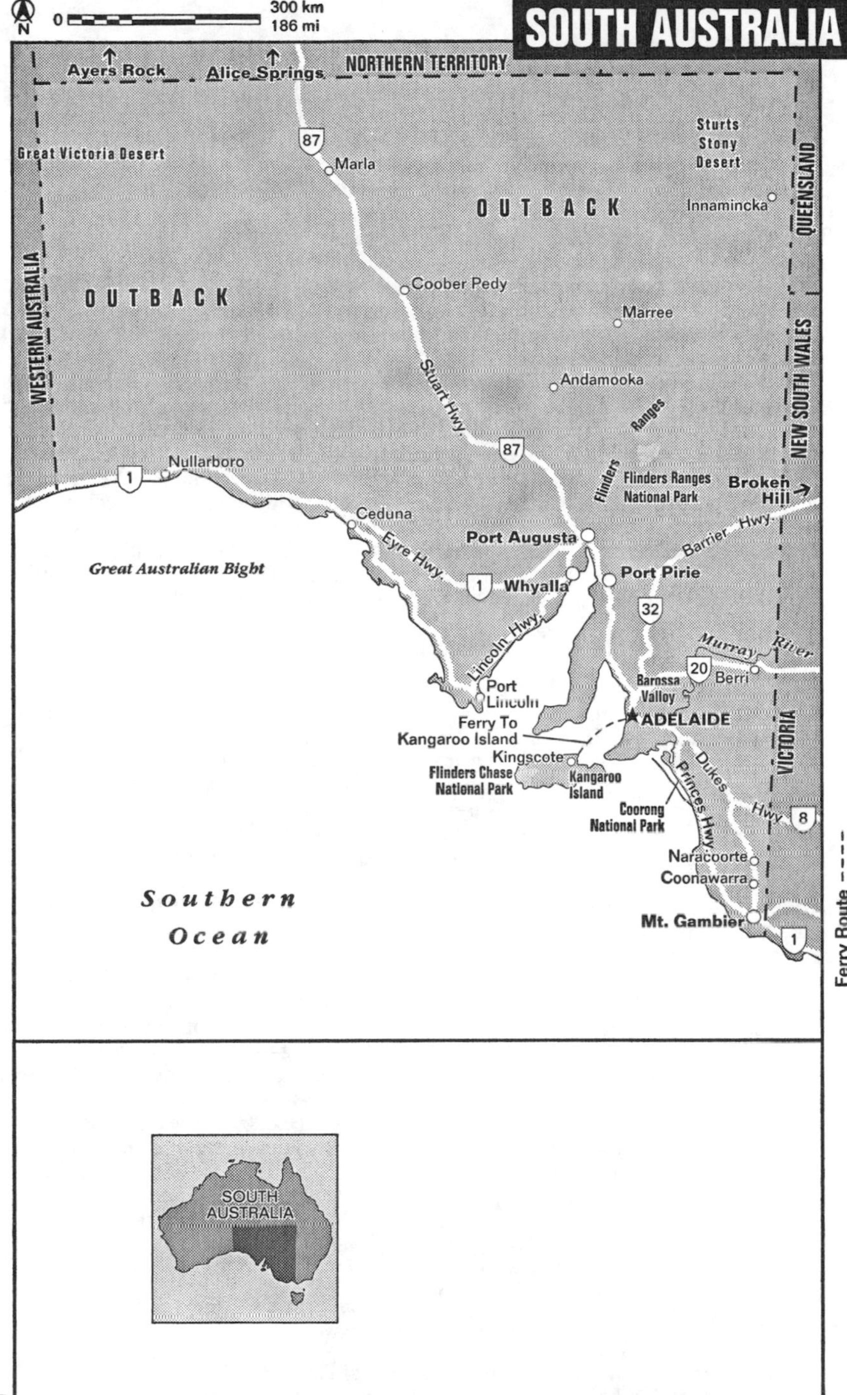
SOUTH AUSTRALIA
0
300 km
186 mi
N
Ayers Rock
Alice Springs
NORTHERN TERRITORY
Great Victoria Desert
Marla
87
Sturts
Stony
Desert
QUEENSLAND
OUTBACK
Innamincka
WESTERN AUSTRALIA
OUTBACK
Coober Pedy
Marree
NEW SOUTH WALES
Andamooka
Stuart Hwy.
Flinders Ranges
87
Nullarboro
1
Flinders Ranges
National Park
Broken
Hill
Ceduna
Port Augusta
Barrier Hwy.
Great Australian Bight
Eyre Hwy.
1
Whyalla
Port Pirie
32
Lincoln Hwy.
Murray River
20
Berri
Port
Lincoln
Barossa
Valley
ADELAIDE
Ferry To
Kangaroo Island
Kingscote
Flinders Chase
National Park
Kangaroo
Island
Dukes Hwy
Princes Hwy
VICTORIA
Coorong
National Park
8
Naracoorte
Coonawarra
Southern
Ocean
Mt. Gambier
1
Ferry Route
SOUTH
AUSTRALIA
6751

attractions with a distinct Aussie flavor that are hard to resist for anyone under the age of 120. You can try the Sleepy Lizard Races, ride the whacky bronco, do the Wombat Wobble and Kangaroo Hop, admire the miniature fairy-tale world behind the little green door, and visit live animals as well. Admission covers both attractions: $A4.50 for adults, $A2.50 for children. Open daily from 10am to 5pm.

About two miles south of Tanunda lies **Halletts Valley,** home ground of the Lindner wine family. Their winery, **St. Halletts,** is shaded by immense red gum trees and is a famed treasure trove for port lovers. Beyond the tasting room you'll find the keg factory; however, *factory* is hardly the right term for a workshop where they make casks in the old style—with hand tools. This is a genuine cooperage, the kind beloved by Falstaff and Co., where oaken hogsheads of sherry, port, and brandy lie in promising rows, awaiting maturity. The craftspeople welcome visitors and have no objections to anyone peering over their shoulders, unlike certain other professional tradespeople—for instance, plumbers.

In **Dorrien,** just north of Tanunda, lies a portion of the Seppelt empire. This is **Seppeltsfield** (tel. 085/62-8028), a vast winery spreading over many acres and surrounded by vineyards. All of it grew from a small patch of land on which Joseph Seppelt unsuccessfully tried to raise tobacco in the 1850s. When the soil proved unsuitable for smoking crops, he turned to the drinking variety and built his first wine cellar over and around his wife's dairy. The old cellar still exists, so well constructed that even after 110 years the heavy timbers haven't given an inch. The hospitality of the Seppelt family was proverbial and continues today. Visitors are welcome to gardens and picnic grounds, with tables, benches, and gas barbecues provided—plus, of course, chilled wines and glasses to clink among the palms and date trees.

NURIOOTPA

This township has been called the heart of the wine country, but that's purely geographical. In fact, Nuriootpa is simply another delightful stop along the Sturt route through the valley, offering pleasures very much the same as those mentioned before.

It does, however, boast the oldest house in the Barossa, built in 1840. Today the quaintly ramshackle little structure contains the **Barossa Gem Centre,** where you can browse among a collection of opals brought directly from Andamooka. There's always a chance—a pretty faint one—that you'll make a "find," assuming that you know one when you spot it. The stones sell from about $A10 upward.

On the lawn outside, **Coulthard House,** another museum, is the permanent parking place for the first caravan built in Australia. It looks exactly like a cottage on wheels, complete with red tile roof, but any resemblance it bears to contemporary recreational vehicles is purely coincidental.

The most imposing winery here is **Kaiser Stuhl,** its name meaning "Emperor's Chair" and arousing visions of some bearded monarch squatting on a wine barrel. Kaiser Stuhl is a new outfit by valley standards, founded as a cooperative in the early 1930s. But its château—red brick with white facing—has all the regality of a century-old mansion, and the tasting room is among the most attractive in the area. The wine-making facilities offer a fascinating contrast to the old-world air of the château. The bottling plants (with a capacity of 12,000 bottles per hour), the stainless-steel tanks storing two million gallons of young wine, and the laboratory where wines are tested and analyzed are technological marvels. The winery offers six tours daily, Monday to Saturday.

Nuriootpa (in case you've wondered, it's an Aboriginal word for "meeting place") has an outstanding German bakery serving made-on-the-premises apple strudel, Bienenstich, and other diet-killing delights. It's also a good place to spend the night if you're trying to preserve your energy for another day's tasting.

Where to Stay

The **Caravan and Camping Park,** Centennial Park (tel. 085/62-1404), offers the most economical lodgings in the area. Nestled in 40 acres of trees and lawns near the Para River, the park offers showering-and-toilet facilities; washing machines; a kiosk selling milk, bread, and so on; and 20 cabins that cost $A28 per night.

ON DOWN THE VALLEY

The Barossa Valley Highway stretches on to **Angaston** (follow the signs), which has a wonderful boulevard restaurant called **Unter der Laterne,** with tables set beneath an arched street colonnade, exactly as you'd find in the Rhineland. Continue on over to Keyneton and Springton, to Birdwood (watch for the interesting museum of old transport), then to Cudlee Creek.

If you're driving, you can take the winding Gorge Road back into Adelaide. But, as previously mentioned, there are any number of tours from Adelaide in which the coach driver is the only one forced to stay sober, and, under the circumstances, they might be the ideal form of locomotion.

COOBER PEDY

This spot is unique not only in Australia but also in the world. The Aboriginal name means "white man live underground." And that's precisely how the locals live, because of the climate. Coober Pedy lies in a lunar landscape of flat-topped sandstone ridges 590 miles northwest of Adelaide, where daytime temperatures soar to 130°F and nights often drop to the freezing point. By burrowing like human moles, the locals escape these drastic extremes of climate and achieve amazingly comfortable conditions.

But why would anyone live there at all? The answer is simple: Coober Pedy sits on the largest opal deposits in South Australia. And that's the raison d'être for this town of over 2,000 people where the only aboveground structures are the post office, school, police station, stores, and air-conditioned motels. Every morning the citizens emerge from their burrows to dig out about 90% of all the opals produced in the world!

Some of these cave homes are amazingly elaborate, complete with modern furniture, carpeting, pictures on the walls, and audio players on the liquor cabinets. The town even has a subterranean Catholic church, reminiscent of the Roman catacombs in which the earliest Christians held their services. You can join tours of this "underworld," which conclude with a visit to a fully operating opal mine.

Or, better still, do a bit of fossicking yourself. All it takes are a pick and shovel, a strong back, and an eye for a dusty pebble emitting a strange fiery glitter. But take my advice and try it between May and August: it's cooler then. **Bull's Tourist Services** runs daily buses from Adelaide to Coober Pedy, a 15-hour trip, or you can fly on **Kendell Airlines,** the trip taking about 3 hours.

KANGAROO ISLAND

A wildlife paradise just off the coast southwest of Adelaide, this is everything a holiday isle should be—cooler than the mainland in summer, balmier in winter; developed enough to offer every tourist comfort yet primitive enough to harbor legions of furred-and-feathered beasties in their natural environment (notably in Flinders Chase National Park); and small enough to explore in a couple of days yet large enough to keep you engrossed for a year.

Kangaroo Island has luxury hotels and budget hostelries, 50 species of wild orchids, hundreds of seals romping over salt-sprayed rocks, regiments of waddling fairy penguins, sheltered swimming pools, and some of the finest big-game fishing in Australia (including expeditions for the legendary great white shark), plus, of course, kangaroos. Officially they're "wild," but in reality they'll take your picnic apples right out of your hand. The dragonlike goanna lizards don't care for apples, but they'll gladly steal your ham sandwiches. The emus might swallow your motel key if you're foolish enough to offer it. But the koalas stick to gum leaves high up in the trees, and if you're very discreet and quiet you might be able to watch the shy duckbilled platypuses playing in the pools of the Rocky River.

There's a daily (weekday) Kangaroo Island passenger and vehicle **ferry** connecting Cape Jervis (on the mainland) with Kangaroo Island. The crossing takes 1 hour and costs $A40 round-trip. Call 13-1301 for ferry information. **Air Kangaroo Island** flies you over in 40 minutes.

CRUISING DOWN THE MURRAY

Three states share the wide, warm, leisurely Murray River, but South Australia makes the best use of its portion. This is a river to play on, to dream by, and to fish in; South Australia facilitates all three pastimes with rare generosity—by, for instance, not insisting that you buy a fishing license.

Have you ever dreamed of cruising down a river in an air-conditioned steamer? Well, the **Murray River Queen** is a luxury craft that you could imagine chugging along the Mississippi with Scarlett O'Hara mooning by the railing and Rhett Butler fanning a deck of cards in the saloon. But this version has a modern twist: The cabins come with either hot-and-cold water or private showers, and there are streamlined dining rooms and sun decks, excellent meals, and a well-stocked bar. The *Murray River Queen* is based at Murray Bridge, east of Adelaide, and cruises for two days past glorious bush scenery, basking lizards, and multicolored birdlife. It also offers deck games, parties, barbecues on shore, unlimited fishing, and the chance to acquire a perfect suntan. The cruise costs from $A190. Contact **Murray River Cruises,** 151 Franklin St., Adelaide, SA 5000 (tel. 08/211-8333).

HOUSEBOATS

But perhaps you'd like to play skipper yourself? Preferably on a virtually unsinkable, "all-mod.-cons." craft that requires no more operational know-how than that required to drive a car. Well, there are more than 400 of these available at seven river towns along the Murray. They are drive-yourself houseboats equipped with paddle wheels or stern motors that push them along at an easy five miles per hour.

The fittings of these craft vary according to size and price. The deluxe models even have two-way radios for summoning "room service"—which comes by way of a fast courtesy boat from the rental base. All of the boats boast cooking facilities, hot water, electricity, showers, gas refrigerators, and ample sleeping accommodations. Some also provide free fishing gear. You have 400 miles of picturesque river for a highway, scores of idyllic mooring spots beneath willow branches, or the choice of tying up at the wharf of a different little town each night. The riverbanks slide past—varying between sandstone cliffs; gum forests; irrigated orchards; and vast marshes alive with pelicans, ducks, cormorants, ibis, herons, and cranes.

These houseboats offer berths for 4 to 10 people and can be rented at rates ranging upward from about $A370 per off-season weekend. The **South Australian Tourism Commission,** 1 King William St., Adelaide 5000 (tel. 212-1505), has detailed literature and will arrange bookings for all of them.

FLINDERS RANGES

They rise abruptly near Crystal Brook, 120 miles north of Adelaide, and go on and on, one towering range after another, the stark grandeur of the peaks contrasting with the sun-drenched, multicolored gorges in between. This is the most ruggedly beautiful mountain country in South Australia, an inspiration to dozens of landscape painters and millions of visitors. Despite good roads from Adelaide and clusters of motels in the townships, the ranges still have more wildlife than people: kangaroos and rock wallabies, earthbound emus, soaring wedge-tailed eagles, screeching parrots and cockatoos, and frilled mountain lizards that look like pocket dragons but are quite harmless. The core of this mountain glory is Wilpena Pound, just beyond Hawker, where the peaks form a complete circle around an emerald-hued valley.

You can explore the ranges by yourself or join one of the half-dozen tours offered by **Stateliner,** 111 Franklin St., Adelaide, SA 5000 (tel. 415-5555). They take from four to eight days. Flinders Ranges National Park, near Blinman, includes an information center.

CHAPTER 6

BRISBANE & THE GOLD & SUNSHINE COASTS

- WHAT'S SPECIAL ABOUT BRISBANE & THE GOLD & SUNSHINE COASTS
1. FROM A BUDGET TRAVELER'S POINT OF VIEW
2. ORIENTATION
- NEIGHBORHOODS IN BRIEF
3. GETTING AROUND
- FAST FACTS: BRISBANE
4. WHERE TO STAY
- FROMMER'S COOL FOR KIDS: HOTELS
5. WHERE TO EAT
6. ATTRACTIONS
- FROMMER'S COOL FOR KIDS: RESTAURANTS
- DID YOU KNOW . . . ?
- FROMMER'S FAVORITE BRISBANE & GOLD COAST EXPERIENCES
7. SPORTS & RECREATION
8. EVENING ENTERTAINMENT
9. GOLD COAST
10. SUNSHINE COAST

The moment you enter Brisbane you'll realize that you're in holiday land—tourist territory—the capital of a state that counts tourism as a major industry. The subtropics start here, the sun shines with patriotic persistence, and the air is balmy when it isn't hot.

Although Brisbane is now a metropolis of some 1.3 million people (larger than Boston), the superabundance of ultraviolet rays keeps the rat race down to a comfortable crawl, infused with a pleasant dash of mañana spirit. The shops are loaded with cheap tropical fruit and sugarcane, and everybody has a tan.

It's a condition that carries drawbacks as well as advantages. On the one hand, there are few places in the world where visitors are made more welcome; the whole town seems to cater to them, woo them, and seduce them to stay permanently (which they do in vast numbers, thus accounting for Brisbane's tremendous rate of growth). On the other hand, certain penalties come attached to this semitropical languor: Queensland's politics and attitudes remain somewhat behind the times; environmentalism is regarded with suspicion, and films and magazines are strictly censored.

And city planning is not exactly Brisbane's strong point. Traffic conditions resemble those in a Keystone Kops epic—hell on motorists and not so cozy for pedestrians either. Downtown is a jigsaw jungle of one-way streets, railroad tracks, and freeway entrances so badly marked that you find yourself zooming off to Sydney instead of your hotel. The adjoining **Fortitude Valley** has some fine restaurants and entertainment spots and the *potential* of becoming a nightlife center.

In the leap from small-town somnolence to metropolitan dynamism, Brisbane seems to have missed the mark. Although it boasts a number of

WHAT'S SPECIAL ABOUT BRISBANE & THE GOLD & SUNSHINE COASTS

Architectural Highlights
- ☐ Parliament House, built in French Renaissance style but set among palm trees.
- ☐ City Hall, a classical structure housing a grand pipe organ.
- ☐ Queensland Cultural Centre, a complex housing performance stages, an art gallery, a museum, a concert hall, cafés, shops, and restaurants.

Beaches
- ☐ Dozens of the finest are along the Gold and Sunshine coasts.

Museum
- ☐ Queensland Art Gallery, with some fine contemporary paintings and a spectacular water mall.

Events/Festivals
- ☐ Warana, Brisbane's September carnival, with street fairs, parades, clowns, and strolling minstrels.
- ☐ Indy Grand Prix Motor Race, roaring along the Gold Coast in March.
- ☐ Surf Carnivals on the Gold and Sunshine coasts.

For the Kids
- ☐ Australian Woolshed, a vast playground with rustic Oz attractions, such as sheepshearing.
- ☐ Lone Pine Sanctuary, the first koala sanctuary in Australia.
- ☐ Bunya Park, where you can wander freely among the wildlife.

Shopping
- ☐ The Queen Street Mall and Wintergarden.
- ☐ Myer Centre, an immense complex with a rooftop amusement park.
- ☐ Rowes Arcade, Brisbane's most stylish enclave of specialty stores.
- ☐ Post Office Square, an ultramodern complex with shops and eateries.

Streets/Neighborhoods
- ☐ Queen Street, with the splendid pedestrian mall.
- ☐ Fortitude Valley, filled with the best and most varied restaurants in town.
- ☐ South Brisbane, site of World Expo '88 and the Queensland Cultural Centre.
- ☐ Gold Coast Highway, snaking along the entire length of the Gold Coast.

Parks
- ☐ Botanic Gardens, a paradise of tropical greenery.

After Dark
- ☐ Jupiters Casino, which combines gambling with star-spangled floor shows.

handsome buildings, several striking vistas, superlative weather, and a relaxed atmosphere, it does not have a single genuinely attractive street. The parks and gardens and riverbanks glow in lush colors, but what lies in between is frankly blah. From the tourist point of view, Brisbane's main function is as a gateway to the scenic wonders of Queensland—perhaps the most spectacular, and certainly the most controversial, state in the Commonwealth.

Like other Australian capitals, Brisbane was founded as a convict settlement in 1824. Unlike most others, however, it was established some 25 miles inland, on the banks of the winding **Brisbane River,** which flows into Moreton Bay. The river links the city with the ocean and carries large vessels, but Brisbane was deprived of a harbor setting that might have enhanced its charms.

The penal-colony memories still linger—carefully preserved as tourist attractions. The meteorological station known as **Old Observatory,** for instance, was originally constructed in 1829 as a convict punishment treadmill and later became a signal post before mellowing into a popular landmark.

1. FROM A BUDGET TRAVELER'S POINT OF VIEW

BUDGET BESTS Brisbane has no beaches—worse luck—but it does have a miniature nature reserve about four miles from the city center: Brisbane Forest Park, which is a bit of bushland harboring thousands of exotic birds and enough winding hiking trails to make you think you're on safari. Brisbane's public swimming pools are famous—the Oasis and Centenary Pool have lush garden settings and in no way resemble the municipal swimming slums you may have splashed in at home.

WORTH PAYING FOR You can take some wonderful river trips in, around, and out of Brisbane (see "Organized Tours"). Best of all is the ride to Lone Pine Sanctuary, Australia's first koala colony (see the "Attractions" section).

2. ORIENTATION

Read this section carefully because Brisbane is one of the worst (and least) signposted cities in Australia. Queenslanders have a deplorable habit of obliterating street names at important thoroughfares and not bothering to mark the less important ones at all. They figure that visitors can always ask the friendly natives for directions. The trouble is that frequently there's nary a native in sight—everyone you ask turns out to be another tourist!

ARRIVING

BY PLANE **Brisbane Airport** is about 2½ miles northeast of the city center. Airport coach fare is $A5.40 to downtown hotels, while a taxi would cost approximately $A15.

At the airport you'll find a buffet open for all arriving-and-departing flights. In the terminal you'll find the duty-free shop, bank and car-rental facilities. There is also a tourist information booth.

Don't miss the glass-walled building, just inside the entrance, housing the *Southern Cross*—the celebrated aircraft that made the first air crossing of the Pacific Ocean in 1928. Commanded by Brisbane-born Sir Charles Kingsford Smith (known as Smithy), this antediluvian trimotored Fokker monoplane did the trip from Oakland, California, to Brisbane—7,347 miles—in 83½ hours' flying time. Two of the four-man crew were Australians and two were Americans. The plane they used was outdated even 50 years ago and affectionately dubbed "the Old Bus" by its crew. Smithy was killed in 1935 while trying to establish a new record for the England-Australia flight.

BY TRAIN & BUS Brisbane has the most centralized and handiest rail-and-bus terminal of any Australian city. This is the **Brisbane Transit Centre** (tel. 235-2222) on Roma Street, downtown, the arrival-and-departure point for all cross-country, in-state, and local trains and buses. There are separate rail, coach, and mall levels, each with computerized video information screens. The pedestrian mall level has a tourist information center; for good measure the complex also boasts a hotel, restaurants, a café, and a pharmacy.

BY CAR If you're coming from Sydney, the closest state capital, you'll most probably be driving on the scenic route, the coastal Pacific Highway. This means you will enter the city from the south, cross Captain Cook Bridge, and enter the Riverside Expressway. Turn right at Queens Park and you'll be on Elizabeth Street, which leads one-way to the city center.

TOURIST INFORMATION

The **Queensland Government Travel Centre,** centrally located at the corner of Adelaide and Edward streets, Brisbane, QLD 4000 (tel. 07/221-6111), has full free-of-charge travel, accommodation, and tour-booking service. For information on current activities in town, consult *This Week in Brisbane,* free from the Travel Centre.

CITY LAYOUT

The best spot for an overall view of the city is the lookout on the tower of the **City Hall,** a vaguely Florentine edifice on **King George Square** that backs the impressive **City Plaza** shopping center. From up there you get a real taste of the fabulous mishmash of Victorian, Edwardian, 1930s, and glass-walled contemporary architecture that characterizes the town.

If you look toward the huge **Central Railway Station** you'll be looking due north. Immediately below you run Brisbane's main commercial streets: Ann, Adelaide, Queen, Elizabeth, Charlotte, Mary, and Margaret, running south to north, and George, Albert, Edward, and Creek, running west to east. Northeast is the direction of **Brisbane Airport,** some 2½ miles away.

To your right (that's east) the **Brisbane River** makes an A-shaped bend. At the tip of this bend the beautiful **Story Bridge** crosses the water, and to the southwest the Custom House Ferry runs across the river. Another ferry leaves from the foot of Edward Street, farther south. Continuing south, the **Botanic Gardens,** containing the **State Parliament,** nestle in the opposite bend of the river. This is the direction of the **Gold Coast,** the sun-drenched chain of beach resorts we'll visit later in this chapter.

The second loop of the river (south of you) separates South Brisbane from the city center. The southside embankment is delightfully landscaped and the site of the Queensland Cultural Centre. Here the river is spanned by the **William Jolly, Victoria,** and **Captain Cook** bridges. The Victoria Bridge serves as a landmark because the spectacular **Elizabeth II Jubilee Fountain** nearby throws a sparkling pillar of water high above the surface. Below this loop, fitted into yet another river curl, stretches the vast green pocket that surrounds **Queensland University.**

Beyond the river, to the southwest, rises **Brisbane Forest Park,** about four miles from the city, embracing the new Botanic Gardens and offering a panoramic view of the metropolis. Due west stands the **Brisbane Transit Centre** on Roma Street, and still farther west is **Government House.** Northwest stretches the huge green enclave of **Victoria Park,** next to **Bowen Park** and the **Exhibition Grounds.** The whole vast and beautiful complex contains the **Municipal Golf Links;** the **Queensland Museum;** and the **Centenary Pool** (at Gregory Terrace), among the finest swimming-and-diving facilities in the country. **Gregory Terrace,** which forms the borderline of these parks, is an important street to remember. It winds uphill and down from College Road to Fortitude Valley and has some of the best budget accommodations in town.

NEIGHBORHOODS IN BRIEF

Brisbane is a boomtown that has expanded rapidly over an enormous area. Most of this is gigantic suburban sprawl. The areas of interest to visitors are quite small—until you reach the surrounding nature parks.

Eagle Street Brisbane's downtown financial center is also the location of her newest attractions. Waterfront Place is a huge shopping, leisure, and business complex on the river. It is a venue for music and entertainment on weekends and "home port" of the *Kookaburra Queen* riverboat. Also here is the Cat's Tango Riverside Market, a highly original arts-and-crafts market in action every Sunday and adding quite unexpected color to the world of lucre.

Fortitude Valley Bordering the city to the northeast, Fortitude Valley includes Brisbane's Chinatown as well as its best eating enclave. The main drag is Brunswick

Street, roaring with traffic and distinctly unbeautiful but crammed with intriguing shops and good restaurants and flanked by an immense, air-conditioned, and colorful complex called McWhirters Centre.

Kangaroo Point The tongue of land sticking into the Brisbane River from the south has some pleasant parks and walkways along the riverfront, an excellent lookout station, and a number of economy-priced guest houses and hostels on quiet streets.

South Brisbane Reached by the William Jolly or Victoria bridges, this is home to the Queensland Cultural Centre, site of World Expo '88, as well as the sports facilities of Musgrave Park, which include a much-needed swimming pool.

Newstead A suburb drenched in history, as witnessed by Newstead House, this is Brisbane's premier colonial showplace. At the modern end of the spectrum there's The Boardwalk, a very attractive complex with its own marina and an array of specialty shops and cosmopolitan restaurants.

3. GETTING AROUND

BY PUBLIC TRANSPORTATION

TRAIN Brisbane has an extensive network of electric trains run by **Citytrain** and **Traveltrain** (tel. 235-1632). A detailed display at the Central Railway Station (tel. 235-2222), 69 Ann St., shows the timetable for services.

BUS The **Brisbane Transit Centre** on Roma Street contains a level for buses which also displays information on routes. Fares are by zone and in the City Heart zone you can ride for just A50¢. Your best bet is to buy a Weekly Ticket allowing unlimited travel on buses and ferries within specified zones for $A9 adults, $A4.50 children.

FERRY Ferries cross the Brisbane River from Riverside and Edward Street in the City. A cross river return ticket costs $A1 for adults, A60¢ children. Bicycles are carried free on all ferries at all times. For schedule information, call 13-1230.

TAXI Brisbane taxis are notoriously difficult to hail (allegedly, they also dissolve in the rain). Better get one from the various ranks or phone one of the following round-the-clock services: **Ascot** (tel. 360-0000), **Blue and White** (tel. 238-1000), or **Yellow Cabs** (tel. 391-0191).

BY CAR

For budget car rentals there's **Thrifty,** 325 Wickham St., Fortitude Valley (tel. 252-5994). They have a special weekend deal in which you get a car for three days but pay for only two.

BY BICYCLE

Although biking is not recommended downtown, where traffic is dense, chaotic, and brutal, all of Brisbane's larger parks have special bike lanes that make riding a safe pleasure. You can rent 12-speeds, mountain bikes, and childrens' steeds at **Brisbane Bicycle Sales,** 87 Albert St. (tel. 229-2592), daily from 8:30am to 5:30pm.

BRISBANE

American Express The Amex office is located at 131 Elizabeth St. (tel. 229-2022).

Area Code The telephone area code is **07.**

Babysitters Call **Anytime** (tel. 263-3807).

Car Rentals See "Getting Around," in this chapter.

Climate See "When to Go," Chapter 2.

Consulates The following countries have consulates in Brisbane. **New Zealand:** 288 Edward St. (tel. 221-9933). **United Kingdom:** 193 North Quay (tel. 236-2575). **United States:** 383 Wickham Terrace (tel. 839-8955).

Currency See "Information, Entry Requirements & Money," Chapter 2.

Currency Exchange Traveler's checks can be exchanged at **American Express** (see above) or **Thomas Cook,** Myer Centre, Elizabeth Street (tel. 221-9749).

Dentist For dental emergencies, go to the **Dental Hospital,** corner of Turbot and Albert streets (tel. 231-3777).

Doctor See "Hospitals," below.

Drugstores Try **Cityheart,** Post Office Square (tel. 229-9696), or **Day and Night Pharmacy,** corner of Queen and Albert streets (tel. 221-4585).

Emergencies To reach an ambulance, the fire department, or police, dial **000,** or contact the **State Emergency Service** (tel. 224-2111).

Eyeglasses Try **OPSM,** Shop 137, Wintergarden (tel. 221-1158).

Hairdressers/Barbers Catering to both men and women is **Bonnie and Clyde,** 270 Adelaide St. (tel. 229-2036).

Holidays See "When to Go," Chapter 2.

Hospitals The **Royal Brisbane Hospital** is located on Herston Road, Herston (tel. 253-8111). To reach a doctor after hours, call 831-9999.

Hot lines **Life Line Counselling Service** (tel. 252-1111) can be reached 24 hours a day. **Rape Crisis Line** (tel. 844-4008).

Information See "Tourist Information," in this chapter.

Laundry/Dry Cleaning Try **City Valet,** 99 Elizabeth St. (tel. 210-0732).

Libraries The **Municipal Library** is located at City Hall (tel. 225-4166).

Lost Property Contact the police or the Brisbane Transit Centre (see above).

Luggage Storage/Lockers Lockers are available at **Brisbane Airport** and at the **Brisbane Travel Centre** on Roma Street.

Newspapers/Magazines The *Courier Mail* is the major metropolitan daily. The *Australian* is a nationwide daily. A wide range of overseas-and-domestic newspapers and magazines is available at **Currans Corner Souvenirs,** corner of Adelaide and Edward streets (tel. 229-3690). Open daily 8am to 9pm.

Photographic Needs Try **Ted's Camera Store,** 146 Adelaide St. (tel. 221-9911).

Police For nonemergencies, contact police headquarters, 100 Roma St. (tel. 364-6464).

Post Office The **Brisbane Post Office** is located at 261 Queen St. (tel. 224-1202). It's open Monday to Friday 7am to 7pm.

Radio Classical, 106.1 FM or 103.7 FM; country western, 101.1 FM; news and weather, 612 AM; rock, 105.3 FM, 104.5 FM, or 1008 AM.

Religious Services You'll be able to attend services at the following locations. **Anglican:** St. John's Cathedral, 417 Ann St. (tel. 839-2420). **Baptist:** City Tabernacle, Wickham Terrace (tel. 831-1613). **Christian Scientist:** First Church of Christ Scientist, 273 North Quay (tel. 236-2023). **Greek Orthodox:** Church of the Assumption, Creek Road, Mount Gravatt (tel. 343-7304). **Jewish:** Brisbane Synagogue, Margaret Street (tel. 229-3412). **Lutheran:** St. Andrews, 25 Wickham Terrace (tel. 831-9106). **Muslim:** 309 Nursery Rd., Holland Park (tel. 343-4748). **Presbyterian:** 145 Ann St. (tel. 221-0238). **Roman Catholic:** St. Stephen's Cathedral, Elizabeth Street (tel. 229-4827). **Uniting Church:** corner of Albert and Ann streets (tel. 221-6788). **Seventh-Day Adventist:** corner of Eagle and Quay streets (tel. 221-7972).

Restrooms Public restrooms are available at the airport, the Brisbane Transit Centre, public parks, and in all shopping complexes.

Shoe Repairs Try **Budget,** 280 Adelaide St. (tel. 229-4146).

Taxes There are no taxes added to purchases or restaurant-and-hotel bills.

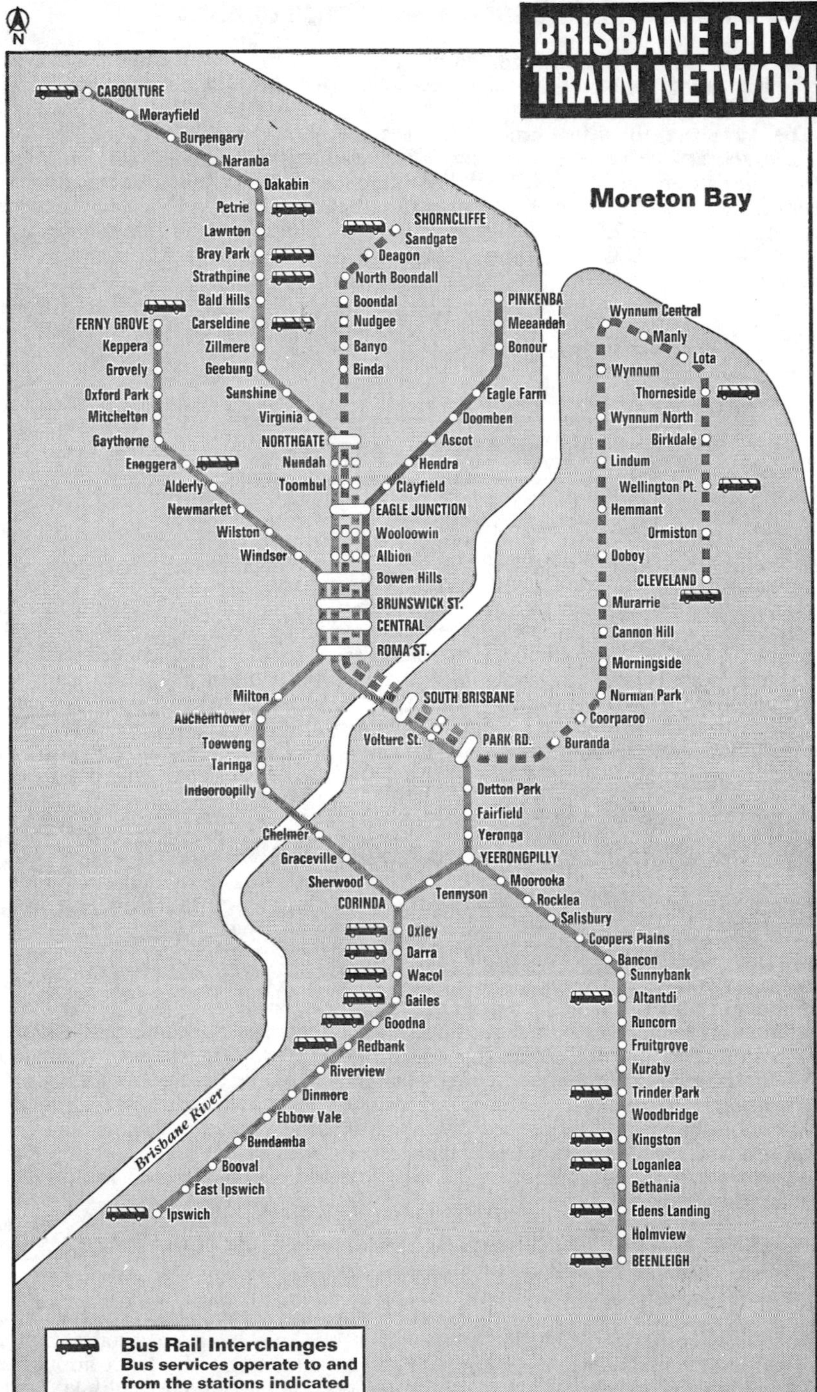
BRISBANE CITY TRAIN NETWORK
N
Moreton Bay
CABOOLTURE
Morayfield
Burpengary
Naranba
Dakabin
Petrie
Lawnton
Bray Park
Strathpine
Bald Hills
Carseldine
Zillmere
Geebung
Sunshine
Virginia
SHORNCLIFFE
Sandgate
Deagon
North Boondall
Boondal
Nudgee
Banyo
Binda
PINKENBA
Meeandah
Bonour
Eagle Farm
Doomben
Ascot
Hendra
Clayfield
FERNY GROVE
Keppera
Grovely
Oxford Park
Mitchelton
Gaythorne
Enoggera
Alderly
Newmarket
Wilston
Windsor
NORTHGATE
Nundah
Toombul
EAGLE JUNCTION
Wooloowin
Albion
Bowen Hills
BRUNSWICK ST.
CENTRAL
ROMA ST.
Wynnum Central
Manly
Lota
Wynnum
Thorneside
Wynnum North
Birkdale
Lindum
Wellington Pt.
Hemmant
Ormiston
Doboy
CLEVELAND
Murarrie
Cannon Hill
Morningside
Norman Park
Coorparoo
Buranda
SOUTH BRISBANE
Volture St.
PARK RD.
Milton
Auchenflower
Toowong
Taringa
Indooroopilly
Chelmer
Graceville
Sherwood
CORINDA
Tennyson
Dutton Park
Fairfield
Yeronga
YEERONGPILLY
Moorooka
Rocklea
Salisbury
Coopers Plains
Bancon
Sunnybank
Altantdi
Runcorn
Fruitgrove
Kuraby
Trinder Park
Woodbridge
Kingston
Loganlea
Bethania
Edens Landing
Holmview
BEENLEIGH
Oxley
Darra
Wacol
Gailes
Goodna
Redbank
Riverview
Dinmore
Ebbow Vale
Bundamba
Booval
East Ipswich
Ipswich
Brisbane River
Bus Rail Interchanges
Bus services operate to and from the stations indicated

Taxis See "Getting Around," in this chapter.

Telegrams/Telex/Fax The post office (see above) and some hotels offer these services.

Television Brisbane receives channels 2, 7, 9, 10, and SBS.

Useful Telephone Numbers For weather information, call 1196. Time: 1194. Tourist Infoline: 11-654. B105 FM News Service: 1197. Brisbane Entertainment Centre: 11-611. Women's Community Health Centre: 844-1935. Women's Information Service: 229-1580. Gay and Lesbian Counselling and Information Service: 844-2967. RACQ Breakdown Service: 340-1122. YHA Travel Centre: 236-1680.

4. WHERE TO STAY

The economy-lodgings scene in Brisbane has improved vastly since the closing days of World Expo '88. This is partly due to the mushrooming backpackers hostels but mainly due to a general recognition of the fact that tourists need alternatives to deluxe high-rises. The improvement occurred despite the on-again, off-again perambulations of the local Y (which has entered the "no accommodations" phase once more), generated solely by the commonsense enterprise of small-scale operators with the courage to compete against the big hotel chains. Further on the plus side, nearly all our budget spots are located downtown or just a couple of bus stops out of town.

When it comes to finding rooms (or anything else) for weary travelers, try the invaluable **Queensland Government Travel Centre,** corner of Edward and Adelaide streets, Brisbane, QLD 4000 (tel. 07/221-6111). They will bend over backward to be of service.

DOUBLES FOR LESS THAN $A65

ASTOR MOTEL, 193 Wickham Terrace, Brisbane, QLD 4000. Tel. 07/831-9522. Fax 07/831-7360. 47 rms (all with bath). A/C TV TEL

$ Rates: $A45–$A69 single, $A49–$A69 double. AE, BC, MC, V.

The Astor Motel doesn't look in the least like a motel. A tropical-style white building with open verandas, it stands in a quiet neighborhood, bordered by parklands on one side, five walking minutes from the city center. The Astor is divided into deluxe suites, which are outside our budget range, and 28 budget units that represent very good value for the price. The lobby is large and pleasantly cool, the elevator service is good, and the corridors are well kept. Budget units come with private bathrooms, carpeting, refrigerators, good-sized wardrobes, clock radios, and electric toasters.

A restaurant is on the premises. Breakfast, which costs from $A4, is served either in your room or on an outdoor verandah. The motel also has a guest laundry and airport coach service.

MAJESTIC HOTEL, 382 George St., Brisbane, QLD 4000. Tel. 07/236-2848. Fax 07/236-1372. 32 rms (all with shower). A/C TV TEL

$ Rates: $A48 single, $A64 double. AE, BC, DC, MC, V.

The Majestic Hotel is a white-and-blue corner building downtown at the corner of Turbot and George streets. The lobby is small, but the hotel has a smart coffee shop, a seafood restaurant, and a cocktail bar with romantic lighting and a dance floor. The furniture is good standard hotel style, and the decoration is in cheerful hues, with large mirrors, fair lighting arrangements, and sufficient wardrobe space. And although plenty of bar activity goes on below, the guest portions are pleasantly quiet.

MARRS TOWN HOUSE, 391 Wickham Terrace, Brisbane, QLD 4000. Tel. 07/831-5388. Fax 07/839-0060. 52 rms (20 with bath). A/C TEL

$ Rates: From $A40 single, from $A55 double. AE, BC, MC, V. **Parking:** Off street.

Marrs Town House looks like a modern office building, and the ground floor actually *is*. The rest, however, constitutes one of the newest and possibly finest budget establishments in Brisbane. The reception area is on the second floor. The whole place, in a delightfully soothing brown decor, breathes the restful quiet that comes from good carpeting and management. The lounge resembles a private club with a pool table and TV; there are a restaurant and a view of the park opposite, and even the elevator comes carpeted. Twenty of the bedrooms have private bathrooms; the rest are served by sparkling public bathrooms. The four hotel floors are air-conditioned. All rooms bear the stamp of comfortable good taste, with ceiling fans, fluorescent lighting, hot- and cold-water basins, large wardrobes, and radios. They also have coffee- and tea-making facilities, bedside lights, and walnut cabinet fixtures. The house offers a guest laundry; a restaurant; plus some truly thoughtful touches, such as special luggage trolleys to ease transport pains. (Other hotels, *please* copy.)

SOHO MOTEL, 333 Wickham Terrace, Spring Hill, QLD 4000. Tel. 07/831-7722. Fax 07/831-8050. 51 rms (all with bath). A/C TV TEL

$ Rates: $A46 single, $A49 double, $A59 triple. AE, BC, MC, V.

A reddish brown four-story brick building with a striped awning, standing opposite Wickham Park, the Soho offers a lot for its rates: direct-dial telephones, a covered parking lot, a guest laundry, in-room refrigerators, a cocktail bar, plus a restaurant in the building. Bedrooms are modern, with heavy drapes, good carpeting, and ample wardrobe space; however, the lighting arrangements are strictly motel standard—that is, insufficient (reading lamps available on request). The hotel is within a few strolling minutes from downtown, and because of its hillside position you get lovely views all around.

SPRING HILL TERRACES, 260 Water St., Spring Hill, QLD 4000. Tel. 07/854-1048. Fax 07/839-0060. 29 rms (17 with bath). A/C TV TEL

$ Rates: $A40 single or double without bath, $A50 single or double with bath. AE, BC, MC, V.

Spring Hill is a modern brick terrace structure about a mile from the city. You step into a neat blue gray lobby and from there into an airy open layout framed around a central yard. There is a dining room on the premises, and the shared bathrooms are excellent. The rooms are divided between standard and budget, the latter with ceiling fans instead of air-conditioning, shared bathrooms, and less space. All rooms, however, have hot- and cold-water basins. Wardrobes are on the small side, the beds and the lighting are good, and refrigerators are in most rooms. There are also a swimming pool and a guest laundry.

BED & BREAKFASTS

Thanks to its tourist mindedness, Brisbane has a much larger array of bed-and-breakfast facilities than most Australian cities. The culinary standard of the breakfasts is generally high, although the quantities served vary.

ANNIE'S SHANDON INN, 405 Upper Edward St., Brisbane, QLD 4000. Tel. 07/831-8684. Fax 07/831-3073. 19 rms (4 with bath). TEL

$ Rates (including continental breakfast): $A36 single, $A46 double without bath; $A46 single, $A56 double with bath. AE, BC, MC, V.

This is not an inn at all but a small and pretty private hotel. A trim blue-and-white two-story structure with geranium boxes in the upper windows, Annie's is a particularly well-run place where the management aims to please. Four of the guest rooms come with private showers and toilets and rates beyond the economy range. The others have hot- and cold-water basins and share four impeccable bathrooms.

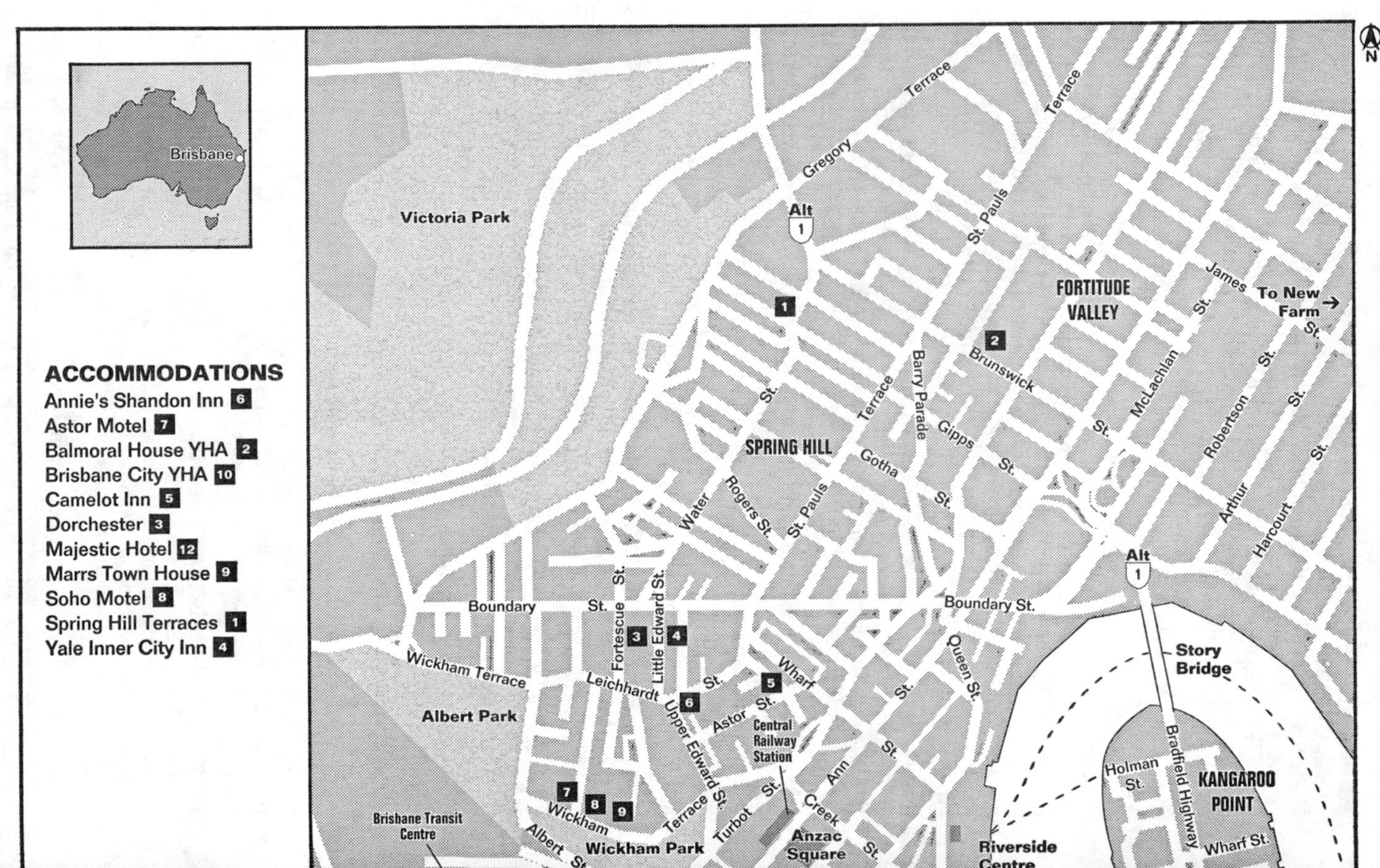
ACCOMMODATIONS
Annie's Shandon Inn 6
Astor Motel 7
Balmoral House YHA 2
Brisbane City YHA 10
Camelot Inn 5
Dorchester 3
Majestic Hotel 12
Marrs Town House 9
Soho Motel 8
Spring Hill Terraces 1
Yale Inner City Inn 4
Brisbane
Victoria Park
Albert Park
Wickham Park
Brisbane Transit Centre
Central Railway Station
Anzac Square
Riverside Centre
Story Bridge
Kangaroo Point
Fortitude Valley
Spring Hill
To New Farm →
Gregory Terrace
St. Pauls Terrace
Boundary St.
Wickham Terrace
Leichhardt St.
Fortescue St.
Little Edward St.
Upper Edward St.
Wharf St.
Astor St.
Ann St.
Creek St.
Turbot St.
Albert St.
Queen St.
Water St.
Rogers St.
Gotha St.
Barry Parade
Brunswick St.
Gipps St.
McLachlan St.
James St.
Robertson St.
Arthur St.
Harcourt St.
Bradfield Highway
Holman St.
Wharf St.
Alt 1
N

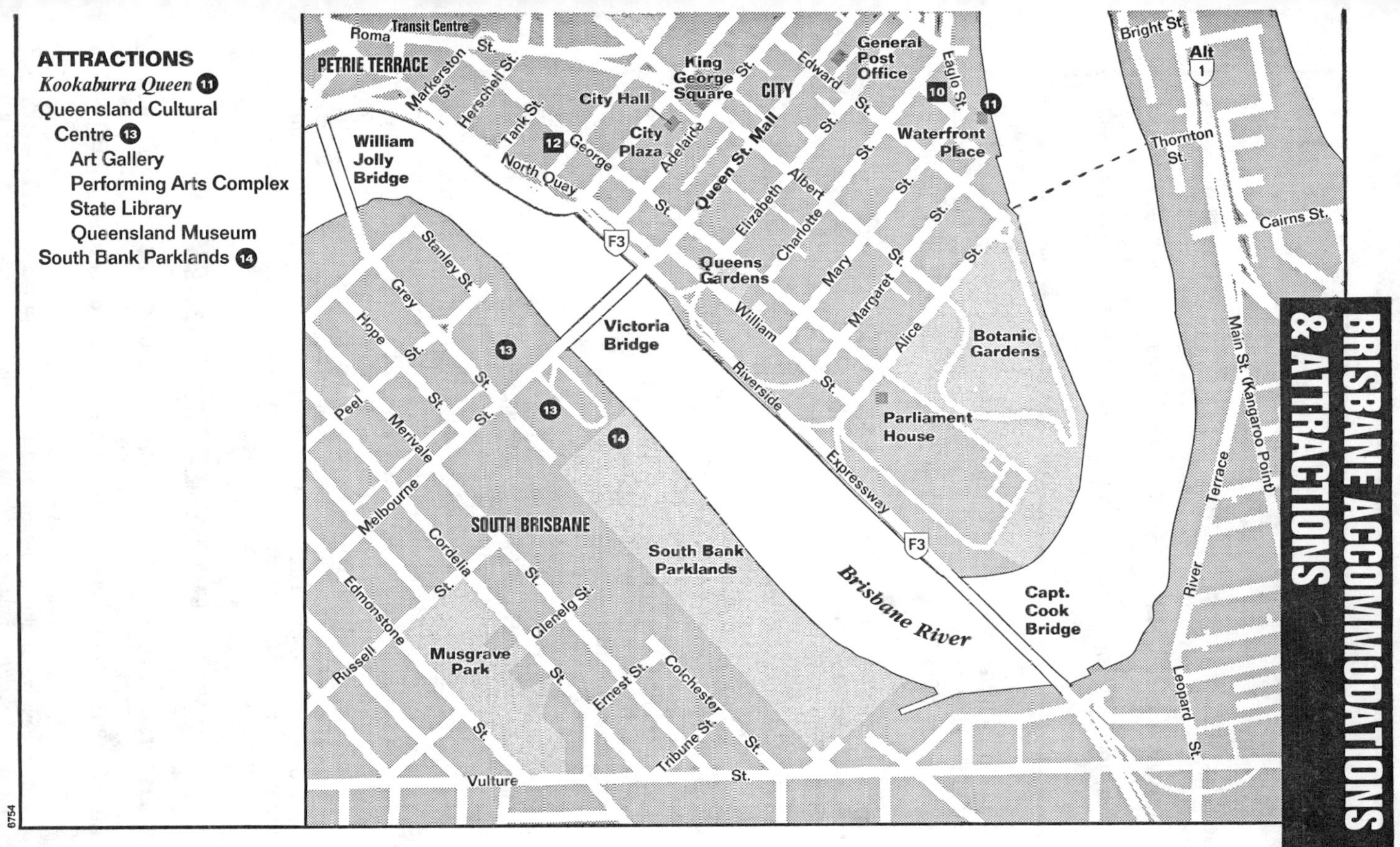
BRISBANE ACCOMMODATIONS
& ATTRACTIONS
ATTRACTIONS
Kookaburra Queen 11
Queensland Cultural
Centre 13
Art Gallery
Performing Arts Complex
State Library
Queensland Museum
South Bank Parklands 14
Roma
Transit Centre
PETRIE TERRACE
Markerston St.
Herschell St.
Tank St.
City Hall
King George Square
CITY
Edward St.
General Post Office
Eaglo St.
Waterfront Place
City Plaza
Adelaide St.
Queen St. Mall
George
North Quay
William Jolly Bridge
Elizabeth St.
Albert St.
Charlotte St.
Mary St.
Margaret St.
Alice St.
Queens Gardens
William St.
Riverside Expressway
F3
Victoria Bridge
Botanic Gardens
Parliament House
Brisbane River
Capt. Cook Bridge
Bright St.
Alt 1
Thornton St.
Cairns St.
Main St. (Kangaroo Point)
River Terrace
Leopard St.
Stanley St.
Grey St.
Hope St.
Peel St.
Merivale St.
Melbourne St.
Cordelia St.
SOUTH BRISBANE
South Bank Parklands
Edmonstone St.
Russell St.
Musgrave Park
Glenelg St.
Ernest St.
Colchester St.
Tribune St.
Vulture St.
6754

FROMMER'S COOL FOR KIDS: HOTELS

Spring Hill Terraces *(p. 215)* There's a swimming pool as well as an open area, providing plenty of splashing-and-romping space.

Camelot Inn *(below)* The inn offers not only a special children's rate but also a fenced-in swimming pool equipped with a trick opening that makes it virtually toddler proof. Swings and slides keep youngsters occupied in a safe play area.

There are also a guest laundry, a TV lounge, and a little garden area with shady umbrellas. The fair-size rooms have ceiling-and-bedside lamps, pink-and-white decor, and tea- and coffee-making equipment. Continental breakfast is served in the dining room.

TOURIST PRIVATE HOTEL-MOTEL, 555 Gregory Terrace, Fortitude Valley, Brisbane, QLD 4000. Tel. 07/252-4171. 40 rms (10 with bath).
$ **Rates** (including full breakfast): Hotel, $A30 single, $A43 double. Motel, $A37 single, $A52 double. BC, MC, V.

Located opposite Brisbane's Exhibition Grounds is the Tourist Private Hotel-Motel. A pretty white weatherboard house with an inviting veranda, this hostelry consists of a bargain hotel portion and a costlier motel part. The hotel is a very relaxed and homey place, not elegant by a long shot but delightfully friendly. Breakfast only is served, but the guest kitchen provides cutlery and crockery. The bedrooms are rather narrow and the furnishings old-fashioned, but they include hot-and-cold running water, bedside lamps, ceiling fans, and wall-to-wall carpeting. Each motel unit has its own toilet and shower, refrigerator, and tea- and coffee-making facilities. The management also provides a TV lounge and laundry and ironing facilities.

YALE INNER CITY INN, 413 Upper Edward St., Brisbane, QLD 4000. Tel. 07/832-1663. Fax 07/831-7318. 60 rms (3 with bath).
$ **Rates** (including continental breakfast): $A30 single, $A42–$A52 double. AE, BC, MC, V.

This inn is strictly an economy lodging. A red-brick structure, made attractive by the greenery outside, this is a rather plain establishment that charges among the lowest rates in town. No frills are wasted on the reception room and hallways. The small dining room serves breakfast only, but there's an upstairs TV lounge for the use of residents. The bedrooms are likewise small and fairly basic but absolutely spotless. Most are equipped with hot- and cold-water basins; some have air-conditioning; and all have fans, wall-to-wall carpeting, and good-size wardrobes, but only ceiling lights. Each of the four floors has two bathrooms. Guests can also use the communal laundry, which has ironing facilities.

WORTH THE EXTRA MONEY

CAMELOT INN, 40 Astor Terrace, Brisbane, QLD 4000. Tel. 07/832-5115. Fax 07/832-3775. 70 rms (all with bath). A/C TV TEL **Parking:** Free.
$ **Rates:** $A80 single or double. Weekend special of $A65 per room. AE, BC, MC, V.

Standing on a hillside—almost downtown—this is a handsome modern structure with a bright red awning and a wide range of facilities. All rooms have kitchenettes, large balconies, refrigerators, bedside clock radios, and good-sized mirrors. Bathrooms are small but well fitted. The walls are cool brick, the drapes are heavy enough to keep out the sun, and there is plenty of strategically placed lighting. The inn also has a swimming pool with a spa, swings and slides, barbecue facilities, and full equipment for the kitchens. The restaurant downstairs serves breakfast and dinner seven days a week.

HOSTELS & DORMS

Advance bookings can be made at any Australian hostel. Brisbane also currently has about 20 Backpackers establishments and more in the budding stage. The Aussie Way and Durham Villa are the most centrally located.

THE AUSSIE WAY, 34 Cricket St., Petrie Terrace, QLD 4000. Tel. 07/369-0711. 20 rms (none with bath).

$ Rates: From $A12 per night. AE, BC, MC, V.

The Aussie Way is centrally located and downright stylish, boasting carpeted rooms, a TV lounge, a pool table, and laundry facilities. Free pick ups from the Transit Centre are also available.

DURHAM VILLA, 17 Laura St., Highgate Hill, QLD. Tel. 07/844-6853. 8 rms (1 with bath), 6 dorms.

$ Rates: $A28 single or double, $A12 dorm. MC, V.

The Durham is a large red-roofed establishment with an upstairs balcony and a welcoming air of Irish hospitality. It is located five minutes from downtown and offers a big saltwater swimming pool, a spacious guest kitchen, TV lounge, laundry facilities, and exceptionally amiable hosts. The place also runs a free pick-up service from the Brisbane Transit Centre. Ask about the very economical weekly rate.

INTERNATIONAL HOUSE, 5 Rock St., St. Lucia, QLD. Tel. 07/870-9593.

$ Rates: $A39 per nonstudent with breakfast, $A50 per nonstudent with breakfast and dinner. AE, BC, MC, V.

Rooms at the University of Queensland are good, and the establishment is conveniently located three miles from downtown. There is excellent public transportation, and rooms are open all year. *Vivat Professoria!*

YOUTH HOSTELS

BALMORAL HOUSE, 33 Amelia St., Fortitude Valley, QLD 4006. Tel. 07/252-1397. Fax 07/252-5892. 39 beds, double and family rooms.

$ Rates: $A40 dorm (for 4 persons), $A28 single, $A32 double. BC, MC, V.

Located in Chinatown, close to legions of restaurants and a train station, Balmoral House is a newish brick structure with a guest kitchen, a public phone, and an airport bus stop at the front door. Some rooms come with private bath at $A45 single or double.

BRISBANE CITY, 53 Quay St., Brisbane, QLD 4000. Tel. 07/236-1004. Fax 07/236-1947. 80 dorm beds, 18 doubles. (none with bath).

$ Rates: $A13 dorm, $A16 per person double. BC, MC, V.

The most modern hostel in town, this is a no-smoking establishment about a 10-minute walk from the Brisbane Transit Centre. It is very well equipped—with spacious lounges, new bathrooms, a cafeteria serving economy meals, a guest kitchen and laundry, plus parking facilities. The twin rooms are large enough for family groups.

SERVICED APARTMENTS

Brisbane doesn't offer much in this bracket—worse luck. Most of Queensland's serviced flats are concentrated in the beach-resort areas, where the tourist trade is thickest.

DAHRL COURT, 45 Phillips St., Spring Hill, QLD 4000. Tel. 07/832-3458. Fax 07/839-2591. 16 apts (all with bath). A/C TV TEL

$ Rates: $A55 single, $A65 double. BC, MC, V.

This is a block of apartments on a quiet street, set among landscaped surroundings. The Dahrl offers self-contained suites, serviced daily, each consisting of a large living room, separate dining room, and modern kitchen and bathroom. These units can hold a family of four comfortably and five at a squeeze, and they come with built-in closets, tasteful furnishings, telephones, and radios. Full laundry facilities are in the building, including a dryer and ironing equipment. There are also a swimming pool, video equipment, and a gym.

DORCHESTER, 484 Upper Edward St., Brisbane, QLD 4000. Tel. 07/831-2967. Fax 07/832-2932. 12 apts (all with bath). TV

$ Rates: $A60 single, $A70 double. BC, MC, V.

This is a real bargain establishment for two persons. The location is fine: within a few walking minutes of the main shopping streets yet far enough away to avoid the traffic noise. It's a small white building, newly decorated, housing 12 apartments (flats), each completely private and self-contained. The hallways are full of greenery, the apartments well maintained and equipped, although not luxurious. Each consists of a bed-sitting-room and a surprisingly spacious kitchen. The management provides microwave, refrigerator, cutlery, crockery, linen, towels, a guest laundry, and a weekly floor-cleaning service. Each apartment has two beds (an extra bed or cot can be rented) and a dinette in the kitchen. Furnishings are good—you get a dressing table, a wardrobe, bedside lamps, and a tub as well as shower. Off-street parking is available with the accommodation.

CARAVAN (R.V.) PARKS

Queensland is an ideal state for camping and caravaning and has a lot of facilities catering to both. Most of Brisbane's caravan parks are better situated than those in other state capitals, at least as far as proximity is concerned. Those listed below are all within a 10-mile radius of the city center and feature on-site vans for rent. The rates charged are between $A18 and $A28 for two people per day. Fees for parking your own van are between $A6 and $A11 per day. Unfortunately the Brisbane City Council has a ruling banning the erection of tents within a radius of roughly 15 miles around the General Post Office. This does not apply to "lean-tos" or canvas verandas attached to vans. For an excellent and comprehensive guide to Queensland camping grounds, ask for the brochure issued by the Government Tourist Bureau. Two to try are **Aspley Acres,** 1420 Gympie Rd., Aspley (tel. 07/263-2668); and **Sheldon Caravan Park,** 27 Holmead Rd., Eight Mile Plains, QLD 4113 (tel. 07/341-6601).

Most of these parks are equipped with hot- and cold-water showers and toilets, a kiosk or store, a community laundry, a barbecue, and ice dispensers. Some feature TV lounges and game rooms. Some also provide linen and blankets as part of their van equipment; others charge extra for them. Find out by telephoning beforehand.

5. WHERE TO EAT

Brisbane boasts far fewer quality restaurants than Adelaide—which is passing strange because Brisbane is the bigger of the two. Even stranger is the time schedule maintained by many eateries. All over the world the general rule applies that the warmer the climate, the later the dinner hour. But not in Brisbane, where they've reversed the custom. Blessed with the balmiest weather of any Australian metropolis, they insist on eating *earlier*. Most Queenslanders seem to consider dining around 9pm as vaguely decadent. And visitors willy-nilly must follow suit or risk finding a locked door and dark premises when they arrive for a meal.

While culinary standards here generally are below those of Melbourne, Sydney, or Adelaide, Brisbane does possess a number of good budget choices and a couple of outstanding "big splurge" spots. Hotel lunches are mostly excellent as well as cheap. All in all, it's not a bad tucker town.

Most restaurants are concentrated in two main areas—the city and Fortitude Valley, just a little hill apart. Why eateries should cluster in a region as unprepossessing as the valley, I cannot fathom, but this concentration certainly makes eating easier for tourists. And as is the case throughout Australia today, the selection is lavishly cosmopolitan: from Spanish to Indonesian and points in between.

MEALS FOR LESS THAN $A12

CAFE LUNAR, 681 Brunswick St., New Farm.

Cuisine: INTERNATIONAL. **Reservations:** Not necessary.
$ Prices: Appetizers $A3–$A4, main courses $A6–$A9.50. AE, BC, MC, V.
Open: Tues–Sun 10am–midnight, Mon 10am–2pm.

Café Lunar has a charming courtyard for al fresco dining and serves outstanding and unusual fruit juices (such as melon) for starters. Unlike most local restaurants, the fare here accentuates light dishes, well in tune with the climate. Try the spinach pie as a main course (the best in Queensland), and for dessert have the hot apple crumble with country-fresh cream. Brunswick Street, incidently, runs from Fortitude Valley to New Farm.

COSMOPOLITAN CAFE, 322 Brunswick St., Fortitude Valley. Tel. 252-4179.

Cuisine: CONTINENTAL. **Reservations:** Accepted.
$ Prices: Appetizers $A2–$A6, main courses $A8.50–$A14. AE, MC, V.
Open: Mon–Wed 7:30am–6pm, Thurs–Sat 7:30am–midnight.

This large, handsome, European-style café has tile floors and French impressionist prints on the walls. The spacious outdoor section spills into the pedestrian mall and is shaded by colored umbrellas. It makes an ideal people-watching vantage. You place your order at the service counter, then carry it to your table—hoping that the seat you've picked is still unoccupied. The special here is a heaped combination of salami, artichoke, olives, eggplant, tomatoes, and mozzarella for $A6. Also recommended: the veal with mushrooms, followed by apple-blossom cake.

FOX AND GRAPES, Spring Hill Hotel, corner of Leichhardt and Little Edward Sts., Spring Hill. Tel. 831-0102.

Cuisine: INTERNATIONAL. **Reservations:** Accepted.
$ Prices: $A3.50–$A9.50. No credit cards.
Open: Mon–Sun noon–2pm, 6–8:30pm.

The bistro portion of this real Aussie pub is a surprise: an open but roofed courtyard with an inside bar decorated with classic French photographs and a menu that includes Mexican nachos, tacos, and burritos (beef or chicken) for $A6.50. There are no appetizers, but an excellent leek and sweet corn soup. Follow through with the seafood basket containing a bit of nearly everything from the ocean.

JENNY'S, 334 Brunswick St., Fortitude Valley. Tel. 252-8036.

Cuisine: CHINESE. **Reservations:** Accepted.
$ Prices: Appetizers $A3–$A6, main courses $A6–$A9.50. AE, BC, MC, V.
Open: Daily 11am–11pm.

Located in Brisbane's Chinatown, this Cantonese eatery offers maximum elbow space and a minimum of Asian ornamentation. An air-conditioned BYO, Jenny's has a sliding-door front entrance, a gleaming tile floor, and an aura of attractive simplicity. There is an unusually large selection of prawn dishes, and I can also recommend the Mongolian chicken, the light and flavorful vegetable delight, and the hefty Singapore noodles with pork.

PANCAKES AT THE MANOR, 18 Charlotte St., Brisbane. Tel. 221-6433.

Cuisine: PANCAKES. **Reservations:** Accepted.

$ Prices: $A6.95–$A13.95. AE, BC, MC, V.
Open: 10am–2:30am.

Another link in the golden chain of pancake dispensaries that winds around Australia, this downtowner dishes them up in every imaginable form: for breakfast with bacon and hash browns; Mexicana, with chili; Greek style, with feta cheese and spinach; and for dessert, with brandied apricots. In between you can choose from about 20 other variations. Also on the menu are Swiss shakes, milk shakes, ice-cream sodas, and smoothies—the classic libations of kids' conventions. The service is as smooth as the shakes and you get "Customer Evaluation Cards" to keep it so.

MEALS FOR LESS THAN $A15

CUBANA, in the Wallace Bishop Arcade, 239 Albert St., Brisbane. Tel. 221-8680.
Cuisine: LATIN. **Reservations:** Accepted.
$ Prices: Appetizers $A3–$A6.50, main courses $A10–$A14.50. AE, BC, MC, V.
Open: Daily 8am–10pm.

There's nothing particularly Cuban about the Cubana, but this midtown eatery is wonderfully versatile: doubling as a coffee lounge or restaurant and serving breakfast, lunch, and dinner. In between you can relax over coffee or a drink; it's licensed as well. The big draw here is the fixed-price lunch for $A9.95—a real bargain that includes a drink of your choice.

GIARDINETTO, 366 Brunswick St., Fortitude Valley. Tel. 252-4750.
Cuisine: ITALIAN. **Reservations:** Accepted.
$ Prices: Appetizers $A5–$A9.50, main courses $A9.80–$A17.80. AE, BC, MC, V.
Open: Lunch, Tues–Fri noon–12:30pm; dinner, daily 6–10pm.

In Fortitude Valley is the solidly Italian Giardinetto. Popular with the locals, Giardinetto divides its fare between general Italian dishes and pizza, and it's hard to decide which category is better. A small BYO with kitchen-type chairs, ceramic-top tables, and latticework strung with bunches of plastic grapes and genuine Chianti bottles, it also offers a courtyard for al fresco dining. Most of the dishes here come in large or small portions, and you'll need a healthy appetite to polish off the biggies. The homemade gnocchi costs $A8.50, cannelloni and ravioli the same. The spaghetti carbonara (bacon egg) comes in an immense portion. A dozen varieties of pizza–including a positively poetic combination of ham, salami, mushrooms, mozzarella, capsicum, and garlic covered in tomato sauce—are also offered.

JIMMY'S ON THE MALL, City Mall, Queen St., Brisbane. Tel. 229-9999.
Cuisine: ASIAN-ITALIAN. **Reservations:** Not necessary.
$ Prices: Appetizers $A5–$A6, main courses $A9–$A12. No credit cards.
Open: 24 hrs.

There may be some confusion here because there are actually *three* Jimmy's, at opposite ends and in the middle of the beautiful City Mall (Queen Street). The second specializes in crêpes and other light victuals. It's the first I'm talking about here. An outdoor-indoor restaurant with smart marble-top tables sheltered by purely ornamental umbrellas, Jimmy's is a patch of transplanted Paris set amid Brisbane's busiest shopping bustle. Potted plants sprinkled among the tables make for greenery. Besides the shopping throngs, you can watch live crabs wandering around their tanks before they make the menu. The atmosphere is delightful. And the fare amazingly varied: fettuccine carbonara or Singaporean noodles for $A13.90. Seafood dishes are also offered. The place is licensed to sell alcohol.

LOTUS ROOM, 203 Elizabeth St., Brisbane. Tel. 221-8546.
Cuisine: CHINESE. **Reservations:** Accepted.
$ Prices: Appetizers $A2.80–$A4.20, main courses $A7.90–$A12.50. AE, BC, MC, V.
Open: Mon–Sat 5–10pm.

You walk downstairs into an air-conditioned, somewhat gaudy dining room, with glowing red wall lighting and scarlet table linen. Glass cases display rows of choice liquor bottles, and a rear mirror makes the place appear twice as large. You dine surrounded by Chinese family groups—always a reassuring sight. Try the subtle steamed dim sums for starters. Then have either the duck and mushrooms or the sweetly piquant honey prawns. This meal will cost $A13.30. Service is fast and smooth, and the restaurant is licensed.

MEDITERRANEO, 25 Caxton St., Petrie Terrace. Tel. 368-1933.

Cuisine: MEDITERRANEAN. **Reservations:** Recommended.
$ **Prices:** Appetizers $A4.95–$A6, main courses $A9.50–$A15. AE, BC, DC, MC, V.
Open: Daily noon–2:30pm, 6–11:30pm.

Mediterraneo is a bright, airy, relaxed establishment that appears more expensive than it is. This is largely due to the art collection on the walls and the impressive wood-fired oven in the back. The Med, as patrons call it, has a semioutdoor area in the rear and is one of the very few places in Brisbane that serves genuine American Caesar salad. Otherwise there is a selection of Greek dips for starters, served with pita bread at $A5.95, and a range of intriguingly "different" pizzas—some topped with seafood—and "mod Med" delicacies like fettuccine with Cajun squid and grilled fish with marinated eggplant, peppers, and scallop salad. Australian wines by the glass.

MUNICH STEAKHOUSE, corner of Albert and Charlotte Sts., Brisbane. Tel. 229-6472.

Cuisine: GERMAN. **Reservations:** Accepted.
$ **Prices:** Appetizers $A2–$A8.95, main courses $A12.20–$A17.45. AE, BC, MC, V.
Open: Daily 5:30pm–9pm.

This is one of a chain of restaurants, all serving a very modified form of German cuisine: a few Teutonic dishes, a vast beer selection, but with the main accent on steaks. The Bavarian atmosphere is supplied by skis and antlers on the walls, wooden peasant tables, and ceiling lights mounted on wagon wheels. The entertainment is a pianist playing jazz. You get truly giant Bockwurst for $A12, a traditional Bavarian mixed-meat platter (heaping) for $A13.90. Beer costs $A1.70 per glass. Ordering is done by marking your menu, which the waiter takes and returns with the food. A big draw here are the children's meals for just $A2.50.

WORTH THE EXTRA MONEY

NED KELLY'S, Boardwalk, South Bank Parklands. Tel. 844-4139.

Cuisine: AUSTRALIAN. **Reservations:** Recommended on weekends.
$ **Prices:** Appetizers $A8.50–$A14.50, main courses $A17.50–$A27.50. AE, DC.
Open: Daily 7:30am–9:30pm.

This is our splurge restaurant, the above-budget prices justified by the near-unique fare. Ned Kelly, of course, was Australia's most celebrated bushranger (see "History," Chapter 1), and his armor-clad, gun-toting figure welcomes you at the entrance. The inside decor is movie-set outback complete with corrugated iron ceiling and log walls, but the best seating is outdoors on the boardwalk along the river.

The restaurant serves Aussie "bush tucker," called "rarkee" on the menu. Delectables like sizzling pans of witchetty grubs, crocodile chowder, Cajun camel (I kid thee not), buffalo steaks, kangaroo tail, and witchetty ice cream, which tastes like hazelnut. If you want to get the lot in one course, order the bush kebab, a skewered combination of chunks of emu, kangaroo, buffalo, camel, and crocodile. For less adventurous diners the Ned Kelly also offers the customary rib-and-rump steak, seafood, and a very rich steamed pudding marinated in port.

SPECIALTY DINING

FOR VEGETARIANS $ **Govinda's,** on the 1st floor at 99 Elizabeth St. (tel. 210-0255), is a small lunchtime restaurant and gift shop operated by the Hare

Krishnas. Meatless, smoke free, and one of the most economical eateries in town, it offers an all-you-can-eat menu for just $A5 and free reading material in the form of rows of brochures on Eastern religions. The patrons are mostly young New Age types and the atmosphere is suitably tranquil. It's open Monday to Friday 11:30am to 2:30pm.

A DINING COMPLEX In Fortitude Valley, which includes Brisbane's Chinatown, you'll find the superlative **Food Mart,** McWhirters Centre, on Brunswick Street, one of the finest of its kind anywhere. A giant air-conditioned food-and-produce market built in a shopping center, it consists of dozens of stalls selling cosmopolitan comestibles, cooked and otherwise, ranging from the simplest to the gourmet. Several offer vast varieties of fruit-and-vegetable salads, among the best you've ever nibbled for $A2.50 per bowl, with or without yogurt. The **Stockman Carvery** has hot lamb, beef, turkey, or ham sandwiches for between $A3 and $A4. Other counters offer pasta dishes, kebabs, German wurst, and such delicacies as venison cooked in Bordeaux. This is one of our top luncheon bets. It opens around 10am and closes at 6pm weeknights, but on weekends you can have dinner there as well because it stays open until 9pm.

AFTERNOON TEA The ideal place to rest your weary sightseer's feet at a festive afternoon tea is the **Shingle Inn,** 254 Edward St. (tel. 221-9039), a beautiful English inn with Tudor-style beamed walls, sparkling chandeliers, rich red carpets, and lovely old pieces of pottery. Casement windows with boxes of flowers and greenery and waitresses dressed like Ruritanian milkmaids enhance the illusion of rusticity in the midst of downtown. The atmosphere is genteel and soothing, the accent on desserts. The inn serves an exceptional lemon meringue pie and waffles with butterscotch sauce and ice cream, each $A4.20. Tea comes in old silver pots. This could be a grand spot for after-theater snacks, but why, alas, does it close its handsome doors at 7:30pm sharp?

6. ATTRACTIONS

The Queensland Tourist Bureau has compiled an informative brochure, "Travel Through History," which you can use as a guide to historic sites and buildings throughout Queensland.

The **City Hall,** King George Square, is one of Brisbane's showpieces. It contains art collections as well as the Tower Lookout (above the clock), which you reach by elevator. Conducted tours for groups can be arranged by phoning 225-4360.

A must for American visitors is the memorial titled *They Passed This Way.* Located at Lyndon B. Johnson Place, Newstead Park, it was erected by the people of Queensland as a tribute to the United States. During the Pacific crisis stage of World War II, General MacArthur made his headquarters in Brisbane.

Rowes Arcade, which runs off Edward Street, is Brisbane's chic shopping arcade, centered by a beautiful and noisy fountain and lined with subtly lit, expensive stores.

QUEENSLAND CULTURAL CENTRE, South Bank, South Brisbane. Tel. 840-7200.

On the south bank, just across Victoria Bridge and next to the World Expo '88 site, stands the Queensland Cultural Centre, pride of the city and one of Australia's major visitors' magnets. Opened in 1985, it is a gleaming giant of many facets, combining aesthetic beauty with remarkable architectural ingenuity. The vast foyers are art exhibitions in their own right, hung with changing collections and simultaneously offering superb views of the Brisbane River and the city.

The jewel of this cultural edifice is the **Performing Arts Complex,** containing three world-class theaters, each designed for excellent acoustics as well as maximum audience comfort. One of them, the **Cremorne Theatre,** is also a unique

FROMMER'S COOL FOR KIDS: RESTAURANTS

Pancakes at the Manor *(p. 221)* Serving a standard favorite, no other establishment caters as consciously to kids' tastes, whims, and comforts.

Jimmy's on the Mall *(p. 222)* Kids love the action going on all around while they're spooning away.

Food Mart *(p. 224)* This place usually holds them spellbound by the sheer variety of tidbits offered, both cooked and raw.

achievement of showcase versatility. With a few internal transfigurations it functions in five different modes: as a concert hall, a movie house, a fashion display stage, an intimate theater-in-the-round, and a cabaret with dance floor.

If you can't attend a show in the complex, take one of the conducted tours of this cultural marvel. The tours leave from the foyer every hour on the hour Monday to Saturday until 4pm. They last about 45 minutes and cost $A5 for adults, $A4 for children, $A2.50 for students.

Another part of the center is the **Queensland Art Gallery.** Bordered by a spectacular water mall, it houses a fine collection of contemporary Australian and European art, including a Picasso. The gallery also hosts guest exhibitions. It's open daily from 10am to 5pm. Admission is free.

The **Queensland Museum,** likewise part of the complex, has contrasting exhibits of old-time utensils and contemporary designs. The most fascinating section, a natural history showpiece called "Dragons and Diprotodons," is the only robotic display of its kind in Australia.

Admission: Free.

Open: Daily 9am–5pm. **Bus:** 502 to South Brisbane Station. **Train:** To South Brisbane Station.

SOUTH BANK PARKLANDS, South Brisbane. Tel. 867-2000.

Parklands isn't quite the right label for this remarkable development of a strip of shoreline along the south bank of the Brisbane River, adjoining the Queensland Cultural Centre. There are plenty of trees and lawns, but the area is really a joyous hodgepodge of theme park, playground, restaurant strip, and showground, with wandering entertainers thrown in for good measure.

There is the **Gondwana Rainforest Sanctuary,** housing 100 species of wildlife and an elevated boardwalk over a crocodile pond. There is **Our World Environment,** which takes you through subzero ice shelves and real snow a few steps from burning deserts and ocean depths. There is an **Insect House,** with magnificent tropical butterflies, barking spiders, and giant tree bugs. There are waterways to cruise on, a beach to swim from, a childrens' theater, 16 restaurants, cafés and taverns to eat and drink in, picnic grounds with barbecue pits, and a **Crafts Village** offering designer togs, delectables, and collectibles. And there is a cavalcade of street performers, from jugglers and clowns to jazz pianists and trumpet tooters, to keep the vibes happy.

Admission: Free.

Open: Daily 9am until "late." **Train:** To South Brisbane Station. **Ferry:** To BCC Terminal.

MARITIME MUSEUM, South Bank, South Brisbane. Tel. 844-5361.

This collection of ships, models, and maritime memorabilia stands just outside the South Bank Parklands. It houses, among many other items, an entire Australian-built

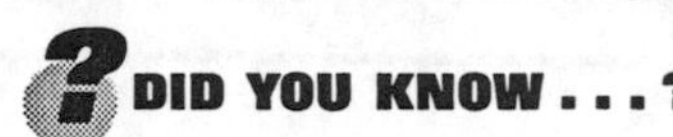

- Brisbane's convict-built Old Windmill was one of the first images ever beamed on a TV screen (during experiments conducted in 1934).
- The Battle of Brisbane took place during World War II, but between allies—it was a gigantic street brawl that erupted in November 1942, pitching GIs against Australian Diggers. The MPs won.
- The first flight across the Pacific Ocean was made from Oakland, California, to Brisbane in 1928—in a trimotored Fokker, which was considered obsolete even then.
- Until its recent abolition, Queensland had a state law forbidding bartenders to serve men dressed in drag.
- Although ginger originated in the Far East, the world's largest ginger-processing plant is on the Sunshine Coast.
- There is a well-attended Muslim mosque in the Brisbane suburb of Holland Park.

frigate that fought in the South Pacific during World War II. It also contains a century-old dry dock, a Thursday Island pearling lugger, and a tiny aluminum yacht that sailed from New Caledonia to Australia.

Admission: $A4 adults, $A2 children.

Open: Daily 9:30am–5pm.

QUEENSLAND ABORIGINAL CREATIONS, 135 George St. Tel. 224-5730.

The curio section of the Department of Community Services, it offers a fascinating display of tribal masks, weapons, fire sticks, and the strange musical instruments known as "bullroarers." There are also bark paintings, oils, and pencil sketches, some outstanding. The artworks shown are for sale.

Admission: Free.

Open: Mon–Fri 9am–4:30pm.

OBSERVATORY [Old Windmill], Wickham Terrace, Brisbane.

The Observatory was originally built by convicts as a windmill, but the sails couldn't be made to operate, so the structure was converted into a (human-propelled) treadmill. Later it became a meteorological station and still later a test lab for TV experiments. In 1934, the first picture ever televised in Australia was the image of the Observatory, transmitted to Ipswich over 20 miles away.

Admission: Free.

Open: Daily 10am–6pm.

NEWSTEAD HOUSE, Newstead Park, Breakfast Creek Rd. Tel. 52-7373.

This is Brisbane's oldest historical building, with a display of relics from the early colonial settlers' days. The residence itself is a museum.

Admission: $A2 adults, $A1 children.

Open: Mon–Fri 11am–3pm, Sun 2–5pm.

SCIENCENTRE, William St. at Stephen's Lane, Brisbane. Tel. 224-6003.

A Victorian red-brick facade hides a wonderfully futuristic collection of scientific marvels, most of which can be touched, explored, and played with. You can make a ball spin in midair, see a cone roll uphill, watch walls expand and contract, become part of a battery, see the sound of a flute, lose your shadow, and experience a dozen other phenomena. It's hands-on learning for all ages in what used to be the government printing office.

Admission: $A4 adults, $A2 children.

Open: Mon–Fri 9:30am–4pm, Sat 1–5pm, Sun 9:30am–5pm.

AUSTRALIAN WOOLSHED, 148 Samford Rd., Ferny Hill. Tel. 351-5366.

This vast playland about 10 miles from the city is centered around the Ram Show. Staged daily at 11am and 2pm, this woolly cavalcade features sheep being herded—and ridden—by superbly trained dogs; sheep being shorn by "gun" shearers; and sheep performing tricks you'd never expect from them. The layout includes a restaurant, waterslides, miniature golf, and picnic areas.

Admission: $A9 adults, $A4 children.
Open: Daily 9:30am–5pm. **Train:** Go to Ferny Grove Station.

BRISBANE FOREST PARK, Mount Coot-tha Rd.

This park is a miniature nature reserve right in the center of a metropolis (the entrance only about four miles from the GPO). It is a wonderful, lofty oasis of towering eucalyptus, tropical shrubs, and millions of birds. Within this complex stretch the new, landscaped **Botanical Gardens,** plus an adjoining park with picnic grounds, barbecues, and a series of cascades. Carefully graded walking tracks snake through the entire area, and strategically placed gaps in the timber provide constantly changing views of the city, suburbs, distant mountains, and sea.

Admission: Free.
Open: Daily 8am to 5pm.

Also in the park is the **Sir Thomas Brisbane Planetarium,** the largest of its kind in Australia, seating 130 people and featuring a regular observatory. General programs dealing with the enthralling movements of the cosmos are staged at the **Star Theatre** Wednesday to Sunday two or three times daily. The observatory houses an excellent 150-millimeter refracting telescope available for public use on a booking basis. Visitors should phone 377-8896 for bookings. Sky shows cost $A6.40 for adults, $A2.95 for children.

Admission: $A7 adults, $A3.50 children.
Open: Daily 10am–4:30pm.

LONE PINE SANCTUARY, Fig Tree Pocket, 15 minutes west of city. Tel. 378-1366.

FROMMER'S FAVORITE BRISBANE & GOLD COAST EXPERIENCES

Brekky at Brekky Creek On the boardwalk of a place called Brekky Creek, you can enjoy a somewhat unusual lobster brekky (the endearing Oz diminutive for *breakfast,* which sounds far too solemn).

Meeting Man's and Koala's Best Friend At the Lone Pine Sanctuary, the German shepherd who patiently carries a fat koala on his back is more than happy to shake paws.

Dining at Crazies Enjoy the manic nuttiness of the "Crazies" show at this comedy restaurant.

Sunday at Cat's Tango Riverside Market This is a bargain-hunting paradise on Sunday afternoon.

Cliff Climbing on Fraser Island The world's largest island composed entirely of sand, it features multicolored sand cliffs.

Feeding Time at Currumbin Bird Sanctuary A cloud of tiny rainbow lorikeets softly descends around you to feed on the bread and honey below.

A Day at the Warana Festival Queen Street Mall comes to life with costumed strolling minstrels, bards, and vagabonds.

The View from Mt. Coot-tha Lookout Take in the breathtaking panoramic view of Brisbane in the cool early morning.

The first koala sanctuary established in Australia, it now has a colony of around 130 of these cuddlies. There's even a photographer on the grounds to snap you and yours with one of the live teddy bears in your arm. But koalas are merely part of Lone Pine's charms. The sanctuary on the banks of the Brisbane River houses a large cross section of Australian fauna, including kangaroos and emus you can feed by hand. Others you certainly can't—Queensland pythons, Tasmanian devils, dingoes, and echidnas (spiny anteaters), for instance. The beautiful layout includes barbecue-and-picnic areas, and there's a special lecture spot where you can learn all about koalas from someone who knows.

You can ride the bus to Lone Pines, but it's more fun to take the 14-mile route by river ferry. The launch leaves **Mirimar Cruises,** at North Quay, daily at 1:30pm. Chugging leisurely down the Brisbane, you get a running commentary on the various features of the river and developments on the banks. The return trip leaves 2¼ hours later. Round-trip tickets cost $A15 for adults, $A8 for children.

Admission: $A10.50 adults, $A6 children.

Open: Daily 8:45am–4:45pm. **Bus:** No. 518, Myer Centre, Queen Street Mall.

BUNYA PARK, Bunya Park Dr., Eatons Hill. Tel. 264-1200.

Bunya Park, about 10 miles from the city, is another outstanding wildlife sanctuary, consisting of natural bushland surrounding an artificial lake. You can move freely among the birds and animals. The park is designed around a "bush walk" leading through various reserves where the inhabitants live in habitats as similar as possible to their natural ones. Kangaroos to koalas, crocodiles to wombats—all ready for your camera. You can cuddle a koala as part of the service, if you don't mind smelling like a eucalyptus cough drop afterward.

Admission: $A9.50 adults, $A5 children.

Open: Daily 9am–5pm.

PIONEER VALLEY PARK, Beenleigh Rd., Kuraby.

Heading south toward the Gold Coast, some 15 miles down the main highway, you reach Pioneer Valley Park, which has the world's largest collection of horse-drawn vehicles on display, plus an awesome array of old coach lanterns, bridles, harnesses, and pioneer tools. You can also go on steam-train, buggy, hay, horse, and canoe rides.

Admission: Free.

Open: Daily 9am–4:30pm.

ORGANIZED TOURS

BUS TOURS The best organized tours are often the least organized ones. That's the case with **Brisbane Citysights** (tel. 13-1230). Operated by the city transport authorities, they use open streetcar-style buses to make a complete city circuit. The buses stop at 20 points, each at a certain attraction, and run every half hour on Wednesday to Monday from 9am to 4pm.

You simply get on a bus at a marked stop (they start at Post Office Square outside the GPO) and get off at any attraction you fancy, look around for as long as you want, then catch the next bus running the circuit. You can do this all day on one ticket.

The attraction stops include City Hall, the Old Windmill Observatory, Waterfront Place, the Sciencentre, Chinatown, and the Edward Street Ferry. And your ticket includes a free ferry trip, plus discounts at several of the attractions. Buy your ticket from the driver. It costs $A10 for adults, $A8 for children.

BAY & RIVER CRUISES **Adai Cruises,** BP Marina, Breakfast Creek (tel. 262-6978), have a motor launch chugging over to **St. Helena Island** for a guided tour of the old Penal Settlement, followed by a barbecue lunch—all for $A20. They operate Saturday and Sunday from 9am to 4pm.

The ***Kookaburra Queen*** is a splendid white paddle wheeler with tall green funnels, fitted with hand-timbered decks and majestic staircases. This floating palace, moored in the Brisbane River, undertakes 15 different cruises, priced from economy to deluxe. The simplest, a jaunt up and down the river, runs daily and costs $A9.90. For $A13.90 you can go on the Morning Devonshire Tea Cruise, offered Sunday at

3:30pm. The departure point is the Pier at Waterfront Place, Eagle Street. Reservations are a must (tel. 07/221-1300).

7. SPORTS & RECREATION

Although lacking the beaches of Sydney and without the football frenzy of Melbourne, Brisbane still has a few options to attract sports lovers.

CRICKET Cricket is one of the major spectator sports in Queensland. The top matches are played in summer at the Woolloongabba Ground (which the Aussies mercifully shorten to "Gabba") on Vulture Street (tel. 391-6533). This is also the locale of the Queensland Cricketers' Club, which has a bar, bistro, and poker machines and welcomes overseas visitors.

GOLF For golfers there's the Ashgrove Golf Club on Waterworks Road, the Gap (tel. 366-3438). Located only five miles from downtown, this offers a picturesque 18-hole course at $A15 per round. There's equipment for hire.

RUGBY Rugby Union, the English derivation of football most familiar to Americans, is fought at Ballymore Oval on Clyde Road, Herston (tel. 356-7584).

SWIMMING Metropolitan Brisbane has no beaches, but a string of superlative swimming pools instead. For anyone accustomed to the dreary municipal pools of America, these are eye-openers. The Centenary Pool, Gregory Terrace, the Oasis, and the Acacia Tourist Garden at Sunnybank are deep blue, fringed with palms and shrubs, and surrounded by vast lawns and flower beds.

TENNIS Dozens of public tennis courts are scattered throughout the metropolitan area. To find out which are currently available, where, and when, call the Lawn Tennis Association on Milton Road, Milton (tel. 368-2433).

8. EVENING ENTERTAINMENT

Brisbane's movie scene is rather handicapped by a frenetic local censorship that uses its "cutting shears" with far more enthusiasm than finesse. But the city has good live theater, both professional and amateur. The *Courier Mail* and *Telegraph* give a good roundup of nighttime doings.

THE PERFORMING ARTS

THE MAJOR PERFORMING ARTS COMPANY

The **Royal Queensland Theatre Company,** which stages anything from Broadway comedies to contemporary Australian drama, offering the best theater in Brisbane, is housed in the luxurious SGIO Theater, Turbot Street (tel. 221-5177).

A MAJOR CONCERT HALL

PERFORMING ARTS COMPLEX, in the Queensland Cultural Centre, South Bank, South Brisbane. Tel. 846-4646.

The city's premier showcase is the Performing Arts Complex, located in the heart of the impressive Queensland Cultural Centre. Offerings there can be anything from a Vienna Pops concert to the Queensland Philharmonic, from the Royal Ballet and Shakespeare companies to Australian avant-garde drama to a Broadway hit.

THEATERS

THE ARTS THEATRE, 210 Petrie Terrace. Tel. 369-2344.

Comedies, drama, occasional pantomimes, and sometimes imported translated productions are staged here, Brisbane's leading little theater.

Prices: Tickets $A12–$A15.

LABOITE THEATRE, 57 Hale St., Brisbane. Tel. 369-1622.

Slick, topical satires and parodies, interspersed with more general productions, are usually shown here. Previews are often run on Thursday at sharply reduced prices.

Prices: Tickets usually $A25.

COMEDY, DINNER THEATER & CABARET

CRAZIES, corner of Caxton and Judge Sts., Petrie Terrace. Tel. 369-0555.

The most sparkling theater restaurant is undoubtedly Crazies. Along with a four-course meal you get 10 acts of stand-up comedy; up-tempo song-and-dance numbers; and several interludes that fall into no known category—a cocktail of cornball, satire, and Marx Brothers madness. Reservations are required.

Prices: Dinner and show cost $A28–$A36, depending on the night.

JOLLY JUMBUCK, 40 South Pine Rd., Alderley. Tel. 356-9913.

This dinner theater presents historical humor, contemporary satire, plus rock bands along with a four-course dinner.

THE CLUB, PUB & MUSIC SCENE

There's a bumper crop of thumping discos spread over town. Like most Aussie establishments going by that label, they happily mix live bands with the serving platters so as to be indistinguishable from dance halls or nightclubs. Sort it out yourself. Unlike most restaurants here, they keep late hours.

There's also quite a lot doing in the rock, jazz, and folk fields. Most numerous are the rock pubs: simply taverns that provide gigs for an immense and constantly changing array of instrumental groups that span the musical gamut from great to dismal.

FOLK, ROCK & JAZZ

BRITANNIA INN, Wintergarden Complex, Queen Street Mall. Tel. 221-1750.

Originated as an attraction for World Expo '88 but having proved so popular that it continued reveling, this is a London-style pub festooned with beer posters and gushing English ale from every tap. It holds rollicking sing-alongs of Cockney favorites, with a tremendously enthusiastic and slightly off-key audience joining in.

Prices: No cover charge.

Open: Daily 11am–midnight.

DOOLEY'S HOTEL, 394 Brunswick St., Fortitude Valley.

Dooley's, at the corner of McLachlan Street, features rock three nights a week. There's no cover charge, and drinks come at bar prices.

KELLY'S HOTEL, 521 Stanley St., South Brisbane. Tel. 844-9777.

The entertainment here alternates between soul groups, pianists, and—at Sunday brunch—a genuine string quartet.

CAXTON HOTEL, 38 Caxton St., Petrie Terrace. Tel. 369-5971.

The Caxton starts rocking and goes on until 3am, with Saturday and Sunday devoted to jazz.

Open: Daily 7pm–3am.

BRISBANE JAZZ CLUB, 1 Annie St., Kangaroo Point. Tel. 391-2006.
Dispensing excellent jazz by the riverside on Saturday and Sunday from 8pm, the club caters to all tastes: traditional, mainstream, Dixieland, and big-band swing. You can dance or just listen. The cover charge varies; sometimes there's none.

DANCE CLUBS/DISCOS

TOUCAN CLUB, 16 Park Rd., Milton. Tel. 368-3626.
Very much upmarket and rather svelte, this nightclub/restaurant combines an open deck overlooking the Brisbane River with a disco on the second floor. This is the hunting ground of Brisbane's junior "smart" set.
Admission: $A5 (only on weekends).
Open: Mon–Sat until 3am.

TRANSFORMERS, 127 Charlotte St., Brisbane. Tel. 221-5555.
Named in memory of the old power station in which it is housed, the "Trannie" two-level disco is decorated with pieces of electrical junk and attracts a young crowd with its high decibels.
Admission: $A4–$A7.
Open: Wed–Sat until 4am or thereabouts.

ROSIES TAVERN, Rowe's Arcade, Edward St., Brisbane. Tel. 229-4916.
Rosies has disco dancing and caters to an upmarket over-25 set.
Open: Wed–Sat 8pm "until late."

ALICE'S ROCK CAFE, 15 Adelaide St., Brisbane. Tel. 221-7719.
Alice's has disco dancing to live or recorded music and insists on "smart casual" dress (whatever that is).
Open: Tues–Sat until 3am or later.

9. GOLD COAST

GETTING THERE By Plane There is direct air service from Sydney to Coolangatta.

BY BUS There is direct bus service from Brisbane and regular service between all points along the coast and to most of the attractions. **Greyhound** buses (tel. 36-9966) operate from Brisbane 15 times a day. The trip costs $A11.30 for adults and $A6.50 for children to Southport, Surfers Paradise, or Coolangatta. In addition, all Brisbane touring companies feature a Gold Coast excursion on their agendas.

ESSENTIALS Time For a few years Queensland fell in step with the other Australian states by going on daylight saving time in summer. But in 1992, a local referendum had a majority voting in favor of returning to standard summer hours, so Queensland again lags one hour behind the rest of the country during the hot season. (Western Australia and Northern Territory also do not observe DST.) This means that if you happen to be in Coolangatta, you must adjust your watch whenever you cross Boundary Street into Tweed Heads, and vice versa on the way back.

Southeast of Brisbane, along the surf-wreathed beaches of the warm Pacific, lies Australia's premier tourist resort, the **Gold Coast.** I use the singular *Coast* deliberately because the entire 20-mile chain of beach resorts is technically *one* town, with one mayor—even though it keeps changing its name every few miles. The Gold

Coast starts at **Southport** and runs all the way past **Coolangatta** and across the New South Wales state border to **Tweed Heads.** Surfers Paradise is the unofficial capital.

The native population of the Gold Coast is only around 220,000, but during holiday seasons this swells to well over two million, and "natives" become as hard to find as proverbial needles in haystacks. The reasons are obvious: idyllic climate; perfect beaches; warm water; magnificent surf; and, as a backdrop, some of the most spectacular mountain scenery in Australia, the **MacPherson Ranges.** A bunch of very astute entrepreneurs have wrapped all these natural advantages into one big glittering tourist package, expertly gauged for mass appeal, backed by a year-round publicity campaign that generates ever-bigger throngs of visitors and a permanent air of expansion.

The Gold Coast is such a perfect replica of Miami Beach that you can't tell the two apart until you hear the prevailing accents: the same high-rise hotels and apartment blocks fronting the ocean; the same aromatic mélange of saltwater air, gasoline fumes, frying hamburgers, and sizzling suntan lotion; the same din of car engines, outboard motors, screeching transistors, and whooping beach crowds; the same dazzle of neon when velvety darkness descends. If you like Miami, you'll love the Gold Coast. If you don't, well, skip to the last part of this chapter.

There are, of course, variations within the area. Surfers Paradise is simultaneously the largest, flashiest, noisiest, and liveliest resort. Coolangatta comes on like a poorer and more subdued relative. And in between you can find some fairly peaceful and serene ocean spots, although peace and serenity are *not* what the tourists come here for. There are also decided advantages for the budget traveler. Because local competition is fierce, the region offers an astonishing number of economy lodgings, eateries, and entertainment spots, most a very good value for their prices. Nightlife, furthermore, is plentiful and not expensive. And the glorious beaches are free—the Gold Coast has not copied the pernicious Riviera custom of allocating choice strips of sand to the luxury hotels. But why are they studded with loudspeakers pouring out an incessant barrage of pop music and awful commercials over their captive audience?

More serious than this sound pollution is the threat of an increasingly solid row of high rises blocking off the Surfers Paradise beach. The shadows they cast over the sand by midafternoon are forcing sunbathers to keep moving in order to catch whatever rays manage to streak between the buildings.

GETTING AROUND

BY BUS **Surfside** (tel. 36-7666) provides local bus service on the coast and issues its own **Rover Tickets,** which allow you unlimited travel up and down the Gold Coast, from Southport to Tweed Heads, getting on and off as often as you please. One-Day Rovers cost $A6.35 for adults, half price for children; Seven-Day Rovers run $A23.10 for adults, $A11.55 for children.

BY CAR **Thrifty Car Rentals,** 3033 Gold Coast Hwy., Surfers Paradise (tel. 38-6511), offers a warm-weather specialty in the shape of the Funtop or Soft-top or Topless (the labels are optional) Suzuki Sierra. Looking and sounding like an underpowered Jeep, these critters have removable tops that give up to four people natural air conditioning from all sides. Great fun to drive, they rent at $A55 per day.

BY BICYCLE & MOPED You can rent bicycles (solo or tandem) all over the coast. But this is one of the areas where weather conditions are nearly ideal for riding mopeds—with due caution. These lightweight motorscooters sound like chain saws and get very inconsiderate treatment from four-wheel motorists. They make up for such drawbacks by being cheap and handy. One place to get them at is **Surfers Blades,** 10 Hanlan St. (tel. 38-3483). They cost $A25 for the first two hours, then $A5 per additional hour.

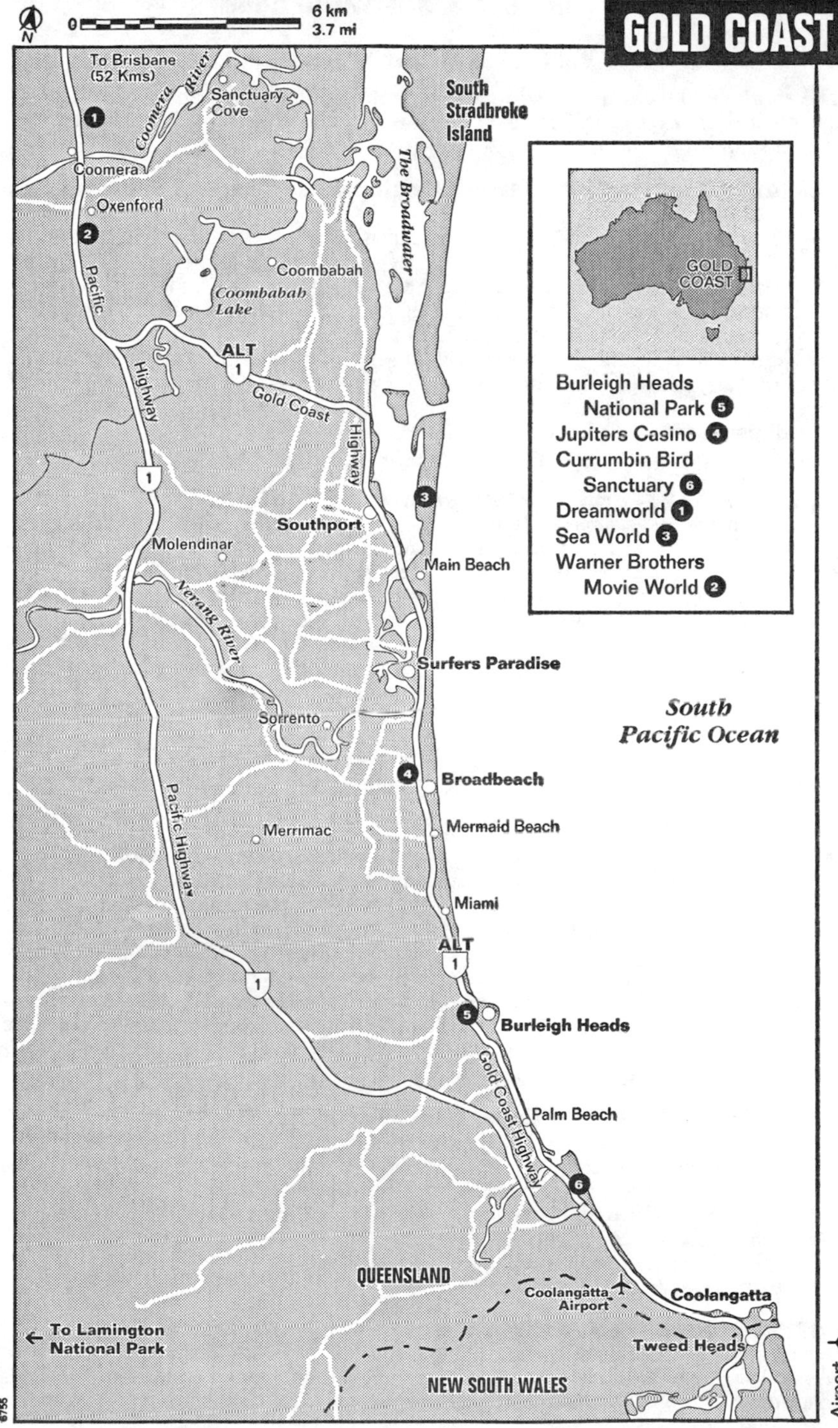
GOLD COAST
0
6 km
3.7 mi
N
To Brisbane (52 Kms)
Coomera River
Sanctuary Cove
South Stradbroke Island
Coomera
Oxenford
The Broadwater
Coombabah
Coombabah Lake
Pacific Highway
ALT 1
Gold Coast Highway
1
Southport
Molendinar
Main Beach
Nerang River
Surfers Paradise
Sorrento
South Pacific Ocean
Broadbeach
Mermaid Beach
Merrimac
Pacific Highway
Miami
ALT 1
1
Burleigh Heads
Gold Coast Highway
Palm Beach
QUEENSLAND
Coolangatta Airport
Coolangatta
Tweed Heads
To Lamington National Park
NEW SOUTH WALES
Airport
GOLD COAST
Burleigh Heads National Park 5
Jupiters Casino 4
Currumbin Bird Sanctuary 6
Dreamworld 1
Sea World 3
Warner Brothers Movie World 2
6755

WHAT TO SEE & DO

The entire Gold Coast is geared to keeping tourists happy—meaning busy. Consequently it offers a dazzling array of attractions over and above its principal ones: sun, sea, and sand.

SEA WORLD, at the Spit, between Southport and Surfers Paradise. Tel. 88-2222.

Sea World ranks among the greatest aquatic show spots anywhere. It is, as the name implies, almost a world by itself—a miniature Disneyland of 61 acres packed with land, sea, and sky rides; viewing pools; a 3-D movie theater; bars; restaurants; and gift shops. There are dolphin and sea lion shows; waterski acrobatics; divers feeding sharks underwater; a climbable replica of Captain Cook's ship *Endeavour;* an Adventure Island cruise; and live marine exhibits including turtles, rays, little fairy penguins and giant groupers; as well as Australia's first flume, a kind of roller-coaster ride on water.

Admission: $A32 adults, $A21 children.
Open: Daily 10am–5pm.

DREAMWORLD, Parkway, Coomera. Tel. 73-1133.

The Gold Coast's largest playpen opened in December 1981. It's the biggest, liveliest, most gee-whizzing theme park in the southern hemisphere, a happy mélange of Disneyland and Coney Island, with a few authentic Aussie touches thrown in. You can chug around it in antique model cars, scream your lungs out on a looping roller coaster, take a log ride through a dizzying flume, bounce on an old-fashioned merry-go-round, explore pioneer cabins, run riot in penny arcades, let out your aggressions in bumper cars, and gorge yourself in a dozen eateries. There's a magic shop, an antique-car museum, theaters, craft shops, shooting galleries, and realistic lions and crocodiles lurking on the lawns. The "theme" is kind of vague, but the fun is absolutely genuine, and the number of souvenirs for sale is overwhelming.

Admission (including all rides): $A29 adults, $A18 children.
Open: Daily 10am–5pm.

TRIBAL ARTS, 2797 Gold Coast Hwy., Broadbeach. Tel. 38-2121.

This is a wondrous emporium displaying and selling authentic artifacts of the South Pacific region. As much a museum as a store, the place has a resident specialist with an encyclopedic knowledge of tribal lore and crafts. You can admire or buy carved canoe paddles from the Sepik River region of New Guinea, ebonywood sharks from the Solomons, grotesquely beautiful carvings of ancestral spirits, dance masks from Papua, or the bark paintings of Australian Aborigines. Prices—all marked—range from $A5 to $A50,000. You can choose, browse, or take photos.

Open: Daily 9am–5pm.

LAND OF LEGEND, Gold Coast Hwy., Tugun. Tel. 34-4644.

Behind a fairy-tale castle front lies a series of miniature to life-size displays, all minutely detailed and some so lifelike that you'd swear you can see the figures breathing. They present a happy mélange of history and legend: King Arthur and his knights, Henry VIII and his wives, a scene from Pioneer Australia, Cinderella's ballroom, and a model railroad landscape.

Admission: $A6 adults, $A2.50 children.
Open: Daily 9am–5pm.

MOVIE WORLD, Pacific Hwy., Oxenford. Tel. 733-999.

This is a Warner Bros. spectacular transported lock, stock, and Bugs Bunny to Australia. Movie World is strictly matinee stuff, but on a grand scale. You can ride a Batmobile to the Batcave and battle the evil Penguin; watch the live Police Academy

Stunt Show; visit the Young Einstein Gravity Homestead and bang away at the Blazing Saddles Shooting Gallery; whirl through a fantastic journey that takes you into a special effects fourth dimension; and you can actually see movies being produced in the studio. The live stage presents the Looney Tunes characters, with Daffy Duck, Yosemite Sam, Tweety, and Porky mingling with the audience. The cafés, food stands, candy stores, and ice-cream parlors that dot the landscape are tailor-made for juvenile palates.

Admission: $A32 adults, $A21 children.
Open: Daily 10am–5pm.

RAP JUMPING, corner of Gold Coast Hwy. & Staghorn Ave., Surfers Paradise. Tel. 450-120.

A new twist in the great Australian lunacy called bungee jumping. In this one you jump from a high rise instead of a bridge. Your ankles are attached to an elastic rope that will feather you to a stop just before you break your neck. Guaranteed to get your adrenaline pumping at record rate, and you're encouraged to scream as well. The equipment is government inspected and I was assured of its absolute safety. You can have your photo taken and obtain a T-shirt to commemorate the moment. One jump costs $A50, two jumps $A80.

RIPLEY'S BELIEVE IT OR NOT, Raptis Plaza, Cavill Mall, Surfers Paradise. Tel. 92-0040.

This is a museum of the famous Ripley curiosities combined with a huge arcade of electronic games. It contains three theaters, one of them showing rare film footage of daredevil stunts. The Magic Show has a leprechaun spinning a ghostly yarn, the Illusion Room invites you to grab hold of "free money" that can't be grabbed, and the Revolving Room plays havoc with your senses. In between are the hallowed Ripley standbys—a genuine shrunken head, the boy who died of old age, the world's tallest man . . . and so forth. Fun for a rainy day.

Admission: $A9.50 adults, $A5 children.
Open: Daily 9am–11pm.

WAR MUSEUM, Springbrook Rd., Mudgeeraba. Tel. 305-222.

The War Museum offers a mixture of weaponry displays and participation games. The former include aircraft, tanks, armored cars, artillery, and infantry weapons. The latter let you try your hand at a live-ammo shooting range, take a cautious stroll down "booby-trap lane," or play at bush warfare toting guns that fire paint-filled gelatin capsules.

Admission: $A4 adults, $A2 children.
Open: Daily 9am–5pm.

WET 'N' WILD, Pacific Hwy., Oxenford. Tel. 73-2255.

Australia's top water park, a replica of the original one in Orlando, Florida, has a hydrotwist water slide that catapults you through 360-degree spiral tubing. There are also a wave pool that runs 3-foot waves, a seven-story speed slide, and a play pool where kids have water-cannon battles with a pirate ship.

Admission: $A15 adults, $A10 children.
Open: Daily 10am–5pm.

BOOMERANG FARM, Springbrook Rd., Mudgeeraba.

The Boomerang Farm sells, displays, and makes boomerangs and teaches visitors the art of throwing them.

Admission: $A5 adults, $A3 children.
Open: Sun–Fri 9am–5pm.

FLEAY'S FAUNA CENTRE, West Burleigh Rd., Burleigh Heads. Tel. 76-2411.

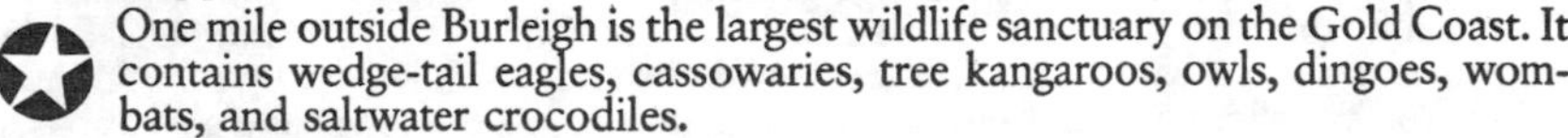

One mile outside Burleigh is the largest wildlife sanctuary on the Gold Coast. It contains wedge-tail eagles, cassowaries, tree kangaroos, owls, dingoes, wombats, and saltwater crocodiles.

Admission: $A7.50 adults, $A3.50 children.
Open: Daily 9am–5pm.

CURRUMBIN BIRD SANCTUARY, 28 Tomewin St., Currumbin. Tel. 34-1266.

The sanctuary, half a mile south of Currumbin Creek, is the site to which hundreds of wild tropical birds flock every morning and afternoon to feed on plates of bread and honey. The birds, mostly multicolored rainbow lorikeets, are quite unafraid and can be fed by visitors when they come down from their bushland habitat. The sanctuary also has koalas, kangaroos, emus, water birds, and Tasmanian devils.

Admission: $A12.50 adults, $A6.50 children.
Open: Daily 8am–5pm.

GRUNDY'S, Paradise Centre, Cavill Mall, Surfers Paradise. Tel. 38-9011.

Located in the heart of Surfers Paradise, this is one of the few *indoor* attractions hereabouts. A giant childrens' playground, it occupies the first floor of the town's largest shopping complex and features a speedway for toy cars, half a dozen amusement rides, a mini–golf course, plus a head-spinning array of video machines, some with positively symphonic sound effects. It's just the place to take the kids when it rains—which it does, periodically.

Admission: Free.
Open: Daily 10am–10pm.

NEARBY ATTRACTIONS

THE HINTERLAND.

It's easy to forget that the Gold Coast is just a narrow strip of oceanfront, a ribbon of artificial glitter flanked on the land side by one of the most majestic mountain ranges in all Queensland—the MacPherson Ranges. Barely 20 miles inland from the neon wilderness rises the real wilderness: a world of rain forests and waterfalls, of jungle trails, silent pools, and sudden views of absolutely stunning beauty.

There are nine National Parks in that region, each open for exploration, all habitats for native animals. The most popular is **Tamborine Mountain**—famous for hiking trails; dozens of individual art, crafts, and antiques shops; and sprinkled with restaurants, tea shops, and bakeries. Much of the food sold is grown right in the area; you can't get it any fresher. And if you'd like to linger, there are small country-style motels and private cabins.

Tamborine is the most developed of the park regions, so you'll find even more nature balm in the others—Witches Falls, Cedar Creek, the Knoll, or Panorama Point. Heading into the Hinterland from the Gold Coast means exchanging the blare of rock tapes for the call of the lyrebird, and the hysteria of neon signs for the green grandeur of giant beech and cedar trees, their tops shrouded in mist.

Most Gold Coast touring outfits include a trip to the Hinterland in their programs. **Coachtrans** (tel. 923-488) offers a drive that takes in the Tamborine Plateau, Orchid Farm, Eagle Heights, Sanctuary Cove, and other beautiful spots. Coaches depart from the terminal at Beach Road, Surfers Paradise, on Wednesday and Sunday only at 12:30pm. Adults pay $A19, children $A10.

ORGANIZED TOURS

If you only have time for one jaunt, make it the full-day trip to **Stradbroke Island,** a patch of (almost) unspoiled paradise just off the coast. **Jetaway Cruises** (tel. 38-3400) operates a truly memorable and economy-geared outing to the place. They use a specially built craft, 89 feet long and shiny white all over, and you're welcomed aboard by the friendliest bunch of tanned T-shirts you've ever met. Lunch is T-bone steak and tropical salad—and it's free. At the island, 14 miles of virgin beach await you. You can swim or loaf around, and if that's too tame the tour has a speedboat for waterskiing or toboggan rides. Dinner comes from a wood barbecue . . . more steak, and again free. The entire outing costs $A45 for adults, $A23 for children.

Shangri-la (tel. 91-1800) is something of a misnomer for a little motor cruiser bedecked with Coca-Cola signs that takes you on a 2-hour canal and harbor jaunt. The boat departs daily at 10am and 1:30pm from Fisherman's Wharf and sails past the sumptuous homes and human-created islands of the Pleasure Coast, accompanied by very knowledgeable commentary. You get complimentary wine or fruit juices en route, plus a thorough look at the Gold Coast from the seaward side. Tickets cost $A22 for adults, $A16 for children.

Gray Line (tel. 923-488) has a full-day tour that shows you the high, isolated beauty spots away from the coastline. The trip goes to **O'Reilly's Green Mountain,** a region of calm and magnificent scenery, of bushwalks, wildlife, and bird watching. You travel up the northern spur of Tamborine Mountain to **Palm Grove National Park.** Morning tea is served at the village of Eagle Heights, then it's on to the century-old logging town of **Canungra** and higher up to lunch at the **Green Mountain** kiosk, where you feed yourself as well as swarms of rosella and king parrots. The tour goes on Mondays and includes free hotel pick ups and returns at 5:30pm. Adults pay $A29, children $A15.

SHOPPING

Pacific Fair, Gold Coast Highway and Hooker Boulevard, Broadbeach, is perhaps the biggest shopping complex on the continent, sprawling just beside the Hotel Conrad and Jupiters Casino. It's a shopping metropolis with lily-laden lagoons and garden fountains, an arcade mall, food hall, children's play park, some 260 retail stores, and a car park in which you could easily lose half an armored division. The shops run the entire gamut from supersvelte to middling economy and sell everything from Australian safari togs and haute fashion to books, photographic equipment, toys, health food, and hardware. Other appetites are catered for at a Tex-Mex café, an Italian deli, a seafood hut, and a pancake parlor. The fair hums daily from 9am till 5:30pm.

Jupiters Casino across the road keeps later hours. You can see their sumptuous Broadway-style stage show for a dinner/show package of $A50. There are Wednesday matinees for $A35. Book by calling 92-8303.

WHERE TO STAY

This is the frosting on the Gold Coast gingerbread, the benefit you get from overcommercialization. The Coast lives and breathes tourists and has the facilities to put them up and bed them down in every notch of the price scale.

Heading south along the Gold Coast Highway, you come into the "frontier region" between Queensland and New South Wales. The state border, in fact, runs through the highway, dividing what is practically the same town into Coolangatta, Queensland, and Tweed Heads. Luckily you don't need a passport to walk across the road. These resorts are considerably quieter than Surfers Paradise, boasting neither the bustle nor the nightlife of their hedonistic neighbor. They are also cheaper, in both the food and the lodgings department. You even get a few old-style bed-and-breakfast places, a commodity that seems to have become extinct in the flashier north.

DOUBLES FOR LESS THAN $A55

ACAPULCO, 2823 Gold Coast Hwy., at Monaco St., Surfers Paradise, QLD 4217. Tel. 075/39-0142. 8 units (all with shower). TV

$ Rates: $A40–$A150 per unit. BC, MC, V.

A real bargain—and booked accordingly—is the shiny pink Acapulco. Resembling a Mexican villa with a pool in front, the Acapulco houses only eight units. Several have bunk beds and folding divans and can sleep four comfortably. All have a lot of hanging-and-folding space in large wardrobes and drawers, kitchenettes, toilets, large refrigerators, sinks, ceiling fans, and silverware and dishes. You'd better book ahead.

QUEENSLAND HOTEL, Boundary St., Coolangatta, QLD 4218. Tel. 075/36-2600. 19 rms (5 with bath).

$ Rates (including breakfast): $A25 single, $A45–$A55 double. MC, V.

This is a modern two-story brick building with plenty of bar facilities. There are two bars, a nightclub, a very attractive TV lounge with ultracomfortable armchairs, a restaurant, and pool tables. Most of the rooms come with hot- and cold-water basins only. But all are neatly compact; nicely furnished in light wood; and equipped with bedside mirror tables, wall-to-wall carpeting, fluorescent lighting, good-size wardrobes, and springy new beds.

RED LION MOTEL, 3016 Gold Coast Hwy., Surfers Paradise, QLD 4217. Tel. 075/39-9021. 13 units (all with bath). A/C TV

$ Rates: $A40–$A45 single or double. MC, V.

A cream-colored two-story building, the Red Lion—despite its rustic inn label—is a modern and very comfortable establishment. There's a swimming pool on the grounds but no restaurant. Some of the units have air-conditioning; the rest have ceiling fans. All, however, contain refrigerators, tea- and coffee-making equipment, fluorescent ceiling lights, bedside lamps, and wall-to-wall carpeting. Wardrobes tend to be rather small, and the units have no telephones.

SILVER SANDS MOTEL, 2985 Gold Coast Hwy. at Markwell Ave., Surfers Paradise, QLD 4217. Tel. 075/38-6041. 11 units (all with bath). TV

$ Rates: $A50–$A65 single or double. MC, V.

The Silver Sands Motel has a swimming pool, a sun deck, and self-contained guest units. All come with their own refrigerators, kitchenettes, and ceiling fans. Furnishings are both modern and ample, including armchairs as well as fluorescent bedside lamps by which you can actually read. For good measure, the motel offers barbecue facilities and a spa.

WHITEHALL LODGE, 7 Stuart St., Tweed Heads, NSW 2444. Tel. 075/36-3233. Fax 075/36-9244. 32 rms (none with bath). TV TEL

$ Rates (including breakfast): $A27 per person. MC, V.

Across the border in Tweed Heads lies the Whitehall Lodge, a quiet little hotel on the fringe of the Gold Coast but only a few blocks away from the ocean. The lodge is a modern beige-brick structure fronted by a small garden with shrubs and multicolored umbrellas. There's a bright, airy guest lounge with color TV. If you don't care about a private shower or toilet, this is one of the best bargains in the area. All nine public bathrooms are immaculately kept. The bedrooms have tea- and coffee-making facilities, good carpeting, and excellent beds. Above all, they're quiet. Rates here include either breakfast or full board—that is, dinner as well. All meals are taken in the adjacent dining room.

DOUBLES FOR LESS THAN $A65

ADMIRAL MOTOR INN, 2965 Gold Coast Hwy., Surfers Paradise, QLD 4217. Tel. 075/39-8759. 16 rms (all with bath). TV

$ Rates: Motel, $A60 single or double per night, $A315 single or double per week. AE, DC, MC, V.

The Admiral Motor Inn is another very attractive hybrid creation. Palm fringed and vaguely Spanish looking, with a swimming pool in front, the Admiral houses 16 self-contained units and has a separate rear building for backpackers. The motel suites come with one, two, or three bedrooms; some come with kitchens, but all have TVs, refrigerators, and ceiling fans. There are a sun deck and a tour desk; also available are boogie boards for rent (these are small surfboards on which you can shoot waves in a prone but not a standing position).

CHELSEA MOTOR INN, 2990 Gold Coast Hwy., Surfers Paradise, QLD 4217. Tel. 075/38-9333. Fax 075/92-3709. 17 rms (all with bath). A/C TV TEL

$ Rates: $A65 single or double. MC, V.

The Chelsea Motor Inn is a low-slung beige structure with a small pool in front, flanked by young palm trees plus several umbrella-shaded tables. It has nicely furnished and well-equipped units: Nine are air-conditioned, the others have ceiling fans; all have large sliding-door wardrobes, refrigerators, and writing desks. Heavy blinds ward off the sun, there's plenty of drawer space, and the bathrooms have sink surfaces large enough for *all* your toiletries. You get tea- and coffee-making equipment, an on-premises laundry, and breakfast in your room if desired. For singles the Chelsea is above our budget bracket, but it's a bargain for two persons.

DELILAH MOTEL, 72 Ferny Ave., Surfers Paradise, QLD 4217. Tel. 075/38-1722. 25 rms (all with bath). TV

$ Rates: $A40–$A55 single, $A45–$A65 double. BC, MC, V.

A small, friendly light-brown complex one block away from the beach, the Delilah shows the sharp seasonal price variations typical for a resort region. The units are pleasantly bright and airy, equipped with cane furniture, ceiling fans, radios, refrigerators, and toasters. The building also has a good-sized pool, a guest laundry, a games room, and underground parking. There is no restaurant, but clusters of them are close by. There are a barbecue and umbrella-shaded tables at the poolside.

THE HUB, Cavill Ave., Surfers Paradise, QLD 4217. Tel. 075/31-5559. 16 rms (all with bath). A/C TV TEL

$ Rates: $A45 single, $A55 double. MC, V.

This is the most central and busiest hostelry of the entire region. These serviced motel apartments are built into a shopping arcade, which puts everything you may need within arm's reach, so to speak: stores, cafés, and restaurants right, left, and below, plus the crowds that go with them. The beach runs a few yards from your apartment. The units are very small, ultramodern, and decorated in standard motel style. But they contain every facility: balconies, refrigerators, electric toasters and jugs, cutlery, crockery, fluorescent ceiling lights, individual bedside lamps, and wall-to-wall carpeting. There's an on-premises laundry. Parking is available.

SERVICED APARTMENTS

Holiday apartments on the Gold Coast may be either completely independent units or parts of a motel. Either way, they're usually superior to their big-city equivalents (newer furniture and better facilities) and can be ideal, price wise, for two or more people, less so for singles.

ANTONIO'S REX MOTEL & RITZ FLATS, 104 Marine Parade, Greenmount Beach, Coolangatta, QLD 4225. Tel. 075/36-2175. 28 units (all with bath). TV

$ Rates: From $A55 single or double, from $A295 single or double weekly. $A20 for each additional person. No credit cards.

Antonio's is an attractive modern dual establishment consisting of a motel part and an apartment block. The 16 apartments come in one to three bedroom versions, each with fully equipped kitchens, and sleep up to six people comfortably. The motel units have small kitchenettes and refrigerators and can accommodate up to three people. Both have generous wardrobe space and fans, and there is a laundry and beauty salon on the premises. Greenmount Beach is the most desirable section of Coolangatta, just across the street from the interstate bus depot and a 5-minute drive from the Gold Coast Airport.

SUNNY SKIES MOTOR INN, 2963 Gold Coast Hwy., Surfers Paradise, QLD 4217. Tel. 075/38-5968. 7 units (all with bath). A/C TV

$ Rates: $A40 double, from $A350 weekly. BC, MC, V.

This inn is one of the best deals of its kind on the entire coast—providing there are two of you. Strictly utilitarian on the outside, it has almost luxurious interiors and a large swimming pool to boot. The units are completely self-contained, each with one or two bedrooms, a kitchen with electric appliances, a garage, and ceiling fans. Only the lack of telephones makes them impractical year-round living quarters. Furnishings are modern with a touch of elegance; the built-in wardrobes provide ample hanging space; the decor is both tasteful and cheerful; and the kitchens boast refrigerators and all the cutlery, crockery, and utensils you could need. There's a coin laundry on the premises, and every apartment comes with a charming little balcony. The units rent by the night or week for doubles—no singles here.

WORTH THE EXTRA MONEY

HAPPY HOLIDAY INN, 2 Albert Ave., Broadbeach, QLD 4218. Tel. 075/70-1311. Fax 075/70-2021. 41 apts (all with bath). TV TEL

$ Rates: $A90–$A95 single or double. MC, V.

A bright, modern "all-suites inn," this is a very good bet for couples or groups. Rates go up to $A120 during holiday season, but this lasts only 21 days, from December to January. All the units have kitchens with electric appliances (and handy serving counters), and come complete with two or three balconies, radios, whispering (quiet) fans, hair dryers, electric irons, and cooking utensils. Bathrooms are generously proportioned, and the hanging space for clothes is adequate. The inn boasts a great array of facilities: a swimming pool, a sauna, a spa, a games room, a guest laundry, underground parking, an on-site car wash, and barbecue facilities. The place adjoins the huge Oasis Shopping Center, has its own restaurant and bar, and stands a few steps away from Jupiters Casino. A nice added feature is the inn's garden, aglow with tropical hibiscus bushes.

BACKPACKERS

These lodgings are relative newcomers on the Gold Coast accommodations scene but are multiplying so fast that those listed below are mere samples of the species.

BACKPACKERS INN, 45 McLean St., Coolangatta, QLD 4225. Tel. 075/36-2422. 65 beds (shared bathrooms). TV TEL

$ Rates: $A19 single, $A28 double. AE, MC, V.

The Backpackers Inn is among the best of its breed. At least it's the only hostel I've ever found that has a licensed restaurant and bar on the premises. Located in a beautiful mansionlike building atop a slight hill, surrounded by lawns, and two minutes from downtown and the beach, the inn/hostel has 65 beds in double rooms (no dormitories), an excellent music system, a TV lounge, a swimming pool, and barbecue facilities. The rooms are airy and rather nicely furnished, the restaurant provides economy-priced breakfasts and dinners daily, and the obligatory bed sheets can be hired. The management arranges discount prices to all Gold Coast attractions, and guests get free use of bikes and surfboards.

COOLANGATTA YHA HOSTEL, 230 Coolangatta Rd., Bilinga, QLD 4225. Tel. 075/36-7644. 80 beds, 3 family rms.

$ Rates: $A11 dorm, $A13 per person double, $A35 family room (for 4). BC, MC, V.

A modern hostel in a handy location, it has a small shop on the premises and the beach a few minutes away. But there are not many facilities, apart from a kitchen with refrigerators and a swimming pool on the grounds.

SURF & SUN, Gold Coast Hwy. & Ocean Ave., Surfers Paradise, QLD 4217. Tel. 075/922-363. 16 dorms.

$ Rates: $A14 per person. MC, V.

Although this place is just across the road from the beach it has its own swimming pool (mainly as a socializing spot). A pleasant beige-brick structure, with a bus stop in front, it also provides bathrooms, TVs, and refrigerators for all dorms, plus discount rates for nearby gyms, squash courts, and nightclubs, Call ahead for the courtesy pick up from your transport stop.

CARAVAN [R.V.] PARKS

With an ideal camping climate, it's not surprising that the Gold Coast abounds in caravan parks. Not all of them, however, rent on-site vans (known as "fixed vans" hereabouts), and only some offer tent facilities. All the places listed below provide on-site vans for about $A17 to $A27 per night for two persons, but you'd better call to inquire about tenting, since that situation seems to change rather rapidly.

Florida Car-O-Tel, Redondo Avenue, Miami (tel. 075/35-3111), has hot- and cold-water showers, laundry facilities, a restaurant, two swimming pools, TV rooms, and a squash court.

Gold Coast, Gold Coast Highway, Palm Beach (tel. 075/34-2290), has hot- and cold-water showers and baths and laundry facilities.

Border Caravan Park, Boundary Street, Tweed Heads (tel. 075/36-3134), has hot- and cold-water showers, laundry-and-ironing facilities, and a store opposite the grounds.

WHERE TO EAT

The Gold Coast culinary scene has been described as "wall-to-wall junk food," which is reasonably accurate but only partly so. There is, indeed, such a superabundance of "snackeries" that at first glance you get the impression that they've muscled out every other form of nourishment. Luckily that isn't so. In between and behind and around the serried ranks of hot dogs, hamburgers, pies, and french fries, you'll find a goodly sprinkling of restaurants serving food fit for folks who have not had their taste buds amputated. Some, in fact, are downright excellent, although they take a bit of tracking. The following listings are aimed at easing that task.

Down in Coolangatta, gastronomics are less varied but cheaper. The best daytime deals here are the pub lunches put on by the competing watering holes for around $A6.50. **Beach House** in Marine Parade is the elegant mall in Coolangatta. Studded with palms and greenery, it conveniently houses the Visitors Information booth as well as several cafés providing indoor/outdoor tables and umbrellas.

MEALS FOR LESS THAN $A14

CHARLIE'S, in the Paradise Centre, Cavill Mall, Surfers Paradise. Tel. 385-285.

Cuisine: AUSTRALIAN. **Reservations:** Accepted.

$ Prices: Appetizers $A4–$A7, main courses $A9.90–$A12.50. MC, V.

Open: 24 hrs.

Opposite the giant chessboard is Charlie's, a very handy eatery that stays open round-the-clock. The large outdoor patio also makes it a prime people-watching grandstand. Other than that it's fairly plastic, though dedicated to the memory of silent-movie celebrities, whose pictures and posters provide the decorative touches. Charlie's serves everything from quick snacks to three-course meals, all at economy prices. You get rib filet, steak-and-mushroom pie, or seafood in a basket for $A10; hefty crêpes with chicken or seafood fillings cost $A8.50.

DANG, corner of Tedder & Woodroffe Aves., Main Beach. Tel. 310-600.

Cuisine: VIETNAMESE. **Reservations:** Accepted.

$ Prices: Appetizers $A4.50, main courses $A8.90–$A13.90. AE, DC, V.

Open: Tues–Sat lunch; daily 5–10pm.

A fairly large and formerly Mexican restaurant, Dang is one of the very few Vietnamese establishments on the Gold Coast. The fare, while somewhat hotter than Chinese cooking, is by no means palate searing, and diners get free sangría with their meals for cooling effect. No MSG is used in the cooking, and patrons are asked whether they prefer mild or fiery condiments. Try the excellent lemongrass chicken braised with onions in a special sauce.

JACKSONS, in the Paradise Centre, Ground Floor, Surfers Paradise.

Cuisine: AUSTRALIAN. **Reservations:** Not accepted.

$ Prices: Appetizers $A4, main courses $A6–$A8. No credit cards.

Open: Daily 10am–9pm.

Inside the Paradise Centre, the shopping heart and focal point of Surfers Paradise, is Jacksons. You might call it an indoor eatery disguised as an outdoor one, because although the entire shopping arcade is roofed, Jacksons consists of a self-service buffet and a charmingly incongruous eating enclosure equipped with "shady" umbrellas. Paradise Centre, incidently, is air-conditioned. Amid potted greenery, you can sit on very comfortably upholstered chairs, listen to local pop guitarists and folksingers, and watch the parade of lightly dressed shoppers flow by. Menu choices are limited, but the quality is good and the prices are economical. Most meat dishes go for $A8; the roast beef is great and the roast pork abounds with cracklings. The vegetables, however, tend to be dull and overcooked, but you also get a choice array of salads and quiches. Drinks are BYO.

SWEETHEARTS, 3 Orchid Ave., Surfers Paradise. Tel. 386-299.

Cuisine: VEGETARIAN. **Reservations:** Accepted.

$ Prices: Appetizers $A4.95, main courses $A5.25–$A6.95. No credit cards.

Open: Daily 8:30am–8pm.

With a smiling angel topping the menu, Sweethearts takes pride in the fact that it uses no animal flesh products and its food is never microwaved. The veggie burgers are prepared before your eyes and there is an array of dairy-wheat-sugar-free items served daily. Hot dishes include cabbage rolls, lentil pies, and Mexican nachos, and there is a large dessert range including a nonallergy fruitcake made minus eggs, sugar, and wheat.

MEALS FOR LESS THAN $A20

BAVARIAN STEAK HOUSE, corner of Cavill Ave. and Gold Coast Hwy., Surfers Paradise. Tel. 31-7150.

Cuisine: AUSSIE-GERMAN. **Reservations:** Accepted.

$ Prices: Appetizers $A3.95–$A9.95, main courses $A11.95–$A17.45. AE, BC, MC, V.

Open: Daily 10am–10:30pm.

A big semitropical eatery with a Bavarian shingle peering rather incongruously over palm trees, this establishment specializes in grain-fed beef reinforced by five traditional German dishes. It has a pleasant sidewalk terrace, a balcony area, and lots of elbow space for indoor dining. Evenings around 7 a "lederhosen" show band starts blowing, and there's a dance floor as well. The menu is huge, with an all-you-can-eat soup, salad, and pasta bar as a special attraction. Otherwise the fare ranges far and wide from chicken burgers to jäger schnitzel to Moreton Bay bugs to New York steak with prawns. The ordering procedure is a bit convoluted and involves filling in a form that could pass as a customs declaration.

BUNGA RAYA, 3110 Gold Coast Hwy., Surfers Paradise. Tel. 503-766.

Cuisine: MALAYSIAN. **Reservations:** Accepted.

$ Prices: Appetizers $A3.20–$A6.80, main courses $A10.80–$A16.80. AE, BC, DC, MC, V.

Open: Daily lunch, then 5:30–10:30pm.

Over to Malaysia and the Bunga Raya. . . . Waiting for a table here is almost a pleasure in its special area equipped with armchairs, couches, and a bamboo-roofed ornamental fish tank. You can choose from a vast array of Malaysian specialties, including the traditional satays (skewered-and-marinated meat or seafood tidbits served in spicy peanut sauce). The curries include *asam sotong* (squid), *rendang daging* (beef), and *asam ikan* (fish).

GEORGE'S PARAGON, Peninsula Building, Clifford St., Surfers Paradise. Tel. 92-2775.

Cuisine: SEAFOOD/GREEK. **Reservations:** Accepted.

$ Prices: Appetizers $A4.45–$A7.95, main courses $A8.45–$A15. AE, DC, MC, V.

Open: Daily lunch, 6:30–10:30pm.

This is an airy atmospheric place, wreathed in greenery, with a courtyard that gives you a choice of indoor or al fresco dining. You get a warm welcome and a menu roughly two-thirds marine edibles, one-third Greek traditionals. There is also a kids' corner that presents favorites like spaghetti for $A4.90. The Greek items include excellent dolmathes, moussaka, and a very fine octopus dish. At the time of writing lunch goes for half the price of the dinner fare.

LA CUCINA, Railway St., Southport. Tel. 314-093.
Cuisine: ITALIAN. **Reservations:** Accepted.
$ Prices: Appetizers $A5–$A9.95, main courses $A11.95–$A15.95. MC, V.
Open: Mon–Sat 6–10pm.

The name is Italian for "the kitchen," but the setting—subdued lights, subtle color schemes, and candle-lit tables—doesn't reflect the label. The fare, on the other hand, does: solid Italian home cooking, with a few gourmet frills added. Servings are so generous that the appetizers could easily pass for main courses. You get outstanding fettuccine marinara for $A13.95, but if you want to go for the frills try the unusual veal mango for $A15.95. Desserts include exceedingly *dolce* profiteroles. It's BYO and charges $A1 corkage.

LA RUSTICA, 3118 Gold Coast Hwy., Surfers Paradise. Tel. 70-1153.
Cuisine: ITALIAN. **Reservations:** Accepted.
$ Prices: Appetizers $A7, main courses $A10–$A14. MC, V.
Open: Daily 5–10pm.

La Rustica comes as close to Italian rusticity as a relatively new establishment can. With cool tile floors; bare light-wood tables; wood-paneled walls decorated with prints, guitars, and wine bottles; and charmingly personalized service, the place is a leisurely haven in the fast-food hurricane raging all around. Although it doubles as a pizzeria, its accent is on the outstanding Italian main courses. You can't go wrong with the scaloppine al vino or marsala, tenderly cooked in wine sauce, and followed by the superb homemade gelati. The meal will cost you $A17, but if you stick to the pasta plates you'll get by for $A11. It's BYO.

MANDARIN COURT, 2374 Gold Coast Hwy., Mermaid Beach. Tel. 72-3333.
Cuisine: CHINESE. **Reservations:** Accepted.
$ Prices: Appetizers $A6.50–$A7.90, main courses $A0.50–$A18.90. AE, DC, DC, MC, V.
Open: Daily noon–3pm, 5–11pm.

Ornate and glittering, this restaurant is a repeated award winner, though not strictly Mandarin in its fare. The dining room is elaborately decorated and has wall mirrors on all sides in which to admire the way you can handle chopsticks. Service is exceptionally smooth, even in high-pressure periods. I can recommend the shark-fin soup, followed by either Mongolian lamb or king prawns in plum sauce. A fine combination, but not within budget borders.

EVENING ENTERTAINMENT

The small strip of Gold Coast offers more nightlife than the rest of Queensland together. The variety is quite remarkable, but sophistication is not exactly the keynote here. Most of the attractions are geared to the holidaymakers' market, where tastes run to pop rock, bare skin, and maximum sound effects.

DINNER THEATER/CABARET

MUSIC HALL, in the Selections Brasserie, Islander Resort Hotel, corner of Beach Rd. and Gold Coast Hwy., Surfers Paradise. Tel. 38-800.

A variety show with lots of singing, dancing, and comedy, nicely geared for the holiday crowd, is presented Wednesday through Friday nights with matinees on Wednesdays.

Prices: Show only $A15; with seafood buffet $A32.50.

GOLD COAST ARTS CENTRE, 135 Bundall Rd., Bundall. Tel. 81-6900.

This is the Coast's own showcase and puts on an astonishing mixture of presentations. Offerings range from musical extravaganzas from the Roaring Twenties to pops orchestral performances, Tchaikovsky medleys, and waltz nights.

Prices: Tickets vary.

GOLD COAST LITTLE THEATRE, 21A Scarborough St., Southport. Tel. 32-2096.

This is live theater in the broadest sense, with plays performed Tuesday through Saturday at 8pm. The repertoire runs from *The Hound of the Baskervilles* to the *Rape of the Belt* to several points in between. Buy tickets in advance.

Prices: Tickets vary.

ROMA VILLA, 2341 Gold Coast Hwy., Mermaid Beach. Tel. 72-6466.

Located in a motel, this is a very lively cabaret-restaurant. Offerings vary but always include song-and-dance numbers and nostalgic jaunts down memory lane.

Prices: $A25 for three-course dinner and show.

THE CLUB, PUB & MUSIC SCENE

HOTEL CLUB PACIFIC, Marine Parade, Southport. Tel. 91-5611.

Shows go on seven nights a week and change nightly. You might get a medium-heavy metal rock group on Wednesday, disco dancing on Saturday, a solo singer with band backing on Sunday, and so on. Some of the shows take place in the hotel's beer garden. There is rarely a cover charge.

SURFERS BEERGARDEN, Cavill Ave., Surfers Paradise.

This is undoubtedly the most popular place for the younger crowd. A pub with an outdoor section in daytime, it becomes a pulsating rock machine at nightfall. Then it's bodies wall to wall, a decibel level you can almost bite, and the kind of ambience in which you can see your partner's mouth moving but can't hear what he or she is saying (which may be no great loss).

Admission: $A5.

Open: The music roars until 3am.

THE PENTHOUSE, Orchid Ave., Surfers Paradise. Tel. 38-1388.

The Penthouse is an entire entertainment complex with four floors of nightlife, each with a different angle. Two floors are devoted to disco dancing; the other two have live bands, stage performances, videos, and guest artists.

Admission: Free.

Open: Daily until 5am.

MEETING PLACE, Paradise Centre, Surfers Paradise. Tel. 70-1322.

More drinks and dancing are here at the Meeting Place (and that it is!). This is a disco for the energetic younger set.

Open: Mon–Sat "until late."

TUNNEL CABARET, in the Forum Building, Orchid Ave., Surfers Paradise. Tel. 38-6400.

The Tunnel Cabaret combines a disco reinforced by huge video screens with a serenely relaxing VIP bar.

Admission: $A5–$A7.

Open: Tues–Sun 9pm–5am.

DRACULA'S, 1 Hooker Blvd., Broadbeach Waters. Tel. 75-1000.

Dracula's is a night haunt starring ghouls, ghosts, freaks, frights, the famous Morticia Addams, and the celebrated Count. It promises "nights of blood-curdling madness" including Igor's (remember him?) funk-and-jive disco, all set in the dungeons of Count Dracula's castle.

Admission: $A32–$A41 (including four-course dinner).

Open: Tues–Sat 6pm–midnight.

MORE ENTERTAINMENT

Queensland does not permit slot machines. New South Wales does—and it so happens that the border between the two states runs along Boundary Street, which divides the twin towns of Coolangatta and Tweed Heads. On the New South Wales side there's a cluster of clubs whose revenues depend on the one-armed bandits. They gladly subsidize meals, transportation, drinks, and lavish entertainment to entice tourists over from Queensland to feed those insatiable slots.

Ostensibly these clubs are "private"—that is, for the use of members only. But in practice they'll admit "bona fide" visitors. Simply call them beforehand, then show some proof of identity (passport or driver's license) to the doorman and the gates will fly open for you. You're welcome to partake of some of the best—and cheapest—victuals on the coast and watch top-class floor shows at no extra charge. And nobody forces you to gamble.

There are direct daily "pokey buses" running from Brisbane and every Gold Coast town. If you're in Coolangatta, you just walk across the border street.

JUPITERS CASINO, in the Conrad International Hotel, Gold Coast Hwy., Broadbeach. Tel. 92-1133.

Jupiters is a deluxe establishment devoted to roulette, blackjack, baccarat, Big Six, craps, sicbo, and two-up (no slots) in the most velvety of settings. The hotel also has a multitiered showroom featuring some of the finest Australian stage and TV talent. The whole place is a stomping ground for celebrities, so many people go there just to see them—and also to ride the Jupiter's own silent-and-smooth monorail.

Admission: Free.

Open: 24 hrs.

TERRANORA LAKES COUNTRY CLUB, Marana St., Tweed Heads. Tel. 90-9223.

This club has a gratis bus service leaving thrice daily from the Coolangatta Post Office. The club features a show band, plus selected solo performers. In the Bistro dining room, roast beef, roast pork, and chicken go for around $A3.

TWEED HEADS BOWLS CLUB, Florence St., Tweed Heads. Tel. 36-3800.

The Tweed Heads Bowls Club does indeed offer bowling (it's a venue for world-class bowls tournaments), but it also has a gorgeous revue show, famous stage and TV comedians, 300 slot machines, a French restaurant, and six bars. Bistro meal prices hover around $A7.

Admission: $A2.

TWIN TOWNS SERVICES CLUB, Pacific Hwy., Tweed Heads. Tel. 075/36-2277; show bookings, 36-1977.

This place puts on a galaxy of Australian and overseas "superstars" every evening in its 1,200-seat auditorium overlooking the water. The lineup changes, but the plush cocktail bar, sports room, and air-conditioned lounges are permanent fixtures. Dinner at the restaurant will cost you $A9.50 and up. The club has over 500 poker machines.

10. SUNSHINE COAST

GETTING THERE By Bus The bus trip from Brisbane takes about one hour, costs $A10.50, and is run by **Skenners Coach Service,** Brisbane Transit Centre (tel. 286-1000).

Some 40 miles north of Brisbane lies what you might call the unspoiled young sibling of the Gold Coast. Unspoiled *as yet,* that is, for the Sunshine Coast is straining hard to catch up with its glamorous relative. But at this point its beaches are still blissfully uncrowded, very few high rises blot its horizon, accommodations are easy to find, and the aroma of hamburgers hasn't yet overwhelmed the scent of the hibiscus.

A string of little and biggish townships, interspersed with long stretches of undeveloped nature, the Sunshine Coast starts at Bribie Island in the south and ends roughly at Fraser Island in the north. In between lie some of the loveliest coastal strips, volcanic mountain ranges, lagoons, waterfalls, and fruit groves in all Queensland.

Noosa is the closest thing to a city the Sunshine Coast has to offer. But the term conveys a wrong image because the place actually consists of several scattered townships like Noosa Heads, Noosaville, Tewantin, and so on, with bus-ride distances between. Noosa, the liveliest locale on the Coast, boasts superb beaches and a mosaic of mangrove-lined waterways called Everglades.

But there are certain drawbacks connected with this area being relatively unspoiled. The Bruce Highway, main artery of the Sunshine Coast, is superb in some parts, terrible in others, under repair in still others, and everywhere too narrow for the traffic it's supposed to carry. Early closing is a general malaise (except in Noosa township), and after dark there isn't very much to do but wait for the next sunrise. But these are minor flaws compared to the wonderful sense of relaxed tranquility that enfolds the coast, the feeling that the urban rat race is being run somewhere on Mars, and the heady sensation of breathing unpolluted sea air. The only question is how much longer all this will last.

GETTING AROUND

Skennars Coach Service, Brisbane Transit Centre (tel. 286-1000), handles transport between the Sunshine Coast towns; the average fare is $A2.

WHAT TO SEE & DO

The Sunshine Coast has none of the Disneylandish razzle-dazzle that permeates the Gold Coast. Most of the attractions here are natural beauty sites; the few human-made showpieces tend to be on the quiet side. But the scenic charmers are so numerous that I can list only a few; there are plenty more where these came from.

GLASS HOUSE MOUNTAINS.

This is a range of peaks rising about 50 miles north of Brisbane on the Bruce Highway, so named by Captain Cook because they resembled English glass-manufacturing plants. Four of the peaks are national parks, popular for bushwalking and scenic forest drives. On the Glass House Mountains Tourist Route, Beerwah, is the **Queensland Reptile Park** (tel. 94-1134), which contains a large collection of native crawlies, including crocodiles, goannas, monitor lizards, pythons, taipans, and death adders. Admission is $A5 for adults, $A2.50 for children.

FRASER ISLAND.

The world's largest sand island and a gem of a wilderness retreat, Fraser Island is nearly 100 miles long and composed entirely of sand but covered with rain-forest vegetation and crisscrossed by crystal-clear freshwater streams meandering through tropical ferns. There are seemingly endless stretches of the whitest beaches you've ever seen, here and there marked by multicolored sand cliffs—an almost untouched nature haven, ideal for camping and fishing. A vehicular barge-ferry runs from Inskip Point, north of Noosa Heads, to the southern tip of the island, but you need a four-wheel-drive vehicle to motor around Fraser (see "Organized Tours," below).

H.M.S. *ENDEAVOUR,* Waterfront Hotel, Maroochy River Resort. Tel. 48-4460.

The H.M.S. *Endeavour* is a two-thirds-scale replica of the wooden windjammer in which Captain Cook explored the South Pacific. You can walk through and marvel at the sheer physical stamina of the men who spent months in unbelievably cramped quarters, charting unknown seas.

Admission: $A3 adults, $A2 children.

Open: Mon–Fri 10am–4pm.

SUPERBEE HONEY FACTORY, Tanawha Tourist Dr., Tanawha. Tel. 45-3544.

The Superbee Honey Factory is a vast spread of gardens, rain-forest walks, and fairy-tale cottages. Every hour you can watch a beekeeping show demonstrating how the honey is produced by bees, then gathered by the keepers. A free tasting follows.

Admission: Free.

Open: Daily 9am–5pm.

FOREST GLEN DEER SANCTUARY, Forest Glen. Tel. 45-1274.

A beautiful wildlife sanctuary embracing forest and pastureland, this is home to 150 deer of 5 species, mingling with kangaroos and wallabies. Since there are no enclosures, you can stroll among the gentle antlered and pouched inhabitants, who don't mind being patted as long as you feed them. Then take a look into the special Nocturnal House, where, through lighting effects, you can watch such Australian night creatures as possums, sugar gliders, and owls. You can also see a colony of koalas with babies.

Admission: $A10 adults, $A4 children.

Open: Daily 9am–4pm.

UNDERWATER WORLD, The Wharf, Park-in Parade, Mooloolaba. Tel. 44-8488.

Underwater World is a transparent tunnel through coral reefs and rocky grottoes, equipped with moving and static walkways. Through the thick glass you can watch giant groupers, razor-toothed moray eels, batlike stingrays, clown fish, angelfish, sharks, and hundreds of other denizens of the tropical marine world. See if you can spot the perfectly camouflaged—and deadly—stonefish, whose erect spines contain poison more potent than a cobra's. Also, this is your chance to watch crocodiles both above-and-below water.

Admission: $A13.50 adults, $A7 children.

Open: Daily 9am–5:30pm.

KONDALILLA NATIONAL PARK.

This national park is set on the crest of the Blackall Range near Montville. The highlight is Kondalilla Falls, a waterfall cascading into a valley of palms and rain forest. There are also magnificent views of a subtropical landscape, bird habitats, bush trails, and picnic grounds and a restaurant.

Directions: Follow the Bruce Highway to Palm Woods. Turn left toward Montville, then follow road signs.

GINGERTOWN, Pioneer Rd., Yandina. Tel. 46-7100.

The largest ginger factory in the world today began production during World War II, when ginger supplies from China were cut off. You are received in a beautiful visitors center, driven around in a little white bus, shown the entire manufacturing process of the spice, and given some free samples.

Admission: Free.

Open: Daily 8:30am–4:30pm.

NOSTALGIA TOWN, David Low Way, Pacific Paradise (at Maroochy Airport). Tel. 48-7155.

This collection of comical memorabilia includes an old-time barber shop (with the inevitable quartet), a bush theater showing silent flicks, a flapper swooning to gramophone jazz, minicars, and a puffing *Nostalgia Express* to take you around.

Admission: Free.

Open: Daily 9am–5pm.

SUNSHINE PLANTATION, Bruce Hwy., Woombye. Tel. 42-1333.

Visible far and wide by its shingle—a 50-foot pineapple made of fiberglass—the plantation actually grows tropical fruit and macadamia nuts and shows you how they are cultivated. Otherwise, it's a large complex of amusement rides, restaurants, and souvenir shops. And, yes, you can climb that megapineapple on the inside.

Admission: Free.

Open: Daily 9am–5pm.

FAIRYTALE CASTLE, David Low Way, Bli Bli. Tel. 48-5373.

This replica of a medieval castle is filled with fairy-tale figures, scenes from legends, dancing dolls, weaponry, and a rather realistic dungeon housing a torture chamber.

Admission: $A5 adults, $A3 children.

Open: Daily 9am–5pm.

AUSSIE WORLD, Bruce Hwy., Palmview. Tel. 074/94-5444.

This is a small theme park with Oz flavor laid out around a picturesque country boozer called **Ettamogah Pub.** The attractions include camel-and-minitrain rides, a reptile house, a motorcycle museum, orchestrated fountains, a glassblower, working blacksmith shop, and simulated Skirmish war games.

Admission: Free.

Open: Daily 10am–5pm.

ORGANIZED TOURS

EVERGLADES CRUISE, Noosa/Fraser Island Tours. Tel. 074/497-362.

This cruise is a tranquil, comfortable chug through the tropical wetlands of the Cooloola National Park along the Noosa River. It includes lush scenery and white pelicans, a barbecue lunch, and time off for a swim in warm water. There is also an amusing commentary on the environment along the way, as well as morning-and-afternoon tea. The boat leaves at 10am and returns around 3pm.

Tickets: $A48 adults, $A27 children.

COLORED SANDS SAFARIS, Noosa Shores Beach Safaris. Tel. 074/49-0300.

This is a four-wheel-drive excursion to the Colored Sands Canyons up the 40-mile beach. You may sight an occasional dingo in the intriguingly wild and open country. You learn how to throw a returning boomerang, swim from the beach, and watch for whales, dolphins, and manta rays offshore. The jaunt includes a solid tea break with homemade goodies and takes half a day.

Tickets: $A40 adults, $A25 children.

TROPICAL COAST TOURS, Noosa. Tel. 074/48-0512.

This is a selection of tours taking in most of the Sunshine Coast. No. 2, departing from Noosa on Tuesdays and Thursdays at 8:30am, visits the Ettamogah Pub, the Deer Sanctuary, Sunshine Plantation, Ginger Factory, and a winery.

Tickets: $A30 adults, $A15 children.

WHERE TO STAY

One of the best aspects of the Sunshine Coast is accommodations. They only are crowded on weekends and are generally cheaper than on the Gold Coast. However, as in all resort areas, the rates go up during special holiday periods.

MAC'S MOTEL, 18 Bowman Rd., Caloundra, QLD 4551. Tel. 074/91-1499. 26 rms (all with bath). MINIBAR TV TEL

$ Rates: $A40–$A54 unit. MC, V.

Mac's Motel is a very attractive spread just off the main road but virtually free from traffic noise. Abundant greenery surrounds a small swimming pool, and the guest units are set beneath sheltering eaves, with tables and chairs outside to enjoy the sea breezes. There's a restaurant on the premises, but breakfast is delivered to the units, all of which have electric toasters so you can make your morning toast fresh and crisp. There are ample furnishings, with large wardrobe and drawer space. Bathrooms are small, but the towel supplies are lavish; all units come with refrigerators and large, effective ceiling fans. The house-proud management bestows much tender loving care on their patrons, providing a guest laundry and two barbecues. The units house up to six comfortably.

MARUTCHI MOTEL, 10 Beach Rd., Maroochydore, QLD 4558. Tel. 074/43-1245. 14 units (all with shower). TV

$ Rates: $A35 single, $A40 double. MC, V.

Set near the riverfront, the Marutchi doesn't look impressive from the outside, but it is an excellent and comfortable resort bargain. The motel lacks decorative touches, but most of the units have their own kitchens. The large rooms have fluorescent ceiling lights and bedside lamps. The wardrobes are new and spacious; the furnishings are basic, but the kitchens have refrigerators, electric stoves, and a full range of cooking-and-eating utensils.

PALM BREEZE, 105 Bulcock St., Caloundra, QLD 4551. Tel. 074/91-5566. Fax 074/91-5115. 21 units (all with shower). TV

$ Rates: $A39 single, $A45 double. AE, BC, DC, MC, V.

A shining white motel a few hundred yards from the beach, this place is also in the center of town with shops and restaurants all around. Fittings are new, the bedrooms bright, airy, and equipped with ceiling fans, refrigerators, electric toasters, clock radios, and user-friendly beds. The Palm Breeze also offers a small swimming pool, hot spa, pool table, and two upstairs apartments that have cooking facilities. Breakfast is extra and delivered to your door.

RIVERSIDE MOTEL, 175 Gymple Terrace, Noosaville, QLD 4567. Tel. 074/49-7551. 14 units (all with shower). TV

$ Rates: $A35–$A40 single or double. BC, MC, V.

The Riverside Motel stands, as the name indicates, by the placidly blue Noosa River. Its units, some with full kitchen facilities, all have electric fans and refrigerators. Furnishings are simple but sufficient; there are a guest laundry and barbecue on the premises, and breakfast and dinner are served to the units. Accommodations are at ground level and spread out, and guests have a swimming pool at their disposal. A bargain.

SANDY COURT MOTEL, 30 James St., Noosaville, QLD 4566. Tel. 074/49-7225. 10 rms (all with shower). TV

$ Rates: From $A40 single or double (if this book is mentioned when reserving). BC, MC, V.

The Sandy Court Motel is one of the Coast's prime budget bargains. A low white-brick structure on a quiet side street, the Sandy Court offers remarkable value for very low rates. All the units large and airy, have their own kitchens and are equipped with wall-to-wall carpeting and newish furniture. Wardrobes are big, offering lots of hanging space; lighting arrangements are good; and you also get bedside clock radios.

VILLAGE MOTEL, 10 Hastings St., Noosa Heads, QLD 4567. Tel. 074/475-800. Fax same. 9 units (all with shower). TV

$ Rates: $A60 single or double. AE, BC, MC, V.

The Village Motel is a small establishment wreathed in foliage alive with tropical birds. It consists of two sections connected by outside stairs. The nine units, however, are marvels of compact comfort: no spare space, but all the essentials. They come with revolving fans, hot- and cold-water basins, and even small but private balconies. Wicker furnishings and little flower jars make for cheerfulness; fluorescent bedside lights provide good vision. The motel serves only breakfast, but there's a restaurant next door, and half a dozen more are down the street.

HOSTELS

NOOSA BACKPACKERS RESORT, 11 William St., Noosa, QLD 4566. Tel. 074/49-8151. 16 rms (2 with bath). TV TEL

$ Rates: $A11 dorm, $A26 double. MC, V.

This establishment is not exactly a "resort" but a good economy lodging, close to the beach and the river and with its own café and swimming pool. Great for socializing. It rents out bikes and runs tours to Fraser Island.

YHA HOLIDAY HOSTEL, 24 Schirrmann Dr., Maroochydore, QLD 4558. Tel. 074/43-3151. 48 beds. TV

$ Rates: $A11 adults, $A8 under 18, $A25 double. No credit cards.

This hostel is about 15 minutes from the surfing beaches and shopping center. It has its own pool as well as a kitchen, showers, and barbecue facilities. The staff will pick up residents from the bus stop if you telephone ahead.

WHERE TO EAT

On the Sunshine Coast you can save a great deal of money by revamping your eating habits—have your main meal at midday. This is quite contrary to the climate, which would indicate a very late dining hour, but it will do wonders for your pocketbook; for the Coast is brimming with little cafés, lunchrooms, and snack shops dispensing excellent food at economy prices. But nearly all of them shut their doors well before sundown, leaving the field to regular restaurants where the cuisine is also good but considerably more expensive. Why this should be so I cannot fathom, but you might just as well make the best of it.

Although Noosa is not the largest township on the Sunshine Coast, it is the undisputed restaurant-and-entertainment capital. Dining choices there not only are more varied and sophisticated but also keep (*cheers!*) reasonably late hours, as befits both the climate and the mirth-making clientele.

MEALS FOR LESS THAN $A14

CHINESE HOLIDAY RESTAURANT, 106 Bulcock St., Caloundra. Tel. 91-6066.

Cuisine: CHINESE/MALAYSIAN. **Reservations:** Accepted.

$ **Prices:** Appetizers $A2.80–$A4.50, main courses $A7.90–$A11.50. AE, DC, MC, V.

Open: Daily 12:30–2:30pm, 4:30–10pm.

This very traditional-looking Chinese eatery has some Malaysian surprise touches, such as Singapore spring lamb. It's large, air-conditioned, fully licensed, and illuminated by tassled lanterns, with vast floral prints covering the walls—a curious mixture of stylishness and economy, because you eat from plain metal tables. The same contrast is reflected in the menu. The house specialties come fairly expensive, but ordinary Cantonese courses run between $A7 and $A10. The dim sum make very good appetizers (three to a plate), and I recommend the braised chicken and almonds.

MEALS FOR LESS THAN $A18

BOON CHUAYS, 16 Sunshine Beach Rd., Noosaville. Tel. 492-1212.

Cuisine: THAI. **Reservations:** Accepted.

$ **Prices:** Appetizers $A5–$A6, main courses $A12. MC, V.

Open: Dinner, Thurs–Tues 6–10pm.

Boon Chuays is a starkly simple Thai BYO with a delightful bamboo garden in the rear. The interior is very plain, enlivened only by the ceiling fan. But the delicacies served are exactly that. You get three curry puffs or the Thai spring rolls called *por pac tod* for $A5.50. Most main dishes go for around $A11.50, including an excellent *larb nuer* consisting of finely minced beef cooked in lemon juice with mint and spring onions.

CAFE LE MONDE, Ocean Breeze, Noosa Heads. Tel. 492-366.

Cuisine: INTERNATIONAL. **Reservations:** Not accepted.

$ **Prices:** Appetizers $A4.20–$A7.90, main courses $A9.50–$A16.90. BC, MC, V.

Open: Daily 7:30am–midnight.

Café le Monde has a distinct Riviera flavor. Half indoors, half out (under canvas), fronted by a small palm fringe, the café serves morning papers along with breakfast and lights up romantically at night. It tries to please every palate: The fare is as international as the wine list is long. You get a glass of fine Riesling, Bordeaux, or Beaujolais for $A2. I highly recommend the chicken Provençale with rice for $A14.90. You also get a range of vegetarian dishes and special kids' meals.

CANTINA, 247 Gympie Terrace, Noosaville. Tel. 49-7497.

Cuisine: MEXICAN. **Reservations:** Accepted.

$ **Prices:** Appetizers $A6.50–$A7.90, main courses $A12.50–$A13.50. AE.
Open: Daily 6pm–"until late."

With a snorting bull wearing a sombrero and cartridge belt as a shingle, the Cantina is about as Mex as you'll get in this region. Picturesquely located on the bank of the Noosa River, it's BYO with an extensive menu and daily specials on a blackboard. Nachos, tacos, and quesadilla for starters, then a difficult main choice between *albondigas* (spicy beef-and-pork meatballs) or Montezuma pie—a fresh seafood pie of local fish, prawns, and scallops with cheese, onions, herbs, and spices between layers of soft tortillas.

LA SABBIA, 6 Hastings St., Noosa Heads. Tel. 49-2328.
Cuisine: INTERNATIONAL. **Reservations:** Accepted.
$ **Prices:** Appetizers $A4.80–$A8.50, main courses $A9.20–$A18.50. AE, BC, DC, MC, V.
Open: Daily 8am–midnight.

La Sabbia is an example of the happy new breed of eatery now springing up all over the Coast. It opens for breakfast, doesn't close until late supper, and serves meals and snacks with equal flourish. The decor is a bit supercontemporary, with a neon-lit bar, but there are tables outside beneath a shady canvas roof and small potted trees for decorations. You have a choice of half a dozen different pizzas or items like fresh catch of reef fish cooked Thai style, Cajun, or meuniére. The garlic prawns are commendable, and a special children's menu comes for $A8.50.

TWO CHEFS, Clubb Coolum Resort Complex, Coolum Beach. Tel. 46-1999.
Cuisine: INTERNATIONAL. **Reservations:** Recommended.
$ **Prices:** Appetizers $A5–$A8, main courses $A10.90–$A18. AE, DC, V.
Open: Daily 9am breakfast, noon lunch, 6:30–10:30pm dinner.

This is, strictly speaking, a splurge restaurant, run by two chefs with a big culinary reputation. But the daily lunch specials fall just within budget range: $A15 for any two courses, coffee included. And the fare is exceptional, though hard to classify. The duo in charge describe it as "spontaneous cuisine." Breakfast here may include eggs Benedict with smoked salmon or veal sausages with poached eggs. At other times you can get a Caesar salad with battered anchovies for extra taste or the fish of the day cooked Cajun style with herb butter sauce and a wreath of gourmet chips. The menu is fairly small but always includes surprise items and changes constantly.

A DINING COMPLEX

The Wharf, Park-in Parade, Mooloolaba, is a waterfront complex of bars, bistros, boutiques, and boats that jostle for space with nightspots, entertainment venues, Underwater World, and the Sunshine Coast Ferry Company. The Wharf also boasts several bargain restaurants, all operating daily from breakfast to dinner. **Fridays** (tel. 448-383) offers different dinner specials almost every night of the week: On Monday it's Mexican for $A7.99; Tuesday it's T-bone steaks for $A9.95; Thursday it's a seafood extravaganza for $A15.99; and so on. **Murphy's** (tel. 448-328) presents splendid ocean views along with the comestibles in an al fresco setting. The big draw here is the Meal of the Month; either rib steak, seafood, or chicken for $A9.99. Also outstanding is the all-you-can-eat salad bar, including pastas, lasagne, and desserts for $A8.99.

CHAPTER 7

THE CAIRNS AREA & THE GREAT BARRIER REEF

1. **CAIRNS**
- **WHAT'S SPECIAL ABOUT THE CAIRNS AREA & THE GREAT BARRIER REEF**
- **FAST FACTS: CAIRNS**
- **FROMMER'S COOL FOR KIDS: RESTAURANTS**

2. **KURANDA, PORT DOUGLAS & COOKTOWN**
3. **GREAT BARRIER REEF**

Cairns started in 1876 as a shipping port for the tin, sugar and gold of the interior. It was a sweating, boozing, brawling harbor patch with a decidedly rough image. An ideal place for "going troppo"—haywire—abetted by heat and rum, and the rowdiest red-light district in Australia.

All this changed with the advent of tourism. Within a decade the city had been polished, sanitized, and velvet-lined almost beyond recognition. What emerged was an antidote to urban stress, a metropolis of laid-back, wrapped in a tropical climate. Even the term "troppo" shed its original meaning. Here it denotes a state of blissful languor in which nothing much matters except the cool drink in your hand and the entertainment in view.

Stretching along much of the Queensland coast is the Great Barrier Reef, a glorious scenic wonderland of innumerable shapes and colors of coral. Cairns, Townsville, and Mackay are tourist gateways to the reef, made up of islets, lagoons, and other structures.

1. CAIRNS

215 miles N of Townsville, 1,107 miles N of Brisbane

GETTING THERE **By Plane** **Cairns International Airport** lies about three miles from downtown. It was built primarily because Qantas now flies here directly from San Francisco and Los Angeles. The airport has everything—well, nearly—an international terminal should have, including banking facilities, self-opening doors, bistro-bar, and good air-conditioning. The airport bus to the city costs $A4.50; a cab comes to around $A10. The air trip from Brisbane (on Ansett or Qantas) takes 2¾ hours and costs around $A265. The Ansett Airlines terminal is at 84 Lake St. (tel. 131-300), and the Qantas terminal is at the corner of Lake and Shields streets (tel. 008/177-167).

By Train The train from Brisbane is the leisurely ***Sunlander,*** which arrives the next day and costs $A116.70. The railway station is on McLeod Street; phone 51-0531 for information. The station is elderly and doesn't offer many facilities, but it's centrally located and a very short cab or bus ride away from most hotels. Remember, though, that in tourist season the Brisbane-Cairns run is heavily booked. Reserve tickets well in advance.

By Bus The bus from Brisbane rolls 24 hours and costs $A125. All coaches arrive at the new and well-equipped **Trinity Wharf terminus,** a mere couple of blocks

WHAT'S SPECIAL ABOUT THE CAIRNS AREA & THE GREAT BARRIER REEF

Events/Festivals

- ☐ Fun in the Sun Festival, with parades, dances, and costumes.
- ☐ The Agricultural Show, displaying the finest North Queensland farm animals and products.

For the Kids

- ☐ Wild World, a combination reptile, animal, and bird park containing Australia's largest captive crocodile.
- ☐ Sugarworld, an erstwhile sugar mill converted into a park area with a children's farm, water slides, and hand-feeding kangaroos.
- ☐ Kuranda, reached by a spectacular train trip, with an Aboriginal dance theater and a butterfly farm.
- ☐ Green Island, with rides in glass-bottomed observation boats, superb snorkeling, and an exciting Marineland.
- ☐ The Flying Doctor Centre, world's most unusual medical service.

Shopping

- ☐ Glamorous complexes: Trinity Wharf, Conservatory, Palm Court, Village Lane, and Orchid Plaza.
- ☐ Unusual markets, such as the Pier Marketplace (built over the water), Kuranda Markets, and Rusty's Bazaar.

Natural Spectacles

- ☐ The Great Barrier Reef, the largest coral reef in the world.
- ☐ The high Tablelands, with gorges, rain forests, waterfalls, plus some of the richest farm and dairy land in Australia.
- ☐ Sugarcane fields so vast you can take a steam-train ride through them.
- ☐ Orchid Valley, with a world-famous waterfall.
- ☐ Port Douglas, site of some of the most breathtaking scenery anywhere.

Parks

- ☐ Botanical Gardens, resembling a tropical jungle.

from central Cairns. An unusual feature here are the hostel reps who lie in wait for the buses and try to recruit guests from among the passengers, frequently offering free rides to their abodes. Bus lines include **Pioneer** (tel. 51-2411), **Greyhound** (tel. 51-3388), and **McCafferty's Coaches** (tel. 51-5899), all located at Trinity Wharf.

By Car The road from Brisbane to Cairns is paved but beset by a multitude of driving hazards. My advice would be to take other transport to Cairns and rent a car there.

We're still in Queensland here—locals, in fact, call this the *real* Queensland—but now we've entered the Far North, the Australian tropics. The landscape is incredibly green in different shadings: light emerald in the pasture lands; deep, dark, and sated in the jungle portions. Human habitations fade into insignificance amid the sprawling immensity of the vegetation. From the air it seems as if the lush wilderness could engulf human settlements at any given moment.

Cairns (pronounced *Cans,* as in tin) is the northernmost city in Queensland, a bustling, thriving, humid harbor town just over a century old. The metropolitan population is now around 100,000 but appears much smaller because the streets are so wide that they give an impression of emptiness. This is one of the very few tourist haunts where you never feel jostled or crowded—there's always plenty of elbow room, at least outdoors.

The town has a spectacular setting. Overlooking the radiantly blue waters of Trinity Bay, Cairns lies enclosed in a ring of green sugarcane fields, which form a natural boundary. Farther inland the mountains rise in steep slopes, covered in thick rain forest. During the crushing season—from June to December—the cane fires blaze every night to clean the stalks for the next day's harvest, licking against the dark sky like the campfires of a race of jungle giants. In daytime the fields are noisy with the whistles of miniature trains chugging to the district crushing mills with loads of sweet cane stalks.

Cairns today is a two-faced town—in the literal meaning of the phrase. Nowhere else has the impact of tourism wrought so many changes in such a short time. A decade ago this was a fairly grubby place, with an oceanfront that made you feel like a Joseph Conrad character. It had the kind of tropical architecture that always looks like an outdoor movie set—picturesque but slightly ramshackle. A big night out was dinner in the fading glory of one of the larger hotel dining rooms. The population stood at around 45,000.

Then came the opening of the new airport, replacing the old tin-shed terminal. With it came 50 international flights a week and about 1½ million tourists per year. They grafted a new face on Cairns, or rather half of one, because you can now cross a road and step from a 1990s holiday world, as cosmopolitan as Sydney, into 1930s-style tropicana, complete with verandas on stilts, dogs snoozing in the shade, and roughhouse saloons.

The new face is impressive. Along the Esplanade high rises tower, outdoor eateries jostle, and crowds stroll chattering in twenty languages. Marlin Wharf, once a haven for island luggers, is now a yacht marina, bordered by giant shop-and-restaurant complexes called Trinity Wharf, Orchid Plaza, Village Lane, and Palm Court. Instead of cheap little waterfront hotels, living on the bar trade, there are immense luxury palaces, each with its own shopping center, nightclub, gourmet restaurant, and oceanview cocktail retreat.

Cairns is not a place "where the old blends graciously with the new"—to use a hoary travelogue cliché. The two don't blend, they coexist, largely by ignoring each other—at least during the peak tourist season of May through October. That's when the dollars and yen pour in and shops have special dispensation to stay open from 8:30am until 7pm or later and the big retail complexes trade on Sunday as well.

You can get an impression of both aspects of the town by wandering along busy Grafton Street. This used to be the Chinese quarter with its own Joss House. It was also the red-light district, operating for the benefit of visiting ships' crews. There are still traces of the old environment, but they are vanishing fast. Today the center is Rusty's Bazaar: a multicultural market selling anything from tropical fruit and fish to T-shirts, shell jewelry, and Aboriginal handcrafts to tourist customers, with nary a seaman in the crowd. And the eastern end boasts air-conditioned arcades housing enough shops and food outlets to satisfy a metropolis. But the old homes on stilts still stand here and there, and when you come to the quieter parts you can hear the rustle of the overhead fans, bravely defying air-conditioning and late trading.

Despite its astonishing facelift, Cairns is still regarded as a staging post, a base for exploring what lies beyond, by most visitors. For the town's claims to tourist fame are its proximity to the Great Barrier Reef (Green Island lies a 45-minute launch ride away) and marlin fishing. Black marlin—no good for eating—are probably the world's foremost game fish, fabulous fighters that even when hooked are not caught by a long shot. Every year around September these giant bull fish migrate with the southbound current from New Guinea. They cruise and hunt in the deep waters on the ocean side of the Great Barrier Reef, leaping high above the surface of the Coral Sea as if challenging the big-game fishermen to come and get them. And these fishermen come out of Cairns, home port for the famous "Marlin Meet," which attracts the international set of sea hunters out to break the world black-marlin

CAIRNS

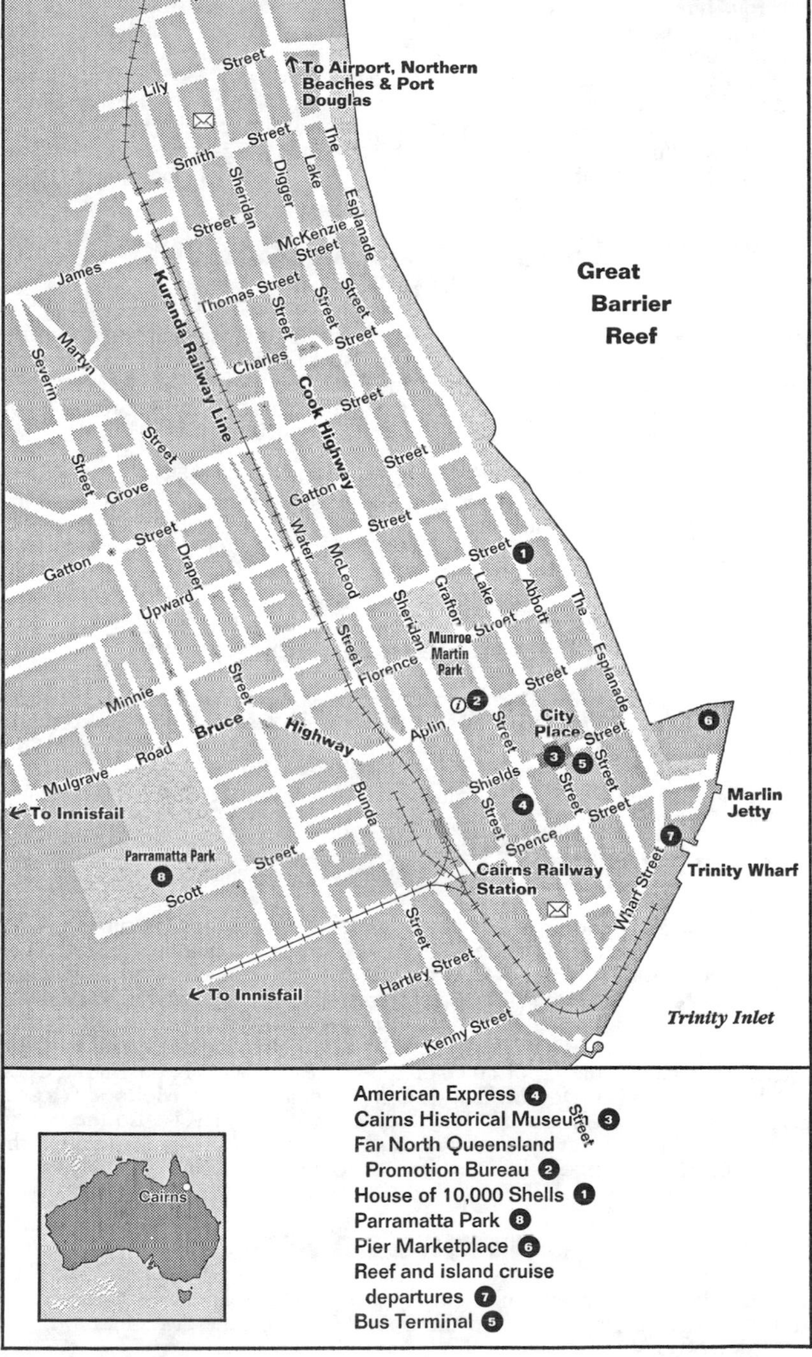

Post Office ☒ Information ⓘ

6756

record. The very rich come in their own craft from across the ocean. The merely prosperous hire them on the spot—the Cairns harbor front has rows of sleek and powerful game-fishing boats for charter. The rest of us watch or go fishing for grouper or coral trout. Marlin fishing is decidedly for the well-heeled: Charters for the specialized launches *start* at over $A300 per day.

Strangely enough, despite its bay location Cairns has no beaches. All the swimming in town takes place in pools. The harbor is only for boating and bird watching—you can see flocks of pelicans, white egrets, and herons while lying on the lawns along the Esplanade. But 15 minutes away, up and down the coast, lie some of the most splendid beaches on earth. We'll visit them in due course.

FROM A BUDGET TRAVELER'S POINT OF VIEW

BUDGET BESTS Cairns is a resort town that lives on tourism and offers very few freebies. But one of them is window-shopping in the brand-new, impressively chic shopping complexes springing up all over the place. The beaches—a long string of them—start a short bus ride away, all flanking the seemingly endless Captain Cook Highway. Trouble is, the buses don't run quite as frequently as they should.

WORTH PAYING FOR Cairns is the gateway to the Great Barrier Reef. You should take a boat ride to at least one of the scores of reef islands. Green Island has the most intriguing sights—but also gets the biggest crowds. Alternatively, there's an enchanting train trip inland to the rain-forest village of Kuranda.

ORIENTATION

TOURIST INFORMATION

The **Cairns Tourist Info Centre** is at 99 Esplanade, Cairns, QLD 4870 (tel. 31-1751). The **Far North Queensland Promotion Bureau** is at the corner of Grafton and Hartley streets (tel. 51-3588), open Monday to Friday from 9am to 5pm and Saturday from 9am to 1pm. The bureau arranges accommodations and tours as well. For information on current activities in town, consult the *Cairns Post,* printed daily.

CITY LAYOUT

Cairns is a small city and requires a minimum of orientation. If you stand at **City Place,** at the junction of Lake and Shields streets, looking up Shields Street, you'll be facing northeast. **Main Street Arcade** is on your right. Two blocks up from you is the **Esplanade,** running along the seafront, flanked on the right by **Fogarty Park,** which adjoins the new and splendiferous **Trinity Wharf** area.

Two blocks behind you runs **Sheridan Street.** This eventually becomes **Cook Highway** and goes to the airport, then on to the ocean beaches of the Marlin Coast (described later) and Port Douglas. The next thoroughfare down is **McLeod Street,** where the train station is located. The direction of the station is also the way to **Parramatta Park** and the outer **suburbs** of Cairns and eventually leads to the **Great Dividing Range,** the magnificent, forested tableland that forms the backdrop of the city.

GETTING AROUND

BY BUS Public transportation is entirely by bus. The beach bus departs at Lake Street Transit Mall and goes out to the Marlin Coast beaches five times a day on weekdays, three times a day on weekends. Fares start at $A2.85 one-way. For schedules, call 57-7411.

BY TAXI You'll usually find cabs at the large luxury hotels (except when you urgently need one). To call a taxi ring **Black and White Taxis** (tel. 51-5333), **Atherton Taxi Service** (tel. 91-1622), or **Mission Beach Taxis** (tel. 68-8266).

BY CAR For car-rental bargains it's worthwhile to study the notice boards outside the backpackers' hostels along the Esplanade. Otherwise try **Aussie Allcar,** 30 Grafton St. (tel. 31-6122); **Cairns Rent-a-Car,** 147 Lake St. (tel. 51-6077); or **Thrifty,** corner of Sheridan and Aplin streets (tel. 51-8099).

BY BICYCLE Being totally flat, with wide streets and light traffic, Cairns is a good biking town—if, because of the heat, you don't mind soaking through your shirt. But beware of the local cab drivers: They drive according to rules of their own. Bikes can be hired at **Bikes for Rent,** 89 Esplanade, for $A8 for 4 hours, $A12 for 24 hours.

CAIRNS

American Express Call toll free **008/02-2461.**
Area Code The telephone area code is **070.**
Babysitters Try **Executive Home Duty** (tel. 55-3439).
Car Rentals See "Getting Around," in this chapter.
Climate See "When to Go," Chapter 2.
Currency See "Information, Entry Requirements & Money," Chapter 2.
Currency Exchange Traveler's checks can be exchanged at **Thomas Cook,** 12 Shields St. (tel. 51-6255), or **NATA Travel,** 91 Grafton St. (tel. 51-6472).
Dentist Call **Baker Steven,** 82 Lake St. (tel. 51-7160).
Doctor Contact **Calvary Hospital,** Upward Street (tel. 52-5200).
Drugstores Try **Civic Centre Pharmacy,** corner of Florence and McLeod streets (tel. 51-1085).
Emergencies To reach an ambulance, the fire department, or the police, dial **000.**
Eyeglasses Try **OPSM,** 182 Grafton St. (tel. 51-1476).
Hairdressers/Barbers For both men and women, try **Hi Profile,** Civic Shopping Centre, Sheridan Street (tel. 51-2746).
Holidays See "When to Go," Chapter 2.
Hospitals **Cairns Base Hospital** is located on the Esplanade (tel. 50-6333).
Hot lines **Lifeline:** 51-4300. **Poisons Information:** 07/253-8233.
Information See "Tourist Information," in this chapter.
Laundry/Dry Cleaning Same-day cleaning can be obtained from **Nu Tone Dry Cleaners,** 149 Lake St. There are laundries at 49 Grafton St., on Lake Street, and on Sheridan Street. One load of wash costs $A1.
Libraries The **Municipal Library** is located at 125 Lake St. (tel. 50-2455).
Luggage Storage/Lockers Lockers are available at the airport and train station.
Newspapers/Magazines The *Cairns Post* is the daily newspaper.
Photographic Needs Try **Smith's,** 86 Lake St. (tel. 51-0433).
Police For nonemergencies, contact the police at 55 Esplanade (tel. 51-2000).
Post Office The **General Post Office** is at the corner of Spence and Abbot streets. Telegrams can be sent from there, and poste restante service is available.
Religious Services The following denominations are represented in Cairns. **Anglican:** St. Johns Cathedral, Lake Street (tel. 51-8055). **Catholic:** St.

Monica's, Abbot Street (tel. 51-2838). **Presbyterian:** St. Andrews, 87 Sheridan St. (tel. 58-1685).

Restrooms Public restrooms are available on the Esplanade, at City Place, and in all parks.

Safety In Cairns, avoid waterfront bars late at night. In the outlying areas of Queensland, observe all crocodile warning signs and avoid swimming at coastal beaches during box-jellyfish breeding season (see "Attractions," below, for more information).

Shoe Repairs Try **Theo's Shoe Hospital,** 56 Shield St. (tel. 51-1334).

Taxes There are no taxes added to purchases or hotel-and-restaurant bills.

Taxis See "Getting Around," in this chapter.

Telegrams/Telex/Fax The post office and some hotels offer these services.

Transit Info Airport bus: 35-9555. Beach bus: 57-7411. Cairns Trans: 53-1120.

Useful Telephone Numbers Community Information: 51-4953. Far North Queensland Promotion Bureau: 51-3588. RACQ Breakdown Service: 51-6543.

WHERE TO STAY

There are at least 20 accommodation places along the seafront Esplanade, a lawn-fringed, palm-lined promenade that runs the entire length of the Cairns waterfront as far as the wharves.

The Ys of Cairns are, sadly, nonexistent. But their places are amply filled by an abundance of hostels, which make this tropical port one of the best budget propositions in the country.

DOUBLES FOR LESS THAN $A50

COSTA BLANCA, 241 Esplanade, Cairns, QLD 4870. Tel. 070/51-3114. 8 units (all with bath). TV

$ Rates: $A40–$A60 double. No credit cards.

A lovely white Spanish villa, made more atmospheric by the cactuses in front, the Costa Blanca has a good-sized pool in the rear, shaded by palms and flanked by pool furniture and a barbecue. All units are large and airy, each consisting of a bedroom, living room, and full kitchen. There is plenty of breathing-and-hanging space, with the closet taking up the entire bedroom wall. Downstairs units open onto the pool area; the four upstairs have balconies overlooking the Esplanade and ocean beyond. Furnishings are new, cheerful, and ample, and the rooms come equipped with ceiling fans and TVs. However, the rates fluctuate sharply with the seasons, and booking ahead here is a near must. Ask for Ms. Julie Forbes and mention this book.

INN THE TROPICS, 141 Sheridan St., Cairns, QLD 4870. Tel. 070/31-1088. Fax 070/51-7110. 54 rms (some with bath). A/C

$ Rates: $35 single or double without bath, $45 double with bath, $41–$51 family rms. No credit cards.

The Inn offers a lot of facilities at economy rates. It has a pleasant courtyard with tables and chairs for socializing, a swimming pool, TV lounge, spacious guest kitchen, games room, and laundry. The beach bus stops nearby. Bedrooms have tile floors, refrigerators, fluorescent ceiling lights (no bedside lamps), small open hanging spaces, and unusual pay-as-you-cool air-conditioning: $A1 gets you three hours of A/C. The place is spotless and patrons give it high marks for the knowledgeable way in which the staff makes tour arrangements for guests. No meals served, but eating utensils are supplied.

MOTEL CAIRNS, 48 Spence St., Cairns, QLD 4870. Tel. 070/51-2271. Fax 070/51-9952. 40 rms (all with bath). A/C TV

$ Rates: Old wing, $A28 single, $A36 double. New wing, $A40 single, $A45 double. AE, BC, MC, V.

Motel Cairns is located downtown. This white, colonial-style structure with an overhanging second story is divided into an old and a new wing: The new wing is air-conditioned, the old wing has ceiling fans. All rooms, however, come with good private bathrooms, refrigerators, and coffee-, tea-, and toast-making equipment. The rooms are quite spacious, but the open clothes-hanging spaces are a bit narrow. There are stone walls for coolness, fluorescent ceiling lights, and bedside lamps—furniture is kept to the essentials. There is no restaurant on the premises, but the pub across the yard offers cheap counter meals (as well as considerable noise at night).

WINTERSUN, 84 Abbott St., Cairns, QLD 4870. Tel. 070/51-2933. Fax 070/31-2627. 20 rms (all with shower). A/C TV

$ Rates: Motel room, $A45 single, $A50 double. BC, MC, V.

Wintersun is a small, pleasant motel/apartment establishment whose accommodations have been sharply upgraded in recent years—as have the rates. The house has a guest laundry, a barbecue, and a small swimming pool.

DOUBLES FOR LESS THAN $A80

CORAL CAY VILLA, 267 Lake St., Cairns, QLD 4870. Tel. 070/31-2377. Fax 070/31-2703. 42 units (all with bath). A/C TV TEL

$ Rates: $A65–$A75 single, $A76–$A86 double. AE, BC, MC, V.

A tropical-style charmer with surrounding greenery and shady verandas, the villa has a simulated "rock pool" in the rear and every modern convenience inside. The units, self-contained and smartly furnished, have in-house videos as well as radios and refrigerators large enough to stock family food supplies. Outside there are several guest laundries, a spa, a barbecue area, plus a cabana. Rates for singles go a bit above the budget bracket, but they fit nicely for doubles and are bargains for families or groups.

WORTH THE EXTRA MONEY

BAY VILLAGE, 227 Lake St., Cairns, QLD 4870. Tel. 070/51-4622. Fax 070/51-4057. Telex 48078. 62 rms (all with bath). A/C MINIBAR TV TEL

$ Rates: $A112–$A130 single or double. AE, BC, MC, V.

Bay Village is a boutique hotel in what resembles a jungle setting, an impression fostered by the dense vegetation all around and between the buildings. The swimming pool lies almost invisibly under drooping palms, and all walkways are fringed with heavy greenery through which the sun gleams in patterns. The "hut" interiors, however, can rank as deluxe because they are wonderfully spacious (the costlier studios have kitchens). Rooms have pink-brick walls and tile floors for coolness, huge rattan ceiling fans that whir purely to provide atmosphere, and lightweight cane furniture. They provide ample wardrobe space, excellent lighting, and large refrigerators. Some units face inward toward the kidney-shaped pool (kept much warmer than real jungle pools, which are mostly freezing cold). There's a restaurant named Jungles on the premises and appropriate jungle juices are dispensed at a poolside bar. You also get a guest laundry, babysitting arrangements, and courtesy transfers to and from the airport.

HOSTELS & DORMS

BACKPACKERS INN, 255 Lake St., Cairns, QLD 4870. Tel. 070/51-9166. Fax 070/51-6604. 16 rms, 10 dorms (shared bath). A/C TV

$ Rates: $A10 dorm, $A20 single, $A24 double. AE, BC, DC, MC, V.

Cozy and scattered, this hostel spreads over three adjoining buildings. A large white bungalow-style building (look for the sign with the hitchhiking kangaroo), the inn features some surprising luxury touches, such as a swimming pool and a volleyball court. There's courtesy bus service to downtown.

CAIRNS CASTAWAY'S, 207 Sheridan St., Cairns, QLD 4870. Tel. 070/51-1238. 16 rms (shared bath).

$ Rates: $A16 single, $A12 per person double, $A10 per person triple. No credit cards.

This is a small, handy, and friendly place, very well maintained and unusual as a backpackers' abode by having no dorms. All rooms house from one to three persons only; the triples paying $A10 each. Hanging space is a bit tight, but the establishment has a TV lounge, fans and fridges in all rooms, a small pool, guest kitchen, and laundry. Air-conditioned rooms available. The management runs a courtesy pick-up service from the airport, rail, and bus station.

CAIRNS GIRLS HOSTEL, 147 Lake St., Cairns, QLD 4870. Tel. 070/512-767. 35 beds (shared bath). TV

$ Rates: $A12–$A15 single or double. AE, BC, MC, V.

This hostel takes only women (of any age) and keeps males out of bounds with several stern notices saying exactly that. The hostel is excellently maintained but rather hard to spot—the entrance is a narrow passage, easily overlooked. There are three bathrooms, a TV lounge, laundry facilities, and three communal kitchens. Bedrooms have bedside tables and wardrobes.

CARAVELLA'S HOSTELS, 77 and 149 Esplanade, Cairns, QLD 4870. Tel. 070/51-2159. Fax 070/31-6320. 40 rms (some with bath). A/C TV

$ Rates: $A25–$A35 single or double, $A10–$A12 in dorm. No credit cards.

Small, red-brick Caravella's, with a nice upstairs balcony, is a real economy establishment. The rooms have bare floors, TVs, and small wardrobes; most have air-conditioning. Furnishings are somewhat sparse but include bedside lamps, and all the rooms come with hot and cold running water. The house has four modern bathrooms, a swimming pool, a guest laundry, a fully equipped communal kitchen, and a games area. No meals are served on the premises.

HOSTEL 89, 89 Esplanade, Cairns, QLD 4870. Tel. 070/317-477. 2 dorms, 20 rms (shared bath).

$ Rates: $A15 dorm, $A25 single, $A30–$A35 double. AE, BC, MC, V.

The 89 has a couple of unusual features: All rooms are air-conditioned and the place has its own diving center and training facility on site. The location is ideal, only two blocks from the bus station and rows of restaurants on each side. The rooms are fairly small and lack hanging space for clothes; fluorescent lights make for brightness. There is a swimming pool, guest laundry with dryer, TV lounge, and a nice courtyard area. This is one of the few hostels that exchanges foreign currency.

PARKVIEW BACKPACKERS HOSTEL, 174 Grafton St., Cairns, QLD 4870. Tel. 070/51-3700. Fax 070/31-4887. 10 rms, 16 dorms (1 with bath).

$ Rates: $A12 dorm, $A26 single or double. MC, V.

This hostel, overlooking the park, is actually a set of two separate houses, which makes for a diversity of accommodations: You get a choice of rooms or dormitories, all nicely maintained. Other nice touches are the printed cards saying "Welcome" in five languages, a courtesy pick-up bus, free video movies, and a swimming pool, and the management lives up to its welcome cards. A park lies in front of the building, with more green lawns in the rear and palms swaying all around. The eight double rooms are fairly small and do not have running water. But the buildings contain 12 shared bathrooms, plus 8 large white community kitchens for the dorms (each housing four to eight persons). You can cook your own meals since all necessary utensils are supplied.

TRACKS, 149 Grafton St., Cairns, QLD 4870. Tel. 070/311-474. Dorms and doubles. TV

$ Rates: $A10 dorm, $A22 double, (including one free meal every night). MC, V.

$ Tracks, at the corner of Minnie and Grafton streets, is a backpackers "resort" with some unusual features. It runs a free courtesy coach that picks you up at the airport or train or bus station and offers discount tickets for local restaurants, attractions, and excursions. It has five kitchens, a dining patio, and a swimming pool, as well as free videos and party nights. The house stands opposite a park, and accommodation is in dorms (including one for women only) or double rooms. The management advises that "the cooking of cane toads is strictly forbidden. We ask that they be eaten *raw*."

WHERE TO EAT

For a town of its size, Cairns has a remarkable number of good eateries, plus a couple of truly great ones. The selection is surprisingly cosmopolitan, too—a far cry from the days when the only foreign cuisine found in northern Queensland was the local chop-suey joint. The price range is the same as in Brisbane, an unusual phenomenon for such a tourist center.

But best of all, Cairns has developed not only Mediterranean dining hours to go along with the fare, but also the wonderful custom of al fresco supping. So far, this is the only Queensland town to have done so on a large scale, and it was a long time in coming. Today all along the beachfront Esplanade you'll see rows of tables and colored umbrellas, some belonging to the deluxe restaurants but most belonging to the little budget buffets that cater to the hostel dwellers of the region. They serve everything from four-course repasts to gelato cones and do so at late and civilized hours. All are thronged with tourists blissfully unaware that the pleasure they take for granted is something many locals still regard as a new and somewhat risqué experiment.

MEALS FOR LESS THAN $A12

COCK & BULL, corner of Grove and Digger Sts. Tel. 31-1160.
Cuisine: ENGLISH. **Reservations:** Accepted.
$ **Prices:** Appetizers $A2.40, main courses $A6–$A9. AE, MC, V.
Open: Daily 5:30pm–midnight, Sun lunch from noon.

This very English and most untropical tavern serves a fine and hearty line of pub grub—apart from 50 varieties of beer. It is an amazing juxtaposition when you step in from the sweltering street—like stepping into Stepney or thereabouts. The menu is short but solid: bangers and mash (sausages and mashed potatoes) for $A7.90, Cornish pasties for $A6.20, shepherds pie for $A7.90 and so on up the ladder all the way to Scotch filet steak. In case you haven't tasted English cider before, this is a good spot to try it.

INTERNATIONAL FOOD HALL, Esplanade.
Cuisine: INTERNATIONAL. **Reservations:** Not necessary.
$ **Prices:** $A4.80–$A6. No credit cards.
Open: Daily 7am–10pm.

$ A long, low hall, usually jammed with hostel dwellers, this is one of the cheapest, speediest, and most varied food establishments in town. A bar on one side and food stalls on the other, with a fish tank for decoration, the place covers the quick comestibles range from vegetarian quiches to German Bockwurst with sauerkraut, from American hotcakes to Chinese noodles—not to forget Danish, French, and Italian specialties, all costing under $A8.

OKEY DOKEY, 64 Shields St. Tel. 51-4744.
Cuisine: GERMAN. **Reservations:** Accepted.
$ **Prices:** No appetizers, main courses $A7.50–$A11.50. No credit cards.
Open: Mon–Fri 7am–8pm.

The name is a puzzling misnomer for what is actually a handsome little Bavarian café. Sidewalk tables are in front, a nicely secluded patio in the rear, and light cane furnishings throughout. There are German illustrated magazines to peruse as well as a chessboard for the use of patrons. The taped oompah music stays soft: this is a spot to relax in. The menu offers Bavarian specialties: Leberkäs panfried with egg, Bratwurst with sauerkraut, champignon Schnitzel with salad, plus genuine Munich Apfelstrudel with whipped cream.

SWAGMAN'S REST, City Place. Tel. 515-075.

Cuisine: AUSTRALIAN WITH ALIEN TOUCHES. **Reservations:** Accepted.

$ Prices: No appetizers; main courses $A10.50–$A13. BC, MC, V.

Open: Daily 8am–9pm.

This place rates a special mention because it was the first outdoor eatery to open in Cairns, at a time when al fresco dining was regarded as an eccentricity one notch odder than tobacco chewing. You eat on a lovely patio in the pedestrian mall, roofed against sunlight and rain showers. The fare includes items like chicken Kiev, seafood baskets, and prawn curry. The Moselle house wine comes at $A2.50 per glass. Special childrens' menu with kids' favorites at $A4.50 per item. Remember to place your order at the counter *before* you sit down, otherwise you'll just wait.

MEALS FOR LESS THAN $A16

FOX & FIRKIN, Central Court, corner of Lake & Spence Sts. Tel. 31-5305.

Cuisine: ANGLO-ITALIAN. **Reservations:** Accepted.

$ Prices: Appetizers $A3–$A7.50, main courses $A7–$A13.50. AE, BC, MC, V.

Open: Mon–Sat 11:30am–midnight, Sun 4pm–midnight.

Located one flight of stairs up, this place is decked out like an English pub (with a ferocious fox demanding ale) but is actually more of a bistro. Either way it's hugely popular. The bill of fare presents a nice mix of English, Italian, and Mexican specialties: Fish-and-chips, beef lasagne, nachos, lamb noisettes, mixed grills, etc. In deference to the English image desserts are listed as "puddings" and include Guinness cake and an excellent Irish apple pie—which I've never seen in Ireland.

GEORGE'S GREEK TAVERNA, corner of Grafton and Aplin Sts. Tel. 411-500.

Cuisine: GREEK. **Reservations:** Recommended.

$ Prices: Appetizers $A3.50–$A8.50, main courses $A13.50–$A18.50.

Open: Tues–Sat from 6pm.

A blue-and-white corner building with a real Aegean air. The atmosphere is truly taverna, complete with checkered table linen, straw-covered chairs, and big welcoming smiles all around. This is a family-run eatery par excellence; owner George Papagelou's mother-in-law even reads the coffee grounds for you when she has time. The whitewashed walls are decked with wine flasks, plates, and family photos and the ambience can best be described as happily laid-back gluttony. For good reasons. The traditional lamb on a spit here is marinated a full five days before being roasted, and you get a choice of char-grilled or pickled octopus, which you may never have tasted before. The bread is home baked and desserts include an irresistible and unpronounceable item called *galactobourico*—semolina custard wrapped in pastry—that you dream about when you're back to weight watching. As the menu says: *kali orexi*—good appetite!

SILVER DRAGON, 102 Lake St. Tel. 31-2828.

Cuisine: CHINESE. **Reservations:** Accepted.

$ Prices: Appetizers $A3.40–$A6.50, main courses $A9–$A14. AE, DC, MC, V.

Open: Daily 5–10pm.

This is probably Cairns's most popular Chinese establishment—and with good reason. The place is lovely, large, and ornate enough to keep you interested while you're waiting for a table at the elegant bar and seating facilities provided in front. The lighting is from traditional Chinese lanterns, casting their glow over Asian statues in glass cases and a gorgeous tropical aquarium. Bar and kitchen quarters are separated from the dining area by a dragon-decorated screen. The overall effect is surprisingly pleasant, and the cuisine better than the average Aussie-Asian standard. There is a long list of lobster and prawn dishes at "seasonal" prices.

STEAK AND PANCAKE HOUSE, 43 Spence St. Tel. 51-6551.

Cuisine: AUSTRALIAN. **Reservations:** Not accepted.
$ Prices: Pancakes $A3.50–$A5.90, steaks $A15.30–$A18.80.
Open: Daily 6:30–10pm.

This restaurant is housed in one of the first permanent structures built in colonial Cairns—originally occupied by a Chinese vegetable store. Today the place leads an intriguing double life as a popular pancake parlor and as one of the finest steakhouses in town. The pancakes—all sweet—are economy priced. The top-quality steaks come a cut above budget range, but include a selection from the extensive fresh fruit and salad bar.

DINING SPECIALS

The Playpen, 3 Lake St., is actually a nightclub (see "Evening Entertainment"), with comestibles secondary to bare skin. But it houses a surprise in the form of **Samuel's** (tel. 51-8211). This features an all-you-can-eat buffet, popular with backpackers, where the price is $A6.

Harbourside Restaurant, 209 Esplanade (tel. 518-999), offers economy dinner specials in which you choose either soup, salad, and pasta or filet steak or carved roasts and trimmings for a standard $A9.95. The restaurant is located inside Harbourside Hotel.

ATTRACTIONS

Virtually all the daylight action in and around Cairns is of the outdoor kind. It's hard to find anything with a roof overhead, except shopping.

THE TOP ATTRACTIONS

HOUSE OF 10,000 SHELLS, 32 Abbott St., Cairns. Tel. 51-3638.

This attraction combines the town's largest souvenir shop with a shell museum. It displays an enormous and fantastically varied range of seashell specimens and coral, as well as shell and coral jewelry and Aboriginal weaponry and bark paintings.

Admission: Free.
Open: Mon–Fri 8:30am–9pm, Sat–Sun until 6pm.

WILD WORLD, Captain Cook Hwy., Palm Cove. Tel. 55-3669.

Some 12 miles north of the House of the 10,000 Shells on the Captain Cook Highway stands the Wild World (take the bus that goes up the coast to the beaches or join one of the many tours heading there). This is a combination reptile, animal, and bird park, containing 100 Australian crocodiles, both fresh- and saltwater species. They range from babies looking like clockwork toys with needle teeth to monsters like Sarge—16 feet long and a century old. Sarge was so christened because she lunged out of Cowal Creek and gobbled up a local police sergeant's dog. After being netted, she had to spend a night in jail before the zoo people transported her to her present enclosure. She's now the only croc extant with a hoosegow record. The park also shows Australia's deadliest snakes, the taipans, plus birds, kangaroos, and giant pythons. You can watch the crocs being hand-fed and the snakes being "milked" and can even do some bird-and-wallaby feeding yourself. Here is also your chance to see cane toad races.

Admission: $A14 adults, $A7 children.
Open: Daily 9am–5pm.

HARTLEY'S CREEK CROCODILE FARM, Captain Cook Hwy., Hartley's Creek. Tel. 55-3576.

For one of the best showplaces you have to go some 25 miles north on the Captain Cook Highway to Hartley's Creek Crocodile Farm. Far more than a menagerie, it's a variety act run with terrific flair, humor, affection, and knowledgeability. The setting is pleasant, with shady walks, little pools, and miniature bridges. But the fascinating part is that all the farm's denizens can be found, wild, within 5 miles of the location. They include cassowaries; tree kangaroos; innocuous-looking taipans, mud-brown and unspectacular but actually the world's most lethal snakes; and flying foxes, the giant Queensland fruit bats with heads like small dogs. You see them fed with apples, and they manage to look very appealing while munching them—upside down. The array of 163 crocodiles includes Charlie, a veteran weighing a solid three-quarters of a ton. The snakes are milked and the crocs fed by a jolly keeper, who maintains a wonderful patter while avoiding getting his hands chewed off. He has Charlie perform the crocodile "death roll"—an acrobatic feat designed to knock prey off its legs—and slam his jaws with a *wham* that can be heard for a mile.

Admission: $A12 adults, $A6 children.

Open: Daily 8am–5pm.

FLECKER BOTANIC GARDENS, Collins Ave., Edge Hill. Tel. 502-482.

The gardens are about two miles from the center but easily reached by bus. Planted back in 1886, they are now wonderfully luxuriant—a kind of harnessed tropical jungle plus parkland, featuring more than 10,000 trees, shrubs, and flowers, among them 200 different species of palms. Also included are magnificent orchids, beautiful ferns, and a collection of exotic flowering trees.

Admission: Free.

Open: Daily 9:30am–4:30pm.

THE ROYAL FLYING DOCTOR SERVICE, 1 Junction St., Edge Hill. Tel. 53-5687.

This offers you a glimpse at the daily routine of Australia's most famous medical institution: the winged "bush angels" who bring help to thousands of outback inhabitants. Guided tours and demonstrations show the small mercy planes used, the pedal-powered radios that provide communications, and some of the original gear and instruments that the service started out with. The earnings from the Visitors Centre help to keep the flying docs flying.

Admission: $A6 adults, $A3 children.

Open: Daily 9am–5pm.

CAIRNS HISTORICAL MUSEUM, School of Arts Bldg., corner of Lake and Shields Sts., Cairns. Tel. 51-5582.

The museum shows some intriguing contrast displays from the early days of Cairns (you wouldn't recognize the place). Also it has a collection of Aboriginal artifacts and weaponry.

Admission: $A2 adults, A50¢ children.

Open: Mon–Sat 10am–3pm.

VIC HISLOP'S SHARK SHOW, Captain Cook Hwy., 5 miles north of Cairns Airport. Tel. 55-0117.

Hislop is one of Australia's greatest shark hunters, and his show exhibits some of the monsters he has caught. And monsters they are—all great whites, the most fearsome of the species, one weighing 2½ times as much as a family car. Since great whites won't live in captivity, these are kept refrigerated. Continuously running movies show Hislop at work catching them.

Admission: $A10 adults, $A5 children.

Open: Daily 8am–6pm.

EDWARD RIVER CROCODILE FARM, Redbank Road (via Gordonvale). Tel. 56-3095.

This is a real crocodile farm, as distinct from an exhibition. Located on Trinity Inlet, 25 minutes south of Cairns, the enterprise belongs to an Aboriginal community. It contains some 12,000 saltwater saurians (the dangerous kind) which are bred for hides and meat. There is a farm tour at 11am daily, and you can watch the feeding at 2pm. A display of hatchlings—4,000 produced annually—a video show on croc farming, and vast numbers of waterfowl and tropical birds around a mangrove walk provide additional attractions. So do the surprisingly tasty crocodile satays on sale at the kiosk. If you don't have wheels there are at least five tours from Cairns with the farm on their agenda.

Admission: $A8 adults, $A4 children.

Open: Daily 8:30am–4:30pm.

NEARBY ATTRACTIONS

Beaches

Captain Cook Highway winds, undulates, and meanders from Cairns northwest to Mossman. It leads through some of the most picturesque country you'll ever see: fields of sugarcane, palm-and-gum forests, and sleepy tropical townships against a backdrop of steep jungle hills that look absolutely magical when partly shrouded by morning or evening mists.

Most of the signposts point to the right, where the beach resorts lie like a string of pearls. They're all beautiful; some are exquisite. Everybody has a different favorite, so take your pick.

MACHANS BEACH Located about 10 driving minutes up the highway, this is the beach closest to Cairns.

HOLLOWAY BEACH Divided from Machans Beach by a tidal lagoon and a creek, Holloway is popular with the fishing-and-netting crowd. The township has a minimarket that sells everything you may need for a beach barbecue.

YORKEY'S KNOB This is the only resort beach I've ever seen that looks even lovelier in reality than on picture postcards. There's a beachfront caravan (R.V.) park and a club with a nine-hole golf course that welcomes visitors.

TRINITY WATERS Located about 12 miles from Cairns, this is my personal favorite. A rather narrow beach, flanked by green hills and backed by rows of shady trees, it has rocks at one end for fishermen to meditate on and kids to climb over. There's a shopping area right on the waterfront, plus a hotel with outdoor tables. You can rent catamarans for $A6 per hour, and the gentle surf provides just enough chop to make sailing them interesting. It's difficult to turn over in these superbly stable craft, but even if you do it doesn't matter unduly. You can right them again with one good heave.

CLIFTON BEACH Next in line and very quiet and serene, Clifton Beach is fringed by the permanent homes of people who like serenity.

PALM COVE This is the base of the Cairns Life Saving Club, and it is aglow with vivid bougainvillea, the foreshore lined with slender palms. It's much livelier than its neighbor, due to the presence of the Reef House, an international luxury pad with a magnificent garden restaurant.

ELLIS BEACH This is the most popular spot for family groups and picnic parties. It has a motel and beachside restaurant and a large caravan park right by the water—well sheltered and gorgeously panoramic against a backdrop of jungled hills.

The beaches go on all the way to **Mossman,** which lies about 50 miles from Cairns. A tranquil and sunbaked little town at the foot of towering Mount Demy, Mossman is the center of the local cane industry. During the crushing season—June to December—you can visit the sugar mill.

Timetables for the **buses** serving the northern beaches are posted at the bus shelter at Anzac Park on the Cairns Esplanade.

Warning: Between May and October you can swim safely on all the Marlin Coast beaches. But from November to April the shore waters become infested with swarms of **box jellyfish**—transparent creatures, almost impossible to see, equipped with trailing tentacles that are highly poisonous. Their sting is extremely painful and can be lethal. During those months you should stay within the confines of the stinger nets supplied at Yorkeys Knob, Holloway, and Trinity Beach.

Jellyfish are inshore breeders, and the waters around the Great Barrier Reef are free of them. Once there, you can swim and dive all year-round.

Organized Tours

The **S.S. *Louisa*,** a quaint little paddle wheeler, departs from Marlin Jetty daily at 10am and 1pm for a leisurely 2½-hour cruise through the Cairns **Everglades.** That's the name bestowed on the maze of creeks, inlets, and waterways branching out of Trinity Bay. They were originally explored by Captain Cook personally, in a ship's whaleboat on Trinity Sunday (hence the label). The shallow-draft paddle wheeler follows in his wake.

The shorescape is green, wild, and swampy, and some of the creeks wind like giant snakes through the mangrove forests. They harbor strange marine life, and many species have not yet been fully classified. One of the strangest is the very common "mud skipper," a fish with huge goggle eyes that can breathe out of water and has been known to climb up mangrove trees. Regularly you see crocodiles sunning on the mud flats at low tide. And you always see the large colony of flying foxes, hanging upside down like clusters of black pears. Clouds of butterflies hover over the greenery. Hunting for prey are night herons, blue cranes, egrets, and sometimes a lone giant sea eagle. The water is mirror calm, the air hot and sleepy. Cost of the jaunt is $A15 for adults, $A6 for children. For information and reservations, call 31-3065 (P.O. Box 7393, Cairns).

For a real taste of the tropics in all their raw splendor you should go on the ✪ **Daintree Connection,** a 1-day coach-and-boat journey cruising along the creeks and backwaters of the Daintree River. You see giant moths and butterflies, wonderful wild orchids, clouds of rainbow-hued birds, and crocodiles basking on the mangrove mud flats. The coach departs Cairns daily at 7:40am and brings you back after 5pm. Morning tea and lunch are included in the price of $A75 for adults, $A40 for children. Book at the Cairns Tour Service, Lake Street (tel. 51-8311 or call 99-5599).

Warning: Northern Queensland is **crocodile** country, and if you intend to see it outside the organized tours you'd better be aware of a few basic facts. There are two types of Queensland crocs: the small, harmless freshwater breed, growing to a maximum size of 5 feet, and the saltwater or estuarine species, which can reach 16 feet, weigh a ton, and become extremely dangerous. At some rivers or ponds you'll see unmistakable warning signs showing open crocodile jaws. They're not put there for decoration—you'll disregard them at the risk of your life. But even where no such warnings are posted you should take some elementary precautions: Don't go swimming alone, camp at least 30 feet from the water's edge, don't stand on logs overhanging deep pools, don't dangle your feet in the water when boating, don't clean fish or prepare food on the water's edge, and don't approach any croc you happen to see. They're ordinarily sluggish but can move like reptilian lightning when they want to.

Wait-a-While Tours (tel. 33-1153) caters to wilderness lovers and takes them "spotlighting" to certain restricted rain-forest trails for surprise encounters with nocturnal animals. Their groups are kept small, and the guides are highly knowledgeable. The company operates two jaunts: one to the high altitude tableland forests west of Cairns, the other to the Mt. Lewis–Daintree jungle country. You'll probably see

FROMMER'S COOL FOR KIDS: RESTAURANTS

International Food Hall *(p. 261)* The tropical fish tanks keep youngsters amused for a limited time, but the variety and hustle of the food stalls will keep their attention longer. But try and usurp a table on the Esplanade outside—the interior is rather accident-prone.

Steak and Pancake House *(p. 262)* The front pancake parlor has a lingering colonial atmosphere and gooey-gorgeous chocolate pancakes.

flying foxes, tiny rat kangaroos, white lemuroid possums, bower birds, tree snakes and—possibly—a platypus. The tours include a grand evening tea with candlelight and port and are taken in air-conditioned four-wheel-drive vehicles. They involve a fair but not overstrenuous amount of walking. Both tours cost $A95 for adults, $A66 for children.

Cairns Reef Charter Services, Marlin Parade (tel. 31-4728), runs a jungle river cruise on the little M.V. *Jungle Queen.* The leisurely chug goes on the Mulgrave and Russell rivers, a wetland region of heavy vine jungle and rain forest, overgrown with giant trees, ferns, and orchids. This is the home of a large range of butterflies, wading birds, scrub turkeys, and cassowaries as well as saltwater crocodiles—but the places you swim in are safe from crocs. En route you can swim, fish, crab, or walk through the mangrove trails. A bus picks you up and returns to your hotel, and you get morning tea plus a sumptuous lunch. Adult fare is $A56, childrens' $A10.

SAVVY SHOPPING

For a town of its size, Cairns has a shopping scene that is downright spectacular, though far from cheap. You have a choice between wandering around the individual stores downtown or strolling through the new glitzy-trendy complexes that have sprouted like concrete mushrooms in the past few years. All of them—**Village Lane, Conservatory, Trinity Wharf, Orchid Plaza,** and so on—operate seven days a week.

The very latest is the **Pier Marketplace,** on Pierpoint Road. Built right on the water, the Pier is an enclosed, air-conditioned collection of specialty shops selling fashions, gifts, jewelry, artworks, and souvenirs—all beautifully displayed and with very few price tags in sight. The Pier is also packed with cafés, bars, restaurants, snackeries, and clubs. Every weekend the locale becomes a real market place, the Mud Market, with dozens of stalls offering handcrafts and artifacts; strolling buskers, minstrels, and musicians provide free entertainment. The Pier is open daily from 9am to 9pm.

Less glamorous but more charming are the old buildings that have been revamped into shopping complexes. **Central Court,** at the corner of Lake and Spence streets, was originally the Central Hotel, built in 1909 but now selling the latest in upmarket gear. **Earl Court,** directly opposite, began life as a venerable bank back in the 1920s.

SPORTS & RECREATION

The many opportunities for swimming and surfing are covered elsewhere in this chapter.

DIVING & SNORKELING Cairns is the undisputed scuba diving and snorkeling capital of Australia. There are so many dive courses available that competition among operators resembles the used-car business. So the same rule applies: Shop around before you buy. Prices and conditions vary sharply; some ventures include boat-and-equipment hire, others don't. Some feed you royally en route, others rely on packaged snacks. If you're a learner one of the important points to watch is the size of the class—6 to 8 divers is ideal. Don't join a class where the numbers are much bigger.

You don't have to worry about dangerous marine critters out on the reef. The reef sharks are quite unaggressive, there are no stinging jellyfish, and the giant clams—despite Hollywood fantasies—can't hold anyone captive underwater. Just follow the precautions given by your instructor and you'll be completely safe.

The outfits listed here are merely samplings from a dozen more of their kind:

Falla, Marlin Marina (tel. 31-3488), is the name of a beautiful traditional pearling lugger converted into a pleasure craft. It sails from the marina at 8:45am for a cruise to a remote sand island on the outer barrier reef. You get a day of diving and snorkeling under expert supervision among coral gardens teeming with tropical fish. The fee of $A39 includes a smorgasbord lunch, diving gear, and a turn at sailing the lugger. Introductory dives are $A45 extra.

Scuba Green Island (tel. 315-559) departs daily from the Pier Marketplace in Cairns for half-day diving jaunts to Green Island. You can choose a morning-or-afternoon trip and get a gratis T-shirt with every dive. Half-day introductory or certified diving cost $A50 and $A45. You pay extra for the transfer to Green Island.

For more extended diving expeditions there are outfits like **Down Under Dive,** 155 Sheridan St., Cairns (tel. 311-288). This one takes you to the outer reef in a luxury catamaran for overnight stays. Rates from $A245 include meals, introductory dives, night diving, and personalized underwater videos.

RAP JUMPING A highly advanced form of rappelling (abseiling) practiced on Magnetic Island, it's a forward descent down a vertical 104-foot cliff face while strapped in a hip harness—guaranteed to send your adrenaline soaring while you plunge head first into the landscape. You get a skilled backup team and the best of safety equipment. The Rap party leaves from Sharkworld daily at 9:30am. Five jumps cost $A30, but the cold beer afterward is free. Book by calling 077/76-5066.

TOAD RACING One of the most peculiar sports on the globe, and one of the most popular events in the backyards of North Queensland, is one in which the contestants are cane toads—huge, ugly, poisonous, and marked with numbers. The toads hop, hurtle, and lumber around a circular racetrack toward the finish line. The official (well, sort of) Cane Toad Racing Association, based in Mackay, produced a rule book for conducting races; the book is hard to get hold of but worth a try. Nobody seems certain whether betting on toads is legal or otherwise, but everybody does it—including some well-heeled gamblers who come all the way from Japan or Singapore for just that purpose.

EVENING ENTERTAINMENT

In recent years Cairns's nocturnal action has zoomed up from about 1 to, say, 7 on a scale of 10. There is even a local publication, the *Barfly,* devoted to nightlife in the widest sense of the term.

Unfortunately the nightspots blossom forth and wither away so fast that it's almost impossible to keep track of them. Between the last and the present edition of this book one particular joint metamorphosized from a deli, to a dry cleaner, to a dance club, and now, I hear, to a restaurant. So show me forebearance if half the places mentioned below have shed their shingles by the time you hit town.

THE CLUB, PUB & MUSIC SCENE

Most of the entertainment is rock oriented and appeals to the younger set, but all the new deluxe hotels feature cocktail bars or dining rooms with live entertainment, usually in the shape of a romantic pianist or smooth dance combo. Some of the older hotels also present musical entertainment but on a less regular basis. You simply have to drop in and see what's on, which can be anything from a tenth-rate guitar basher to a first-class local band. No risk is involved, since none of the pubs puts on a cover charge and drinks sell at bar prices.

TROPOS, corner of Lake and Spence Sts. Tel. 31-2531.

The "in" spot as of this split second is Tropos, which features nonstop rock into the wee hours. Depending on the night, you might get a swimsuit competition, a celebrity band, or two-for-the-price-of-one drinks.

Admission: $A5.
Open: Daily 8pm–3 or 5am.

END OF THE WORLD, corner of Abbott and Aplin Sts. Tel. 51-7788.

The highest decibel range may be achieved here, steeped in darkness and usually packed to the rafters. The place serves jugs of beer for $A5 and surprisingly good meals for the same price.

Admission: $A5.
Open: Daily 6pm–5am.

THE PLAYPEN, Lake St. Tel. 51-8211.

This decidedly adult playground has the kind of video clips and novelty games that go with the label.

Open: Mon–Sat 7:30pm–4 or 5am.

HARBOUR BAR, Pacific International Hotel, corner of Esplanade and Spence St. Tel. 51-7888.

One of the silkiest piano bars, it's on the second floor of the hotel, offering panoramic ocean views along with the music and priced accordingly.

Admission: Free.

Open: Daily 6pm–midnight.

HIDES HOTEL, corner of Lake and Shields Sts. Tel. 511-266.

The hotel's lounge is given over to a changing parade of entertainers. When I dropped in they had the "Working Class Band," an absolutely terrific outfit including one lass with a box fiddle. The numbers, mostly Irish-Aussie folk stuff à la the Clancy Brothers, got the audience clapping and stamping, and a rollicking sentimental time was enjoyed by all—including yours truly.

Admission: Free.

Open: Mon–Sat 8pm–11pm.

MOVIES

Apart from several suburban drive-in theaters, Cairns has two downtown movie houses: the **Capri Cinema,** 88 Lake St. (tel. 51-3817), and the **Odeon,** 108 Grafton St. (tel. 51-1187).

2. KURANDA, PORT DOUGLAS & COOKTOWN

Color Queensland gold like the sun, beach sands, and ripe oranges; red like coral reefs and tropical sunsets; blue like the South Pacific; green like waving palm forests, lush cattle grass, and—if you like—tourist dollars. For this is the **Sunshine State,** the national playground, a region so bursting with Technicolor that it looks as if God had spilled paint pots all over the landscape.

Queensland comes closest to looking the way some foreigners imagine *all* Australia looks. This is the youngest state of the Commonwealth, the second largest, and the most rapidly expanding. By a benevolent freak of geography, Queensland's 667,000 square miles are split exactly in two by the Tropic of Capricorn: The northern half has tropical climate, the southern portion Mediterranean temperatures—adding up to an absolutely ideal holiday environment.

The 2½ million Queenslanders—perhaps the healthiest bunch of people on earth—live in the usual lopsided Australian pattern: more than one million in the capital of Brisbane, the rest thinly scattered over the enormous bulk of the state. Nature has treated them more than fairly: They have one of the natural wonders of the world—the Great Barrier Reef—as well as some of the juiciest pasture land, richest agricultural soil, and greatest mineral resources on the continent. What more do you want—oil? Yes, they have that, too!

Queensland is Australia's tropical fruit basket, the nation's sugar bowl, its principal beef producer, and its greatest copper-and-silver miner. It looks like it's developing into the top coal producer as well. But, above all, Queensland manufactures holiday happiness in fabulous quantities.

Most of that joyous commodity is concentrated along the gently curving coastline lapped by the warm Coral Sea, which provides, among other pleasures, superb year-round fishing. Depending on where you are and how far out you want to go, you can hook anything from estuary whiting, bream, salmon, and barramundi to deep-sea fighting game like tuna, dolphin, marlin, barracuda, shark, and even giant groupers that come truly gigantic—eight feet long, with cavernous mouths large enough to swallow a human being whole.

KURANDA

One of the best, cheapest, and most enchanting outings in all of Australia is the scenic rail trip from Cairns to Kuranda, the "Village of Rain Forest." The motor-train tracks run for 28 miles through spectacular vistas—and the train obligingly stops at the greatest for the benefit of the camera hounds. The mountains of the **Atherton Tableland** rise green, steep, and majestic before you; waterfalls cascade like silver curtains beside the track; and the air is sweet and cool. There are 15 tunnels en route, each opening up on some new panoramic splendor. At **Barron Gorge** the roaring waters of the Barron Falls have been harnessed by a hydroelectric complex, but the trip through the gorge, on high iron girders, is almost as scary as it is dramatic. Kuranda lies on the rim of the Great Plateau and boasts what may be the prettiest railroad station in the world—a cross between a tropical bungalow and a flower garden. The trip costs $A29 round-trip for adults, $A14.50 for children.

Kuranda also offers a couple of unique attractions. One is the **Tjapukai Aboriginal Dance Theater** (tel. 93-7544), featuring an authentic troupe of performers that has won several awards. Shows go on twice daily and cost $A16 for adults, $A8 for children. Bookings are essential. The other is the **Butterfly Farm,** 8 Rob Veivers Dr. (tel. 93-7575). One of the world's largest walk-through flight aviaries, it lets you wander among hundreds of wildly colorful tropical butterflies. Admission costs $A9.50 for adults, $A5 for children, and you can look the place up in the *Guinness Book of World Records*. If you take the regular train from Cairns, you get a voucher providing discounts to these and several other attractions.

PORT DOUGLAS

Some 45 miles north of Cairns along the coast-hugging Captain Cook Highway lies Port Douglas, base headquarters of the Mango Tango. This particular "tango" isn't a dance but the direct opposite—it's a term denoting total relaxation, tropical langor cultivated to a degree where it resembles perambulated snoozing. Please note that this doesn't apply to *all* of the place: The local Sheraton Mirage is one of the glossiest and sleekest luxury resorts around, and there are enough chic boutiques and smart restaurants to impart a kiss of glamour.

But most of Port Douglas still happily does the Mango Tango. The erstwhile fishing village hasn't quite yet learned the tourist trot, and therein lies its special charm. Here you see the rain forest in a nutshell, so to speak. You can walk wreathed by thickets of hibiscus and vines, watch swarms of brilliantly colored birds, and buy big golden mangoes from roadside stalls for A60¢ each. Most of these stalls are unattended: You pick out your mango, leave the money, and go off without ever catching sight of the owner. Long live the Mango Tango!

Port Douglas is the point where the Great Barrier Reef runs closest to the shore, one reason why a good many visitors prefer it to Cairns as a launchpad for reef adventures.

Apart from the plusher eating spots, the town has a sprinkling of good, cheap "fish-and-chipperies" such as **EJ's** on Grant Street (tel. 99-4128). Equipped with outside tables and chairs, EJ's serves fresh, locally caught seafood—grilled, battered, and breaded—to go with the obligatory chips. The standard portion costs $A3.50, but the slightly more exotic prawn kebabs, served with rice and a spicy sauce, come to $A5. Open daily from 10am to 10pm.

COOKTOWN

Cooktown has been called "Australia's living museum." No other place on the continent remains as tangibly linked with its past as this idyllic semi-ghost

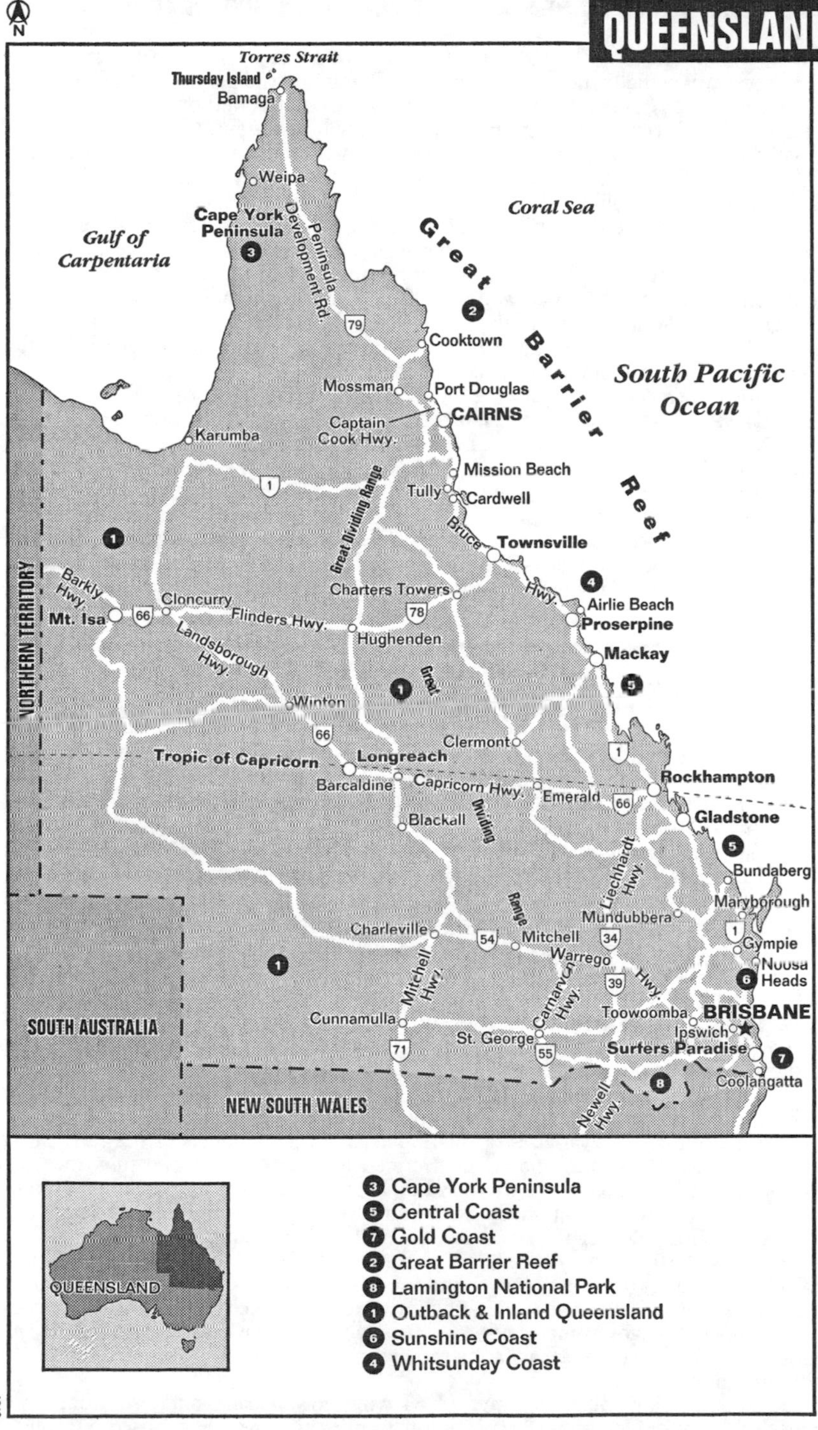
QUEENSLAND
N
Torres Strait
Thursday Island
Bamaga
Weipa
Cape York Peninsula
Peninsula Development Rd.
Gulf of Carpentaria
Coral Sea
Great Barrier Reef
South Pacific Ocean
Cooktown
Mossman
Port Douglas
CAIRNS
Captain Cook Hwy.
Karumba
Mission Beach
Tully
Cardwell
Great Dividing Range
Bruce Hwy.
Townsville
Charters Towers
Airlie Beach
Proserpine
Mackay
Barkly Hwy.
Cloncurry
Mt. Isa
Flinders Hwy.
Hughenden
Landsborough Hwy.
Winton
Clermont
Tropic of Capricorn
Longreach
Barcaldine
Capricorn Hwy.
Emerald
Rockhampton
Gladstone
Blackall
Liechhardt Hwy.
Bundaberg
Maryborough
Mundubbera
Charleville
Mitchell
Warrego Hwy.
Gympie
Noosa Heads
Mitchell Hwy.
Carnarvon Hwy.
Toowoomba
BRISBANE
Ipswich
Cunnamulla
St. George
Surfers Paradise
Coolangatta
Newell Hwy.
NORTHERN TERRITORY
SOUTH AUSTRALIA
NEW SOUTH WALES
QUEENSLAND
3 Cape York Peninsula
5 Central Coast
7 Gold Coast
2 Great Barrier Reef
8 Lamington National Park
1 Outback & Inland Queensland
6 Sunshine Coast
4 Whitsunday Coast
6757

town—mainly because there's not much present to interfere with the memories. Cooktown was actually the *first* British settlement in Australia, but quite involuntarily so. In June 1770, Captain Cook's little *Endeavour* ran aground on a coral reef while exploring the Queensland coastline. By jettisoning his cannons, the captain managed to sail the tiny craft up the mouth of a river, then settled down to a 7-week repair job. This was the historical foundation of Cooktown. The river was duly christened Endeavour, after the ship.

There was no "settlement" to speak of until 103 years later, when gold was discovered on the banks of the Endeavour River. Almost overnight the resultant rush boomed Cooktown into the colony's major seaport: a brawling, sweating, gambling gold metropolis with 94 hotels and 50,000 people, of whom 18,000 were Chinese. The glory lasted only as long as the gold. When the strikes petered out, Diggers and those who depended on them decamped for the south. Today Cooktown is left with a populace of just 550 and a lot of memories.

It's those memories that make the township fascinating. Most of them are on show in the **James Cook Museum** (tel. 69-5386), a beautiful old building containing the world's greatest collection of Cook memorabilia, surrounded by a botanical garden. There are a Chinese shrine; a graveyard for the thousands of Cantonese who labored and died here during the boom; an old colonial bank building; the ruins of once-rip-roaring taverns; and Grassy Hill lookout, where Cook stood and peered for a passage through the mass of reefs. Cooktown lies some 250 miles north of Cairns, and one way of visiting it is by bus—an 8-hour trip costing $A40. But it's more scenic by boat from Port Douglas for $A65. Open daily 10am to 4pm.

3. GREAT BARRIER REEF

Queensland's second-greatest magnet for tourists, the Gold Coast, is covered in Chapter 6 on Brisbane. Its top attraction, however, is undoubtedly the scenic wonder known as the Great Barrier Reef. The reef is the world's largest coral creation—an irregular chain of reefs, lagoons, and islands stretching 1,250 miles along the coast. Covering a total area of 80,000 square miles, it lies between 10 and 200 miles offshore. Close to shore the reef is splintered into a labyrinth of lagoons and pools, up to 200 feet deep and as clearly transparent as fishbowls. And as the tide recedes these pools become showcases of living coral in a hundred rainbow colors and of the thousands of plants, fishes, and mollusks that swim, crawl, hunt, and hide around them.

There are shells ranging from the tiny cowrie to the giant clam—the size of a bathtub and strong enough to trap a careless diver. There are minute coral fish, looking like multihued drops of paint flicked from a palette. There are octopuses; razor-toothed eels; starfish; flat wing-flapping rays; ribbonlike sea snakes; and fluorescent sea anemones, flowerlike but deadly poisonous to their prey.

The most wondrous creature of all may be the corals themselves, although they're only the size of pinheads. Corals are animals, of the polyp species, and the reef harbors more than 350 varieties of them. They are the architects of the reef. Living together in dense colonies, the corals secrete a protective limestone substance that hardens into formations with a thousand different shapes—hands, organ pipes, fans, snails—and scores of color shadings. Infinitely slowly, over millions of years, they formed the Great Barrier Reef and are still at it, still building.

Recently the coral polyps seemed in danger of extermination. Something went haywire in nature's balance of feeder and food. There was a sudden mass incursion of the coral's worst enemy, the crown-of-thorns starfish, which wiped out entire coral communities. But government skin divers fought the spiny invaders and destroyed about 50,000 of them. And, as far as the eye can see, they haven't made much of a dent in the reef.

There are many different ways of viewing this marine paradise from every conceivable angle. One is **reefing**—simply wandering along the exposed portions of

GREAT BARRIER REEF

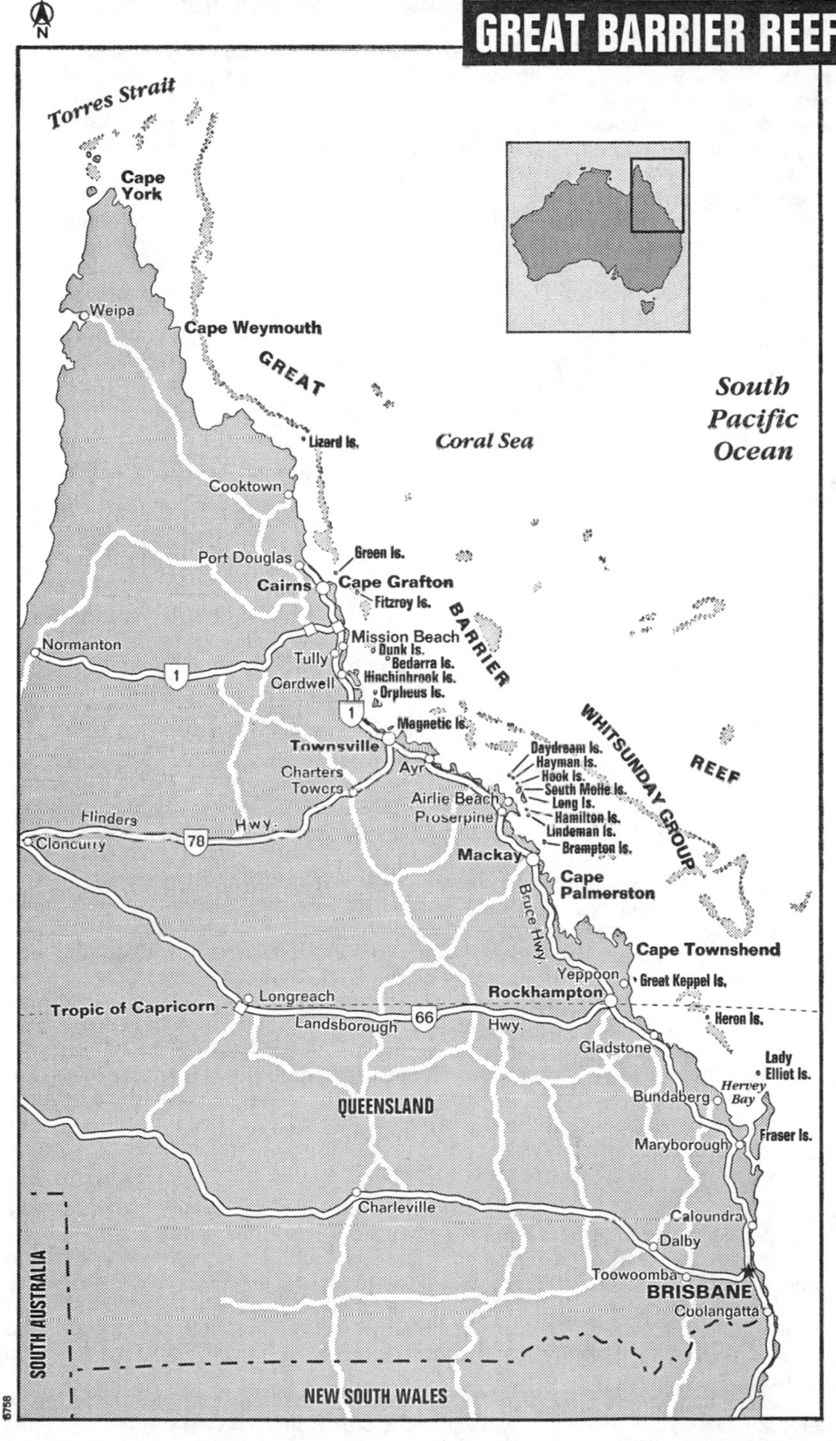
N
Torres Strait
Cape York
Weipa
Cape Weymouth
GREAT
South Pacific Ocean
Coral Sea
Lizard Is.
Cooktown
Port Douglas
Green Is.
Cairns
Cape Grafton
Fitzroy Is.
BARRIER
Normanton
Mission Beach
Dunk Is.
Tully
Bedarra Is.
Hinchinbrook Is.
Cardwell
Orpheus Is.
1
Magnetic Is.
Townsville
WHITSUNDAY GROUP
REEF
Charters Towers
Ayr
Daydream Is.
Hayman Is.
Hook Is.
South Molle Is.
Airlie Beach
Long Is.
Proserpine
Hamilton Is.
Lindeman Is.
Flinders Hwy.
78
Cloncurry
Brampton Is.
Mackay
Cape Palmerston
Bruce Hwy.
Cape Townshend
Yeppoon
Great Keppel Is.
Longreach
Rockhampton
Tropic of Capricorn
66
Landsborough Hwy.
Heron Is.
Gladstone
Lady Elliot Is.
Hervey Bay
Bundaberg
QUEENSLAND
Fraser Is.
Maryborough
Charleville
Caloundra
Dalby
Toowoomba
BRISBANE
Coolangatta
SOUTH AUSTRALIA
NEW SOUTH WALES
6758

the barrier at low tide and peering at the teeming life in the pools. But you *must* observe a few elementary precautions. Put on tennis sneakers or similar footwear since some of the coral is razor sharp. Don't pick up anything unless you know what it is—even tiny creatures can have poison stings or needle teeth. And don't disturb the delicate balance of nature that keeps the reef alive. Always replace rocks you overturn and don't leave behind any garbage. A hundred thousand careless visitors can wreck the ecology of this wonderland.

The entire area is also dotted with underwater observatories and coral museums, enabling you to watch through glass portholes. Then there are cruises in glass-bottomed boats, low-level flights for a bird's-eye view, and—for the more energetic—skin-diving and snorkeling. The best time to explore the reef is from May to November, when the tides are lowest.

Many of the reef islands are tourist resorts, several offering luxury-style accommodations, but even the simpler ones aren't exactly in the economy bracket. If you're planning overnight stops on any of them, it'll run into money. The budget method of seeing them is to take one of the day excursions from Cairns and return the same evening. You have a lot of choice there.

GREEN ISLAND A small coral cay rising about two feet above sea level, densely wooded and lapped by crystal-clear water, this is the most popular of the Great Barrier Reef islands. It offers the most fun facilities and draws the biggest crowds.

Anchored on the seabed offshore stands the **Underwater Coral Observatory,** where you actually walk on the ocean bed and gaze at the submarine scenery through viewing windows. You see the fantastic coral gardens, the clouds of darting rainbow-colored fish, the clams, the starfish, and the ribbonlike water snakes (which are quite timid and unaggressive, but their poison is as lethal as a cobra's). For a view from above you can take a ride in the **glass-bottomed boats,** among the island's top attractions, or you can go snorkeling or scuba diving. There is equipment for rent at the Resort Dive Centre.

On shore there's **Marineland Melanesia,** a sunlit arcade of tanks displaying fabulous fish; live corals; 6-foot giant clams; and possibly the most spectacular collection of crocodiles on view anywhere—monsters up to 16 feet long, whose terrifying jaw power you can observe, safely, when they lunge for dangling chunks of meat ($A5 admission). Next door you'll find the **Castaway Theatre,** showing color movies of underwater reef scenes.

Another major attraction is the **Yellow Submarine.** Not quite a true sub, this intriguing contraption is a semisubmersible coral-viewing vehicle equipped with underwater lights. The skipper noses the craft over the most colorful coral regions and gives a running commentary on the wonders below. Passengers sit in air-conditioned comfort below the waterline and enjoy a diver's view of the ocean scape without getting wet. The sub departs from the Green Island jetty every 45 minutes and you can buy tickets on board. The cost is $A15.

There are several ways of visiting Green Island. The fastest is by seaplane (flying time: nine minutes) with the shuttle service operating from Cairns Airport. Or you can take the ***Big Cat*** (tel. 51-0444), a comfortable 24 meter catamaran with its own bar and glass-bottomed boat. The craft leaves from Pier Marketplace at 9am daily. The round-trip fare is $A28 for adults and $A14 for children, and this includes either a ride in the glass-bottom boat or free snorkeling gear.

DUNK ISLAND Rather plainly named for a dazzling beauty patch, it was developed to the tune of $A2.5 million to make it luxurious. Dunk has everything you'd expect from the proverbial tropical paradise: unspoiled vegetation and homegrown produce; delicate reef fish and top-grade chefs to cook them; vast lonely stretches of sandy beach; a hectic nightlife that breaks loose when the sun dips below the horizon; clear, warm coral waters; landscaped gardens and cool streamlined cabana units; and mangoes, figs, and coconuts on the one hand, imported wines on the other.

The mainland point closest to Dunk is Mission Beach, south of Cairns. From there, at Clump Point Jetty, you can catch the **Dunk Island Cruise** (tel. 68-7211), departing daily at 8:55am and 10:30am. For $A18 for adults and $A9 for kids, you get the trip over, time to explore and swim, plus gratis snorkeling gear. The island is not an economy haven to spend time on.

LOW ISLES This is a small coral cay and a striking contrast to the above—the only residents are a lighthouse-keeper's family. The lighthouse is over a century old; the corals can be viewed from a glass-bottomed boat; the low tide on the reef flat exposes some of the most gorgeous shells in creation (no, you can't collect them, they're protected); and the water is so fishbowl clear that you can almost count the pebbles many feet below while you're floating on top.

HAYMAN ISLAND For the fairly flush, this island is 35 minutes by helicopter from Mackay. Hayman swings and has become at least as famous for its sultry nightlife as for its picturesque mountain scenery and fascinating reefs.

BRAMPTON ISLAND Although it lies some distance from the heart of the Great Barrier Reef, this may be the most paradisical patch of them all. A Twin Otter aircraft flies you over from Mackay in 15 minutes, and when you land you'll think you've been whisked to one of those South Sea Edens they used to create specially for Hollywood sarong epics.

The island has forest-shrouded hills with near-tame kangaroos, groves of coconut palms, romantic little bays, ribbons of dazzling white beaches, some of the finest fishing on the reef, clouds of rainbow lorikeets that will peck from your hand, plus all the champagne-bubble nightlife you can cope with. At low tide you can wade over to neighboring **Carlisle Island,** a national park that contains herds of brumbies—wild horses introduced by early settlers and now roaming free, unsaddled, and very far from tame.

Brampton is a resort par excellence, offering plush-and-semiplush accommodations and every conceivable brand of watersport, plus a few you may never have heard of—like boom netting and water tobogganing. It's not exactly cheap, but Qantas offers a package deal that cuts the cost considerably. You can get a twin share room for $A122, and per person meals costing $A60 extra.

GREAT KEPPEL ISLAND This tiny, fun-filled dot lying some 45 miles off Rockhampton in the blue Pacific is about four flying hours from Sydney and Melbourne. The island has 17 superb beaches, some thronged and some for solitude, all fringed with deep-green tropical vegetation. It also has a disco with a resident band, sporting facilities, a bar, a café, a restaurant, and a hairdressing salon—and young, immensely enthusiastic clientele. Aside from deluxe accommodations in carpeted holiday units, there's a caravan (R.V.) and camping ground for the budget conscious. The on-site vans come with electricity, linen, cutlery, gas stoves, and refrigerators (but no towels).

You reach Great Keppel by taking a coach leaving from the Rockhampton post office every morning on Friday to Wednesday and connecting with a speedy hydrofoil that whizzes across to the island. Round-trip fare is $A16 for adults, $A8 for children. For the Qantas package trip to Great Keppel see Chapter 2, "Getting Around."

HERON ISLAND At the southern tip of the reef lies a tiny and wonderfully unspoilt haven for nature lovers in the shape of this miniature national park. Two hours by catamaran from Gladstone, Heron draws bird-watchers, fossickers, photographers, and snorkelers. The top attraction, however, are the sea turtles who labor up the beach in the early mornings, spend several hours laying their eggs, and, then, utterly exhausted, return to the water. You can stroke their shells as they lumber past, oblivious of onlookers. Island accommodations range from budget lodges (shared bathrooms) to self-contained suites; meals come buffet style.

Qantas has a special holiday package including five nights in a suite, all meals, and passage from Gladstone for $A1,025 per person twin share. To this you must add the Sydney-Gladstone airfare of around $A400.

OTHER ISLANDS These are merely a few of the islands at your disposal. And remember, the reef is so huge and varied that the only way to get an overall view of its beauties is to hang around for a few days and take several cruises. There's no shortage of cruise vessels—they come in all sizes and price ranges, from mass-excursion launches to semiprivate charter yachts. For some of the latter, however, the old adage applies: If you have to ask the price, you can't afford it.

WHITSUNDAY COAST & ISLANDS

The vast expanse of the Great Barrier Reef has several geographical subdivisions. This particular portion is called the Whitsunday Coast (or Coral Coast) and Whitsunday Passage. Don't let the labels confuse you: You're still in the realm of the reef, with the lush splendor of the tropical hinterland reflected in the scatter of islands and islets offshore.

The focus point of the Whitsunday Coast is forest-fringed **Airlie Beach** and nearby **Shute Harbour,** situated some 120 miles north of Mackay. A whole armada of big and little pleasure craft start engines or hoist canvas every morning to cruise the Whitsunday waters, which are picture-postcard blue most of the year.

Airlie Beach has a holiday-village atmosphere and a wildlife sanctuary with glass reptile pens and crocodile enclosures, plus emus, kangaroos, and swarms of exotic birds roaming free. **Whitsunday Village,** a Polynesian-style resort, offers some economy units jokingly called Castaway Cottages (real castaways should be so lucky). The place has a restaurant and bar, swimming-and-wading pools, a recreation arcade, a laundry, playgrounds, and barbecue areas. It holds cocktail parties and arranges scuba and snorkeling lessons.

The offshore islands bear a close resemblance to Robinson Crusoe's involuntary retreat—except that some of them boast swimming pools, tennis courts, golf courses, and air-conditioned beach units. You reach them by either launch or seaplane from Shute Harbour.

DAYDREAM ISLAND Somewhat less stylish but at least as attractive as Airlie Beach, Daydream's secluded beaches and superb waterskiing are its main joys, apart from a Polynesian-style restaurant specializing in local reef seafood.

Daydream houses tourists in the **Polynesian Village,** in either standard units or suites, each equipped with private facilities, radios, and piped-in music. (Air-conditioning, refrigerators, and color TVs are in the VIP suites only). Social life revolves around a huge, free-form, and rather redundant swimming pool with a bar on an islet in the middle.

LONG ISLAND About five miles southeast of Shute Harbour, Long Island is a tranquil little patch of green roughly a million miles removed from the rat race. The place has a budget settlement in the shape of small cabins at **Palm Bay**—not to be confused with the much pricier resort at Happy Bay. At Palm Bay you get cooking facilities and refrigerators but must share the showers; meals are not included in your rates. There are no frills or entertainment, but you do get complete relaxation and all the sand, surf, and sunshine you've ever dreamed about. For information, consult the Queensland Government Travel Centre in Brisbane (tel. 07/833-5255).

MORETON ISLAND A genuine hideaway some 20 miles from Brisbane, the island has only one resort, **Tangalooma,** but several fascinating features. There's the world's largest sandhill to toboggan from, a mystery desert to explore, an antique lighthouse, wild horses, pigs, and goats, plus some of tropical Australia's finest fishing. Tangalooma has a beautiful bushland setting right by the beach and offers cocktail bars, tennis courts, waterskiing, and aquaplaning. All units—standard and deluxe—are completely self-contained.

LINDEMAN ISLAND Easily accessible by either boat or plane from Mackay, Lindeman Island recently underwent an extensive (and very expensive) redevelopment. On this occasion, however, in the right direction. The island resort, **New Lindeman,** sits in the midst of a wondrous national park and blends in so well that you could mistake it for a natural outgrowth. The vegetation remained lush and barely touched, the seven beaches have retained their secluded look, and the palm trees are filled with vibrantly screeching little lorikeets.

Accommodations are divided into the new and luxurious Seaforth Suites and the older Whitsunday Budget rooms. The former are air-conditioned; the latter have ceiling fans. But both come with their own bathrooms, minibars, and tea/coffee makers. The resort also offers restaurant bars, a swimming pool, windsurfers, catamarans, jet skis, paddle skis, and snorkeling gear, plus a swirling social life that bursts into sound the moment the lorikeets fall silent.

TOWNSVILLE

With a population nudging 115,000, Townsville is Australia's largest tropical city as well as the southern gateway to the Great Barrier Reef. Its life-style could be said to offer the best of both worlds: plenty of city action combined with enough tropical lassitude to suggest the ambience of an eternal vacation.

The misnamed **Town Common,** for instance, is actually a wondrous bird sanctuary, flapping ground of the unique dancing brolga. **Flinders Mall,** palm shaded and modernistic, is the hub of a pretty sophisticated shopping-and-restaurant strip. The **Strand,** which follows the curve of Cleveland Bay, is an elegant boulevard created for strolling, cooled by fountains and waterfalls, and lined with some of the lushest garden landscapes in the land. And in case you crave an industrial touch, there's **Victoria Mill,** the biggest sugar mill in the southern hemisphere, where you can inspect operations during the crushing season from June to November.

Five miles offshore—25 minutes as the ferry chugs—lies **Magnetic Island.** This is possibly the most idyllic of the barrier reef islets, with tall hoop pines, rugged headlands, brilliant coral formations, ferns, a sea-life aquarium, and some very velvety resorts. Daily passenger ferries leaving from the Wonderland Complex will get you there and back and let you enjoy the Koala Park Oasis, walking trails, and 25 beaches for a round-trip fare of $A11.

Townsville's top attraction is the new **Great Barrier Reef Wonderland,** Flinders Street East (tel. 21-1793). This is the world's largest coral-reef aquarium—two stories high with giant panoramic windows, an Omnimax theater, and a transparent tunnel that lets you stroll among—and almost rub shoulders with—the darting and cruising marine denizens. Admission is $A18 for adults, $A9 for children. The **Museum of Tropical Queensland** features life-size figures of the marine reptiles that once swarmed in these waters.

The **Sheraton Breakwater Casino,** a plush gambling spot, is located in front of the marina. It has roulette, baccarat, keno, minidice, and crap games daily from 11:30am to 3am, and it insists on a middling strict dress code.

The train from Brisbane to Townsville takes about 28 hours and costs $A104.40. It's a bit quicker by bus—20 hours—with all major coach companies servicing the route. The trip costs $A118.

WHERE TO STAY

Doubles for Less than $A33

FOREST HAVEN, 11 Cook Rd., Arcadia, Magnetic Island. Tel. 077/78-5153. 25 rms (none with bath).

$ Rates: $A12 backpackers, $A26 single, $A28 double. MC, V.

On Magnetic Island, among a lot of deluxe retreats, is the Forest Haven, situated next to the popular beach of Alma Bay and the beautiful national park. The Haven has good kitchen facilities, provides linen and blankets on request, and also has a pool table and bikes and snorkeling gear for hire.

REEF LODGE, 4 Wickham St., Townsville 4810. Tel. 077/21-1112. Fax 077/21-1405. 28 rms (3 with bath).

$ Rates: $A26 single; $A32 double without bath, $A42 double with bath. BC, MC, V.

Standing near the beach, ferry terminal, and Great Barrier Reef Wonderland, the Reef Lodge offers rooms with balconies, a guest kitchen, an adjacent snack bar, and a laundry. Furnishings are basic, but you get a free coach pick up on arrival and discount rates for diving courses, reef cruises, and rain-forest excursions. All rooms have either air-conditioning or ceiling fans.

ROCKHAMPTON

Capital of Central Queensland, this tropical town of 60,000 lies exactly on the invisible demarcation line of the Tropic of Capricorn. A soaring spire indicates the precise spot—although, of course, the "line" is as imaginary as the equator. The entire region, located at the southern end of the Great Barrier Reef, is known as Capricornia.

"Rocky," as the locals call it, sprawls astride the wide, meandering Fitzroy River, about 26 miles inland from the Pacific. The town has an attractive, playful **Central Mall,** packed with 300 specialty shops, overlooked by an ornately Victorian post office. A short way north lies a series of dry limestone caves, **Cammoo Caves** and **Olsen's Caverns**—huge, weirdly formed, and labyrinthine, with guided daily tours through both.

At Koorana, Emu Park Road, half an hour's drive away, is the **Crocodile Farm,** a commercial croc skin farm (tel. 34-4749), where the people eaters range from 12 inches to 12 feet. Here you get a chance to turn the tables on them: The farm sells crocodile steaks. Tours daily at 1pm and cost $A9 for adults, $A4.50 for children.

Rockhampton's **Grosvenor Hotel,** 186 Alma St. (tel. 079/27-1777), fulfills a triple budget function as a Mexican restaurant; an "over-25" nightclub; and a motel where singles cost $A22, doubles $A30.

Just 10 miles from the shore lies **Great Keppel Island** (see above), the closest of 32 barrier reef islands in the vicinity. Great Keppel has a ferry connection with Rockhampton, giving you the opportunity of spending all day on the island—coral viewing, snorkeling, or exploring—then catching the evening ferry back. For overnight stays there's a rather plush resort as well as more economical camping-and-cabin sites.

MOUNT ISA

A thousand miles northwest of Brisbane lies what is—by definition—the largest city in the world. The Mount Isa City Council administers a "municipality" which, while much bigger than the entire Netherlands, houses only about 22,000. "The Isa," as the locals call their phenomenon, also has several other claims to fame: It's the biggest copper producer in Australia and one of the greatest silver, lead, and zinc mining areas in the world; and it enjoys the longest milk run on earth—milk deliveries come from Townsville, 600 miles by rail, every morning.

Mount Isa (take a plane from Brisbane or Cairns) lies surrounded by an immense loneliness studded with ochre-red rock ramparts, astonishingly green valleys and blue lakes, forests of ghost gum trees, and natural springs. Here dingoes prowl and wild camels nibble the scrub while eagles draw slow circles in the deep-blue inland sky. The contrast between the timeless empty solitude of the land and the booming hustle of "The Isa" is almost unreal—a miracle wrought by copper.

CHAPTER 8

PERTH & THE FAR WEST

- WHAT'S SPECIAL ABOUT PERTH & THE FAR WEST
1. ORIENTATION
2. GETTING AROUND
- FAST FACTS: PERTH
3. WHERE TO STAY
- FROMMER'S SMART TRAVELER: HOTELS
4. WHERE TO EAT
- FROMMER'S SMART TRAVELER: RESTAURANTS
5. ATTRACTIONS
- FROMMER'S COOL FOR KIDS: RESTAURANTS
- DID YOU KNOW . . .?
6. SAVVY SHOPPING
7. SPORTS & RECREATION
8. EVENING ENTERTAINMENT
9. EASY EXCURSIONS: WESTERN AUSTRALIA

To tell you that Perth is the world's most isolated major city means to risk evoking a completely false picture of the place. So I'll start by saying that Perth is one of the prettiest cities on earth and probably the most all-around charming town in Australia. Isolated it certainly is—not merely from the Australian mainstream but from everybody else's as well. However, this has somehow worked in its favor. From its remote vantage point, Perth was able to watch other centers grow and then follow suit and avoid most of their mistakes.

Thus Perth acquired liveliness without garishness, beauty without pomposity, modernity without frigidity. Helped along by an ideal Mediterranean climate, an amiable population, and the enormous mineral wealth of its state, Perth developed into the nearest facsimile of an ideal metropolis. How long it will remain so—given its rate of growth—is another question.

Perth's main commercial street, **St. George's Terrace,** ranks among the most elegant thoroughfares in the world. Instead of shopping streets, Perth has shopping arcades and malls, some on two and three levels connected by escalators and elevators. In the City Arcade the elevator emerges from a fountain that surrounds passengers on three sides without splashing them. The shopping areas abound in patios, trees, flowers, benches, and delightful little boutiques. Almost constant glittering sunshine and vast areas of parkland give the city a wonderful *open* look usually reserved for small resorts.

It's a modern town created for pedestrians, not motorists. The core is formed by arcades radiating from a central mall, encircled counterclockwise by one-way streets. This arrangement is tough on drivers, but it pampers them the moment they climb out of their vehicles and start strolling. If you rent a car, don't drive it downtown; in Perth the infantry will get to your destination faster than you.

The first Caucasian settlers arrived here in 1829, but it wasn't until the 1890s gold rush that Perth became a city of sorts. The mineral rush that followed World War II then transformed it from a drowsy backwater into a metropolis. Today the capital of Western Australia, it has about 1.2 million inhabitants (more than San Francisco) and is expanding rapidly, but according to a master plan that matches new building developments with equivalent parks and gardens.

Perth lies astride the **Swan River,** some 12 miles inland from its seaport of **Fremantle.** This is one of its special characteristics: Perth faces the Indian Ocean,

WHAT'S SPECIAL ABOUT PERTH & THE FAR WEST

Architectural Highlights

- ☐ Government House, the Gothic-style residence of the state governor, resembling the Tower of London.
- ☐ Town Hall, built by convicts (1867–70), in English-Jacobean market-hall style.
- ☐ Old Courthouse, Perth's oldest public building (1836), in colonial Georgian style.
- ☐ His Majesty's Theatre, its Edwardian opulence housing the Western Australian Opera Company.

Beaches

- ☐ City Beach and Cottesloe, fronting the Indian Ocean and within easy reach.
- ☐ Canning Bridge and Apple Cross, Swan River beaches offering safe, calm swimming.

Museums

- ☐ Western Australian Art Gallery, with traditional and contemporary exhibitions.
- ☐ The Perth Mint, the oldest coining operation in the world.
- ☐ Western Australian Museum, with an excellent Aboriginal gallery, marine exhibits, and historic displays.
- ☐ Aviation Museum, the largest in the country, displaying historic bombers, fighters, and aircraft engines.

Festivals

- ☐ Festival of Perth, with parades, masquerades, exhibitions, and competitions.
- ☐ Wildflower Season, August to October, when Westralia becomes carpeted with the most spectacular panorama of blossoms.

For the Kids

- ☐ It's a Small World, a collection of miniature everything.
- ☐ Scitech Centre, with activated technical marvels that are also toys.
- ☐ Caversham Wildlife Park, with koalas to cuddle and kangaroos to pet.
- ☐ Underwater World, a submerged tunnel that brings you face to face with giant stingrays, sharks, and porpoises.

Shopping

- ☐ Malls and arcades linked by overpasses and walkways free from vehicle traffic.
- ☐ Street markets, the most historic and colorful located in Fremantle.

Parks

- ☐ Kings Park, the pride of Perth, with walking trails, a lookout tower, and panoramic city views.
- ☐ Supreme Court Gardens, which stages outdoor concerts.
- ☐ Queen's Garden, a restful oasis of greenery with a Peter Pan statue at the center.

After Dark

- ☐ Northbridge, a European-flavored region of bars, clubs, cafés, and restaurants.

while every other Australian capital faces the Pacific. The location gives Perth the advantage of a beautiful riverfront, yet with half a dozen great ocean beaches just a suburban train ride away. On warm evenings, when the cooling breezes fail to arrive, tens of thousands of people flock to the beaches to swim under the stars. And while the suburbs are relentlessly spreading north and south along the coast and inland toward the Darling Ranges, Perth can still boast of thriving vineyards producing quality wines within 10 miles of the General Post Office.

Perth is billed as the "Sunshine City" and can prove the title statistically. It gets more radiance than any other Australian capital—averaging eight hours of sunshine daily throughout the year, a possible world record for a big city. The local temperament reflects the weather: the aptest term for it is "sunny." And perhaps its climate will save Perth from the urban What-Makes-Sammy-Run blight for which it seems destined by the rate of its expansion.

1. ORIENTATION

ARRIVING

BY PLANE Both Qantas and Ansett Airlines run daily air services to Perth from all other capitals. The flight from Sydney takes about four hours and costs roughly $A589.

Perth Domestic Air Terminal lies about seven miles northeast of the city. By hotel bus it's $A5, by cab about $A13. The airport is new, smallish, and cozy. The cafeteria stays open around-the-clock and sells, among other edibles, sandwiches that are infinitely superior to those retailed at U.S., British, or New Zealand airports. The two bars, though, are understaffed and overworked. There are a duty-free shop and a 24-hour gas station. In addition, the airport has a charming welcome touch in the shape of a little stone pond on which black swans sail majestically in circles—black swans are the symbol of Westralia. A separate international terminal is some 11 miles northeast.

BY TRAIN Nothing drives home the sense of Perth's remoteness like the process of getting there. If you want the full taste of it, try the train trip from Sydney: The *Indian Pacific* takes 65 hours (three nights) for the continental crossing. It's shorter and cheaper from Adelaide (Port Pirie) for $A170, but it's still a mighty haul across the tabletop-flat Nullarbor Plain.

BY BUS You can reach Perth on an express bus from Adelaide. It takes some 35 hours and costs about $A160.

BY CAR The Eyre Highway that crosses the Nullarbor was only completely surfaced in 1976. Since then driving or hitching across has become quite popular, although this can be a pretty wearing experience for all parties concerned. Adelaide is about 1,730 miles by road from Perth; Canberra, about 2,460 miles; and Brisbane, about 2,770 miles.

TOURIST INFORMATION

The **Western Australia Tourist Centre** is at Forrest Place, Perth, WA 6000 (tel. 483-1111), and makes a good orientation point. It's open Monday to Friday 8:30am to 5:30pm, Saturday 9am to 1pm.

During summer daylight savings time, Western Australia is two hours behind the other states.

CITY LAYOUT

The W.A. Tourist Centre is at **Forrest Place** (see above), directly opposite the Perth Central Railway Station and the Myers shopping complex. Adjacent to **Wellington Street,** this makes for a good orientation point because Wellington Street runs parallel to the other main thoroughfares: **Murray** and **Hay streets,** and **St. Georges Terrace** (which becomes Adelaide Terrace farther east). In this central section you'll find all the large retail stores and business offices, government departments, and theaters, as well as shopping arcades and malls.

At the head of St. Georges Terrace stands the venerable **Barracks Arch,** one of Perth's landmarks. The other is the **Perth Town Hall,** corner of Hay and Barrack streets, built in the style of the English-Jacobean market hall but with convict labor.

Adjacent to where you're standing is the **General Post Office (GPO).** To the south is the **Esplanade,** and adjoining it is **Barrack Street Jetty,** from where the ferries cross the river to South Perth and also depart for Fremantle and Rottnest Island. The **Swan River** makes a curving bulge around the city, separating the downtown section from the vast suburban sprawl to the south. The two main bridges linking the portions are the Causeway (east of Barrack Street Jetty) and the Narrows (west of it).

West of your position stretches the Indian Ocean with the popular beaches of Leighton, Cottesloe, Swanbourne, City, and Scarborough. Southwest, at the mouth of the Swan River, is **Fremantle.** Northeast, alongside the **Great Eastern Highway,** lies the airport and farther out in the same direction the magnificent **John Forrest National Park.**

2. GETTING AROUND

BY PUBLIC TRANSPORTATION

BUS Perth city buses are possibly the best in Australia with regard to comfort, frequency, and punctuality. The downtown area also has a wonderful free bus service—the **City Clippers.** Remember these colors: Red Clippers circuit the eastern part of the city, Green Clippers travel around West Perth, Yellow Clippers service the inner shopping area, and Blue Clippers do the "cultural" round of museums and art galleries. All Clippers interlink at Perth main bus terminal on Wellington Street. All city bus and rail services are operated by Transperth. For information call the **Transperth Information Office,** 10 Adelaide Terrace (tel. 13-2213).

TAXI Phone **Swan Taxis** (tel. 322-0111) or **Black and White** (tel. 328-8288) for taxi service.

TRAIN Transperth operates the electric trains connecting the city with Fremantle, Midland, Joondalup, and Armadale, and stations en route. All suburban trains leave from the City Station on Wellington Street. Interstate-and-country trains depart from the East Perth Railway Terminal. For bookings, call 326-2222 or the Western Australian Tourist Centre (tel. 483-1111). A Transperth ticket allows you a return trip within two hours on any Transperth train, bus, or ferry.

FERRY Wellington Street ferries to South Perth leave from the Barrack Street Jetty (tel. 231-1222). Same day return tickets cost $A1.40 adults, A80¢ children.

BY CAR

For car rentals, **Thrifty** has a desk at the airport and a main office at 33 Milligan St. (tel. 481-1999).

Despite (or because) of its modernistic layout, however, Perth is not an easy city to drive in—at least not for unwary visitors. It's bisected by rail lines with far too few crossings. These handsome road bridges, overflights, and underpasses make for a pleasing variety of vistas but also for traffic snarls where none need be. One-way streets are poorly marked and street signs are scarce, often hidden behind decorative trees. And once you get out of the main streets, the illumination frequently resembles that of Tombstone in the days of Wyatt Earp. The new freeways look beautiful, but their entry-and-exit system doesn't match their appearance. Some intersections must be navigated by a mixture of cunning, instinct, and faith in one's guardian angel. Put it all down to growing pains.

BY BICYCLE

Perth is possibly the best biking city in Australia: climatically and topographically. The area is interlaced with cycle tracks and dual-use paths (bikes and pedestrians), and you can rent bicycles (as well as tandems and three-wheelers) close to most of the popular bike trails. The wearing of safety helmets is compulsory. Try **Koala Cycle Hire,** Kings Park (rear of Garden Restaurant; tel. 321-3061), which charges $A4 per hour for standard bikes. No deposit is required, but identification and bookings are essential.

PERTH

American Express The Amex office is located at 51 William St. (tel. 322-1177).

Area Code The telephone area code is **09.**

Car Rentals See "Getting Around," in this chapter.

Climate See "When to Go," Chapter 2.

Currency See "Information, Entry Requirements & Money," Chapter 2.

Currency Exchange Money can be changed at the American Express office (see above) or at the airport.

Dentist Contact the **Dental Hospital,** 196 Goderich St. (tel. 325-3452).

Doctor See "Hospitals," below.

Drugstores Try **Cravens Pharmacy** (tel. 325-4375) or **Night Owl Chemist** (tel. 367-1441).

Emergencies Dial **000** for an ambulance or the police.

Hospitals Contact **Royal Perth Hospital,** Wellington Street (tel. 224-2244), or **Fremantle Hospital,** Alma Street (tel. 431-3333).

Hot lines Alcohol and Drug Information: 421-1900. Poisons Information: 381-1177. Samaritans: 381-5555.

Holidays See "When to Go," in Chapter 2.

Information See "Tourist Information," in this chapter.

Luggage Storage/Lockers Both the airport and the Perth Railway Station have storage lockers.

Newspapers/Magazines The *West Australian* and The *Australian* are both morning daily newspapers. Overseas newspapers and magazines are available at Plaza Newsagency, Plaza Arcade, off Hay Street.

Photographic Needs Try **City Arcade Photographics,** City Arcade, Shop H22 (tel. 321-6129).

Police See "Emergencies," above.

Post Office The **General Post Office** is located at Forrest Place; it's open Monday to Friday 8am to 7pm, Saturday 9am to noon.

Religious Services The following denominations are represented in Perth. **Anglican:** St. George's Cathedral, 38 St. George's Terrace (tel. 325-5766). **Baptist:** 10 James St. (tel. 328-6507). **Catholic:** St. Mary's Cathedral, Victoria Square (tel. 325-9177). **Jewish:** Perth Synagogue, corner of Plantation Street and Menora Road, Menora (tel. 271-0539). **Lutheran:** 16 Aberdeen St. (tel. 444-9484).

Taxes There are no taxes added to purchases or hotel-and-restaurant bills.

Taxis See "Getting Around," in this chapter.

Telegrams/Telex/Fax Call 1291 or go to the nearest post office to send a telegram. Telex and fax services are available at some hotels and the General Post Office, at Forrest Place.

Useful Telephone Numbers The **Royal Automobile Club** is located at 228 Adelaide Terrace (tel. 421-4444). For car breakdowns or assistance call 325-0333; help is available 24 hours a day.

3. WHERE TO STAY

Perth is well—almost lavishly—equipped with budget beds, in both the downtown area and the inner suburbs. But it lacks any kind of motel strip where hostelries stand in rows and you can go from door to door and do comparison shopping. It does, however, boast a larger-than-average share of hostel-type places (possibly due to its geographical position), which helps to keep accommodation costs down, since most of them offer comfortable alternatives to the standard hotels.

DOUBLES FOR LESS THAN $A50

CHEVIOT LODGE, 30 Bulwer St., Perth, WA 6000. Tel. 09/227-6817. 18 rms (none with bath). TV

$ Rates: $A13 single, $A28 double. AE, MC, V.

A stately home converted into a guest house, the Cheviot stands in a garden area and exudes quiet friendliness. The place is the handiwork of a tremendously houseproud owner couple who manage to combine many creature comforts and facilities with economy rates. The modular bedrooms, in attractive shades of gray and pink, come with wall-to-wall carpeting, ample clothes-hanging and shelf space, good reading lights, and excellent beds. The seven shared bathrooms are impeccable and have special basins for women to wash their hair in. The lodge has a vast communal kitchen, TV and games rooms, a guest laundry, cheap bike-rental rates, a patio, and courtesy bus service to the downtown shopping district. The rail-and-bus terminal is five walking minutes away, and the Cheviot management picks up arriving guests.

GRAND CENTRAL YWCA, 379 Wellington St., Perth, WA 6000. Tel. 09/221-2682. Fax 09/421-1166. 28 rms (6 with bath), 4 suites.

$ Rates: $A15 dorm, $A25–$A40 single, $A40–$A50 double, $A80 suite. AE, BC, DC, MC, V.

This is an antique hotel, recently taken over, renovated, and restored to splendor by the YWCA. The refurbishing was accomplished while retaining the original period character of the building—except for the ban on smoking, which wouldn't have sat well with the cigar-puffing gentry of 1900. As central as the name implies, the hotel has a restaurant and a café, two TV lounges, and a guest laundry. Furnishings are comfortable, and the management is extremely amiable as well as knowledgeable about the city.

HOTEL REGATTA, 560 Hay St., Perth, WA 6000. Tel. 09/325-5155. Fax 09/325-4176. 63 rms (32 with bath). A/C TV TEL

$ Rates (breakfast included): $A34–$A60 single, $A47.50–$A60 double. AE, BC, MC, V.

The Hotel Regatta, opposite Perth's Town Hall, is a picturesque old Edwardian complex containing two restaurants and three bars magnificently decorated in scarlet and walnut, with a welcoming art-deco lobby. Although the rooms are smallish and the fittings in some old-fashioned, you get overhead-and-bedside lights, lofty ceilings, tiny dressing tables with mirrors, hot- and cold-water basins, and tea- and coffeemaking equipment. Rooms with bathrooms have air-conditioning.

DOUBLES FOR LESS THAN $A76

AIRWAYS HOTEL APARTMENTS, 195 Adelaide Terrace, Perth, WA 6000. Tel. 09/323-7799. Fax 09/221-1956. 157 units (all with bath). A/C TV TEL

$ Rates: $A68 single, $A75 double, $A100 family unit (for 4). AE, BC, MC, V.

This hotel is slightly above our budget range, but it's such an exceptional find for couples or family groups that I felt compelled to include it. It's part hotel; part office building; and an equal mixture of comfort, convenience, and stylishness. Opened in 1981, the centrally located Airways has self-contained units with ultramodern kitchens, plus a grocery store and delicatessen to keep them stocked. A doctor, dentist, dry cleaner, restaurant, coffee shop, newspaper kiosk, and souvenir store are also on the premises. The units have small balconies, wide beds with bedside radios, multitudes of drawers, vast clothes-hanging space, and handy writing desks. The kitchens are equipped with gas ranges (a rarity); refrigera-

PERTH ACCOMMODATIONS, DINING & ATTRACTIONS

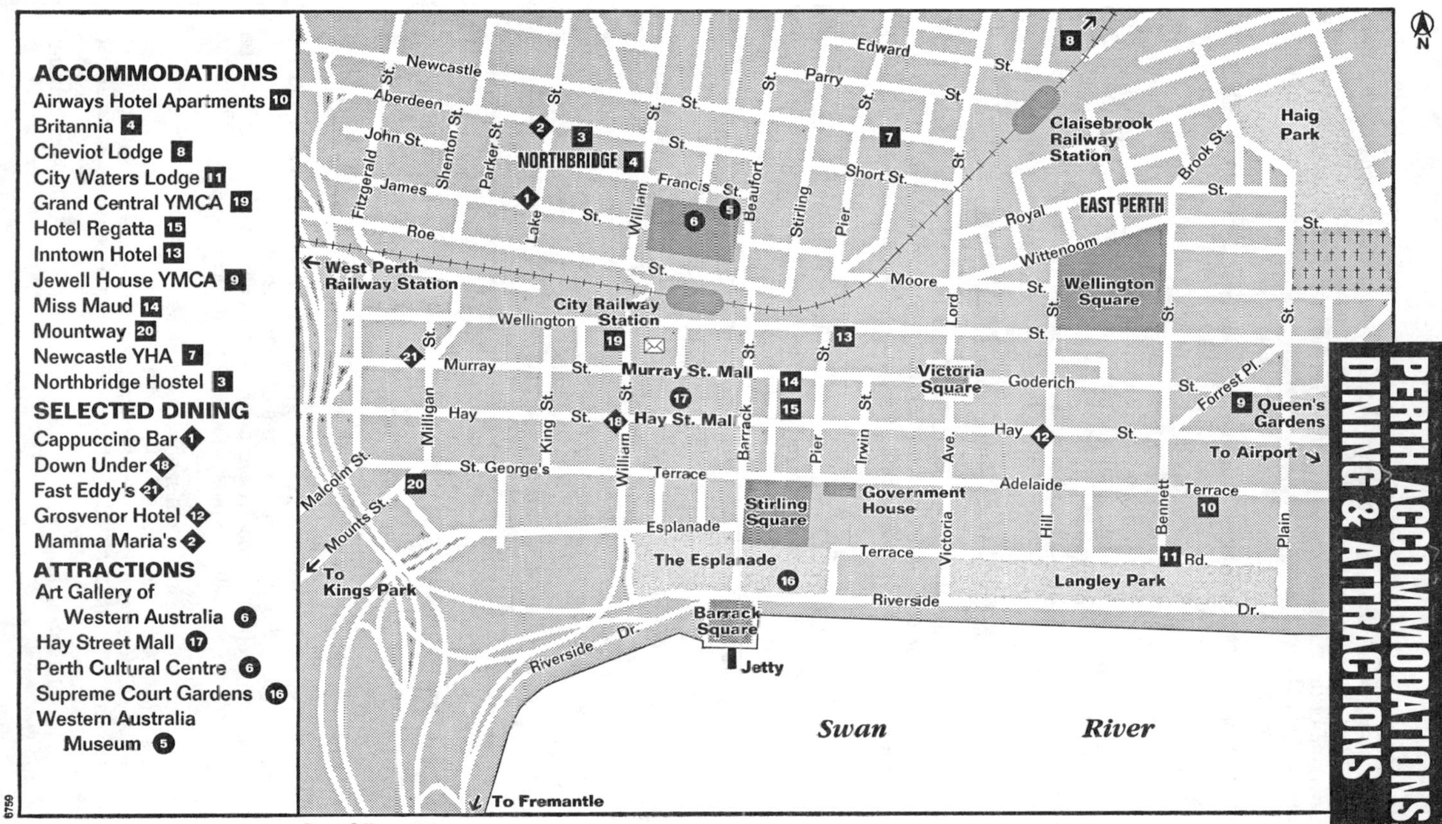

6759

tors; ample sinks; and cooking utensils, complete down to the salt-and-pepper shakers, trays, bread knives, and corkscrews. The compact bathrooms, with fluorescent lighting, are supplied with thick towels. As a crowning touch, the Airways also boasts one of the fastest elevator (pardon me—"lift") services in town. Family units sleep two adults and two children. Cots, bassinettes, high chairs, and baby bathtubs are free.

INNTOWN HOTEL, corner of Murray and Pier Sts., Perth, WA 6000. Tel. 09/325-2133. Fax 09/221-2936. 96 rms (all with bath). A/C TV TEL

$ Rates: $A65 single, $A75 double. AE, BC, MC, V.

Located in the heart of the city's shopping-and-business district, the Inntown is a functional, modern structure with a compact lobby, a pleasant little café, and the kind of cocktail bar you usually find at an airport. Guest rooms are fairly small, with limited wardrobe space but good lighting, refrigerators, and bedside clock radios. The hotel has washing-and-ironing facilities, and there are two huge multistory garages in the vicinity.

SERVICED APARTMENTS

CANNING BRIDGE AUTO LODGE, 891 Canning Hwy., Applecross, WA 6153. Tel. 09/364-2511. Fax 09/364-2477. 31 apts. TV TEL

$ Rates: $A50 1-bedroom unit, $A80 2-bedroom unit (for 4). Weekly discounts available. AE, BC, MC, V.

The suites here accommodate from two to six persons. Every apartment is self-contained and includes all kitchen appliances and utensils, linens, refrigerators, and radios. The beds have innerspring mattresses and individual reading lights. There are a guest laundry, a swimming pool, and a children's playground.

CITY WATERS LODGE, 118 Terrace Rd., Perth, WA 6000. Tel. 09/325-1566. Fax 09/221-2794. 70 units (all with bath). A/C TV TEL

$ Rates: $A67 single, $A72 double, $A77 triple. AE, BC, MC, V.

The lodge occupies one of the choicest locations in the city: overlooking Langley Park and the Swan River, right in the heart of Perth. A motel-style apartment complex, it comprises self-contained units ranging from single to family size, all charmingly furnished. Kitchens have excellent refrigerators and gas ranges, plus all necessary utensils, crockery, and cutlery; linens are also provided. Bathrooms are modern, and there's plenty of wardrobe space. A laundry and

FROMMER'S SMART TRAVELER: HOTELS

1. Ask about the special "weekend packages" with sharply reduced rates at some of the larger hotels.
2. Most hotels will give you a lower rate—10% to 35%—if you stay more than one week.
3. "Parking available" can mean anything from a hotel garage to an empty lot. Always find out *beforehand* if there's an extra charge.
4. A few hotels offer free local phone calls but many charge A50¢ or A60¢ for a call that costs A30¢ from a public phone. Ask the rate and use a public phone if necessary.
5. Most hostels, and some hotels, offer free pick ups from train or bus stations, so let them know your arrival well in advance.
6. Virtually all hotels provide coffee- and tea-making equipment. If you add some pastries or biscuits (cookies) you can organize an inexpensive light breakfast.
7. In most cases an Australian hotel bathroom denotes a shower. Very few budget establishments provide tubs, and there is no price difference between the two.

rental-car office are also on the premises. Present this book and get a 10% discount on the rates.

MOUNTWAY, 36 Mount St., Perth, WA 6000. Tel. 09/321-8307. Fax 09/324-2147. 63 units (all with bath). TV

$ Rates: $A36 single, $A41 double; $A2 per day for children under 12 in parent's room. BC, MC, V.

The Mountway is one of my prime bargain discoveries in all Australia. A handsome, modern six-story building rising just behind a freeway bridge in central Perth, it offers wonderful views of the parklands along the Swan River from the upper floors. The Mountway has furnished units that can comfortably accommodate three people. Each unit has a bathroom with tub and shower and a kitchen with a gas stove, refrigerator, and full cooking and eating utensils. Furnishings are new, carpeting is wall-to-wall, and bathroom fixtures are in excellent condition. The managers go out of their way to please their tenants, and despite the freeway vicinity the units are remarkably quiet.

WESTHAVEN HOUSE, 150 Marine Parade, Cottesloe, WA 6011. Tel. 09/384-4738. 12 apts. TV TEL

$ Rates: From $A30 bed-sitter, from $A40 2-bedroom apartment. AE, BC, MC, V.

This selection is at one of Perth's most popular beach resorts. It offers typical seaside-vacation accommodations in a large building right beside a delightful Indian Ocean beach, with a shopping complex across the road and a reasonably quiet environment. The Westhaven has two types of units: two-bedroom apartments, fully equipped (except for towels) and self-contained, accommodating up to six people; and bed-sitters, which have only hot plates and shared bathrooms but also refrigerators, color TVs, and all utensils. Laundry facilities are available.

HOSTELS, Y's & DORMS

Included in the hostels listed below are the official **Youth Hostels:** four in Perth proper, three more in Fremantle, and another two in the outer hill suburbs—adding up to a virtual embarrassment of riches.

The University of Western Australia, in Crawley, is next to Kings Park and beautifully situated amid the greenery facing a small bay of the Swan River, which widens to lake dimensions in this area. The various colleges have budget rooms available for guests during the holidays (November to February), but they are usually heavily booked. **Kingswood College** (tel. 389-0389) charges $A12 per night. In a similar price bracket are **St. Columba College** (tel. 386-7177), **St. Thomas More College** (tel. 386-5080), and **Currie Hall** (tel. 380-2772).

BRITANNIA, 253 William St., Perth, WA 6003. Tel. 09/328-6121. Fax 09/227-9784. 80 rms (none with bath). TV

$ Rates: From $A13 per person. BC, MC, V.

The Britannia is a converted gold-rush-era hotel located on a wonderfully cosmopolitan restaurant strip. A quaint antique structure with a small corner tower, this YHA establishment gives you a wide choice of dormitories and double or single rooms. There are a guest laundry, a communal kitchen, and a TV lounge. The airport bus stops outside.

BUNDIKUDJI BACKPACKERS, 96 Hampton Rd., Fremantle, WA 6160. Tel. 09/335-3467. 56 beds (shared bath).

$ Rates: $A16 single, $A26 double, $A11 dorm. BC, MC, V.

This hostel is located in a historic building—a family home that became a maternity home and then a nurses' quarters before its present incarnation. A charming, traditional colonial-style building, it has a guest kitchen, TV room, laundry, and is situated close to the America's Cup marinas (yachting fanatics, please note) and within walking distance of downtown. Free taxi fare from Fremantle train station.

JEWELL HOUSE YMCA, 180 Goderich St., East Perth, WA 6000. Tel. 09/325-8488. Fax 09/221-4694. 205 rms (none with bath). TV TEL

$ Rates: From $A26 single, $A34 double, $A55 family room (for 5). AE, BC, MC, V.

Jewell House, a former nurses' quarters converted into a private hotel, stands centrally located on a blessedly quiet street—which is still a hospital zone. A trim building, kept absolutely spick and span, the Jewell accommodates 250 guests in rooms ranging from single to family size (two adults, three children). The free City Clipper, to take you shopping, stops right outside. The hotel has laundry-and-ironing facilities, a TV lounge, and a dining room. The double rooms come with coffee- and tea-making equipment, and the shared bathrooms positively sparkle. Bedrooms are small but comfortable and airy, with overhead-and-bedside lamps, wall-to-wall carpeting, writing tables, and good-size wardrobes. They don't, however, have basins.

LADYBIRD LODGE, 193 Oxford St., Leederville, WA 6007. Tel. 09/444-7359. 34 rms (none with bath).

$ Rates: $A15 per person. No credit cards.

The lodge is a curious whitewashed-brick building in a relatively quiet part of Leederville's main shopping street. City transport stops at the door. The house has a sun deck, a communal kitchen, a large clean dining room looking rather like a gym hall, an upstairs laundry, and a TV lounge. The rooms (all but six doubles) feature wall-to-wall carpeting, large wardrobes, writing desks, and handy shelves—simple but neat furnishings. The rooms have no basins, but the public bathrooms are well fitted and absolutely spotless.

NEWCASTLE YHA, 62 Newcastle St., Perth, WA 6000. Tel. 09/328-1135. 48 beds.

$ Rates: $A11 adults, $A5.50 under 18. BC, MC, V.

This is another YHA hostel, also once a guest house, with rooms holding four, six, or eight beds each. There are a guest laundry, a kitchen with a microwave, and bikes for hire. The place has an old-fashioned but homey atmosphere and is within walking distance of the city center.

NORTHBRIDGE HOSTEL, 42 Francis St., Northbridge, WA 6003. Tel. 09/328-7794. Fax same. 87 beds.

$ Rates: $A12 per person. BC, MC, V.

The Northbridge YHA Hostel is an erstwhile guest house, nicely renovated with kitchen-and-laundry facilities. Rooms are doubles or five beds, and there are barbecue grills, a garden, and rental bikes.

WORTH THE EXTRA MONEY

MISS MAUD, 97 Murray St., Perth, WA 6000. Tel. 09/325-3900. Fax 09/221-3225. 21 rms (all with bath). A/C MINIBAR TV TEL

$ Rates (including breakfast): $A85 single, $A95 double. AE, BC, MC, V.

One reason for including this place is the absolutely terrific smorgasbord breakfast included in the room rates. Another is the sheer charm of this small, European-style establishment, where the staff wears Scandinavian costumes and seems to have graduated from a training college for diplomats. A Swedish-designed corner building with a pinewood-paneled reception area, Miss Maud has rooms that are surprisingly spacious, with subtly blended Nordic decor, broad beds, leisure seating facilities, deep carpeting, refrigerators, and electric hair dryers. Most of the ground floor is taken up by a celebrated Scandinavian restaurant and sinful pastry shop, guaranteed to wreck whatever dietary resolutions you made for your trip. The rye bread sold there is possibly the best in Australia.

CARAVAN [R.V.] PARKS

Perth is as well supplied with caravan parks as it is with all other types of accommodations. There are 29 of these parks within and around the city area: 21 have on-site vans for hire, and the majority permit camping. For a complete list of these facilities, get the brochure at the W.A. Tourist Centre, Forrest Place, Perth, WA 6000. Here are a couple of choices:

COMO BEACH CARAVAN PARK, 4 Ednah St., Como, WA 6152. Tel. 09/367-1286.

$ Rates: From $A14 for on-site vans.
Located three miles from the city, the caravan park is close to the beach with a bus terminal at the entrance. It has vans with four to six berths and all cooking equipment.

PERTH CARAVAN PARK, 319 Hale Rd., Forrestfield, WA 6058. Tel. 09/453-6677.
$ Rates: From $A5 per person.
Located 9½ miles from the city, this park has on-site vans and camping sites.

4. WHERE TO EAT

One reason why the word *isolated* conveys such a false image of Perth is the culinary scene, which happens to be among the best in Australia. Perth boasts a happy profusion of eateries running the scale from Arabian to Yugoslav, many in the economy bracket. What's more, they are heavily concentrated in a distinct area, so they are delightfully easy to track down. The region is James Street/William Street, Northbridge, lying across the railroad tracks, a once-seedy, now-booming neighborhood chockablock with small, cheap, ethnic family-run restaurants providing delicious fare. Vino Vino, Costa Brava, Romany, and Mamma Mia's are all located there. In recent years this has become *the* dining-and-entertainment region of Perth, packed with both budget and plush food dispensaries. The attrition rate, unfortunately, is rapid. So if you find that a particular establishment has vanished, changed names, or turned into a hardware store, simply wander on to the next.

Hotel counter lunches have the usual high Australian standard, sometimes coupled with plenty of atmosphere.

MEALS FOR LESS THAN $A13

FAST EDDY'S, corner of Hay and Milligan Sts., Perth. Tel. 321-2552.
Cuisine: AUSTRALIAN-AMERICAN. **Reservations:** Accepted.
$ Prices: Appetizers $A3.65, main courses $A5.50–$A12. No credit cards.
Open: 24 hrs.
We've already encountered this rapid Edward in Melbourne. The Westralian establishment offers more of the same: fast round-the-clock service, special attention to junior-set palates and pleasures, and a general atmosphere of family fun. The menu lists rows of filling hamburgers and pasta dishes for around $A7; breakfasts in all appetite sizes; and more upscale steaks, ribs, and seafood. This is one of the few Oz eateries to serve genuine American chocolate sundaes and ice-cream sodas.

GROSVENOR HOTEL, Hay St. corner of Hill St., Perth. Tel. 325-3796.
Cuisine: ECLECTIC. **Reservations:** Not necessary.
$ Prices: $A6–$A10. No credit cards.
Open: Mon–Sat 10am–10pm.
This is an intriguingly schizoid place for lunch or snacks: The older portion—white, colonial, and absolutely beautiful—has one of the most pleasant wine gardens in Perth. The new part—tacked on as if by absentminded afterthought—possesses all the subtle charm of an airport passenger lounge. The two halves are shoved together like immobile railroad cars, turning the interior into a maze of bars, lounges, dining rooms, and saloons in which you can get lost for hours. But yet another attachment is a smart Italian restaurant, serving—among other lunches—excellent fettuccine for $A7.

ROMA RESTAURANT, 9 High St., Fremantle. Tel. 335-3664.
Cuisine: ITALIAN. **Reservations:** Accepted.
$ Prices: Appetizers $A3–$A4, main courses $A9–$A10. No credit cards.

Open: Mon–Sat noon–2pm and 5–10pm.

One of the oldest and most beloved eateries in the state, though you couldn't tell by its appearance, the Roma has metal tables and chairs and virtually no decor, but it has a classic reputation. The policy of the place is firmly maintained by the management: "We close Sundays. That's when we go to church." All the artistry goes into the cooking. Patrons come from far away for the big drawing card: roast chicken and spaghetti, which costs $A10 and could feed the average couple.

MEALS FOR LESS THAN $A19

BOBBY DAZZLER'S, 300 Murray St., Perth. Tel. 481-1000.

Cuisine: AUSTRALIAN. **Reservations:** Accepted.

$ **Prices:** Appetizers $A4–$A5, main courses $A8.50–$A17.50. AE, BC, MC, V.

Open: Daily.

Billing itself "The Great Aussie Eatery," this establishment devotes considerable menu space to a translation of such Oz phraseology as "U-right?" for "Can I help you?" A "Bobby Dazzler," incidently, is an excellent, praiseworthy person or object. The entire fare is listed in Aussie idiom, with the standard English translation underneath in small print. Thus you learn that "underground mutton" means rabbit, "black stump" rump steak, and "BBQ chook" charcoal-grilled chicken. The offerings run from "jumbuck pie" (lamb) for $A8.50 to "Great Australian buff" (buffalo filet) for $A17.50. There is also a vast all-you-can-eat salad bar for $A10.50, plus an excellent range of Australian wines starting at $A6.50 per half bottle.

CANTON, 532 Hay St., Perth. Tel. 325-8865.

Cuisine: CHINESE. **Reservations:** Accepted.

$ **Prices:** Appetizers $A3–$A5, main courses $A10–$A15. AE, BC, MC, V.

Open: Daily 5pm "until late."

This softly lit, carpeted Chinese eatery has excellent food and leisurely service. It provides an odd contrast between ornately tasseled chandeliers and severely functional metal tables. I had dim sum for starters, followed by a vegetarian combination with nuts, both highly commendable. The meal came to $A14.

COSTA BRAVA, 137 James St., Northbridge. Tel. 328-6741.

Cuisine: SEAFOOD. **Reservations:** Required.

$ **Prices:** Appetizers $A5.80, main courses $A9.50–$A15. MC, V.

Open: Daily noon–3pm and 6–10:30pm.

The Costa Brava looks like a vaulted wine cellar carpeted in blue. The decor is beautiful, cool, and white—with highly appetizing still lifes of marine delectables on the walls, illuminated fish tanks, and flowers in glass vases on black-lacquered tables (needless to add that the place specializes in seafood). The portions are huge and accompanied by crackling-fresh bread. You dine by the light of lanterns hanging from a low beamed ceiling and imbibe Catalonian atmosphere along with the wine—the Costa Brava is fully licensed. The seafood selection is vast, with prices ranging from $A9.50 to $A15. I had some truly memorable barramundi filets with salad, vegetables, and bread for $A14.50.

FRANCO'S, 323 Hay St., Perth. Tel. 325-4843.

Cuisine: SPANISH. **Reservations:** Accepted.

$ **Prices:** Appetizers $A6, main courses $A12. AE, BC, MC, V.

Open: Daily 6pm "until late."

Franco's is an attractive corner building with two small dining rooms. The establishment has a dual personality—Anglo-Spanish—which even flavors the decor. The walls and ceiling, with oak beams, wagon wheels, and ornate lanterns, give it the Iberian touch. Tables and chairs are strictly utilitarian. The menu and cuisine are split as well: The rice that accompanies the dishes is saffron, but the fresh tomatoes and mushrooms taste very Aussie indeed. I'd recommend the steak Pablo ($A11.50) or the garlic prawns ($A8), with the homemade flan con nata for dessert. This is a BYO—so do.

FROMMER'S SMART TRAVELER: RESTAURANTS

1. Perth's shopping malls and arcades are crammed with little coffee lounges and tearooms serving economy lunches (but rarely dinners).
2. Hotel counter lunches are among the cheapest meals in town.
3. When ordering wine in a restaurant, stick to the house brand. The labels on the wine list are always much more expensive—but not necessarily better.
4. In Australia lamb ranks among the cheaper types of meat. On the other hand, the exotic meat varieties—like buffalo stew and crocodile chops—are the most expensive.
5. Fixed-price meals can save you 25% of your lunch or dinner check—but only if you have a hearty appetite. If you're a one-course eater, you'll do better ordering just a solo dish.

ROMANY, 188 William St., Northbridge. Tel. 328-8042.
Cuisine: ITALIAN. **Reservations:** Accepted.
$ **Prices:** Appetizers $A7–$A8.50, main courses $A9–$A16. No credit cards.
Open: Mon–Sun lunch and dinner.

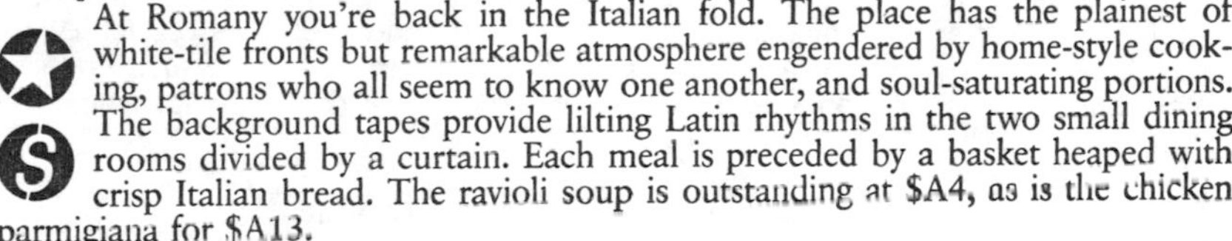

At Romany you're back in the Italian fold. The place has the plainest of white-tile fronts but remarkable atmosphere engendered by home-style cooking, patrons who all seem to know one another, and soul-saturating portions. The background tapes provide lilting Latin rhythms in the two small dining rooms divided by a curtain. Each meal is preceded by a basket heaped with crisp Italian bread. The ravioli soup is outstanding at $A4, as is the chicken parmigiana for $A13.

SASSELLA'S TAVERN BISTRO, City Arcade, 207 Murray St., Perth. Tel. 322-4001.
Cuisine: ENGLISH-ITALIAN. **Reservations:** Not necessary.
$ **Prices:** Appetizers $A4, main courses $A8–$A14.95. AE, BC, MC, V.
Open: Mon–Sat 11am–10pm.

This is one of Perth's most popular watering holes, redolent with Olde English pub charm but air-conditioned as well. The bistro portion functions on a balcony separate from the bar. You place your food order, wander over to the bar for a beer (a middy costs $A2), then sit at your table until your order is called out. The fare is limited, tasty, and economical: fried squid for $A8, lasagne for $A7. Food service is available until 9pm.

VINO VINO, 152 James St., Northbridge. Tel. 328-5403.
Cuisine: ITALIAN. **Reservations:** Accepted.
$ **Prices:** Appetizers $A5.80, main courses $A11–$A17. AE, BC, MC, V.
Open: Dinner, Wed–Mon 6–11pm.

Despite its brand-spanking-new appearance, Vino Vino is an old family restaurant and the fare tastes accordingly. A corner place with viewing windows overlooking two busy streets, the Vino has a cheery, inviting dining room with comfortable light-wood chairs, checked table linen, lace curtains, a cupboard with Italian pottery, and a homey umbrella stand in one corner. The sole disturbing feature is the sometimes overly loud background music. Menu items run $A11 to $A17 and come accompanied by bowls of excellent crisp salad with black olives and onion slices. Highly recommended here is the beef Don Camillo, cooked in herb butter and fresh peppercorns.

DESSERT

CAPPUCCINO BAR, corner of James and Lake Sts., Northbridge. Tel. 328-5426.

Cuisine: PASTRIES. **Reservations:** Accepted.
$ Prices: Gelato, $A6.50. No credit cards.
Open: 10am–1am, Sat and Sun until 4am.

Across the railroad tracks in Northbridge, the large, glittering Cappuccino Bar would look perfectly in place on the Via Veneto. With pink-and-white decor, tables on the pavement in front, globe-shaped lighting, and flirtatious patrons, the place is as much for socializing as for snacking. It serves top-notch coffee and desserts and 36 kinds of "gelati temptations" for $A6.50. Try the Pago Pago—a pineapple, banana, mandarin, and nougat creation.

FOOD HALLS

These cosmopolitan, unglamorous, and wondrously economical grub dispensaries are great for quick lunches and early evening meals—especially when it comes to feeding kids. Here are two of them.

Down Under, at the corner of William and Hay streets, Mall, is open Monday to Saturday from 8am to 7pm. It is a noisy, aromatic array of little stalls selling Chinese, Indian, Mexican, Thai, and Italian specialties for $A5 to $A6, as well as vegetarian meals and subway sandwiches. This BYO has a no-smoking area. **East Fremantle Food Hall,** Shopping Centre, 147 Canning Hwy., East Fremantle, is open Tuesday to Sunday from 11:30am to 8:30pm. It is remarkably spruce and clean—but not quiet. The comestibles here are almost entirely Asian, the highest-priced item being the combination platter piled high with roast lamb, pork, and beef, plus vegetables, for $A6. Most dishes go for $A4 to $A5, including the East Indian *luksa,* Malaysian satays, and Chinese garlic prawns. In deference to fragile taste buds, the spicier choices can be ordered "mild" or "really hot."

WORTH THE EXTRA MONEY

MAMMA MARIA'S, corner of Lake and Aberdeen Sts., Northbridge. Tel. 328-4532 or 227-9828.
Cuisine: ITALIAN-INTERNATIONAL. **Reservations:** Recommended.
$ Prices: Appetizers $A4–$A6, main courses $A8–$A16. AE, BC, MC, V.
Open: Daily "until late."

Just off William Street stands the cottage-style Mamma Maria's. Our splurge restaurant, this is one of the most famous eating houses in town; it's been going strong ever since the days of the original "Mamma"—about 22 years ago. The rustic decor has hardly changed; even the village hand pump is still attached to the stairway. The menu cover bears the autographs of the legion of celebrities who have overeaten here on the richly Italian fare. You can get a two-course à la carte choice from $A16 and up, along with complimentary cheese, olives, greens, and a basket of crusty Italian bread.

5. ATTRACTIONS

THE TOP ATTRACTIONS

Perth is one of the few cities in which the shopping areas can rank as sights. The **Hay Street Pedestrian Mall** is tremendous fun, and **London Court,** linking Hay Street to St. George's Terrace, is a real museum piece. This arcade, built in delightfully ridiculous mock-Tudor style, actually opened in 1937 but pretends to be a kind of medieval fortress. Guarded by iron portcullises, which are lowered at night, it contains two "dungeon towers," the statues of Sir Walter Raleigh and Dick Whittington (plus cat), and moving clockworks showing St. George perpetually slaying the poor dragon and tilting knights having at each other.

FROMMER'S COOL FOR KIDS: RESTAURANTS

Fast Eddy's *(p. 289)* Catering to kids in family groups or large parties, Fast Eddy's has fun surroundings and exactly the kind of solid-and-liquid fare youngsters prefer.

Food Halls in Perth and Fremantle *(p. 292)* Located in Perth and Fremantle, these are a source of culinary fascination for juniors, with immense variety, intriguing aromas, and a lot of noise and activity—and nobody minds kids running from stall to stall.

Just across the Narrows Bridge stands the **Old Mill,** a relic from 1835 that was once used to grind flour but now houses a collection of early colonial tools, artifacts, and mementos.

The small modern **zoo** on Labouchere Road (tel. 367-7988) in South Perth on the other side of the river is interesting because it contains many animals unique to Western Australia. Open daily 10am to 5pm. Admission is $A5 for adults, $A1.50 for children. You can take bus no. 36 from St. George's Terrace or the ferry from Barrack Street Jetty. For more Westralian fauna there's **Lake Monger** in suburban Wembley. This is a haven for the state's famous black swans (and hundreds of other waterfowl), and if you bring a bag of buns the swans will eat out of your hand. Take bus no. 90, 91, or 92 from the Central Bus Station and get off at the corner of Harbourne and Grantham streets.

MORE ATTRACTIONS

MUSEUMS/GALLERIES

ART GALLERY OF WESTERN AUSTRALIA, In the Perth Cultural Centre, James Street Mall. Tel. 328-7233.

This is one of the newest and architecturally most striking museums in the country. Its unusual octagonal shape, bordered by a vast concourse with a waterway, makes it a landmark within the city's cultural precinct. The highlight of the gallery is the collection of early Australian paintings, some showing the tribulations of the pioneer generation with touching poignancy. Also represented are the more sophisticated newer artists, including Dobell, Nolan, Drysdale, and Boyd. There is a changing exhibition of Aboriginal art, plus temporary exhibits.

Admission: Free (except for special exhibitions).

Open: Daily 10am–5pm.

WESTERN AUSTRALIAN MUSEUM, Francis St. Tel. 328-4411.

This is probably the only museum in the world that incorporates an old jail. The prison is now part of the Westralian memorabilia on display here—rather apt because of the colony's penal history. Also on show are an immense blue whale skeleton and an even more immense 11-ton meteorite.

Admission: Free.

Open: Mon–Fri 10:30am–5pm, Sat–Sun 1–5pm.

IT'S A SMALL WORLD, 12 Parliament Place. Tel. 322-2020.

It's a Small World has a delightful collection of miniature trains; dollhouses; fire engines; animated fairy-tale figures; midget shops; and a unique series of children's pedal cars, ranging from antique Fords to sleek Mercedes and Formula 1 racers.

Admission: $A4 adults, $A2 children.

Open: Sun–Fri 10am–5pm, Sat 2–5pm.

PERTH MINT, 310 Hay St. Tel. 421-7277.

The oldest operating mint in the world still housed in its original premises, the mint was founded as a branch of the Royal Mint in London in 1899 and has been "coining" ever since. Exhibits include a huge array of gold-and-silver coins, bars, bullion, and certificates. Also on sale are precious metals, for investors and collectors. The Perth Mint is one of the few global gold refiners whose weights and measures are internationally accepted.

Admission: To be decided.

Open: Mon–Fri 9am–6pm, Sat 9am–1pm.

AVIATION MUSEUM, Bullcreek Drive, Bullcreek. Tel. 332-4444.

This collection of historic aircraft, models, and memorabilia is guaranteed to enthuse flying fanatics of all ages and sexes. It houses one of the legendary Avro Lancaster "Dam Busters," a World War II Dakota and Tiger Moth, as well as one of the last Spitfires ever built.

Admission: $A5 adults, $A2 children.

Open: Daily 11am–4pm.

UNDERWATER WORLD, Boat Harbour, West Coast Dr., Hillarys. Tel. 447-7500.

An underwater glass tunnel lets you walk among 2,500 or so marine creatures ranging from minute to immense. At a special Touch Pool you can feel the texture of starfish and sea slugs, and the Microworld gives you closeups of microscopic ocean inhabitants.

Admission: $A13.50 adults, $A6.50 children.

Open: Daily 9am–5pm.

SCITECH DISCOVERY CENTRE, corner of Sutherland St. and Railway Parade, West Perth. Tel. 481-5789.

A fascinating assembly of "hands-on" displays allows visitors to become participants. You can step inside a giant breathing lung, walk into optical illusions, create a miniature whirlwind, act as part of an electric battery, and do much more with the 160 exhibits.

Admission: $A9 adults, $A5 children.

Open: Daily 10am–5pm.

WILDLIFE & AMUSEMENT PARKS

CAVERSHAM WILDLIFE PARK, corner of Arthur and Cranleigh Rds., West Swan. Tel. 274-2202.

One of three wildlife parks in the Perth region, this one is embedded in the idyllic scenery of the Swan Valley. It is home to rare marsupials and Australian birds, as well as monkeys and deer, which you can feed with tidbits supplied on the spot. Most of the inhabitants roam freely.

Admission: $A6 adults, $A2 children.

Open: Daily 9am–5pm.

KINGS PARK, at the top of Mt. Eliza.

This is the pride of Perth, a 1,000-acre reserve of natural-and-cultivated bushland. The park not only is magically beautiful but also offers a panoramic view of the entire city. Within the area there are a joyously bubbling fountain dedicated to the Pioneer Women; a floral clock; some ancient cannons; and a tragic row of gum trees, each planted by the family of a fallen "Digger" as a living memorial and marked with his battalion colors. There is also an excellent but expensive restaurant with a dining patio, and next to it is a pleasant snack terrace (small tables and self-service) that sells very good sandwiches and afternoon tea. **Bus:** 33 and 34.

ADVENTURE WORLD, 179 Progress Dr., Bibra Lake. Tel. 417-9666.

A vast amusement park, 10 minutes from Fremantle, sprinkled with artificial lakes and cascades and interlaced with tracks, slides, and rides of varying wildness,

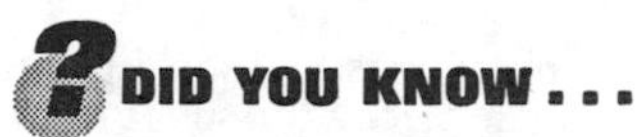

DID YOU KNOW . . . ?

- Perth lies closer to Jakarta, the capital of Indonesia, than to Canberra, the Australian capital.
- The erstwhile pirate William Dampier discovered Western Australia in 1688 and actually landed there. But he gave such a dismal account of the region—calling the natives "the miserablest people in the world"—that the English government lost any interest in seizing it.
- Perth received its proud subtitle, "City of Lights," from astronaut John Glenn. When orbiting Earth in 1962, Glenn saw a shining beacon of lights blazing up from the immense blackness of Western Australia—the people of Perth had turned on every light in their city to greet the wayfarer.
- Western Australia grows 6,580 species of wildflowers—more than in any other area in the world.
- The cooling sea breeze that fans Perth after a summer scorcher blows from the southwest and is known locally as the "Fremantle doctor."

Adventure World also houses a magic castle, a wildlife park, an animal circus, a motor car-racing track, a swimming pool, a toboggan slide, a monorail, a "mystery cave," and a dozen other thrills. You get unlimited rides for the price of your ticket.

Admission: $A19.50 adults, $A16 children.

Open: Daily 10am–5pm.

NEARBY ATTRACTIONS

ARMADALE

Take bus route no. 219 on Pier Street and ask the driver to let you off at the Narrogin Inn in Armadale. Then it's a short stroll to two contrasting attractions. **Pioneer World** at the corner of Albany Street and Highway (tel. 399-5322), S.W. Hwy., is a reconstructed street of the Australian colony a century ago, with traditional craftspeople at work and specialty shops selling colonial wares. The **Elizabethan Village** features replicas of Shakespeare's birthplace and displays English arms and armor, tapestries, needlework, and period furniture. Both attractions are open daily from 10am to 5pm. Admission is $A8.50 for adults, $A6.50 for children.

BEACHES

All the nearest ocean beaches are outside Perth but very easy to get to. The Indian Ocean surf is quite heavy, so you'd better gauge your capabilities before joining the surfboard brigade. But the golden sands offer glorious lounging, and the boys and gals on the boards can be as much fun to watch as to join. Among the most popular ocean resorts are **Scarborough**—catch bus no. 260 at the Central Bus Station, then change to bus no. 268 to reach the foreshore. **City Beach** can be reached directly by bus no. 84 from the Central Station. **Cottesloe** is a large resort with extensive shopping centers, hotels, restaurants, and so forth. Get there by bus no. 72 or 207 from St. George's Terrace.

FREMANTLE

Perth's seaport on the Indian Ocean, called "Freo" in local lingo, is an astonishing place. Founded as the original Swan River Colony by Captain Fremantle in 1829, the town is only a few years older than Perth but looks centuries its senior. Fremantle had a curiously reversed history. It was the first voluntary settlement—that is, the settlers were free immigrants—but they found themselves so desperately short of labor that the infant colony *requested* the government to send them convicts. The authorities obliged and dispatched nearly 10,000 "gentlemen of the broad arrows" to the Swan River, where they constructed most of the fine old buildings that today give the port its quaintly archaic air.

Over the past few years, Fremantle has undergone an astonishing transformation, mainly because it was the site of the 1987 America's Cup challenge race, for which it was spreading the welcome mat for a very cosmopolitan clientele. Its port facilities have always been modern and streamlined, capable of handling 15 million tons of cargo annually. But suddenly the brooding atmosphere of its old-world streets and squares was rejuvenated by a crop of smart shops, "in" restaurants, and sophisticated cafés. They provide some much-needed glitter and make the place a fun spot to stroll around in but haven't changed the basic character of the town—the contemporary touches still appear like a superficial graft. Fremantle's soul remains Victorian—a century removed from Perth, which lies only 12 miles away. It is this oddly appealing schizophrenia, the contrasts that strike you at every corner, that gives Fremantle a unique charm found nowhere else on the continent.

The town was the first to build a bridge across the Swan River, and its official opening in 1866 ranks as the most hilarious episode in the annals of the colony, for the man who cut the ribbon was not a local dignitary but Moondyne Joe, a notorious bushranger who had just escaped from prison! **Fremantle Gaol,** built in 1851 by convicts to house convicts, still stands grimly gray and formidable and still functions as a jail. (You can admire it from the outside.) Despite its Dickensian appearance, however, it is reputedly the most comfortable lockup in Australia. Another jail, the **Round House** on Arthur's Head, is no longer used in that capacity but represents the oldest building in the state and can be inspected daily.

Fremantle has narrow streets, old churches and warehouses, Dutch gables and Gothic cloisters, and a pub at every corner, as befits a harbor town. Most of the watering holes are steeped in seafaring tradition, like the **P & O Hotel** on High Street, looking as if it might have been frequented by the Ancient Mariner. It also puts on excellent counter lunches: chicken soup, grilled snapper for $A6, and a big help-yourself salad bar.

You can get to Fremantle from Perth by catching bus no. 101 or 103 in St. George's Terrace.

FREMANTLE MUSEUM, 1 Finnerty St. Tel. 335-8211.

★ The most famous building in town began as the colony's first lunatic asylum in the 1860s—a stark but beautiful showpiece of convict colonial architecture. Due for demolition in 1900, it was saved by the taste and foresight of the mayor and duly converted into the Fremantle Museum. This is one of the truly fascinating museums Australia has to offer. To make things even better, it's free. The place is actually more than a museum: One of the wings is given over to local artists as work-and-exhibition space, and the courtyard becomes a starlit stage on summer nights. The museum proper is an enchanting mélange of relics, maps, photographs, artifacts, weapons, paintings, documents, clothes, and utensils that tell the story of Western Australia. There are a raised cannon from a 17th-century Dutch East India Company ship and the jewelry worn by fashionable colonial ladies. There are century-old newspaper ads and the harpoons used by Fremantle whalers; the muskets, pistols, swords, and clubs used by Victorian garrison troops and bushrangers alike; evocative old photographs; ancient maps; fashion plates; official proclamations; ladies' sunshades; lighthouse equipment; diving gear; carved whales' teeth; superb early ships models; and on and on. You'll just have to see for yourself.

Admission: Free.

Open: Mon–Thurs 10:30am–5pm, Fri–Sun 1–5pm.

SAILS OF THE CENTURY, B Shed, Victoria Quay. Tel. 335-8211.

Sails of the Century is housed in a converted cargo shed overlooking the historic waterfront. The varied and expertly displayed armada of craft include the America's Cup winner *Australia II,* with its legendary winged keel; a fishing boat dating back to 1875; the little yacht *Ferie Banou* that circumnavigated the globe; a steam launch; rowing fours; sleek racing yachts; sturdy lifeboats; and many other water vehicles.

Admission: Free.

Open: Daily 11am–4pm.

WESTERN AUSTRALIAN MARITIME MUSEUM, Cliff St., Fremantle. Tel. 431-8444.

Probably the only museum to specialize in ancient shipwrecks, it displays a treasure trove of items salvaged from vessels that went down along the uncharted coastline before the founding of the colonies. Most intriguing are the objects brought up from four 17th-century windjammers of the Dutch East India Company: silver coins, cannons, navigation aids, jewelry, cups, and pots—the mementos of the doomed crews and passengers.

Admission: By donation.

Open: Mon–Thurs 10:30am–5pm, Fri–Sun 1–5pm.

FREMANTLE MARKETS, corner of Henderson St. and South Terrace.

These markets have been operating since 1897, when they were established as exact replicas of the European models. They consist of more than 150 variegated stalls selling fresh local seafood, exotic herbs and spices, antiques (genuine and repro), jewelry, gemstones, finery, bric-a-brac, and handcrafted items. The background is an ornate 19th-century colonnade, the air full of music and tangy smells, and the whole scene delightful.

Open: Fri 9am–9pm, Sat–Sun 10am–5pm.

ENERGY MUSEUM, 12 Parry St. Tel. 430-5655.

This museum presents an interesting array of machines and contraptions that produce energy and shows some of the practical uses we make of it. It traces the development of electricity and gas in Westralia by means of hands-on working displays and wax-figure scenes, all under the apt museum slogan: "If you've got the time, we've got the energy."

Admission: Free.

Open: Mon–Fri 10:30am–4:30pm, Sat–Sun 1–4:30pm.

ROTTNEST ISLAND

Rottnest Island was unflatteringly (and wrongly) named by early Dutch explorers who thought the place was swarming with rats. What they actually saw were cute, pint-sized marsupials called quokkas, which were indigenous to the island and still hop around there in furry bunches. Now affectionately known as "Rotto," the island is a patch of tranquil beauty in the deep blue of the Indian Ocean, 12 miles offshore from Fremantle.

Tranquil is the word for Rottnest because there are no motor cars and no mechanical noises. Hardly anyone wears shoes. The air is absolutely pure and mostly balmy; the beach sand like talcum powder; and the only means of transport across its 7-mile length are bicycles whirring softly over smooth roads. It's tons of fun, though. There are peacocks and quokkas on land, herring and skipjack leaping in the water, a big and beautiful pub, fishing from boats or rocks, golf, tennis, bowling, and swimming. "Rotto" is more than a resort, it's a solidified tonic for frayed city souls, although that deep enfolding silence takes a bit of getting used to. You can reach the island in 2 hours by ferry from Perth's **Barrack Street Jetty** ($A17 round-trip ticket) or whiz over in 50 minutes by hydrofoil.

DARLING RANGE

Once the wild stamping ground of Moondyne Joe and dozens of other bushrangers, the Darling today is Perth's favorite excursion goal (take bus no. 297 or 302 from Hay Street). With several small townships nestling in the hills, the area has breathtaking panoramas and—in spring—immense carpets of wildflowers. One of the villages, **Kalamunda,** has a Folk Museum with early steam trains and historic photos. Those sitting on the left side of the bus get the best views. **Yanchep Park,** a 6,000-acre bushland reserve 34 miles north of Perth, offers wildlife, boating, and swimming, and also some spectacular caves in the limestone cliffs rising 270 feet above Loch McNess. **Crystal Cave** contains an enchanting grotto with an underground stream that reflects the images of stalactites and stalagmites in its crystal-clear water.

ROCKINGHAM & MANDURAH

These two pretty, tranquil resort towns lie some 40 miles down the coast from Perth (the bus ride from Perth takes about an hour). Exactly midway between the towns is the **Marapana Wildlife World** (tel. 537-1404). A spread of bushland, sprinkled with picnic areas, where deer, kangaroos, and wombats roam freely, this is one of the few places where you can feed a couple of deer and several kangaroos in unison. The admission of $A5 for adults and $A2.50 for children includes a bag of feed. Open daily 10am to 5pm.

Mandura also has the **Rosella Bird Park** (tel. 535-2104), which is inhabited by swarms of small, brightly colored Rosella parrots. In South Mandurah there's the **Castle Fun Park** (tel. 581-3875), with mini-go-karts, miniature golf, and fairly gentle amusement rides.

ORGANIZED TOURS

Pinnacle Travel Centre, at the corner of Hay and Irwin streets (tel. 325-9455), organizes a day tour to one of the most spectacular—and least known—natural wonders of Australia. This is **Wave Rock,** a solid-granite formation that looks like a titanic wave breaking over the flat countryside, dwarfing the tiny humans standing at its base. Wave Rock is perhaps even more awesome to behold than the much-publicized Ayers Rock. Coaches depart 8am Tuesday through Thursday and on Saturday, returning at 8pm. You get a picnic lunch at Wave Rock and also view other rock formations—the aptly named Hippo's Yawn and The Humps.

One of the nicest ways of seeing the city and environs is by water. There are several economy-priced cruises operated by **Transperth,** Barrack Street Jetty No. 1 (tel. 231-1222). Every Friday morning a ferry cruises to the port of Fremantle and back, departing at 9:15am. Adults pay $A9.60, children $A4.80.

On Thursday it's **Million Dollar Views,** a leisurely float past the sumptuous mansions along the banks of the Swan River known as Millionaires' Row—the costliest stretch of real estate in town. The ferry leaves at 9:30am and tickets cost $A4.80. On Monday and Tuesday there are ferry trips to **Tranby House.** This is a beautifully restored Western Australian heritage home, built on the banks of the Swan in 1839. The boat leaves at 2pm and the trip costs $A12 for adults, half for children.

The **M.V. *Captain Cook,*** No. 2 Pier, Barrack Street (tel. 325-3341), offers a scenic harbor cruise daily, chugging downriver, then through **Fremantle Harbour** and into the **Fishing Harbour,** where the America's Cup yachts prepared for the great race. After the return at 4:45pm, a wine tasting takes place at the Cook's private cellar. The cruise costs $A20 for adults, $A12 for children.

Australian Pacific Tours, 29 Pier St. (tel. 221-4000), has a variety of half-day tours through and around Perth. One includes the city highlights and country hills; takes in Lake Monger, the watershed where the unique black swans of Westralia abound; and goes out to the restored pioneer village of Armadale and on to the crest of the Darling Range. Tours leave daily at 1pm and return in the evening. The tour costs $A27.50 for adults, $A14 for children.

6. SAVVY SHOPPING

THE SHOPPING SCENE

ARCADES Shopping is an undiluted delight in this city of arcades. Along the **Hay Street promenade** you can rest your legs on seats beneath umbrella shades amid little potted trees, undisturbed by traffic. Within ambling distance lie the shopping walkways of **Plaza Arcade, City Arcade, Piccadilly Arcade, Terrace Arcade,** and **London Court**—each with a distinct (sometimes contrasting) style, each filled with elegant, quaint, intimate, or brash little stores. After a shopping tour of Perth you'll find it hard to understand why more cities don't follow suit. (Well, it does mean confining His Sacred Majesty the Automobile to underground dungeons or forcing him—horrors—to make a detour so that people on two legs can enjoy walking.)

STREET MARKETS The Perth area has more street markets than any other Australian city. The most famous one is in **Fremantle,** but at least half a dozen others have sprung up in suburban locales since retail stall markets reappeared on the scene in 1975. *Re*appeared is correct, because street markets operated throughout Australia back in the colonial days before they were driven off by chain stores and myopic municipal regulations.

The suburb of **Subiaco** (take bus no. 3, 4, 6, or 209) boasts two outstanding markets. The one on **Station Street,** with a railroad background, has 130 stalls, a garden courtyard, and a dining area surrounded by rows of international food booths (open Saturday and Sunday from 9am to 5pm). The second is inside the handsome **Subiaco Pavilion,** at the corner of Rokeby and Roberts roads, an erstwhile warehouse, converted and beautified. The market comprises a large food hall, selling cosmopolitan goodies and some 60 specialty stalls specializing in—well, almost anything that you can legally sell (open Thursday and Friday from 10am to 9pm).

DUTY-FREE SHOPS At several duty-free shops you can take advantage of your tourist status to pick up bargains for later use. The **Downtown** is in Wanamba Arcade, Hay Street; the **Compass** is at 237 Murray Street Mall (tel. 321-1433).

BEST BUYS

AUSTRALIAN SPECIALTIES

ABORIGINAL ARTS, Markalinga House, 251 St. George's Terrace.
This is the authorized marketing outlet for authentic Aboriginal artwork, and it operates on behalf of the craftspeople of Western Australia. The items on sale span the entire range of artistic expression: painting, carving, incising, and fiber work.

THE OPAL CENTRE, Shops 1–5, St. Martin's Arcade (off London Court). Tel. 325-8588.
A combination retailer and gem museum, the center lets you step into the lifelike replica of a working opal mine (though this one is air-conditioned). The very knowledgeable staff explains the different qualities of various opal species, between the black opal found in Lightning Ridge and the light opal from Coober Pedy. Yes, you can also buy them—from opal stickpins costing $A7 to gems a thousand times that amount and more.

CONTEMPO, Murray Mews, 329 Murray St. Tel. 322-2306.
This store concentrates on locally crafted souvenirs, such as Jarrah and Mallee made into vases, bowls, and lamps, as well as coffee tables, wall clocks, and unusual chairs produced by Westralian artisans.

AUSSIE THINGS, Shop 65A, Wesley Arcade, corner of William and Hay Sts. Tel. 321-8984.
Aussie Things runs the souvenir gamut from teaspoons to T-shirts.

CITY ARCADE SOUVENIRS, Shop H3, City Arcade. Tel. 321-4586.
Toy kangaroos and koalas, bush hats, posters, tea towels, and scores of other items are here to remind you of where you've been when you're no longer there.

7. SPORTS & RECREATION

Blessed with an ideal year-round climate, Perth can be said to have achieved saturation point in sports facilities. One of them is the **Superdrome,** Stephenson Avenue, Mount Claremont (tel. 441-8222), which ranks among the world's most sophisticated indoor swimming, diving, gymnastic, and athletic venues.

GOLF Perth has an abundance of golf courses, some situated in nature parks where players may find themselves inquisitively watched by stray kangaroos or emus. The latter can be a nuisance because they occasionally snatch—and swallow—golf balls. It's no use chasing them because they can outrun any golf buggy ever built.

Collier Park Golf Course, Hayman Road, Como (tel. 450-6488), is located only a few minutes from downtown and is possibly Perth's most popular public course, so it's fairly heavily booked. You can rent clubs as well as motorized carts and buggies. Greens fees range from $A7 to $A8 for nine holes, depending on the day of the week. Another course is a **Burswood Park,** Burswood Resort Casino Complex, Great Eastern Highway, Riverdale (tel. 362-7576). Call for reservations and fee information.

WINDSURFING & BOATING Watersports, either in the Indian Ocean or on the Swan River, are probably the most popular of the participating kind. You can rent windsurfers at $A11 per hour from **Pelican Point Windsurfing Hire,** Hackett Drive, Crawley (tel. 915-136). Canoes are available at **Carry On Camping Hire,** 129 Burswood Rd., Victoria Park (tel. 362-4455). A two-seater canoe rents for $A20.

Catamaraning on the Swan River costs $A14 per hour from **Funcat Hire,** Coode Street, South Perth (tel. 018/927-971). Full-fledged yachts come rather more expensive, costing from $A50 for up to four people at **Advance Yacht Charter,** Nedlands Jetty, Nedlands (tel. 317-1354).

8. EVENING ENTERTAINMENT

Perth is a surprise package, and that includes its nightlife, which is as varied and jumping as it is unexpected. The outstanding development in the city's impressive nightlife is the blossoming of a concentrated entertainment region in Northbridge (across the railroad overpass) along William Street and the adjoining James and Lake streets. This has become a glittering ribbon of bars, clubs, cafés, restaurants, and strip shows—thronged with pedestrians at all hours—where you can stroll along and drop in on whatever appeals to you.

Check *This Week in Perth* or the "Revue" section of the *West Australian* for a listing of current offerings.

THE PERFORMING ARTS

THEATER COMPANIES

There's a very active live-theater movement, both amateur and professional, with prices generally cheaper than those in the eastern capitals. The **Playhouse,** 3 Pier St. (tel. 325-3500), puts on a full range of professional theater, from musicals to the classics. The **Hole in the Wall Theatre,** 180 Hamersley Rd., Subiaco (tel. 381-2733), goes in for more avant-garde and unusual—at least 50% Australian—material. **Her Majesty's,** Hay Street (tel. 322-2929), gets the tried-and-proved successes. The **Old Mill,** Mends Street, South Perth (tel.), puts on amateur rep in charming surroundings. There are half a dozen more companies, and you can find their programs in the newspapers.

MAJOR CONCERT HALLS & ALL-PURPOSE AUDITORIUMS

Perth has two main auditoriums for musical presentations—in the broadest sense of the word. The **Concert Hall,** 5 St. George's Terrace (tel. 484-1133), presents international ballet companies and musicians, all the way from pop to classical. The **Entertainment Centre,** Wellington Street (tel. 322-4766), is a vast and lavishly modern air-conditioned complex, seating 8,000, where you can see the cream of visiting celebrities and listen to some of the finest concerts performed in the country. It also has a bar.

DINNER THEATER

Perth has quite a collection of dinner theaters, with offerings much the same and tabs slightly lower than those in other capitals.

DIRTY DICK'S ELIZABETHAN ROOMS, 194 Cambridge St., Wembley. Tel. 381-9577.

This is the most elaborate dinner theater in Perth. You get an Elizabethan banquet handed out by buxom, comely serving wenches; presided over by a king and queen; and kept lively by court jesters, jugglers, and musicians. There is also an "all you can eat or your money back" guarantee.

Prices: $A26–$A32 per glutton, depending on the night. Libations extra.

Open: Daily, call for show times. Bookings essential.

CIVIC, 380 Beaufort St. Tel. 328-1455.

The Civic has name entertainers and a bevy of chorus belles, a three-course meal, a 2½-hour show, and dancing to follow, with drinks at bar prices.

Prices: $A28.95 weeknights, $A31.95 weekends.

Open: Daily, call for show times.

THE CLUB & MUSIC SCENE

SHERATON-PERTH HOTEL, 207 Adelaide Terrace. Tel. 325-0501.

This hotel has a dual attraction: a lobby that can pass as a visual feast and an adjoining vibrant disco. The lobby is possibly the most grandiose example of interior decorating in the southern hemisphere—a subtly perfect blending of sumptuousness and functionalism that's simultaneously palatial and supremely comfortable, like the antechamber of a middling oil king. The foyer contains, among other delights, the smartest cocktail bar in town—perhaps in the country. The **Clouds Disco** features a very smooth deejay, elegant decor, and good vibes.

Admission: Free Wed–Thurs.

Open: Wed–Sat until 3:30am.

PINOCCHIO'S, 393 Murray St. Tel. 481-1156.

The largest of the local disco palaces, Pinocchio's is a high-volume, garishly decorated gyration grove that features imported talent along with native fare.

Admission: $A8.

Open: Daily 8pm–3:30am.

THE SITE, 434 William St., Northbridge. Tel. 328-3581.

The Site is the prime strip joint of Perth. Apart from the actual bare-skin performers, the place features "See Thru Waitresses" on Tuesday to Saturday from 9pm to 3:30am. There's also an excellent dance floor for use between the shows.

GOBBLES, 613 Wellington St. Tel. 322-1221.

Gobbles has been described as the local Hard Rock Café and it blasts out the appropriate entertainment.

Admission: Free until 10pm, $A5–$A8 after.

Open: Daily until 3am.

CLUB RUMOURS, 418 Murray St. Tel. 321-6887.

Club Rumours features a changing lineup of rock groups.

Admission: Free–$A10.

Open: Fri–Sat 8pm–6am.

MILLIGAN'S PIANO BAR, corner of James and Milligan Sts., Northbridge. Tel. 328-1488.

Milligan's is large, brassy, and atmospheric.

Admission: $6.

JULES, 104 Murray St. Tel. 325-3638.

A youth-oriented basement club, flickering with lighting effects, Jules offers music that ranges from alternative to funk.

Admission: $A5–$A8.

Open: Wed–Sun 9pm–2am.

SHAFTOS, 397 Murray St. Tel. 321-3258.

Shaftos is a combined bar with a giant video screen and pool tables in the upstairs gallery and a disco in the rear. The lighting effects in the latter are blinding, the overall sound effects deafening; the establishment, one of the most popular in Perth, is usually packed to the rafters.

Admission: Free.

Open: Mon–Sat until midnight.

HAVANA, 69 Lake St., Northbridge. Tel. 328-1065.

This is a place for hip under-30s; no dress code to speak of but whatever you wear has gotta reek attitude. The Havana is a nicely laid-back bar/nightclub, where you can drink, play pool, or hit the dance floor. Definitely for socializing, especially on weekends.

Admission: Free Mon–Thurs, $A6 Fri–Sat from 9pm.

Open: Daily 9pm–3am.

JAMES STREET NIGHTCLUB, 139 James St., Northbridge. Tel. 328-7447.

A happily laid-back nightspot catering to a mainstream crowd with mainstream music and an excellent dance floor, the nightclub also has two private VIP areas more svelte and discreet than the general stamping ground.

Admission: $A8, but with your overseas passport and a copy of this book you get a discount.

Open: Wed 9pm–5am, Fri–Sat 9pm–6am, Sun 8pm–midnight.

THE PUB SCENE

THE MOON & SIXPENCE, 300 Murray St. Tel. 481-1000.

A traditional English country pub in the heart of downtown, complete with shingle roof and oaken cross-beams, it has a large array of British ales that go well with the pub grub on the menu. Musical entertainment is featured most nights.

Open: Daily 11am–midnight.

THE BRASS MONKEY, corner of James and William Sts., Northbridge. Tel. 227-9596.

A tastefully restored and refurbished tavern and brasserie with a pleasantly relaxed atmosphere, it has a charming outdoor beer garden and bars upstairs and down.

Open: Daily 11am–midnight.

SASSELLA'S TAVERN, City Arcade, upper Hay Street Level. Tel. 322-4001.

Up a winding flight of stairs, Sassella's has an agreeably Olde English decor—but without the obligatory drafts of the real thing—including cellar walls, lantern light, horse brasses, and huge Brueghel painting for decor. This is one of Perth's most popular mingling spots.

Open: Daily 10am–11pm.

NOVAKS ALEHOUSE, corner of Lake and James Sts., Northbridge.

Novaks Alehouse is a trendy little watering hole, rather chic but disguised as a neighborhood pub, with mellow vibes aided by nightly live entertainment.

Open: Daily 10am–midnight.

A CASINO

BURSWOOD CASINO, Great Eastern Hwy., Victoria Park. Tel. 362-7777.

It's hard for me to decide where to put this one—it could pass as either daytime or nocturnal entertainment. It forms part of a resort area on a human-created island a few minutes from downtown Perth. The resort also contains a luxury hotel, a superdome indoor sports complex, a very svelte shopping mall, bars, restaurants, golf courses, and cabarets—quite a creation on what used to be a municipal rubbish dump. The gambling facilities include roulette, baccarat, blackjack, craps, and two-up. This, incidentally, is the only *legal* gambling locale in Western Australia, and the continent's biggest casino.

Open: 24 hrs.

9. EASY EXCURSIONS: WESTERN AUSTRALIA

Gigantic is the only word that describes Westralia, the biggest, emptiest state of the Commonwealth. With its million square miles, the state could comfortably engulf all of Western Europe or swallow up Texas four times over. It boasts about three quarters of a square mile of elbow room for every inhabitant—if they were evenly spread. Actually, with about 1.2 million living in the capital of Perth, only some 430,000 are left to sprinkle the enormous remainder.

Westralia has a distinct air of separateness, of thriving apart from the other states: It looks north toward Asia rather than eastward. As the jet flies, it's as far from Perth to Sydney as to Singapore and Indonesia. Between Western Australia and the country's main population centers stretches the dizzying vastness of the **Nullarbor Plain,** flat as a kitchen floor and crossed by the longest straight railroad track on earth.

And "thrive" is what Westralia does. As one of the globe's mineral treasure chests it harbors, among other riches, enough iron ore to supply humankind's industrial needs single-handedly. The west is an immense boom territory, wide open and barely tapped, sprawling from the tropical Timor Sea in the north to the temperate Southern Ocean more than 1,500 miles away.

Western Australia lies off the usual tourist routes but offers some of the most grandiose sights in the hemisphere to those who tackle the distances involved. It also grants the rare thrill of seeing Tomorrowland, of viewing an awakening young titan flexing mammoth muscles.

The climate of the state spans the spectrum from heavenly to hellish. Perth enjoys the balmiest Mediterranean weather on the continent; Marble Bar, on the other hand, is the hottest town in Australia, sizzling in an average daily temperature of 96°F!

The sights beckoning in Westralia cover as wide a range as the climate—from wildflower fields stretching into infinity to mysterious cave paintings allegedly daubed by Aboriginal tribal "spirits" 2,000 years ago.

NEW NORCIA

On our blitz tour of the highlights we'll start with New Norcia. A slice of Spain—cool, ancient, and secluded—rising on the Victoria Plains 82 miles north of Perth, this is perhaps the most unexpected attraction you'll find in Australia; you feel like rubbing your eyes to make sure it's really there. Nova Norcia **monastery** was founded by Spanish Benedictine monks, driven from their homeland in 1846, and created in the exact image of the medieval monasteries they had inhabited in Compostela.

The purpose of the monastery is the same today as it was then—to care for the local Aborigines. But today you'll find it difficult to believe the grinding poverty and backbreaking struggles of the early monks that went into the making of this palm-shaded oasis. The Benedictine fathers proudly show you around, beaming over the orphanage, the gardens and orchards, the library with its medieval manuscripts, and the art gallery boasting some rare religious paintings.

Western Australian Government Railways (WAGR) buses leave Perth every weekday morning for the 2-hour trip on Route 95 to New Norcia and return the same afternoon.

BUNBURY

Western Australia's second city lies roughly 120 miles south of Perth on the coast. You get there either by train (two hours from Perth Central Railway Station for $A17) or by bus (coaches depart Wellington Street Bus Station, the trip costing $A15.50).

Bunbury is a thriving town, but its special tourist attraction romps in **Koombana Bay,** which you reach by a bridge from the city center. There you can meet and mingle with the famous tame/wild **Bunbury dolphins.** They are tame because they nonchalantly interact with people—swimming beside and under them and allowing themselves to be touched, but they're wild insofar as they live in the bay, not in an aquarium, and return to open water when they tire of human company.

This amazing development began back in the 1960s, when Mrs. Evelyn Smith started feeding bottlenose dolphins from a small jetty behind her home. She rang the dinner bell by hitting the water with a rake—and her guests came a-swimming. After her death the process was continued by the Bunbury Dolphin Trust, with dolphin specialist Steve Honnor identifying the animals and swimming among them. The general public was let in on the game in 1990. For visitors this offered the chance of having their picture taken with an ominous triangular dorsal fin slicing the water a few inches away from their legs.

GOLD & GHOSTS

In the desert east of Perth lie the once fabulous Westralian goldfields. During the great 1890s gold rush, some 200,000 prospectors tried their luck there, battling nature and one another for the yellow metal. The town of **Kalgoorlie** sprang up almost overnight, boasting two stock exchanges, seven newspapers, and the swinging, rip-roaring "Golden Mile"—reputedly the richest square mile of real estate in history. The glory lasted until the gold dwindled. Kalgoorlie still mines gold—you can see the 4,000-foot-deep mine shafts in action—however, no longer in legendary quantities. The town has calmed down considerably, but the unique atmosphere of a desert mining community remains strong; the "smell of gold" still lingers.

Twenty-six miles southwest stands haunted **Coolgardie,** once the Queen of the Goldfields, now Australia's most famous ghost town. Of the 15,000 Diggers who brawled in the city's 29 hotels and bars, not a soul remains. But the old covered wagons still stand on the main street, and the Goldfields Exhibition in Bayley Street preserves the relics of the town's wild past. The greatest chunk of gold dug out here weighed 2,000 ounces! And all around the area, now studded with motels and caravan parks, there are the glittering remnants of wealth—flecks of gold and gemstones. These gemstones find their way into the oddest places. A Coolgardie garage has tiled walls sprinkled with them, turning the place into a kind of Aladdin's Cave when the light strikes them.

You can tour the goldfields by air, rail, or coach. For details, call the W.A. Tourist Centre (tel. 483-1111).

WILDFLOWER TOURS

Westralia's wildflowers have to be seen to be believed: They look like multicolored oceans rolling to the horizon in exquisite shades of light blue, deep azure, bright scarlet, and golden orange. From August to October some 7,000 native species of blossoms carpet immense areas of the southwest. Most of these plants are unique, found nowhere else on earth, a phenomenon due to Western Australia's long isolation that allowed hundreds of primeval forms to survive and bloom every year in an unchanged habitat.

The most celebrated wildflower fields stretch around Albany on the southern coast, and Geraldton, about 300 miles north of Perth. You can choose one of several special wildflower tours traveling from Perth during the 3-month blossom season. Both **Pioneer,** 26 St. George's Terrace, Perth (tel. 478-1122), and **Parlorcars** use air-conditioned coaches with wide windows and reclining seats.

THE MIGHTY KIMBERLEY

Rising from the northern corner of Western Australia is the colossal Kimberley Plateau—a region larger than California but housing only 6,000 people. All the Kimberley is spectacular, and some parts are stunning. At Wolf Creek there's a meteorite crater measuring 2,800 feet in diameter; the Ord River Scheme culminates in

WESTERN AUSTRALIA

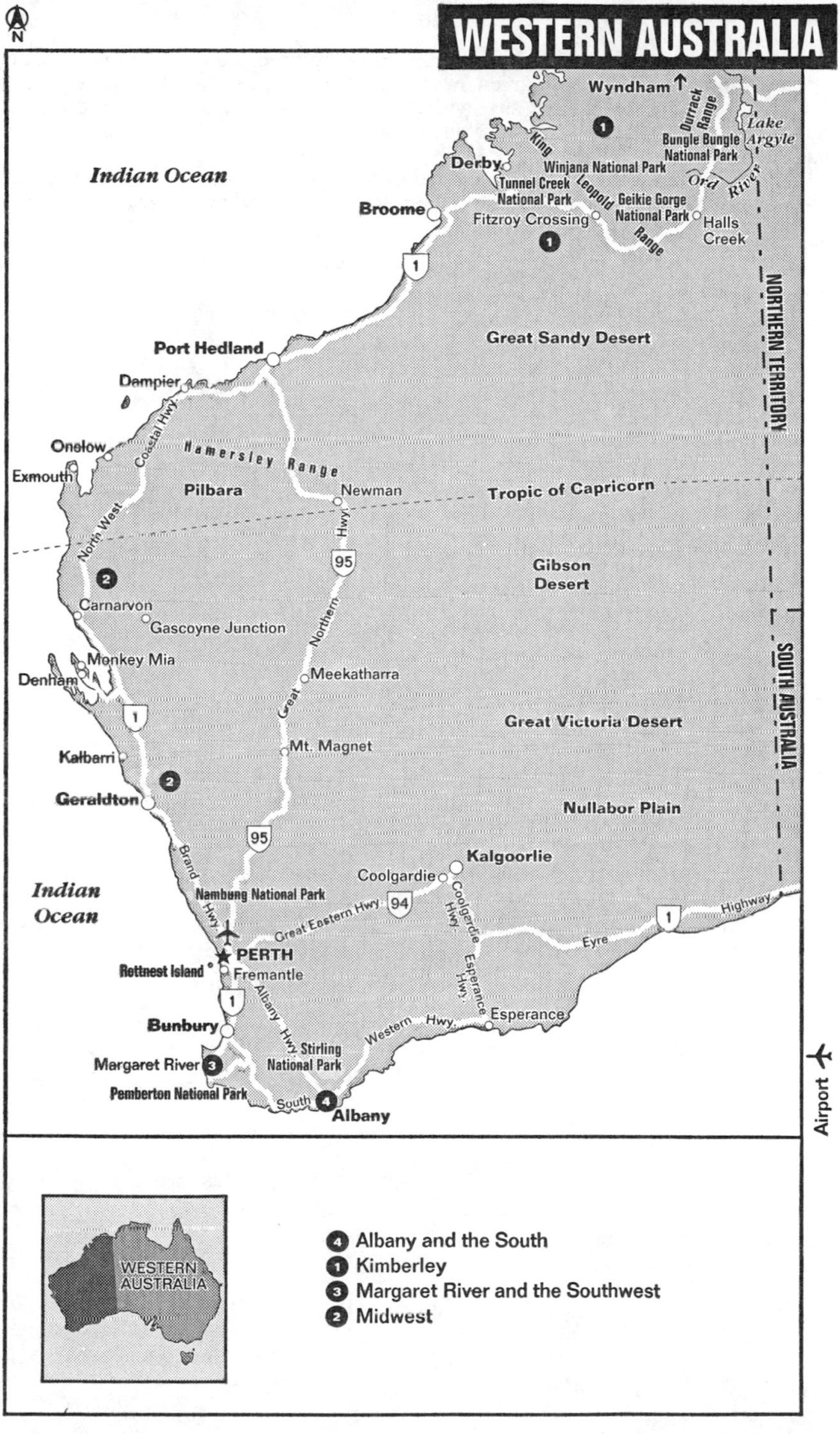

Indian Ocean
Wyndham
Durrack Range
Lake Argyle
Bungle Bungle National Park
King
Derby
Winjana National Park
Tunnel Creek National Park
Leopold Range
Geikie Gorge National Park
Ord River
Broome
Fitzroy Crossing
Halls Creek
1
Great Sandy Desert
NORTHERN TERRITORY
Port Hedland
Dampier
Coastal Hwy
Onslow
Exmouth
Hamersley Range
Pilbara
Newman
Tropic of Capricorn
North West
Hwy
95
Gibson Desert
2
Carnarvon
Gascoyne Junction
Great Northern
Monkey Mia
Denham
Meekatharra
SOUTH AUSTRALIA
Great Victoria Desert
Kalbarri
Mt. Magnet
Geraldton
Nullabor Plain
Brand Hwy
Kalgoorlie
Coolgardie
Indian Ocean
Nambung National Park
Great Eastern Hwy
94
Coolgardie Hwy
Highway
Eyre
PERTH
Rottnest Island
Fremantle
Albany Hwy
Esperance Hwy
Esperance
Bunbury
Western Hwy
Stirling National Park
Margaret River
3
Pemberton National Park
South
4
Albany

Airport

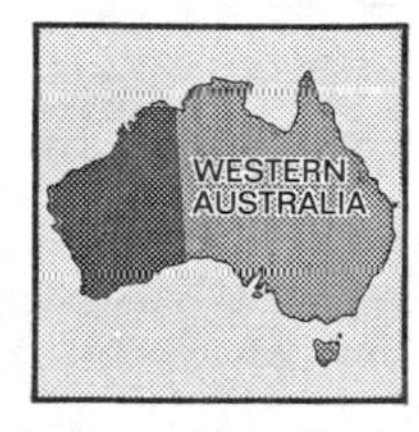

- 4 Albany and the South
- 1 Kimberley
- 3 Margaret River and the Southwest
- 2 Midwest

6760

Australia's largest lake, a miniature human-made ocean of 286 square miles; in the gorge country at Geikie, the green Fitzroy River carves its way through towering limestone cliffs, the warm water alive with stingrays, sharks, and freshwater crocodiles; and at Windjana the cliff caves were once used as Aboriginal burial grounds and are still decorated with wonderful primitive cave paintings.

Although the Kimberley has developed into a popular tourist region, it's too vast to become crowded. MacRobertson-Miller Airlines flies regular jet services up from Perth, doing the hop in less than four hours.

CHAPTER 9

CANBERRA — AUSTRALIA'S CAPITAL

- **WHAT'S SPECIAL ABOUT CANBERRA**
1. **ORIENTATION**
2. **GETTING AROUND**
3. **WHERE TO STAY**
- **FROMMER'S COOL FOR KIDS: HOTELS**
4. **WHERE TO EAT**
- **FROMMER'S COOL FOR KIDS: RESTAURANTS**
5. **ATTRACTIONS**
- **DID YOU KNOW . . . ?**
6. **SAVVY SHOPPING**
7. **SPORTS & RECREATION**
8. **EVENING ENTERTAINMENT**
9. **EASY EXCURSIONS TO SNOWY MOUNTAINS HYDROELECTRIC SCHEME & COOMA**

Canberra is an "artificial" city, an attribute that it shares with some other capitals, such as Washington, D.C.; Brasília; and Ankara. Like them, it was designed with the express purpose of housing a central government under the best possible conditions. Unlike the others, however, Canberra succeeded completely in that aim.

Canberra is a "model capital" in every conceivable respect: a city with no slums, no ugly industrial areas, and no traffic congestion but with clean air, minimal crime, beautiful surroundings, good public transportation, and the nation's two largest cities within easy driving distance. Its layout is an urban planner's dream come true (literally), and all its government departments are comfortably accessible for foot sloggers as well as motorists.

In the past 15 years, Canberra has even overcome its sole major drawback—a paralyzing dullness, enlivened only by periodic political brawls. In the early 1950s a famous local journalist cracked, "You can pronounce Canberra the same way you yawn." He certainly wouldn't say this today. Now the place is sparking on all plugs, generously helped by the fact that the Capital Territory has unlimited licensing laws, with every watering hole open for business as long as it chooses.

Yet Canberra had a remarkably slow start. Its site wasn't even selected until 1908 (diplomatically midway between archrivals Sydney and Melbourne), and not until 1927 did Parliament actually convene there. For the next 30 years the capital developed with the tempo of a drowsy snail. The entire grandiose experiment seemed stillborn, throttled by bickering politicians, financial crises, and world wars. Someone compared Canberra's image to its coat of arms: Supposedly representing two graceful swans supporting a crowned fortress, it actually looks like two angry ducks kicking down a toy castle.

But suddenly, in the late 1960s, the city took off like a rocket. The capital heaved, churned, vibrated, and began to expand at a positively dazzling rate. Today Canberra has a population of some 250,000, and it is the fastest-growing city in the

WHAT'S SPECIAL ABOUT CANBERRA

Architectural Highlights
- ☐ Parliament House, a majestic new edifice that replaced the old "temporary" one.
- ☐ National Library of Australia, in Greek Parthenon style, a site of subtle beauty as well as learning.
- ☐ Australian War Memorial, a splendid, dignified shrine for the dead of two world wars.
- ☐ Foreign embassies, notably those of Indonesia and the United States.

Museums
- ☐ Australian National Gallery, with a fine collection of overseas and native artworks.
- ☐ Royal Australian Mint, where you can see the printing and an excellent exhibit.
- ☐ National Film and Sound Archive, tracing the development of Australia's film industry from the 1890s to the present.
- ☐ National Science and Technology Centre, one of the finest technological displays on the continent.

Parks/Gardens
- ☐ Commonwealth Park, with pools, playgrounds, sculptures, a music bowl, and the world's tallest flagpole.
- ☐ Botanic Gardens, with rain-forest gullies, masses of birds, and sheltered paths among flowering plants.
- ☐ Canberra Nature Park, with 21 bushland areas connected by wildlife corridors.

Festivals/Events
- ☐ Balloon Festival, with armadas of hot-air balloons floating over the capital every March.
- ☐ Canberra Festival, celebrating the founding of the city on March 12, with free concerts, street dances, and parades.
- ☐ Floriade, the Spring Festival, when Canberra becomes one huge flower garden from September to October.

For the Kids
- ☐ Bicycle Museum, a collection of antique velocipedes and rows of video space machines.
- ☐ Canberra Maze, a quiz within a maze, providing genuine challenge and a lot of fun.
- ☐ Cockington Green, a miniature Olde English village, handcrafted down to the smallest detail.

Shopping
- ☐ Monaro Mall, Garema Place, and Petrie Plaza, some of the pedestrian malls and complexes that shelter you from rain and sun and relieve you of parking worries.

After Dark
- ☐ The Theatre Centre, a superb performing-arts complex, staging everything from Shakespeare to pop concerts.

Commonwealth. Yet so perfect was the master plan under which it was conceived that the immense population increase has flowed smoothly into prepared channels, causing no chaos, social problems, congestion, or even clashing architectural designs. Canberra is full of avant-garde buildings and has the highest ratio of cars to people in the country. But all its structures blend beautifully into the city pattern and the countryside around. And the cars neither clog the roads nor foul the atmosphere. Thanks to a wonderfully ingenious network of freeways, underpasses, and parking areas, they hardly intrude at all.

As with the Sydney Opera House, the design of the national capital was set up as an international competition. The winner was a Chicago landscape architect and former associate of the great Frank Lloyd Wright named Walter Burley Griffin. He came to Canberra in 1913 and nearly went out of his mind with frustration at the slow growth of his brainchild. But today the city mirrors his dream: classical public buildings overlooking a huge artificial lake and a core of central circles with broad tree-lined avenues radiating out to landscaped garden suburbs.

The balance between parklands and built-up areas is weighted in favor of greenery. From the air Canberra looks like a vast park sprinkled with patches of city. Wherever you go you're in sight of trees and grass. Native birds and animals live and breed in the vicinity of the city's landmarks, and the real bush lies only a few minutes' drive away. Canberra has no actual shopping streets but a pattern of shopping centers, malls, arcades, and complexes—free of traffic and ablaze with colorful shrubs and flowers. Instead of allowing real-estate developers to build up the core of the metropolis at the expense of open space, Canberra opted for satellite cities farther out, linked with the center by the finest freeway system in Australia.

The capital is unique among large Australian cities by lying 90 miles inland at 1,900 feet above sea level and having no port. But it has its own private lake, right at the core, created artificially strictly for decoration and entertainment. It bears the name of the American who didn't live long enough to see his drawing-board infant grow up—Lake Burley Griffin.

No such memorial exists for the other American who helped to birth Canberra, a highly controversial character named King O'Malley. A former Kansas realtor, O'Malley took advantage of tax concessions granted to religious bodies by founding his own—the "Waterlily Rock-bound Church of the Redskin Temple in the Chickasaw Nation." In Australia he described himself as a bishop of the church, and in order to run for Parliament he claimed to be Canadian born, therefore a British citizen. O'Malley not only won a seat but also became Australia's minister for home affairs at the time of Canberra's foundation. A rabid teetotaller, he pushed through an ordinance prohibiting the sale of alcoholic drinks in the Capital Territory. O'Malley's handiwork lingered long after he left the scene, keeping Canberra in a state of social retardation. On weekends half the population fled their dry kindergarten and made for Queanbeyan, across the New South Wales border, to get a drink. Queanbeyan prospered while Canberra parched. Gossip had it that this was O'Malley's revenge on the wicked journalists who had voiced doubts about his birthplace.

The shades of "Bishop" O'Malley have been happily banished. Canberra now ranks among the best eating *and* drinking spots in the country. And because the inhabitants are predominantly young, single, and prosperous, the place radiates *joie de vivre* to a degree rarely found among civil-service cities.

Finally, unlike most Australian cities, Canberra has distinct seasons: gold and red autumn leaves, blossoming spring flowers, broiling dry summers, and genuinely icy winters with occasional snow flurries.

1. ORIENTATION

ARRIVING

BY PLANE Although one of the busiest in the nation, **Canberra Airport** is rather small and unimpressive—you might say cozy. Located four miles east of the city, it's easy to get to, easy to park in, and impossible to get lost in. There are car-rental desks, a cocktail bar, and a bistro but no banking facilities and no tourist information counter. It does have a weighing machine, though, and is currently being upgraded. A cab ride to town costs $A10.

By Qantas or Ansett it's a 30-minute hop from Sydney at $A143, an hour from Melbourne at $A189.

BY TRAIN By train the journey costs $A30 from Sydney; but the Melbourne choo-choo goes only to Yass, so you have to take a bus the rest of the way.

BY BUS The bus trip from Sydney (Pioneer or Greyhound) takes 4¼ hours and costs $A26. From Melbourne it's $A51.

BY CAR Canberra lies within a 934-square-mile area known as the **Australian**

Capital Territory (ACT). The city is 150 miles southwest of Sydney, 300 miles northeast of Melbourne, and has good traffic connections with both.

TOURIST INFORMATION

The **Australian Capital Territory Tourism Commission Information Booth,** in the Jolimont Centre, Northbourne Avenue, Canberra, ACT 2601 (tel. 274-3838), is open during business hours every day. It provides information, brochures, and a free booking service for accommodations and tours. The **Visitor Information Centre,** Northbourne Avenue, Dickson, is open daily from 8:30am to 5pm. For current activities in town consult *This Week in Canberra,* free from hotels and the tourism commission. The morning *Canberra Times* gives the best roundup of evening doings. For the addresses and phone numbers of foreign embassies, call the tourism commission.

CITY LAYOUT

The core of Canberra is sliced into two roughly equal portions by **Lake Burley Griffin,** and the two halves are connected by the **Commonwealth Avenue** and **Kings Avenue bridges.** Right beside the Commonwealth Avenue Bridge is an ideal orientation landmark: the **Captain Cook Memorial water jet,** which flings six tons of water 450 feet into the air and can be spotted for miles. (On windy days it can also be *felt* from an amazing distance.)

Each of the two portions of the city has its own central core from which all the important avenues of the area radiate. In the northern half this is **City Hill,** in the southern it's **Capital Hill.** The northern part contains the facilities of city life: shops, restaurants, post office, hotels, university, churches, and theaters. The southern half is the political-and-administrative territory, housing Parliament, the prime minister's residence, foreign embassies, the governor-general's mansion, and so on. All around these central portions lie the suburbs and satellite towns, interspersed with enormous parks and recreation grounds. Farther out to the east lies **Canberra Airport;** to the west and south are **Kosciusko National Park** and the **Snowy Mountains;** and to the northeast are **Lake George** and the New South Wales city of **Goulburn.**

Although **Parliament House** is the official center of Canberra, for practical purposes the core is **London Circuit** on the north side, which encloses City Hill and adjoins **Civic Square** and into which run all the main thoroughfares of interest to tourists. The **ACT Tourism Commission Information Booth** is at the corner of London Circuit and West Row, the **Visitor Information Centre** on Northbourne Avenue (see above).

2. GETTING AROUND

Canberra sprawls over an enormous area for its population. Luckily most of the sights, accommodations, eateries, and shops are concentrated in a relatively small space north of the lake. But if you want to play the poker machines, you'll have to cross the New South Wales border into adjacent Queanbeyan (known as "Queen bean"). The one-armed bandits are banned within the Capital Territory.

Apart from sightseeing cruises around the lake, the only transportation in Canberra is by road. **Bus services** are frequent, and the vehicles new and comfortable; fares run to $A1.60. You can get an all-day pass for $A4.60. There is a free service, the Downtowner, in operation around the inner-city shopping areas. For bus information, ask one of the green-uniformed inspectors or call **Action** at 251-6566.

Canberra can also be seen by **bicycle,** but it's advisable to stick to the bike tracks. You can rent a bike at the **YHA Hostel** (see "Where to Stay," below) or at **Mr. Spokes,** Barrine Drive, Acton Park (tel. 257-1188).

For **rental cars,** there is **Thrifty,** Lonsdale Street (tel. 247-7422).

3. WHERE TO STAY

Not only one of Australia's main tourist attractions but its administrative center as well, Canberra is amply supplied with accommodations, although not particularly cheap ones. Budget beds, in fact, are somewhat scarce and becoming more so.

Canberra boasts a real accommodation row—**Northbourne Avenue,** an endless ruler-straight boulevard that runs all the way from the Federal Highway to London Circuit. But the street is so long and the buildings are so generously spaced that you can't talk about lodging houses nestling cheek by jowl—within shouting distance of each other would be a more appropriate term.

If you have difficulties getting a bed, contact the **ACT Tourism Commission,** Northbourne Avenue (tel. 274-3838), and rest assured that they'll find you one. There's also a local specialty called accommodation complexes, places that simultaneously provide motel, caravan, and camping facilities. We'll look at a few toward the end of this section.

DOUBLES FOR LESS THAN $A49

BED & BREAKFASTS

BLUE & WHITE AND SKY BLUE LODGES, 524 and 528 Northbourne Ave., Downer, ACT 2602. Tel. 06/248-0498. Fax 06/248-8277. 18 rms (6 with bath). TV

$ Rates (including breakfast): $A36–$A40 single, $A44–$A65 double. BC, MC, V.

These are double hostelries under one management. The places have breakfast rooms, plus attractive bathrooms with colored tiles. Bedrooms have TVs, refrigerators, and coffee- and tea-making facilities. Guests can arrange free pick ups from the bus depot.

CHELSEA LODGE, 526 Northbourne Ave., Downer, ACT 2601. Tel. 06/248-0655. 12 rms (4 with shower). TV TEL

$ Rates (including full breakfast): $A38 single, $A48 double. BC, MC, V.

Chelsea Lodge is a villalike building with a pleasant veranda and a tiny potted palm. It has a plain little breakfast room (no other meals served). Rooms have built-in wardrobes and electric blankets. The breakfast is exceptionally good.

NORTHBOURNE LODGE, 522 Northbourne Ave., Downer, ACT 2602. Tel. 06/257-2599. 10 rms (3 with bath). TV TEL

$ Rates (including full breakfast): $A38 single, $A46–$A64 double, $A22 per person 4-bed dorm. BC, MC, V.

A charming beige-brick building with colored lights beneath the roof, the Northbourne has coffee- and tea-making equipment, bedside lamps, refrigerator, and a color TV in every room.

VICTOR LODGE, 29 Dawes St., Kingston, ACT 2604. Tel. 06/295-7432. Fax 06/295-7432. 28 rms (none with bath).

$ Rates (including breakfast): $A15 hostel rooms, $A35 single, $A40 double. MC, V.

Standing right next to the Canberra railway station, this is actually a modern guest house. A pleasant, awning-shaded two-story building, the Victor has guest rooms and a dining room that are all comfortably if not lavishly furnished. Lighting arrangements vary according to habitat. There are single, double, hostel-style, and family rooms; the less expensive ones with bunk beds cost $A55. Guests can be picked up at the bus station.

DOUBLES FOR LESS THAN $A61

MACQUARIE, 18 National Circuit, Barton, ACT 2600. Tel. 06/273-2325. 530 rms (none with bath).

$ Rates (including breakfast): $A35 single, $A60 double. AE, BC, MC, V.

The Macquarie, located south of the lake (one of the few hostelries that is), is a modern four-story brick structure, about three miles from the city and adjacent to the National Press Club. The Macquarie offers many amenities: a color TV in the lounge, special billiard and table-tennis rooms, a book-and-magazine kiosk, a cafeteria-style dining room, a bar, and an outdoor barbecue service where you can cook your own meat. The bedrooms are decorated in bright pastels, with colorful rugs, built-in wardrobes, wonderfully handy writing tables, excellent lighting, and hot-and-cold water. There's also a guest laundry with irons.

HOSTELS & DORMS

Australian National University has a vast and varied selection of residential places, but the situation is rather confusing. Some colleges take only students, others accept nonstudents as well; some prefer groups, others don't. The accommodations are excellent and cheap—when you can get them. One of the best is **Toad Hall** (see below), but also try **Bruce Hall** (tel. 06/249-5524), **Ursula College** (tel. 06/248-9055), or **Burgmann College** (tel. 06/247-9811).

TOAD HALL, Kingsley St., Acton, ACT 2601. Tel. 06/249-4722. 16 rms (none with bath). TV TEL

$ Rates: $A14.50 students, $A20 nonstudents. No credit cards.

Toad Hall has single study-bedrooms grouped around lounge, kitchen, and bathroom areas, and the residents cook for themselves. The accommodations are available only during the vacation period from November to February.

YHA HOSTEL, 191 Dryandra St., O'Connor, ACT 2601. Tel. 06/248-9155. Fax 06/249-1731. 28 rms (4 with bath). TV TEL **Bus:** No. 380 leaves every half hour from the city terminal. Take it to Scrivener St., then follow the YHA signs.

$ Rates: $A15 per person senior, $A20 per person double, junior half price. BC, MC, V.

The Canberra YHA Hostel is about 3½ miles from the city. A one-story brick building extending over a second, newer building, the place has a fully equipped communal kitchen, hot showers, a small food store, and bike rentals. YHA members receive discounts for many local attractions, tours, and restaurants.

MOTEL-CARAVAN [R.V.] COMPLEXES

CANBERRA CAROTEL, Federal Hwy., Watson, ACT 2901. Tel. 06/241-1377. Fax 06/241-6674.

FROMMER'S COOL FOR KIDS: HOTELS

Canberra Carotel *(above)* Kids have plenty of romping space here, apart from playground facilities and a swimming pool. For rainy weather there's the recreation room equipped with games.

Canberra Motor Village *(p. 314)* The bushwalking trails of Black Mountain are at its doorstep and it virtually blends into the open country. Inside the village, youngsters have a swimming pool, playgrounds, tennis courts, and table-tennis equipment.

Kythera Motel *(p. 314)* There's a large pool in the rear of the establishment, well away from street traffic.

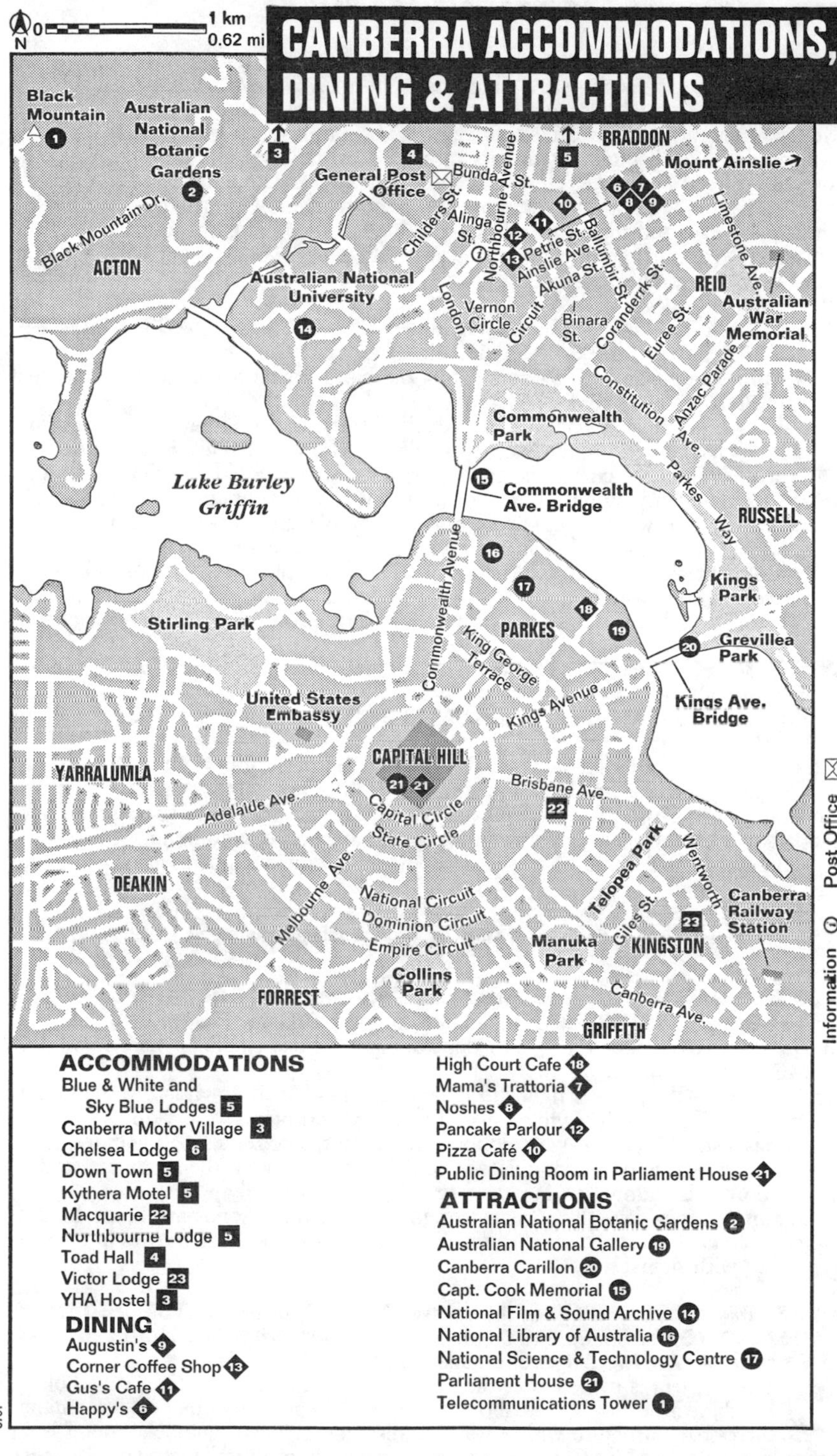
CANBERRA ACCOMMODATIONS, DINING & ATTRACTIONS
N
0
1 km
0.62 mi
Black Mountain
Australian National Botanic Gardens
BRADDON
Mount Ainslie
General Post Office
Bunda St.
Northbourne Avenue
Childers St.
Alinga St.
Petrie St.
Ballumbir St.
Ainslie Ave.
Akuna St.
Limestone Ave.
Black Mountain Dr.
ACTON
Australian National University
London Circuit
Vernon Circle
Binara St.
Coranderrk St.
Euree St.
REID
Australian War Memorial
Constitution Ave.
Anzac Parade
Commonwealth Park
Parkes Way
Lake Burley Griffin
Commonwealth Ave. Bridge
RUSSELL
Kings Park
Commonwealth Avenue
Stirling Park
PARKES
King George Terrace
Grevillea Park
Kings Avenue
Kings Ave. Bridge
United States Embassy
CAPITAL HILL
YARRALUMLA
Brisbane Ave.
Adelaide Ave.
Capital Circle
State Circle
Telopea Park
Wentworth
Melbourne Ave.
DEAKIN
National Circuit
Dominion Circuit
Empire Circuit
Giles St.
Canberra Railway Station
Manuka Park
KINGSTON
Collins Park
FORREST
Canberra Ave.
GRIFFITH
Post Office
Information
ACCOMMODATIONS
Blue & White and Sky Blue Lodges 5
Canberra Motor Village 3
Chelsea Lodge 6
Down Town 5
Kythera Motel 5
Macquarie 22
Northbourne Lodge 5
Toad Hall 4
Victor Lodge 23
YHA Hostel 3
DINING
Augustin's 9
Corner Coffee Shop 13
Gus's Cafe 11
Happy's 6
High Court Cafe 18
Mama's Trattoria 7
Noshes 8
Pancake Parlour 12
Pizza Café 10
Public Dining Room in Parliament House 21
ATTRACTIONS
Australian National Botanic Gardens 2
Australian National Gallery 19
Canberra Carillon 20
Capt. Cook Memorial 15
National Film & Sound Archive 14
National Library of Australia 16
National Science & Technology Centre 17
Parliament House 21
Telecommunications Tower 1
6761

$ Rates: Chalet $A40–$A45 single, $A45–$A95 double; bungalows, $A70–$A95 single or double; $A30–$A55 caravans (4 berths). BC, MC, V.

The Canberra Carotel lies four miles north of the city, just off the highway from Sydney. An unusually versatile complex, it has motel units with private facilities, two-room holiday flat units, stationary caravans, caravan sites, and camping sites. The rows of little red-brick units along a street form a village with a fast-food bar, general store, playground, car wash, swimming pool, and recreation lounge with pool tables. The brick lodges and chalets have both cooking facilities and bathrooms. The on-site (four-berth) caravans come with stoves and refrigerators but do not have bedding. Rates vary according to season.

CANBERRA MOTOR VILLAGE, Kunzea St., O'Connor, ACT 2601. Tel. 06/247-5466. Fax 06/249-6138.

$ Rates: Motel from $A73 single, $A94 double, caravan from $A39 double, tent from $A13 double. AE, BC, MC, V.

Canberra Motor Village lies in a beautiful tree-shaded setting five minutes from the city center on the slopes of Black Mountain. This is a multichoice accommodation complex, meaning that you can pick either a motel unit with an optional kitchen, a mobile home, or a trailer. Whatever your choice, you get a lot of extra facilities thrown in, including tennis courts, playgrounds, table tennis, barbecues, and a swimming pool. The complex includes a restaurant and backs onto the bush-walking trails of the Black Mountain reserve. There are also a shop, a laundry, and excellent transportation connections to Canberra. The tariff structure is fairly complicated and varies according to the season. A free communal kitchen is available.

WHITE IBIS, 1520 Bidges Rd., Sutton, NSW 2620. Tel. 06/230-3433. Fax 062/230-3483.

$ Rates: $A48–$A53 cabin, $A13–$A15 powered caravan site. AE, BC, DC, MC, V.

A tourist village prettily situated just over the state border, about eight miles northeast of downtown off Federal Highway, the White Ibis has cabins, caravan sites, and landscaped campgrounds well removed from traffic noise. There are also a coffee shop, supermarket, laundry, swimming pool, barbecue, and tennis court. The self-contained cabins hold up to seven people and come equipped with TVs, linens, and bathroom.

WORTH THE EXTRA MONEY

DOWN TOWN, 82 Northbourne Ave., Canberra, ACT 2601. Tel. 06/249-1388. Fax 06/247-2523. 65 rms (all with bath). A/C TV TEL

$ Rates: $A70 standard single or double, $A90 deluxe single or double. AE, BC, MC, V.

Aptly named—the place is right in the city center—Down Town is a very modern, functional building with a white-pillared frontage and plenty of parking space. The motel has a small blue-and-white lobby, a restaurant, a coffee shop, a laundry, and a dry-cleaning service on the premises. The difference between the 20 deluxe and 45 standard units is mainly size. Standard rooms are fairly small and furnishings strictly utilitarian, but they have all conveniences, including refrigerators, bathrooms, bedside lights, open hanging space for clothes, clock radios, and in-house movies in case you get bored with sightseeing.

KYTHERA MOTEL, 98 Northbourne Ave., Canberra, ACT 2601. Tel. 06/248-7611. Fax 06/248-0419. 74 rms (all with bath) A/C TV TEL

$ Rates: $A77–$A79 single or double. AE, BC, MC, V.

The Kythera is named after the birthplace of Aphrodite in Greek mythology, but there is nothing Greek about the place. An eminently practical, streamlined three-story structure within walking distance of downtown, the motel has a smart lobby, flanked by a Chinese restaurant on one side, an Italian one on the other.

There is a good-size oval swimming pool in the rear, and the building is air-conditioned. The management also runs a gratis airport shuttle service for guests.

The decor of the units is cream colored, and the rooms are bright but have rather weak lighting arrangements. Furnishings include plain metal tables and chairs, comfortable couches, and ample clothes-hanging space in wardrobes equipped with sliding doors and mirrors. The rooms have refrigerators, and the bathrooms come with American voltage plugs—a great rarity. Motel service is friendly and efficient, and the reception quite unflappable, even in high-pressure periods.

4. WHERE TO EAT

The dining scene is as cosmopolitan as you would expect in a city housing a score of foreign embassies and hundreds of overseas students. Prices are generally high, but there's a fair sprinkling of budget choices, most in and around **Civic Square. Garema Place,** a shopping area between Mort and Petrie streets, is also dotted with good, fairly economical dining spots.

If you're out and hungry late at night, watch for the **Tuckerbuses.** These are old Sydney double-decker monsters. The drivers say they park "anywhere we can make a buck" to dispense hot dogs, hamburgers, and the like until all hours. The last time I spied them they were in Belconnen Way.

A final and glorious Canberra specialty: Lake Burley Griffin is stocked every year with 25,000 trout. Fishing is free, and you don't need a license. So rent a boat and catch your own lunch, then take it to one of the numerous picnic grounds and grill it over the coin-in-slot gas barbecues you'll find in all of them. You'll have a memorable al fresco feast. There are picnic areas all around the lakeshore. My favorite is in **Weston Park,** Yarralumla, south of the lake. It has treehouses, a minirailroad; and an area specially developed for kids to climb, hide, paddle, and run.

MEALS FOR LESS THAN $A12

CORNER COFFEE SHOP, corner of London Circuit and East Row. Tel. 247-4317.

Cuisine: SANDWICHES/SNACKS. **Reservations:** Not necessary.
$ **Prices:** $A3–$A6. AE, BC, MC, V.
Open: Daily 8am–6pm.

The Corner Coffee Shop is a small, simple but rather cozy establishment that's strictly for daylight eating: outside, at tables under shelter, or inside, amid artistic photos and posters and a mostly student clientele. It serves standard sandwiches on outstanding wheat bread; good pork and veal pies (all within the $A3 to $A4 range); and classic continental desserts, including homemade cannoli.

GUS'S CAFE, Garema Arcade, Bunda St. Tel. 248-8118.

Cuisine: CONTINENTAL. **Reservations:** Not necessary.
$ **Prices:** Appetizers $A4–$A4.50, main courses $A7.50. No credit cards.
Open: 24 hrs.

Gus's Café is a tiny restaurant with a much larger outdoor dining terrace, partly glassed in and wholly delightful. One tree is in the middle, and flower boxes are all around the gaily multicolored tables. It offers a free selection of newspapers and magazines to read at your table—a European custom that has been *slowly* catching on elsewhere. Interior decoration is devoted mainly to dozens of framed mottoes, slogans, and extracts dealing with pollution (moral and physical), the evils of drug abuse, and the virtue of things small as opposed to things big. Gus's serves indubitably the finest cheesecake in Canberra, at $A3 a slice. The heartier dishes are likewise excellent and wallet-pleasingly cheap, like fettuccine with spinach and mushrooms for $A7.50.

NOSHES, in the Trump Centre, Garema Place. Tel. 257-3750.
Cuisine: INTERNATIONAL. **Reservations:** Not necessary.
$ Prices: Appetizers $A4, main courses $A6–$A10. No credit cards.
Open: Daily 7am–midnight.

Despite its snackish shingle, Noshes could pass as a full-fledged restaurant. Located in a busy arcade, with tables overflowing onto the charming plaza outside, Noshes lures you with lilting jazz, waltz, and classical tapes. The interior—simply a row of tables set in the arcade—is decorated with changing art exhibits of surprisingly good quality. The "noshes" are chalked on a blackboard, all hovering within the $A6-to-$A8 range. You get vegetable curries; mushroom-and-spinach lasagne; pâté with salad; fettuccine bolognese; or gourmet avocado, bacon, and cheese sandwiches. Hours here are the touristic ideal.

PANCAKE PARLOUR, corner of East Row and Alinga St. Tel. 247-2982.
Cuisine: PANCAKES. **Reservations:** Accepted.
$ Prices: Appetizers $A5.90–$A6.90, main courses $A6–$A11.20. AE, BC, DC, MC, V.
Open: 24 hrs.

Pancake Parlour is the local link in a chain that benevolently girdles Australia. This particular link lies tucked beneath the Canberra City Pharmacy. The early colonial decor features the chain's trademark: a soulful Victorian damsel holding up a fork and exclaiming, "Lovely!" The great thing about all the Pancake Parlours are the serving hours—round-the-clock. The pancakes they dish up are hefty, the crêpes somewhat lighter, but neither is designed for weight-watchers' banquets. You can get them meaty and savory or sweet; they make solid meals in both shapes at prices ranging from $A6.80 to $A9.50. The place has a pleasantly relaxed atmosphere and cheerful staff, even in the wee hours.

PIZZA CAFE, Shop 11, Garema Arcade, Bunda St. Tel. 248-9131.
Cuisine: PIZZA. **Reservations:** Not necessary.
$ Prices: $A6.90–$A16.50. No credit cards.
Open: Daily 8am–midnight.

The café has the reputation of serving the best pizza in the territory, which you can take out or eat there, indoors or outdoors. Small, modern, and functional, with a window facing the square and a permanent throng inside, it offers 12 varieties—small for $A6.50, medium for $A11.50—and a 10% discount for YHA members on orders over $A10.

MEALS FOR LESS THAN $A16

AUGUSTIN'S, 23 Garema Place. Tel. 257-7559.
Cuisine: CONTINENTAL. **Reservations:** Accepted.
$ Prices: Appetizers $A3.50–$A8.80, main courses $A8–$A9. AE, MC, V.
Open: Daily 8am–2am.

Augustin's has the most intriguing decor in all Canberra: furnished partly with upholstered settees, partly with metal chairs and marble-top tables. Patrons can choose from an entire library of reading matter, ranging from hardcover classics to English magazines dating back to 1914 (I kid thee not). One wall is devoted to art-nouveau prints, the other to letters to newspaper editors praising outdoor cafés. Service is leisurely, but the food is worth waiting for. There are excellent soups and such European specialties as veal goulash, paprika chicken, and spicy meat loaf for $A8 to $A9.50. The menu is chalked on a blackboard that gets carried from table to table. Try to leave room for one of the memorable desserts.

CURTIN GREATER INDIAN RESTAURANT, Curtin Shopping Centre, Curtin Place, Curtin. Tel. 285-2425.
Cuisine: INDIAN. **Reservations:** Accepted.
$ Prices: Appetizers $A5–$A9, main courses $A8–$A15. AE, BC, MC, V.
Open: Daily 11:30am–2pm and 6–10:30pm.

Located about five minutes from downtown, this big, modern, friendly establishment serves "Indian home cooking." It's also one of the few Canberra eateries with an extensive vegetarian menu, including excellent West Bengal *kofta* curry. I can recommend the unusual fish kebab, followed by either the lamb tandoori or the Madras chicken vindaloo. The place is licensed and BYO, but there's $A1 corkage fee.

HAPPY'S, Garema Place. Tel. 49-7015.
Cuisine: CHINESE. **Reservations:** Accepted.
$ **Prices:** Appetizers $A4–$A5, main courses $A6.50–$A12. AE, BC, MC, V.
Open: Daily 5–10pm.

Located in a small basement, down a flight of stairs that's easy to miss, Happy's is illuminated by ornate tasseled lamps and has an entire wall devoted to a huge mural depicting the Great Wall of China. Standard Cantonese chicken, beef, and pork dishes cost around $A7.50; duck and seafood come higher. Try the banana chicken (yes!), the beef and sweet ginger, or the pork ribs in black-bean sauce; for dessert have the deep-fried ice cream.

HIGH COURT CAFE, High Court Bldg., King Edward Terrace, Parkes. Tel. 270-6828.
Cuisine: AUSTRALIAN. **Reservations:** Accepted.
$ **Prices:** Appetizers $A4–$A6, main courses $A7.80–$A10. No credit cards.
Open: Daily 9:45am–4:15pm.

You don't expect a cozy café in a high court building, but here is one. With a nice view of Lake Burley Griffin and a generally beautiful setting, this café caters to an awesome array of legal eagles, who traditionally know where to find a good bite. The excellent quiches (made on the premises) are served with salad ($A9.20). For $A10 you get grilled salmon with french fries and salad. A stubbie of beer sets you back $A2.50.

MAMA'S TRATTORIA, Garema Place. Tel. 248-0936.
Cuisine: ITALIAN. **Reservations:** Recommended.
$ **Prices:** Appetizers $A5, main courses $A10. No credit cards.
Open: Daily noon–3pm and 6–11pm.

Warm, atmospheric, and so popular that it's wise to book a table, Mama's is Italian to the core. Short on decorations, long on ambience, the trattoria has light-wood tables and chairs interspersed with potted plants, hanging ferns, and a few fine-art prints on the walls. A BYO—one of the few that charges for corkage—it serves a famous soup of the day (the house specialty) as well as main courses for around $A9, among them *mistoo di mare* (mixed seafood in white-wine sauce) and *paglia-e-fieno* (fettuccine in cream sauce with ham). All taste exactly as if Mama had cooked them, which she has.

STOCKADE, 13 Lonsdale St., Braddon. Tel. 247-0848.
Cuisine: AUSTRALIAN. **Reservations:** Accepted.
$ **Prices:** Appetizers $A2–$A5, main courses $A5–$A11. BC, MC, V.
Open: Mon–Sat 11:30am–10:30pm.

On a thoroughfare otherwise given over to lots for secondhand cars, the Stockade is a very large, extremely lively bar-restaurant decked out like a cross between a stable and a country hoosegow. The bar in front is festooned with framed prison regulations

FROMMER'S COOL FOR KIDS: RESTAURANTS

Gus's Café *(p. 315)* There's a whole range of games for kids, including draughts, Scrabble, Stratego, and checkers.

The Woodstock *(p. 318)* Priding itself on being a family restaurant, the Woodstock supplies high chairs, has a childrens' menu, and caters to special culinary wishes kids might have.

from the colonial days, some of them pretty scary. The patrons happily ignore the strict "No Speaking" rule, because the problem here is to make yourself heard at all. The dining room in the rear contains a lot of rustic gadgetry, plus a huge open electric grill. You select your victuals from glass cases filled with meats, sweets, and salads, then take them to the center grill and cook them according to your fancy. The meat is top grade; ham steak goes for $A5, and rump steak for $A8.50. That grandiose dessert import from New Zealand—Pavlova—costs $A2.

WAFFLES, 46 Northbourne Ave. Tel. 247-2913.
Cuisine: INTERNATIONAL. **Reservations:** Accepted.
$ Prices: Appetizers $A5–$A8.50, main courses $A8.50–$A13. AE, DC, MC, V.
Open: Daily 8am "until late".

Housed in a historic landmark building but with a sleek modern interior, Waffles manages to combine mellowed charm with fast-paced service and an amazingly multicultural menu. The name is somewhat misleading—Waffles *does* offer waffles, plus freshly baked bread and French pâtisserie, but its main trade are solid breakfasts, lunches, and dinners. Dishes range from barbecued spareribs and kangaroo burgers to veal schnitzel, quiches, lasagne, ravioli, and pâté maison. The big drawing card here is the "Express Menu" for $A12.50, which includes a main dish (in my case pork filet with prunes), salad, pâtisserie, a glass of wine, and coffee. The actual waffles, by the way, come with eight different toppings. I recommend the mocha.

THE WOODSTOCK, 185 City Walk. Tel. 249-7969.
Cuisine: AUSTRALIAN. **Reservations:** Accepted.
$ Prices: Appetizers $A4–$A6.95, main courses $A9.95–$A15.95. AE, BC, MC, V.
Open: Daily 11:30am–10pm.

The Woodstock is a comfortable and highly congenial eatery without any trace of Woodstock flavor. A long room with brown-on-brown decor, dimly lit and featuring wooden eating nooks, it has a huge counter selection of edibles for your perusal. Table service is very fast and efficient. Lasagne or spaghetti bolognese costs $A7.95 and a three-course dinner is around $A25.

READERS RECOMMEND

Before leaving the restaurant scene, I want to mention two establishments that were specially recommended by readers. The first is **Mr. Spokes,** Barrine Drive, Acton Park (tel. 257-1188). To my knowledge this is the only café attached to a bike-rental shop. Located on the shore of Lake Burley Griffin, the place invites you to snack either before you start your bicycle jaunt around the lake or after you return. Open daily from 9am to 6pm.

The second is **Chevy's Car,** Woden Plaza, Woden (tel. 81-2054). Decked out like a 1950s U.S. diner, Chevy's dishes up American roadside specialties: hamburgers and cheeseburgers, spareribs, chili burgers, potato skins, and mud pies. Its neon-lit interior is loaded with nostalgia for the age of Ike.

5. ATTRACTIONS

Canberra is a city of "sights"—so many of them that it's difficult to decide where to start.

In addition to the attractions listed below, there are many areas ideal for strolling. Among them is **Australian National University,** which covers an area of 320 acres north of the Civic Centre and enrolls more than 6,000 students. The campus is beautifully landscaped, sprinkled with modernistic fountains and sculptures. In addition, over 50 countries maintain **embassies** in Canberra, and their mission

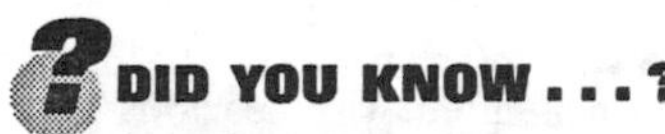

DID YOU KNOW . . . ?

- Canberra was planned as a "perfect habitat" for 140,000 people—it has almost twice as many today.
- Canberra is the only city with a Story Tellers Guild. No, they're not politicians but a group of yarn spinners who recite childrens' tales every Saturday at a local bookstore.
- One person in three of Canberra's population was born overseas.
- The first pictures of man walking on the moon were transmitted to the Tidbinbilla Space Tracking Station, southwest of Canberra.
- The average household income in Canberra is nearly $A5,000 higher than that of the rest of Australia, and the median age of Canberrans is three years younger than the national average.
- Nearly one-half of Canberra's work force are government employees.
- Among the innumerable names suggested for the national capital were Sydmcladperbrisho and Marsupalia. Another was Cac (Commonwealth Administration Centre).

buildings form a tourist attraction all their own. The architectural styles range from tasteful to terrible (the Thai embassy looks like Fu Manchu's castle dipped in whitewash), but a glimpse of them is an established part of "doing" the capital. It can be surprising. The British High Commission, for instance, is housed in a depressingly functional building resembling an upper-class college dorm, while the U.S. ambassador dwells in an enchanting Virginia mansion, the site of which, incidentally, was leased on the day Pearl Harbor was bombed. Most of the embassies are in the suburbs of Red Hill, Forrest, and Yarralumla, and you can't inspect them from the inside unless you wish to cause a diplomatic incident. But the **Indonesian Embassy,** Darwin Avenue, Yarralumla, has a charming pavilion containing a display of artifacts, puppets, and musical instruments and is open daily from 9am to noon and 2 to 4pm.

Canberra is also dotted with **public artworks:** artistic sculptings and statuary, sometimes combined with fountains or acting as children's playthings. All are modernistic, and most are symbolic. The National Capital Development Commission authorizes and buys major artworks—sculptures, paintings, stained glass, tapestries, and ceramics—from local or overseas artists and distributes them around the city. Because of this central guiding body (and because that body has excellent taste), there's a sense of unity of theme and purpose linking all these objects that make a special tour of them worthwhile. The only other city I have seen make equally splendid use of public ornamentation is Rotterdam in Holland. Among the really great works are Henry Moore's *Reclining Figure,* Tom Bass's *Ethos* (in Civic Square), and the fountain of *Thespis* by the American Robert Cook, at the Theatre Centre. Get hold of the excellent pamphlet guide "Artworks in Canberra," produced by the Development Commission. It is available from the ACT Tourism Commission.

THE TOP ATTRACTIONS

PARLIAMENT HOUSE, Capital Hill. Tel. 277-5399.

The new Parliament House, begun in 1979, opened in 1988 as part of Australia's Bicentennial celebrations. This is the executive heart of the Commonwealth, created at a cost of $A439 million to replace the old "temporary" structure from which the country had been governed for more than 60 years.

Set on Capital Hill, the symbolic center of Canberra, the white, majestically colonnaded edifice was designed to blend in with rather than dominate its surroundings. The low-profile building stands surrounded by vast and beautifully landscaped grounds that give the impression of a somewhat formal recreation area instead of a governmental stronghold.

The interior is palatial but in a subdued style that welcomes visitors without dwarfing them. The public entrance is through the Grand Verandah, white pillared with marble floors and broad stairways leading up to the first floor. This is the main public area, containing a restaurant, exhibition space, and a theatrette, as well as an open veranda offering panoramic views of the city.

The actual engines of government, so to speak, are housed in two halls: the **House**

of Representatives to the east and the **Senate Chamber** to the west. Together these two elected bodies make up Parliament. Each is fitted with spacious public galleries where visitors can observe their members in action. Behind the scenes, to the south, stretch the prime minister's and other ministerial offices, where the day-to-day tasks of government are performed. The top floor is given over to the Parliamentary Library and the Committee Rooms, where matters are thrashed out before they reach the debating chambers.

Most of Australia's parliamentary procedures were taken over *in toto* from the "Mother of Parliaments" in London. (The title, though generally used, is not quite correct. It actually belongs to Iceland, which boasts the world's oldest existing parliament.) And some of the exhibited trappings are fully English, among them one of the only three surviving exemplars of the Magna Carta, issued in 1297. (The original charter, arm-twisted from "Bad King John" at Runnymede, was annulled after only nine weeks.)

Tours of inspection take place when only one chamber is in session—then the other one gets inspected.

Admission: Tours, free.

Open: Daily 9am–5pm. **Closed:** Christmas.

AUSTRALIAN WAR MEMORIAL, Anzac Parade, corner of Limestone and Fairbarin Aves. Tel. 243-4238.

Canberra's biggest tourist attraction, standing at the foot of Mount Ainslie, is an absolutely splendid edifice in honor and memory of the 100,000 men and women who died for the Commonwealth in the two world wars. The memorial contains exhibition galleries and one of the finest libraries in the country.

It's hard to say which exhibits are more fascinating: the vast dioramas of combat or the mechanical relics of it. The former show the gruesome, slogging trench warfare of World War I and the African desert struggles of World War II in minute detail and brutal realism. The latter include **Aeroplane Hall,** with the strutted biplanes, sleek Spitfires, and hulking bombers flown by Australian airmen in both wars; also displayed are the artillery pieces, tanks, landing barges, shells, bombs, and torpedoes used by the men from Down Under. Also among the relics is the colossal German Amiens gun (the barrel weighs 45 tons) and the toylike Japanese midget submarine, reconstructed from the two sunk in the attack on Sydney Harbour in 1942. And then there's the memorial showing the cost of it all—the bronze panels inscribed with the awesome roll of names of the fallen, covering two huge walls.

Admission: Free.

Open: Daily 9am–4:45pm.

CANBERRA CARILLON, near Kings Avenue Bridge.

One of the largest musical instruments in the world, the Canberra Carillon was a gift from Britain to Australia to mark Canberra's Jubilee. A tall white pillar, it stands near the northern end of Kings Avenue Bridge and is played in regular Sunday and Wednesday recitals. A carillon is an instrument in which tiers of bells are played from a "clavier"—an organlike keyboard. The Canberra version has 53 bells, the largest weighing more than 6 tons, the smallest only 15 pounds. Playing them requires considerable strength and tremendous skill: The performing artists have to wear padding on their little finger, which strikes the hand batons that sound the bells by means of a long steel wire connected to a soft metal hammer.

Admission: Free.

Open: Sat 1–4pm, Sun 9am–2pm.

AUSTRALIAN NATIONAL GALLERY, King Edward Terrace, Parkes. Tel. 71-2411.

Rising on the shores of Lake Burley Griffin, this majestic gallery houses permanent exhibitions of some of the world's greatest artists—Australian and international. It's something of a surprise to find America's Jackson Pollock so well represented along with France's Claude Monet and Italy's Mimmo Paladino. The gallery also houses a wide selection of Australian artists including Sidney Nolan and Arthur Boyd, plus an excellent range of Aboriginal artwork. The gallery is a surprise package, not least because of its first-rate restaurant overlooking the waters of the lake and the al fresco eatery in the Sculpture Garden.

Admission: $A3 adults; students and seniors free.

Open: Daily 10am–5pm.

ROYAL AUSTRALIAN MINT, Denison St., Deakin. Tel. 202-6999.

The mint is the place where they make the filthy lucre. You can watch the operation of the production floor through plate-glass windows in the visitors gallery and can see the large coin exhibition in the foyer. (No, they don't hand out free samples, but you can make your own coin or token on the public coining presses.)

Admission: Free.

Open: Mon–Fri 9am–4pm, Weekends 10am–3pm.

BICYCLE MUSEUM, in the Canberra Tradesmen's Club, 2 Badham St., Dickson. Tel. 248-0999.

This museum contains the largest collection of antique and unusual velocipedes in Australia. You can admire the sheer ingenuity (and heroic disregard for comfort) of some of these muscle-propelled contraptions. Have your picture taken riding a genuine penny-farthing. A bistro, coffee shop, and bar are on the premises.

Admission: Free.

Open: Daily 9:30am–midnight.

AUSTRALIAN NATIONAL BOTANIC GARDENS, Clunies Ross St. Tel. 250-9540.

The gardens, situated on the lower slope of Black Mountain, are devoted entirely to native Australian flora. They are crisscrossed by beautifully designed walks through green and shady glens over bridges and small ponds, with no playgrounds or picnic areas to disturb the hushed peace. This is an excellent place for bird watching.

Admission: Free.

Open: Daily 9am–5pm.

BLUNDELL'S COTTAGE, Wendouree Dr. Tel. 273-2667.

This farmhouse was built in 1860 as a plowman's cottage. Four rooms are furnished in the old pioneer style.

Admission: $A1.50 adults, A50¢ children.

Open: Daily 10am–4pm.

ROYAL MILITARY COLLEGE, Jubilee Ave., Duntroon. Tel. 275-9545.

Located in suburban Duntroon, this is the training establishment of Australia's regular army officers. It's open to vehicle tours every day.

NATIONAL FILM AND SOUND ARCHIVE, McCoy Circuit, Acton. Tel. 267-1711.

The purpose of this very-much-alive archive is to preserve Australia's radio, film, and television heritage, which is much older and more extensive than most visitors realize. Australia, in fact, was making full-length feature films around 1908 and regular newsreels during World War I. The archive features continuous screenings of historic footage, including a Melbourne horse race filmed in 1896 and some of the superb action reels shot by Damien Parer during the World War II fighting in the Pacific (he was killed in the process).

Admission: Free.

Open: Daily 9:30am–4pm.

POKER MACHINE MUSEUM, West Belconnen Leagues Club, Hardwick Crescent, Holt. Tel. 54-1044.

This museum displays an assembly of historic poker machines (or slots or one-armed bandits). These dough-devouring robots were first manufactured in San Francisco in the 1880s and have taken on an astonishing variety of guises. My personal favorite is the so-called Irish machine (made in Australia) on which you push the handle instead of pulling it and the reels spin backward and drop in sequence from right to left. Rumor has it that if you hit the jackpot on this contraption, *you* must pay the machine.

Open: Daily 10am–6pm.

CAPTAIN COOK MEMORIAL, near Commonwealth Avenue Bridge.

The Captain Cook Memorial hurls six tons of water into the air at any given moment. Part of the memorial is a 9-foot terrestrial globe on the shoreline, showing and describing the routes of exploration followed by the illustrious navigator.

Admission: Free.

Open: Water jet operates daily 10am–noon and 2–4pm.

NATIONAL SCIENCE AND TECHNOLOGY CENTRE, King Edward Terrace. Tel. 270-2800.

The centre is an astonishing structure built around a huge cone from which a spiral walkway leads to five galleries. Each gallery features a different aspect of science or technology. The exhibits are of the hands-on kind: beams, wheels, rays, and spectrums you can operate or touch, producing some astonishing effects. It is one of the most enthralling spots in town.

Admission: $A7 adults, $A3.50 children.

Open: Daily 10am–5pm.

CANBERRA MAZE, in Weston Park, Yarralumla.

The Canberra Maze contains puzzles within the puzzle. While you're wandering around the actual maze, you'll see signs—each with four questions—that make up a quiz to be answered while looking for the exit. The maze is fairly easy, but the quiz is not.

Admission: $A2.50.

Open: Sat–Sun and school holidays 10am–5pm.

NATIONAL LIBRARY OF AUSTRALIA, Parkes Place. Tel. 62-1111.

The National Library of Australia, near the south side of Commonwealth Bridge, is one of the newest and most beautiful of Canberra's public buildings. Based on the Greek Parthenon, it's a clean and subtly dramatic structure in the neoclassic tradition, fronted by two gushing fountains. The library houses some 2 million books, over 300,000 maps, 390,000 photographs, 65,000 films (including the earliest ever shot in Australia), and 440,000 sound recordings. Only the foyer and exhibition areas are open to visitors, but guided tours of the building are available.

Admission: Free.

Open: Mon–Thurs 9am–10pm, Fri–Sun until 4:45pm.

NEARBY ATTRACTIONS

MOUNT STROMLO OBSERVATORY, Cotter Rd., Mt. Stromlo, Woden (10 miles west of Canberra).

Large science-fictionish silver domes house the telescopes and measuring instruments of the Department of Astronomy of the National University. The observatory is one of the biggest and best equipped in the southern hemisphere. The visitor center is at the 74-inch telescope.

Admission: Free.

Open: Daily 9:30am–4pm.

BYWONG TOWN, off Federal Hwy., Bywong Town (20 miles north of Canberra). Tel. 236-9183.

Bywong Town is an exact and altogether fascinating restoration of a gold-mining township. The Bywong gold rush began in 1894 and ended when the last Digger stopped prospecting in 1964. What lay between was mostly hardship, privations, and remarkable feats of human grit and endurance. Today many of the town's primitive dwellings have been restored—a collection of mud, bark, and slab huts that once housed some 300 people. A conducted and excellently narrated tour takes you around the huts, the abandoned farm machinery, the old gold mine and panning sites, the blacksmith-and-wheelwright shops, and the well dug by Chinese laborers. You get the feel of the town as it was when 300 people toiled and sweated for the sake of the golden dust that proved so elusive and made nobody rich.

Admission: $A7 adults, $A4 children.

Open: Daily 10am–4pm.

TIDBINBILLA NATURE RESERVE, Tidbinbilla (25 miles southwest of Canberra). Tel. 237-5120.

Tidbinbilla Nature Reserve, stretching over a valley by the same name, embraces 12,000 acres of unspoiled bushland. Offering scenic walks and picnic sites (but no gas stations) in a region that sometimes wears a light snow mantle during winter, it abounds in native flora and fauna and offers an opportunity to hand-feed kangaroos kept in a special enclosure. The kangaroos are gentle nuzzlers. The fur and feather enclosure can also be visited.

Admission: Free.
Open: Daily 9am–6pm.

LANYON, Tharwa Dr., off Monaro Hwy., Tharwa (19 miles south of Canberra). Tel. 293-5296.

Lanyon, a gracious colonial homestead (built in 1859) stands on the east bank of the Murrumbidgee River. Now a National Trust building, Lanyon has the original kitchen, stables, and furnishings of the period. On the grounds you'll find the **Nolan Gallery,** showing the works of that superb Australian artist Sir Sidney Nolan, whose bush scenes will imprint themselves on your visual memory like very few other paintings.

Admission: $A3.70 adults, $A1.85 children.
Open: Tues–Sun 10am–4pm.

TELECOMMUNICATIONS TOWER, Black Mountain Dr. Tel. 248-1911.

The tower at Black Mountain is the capital's landmark, stabbing skyward west of the city like an immense fine-pointed needle encrusted with electronic doodads. The purpose of the tower is to centralize TV and radio transmitters and radiotelephone communications, but it also makes a superb viewing platform. There are three levels of technical equipment, plus two enclosed and two open levels for public pleasure. They contain a revolving restaurant, a stationary snack bar, a glassed-in viewing gallery, and two floors for open viewing. The panorama below is absolutely spectacular—you think you can see the entire continent and a bit of next week as well.

Admission: $A3 adults, $A1 children.
Open: Daily 9am–10pm.

REHWINKEL'S ANIMAL PARK, Mack's Reef Rd., off Federal Hwy. (18 miles northeast of Canberra). Tel. 230-3328.

In this 50-acre spread of natural bushland with free-roaming inhabitants, you can mingle with wallabies, wombats, emus, camels, deer, and ponies and have a barbecue picnic or snacks from the park kiosk. You can feed almost everybody except the koalas—they stick to the trees and their gum-leaf diet.

Admission: $A7.50 adults, $A3.75 children.
Open: Daily 10am–5pm.

CANBERRA SPACE CENTRE, Tidbinbilla (32 miles southwest of Canberra). Tel. 201-7800.

The Canberra Space Centre contains a fascinating array of model spacecraft, space photos, and space research equipment. The audiovisual displays give you an insight into the mysteries of deep-space tracking and the complexities of space exploration.

Admission: Free.
Open: Daily 9am–5pm, until 8pm in summer.

COCKINGTON GREEN, Gold Creek Rd., Gungahlin (5 miles northwest of Canberra). Tel. 230-2273.

Cockington Green is a miniature patch of Britain set into the green-brown Australian landscape—an entire Olde English village studded with historical buildings that were lovingly handcrafted on a scale of 1:12. Thatched cottages, a forbidding gray castle, country inns, and a scale-model speed train have been individually wrought down to every tiny brick, tile, wheel, and window, as have been the teensy clay-model people and animals.

Admission: $A5.75 adults, $A2.75 children.
Open: Daily 9:30am–4:30pm.

ORGANIZED TOURS

BY BUS **Murrays,** in the Jolimont Centre, Northbourne Avenue (tel. 06/295-3611), runs a variety of excursions, including half-day City Sights Tours, visiting different attractions on each. The afternoon round, starting at 1pm, takes in the university, Australian War Memorial, Carillon, Parliament, Telecom Tower, Captain Cook Memorial, and a scenic drive, costing $A22 for adults, $A18 for children.

The company's Day Tour gives you virtually all the sights of Canberra—and adjoining areas—in one very full day. Coaches depart from the Jolimont Centre at 10am. Adults pay $A48, children $A32.

BY BOAT Various water excursions on the capital's large central lake are run by **Canberra Cruises** (tel. 295-3544). All start and finish at the Acton Ferry Terminal. The 1½-hour cruise circles the entire lake, then glides into the Molonglo River and the oddly wild Jerrabomberra Wetlands, which teem with birdlife. It departs twice daily and costs $A10 for adults, $A5 for children.

For those with limited time there is the 1-hour **Parliamentary Triangle Cruise,** viewing all major buildings and foreshores from the water. The cost is $A8 for adults, $A4 for children.

6. SAVVY SHOPPING

Canberra's commercial center consists of a series of shopping complexes either adjoining or close to Civic Square. They house large department stores as well as scores of little boutiques, cafés, and gift shops; I can't think of any other form of retail design that spoils shoppers so thoroughly: no parking worries, no chance of getting wet when it rains, and no distances to tire your feet. The only drawback is that the range of goods isn't quite as great as in Sydney or Melbourne.

The largest complex is **Monaro Mall,** between Petrie Street and Alinga Street. Fully enclosed and air-conditioned, the three-level mall contains two separate department stores and dozens of specialty shops. Others are **Garema Place** and **Petrie Plaza,** which occupies a special niche in the hearts of Canberra kids. It boasts a wonderful old merry-go-round that twirls during business hours to the strains of the real traditional tweedle-zing-oompah-pah orchestreon music, guaranteed to awaken nostalgia in most hearts. Ticket prices, unfortunately, no longer reflect the music: One spin now costs $A1. The **Boulevard** is a beautifully landscaped open plaza facing Akuna Street. Strongly cosmopolitan, as the name indicates, the Boulevard has three ultramodern levels filled with international boutiques, a couple of movie theaters, and several gourmet-food stores.

Canberra also has an entertaining commercial throwback in shape of the **Trash and Treasure market.** This is an open-air, open-ended market held on Sunday morning at the Jamison shopping center car park, organized by the local Rotary club. It offers exactly what the name promises—you can buy or sell virtually anything there. There are heaps of trash and an occasional treasure; half the fun is hunting for it.

7. SPORTS & RECREATION

The Capital Territory is glutted with playing fields, jogging trails, and biking paths, not to mention a plethora of tennis courts and golf courses.

The shrine of Canberra's athletic world is the **Australian Institute of Sport,** Leverrier Crescent, Bruce (tel. 252-1111). A truly spectacular complex of indoor-and-outdoor stadiums, it's a showpiece as much as training ground. Public tours of the facilities are held daily at 2pm.

BOATING Lake Burley Griffin is the focal point for a variety of sports (including the most popular cycling trail that describes a 25-mile circuit around the lakeshore). You can rent catamarans, windsurfers, rowboats, and canoes from **Dobel Boat Hire,** Barrine Drive, Acton (tel. 249-6861).

GOLF & TENNIS There are plenty of golf courses and tennis courts, but bookings tend to be heavy on weekends and during holiday periods: **Capital Golf Club,** Jerrabomberra Avenue, Narrabundah (tel. 295-8048); **Federal Golf Club,** Red Hill (tel. 281-1888); **National Sports Club,** tennis courts, Mouat St., Lyneham (tel. 247-0929).

SWIMMING The capital has no beaches, but there are an ample number of swimming pools: **Civic Olympic Pool,** Allara Street, Reid (tel. 247-9321); **Dickson Olympic Pool,** Cowper Street, Dickson (tel. 247-2972); and **Swimming & Ice Skating Centre,** Irving Street, Phillip (tel. 282-1036).

8. EVENING ENTERTAINMENT

THE PERFORMING ARTS

Canberra has what many much larger cities lack: a performing-arts complex in a central position. It couldn't be more central, because the Civic Square, off London Circuit, is the geographical core of the capital. The **Canberra Theatre Centre** (tel. 257-1077) contains the Theatre, the Playhouse, the Centre Gallery, and the Rehearsal Room (for lunchtime performances). It can (and does) put on everything from Shakespeare to rock festivals. Usually there's a visiting professional group and various amateur theatrical and musical units. You get modern-and-classical dramas, grand opera, symphony and pop concerts, ballet, modern dance, choral works, chamber music, and operettas. (There's also an adjoining restaurant.)

Consult the daily press or *This Week in Canberra* for current offerings. Ticket prices vary but lean toward expensive. For a production by a visiting professional theater group you'll pay around $A35.

THE CLUB & MUSIC SCENE

Canberra now boasts some fairly swinging discos, swarming with young and fairly young government functionaries of all sexes. Other kinds of nightlife are concentrated mainly in the large hotels, like the sumptuous Lakeside International, and they tend to be costly, as well as somewhat more formal than the usual Down Under style. This is probably due to the heavy diplomatic influx into the capital's nightlife.

In addition to the establishments listed below, there are at least 20 more nightspots in downtown Canberra and the closer suburbs.

PRIVATE BIN, 50 Northbourne Ave. Tel. 247-3030.

An entertainment complex cum meeting place and one of the busiest spots in town, the Private Bin caters to four taste varieties simultaneously. It includes a nightclub (dance music), a tavern (rock 'n' roll), a piano bar (romantic intimacy), and a restaurant (palate pleasures). For good measure it also has a pâtisserie in which to put on the weight you later dance off. Entertainment comes in the form of live bands, name comedians, and fashion parades—when I witnessed one, the models apparently could choose any color providing it was black.

Admission: Free five nights, $A5 Friday and Saturday.

Open: Daily; tavern midday "until late," nightclub 9pm "until *very* late."

RASCALS, 33 Petrie Plaza. Tel. 257-1110.

Rascals swings nightly as a restaurant early in the evening, as a nightclub later. It's very much a meeting spot with a fine dance floor.

Admission: $A5.
Open: Daily 5pm "until late."

SCHOOL OF ARTS CAFE, 108 Monaro St., Queanbeyan. Tel. 297-6857.

This place has chameleon qualities: In the daytime it's a real café, serving the reputedly best cuppa in Canberra; at night, it becomes a mixed-bag showcase. Offerings range from multitalent cabaret programs to solo performers warbling blues or intoning Coward. Thursday to Sunday, starting at 7:30pm, you get supper and a show, along with the kind of laid-back vibes you don't expect in the Capital Territory. Not surprisingly, advance bookings are essential. The real surprise lies in the fact that this is a BYO.

Admission: Dinner and show $A29.50–$A35.

PANDORA'S, corner of Mort and Alinga Sts. Tel. 248-7405.

Located in the heart of the city, this is the upper-level disco of a bar and restaurant complex and is a pleasantly uninhibited mingling spot for embassy and government-department personnel as well as lesser mortals. It's lively, noisy, and flirtatious.

Admission: $A5.
Open: Wed–Sat 9:30pm–5am.

MOVIES

Most of the standard movie theaters are around the Civic Square area. Special screenings of foreign-language films and others classed as not standard commercial fare are held at various cultural centers: the **National Library of Australia** (free), the **Maison de France,** and the **Goethe Centre.** For information call the Multicultural Office (tel. 245-6413) or the Ethnic Communities Council (tel. 249-8994).

9. EASY EXCURSIONS TO SNOWY MOUNTAINS HYDROELECTRIC SCHEME & COOMA

SNOWY MOUNTAINS HYDROELECTRIC SCHEME

To the southwest of Canberra is the Snowy Mountains Hydroelectric Scheme, one of the most grandiose showpieces of the entire hemisphere. The "Snowy Scheme," as the Aussies call it, was named by the American Society of Civil Engineers as one of the "Seven Wonders of the Engineering World." It is the mightiest technological task ever accomplished in Australia and has become an almost mystical focal point of national pride. For sheer magnitude the "Snowy" can only be compared with America's Tennessee Valley Authority water scheme.

The significance of the SMA (Snowy Mountain Authority) stems from the fact that Australia is the driest of all continents, mainly because it has few massive mountain ranges to precipitate rain and give rise to rivers. The basic idea of the scheme was to divert the Snowy River from its original path into three rivers that would flow west into water-needy country, and in so doing provide not only irrigation and thus fertility but also a colossal amount of water-generated electricity for power and light for homes, industries, and transportation in the plains below.

Begun in 1949, the project took 25 years to complete and cost $A800 million, the labor of 6,000 men, and the lives of 54 killed by rockfalls and misfiring tunnel blasts. This was the price paid for the astonishing speed of the tunneling operations, which frequently reached a rate of 541 feet per week. (The previous world record, set by the Swiss, was 362 feet of tunneling per week.)

The SMA boasts a mass of dazzling statistics: 90 miles of tunnels hewn through the mountains; 80 miles of aqueducts constructed; 1,000 miles of road laid down; and seven power stations in operation, producing 4,000,000 kilowatts of electricity! The entire scheme involves an area of over 2,000 square miles and has created a chain of huge artificial lakes, the largest of them, **Eucumbene,** containing nine times the volume of water in Sydney Harbour!

But better than all these figures is the loving care with which the whole undertaking has been blended into the scenery. Far from marring the beauty of the mountain ranges, the "Snowy Scheme" has enhanced it. Many of the power plants are underground and invisible until you reach the entrance. The immense silvery-white dams blend with the snowcapped peaks like natural waterfalls. The lakes, cold, blue, and crystal clear, have been stocked with rainbow trout and provide some of the finest **game fishing** in the country. And somehow, even the masses of sightseers attracted by the project are absorbed with a minimum of blatantly commercial tourism.

COOMA

Gateway and launching pad for a tour of the Snowy, this formerly drowsy little mountain hamlet burst into new cosmopolitan life when it became Snowy Scheme headquarters. Today it proudly flies the flags of 27 nations—one for each country whose sons took part in the project.

Cooma lies 30 minutes by air from Canberra, about an hour from Melbourne or Sydney, and it can also be easily reached by bus, train, or car. I would advise you to take one of the conducted tours of the Scheme—it's impossible to view the magnitude of the project without expert guidance.

Tours lasting one to three days leave Canberra and Cooma several times a week. Typical of the budget range is the 1-day jaunt run Wednesdays from Canberra by **Deane's Tours** (tel. 06/299-3722). This includes a fascinating film show of the SMA; visits to Lake Eucumbene, a dam, and an underground power station; and lunch at Thredbo, the highest township in Australia. Adults pay $A38, children $A28.

CHAPTER 10

ALICE SPRINGS — THE "RED HEART"

- **WHAT'S SPECIAL ABOUT ALICE SPRINGS & NORTHERN TERRITORY**

1. ORIENTATION

2. GETTING AROUND

3. WHERE TO STAY

- **FROMMER'S COOL FOR KIDS: HOTELS**

4. WHERE TO EAT

- **FROMMER'S COOL FOR KIDS: RESTAURANTS**

5. ATTRACTIONS

- **DID YOU KNOW . . .?**

6. SAVVY SHOPPING

7. EVENING ENTERTAINMENT

8. EXCURSIONS AROUND THE RED CENTRE

9. OTHER EXCURSIONS IN NORTHERN TERRITORY

"The Alice," as locals affectionately call this town, lies at almost the exact geographical center of Australia—a long way from *anywhere.* It is certainly the most contradictory town on the continent: Everything said about it is right on the one hand and wrong on the other. It has aspects of movie-land and picture-book Australia: streets sprinkled with reddish desert dust, sun-baked pubs propped up by tall men in khaki shirts, drifting groups of Aborigines, and an infinity of blue-hazed sky with wedge-tail eagles floating motionless on the air currents. And all around is an endless expanse of surrealistic wilderness—harsh, primeval, barely touched by humankind, wrinkled and split, churned and clefted by cataclysmic upheavals in ages before human reckoning . . . the landscape of Dreamtime.

Yet Alice Springs is also a modern desert town of about 26,000 people; a tourist resort with elegant hotels, air-conditioned shopping malls, and surprisingly sleek restaurants; and a rapidly growing government center that expects to quadruple its population in the next 20 years. Perhaps the oddest detail about the Alice is that while foreigners find it completely in accordance with their image of Australia, the Aussies consider it quaintly "different."

The Alice is an incredibly young city. In 1911 the area was still being supplied by camel caravans driven by Afghans. In 1929, when the railroad reached the town, it numbered 200 inhabitants. The passenger train from Adelaide was promptly christened *The Ghan* in tribute to the Afghan camel drivers. The railroad terminates here; it can't go anywhere else. Alice Springs is the only sizable community in Central Australia. Darwin, the territorial capital, lies 954 miles to the north.

The center forms the southern portion of the **Northern Territory** (not a state), a region of over half a million square miles with under 150,000 people—of whom 22,000 are Aborigines. After the polar caps, this is the most sparsely settled patch of land on earth. There's a saying that "One Territorian is a village. Two Territorians are a town. Three Territorians are a population explosion."

In 1860 explorer John McDouall Stuart became the first white man to set foot on the present town site. In 1871 a surveyor came on a large waterhole and christened it Alice Springs, after his employer's wife. This occurred during the building of the Overland Telegraph Line, linking Port Augusta with Darwin. A telegraph repeater station was built at the site, followed by a settlement of sorts about two miles south.

WHAT'S SPECIAL ABOUT ALICE SPRINGS & NORTHERN TERRITORY

Natural Spectacles

- ☐ Ayers Rock, the world's largest monolith, steeped in Aboriginal mystique and about 600 million years old.
- ☐ Kings Canyon, an immense cleft in the George Gill Ranges, with walls of pink sandstone reflected in hundreds of rock pools.
- ☐ Palm Valley, a fauna reserve containing some of the oldest plant life on earth.
- ☐ Kakadu National Park, Australia's most spectacular wildlife region and scene of *Crocodile Dundee*'s animal adventures.
- ☐ Litchfield Park, the second great wildlife reserve, with magnificent waterfalls and jungle landscapes.

Festivals/Events

- ☐ Camel Cup, a race held with camels instead of horses.
- ☐ Alice Springs Rodeo, with cowboys and cowgirls from all over Australia competing for top prize money.
- ☐ Henley-on-Todd, the world's most hilarious boat race, run (literally) on the Todd River—which has no water.

The settlement, then called Stuart, numbered exactly 40 souls by 1926. It was renamed Alice Springs when the railroad went into operation.

The old telegraph station is now a museum, preserved exactly as it looked when the telegraph wire represented the territory's only link with the civilized south and the world beyond. But Alice Springs has meanwhile shed its shantytown image, at least in parts. Yet you're always conscious of the fact that this is an oasis in the midst of the "Never Never." The wilderness laps on all sides; there's an unmistakable whiff of desert in the air; and you have to drive only a few blocks to find yourself alone with the limitless horizon.

Once the wide red land all around belonged to the Arunta, the Pintjantjarra, and the Gurindji, and their descendants are still there. You see them in little bands drifting through the alien streets, always moving, always going somewhere and from there to somewhere else, as if searching in circles for some destination that eternally eludes them. The ancient nomadic urge still flickers, even though their water-and-food supply is now stationary and they wear more conventional clothing, receive medical treatment, and know how to drive trucks. Perhaps beer and automobiles and brick shelters are no substitute for the harsh majesty of the bush, and canned meat doesn't taste like the kangaroo they tracked and speared. Or perhaps it's just a fading memory of a time with no roads or houses or fences, when they walked as far as their feet would carry them and slept in the open with their mates under stars as ageless and unchanging as the earth beneath.

The desert climate is a reminder, too. There is a kind of brute violence in its extremes that no amount of air-conditioning can tame. From November to March the town sizzles; the landscape glimmers with heat. From April to October the days are sunny—sometimes hot—but the temperature drops steeply as soon as darkness falls. Overnight frosts are common, and early in the morning it can be several degrees below freezing! When a heavy rainstorm strikes, dry riverbeds become foaming torrents, and the first touch of wet brings out an explosion of flowers and shrubs in the arid hills. Then the landscape turns into a scene of magic beauty, of colors so vivid and contrasts so pure and clear that you begin to understand what Territorians mean when they say this about their grim and gorgeous land: "There's no place like her."

Northern Territory consists of two quite distinct regions, which share extremes of climate, sparse population, and a dramatic sense of isolation. One is the **Top End,** with the territorial capital of Darwin, a wild tropical jungle coastline, and monsoonal rains that drop an annual average five feet of lukewarm water on the landscape. The other is the **Red Centre,** with Alice Springs in the middle, a region of ocher-colored desert, meager vegetation, and phantasmagoric rock formations.

But the handful of Territorians who inhabit both portions bear the same characteristics. They are by far the heaviest beer drinkers in Australia; they breed more eccentrics than any other part of the continent; and they supposedly invented Australia's national salute—one hand waved in front of the face (to ward off flies). They also share an inherent distrust for government regulations; a slow, deliberate way of moving and talking; and the spontaneous hospitality toward strangers that is the hallmark of all people who dwell in rugged corners of the earth.

CLOTHING Sunglasses are an essential in the Alice any time of the year, and a shady hat is needed if you're sensitive to ultraviolet exposure. Also you need *sturdy* walking shoes if you plan to visit scenic attractions. Elastic-sided boots are ideal for keeping out sand and burrs. If you come in winter, bring at least one warm sweater or coat. Alice Springs men usually wear short-sleeved shirts, shorts, long socks, and shoes in daytime, the women light cotton frocks or pants. In the evening "Territory Formal" means a long-sleeved shirt, long slacks, and a tie for a man (coat optional, depending on the season); for a woman, anything from a caftan to a pantsuit can be worn with shoes or sandals. "Out bush" the most common outfit is jeans and a long-sleeved shirt. Going bare armed and bare legged leaves you unprotected against insects and prickles—and the territory has a superabundance of both. The one garb you'll hardly ever see is tropical whites. Red dust plays havoc with them.

1. ORIENTATION

ARRIVING

BY PLANE Alice Springs lies 820 air miles north of Adelaide, the closest city. Flying time is nearly two hours, and the trip costs $A360. The **Alice Springs Airport** is a small affair—but it takes jets. It doesn't boast much by way of facilities: a bar, an information booth, a snack counter, and the car-rental desks. But it's delightfully easy to get to, from, and around in. The cab fare to the city comes to about $A14. Or for $A7 you can take the airport shuttle, which meets all flights and does hotel pick-ups.

BY TRAIN If you're a railroad buff, you've missed a historical moment—the demise of the legendary *Ghan,* the train that first connected the Alice with civilization in 1929 by starting a fortnightly freight-and-passenger service to Adelaide. Until then goods and people were hauled back and forth in camel caravans by Afghan drivers. The train was nicknamed *Ghan* after those hardy cameleers. Riding *The Ghan* was likely more of an adventure than the passengers had bargained for. The builders of the track had figured that this was permanently dry desert country, and consequently they laid rails and sleepers flat on the ground without the ballast considered essential in wetter climes. They didn't realize until too late that they had laid the track through one of the most flood-prone regions in Australia. The result was that the entire train was frequently marooned for several weeks in a flood in the middle of a desert! The passengers, it was said, got to know one another pretty well during those castaway periods.

Otherwise, the old *Ghan* was a comfortable affair, air-conditioned and slow enough to give you plenty of opportunity to admire the wild horses, buffalo, and camels often seen through the windows. The journey from Adelaide took nearly 48 hours northward but a good 10 hours less going back—it's downhill then, because Alice Springs lies 2,000 feet above sea level.

A new train started service late in 1980, running on a line built about 100 miles west of the former track; it is immune to lightning, floods, and washouts and is considerably faster and much less exciting. Already veteran travelers are murmuring that there was "nothing like the old *Ghan*." And with a little bit of luck, they'll be right. But the wild desert animals are still there to provide entertainment. The fare on the new *Ghan* from Adelaide is $A139. The new train runs twice a week and takes 20 hours.

BY BUS & CAR The bus trip from Adelaide to Alice is an overnight 20-hour haul costing $A168. If you're coming from Adelaide by car, you'll be on the Stuart Highway—"The Track" to Territorians—the only road running into Alice Springs from the south. Make sure to read the desert driving tips in "Excursions Around the Red Centre," at the end of this chapter, before starting, and figure on about 24 hours for the journey. The bus drivers know the road conditions, you don't.

TOURIST INFORMATION

Possibly the most important address in town is the **Northern Territory Government Tourist Bureau,** Ford Plaza, Todd Mall (tel. 51-5470). They not only arrange accommodations and tours, but also are a living encyclopedia of territorial know-how and lore.

CITY LAYOUT

On the map on page 333 you'll see that Alice Springs is divided into two sections by the **Todd River.** Most of the year, however, this is merely a dry sandy riverbed. The locals go wild with excitement when rains momentarily transform this gully into a genuine torrent, which can be pretty strong while the water lasts. The town has one main street: **Todd Street,** starting off as **Gap Road** and changing its name about halfway down its length. **City Center** is the square formed by **Stuart** and **Wills Terrace** in the south and north, and **Todd Street** and **Railway Terrace** in the east and west. Nearly every hostelry, eatery, and office can be found in this small area.

The **Stuart Highway** branches off Railway Terrace and runs northward out of town all the way to Darwin. Also at the northern end of town lies the **Alice Springs Telegraph Station,** the site of the original telegraph post. The Stuart Highway actually enters the city from the south, running alongside the railroad line, but it becomes Railway Terrace before regaining its identity at the exit point. At the southern tip lies the **Alice Springs Airport** and the **Pitchi Ritchi Sanctuary.** On both sides stretch the **MacDonnell Ranges,** whose fantastic red-rock formations leap into view wherever you go.

2. GETTING AROUND

Alice Springs has no public transport and doesn't need it—as yet. Bus services are confined to schoolchildren. But there are plenty of **taxis** (tel. 52-1877). Also, there are several **car-rental** firms: **Territory** has a desk at the airport and an office at the corner of Stott Terrace and Hartley Street (tel. 089/52-9999). You can rent minimokes for $A28 per day, Toyotas for $A55 per day.

3. WHERE TO STAY

Alice Springs' economy depends heavily on tourism, so there's no shortage of guest rooms in a variety of price ranges. The peak tourist season runs from March to October—the winter months—and during that period it may be wise to book ahead through the tourist bureau. Standards are generally good (not great), and *most* hostelries provide air-conditioning. In the guest-house-and-hostel category the rates are pretty reasonable, but once you get into the hotel-and-motel range they climb steeply. There is also a 5% government tax on accommodations.

Fortunately Alice Springs is geared more for family tourism than for business travel. This is why, even in the budget bracket, the town provides more facilities for youngsters than other, much larger places: A good half of the establishments listed below boast swimming pools ranging from splash size to Olympic dimensions.

Also, note that many of the lodges listed below offer dormitory accommodations for less than $A12.

DOUBLES FOR LESS THAN $A68

ALICE LODGE, 4 Mueller St., Alice Springs, NT 0870. Tel. 089/53-1975. 8 rms (none with bath). A/C TV

$ Rates: $A10 dorm, $A20 single, $A26 double. AE, BC, MC, V.

An old outback home converted into a modern lodging house, the Alice is fully carpeted and air-conditioned. There are a good communal kitchen, a saltwater pool, a shady garden, barbecue facilities, and bikes for hire. House rules forbid smoking in the rooms. No hot- and cold-water basins are in the rooms, but there are attractive wood paneling, private refrigerators, tiny cupboards with drawers, and hanging rails for clothes.

LARAPINTA LODGE, 3 Larapinta Dr., Alice Springs, NT 0870. Tel. 089/52-7255. Fax 089/52-7101. 22 units (all with bath). A/C TV TEL

$ Rates: $A57 single, $A67 double. BC, MC, V.

Highly practical though not glamorous, the units are housed in a modern two-story building about five walking minutes from midtown. The lodge facilities include an Olympic-size pool, a children's play area, a guest laundry, and recreation equipment. Standard units come with refrigerators, cutlery, crockery, plus basic cooking utensils and microwave ovens. There is also a large communal kitchen, designed for more elaborate meals.

THE LODGE, 16 Bath St., Alice Springs, NT 0870. Tel. 089/52-3108. 14 rms (2 with bath). A/C

$ Rates: $A19 dorm, $A23 single, $A35 double. No credit cards.

Equipped with a small swimming pool, plus cooking-and-laundry facilities, this simple budget place has an easy-going atmosphere and a cosmopolitan clientele.

MELANKA LODGE, 94 Todd St., Alice Springs, NT 0870. Tel. 089/52-2233 or toll free 008/89-6110. Fax 089/52-3819. 205 rms (49 with bath). A/C TV TEL **Transportation:** The Melanka's shuttle bus will meet bus-and-rail arrivals.

$ Rates: Backpacker, $A10 dormitory, $A26 twin; budget, $A36 single, $A47 double; standard $A30 single or double, deluxe, $A40 single, $A45 double. AE, BC, MC, V.

The most versatile establishment in town not only offers deluxe, standard, and budget rooms but incorporates the local backpackers haven as well. A low-slung, lawn-fronted, very attractive row of buildings right next to the main shopping drag, the Melanka (Aboriginal for "resting place") boasts two pools, a bistro, a TV lounge, a recreation hall, a guest laundry, a currency exchange, an aviary, and a bike-rental service. It's like a self-contained village, although accommodation comforts vary sharply according to price. Deluxe rooms have refrigerators; all *new* rooms have air-conditioners, TVs, telephones, radios, carpeting, and private toilets/showers. The rest share bathroom facilities.

OUTBACK MOTOR LODGE, South Terrace, Alice Springs, NT 0870. Tel. 089/52-3888 or toll free 008/89-6133. Fax 089/53-2166. 60 rms (all with bath). A/C MINIBAR TV TEL

$ Rates: $A67 double. Extra person $A10. BC, MC, V.

The relatively new Outback Motor Lodge is a genuine bargain *for two persons*, offering a whole range of deluxe facilities, including private bathrooms, fully equipped kitchenettes, air-conditioning, and color TVs. A large rectangle of brick units about a mile from town, the Outback is fronted by lovely strips of lawn with chairs, tables, and sunshades and has a fair-size pool. Fittings are very modern,

ALICE SPRINGS

N

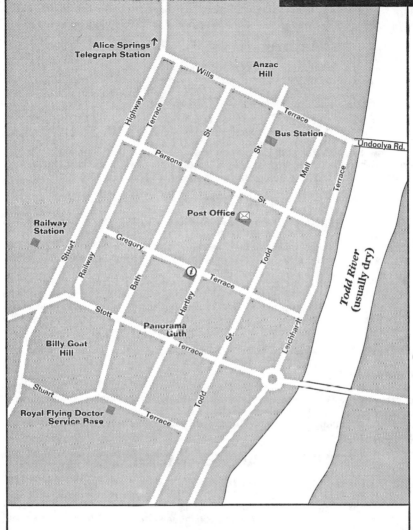

Alice Springs Telegraph Station ↑

Anzac Hill

Wills Terrace

Highway

Terrace

St.

St.

Bus Station

Undoolya Rd.

Parsons St.

Mall

Terrace

Post Office

Railway Station

Gregory Terrace

Stuart

Railway

Bath

Hartley

Todd

Todd River (usually dry)

Stott Terrace

Panorama Guth

St.

Leichhardt

Billy Goat Hill

Stuart Terrace

Royal Flying Doctor Service Base

Todd

Post Office ⊠ Information (i)

6762

including comfortable armchairs, bar stools at the kitchen counter, double wardrobes, and all necessary cooking-and-eating utensils. The management is exceptionally attentive and helpful. Most of the units can easily sleep up to six.

CARAVAN (R.V.) PARKS

There are half a dozen caravan parks in the Alice Springs area, all very close to town. You can camp at every one, and the majority have both tourist cottages and on-site caravans for hire.

Wintersun Caravan Park (tel. 089/52-4080) is about 1½ miles north on the Stuart Highway. On-site vans, fully equipped with kitchen utensils and air-cooled, hold a maximum of seven. Hot and cold running water and three laundries are in the park.

Carmichael Motel and Caravan Park, Larapinta Drive, Tmara Mara, about 2½ miles west of Alice (tel. 089/521-200), has cabins for two to six. It has kitchens as well as a laundry and a swimming pool.

HOSTEL & Y

STUART LODGE, Stuart Terrace, Alice Springs, NT 0870. Tel. 089/52-1894. 31 rms (none with bath). A/C TV

$ Rates: $A27 single, $A38 double. Discounts available for children. BC, MC, V.

Ⓢ The home of the YWCA is a nice modern building, completely air-conditioned, 10 walking minutes from the town center. The place has spacious grounds, three TV lounges, a guest laundry, a community kitchen, and coffee- and tea-making facilities. Accommodations are in single, double, and triple rooms. The rooms are bright, nicely furnished, and cheerful, with good wardrobe space and individual bed lamps as well as ceiling lights. No hot and cold running water is in the rooms, but plenty of bathrooms are on the premises.

YOUTH HOSTEL, corner of Todd St. and Stott Terrace, Alice Springs, NT 0870. Tel. 089/52-5016. 48 beds. A/C

$ Rates: $A19 per person. BC, MC, V.

The Youth Hostel is located in a brand-new building next to the Todd River and gets rather crowded. The 48-bed establishment comprises four dormitories and provides full kitchen facilities. Amenities include a piano in the main hall, a pool table, a guest laundry, a swimming pool, and a foreign-currency exchange desk. You're strongly advised to book ahead.

TOURIST CABINS & CAMPSITES

RED CENTRE RESORT, North Stuart Hwy., Alice Springs, NT 0871. Tel. 089/52-8955. Fax 089/528-300. A/C TV TEL **Transportation:** Courtesy bus to and from Alice Springs runs until 4:30pm.

$ Rates: Campsite $A8.50 per person, bunkhouse (for 4) $A19.50 per person. AE, BC, MC, V.

The Red Centre Resort is set on 18 picturesque acres 3 miles from town. A resort complex with luxury touches like a bistro, two pools, a poolside bar, a laundry, a tennis court, and a kiosk, plus an unlimited amount of ice, the village consists of a motel, bunkhouse, and camping site. The motel rates are above the budget bracket, but the bunkhouse and the campsites are affordable—and you get to enjoy all the amenities.

TODDY'S HOLIDAY ACCOMMODATIONS, 41 Gap Rd., Alice Springs, NT 0870. Tel. 089/52-1322. Fax 089/52-1767. 30 rms (16 with bath). A/C TV

$ Rates: $A10 bunkhouse; $A28 single or double without bath, $A39 single or double with bath. BC, MC, V.

Ⓢ Toddy's consists of modern rooms and a dormitory "bunkhouse," all air-conditioned but fairly basic in their furnishings. The establishment maintains excellent and spotless bathrooms; two large, well-equipped community kitch-

FROMMER'S COOL FOR KIDS: HOTELS

Larapinta Lodge (*p. 332*) It has an Olympic-size pool as well as a children's play area.

Melanka Lodge (*p. 332*) The Melanka offers a recreation hall, two pools, and—irresistibly—a pair of pet kangaroos loose on the grounds.

Youth Hostel (*p. 334*) This hotel charges half rates for "juniors" (guests under 18).

Red Centre Resort (*p. 334*) This hotel has a games room and tennis courts.

ens, and a coin laundry. The cabins have basins, refrigerators, and bedside lamps but come with open hanging closets. There is a courtesy bus to and from town.

WORTH THE EXTRA MONEY

OASIS FRONTIER RESORT, 10 Gap Rd., Alice Springs, NT 0870. Tel. 089/52-1444. Fax 089/52-3776. 102 rms (all with bath). A/C TV TEL

$ Rates: $A80 single or double. AE, BC, MC, V.

A real oasis a few minutes from the main shopping mall, the resort backs onto a large lawn and shrubbery area, featuring an aviary of exotic birds, two swimming pools, a spa, sauna, and a scattering of attractive garden furniture. The adjoining restaurant and tropical cocktail bar have so much greenery that they seem continuations of the garden—which was once an orchard. All the rooms are spacious, airy, and equipped with small private balconies. The refrigerators are stocked with fresh milk, the bedside-and-overhead lights provide good illumination, there is plenty of hanging space in the slotted wardrobes, and TV sets come with in-house movies. Heavy drapes keep out the sun, and you get thoughtful extra touches like a writing desk fitted with fluorescent lights as well as bedside radios. Room service provides breakfast as early as 6am—a rare hour.

NEARBY RESORT

ROSS RIVER RESORT About 55 miles east of Alice on Ross Highway, this old territory homestead white fenced and tree shaded, has been restored and gussied up for tourist accommodation, each guest cabin with its own air conditioner. Horseback riding and swimming are the main pleasures, and the resort acts as springboard for jaunts to various beauty spots in the vicinity. **N'Dahla Gorge** has Aboriginal rock carvings estimated to be 30,000 years old. **Aritunga** is a crumbling little ghost town that was once a gold-mining center, until the stuff petered out around 1912. Almost as many prospectors perished getting to the place as eventually worked there. **Trephina Gorge** and the **Valley of the Eagles** are a region of tranquil water holes forming chains, edged by sandy white "beaches" and giant river gums. You can watch the mighty wedge-tail eagles circling high in the sky, occasionally pouncing on rabbits or lizards they spot with their bomb-aimers' eyes.

4. WHERE TO EAT

Alice boasts several surprisingly sophisticated eateries. Less surprising is the fact that they aren't exactly cheap. In the economy range (which is only slightly more expensive than the equivalent down south) you have a fairly extensive choice. The food generally is at least as good as the fare offered by American, English, Canadian, or New Zealand cities of similar size, although it's nowhere near the quality encountered in Sydney or Melbourne. Some of the swankier restaurants strike a formal note and insist that gentlemen wear ties at the table—although not necessarily coats.

MEALS FOR LESS THAN $A16

BOJANGLES, 80 Todd St. Tel. 52-2873.

Cuisine: AUSTRALIAN. **Reservations:** Accepted.
$ **Prices:** Appetizers $A7.50, main courses $A8–$A25. AE, BC, MC, V.
Open: Daily 11:30am–6am.

This bar and restaurant with a plain frontage has a pleasant interior and a nice beer garden in the back. A sign in front announces "Strine, German, Swiss Spoke 'ere," and this pretty much sets the tone of the place. The wall murals depict rather intriguing Territorial "types." At the counter you can order kangaroo-tail soup and damper (bush bread) for $A4.50 or the more expensive and very tasty kangaroo, buffalo, or camel steaks. Draft beer goes for $A4.50 per mug. Bojangles also serves children's menus, such as fish-and-chips for $A6.50. After dark, the establishment—like several in Alice—doubles as a "nightclub" of sorts.

CAMEL'S CROSSING, Fan Arcade off Todd Mall. Tel. 52-5522.

Cuisine: MEXICAN. **Reservations:** Accepted.
$ **Prices:** Appetizers $A3.80–$A6, main courses $A10–$A16.50. AE, BC, MC, V.
Open: Mon–Sat 5:30–10pm.

The decor is not particularly Mexican, but the ambience is delightful. The patrons are strongly cosmopolitan, possibly attracted by the (for Alice) late dining hours. You can choose between eating inside or at the cluster of outdoor tables in the arcade (which unfortunately go fast). Starters here include a tangy frijole dip ($A4.80), and the main courses offer a variety of chicken, spinach, bean, or beef enchiladas, covered with salsa and sour cream ($A10). The fare is modulated for gringo palates, but you can add a dash of liquid fire by ordering the special "hot sauce."

JOLLY SWAGMAN, Todd Plaza, Todd Mall (opposite the Flynn Church). Tel. 52-3633.

Cuisine: AUSTRALIAN. **Reservations:** Not necessary.
$ **Prices:** Appetizers $A2.50, main courses $A6. AE, BC, MC, V.
Open: Daily 5:30am–10:30pm.

Jolly Swagman is a handy little restaurant and snack bar. The menu is limited, but no meal costs more than $A7, and the fare includes vegetarian dishes—rare in these here parts. This is also a place to try dampers, the traditional unleavened Australian bush bread, which is surprisingly hard to come by.

LA CASALINGA, 105 Gregory Terrace. Tel. 52-4508.

Cuisine: ITALIAN. **Reservations:** Accepted.
$ **Prices:** Appetizers $A4–$A5, main courses $A6–$A14. AE, BC, MC, V.
Open: Daily 6–10pm (pizza bar until 1am).

Artificial tree stumps and electric "oil lamps" that cast a mellow light create a "bush" effect. For contrast you can gaze at the framed photo of the Italian World Champion soccer team that occupies a place of honor above the bar. The fare is divided into pizza and pasta, the former in 10 varieties from $A5 to $A14, the latter costing $A6 to $A8. Try one of the excellent ice-cream desserts for $A3.50, with a powerful cappuccino to finish off your meal. You have to order at the counter, then retire to the tiled dining section to await the vittles.

STUART ARMS BISTRO, upstairs in Todd Plaza. Tel. 52-7131.

Cuisine: AUSTRALIAN. **Reservations:** Not necessary.
$ **Prices:** Appetizers $A5.50–$A6, main courses $A6.50–$A11.50. AE, BC, MC, V.

Open: Daily noon–2pm and 6–8pm.

Up a flight of stairs from the shopping plaza, this is a large, rather noisy eatery with a skylight and a nice view of the town through picture windows. An antique Territory van forms the centerpiece, surrounded by clusters of indoor ferns and plants. The dining area has cane chairs and plastic-top tables, and the wall menu bears the heading "Gourmet Grub." Under this description come buffalo-and-kangaroo filets ($A10.50), steaks, schnitzels, and mixed grills. You help yourself from a copious salad bar.

MEALS FOR LESS THAN $A18

CHOPSTICKS, in the Yeperenye Shopping Center, Hartley St. Tel. 52-3873.

Cuisine: CHINESE. **Reservations:** Accepted.

$ **Prices:** Appetizers $A2–$A5, main courses $A14.50–$A16. AE, BC, MC, V.

Open: Daily 5:30–10:30pm.

This is one of only two Chinese restaurants in town. Surprisingly elegant and astonishingly formal, it welcomes you with a tuxedoed receptionist. There's a small, smart bar in front, plus an illuminated aquarium with tropical fish. Dimly lit by globular lamps, with deeply carpeted floors and beautifully paneled walls, the place is a picture of stylish repose; its soft background music blends into your sweet-and-sour pork. The menu and wine list are impressively leatherbound, and the red napkins pyramided on the gold tabletops make a very attractive showing. The cuisine is superior by Aussie-Asian standards. I can highly recommend the braised beef in garlic sauce. Chinese tea costs $A2. Open "until closed," as the menu puts it with suitable inscrutability, and that includes Sunday.

FLYNNS ON THE MALL, Todd Mall. Tel. 52-2066.

Cuisine: INTERNATIONAL. **Reservations:** Accepted.

$ **Prices:** Appetizers $A6.90, main courses $A9–$A16.90. AE, BC, MC, V.

Open: Daily 6am–9pm.

This handsomely furnished bistro has stately dark-wood tables and chairs, a cool tile floor, and a beamed ceiling. The wall decorations consist of "classic" photographs showing old-time Territory scenes. This is probably the most versatile restaurant in town, serving breakfast, lunch, dinner as well as morning-and-afternoon tea. The menu ranges from pâté and beef stroganoff for $A6.90 to American ribs, Australian buffalo stew, and fettuccine Sicilia. Drinks are equally catholic: from chocolate malteds to brews from wines to exoticas like the Todd River cocktail (containing coffee liqueur, brandy, and ice cream).

WORTH THE EXTRA MONEY

OVERLANDERS, 72 Hartley St. Tel. 52-2159.

Cuisine: INTERNATIONAL. **Reservations:** Recommended.

FROMMER'S COOL FOR KIDS: RESTAURANTS

Bojangles *(p. 336)* Items on the special children's menus go for $A6.50.

Stuart Arms Bistro *(p. 336)* Youngsters are entertained by the TV left permanently on. They also offer half-servings for children at $A5.

Flynns on the Mall *(above)* The restaurant has a whole listing of children's meals—all for $A5.50—which includes miniburgers, sausages, chicken, and fried fish, all with the inevitable chips. There's also an array of milk shakes, banana splits, thick pancakes, and other kid-pleasing items.

$ Prices: Appetizers $A7–$A14, main courses $A13–$A21. AE, BC, MC, V.
Open: Daily noon–2pm and 6–10pm.

Overlanders is a plush steak house masquerading as a rustic barn but with every curlicue of comfort thrown in: a large and stately fireplace for crisp nights; pretty, polite, and attentive waitresses in chic "bush attire"; and an extensive wine list to browse over. The establishment has few windows, and the barn atmosphere is maintained by massive oak rafters, whitewashed walls hung with cattle hides, antique telephones, rifles, pistols, branding irons, and several oil portraits depicting what you're eating. Succulent filet steak costs $A18.95, and there's also the territorial classic—"buffalo à la witchetty," as well as witchetty grub soup.

ROSSINIS, in the Diplomat Motor Inn, corner of Hartley St. and Gregory Terrace. Tel. 52-8977.

Cuisine: INTERNATIONAL. **Reservations:** Recommended.
$ Prices: Appetizers $A8, main courses $A15–$A20. AE, BC, MC, V.
Open: Daily 6:30pm "until late."

Rossinis, a rather swank fine-dining establishment, has pasta specials every Wednesday and Thursday night. At $A13 per head, you can tuck away all the pasta dishes you can hold. The velvety background comes gratis. Sample the outstanding tornedos Rossini if you can manage $A17. This restaurant is a gourmet award winner.

5. ATTRACTIONS

You might want to begin your sightseeing with a panoramic view of the town by climbing the northern end of **Anzac Hill,** off Stuart Highway. There's a war memorial on top and a superb view of the entire city and the desert beyond at your feet. *Climb* is rather hyperbolic—it's more of a gentle uphill stroll. And it doesn't cost a cent.

ROYAL FLYING DOCTOR SERVICE [RFDS], Stuart Terrace, between Todd and Simpson Sts. Tel. 52-1129.

Books, movies, and a TV series have turned the Flying Doctor into an almost legendary institution and its founder—the Rev. John Flynn—into a kind of outback saint. The reality is both more mundane and more impressive: Instead of daily heroics and hairbreadth adventures, there's daily grind and an organization that depends on meticulous planning and maintenance far more than on daredevilry. The adventures are taken in stride, as part of the routine. You'll appreciate them only after you've seen some of the so-called airstrips on which those little prop planes land in order to take patients to emergency treatment. You can only hope that you'll never experience the flying conditions under which some of those evacuations take place.

The main mission at the RFDS base is to keep going the radio network on which the whole service depends. And the chief function of the network is to facilitate the 6,000-or-so medical consultations given each year over the air between the sophisticated equipment at the base and the far more primitive transceivers out in the bush. Without those transceivers—and the painstaking routine devotion that keeps them operational—the aerial medicos would be useless stuntmen.

The base you see has come a long way from the pedal-generator sets and mothlike DH50 biplanes used by the pioneer flying doctors of Flynn's Australian Inland Mission back in 1929, when the service started. Today the bases in Alice and Port Augusta fly dentists to bush clinic centers as well and conduct air search and rescue operations when requested by the Department of Civil Aviation. You can see the whole fascinating works by taking one of the tours offered every hour.

Admission: $A2.50 adults, A50¢ children.
Open: Mon–Sat 1–4pm.

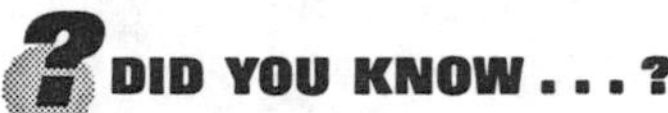

- Northern Territory covers one-sixth of Australia but contains less than 1% of its population.
- N'Dahla Gorge's Aboriginal rock carvings are estimated to be 30,000 years old.
- Alice Springs gained international fame through the TV miniseries *A Town Like Alice*—most of which took place elsewhere.
- Ayers Rock is the world's oldest monolith.
- Katherine Gorge has been 1,400 million years in the making.
- "Bulldust," in Territorian lingo, means the itching, blinding, and pervasive fine red dust stirred up when driving over unsealed roads. But careful—it means something entirely different outside the Territory.

ADELAIDE HOUSE, Todd Mall. Tel. 52-1856.

Adelaide House was actually Alice Springs' first hospital. Built by the Inland Mission in the early 1920s, the place was ingeniously "air-conditioned" by a system of air tunnels combined with wet burlap, which kept it reasonably cool. In the rear you'll see the primitive stone hut from which the first field radio signals and telegrams were sent in 1926. The next step—pedal-powered radio—didn't come until later.

Admission: $A2.50 adults, $A1 children.

Open: Mon–Fri 10am–4pm, Sat 10am–noon.

SCHOOL OF THE AIR, 80 Head St. Tel. 52-2122.

School of the Air is actually a service conducted from radio studios in which teachers help and advise unseen pupils whose homes are widely scattered and spread over thousands of square miles of outback. The school supplements these children's correspondence classes—the only means of educating them as long as they live at home. Their parents are supplied with transceivers at a nominal charge that covers their maintenance as well.

Admission: $A2 per adult; children free.

Open: Mon–Fri 8am–noon.

JOHN FLYNN MEMORIAL, Todd Mall.

This is a beautiful, simple modern church dedicated to the founder of the Royal Flying Doctor Service—a shrine and a museum at the same time. Erected by the Australian Inland Mission, it commemorates the great, gentle, and wonderfully stubborn padre with the twangy voice, round spectacles, and a dream in his heart. The dream was to spread "the mantle of safety over inland Australia," and it took an awful lot of scrapping and flying and crashing before that dream came true. Flynn died in 1951, but in a way he flies with the little bush buzzers every time they take off on another mercy mission. The western annex of the church is devoted to the actual relics of John Flynn's life and work: the first pedal-generator set used with the first transceiver; the old Morse keyboard; a scale model of the biplane that inaugurated the service; Flynn's maps; some of his writings; and the smoky, battered old billy in which he brewed his tea when out "on the wallaby."

Admission: Free.

Open: Daily 9am–5pm.

PITCHI RICHI ABORIGINAL CULTURAL EXPERIENCE, Ross Hwy. Tel. 52-1931.

Pitchi Richi—an Aboriginal term meaning "break in the range"—is an outdoor museum and bird sanctuary just across Heavitree Gap on the southern fringe of Alice. The museum part, blending with the open bushland all around, is a delightful mixture of art and artifacts. The art is that of sculptor Bill Ricketts, who carved his dreamlike Aboriginal faces and figures into trees and rocks so that they seem to be *growing* out of nature and become integral portions of the landscape. The sheer melancholy yet serene beauty of his *Emu Spirit Children* and *Arunta Men* would lose their haunting quality if they were placed indoors, surrounded by walls.

The folk museum features the implements used by the territorial pioneers—tools, weapons, and vehicles, including an antique Minerva car converted into a camel wagon.

Admission: $A8 adults, $A5 children.

Open: Daily 9am–2pm.

PANORAMA "GUTH," 65 Hartley St. Tel. 52-2013.

This museum is built around the colossal work of Dutch artist Henk Guth, who came to Alice Springs in 1966. He conceived the idea of a panoramic painting of his new home, inspired by a similar project in The Hague, Holland. The Alice Springs panorama is a canvas 20 feet high and 200 feet around, with a foreground of natural sand and shrubs that gives the painting an uncanny air of realism. You view it from a platform and could swear you're gazing at a real sunlit landscape all around you. The rest of the museum features artistically arranged showcases with Aboriginal artifacts, weapons, and tools, and watercolors by native Arunta painters.

Admission: $A3 adults, $A1.50 children.

Open: Mon–Sat 9am–5pm, Sun 2–5pm.

CAMEL FARM, Ross River Rd. Tel. 53-0444.

Australia's first Camel Farm is five miles southeast of the city. Camels were originally imported as domesticated beasts of burden to Australia, but a number escaped into the desert, where they adapted, survived, multiplied, and became a very *wild* part of the native fauna. There have even been cases of "killer camels" terrorizing outback settlements.

Noel Fullarton got the idea of reversing the process. He began capturing wild camels, breaking them in—a grueling task that takes three to four months—and utilizing them again as riding animals. Today his camel farm not only breeds the animals but also actually exports them to Iran and Saudi Arabia! The reason for this is the uniquely tough and sturdy species produced by the Australian desert strain. Fullarton himself is a Kiplingesque graybeard who occasionally stars in movies requiring camel drivers. He also supplies the necessary camels. Visitors get a fascinating lecture on camel lore (they aren't as strictly vegetarian as the textbooks have it) and a tour of the farm, which also has a fascinating collection of desert reptiles, from large pythons to pygmy lizards. (For more camel capers, see "Organized Tours," later in this chapter.)

Admission: $A8 adults, $A4 children (includes a camel ride).

Open: Daily 9am–5pm.

OLD TELEGRAPH STATION, about 1½ miles north of Alice off the Stuart Hwy. Tel. 52-1013.

The Old Telegraph Station was the birthplace of Alice Springs. The original spring is still there, and so are the simple but attractive little station buildings. The whole area is now a national park. The first message on the newly completed overland telegraph line—spanning the continent from Darwin in the north to Port Augusta in the south—was sent in January 1872. It was a momentous day for Australia, because the wire, linked to submarine cables, connected the colony with the Dutch East Indies as well as Europe. The Conservation Commission of Northern Territory now displays some interesting old-time photographs and documents in glass cases in the station building. Just across the railroad track lies the Alice's first cemetery, with the graves of the earliest pioneers who settled the region—and mostly died young.

Admission: $A2.50 adults, $A1 children.

Open: Daily 8am–5pm.

DIORAMA VILLAGE, Larapinta Dr. Tel. 52-1884.

An unusual combination of museum, shopping arcade, sidewalk café, diorama, and incongruously misnamed bistro, the center is also a beautiful architectural oasis—with a sculptured garden; a playing fountain and serene pool; and interiors that are in turn modernistic, artistic, and strangely haunting. The diorama is the focal point: a winding darkened corridor with a series of eerily illuminated caves that depict Aboriginal legends—the creation of the earth, how the desert was made, the origin of the Southern Cross and the evening star, the first sunrise, the birth of the sun, and so on. The figures are fairy-tale-like yet realistic, the lighting effects highly sophisticated;

the background music—authentic corroboree wails and hums—blends into a strikingly effective whole. The complex also houses one of the largest souvenir shops in the Territory.

Admission: $A2.50 adults, $A1 children.

Open: Daily 10am–5pm.

STUART AUTO MUSEUM, Emily Gap Rd.

This museum houses a collection of beautifully restored "horseless carriages," the types and makes used to open Central Australia in the early days—although how they ever managed to run along the roads then in existence remains a mystery. (Many of these roads prove impossible for *today's* vehicles, unless they have four-wheel drive.) Also on view are some antediluvian stationary steam-driven engines used for pumping water on cattle stations and a collection of early "talking machines." Fully air-conditioned, the place also features a licensed restaurant.

Admission: $A2 adults; children free.

Open: Daily 9am–5pm.

AVIATION MUSEUM, Memorial Dr. Tel. 52-4241.

The Aviation Museum is housed in an erstwhile hangar, next to the Kookaburra Memorial. You can view photographs of the adventurous pioneering era of desert flying and some of the planes and engines that took part in it, including one recovered after a crash landing.

Admission: Free, but donations welcome.

Open: Daily 10am–4pm.

CHATEAU HORNSBY, Petrick Rd., 8 miles southeast of Alice. Tel. 089/55-5133.

This is something to make you blink with disbelief—a winery in the middle of the desert! With spreading green vines over the red soil, this desert miracle was the creation of Dennis and Miranda Hornsby. They refused to believe the ancient dictum that you can't grow grapes in a summer temperature of 125°F. They did just that, using irrigation water pumped from beneath the sand and refrigerating the grapes as soon as they're harvested so they won't shrivel into raisins. The vineyard started in 1972 and today produces some 1,000 cases of wine annually—including the Early Red label, the first wine in the world every year, because it's made from grapes picked at one minute past midnight on New Year's Day.

The white-roofed château has expanded into an entire entertainment complex, featuring an excellent restaurant, music by local jazz and folk groups, campfire bush nights, and wine tastings. Combined vineyard tours and tastings are daily at 11am and 1 and 2:30pm.

Next door to the château is **Wintercarn Flower Farm.** Another example of how to make the desert bloom, Wintercarn is the first commercial flower plantation in the Northern Territory. It's open for tours Monday to Friday from 7am to 3pm. Admission is $A1.

OLD STUART GAOL, Parsons St.

Once the town lockup, dating from 1907, and one of the oldest buildings in the Alice area, this is a stifling hot, unventilated coop with tiny barred windows. It was a hellish spot to spend a week in.

Admission: $A2.

Open: Tues, Thurs, and Sat 10am–12:30pm.

GHAN PRESERVATION SOCIETY, 6 miles south of Alice on Stuart Hwy., MacDonnell Siding. Tel. 55-5047.

Ghan Preservation Society keeps the steam locomotives and wooden carriages of the grand old train in working order. A sentimental shrine for steam-railroad buffs, the siding has a museum, a souvenir shop, a refreshment kiosk, and barbecue facilities. Train trips leaving at 10am Wednesday to Friday and on Sunday can be booked through the Northern Territory Government Tourist Bureau (tel. 51-5470).

Admission: $A3 adults, $A1.50 children.

Open: Daily.

MECCA DATE GARDENS, Palm Circuit. Tel. 52-2425.

Some four miles south of Alice, en route to the airport, is Australia's first commercial date garden. Walk among the palms and buy fresh dates from the plantation, plus the varied confections made from them.

Admission: Free.

Open: Mon–Sat 9am–5pm.

ORGANIZED TOURS

For a town its size, Alice Springs offers a larger choice of jaunts, trips, and organized excursions than any place in the hemisphere—partly because the territory depends on tourism for the jam on its bread, partly because it's not an easy country to cover on your own. For the remoter points, at least, you'd do better to join one of the group tours and leave the driving to the guides.

Frontier Camel Tours, P.O. Box 2836, Alice Springs, NT 0871 (tel. 53-0444), works in conjunction with the Camel Farm and offers an array of intriguing jaunts on camelback. On safari the camels travel in a tethered string, so you need no riding skills whatever. These riding camels don't bite, spit, or kick (only ill-treated camels do); they make more comfortable mounts than horses; and they kneel on command—more or less. The economy ride is the "Todd River Ramble," a trot along the sandy course of the Todd River, costing $A29 per adult per hour, $A15 per child. But you can also "Take a Camel Out to Lunch," "Take a Camel Out to Dinner," "Spend a Night with a Camel" (desert camping), or "Take a Camel Back in Time" (a half-day safari to the old Telegraph Station). My personal favorite was the dinner date: a 1-hour sundown trot to the Château Hornsby winery. The dinner was excellent, the wine likewise, and both are included in the price of $A69 per person.

A. A. T. King's, 74 Todd St. (tel. 52-5266), has a 1-day "Palm Valley Safari." You ride in a four-wheel-drive vehicle through the impressive MacDonnell Ranges to Hermannsburg Mission to view the historic buildings, then on to Palm Valley, an area seen by few whites before the 1960s. Some of the palms standing there are survivors of a plant age thousands of years ago. The tour departs daily at 8am and costs $A79 for adults, $A67 for children.

The same company also conducts a 4½-hour "Dreamtime Tour" using a specialist guide. You watch demonstrations of Aboriginal hunting-and-gathering methods, see a corroboree and boomerang throwing performed by experts, and sample bush cakes and billy tea. It starts daily at 8am. Adults pay $A62, children $A39.

Outback Experience, P.O. Box 688, Alice Springs, NT 6750 (tel. 089/532-666). This is a small outfit with a great deal of desert experience that keeps its tours down to a maximum of six persons. A daily full-day tour leaves at 7am and follows the legendary old *Ghan* tracks into the desert along the routes pioneered by Afghan camel drivers. There are no crowds and no rigid timetables on this jaunt that shows you Aboriginal rock carvings, cattle stations, ancient fossils, fantastic sandstone formations, the Rainbow Valley, and the flora and fauna of the harshly beautiful outback. There are no tours between December 10 and February 1, when the driver-guide-commentator takes his annual holidays. The trip costs $A95 for adults, $A85 for children.

6. SAVVY SHOPPING

Australia's original inhabitants have been producing artwork for over 40,000 years, but it's only quite recently that the white world has deigned to take more than condescending notice of it. Aboriginal art became fashionable with the advent of Albert Namatjira, an Arunta watercolorist trained at the Hermannsburg Mission, whose landscapes won a string of awards and focused international attention on Australian "primitives." Namatjira died young and lies buried in the city cemetery. He founded a specific school of painting that is being followed by scores of imitators, most of them way below his class.

But although the Europeanized Namatjira-style bushscapes sell best, they form only a very small portion of Aboriginal art output. Most Aboriginal visual-arts expression is religious and deals with the myths and totemic beliefs connected with their spirit ancestors. Traditionally the tribes had no professional artists. Everybody participated in the work, which—together with ceremonial dancing, music, and song cycles—was inextricably linked with daily life. Thus only those works expressing a tribal *theme* can be called genuinely Aboriginal. Everything else is a copy of the white man's art. This isn't so bad, considering that American painters, for instance, spent centuries copying the styles of European masters.

Alice Springs is a major market for Aboriginal artwork in all its forms. A dozen or more shops and galleries retail the output or what passes as such. If you're interested in the genuine article you can't do better than browse around the **Centre for Aboriginal Artists,** 88 Todd St. (tel. 52-3408). This was the first gallery in Australia designed and built solely for the display of Aboriginal handwork. It's a government enterprise, operated on behalf of Central Australia's native artists.

The exhibits—all for sale—are divided into "Authentic Traditional" and "Adapted and Contemporary." The former embrace bark paintings, weapons, carvings, musical instruments, burial poles, and string bags; the latter include woven rugs, pottery, leather crafts, sand paintings, wall hangings, watercolors, and screen prints. All are interesting, some outstandingly beautiful. No one will hassle you to buy, but you can get baskets from $A20 and up, paintings from $A18, and carvings from $A5 to $A50. Open daily from 10am to 5pm.

7. EVENING ENTERTAINMENT

Most of the nocturnal action takes place at the large, swank hotels, but a few spots around town burn a little midnight oil. One of them is **Bojangles** (see "Where to Eat," earlier in this chapter), which puts on live bands nightly from 10:30pm.

Old Alice Inn, 1 Todd Mall (tel. 52-1255), is a bit of everything, including an architectural charmer. The pink-roofed building with shady verandas running all around fills a triple role as a budget hotel, a bar and restaurant, and an entertainment complex. It houses a piano bar where the ivories tinkle Wednesday through Sunday; a didgeridoo virtuoso performs nightly in the restaurant; locally famous jam sessions are held Monday until 4am; and live bands, deejays, and fairly hectic parties take place Friday and Saturday.

MOVIES & A CASINO

Alice Springs boasts two movie houses—the **Pioneer Theatre,** an open-air cinema in town, and a **drive-in** on Airport Road. There's also an amateur live-theater group that puts on performances irregularly. For these and all other after-dark activities, check the weekly *Centralian Advocate* or *This Fortnight in Alice,* available free at hotels and the tourist bureau.

Lasseters Casino in the Diamond Springs Hotel, Barrett Drive (tel. 52-5066), enables Alice Springs, of all places, to glory in one of Australia's legitimate gambling casinos. Opened in 1981, this $A12-million playground resort has the most spectacular setting of any such institution on the globe. Ringed by granite hills that change color every hour with the movements of the sun, this is a superbly adapted scattering of low, white, red-roofed, safari-style buildings, modestly concealing their splendiferous interior.

Apart from a luxury hotel, the resort features an around-the-clock coffee shop (the gourmet restaurant is a mite costly for budget bedouins), a swimming pool, an open-air amphitheater concert bowl, and the gaming rooms. You can test your lucky streaks at American roulette, minidice, blackjack, punto banco, or keno, or you can get a spinning acquaintance with the Australian ritual of two-up.

The casino, incidently, was first run by Rosemary Nin, a tall, supremely chic woman from Birmingham, England, who has a lifelong background in the hotel business. It was the only such enterprise anywhere run by a woman. So much for Australia's alleged macho fixation.

8. EXCURSIONS AROUND THE RED CENTRE

There are organized tours to every one of the attractions described below. But should you decide to strike out on your own, you must observe a few simple rules. By and large the territory in general, and Central Australia in particular, is considerably safer than, say, the streets of New York. But just as you automatically look both ways when crossing a city street, you have to take some elementary precautions when heading into an enormous empty desert. As I said, the territory is pretty safe country, but it's *not* rural Iowa or Sussex. You might pay dearly for ignoring this.

First you must check your vehicle for mechanical defects. Take a tool kit along: There are few service stations where you're going. Make sure, by asking, that your destination doesn't require a four-wheel-drive vehicle. In any case, you'll need a spare tire (two are better), a fan belt, a coil, and a condenser. If you intend to leave the main roads, take an extra jack, a gallon of engine oil, and a shovel. Also take some reserve gas but only in a proper container. Plastic containers are likely to expand and burst from the heat.

The most important item is water. Apply the rule of always taking twice as much as you think you'll need. This goes even for a day trip. One gallon per person per day is regarded as a minimum for survival in summer, and a child needs as much water as an adult.

The territory is renowned for kangaroos, wild camels, wild horses (brumbies), and buffalo. Watch out for them on the roads. A collision with a buffalo is no joke. Above all, watch out for road floodings. In a predominantly arid country, even a little rain can have devastating effects on road conditions. *Never* try to drive through a washaway—if your car stalls, you're in real trouble.

The Northern Territory Tourist Bureau has an excellent pamphlet, "Driving in the Northern Territory." Get it and read it before setting out.

Most of the animals you may encounter are completely harmless, although snakes are always best left alone. Dingos—the wild yellow dogs of the territory—will give you a wide berth. Even the giant perentie lizard—a species of goanna that grows to seven feet in length—is shy and unaggressive unless cornered. The so-called mountain devil, or horned dragon, is a 7-inch lizard covered with sharp spines that give it a rather ferocious appearance. Actually it's a gentle critter that makes quite a good pet. Plants are much more likely to be dangerous, so don't chew any. Two or three seeds of the castor-oil plant, for instance, can kill you.

Since you'll probably get very hot and dusty on the road, a swim in a water hole or gorge looks tempting. It can also be very risky. Desert water is often *freezing cold* and can induce sudden fatal cramps. The water on top is usually the warmest—so check the temperature *below* the surface before plunging in. These holes are often much deeper than they look, so check the depth as well. Also check for hidden snags in the water.

The main rule to remember at all times is this: Treat the territory with respect. It's no jungle—but it's not your backyard either.

KINGS CANYON

The largest and most spectacular in Central Australia, this is a mighty cleft in the George Gill Ranges, about 130 miles southwest of Alice. Until recently it was quite inaccessible to tourists, but now it forms one of the territory's top attractions.

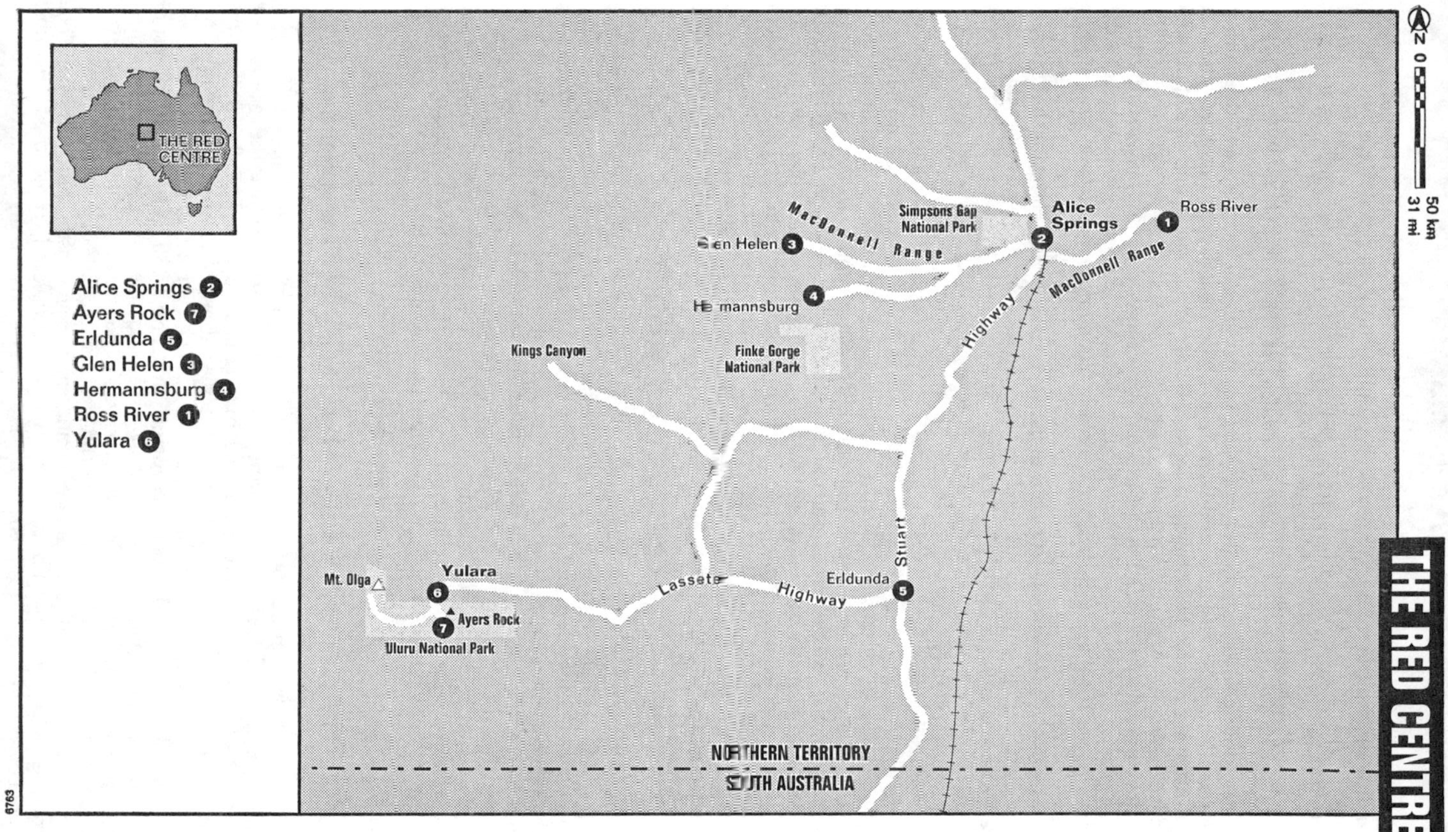
THE RED CENTRE
THE RED CENTRE
Alice Springs 2
Ayers Rock 7
Erldunda 5
Glen Helen 3
Hermannsburg 4
Ross River 1
Yulara 6
N
0
50 km
31 mi
Ross River
Alice Springs
Simpsons Gap National Park
MacDonnell Range
MacDonnell Range
Glen Helen
Hermannsburg
Finke Gorge National Park
Kings Canyon
Highway
Stuart
Erldunda
Highway
Lassete
Yulara
Mt. Olga
Ayers Rock
Uluru National Park
NORTHERN TERRITORY
SOUTH AUSTRALIA
6763

Immense walls of pink sandstone reflect in hundreds of rock pools, creating fantastic color combinations from cream to deep purple. This is an oasis of wildlife—birds, huge lizards, and rock kangaroos hunting and feeding in the lush vegetation. And all around the cliff walls rise to 700 feet and more.

HERMANNSBURG HISTORIC PRECINCT

Located some 93 miles southwest of Alice on Larapinta Drive, this was originally a German Lutheran mission, established in 1877 on traditional Aboriginal lands. In 1982 the land was handed back to its historic owners, the Aranda, and the community called Ntaria has been run by them ever since.

The mission has been a training ground for some of the most famous Aboriginal painters and craftspeople, and some of their work can be seen there. The core of the mission, the Historic Precinct, contains the old buildings registered on the National Estate. There is the original church, the schoolhouse, a small museum, and the Art Gallery housing some excellent representative samples of the Hermannsburg watercolorists. The old missionary houses are now the Kata Anga Tea rooms, which serve refreshments as well as selling local art and artifacts at very reasonable prices. Open daily 9am to 5pm. Entry to the Historic Precinct is $A2 for adults, half for children. For limited summer hours, call 089/56-7411.

Across the Finke River, 15 miles to the south, lies **Palm Valley.** The track leading there, going through the sandy riverbed, can be a stretch of sheer hell, so be sure to inquire about its current condition at Hermannsburg. The valley is a flora-and-fauna reserve and perhaps the most beautiful oasis of the center, all the more striking because of the arid wilderness surrounding it. The vegetation includes some of the oldest plant forms on earth—tall palms, ferns, and cyads, sheltered by towering cliffs, casting their reflections into mysterious rock pools. Despite its beauty, the place has a strange eeriness, like a patch of another planet grafted into the desert. It won't surprise you to learn that the valley is a focal point of Aboriginal tribal myths, populated by phantom creatures and supernatural totem animals.

STANDLEY CHASM

Thirty-six miles west of Alice Springs on Namatjira Drive, this cleft in the MacDonnell Ranges, 15 feet wide and more than 250 feet high, which glows dark red under the midday sun, draws camera buffs from every part of Australia. You can walk through the entire fissure and feel those soaring ochre-red walls closing above you. Aborigines from the nearby **Jay Creek Settlement** run a refreshment stall, and the site is quite touristy—toilets and all, as well as a A50¢ admission fee. The Aborigines also organize trail rides through the surrounding countryside. The trail boss is a mine of information about tribal legends, and the rides are fascinating if you're an average horseperson. Open daily 8:30am to 4:30pm. Admission is $A2.

AYERS ROCK

This is *the* landmark of the territory and one of the most stunning natural marvels in the world. It is the summit of a buried mountain, the largest monolith on earth, rising unbelievably huge and abrupt from the flat scrub desert that surrounds it. Towering 1,143 feet above the plain and measuring 5½ miles in circumference, the rock is twice the size of central London. The wind playing around its titanic flanks gives the monolith a strange moaning "song" that the Aborigines—who venerated it for centuries—believed were spirit voices. They called the rock Uluru.

Ayers Rock lies amid **Uluru National Park,** about 280 road miles southwest of Alice. The sight takes your breath away—the suddenness with which this monster looms before you, the sheer silent immensity of its bulk catches your throat before you become aware of its colors. The colors change with the time of day: from deep scarlet to molten gold to delicate lilac, presenting entirely new vistas with every hue. The rock is honeycombed with caves, many still unexplored, some used for tribal ceremonies and burial chambers. There is an aura of ageless mystery about the rock that no amount of camera clicking and no tourist buses and airplane roars can dispel.

It's as if the stone is aware that it will still be there, unchanged and eternal, when all of us have vanished.

You can climb all the way up, but I wouldn't advise it unless you're in very good physical condition. The desert sun beats down, it's steep, and for the first 280 feet there are no handholds. At the top you sign your name in the park ranger's book and get your reward in the form of a fabulous view—the crystal clarity of the air shrinks distances in an amazing fashion.

Twenty miles west of the rock stands a cluster of striking blue domes called the **Olgas.** These are huge round monoliths topped by Mount Olga, rearing 1,800 feet and encircling some of the most beautiful bushland in the centre. These rocks, too, change their coloring and glow like red-hot iron in the morning. Ayers Rock and the Olgas are parts of the same national park, so most visitors combine these sights in one trip. There's an $A8 entry fee; children are admitted free. Permits are valid for five days. Open daily from 5:30am to 8:30pm.

The park has a large variety of wildlife, from big goannas to tiny marsupial mice. Unfortunately it also has flies—millions of them. These flies are the curse of the Australian bush, for they seek body contact with a persistence that borders on the maniacal. Veterans like the park rangers have learned to ignore them, more or less, but they keep the rest of us slapping away at our arms and faces. The park rangers are a philosophical lot. I asked one of them how often he'd climbed the rock. His smile wrinkles deepened. "Me? Never. D'you think I'm crazy? I work here."

A further word concerning Ayers Rock: Bring a sweater along; desert mornings can be quite nippy, and nothing can ruin a sunrise better than goosebumps. If you want to climb up you *must* wear rubber-soled shoes. Even then it's pretty tough going, so don't play Edmund Hillary unless you're physically fit.

WHERE TO STAY

Ayers Rock ranks almost with the Great Barrier Reef as a tourist attraction. In order to accommodate the swelling tide of visitors, the Northern Territory government, together with private developers, has constructed the $A160-million **Ayers Rock Resort** (tel. 089/56-2144). A desert oasis of inspiring proportions, the resort is entirely self-contained, offering swimming pools, a shopping mall, a supermarket, a tavern, bars, banks, a spectacular multilevel Information and Display Centre, an 800-seat amphitheater, and a miniature theatrette. The resort has been thoughtfully planted just outside the national park area so as not to spoil the rock's grandiose wilderness effect. It's located about 4½ driving hours from Alice Springs on a highway some 13 miles from Ayers Rock itself. A recent suggestion by a politician to build a monorail across the landscape was luckily howled down by a nationwide chorus of protests. There are cabs and charter buses to the rock. By car, take Stuart Highway to Eridunda, then turn right onto Lasseter Highway.

The resort can accommodate up to 5,000 people per day in various degrees of comfort. Admittedly, it's top-heavy on the luxury side—at the multistar Sheraton and Four Seasons hotels guests pay around $A123 to $A230 per night per room. But there is also the **Outback Pioneer Hotel,** P.O. Box 10, Yulara, NT 0872 (tel. 089/56-2170), offering good dormitory-style accommodations (four-bedded) at $A18 per person, cabins for $A84 for up to four people. The lodge has air-conditioning, bedding for hire, a separate ablution block, meal service, an excellent pool, and gas-fired barbecue sites. All buses from Alice and to the rock stop there. Even cheaper is the **camping ground,** P.O. Box 96, Yulara Drive (tel. 089/56-2055), with electricity, showers, toilets, hot-and-cold water, on-site caravans, and barbecue pits; you can rent vans for $A60, powered camping sites for $A22.

TOURS

There are many activities around the rock, including **motorcycle tours** with passengers riding pillion on heavy Harley-Davidsons, and the Southern Skies Observatory, which takes advantage of the very clear, pollution-free air to show visitors the highlights of the firmament. Perhaps the most intriguing is the **"Edible Desert" Tour.** Participants learn the basics of desert survival by studying the knowledge and techniques of the Aboriginal desert wanderers. It's getting to know "bush tucker" at the source. You book for this tour at the **Ayers Rock Resort Visitor Centre,** Yulara Drive (tel. 089/56-2240), open daily 8am to 9pm, and pay $A35 for adults, $A25 for children.

From Alice Springs a whole batch of tours head for Ayers Rock, several run by hostels. They range from luxurious to basic. One of the most economical is a 2-day camping excursion operated by **Central Australia Tours,** P.O. Box 8369, Alice Springs, NT 0870 (tel. 089/53-1733). For $A165 you get transportation, meals, tents, and camping equipment. The price does not include the entrance fee to the National Park. There is also a **Backpacker Special** with dorm accommodations costing $A125 for two days. Book at the Alice Springs Tourist Bureau, Ford Plaza, Todd Mall (tel. 51-5470), or by calling toll free 008/89-1121.

9. OTHER EXCURSIONS IN NORTHERN TERRITORY

The road running north from Alice Springs to Darwin is officially named Stuart Highway. The Territorians never call it that. For them it's either "The Bitumen" or "The Track." But whatever label you give it, this is the high road to adventure, the path through the "Never Never," the 954-mile-long spear of civilization stabbing into one of the remotest, least known, and most exciting frontier lands on the globe.

Northern Territory hasn't achieved statehood yet. With fewer than 170,000 people inhabiting an area twice as large as Texas, the process may take a good many years. But meanwhile the territory is surging ahead at a pace that seems dizzying after its 150 years of Rip van Winkle sleep.

Until the construction of the Overland Telegraph Line in the 1870s, the north slumbered undisturbed, isolated and mysterious as the valleys of the moon. With the telegraph wire—stretching from Port Augusta in South Australia to Darwin, clear across the continent—came a track. Then a road of sorts, trodden mainly by adventurers and gold seekers hearty enough to brave it. But during World War II, with the tide of Japanese conquests surging toward Australia's northern shores, "The Track" suddenly became a lifeline, a vital military artery. Hundreds of thousands of Australian and American soldiers passed up and down that sun-scorched bitumen ribbon, and at last Australia learned that it was neglecting the north at its peril.

One of the few blessings of the war was the tremendous improvements it brought to "The Track." And these, in turn, resulted in a steady flow of tourists, lured by hunting thrills, nomadic tribes of Aborigines, and the wild surrealistic grandeur of the landscape.

In places the scenery resembles a canvas by Salvador Dalí: gigantic meteor boulders, some as perfectly round as cosmic marbles; magnetic anthills towering 20 feet high; white ghost gum trees reflected in lagoons of incredibly clear blue water; rice grass that closes over a horseman's head; rust-brown deserts; darkly mysterious rock chasms; immense lushly green mangrove swamps . . . all this is the Top End.

Regardless of whether you go armed with a gun, a rod, or a camera, the territory provides action. Flocks of emus race through the mulga, wild buffalo muster you warily, dingoes howl around the campfires at night, huge pythons slither over the rocks; the rivers and sea contain catfish and sharks, harmless freshwater crocodiles, and the dangerous saltwater kind. Kangaroos and wallabies—from little dwarf hoppers to "big red" six footers—flee in fantastic leaps. And in the air teem swarms of parakeets, ducks, geese, tiny wrens, and occasionally a mighty wedge-tail eagle.

The territory knows only two seasons—"wet" and "dry"—and only the dry is suited to tourist activities. It lasts from early April to October and comes close to being ideal, with cloudless skies day after day, the average daytime temperatures hovering around 80°F, and the nights pleasantly cool, sometimes even chilly.

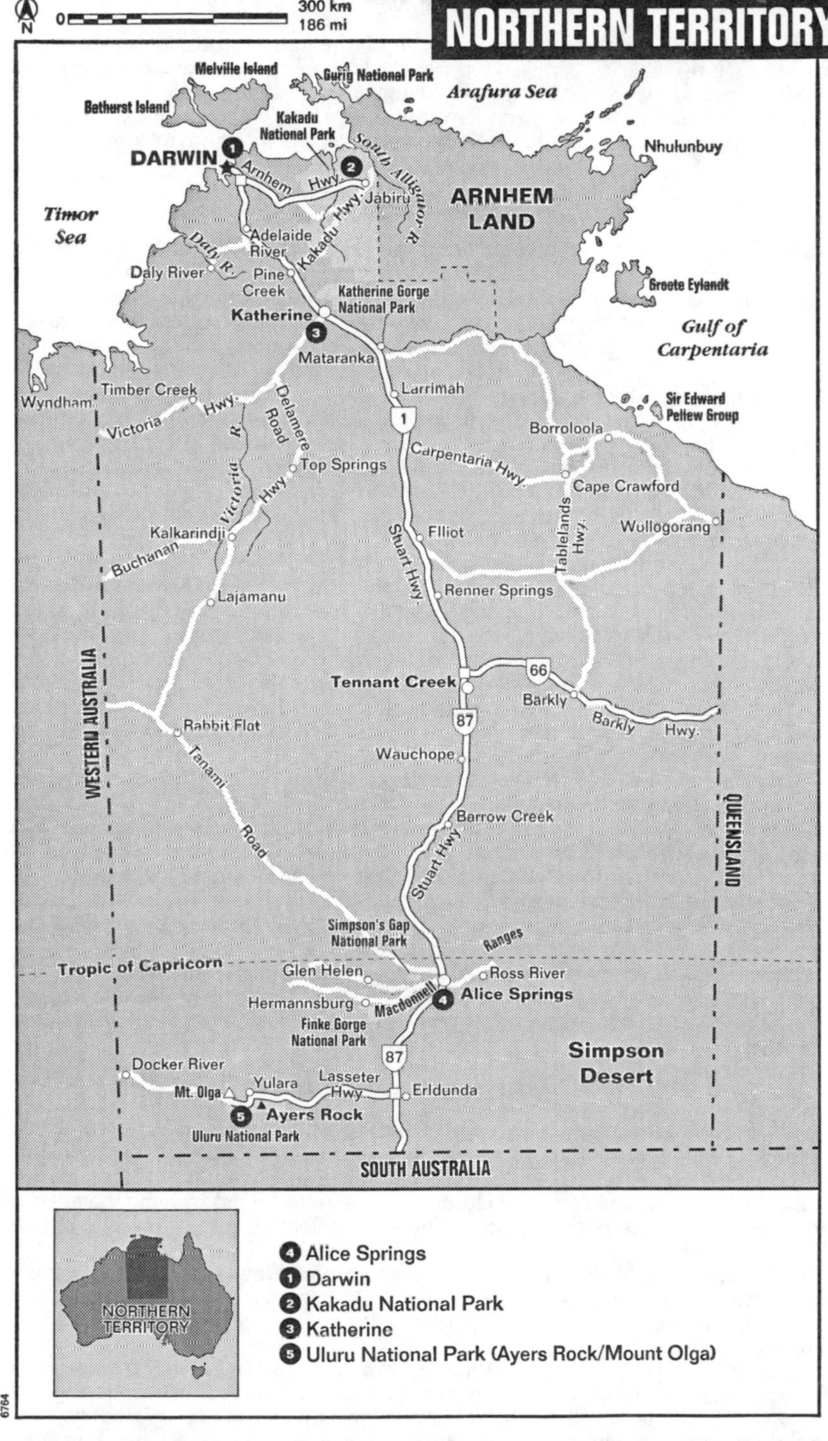

NORTHERN TERRITORY
0
300 km
186 mi
N
Melville Island
Gurig National Park
Arafura Sea
Bathurst Island
Kakadu National Park
South Alligator R.
DARWIN
Arnhem Hwy
Jabiru
ARNHEM LAND
Nhulunbuy
Timor Sea
Adelaide River
Kakadu Hwy
Daly R.
Daly River
Pine Creek
Katherine Gorge National Park
Groote Eylandt
Katherine
Gulf of Carpentaria
Mataranka
Larrimah
Wyndham
Timber Creek
Victoria Hwy.
Victoria R.
Delamere Road
Sir Edward Pellew Group
Borroloola
Carpentaria Hwy.
Top Springs
Cape Crawford
Tablelands Hwy.
Wollogorang
Kalkarindji
Buchanan Hwy
Elliot
Stuart Hwy
Renner Springs
Lajamanu
WESTERN AUSTRALIA
Tennant Creek
Barkly
Barkly Hwy.
Rabbit Flat
Tanami Road
Wauchope
Barrow Creek
QUEENSLAND
Simpson's Gap National Park
Ranges
Tropic of Capricorn
Glen Helen
Ross River
Alice Springs
Hermannsburg
Macdonnell
Finke Gorge National Park
Simpson Desert
Docker River
Lasseter Hwy.
Erldunda
Mt. Olga
Yulara
Ayers Rock
Uluru National Park
SOUTH AUSTRALIA
NORTHERN TERRITORY
4 Alice Springs
1 Darwin
2 Kakadu National Park
3 Katherine
5 Uluru National Park (Ayers Rock/Mount Olga)
6764

Wedged between is the so-called "Build-up," the humidly broiling period from October to November that weighs on people like a hot, itching shroud, making tempers flare and fists fly rather like the khamsin wind of the Middle East. That's when the thunderstorms strike, and if you fly into Darwin then, you can expect a pretty bumpy descent. Darwin holds a continental record with a yearly average of 88 thunderstorms.

DARWIN

This small tropical port on the Timor Sea is the territorial capital and something of a phoenix among cities. In its brief history Darwin has risen twice from almost total destruction. Before World War II, Darwin was a sleepy little outpost, drowsily uninterested in becoming anything else. But the Japanese bombers that virtually flattened the place also gave it the spark of new life. Darwin was reborn as a model of town planning, blossoming out in tree-lined streets, shady parks, and cool ultramodern public buildings. Then—during Christmas 1974—Cyclone Tracy did as thorough a destruction job as the Japanese. And for the second time Darwin rose from the debris, picked up the pieces left by the hurricane, and built anew.

The city now contains some 73,000 people, nearly half the entire population of the north, and today it boasts one of the fastest expansion rates of any Australian community. It currently houses over a dozen air-conditioned hotels and at least six first-rate restaurants. There are also a Chinese temple, a superb Botanic Garden, and a string of silver-sand beaches on its doorstep.

In 1982 it got an additional magnet in the shape of the **Diamond Beach Hotel-Casino** (tel. 46-2666). Looking somewhat like an architect's dream from the *Arabian Nights,* this gleaming white edifice is set on acres of tropical gardens, right on the coast so as to provide a panoramic view across the ocean. Most of the clientele, however, is less interested in views than in the roulette, blackjack, minidice, punto banco, and keno action in the gaming rooms. The hotel also houses a top-ranking cabaret, two top-line restaurants, and a 24-hour coffee shop, which Darwin can do with very nicely.

Darwin's special allure, however, doesn't stem from buildings or entertainment ventures. It lies in a quite unique life-style for which the term *laid-back* is a pale understatement. It lies in midcity streets heavy with the scent of jasmine and frangipani; in a suburbia blazing purple with bougainvillea flowers; in miles of silvery beaches on one side of town and tropical forest on the other; and in a pattern of mangrove-fringed rivers winding into an immense harbor. This is the only place in Australia where you can see business executives holding a conference on the lawn of a public park.

Darwin lies closer to Indonesia than to Alice Springs, and the Asian and Melanesian influence hits you immediately. The town has had two Chinese mayors, and of the 40 or so nationalities that make up the population more than half are Timorese, Vietnamese, Chinese, and Laotian.

WHAT TO SEE & DO

The chief tourist attraction is a daily **fish-feeding** ritual whose timing, governed by the tides, is announced in the newspaper. It takes place at **Aquascene** at Doctors Gully, in the heart of the city. There, as if on command, thousands of catfish, mullet, bream, and batfish come crowding close to the shore to be fed by hand, competing with one another in a positive frenzy. The gully is located just below the YMCA building.

Two miles north of downtown, in the **East Point Reserve,** you can wander among entire herds of wild kangaroos and wallabies that emerge from the bushland beyond to browse, tussle, snooze, and get in the way of sweating joggers and picnicking families.

Somewhat less gentle are the inhabitants of the **Crocodile Farm,** 30 miles south on Stuart Highway (tel. 88-1450). Here are more than 7,000 crocs in various stages of development; although, even the babies are equipped with rows of needle teeth. The reptiles are bred for both leather and food—this is where most of the Territory's crocodile steaks originate. It's open daily from 9am to 5pm, and admission is $A6 for adults, $A2.50 for children.

The **Territory Wildlife Park** (tel. 88-6000) is some 45 miles south of Darwin. A 960-acre patch of natural bushland, the park also has a walk-through aquarium and a "nocturnal village" in which you can observe scrub-and-treetop denizens that shy from daylight. Open daily from 8:30am to 4pm. Admission is $A10 for adults, $A5 for children.

A variety of organized **safari tours** head for the creeks, lagoons, and nature parks east and south of the city. These jaunts cater to a wide range of interests, purses, time schedules, and stamina. This means that you can shoot, fish, film, watch, stalk, or just laze around—according to your fancy. Ducks and geese can be hunted all year, and your safari guide can arrange permits to shoot red kangaroos and buffalo. For fishermen there's the giant barramundi—one of the finest table delicacies on earth, apart from saratago, mullet, and sawfish. But for most tourists the thrill lies in observing the wildlife, flora as much as fauna, and in seeing a slice of nature still very much in the raw.

Safari accommodations run from elaborate cabins with electricity, showers, and septic-tank toilets to simple tents for bush camping. The time involved varies from one morning to four days and nights.

Jumping Crocodiles! For a nature spectacle you won't see anywhere else on the globe, board the ***Adelaide River Queen,*** P.O. Box 37913, Winnellie, NT 0821 (tel. 089/88-8144). The *Queen* is moored in the Adelaide River, along the Arnhem Highway, about 50 miles southeast of Darwin. A specially constructed two-decker turbo-powered craft, it has an open-air upper deck and an air-conditioned, glass-walled lower portion.

The *Queen* noses slowly and silently along the brownish green river until it draws close to a cruising croc. From the lower deck you're eye to eye with the monster—you can *see* it contemplating you for the dinner menu and feel grateful for the thick polarized-glass partition between you. Then the guide dangles a chunk of meat on a pole from the upper deck. The croc leaps like a leather bullet out of the water, its jaws slamming shut with a bang on the morsel. There's a tremendous flurry of water . . . then just ripples. This is repeated again and again with different crocs—some 10 feet long—and I guarantee you won't forget that explosive *whack* of toothed maws slamming on prey. And you certainly won't ignore the warning symbols of crocodile jaws posted by the rivers and creeks of the territory.

If you drive down to the *Queen* yourself, the 2-hour tour costs $A26 for adults, $A14 for children. The half-day tour, including coach pick up at your hotel, costs $A48 for adults, $A35 for children.

Finally, the Northern Territory is renowned for its bizarre **festivals** and contests, and Darwin offers two prime examples, both held every August. The first is the **Mud Crab Tying Championship.** Contestants can use only their bare hands and feet to neatly tie up huge slippery crabs whose snapping claws can take off a finger. (The trick is to hold down with your toes and tie with your hands.) Older and more traditional is the **Beer Can Regatta,** in which Darwinites utilize their immense consumption of the amber brew by making ships from the containers and racing them on the harbor. It's an inspiring spectacle: Viking boats, Spanish galleons, Chinese junks, American clippers, pearling luggers, and fishing craft—all made from beer cans and battling for the victory cup. In the subsequent festivities more shipbuilding material is amassed for the following year.

WHERE TO STAY

The Top End of Australia is not exactly cheap. But it does have budget accommodations once you get there. One of the best bets is the **YMCA,** Doctors Gully, Darwin, NT 5790 (tel. 089/818-377). In a downtown location, very simple but spotless, the Y offers 100 beds (with shared bathrooms), a TV lounge, and a pool at $A28 for single, $A38 for double (no credit cards).

The rather oddly named **Air Raid,** 35 Cavenagh St., Darwin, NT 0801 (tel. 089/81-9214), is a well-equipped lodge standing opposite the GPO. All rooms have air-conditioning, private showers, and TVs, and there is a communal kitchen and guest laundry on the premises and a budget-priced restaurant downstairs. Singles cost $A48, doubles $A58; "small families" (six maximum) pay $A78.

Inner-City Lodge, 112 Mitchell St., Darwin, NT 0801 (tel. 089/81-8399), has a pool, kitchen-and-laundry facilities, and barbecue pits. It offers special rates for backpackers, starting at $A11 per night.

Darwin City YHA Hostel, 69A Mitchell St., Darwin, NT 0801 (tel. 089/81-3995), is located within the Darwin Transit Centre, the terminus for all buses as well as a shopping-and-restaurant complex and pick-up point for all coach touring companies. The YHA has 90 dorms and double rooms, a pool, and a coin laundry; it is housed in a former hostel for government employees. Charges vary according to season: $A10 to $A12 for adults, $A5 to $A6 under 18, with double rooms going for a standard $A22 per couple (BC, MC, and V are accepted).

KAKADU NATIONAL PARK

This is the most wildly exotic of all Australian nature reserves. Sprawling some 150 miles east of Darwin off Arnhem Highway, this World Heritage treasure represents the very essence of the tropical north. Densely forested and sprinkled with Aboriginal rock paintings, Kakadu is swarming with furred, feathered, and scaled wildlife. Huge black buffalo graze near the riverbanks and wild pigs root in the tall grasses. The waters teem with more than 100 species of reptiles, and high above circle hawks, geese, kingfishers, brolgas, jabirus, ibis, and corella parrots. But the Kakadu is not entirely untamed wilderness. At the National Park Headquarters there's a unique crocodile-shaped resort hotel, stocked with iced drinks, that serves very civilized food and offers air-conditioned sleeping quarters.

AKT Tours, GPO Box 1397, Darwin, NT 0801 (tel. 089/81-5144), runs an excursion to Kakadu National Park that includes a boat cruise on Yellow Waters and visits to Aboriginal "Dreamtime" rock paintings. It leaves Darwin daily at 6:30am and returns at 7:30pm. The cost is $A92 per person, plus the park entrance fee.

KATHERINE GORGE

Located some 160 miles south of Darwin on the Stuart Highway, this is a mighty waterway cut through a rock plateau by the Katherine River. It is also one of the most awesomely impressive nature spectacles on earth . . . and an estimated 1,400 million years old. The ocher rock walls tower above the azure-and-emerald water populated by crocodiles, tortoises, marine monitors, goannas, and 30 species of fish. Ashore and in the sky flutter and stalk 160 breeds of birds. The jungle garden setting all around is criss-crossed by hiking trails and marked with ancient Aboriginal rock art. The gorge is one of 13 similar cuts contained in **Katherine Gorge National Park** (tel. 089/72-1886)—a region made famous through the classic novel *We of the Never Never* and the film version.

The most enjoyable way of seeing the gorge is by cruising through it. This is done in beautiful white streamlined motor vessels, specially designed for the purpose, with all-round vision decks, ice-water dispensers, and toilets. Book your scenic ride with **Frontier Cruises,** GPO Box 4665, Darwin, NT 0801 (tel. 089/81-3173 for Darwin or 089/71-1381 for Katherine). The shortest cruise (two hours) costs $A17 for adults, $A7 for children.

CHAPTER 11

TASMANIA — THE ISLAND STATE

- WHAT'S SPECIAL ABOUT TASMANIA
1. LAUNCESTON
2. HOBART
3. DEVONPORT

Tasmania hangs like a heart-shaped pendant 150 miles south of the Australian mainland coast, separated by a very turbulent stretch of water called Bass Strait. On some world maps the island gets left off altogether, and it certainly is the state foreign visitors know the least about. Yet in some respects it is the most fascinating component of the Commonwealth.

There is something oddly un-Australian about Tasmania, a sense of not belonging where it is. You get the feeling that during the immemorial past it had been towed from the northern hemisphere and left anchored here by mistake. Tasmania's climate, vegetation, topography, and general appearance don't belong in the antipodes. But historically this is part of Australia's cradle—the grimmest and most tragic part.

The smallest and, with fewer than half a million inhabitants, least populous Australian state, the island is affectionately known as Tassie among mainlanders, and the diminutive denotes its status in the political pecking order. As a tourist attraction, however, Tassie enjoys big advantages. Its size—with 26,383 square miles, a bit smaller than Ireland—brings everything within easy reach. Its scenic beauty is fabulous in parts and well watered, green, and lush everywhere. Its climate is mildly European, without extremes in either direction. And it has preserved its historical heritage so well that the island is a treasure trove for those interested in the white man's "fatal impact" on the region.

Most of that heritage is brutal, some of it hideously so. The island was discovered by the Dutch seafarer Abel Tasman in 1642, who named it Van Diemen's Land. (Eventually it was renamed after *him.*) But the British under Captain Cook were the first to explore and take possession of the place in 1777. Lt. William Bligh of the *Bounty* (who later achieved fame of sorts as captain of the same ship) planted the first apple tree on the island—forerunner of its major export crop today.

Hobart, the capital, was founded in 1803—some 15 years after Sydney—and ranks as Australia's second-oldest city. But the island's chief role was a dumping ground for "unmanageable" convicts from the mainland, a kind of penal settlement within a penal colony. The treatment meted out to these men and women was reflected in the name the convicts bestowed on the Bass Strait: "The passage between earth and hell on earth." Today the ruins of the old penal stronghold of Port Arthur are a top tourist attraction. Then they meant a living death for thousands of human beings in chains, driven to work by the constant cracking of rawhide whips across their backs.

If the treatment of whites was gruesome, that of blacks was unspeakable. The Aborigines of Van Diemen's Land weren't merely decimated, they were exterminated in what must pass as a 19th-century experiment in genocide. After repeated clashes with the natives, the administration decided to get rid of them all. The original Tasmanians were even less advanced in technology than the mainlanders and therefore even more helpless. After a concerted drive across the entire island failed, they were

WHAT'S SPECIAL ABOUT TASMANIA

Cities/Towns
- ☐ Hobart, the capital, a historic charmer and the second-oldest city in Australia.
- ☐ Launceston, relaxed and tranquil, enlivened by a country-club casino.
- ☐ Devonport, a bustling little harbor town and the island's richest farming region.
- ☐ Port Arthur, a semi-ghost town filled with haunting mementos of its past as the most hellish prison on the continent.

Architectural Highlights
- ☐ Wrest Point, an ivory tower pointing up from Hobart, site of Australia's first legal gambling casino.
- ☐ Penny Royal World, an old quarry in Launceston transformed into a miniature theme park.
- ☐ Anglesea Barracks, the oldest still-functioning military establishment in Australia.

Park
- ☐ Tasmanian Devil Park, a small nature reserve harboring the only pattable "devils" on the globe.

Festivals/Events
- ☐ The finish of the Sydney-Hobart Yacht Race, top sailing event of the hemisphere.
- ☐ Australian Jazz Convention held in Launceston.
- ☐ Hobart Summer Festival, when the waterfront breaks out with strolling minstrels, dancing groups, concert parties, and open-air dining.

captured or coaxed out in little groups and either killed or deported. The last pure-blooded Tasmanian Aborigine died in 1876. There is *not one* left.

The convicts left their marks in the form of carefully preserved buildings and bridges. The Aborigines left nothing except a memory that's fading fast.

For many visitors, however, the real interest of Tasmania does not lie in historical mementos but in the scenery. The island is one of the most mountainous on earth, and much of the southwest is a barely mapped, hardly explored wilderness of towering peaks and dense forests broken by roaring streams—a wonderful challenge for mountaineers and bush walkers, but a rugged one. Sir Edmund Hillary, the conqueror of Mount Everest, used to come here to sharpen his skills. It's also a paradise for fishermen who flock from all over Australia to tackle the river and lake trout.

The wilderness also harbors animals that have become extinct on the mainland. One is the Tasmanian devil, a carnivore about the size of a fox terrier with huge teeth and an extremely ugly disposition. The other is probably the rarest-known beast in the world today: The marsupial wolf—or tiger—is built like a German shepherd, with blackish brown stripes across the hindquarters. A lone nocturnal hunter, it captures its prey by outrunning it, loping along tirelessly until the victim drops with exhaustion. These wolves are now so rare that none has been sighted in recent years.

Around the well-trodden tourist trails (the ones we will tread) the landscape is rolling and gentle, redolent with fruit trees and sprinkled with tranquil villages that call themselves towns. Tassie has only one real city, Hobart, but that packs a real surprise. It boasts one of Australia's legal gambling establishments, the Wrest Point Casino—as distinct from hundreds of illicit ones flourishing on the mainland.

SEEING TASMANIA

The best way to see Tasmania is to make a circuit of the island, which is the way in which this chapter proceeds. Ideally, you should begin your jaunt in Launceston (see the "Launceston" section for information about getting there), then move on to

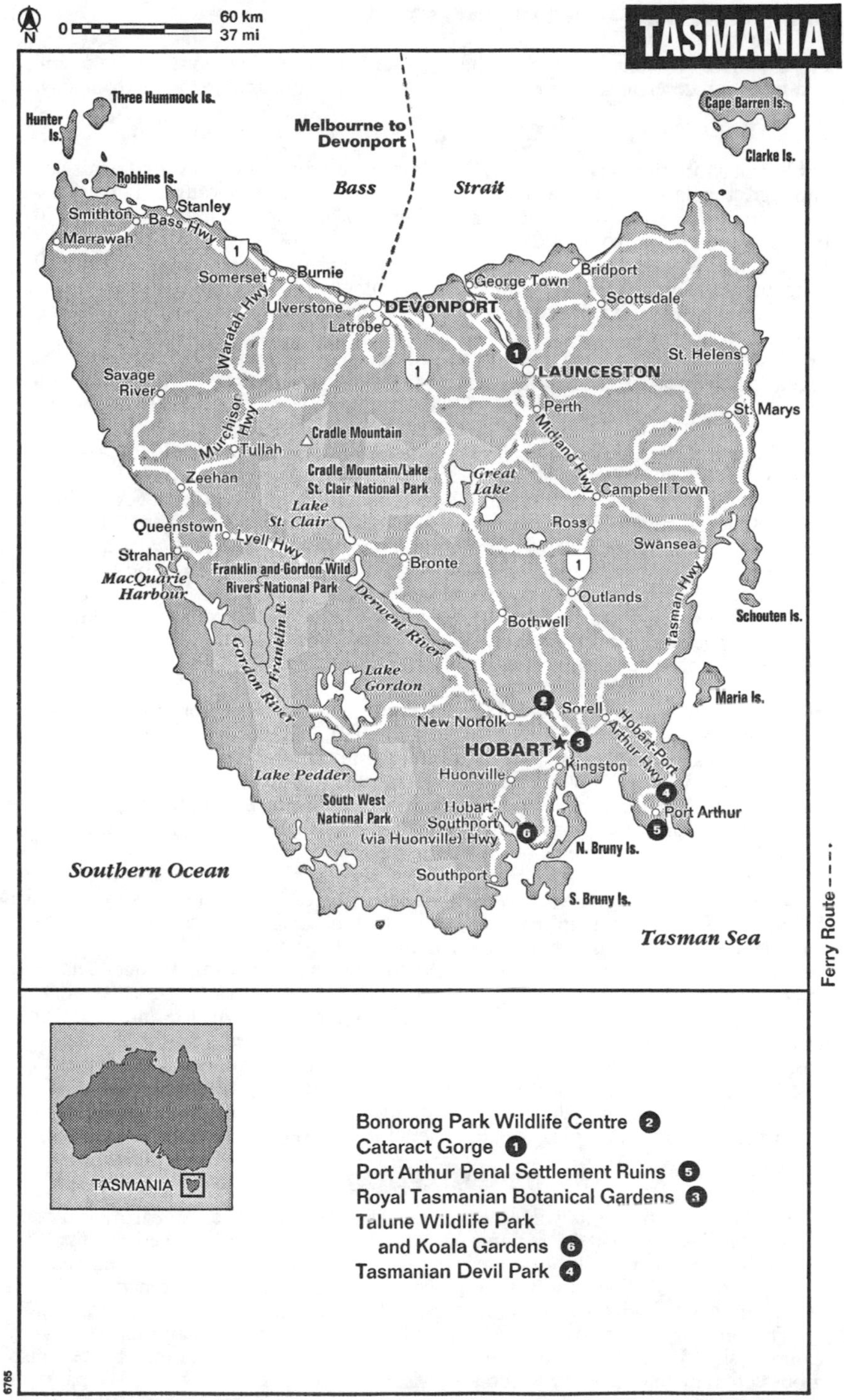

TASMANIA

Three Hummock Is.
Hunter Is.
Robbins Is.
Melbourne to Devonport
Bass Strait
Cape Barren Is.
Clarke Is.
Smithton
Stanley
Bass Hwy
Marrawah
1
Somerset
Burnie
George Town
Bridport
Ulverstone
DEVONPORT
Scottsdale
Latrobe
Waratah Hwy
St. Helens
Savage River
1
LAUNCESTON
Perth
St. Marys
Cradle Mountain
Murchison Hwy
Tullah
Midland Hwy
Cradle Mountain/Lake St. Clair National Park
Great Lake
Zeehan
Campbell Town
Lake St. Clair
Ross
Queenstown
Lyell Hwy
Swansea
Strahan
Bronte
MacQuarie Harbour
Franklin and Gordon Wild Rivers National Park
1
Outlands
Franklin R.
Derwent River
Tasman Hwy
Schouten Is.
Bothwell
Gordon River
Lake Gordon
Maria Is.
2
Sorell
New Norfolk
Hobart-Port Arthur Hwy
HOBART
3
Kingston
Lake Pedder
Huonville
4
Port Arthur
South West National Park
Hobart-Southport (via Huonville) Hwy
6
5
N. Bruny Is.
Southern Ocean
Southport
S. Bruny Is.
Tasman Sea

Ferry Route - - - -

Bonorong Park Wildlife Centre 2
Cataract Gorge 1
Port Arthur Penal Settlement Ruins 5
Royal Tasmanian Botanical Gardens 3
Talune Wildlife Park and Koala Gardens 6
Tasmanian Devil Park 4

6765

Hobart and Devonport, stopping at the suggested en route attractions as time permits, and using whatever means of transportation best fits your intended length of stay.

GETTING AROUND

Public transportation on the island is first class, giving you a choice of road or air hops, although the last is no way of seeing the country. But because of Tasmania's mountainous personality, surface travel always takes considerably longer than the mileage on the map would indicate.

Several years ago Tasmania scrapped its wonderful rail service—for the usual "economy reasons." (The Railway Department would rent you an entire railroad train, just in case you happened to need one.) So let's all heave a concerted sigh for the snows of yesteryear.

However, the island has a nice little airline specializing in the grasshopper leaps required. **Airlines of Tasmania** (tel. 003/91-8755) connects all the major and some of the minor population points. These are sample airfares from Hobart: to Launceston $A52, to Queenstown $A93, to Devonport $A93.

All main centers are connected by bus services operated by **Redline Coaches,** 199 Collins St., Hobart (tel. 31-3233), and 112 George St., Launceston (tel. 31-3233). Sample fares are Hobart-Launceston $A16.80, Launceston-Devonport $A11.80, and Burnie-Queenstown $A25.60. You can, in fact, make the complete loop of the island for about $A110. There is also the Redline **Tassie Pass,** costing $A99 for adults and $A80 for children, which gives you unlimited bus travel around the island for a week.

Best of all, if you can swing it, is to rent a car. Here you benefit by Tasmania's small size. Unlike their mainland colleagues, who have to contend with enormous distances, the local drive-yourself firms usually offer one-way rentals, enabling you to drop your vehicle wherever your trip terminates.

In conjunction with Hertz Rental Car, 119 Harrington St., Hobart (tel. 002/34-5555), you can get a very good travel/accommodation package from **Cosy Cabins,** P.O. Box 304, Rosny, TAS 7018 (tel. 002/44-7070). The Cosy outfit has a chain of cabins girding the island; all are modern and simple, and they are equipped with bathrooms, TVs, and cooking facilities. They sleep up to five people. The package includes the use of a cabin, plus a Hertz car, for $A49 per night per person. The minimum package voucher is for seven nights twin share. You can see most of the island by driving from one cabin to the next.

Tasmania is the only state you can also see by bicycle, providing that you're reasonably fit. Distances are short, but the hilly roads can be strenuous, so you'll have to make sure of a mountain machine. By and large, Tassie motorists are much more considerate of pedal pushers than their mainland brethren.

Keep in mind, though, that many of the townships are very small indeed and tend to go into semihibernation outside the peak tourist season—that is, from around May to September. When I got to Bridport, billed as a resort town, I found that all my traveler's checks wouldn't buy me a meal. The one restaurant was booked for a private wedding reception. The manager of my hotel wouldn't hear of cooking dinner "for just one guest." And the local snack bar served only take-out food—and I had no place to take it to and nought to eat it with. I went to bed hungry that night, thinking that this would make an ideal headquarters for the Weight-Watchers Association.

ORGANIZED TOURS

Tasmania has cherished its wilderness regions like few countries on earth, attracting visitors but keeping out developers. As a result, UNESCO has named no less than one-fifth of the island as a World Heritage Area—a region to be carefully maintained in its present state. The area concerned consists of three interlinking national parks, stretching from Cradle Mountain in the north to Port Davey on the south coast.

The parks are crisscrossed by hiking trails (some pretty rugged) and sprinkled with camping sites. In the towns on the periphery there are hotels and hostels. There is also a bus company that specializes in taking visitors to isolated spots within the parks or driving them around the area on week-long passes. **Tasmanian Wilderness**

Transport, 60 Collins St., Hobart (tel. 008/030-505), runs six different trips, costing from $A35 to $A80, depending on where you start and want to go. Alternatively you can buy a Wilderness Pass for $A159, giving you 14 days of unlimited travel.

There is an immense selection of tours taking you around, across, and to certain points in Tasmania, as you'll notice the moment you set foot on the island or even before. The most economical are the brief jaunts arranged by the **Tasmanian Travel Centres,** 80 Elizabeth St., Hobart, TAS 7000 (tel. 002/30-8222). They offer, for example, a 1-day coach tour from Hobart to Port Arthur, leaving three times per week and costing $A33.

There are lots of packaged or organized tours for different routes, which we'll study throughout this chapter. To help you choose, get a current copy of *Tasmanian Travelways,* a bimonthly newspaper published by the **Department of Tourism**—the finest periodical of its kind I've ever perused. It's invaluable, and they hand it out gratis at every tourist bureau.

1. LAUNCESTON

123 miles N of Hobart

GETTING THERE **By Plane** Qantas and Ansett fly from Melbourne. The trip takes an hour and costs $A187.

Launceston Airport is small but modern. The Redline bus to the city costs $A6. A taxi ride comes to around $A17. Both Qantas and Ansett have offices at the corner of Brisbane and George streets.

ESSENTIALS **Orientation** Launceston is Tasmania's second-largest city, although with 85,000 people it can hardly be called a city. It lies 35 miles inland at the head of the **River Tamar,** a small commercial-and-industrial complex surrounded by immense garden tracts. The Tamar and South Esk rivers join right in the heart of the city.

The **downtown** section consists of a few blocks between Bathurst and Tamar streets, east of the river junction, although the **Railway Terminal** lies on the west side, across **Victoria Bridge.** The **post office** is at the corner of Cameron and St. John Streets, one block away.

Information **Tourism Tasmania** is at the corner of Paterson and St. John streets (tel. 36-3122).

Getting Around **Metropolitan Transport Trust (MTT)** buses serve Launceston and its surrounding areas. Drivers sell unlimited-travel tickets (all MTT routes) for $A1.60. For rental cars, **Thrifty** is located at Launceston Airport (tel. 003/91-8105). They also rent camper-vans. **Bicycles** can be rented at the Launceston City Youth Hostel, 36 Thistle St. (tel. 44-9779).

Fast Facts The telephone **area code** is 003. The **post office** is at the corner of Cameron and St. John streets.

Looking at the north coast of Tasmania from the air, you might think that you're approaching rural England or Ireland instead of an island in the South Pacific. Below you stretch green velvet hills broken by brown rectangles of plowed land, ribboned with winding country lanes; little fishing villages dot the seashore, white stone farmhouses nestle among the fields, and a cooling mist hangs over the scene.

WHAT TO SEE & DO

Launceston's **City Park,** stretching east of Tamar Street, is the most centrally located of the town's parklands. A beautiful oasis, it harbors a miniature zoo and a conservatory with a display of begonias, cyclamens, and other hothouse blooms.

QUEEN VICTORIA MUSEUM AND ART GALLERY, Wellington St. Tel. 31-6777.

This museum houses a unique collection of Tasmanian fauna, Aboriginal relics, colonial-period paintings, and historical weapons and artifacts. The vintage firearms—crude and heavy but devastatingly effective—are particularly interesting. The museum also has the Zeiss planetarium, which has an admission fee of $A1.50.

Admission: Free (museum only).

Open: Mon–Fri 10am–5pm, Sun 2–5pm.

FRANKLIN HOUSE, in Franklin Village, Hobart Rd., South Launceston. Tel. 44-7824.

Franklin House, five miles south of town, was originally erected in 1838 as a schoolhouse. The restored interior now contains the furniture and fittings of the period.

Admission: $A5 adults, $A2.50 children.

Open: Daily 9am–5pm.

CATARACT GORGE, 1 mile from city center.

Cataract Gorge, a few minutes by bus from the city center, ranks as one of Australia's foremost beauty spots. A long pathway on the face of a towering cliff leads to the First Basin in the Cataract Cliff Grounds—a scene of gardens, picnic areas, and panoramic vantage points, with an Olympic-size pool across the river and peacocks strutting conceitedly around the lawns. The gorge is spanned by a scenic chair lift, which gives you a dizzying, exciting, but eminently safe 6-minute ride across the 1,450 feet l'nking the two sections of the reserve.

Admission: Chair-lift ride $A3 adults, $A2 children.

Open: Dec–Apr 9am–5pm, May–Dec until 4:30pm.

DESIGN CENTRE OF TASMANIA, corner of Tamar and Brisbane Sts. Tel. 31-5506.

Located in the City Park, the Design Centre features the work of Tasmania's foremost craftspeople and furniture designers. All the exhibits are made of timber from the state's forests. You'll see some of the finest and most individualistic contemporary furniture turned out in Australia today.

Admission: Free.

Open: Mon–Fri 10am–6pm, Sat until 1pm, Sun until 5pm.

PENNY ROYAL WORLD, 147 Paterson St. Tel. 31-6699.

Penny Royal World is an odd name for an unusual tourist attraction: a replica of an 18th-century powder mill, situated in an old quarry and driven by water power. The artificial-lake setting also contains an underground cannon foundry and an island fort, complete with dungeon. A 10-gun "sloop of war" sails around firing broadsides at the fort. Nearby stand an ancient windmill and corn mill and a fantasy "molehill" through which you can walk and see the residents spinning thread, baking bread, and so on.

Admission: $A19.50 adults, $A9.50 children.

Open: Daily 9:30am–4:30pm.

WAVERLEY WOOLLEN MILLS, Waverley Rd. Tel. 39-1106.

About three miles north of downtown is one of Australia's most prestigious manufacturers of wool products, still standing on the site of the original mill built in 1874. Waverley turns out the largest range of wool products produced by any manufacturer in the southern hemisphere. You can see huge automatic looms banging out miles of supreme-quality textiles, plus the showrooms displaying and selling the famous Waverley blankets, rugs, tartans, mens' jackets, womens' skirts, caps, and ties. There are guided tours every day.

Admission: $A3 adults, $A2 for children.

Open: Mon–Fri 10am–4pm.

NATIONAL AUTOMOBILE MUSEUM, Waverley Rd. Tel. 39-3727.

At this museum the exhibits are *not* for sale. Just stand and admire those superbly

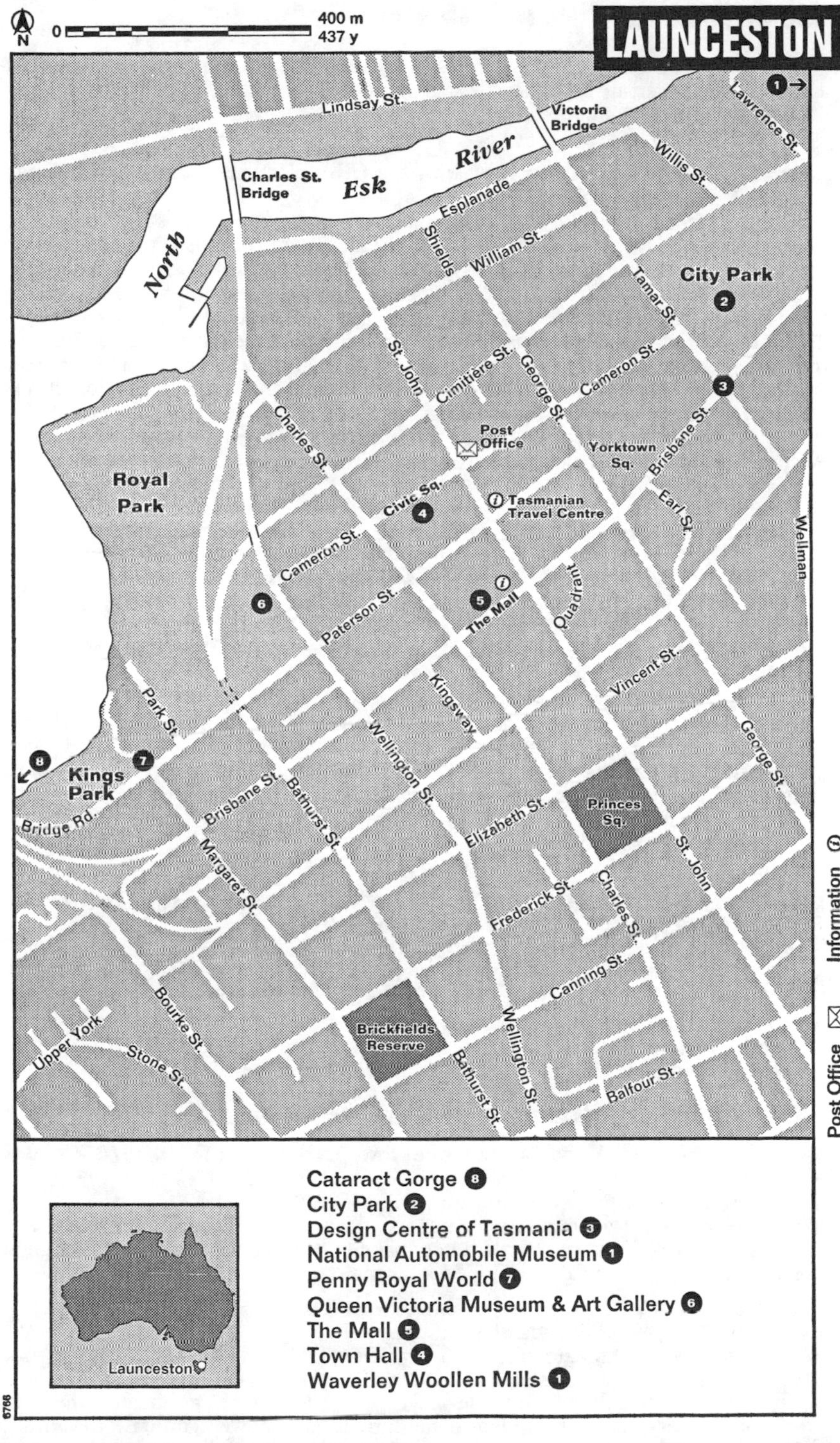
LAUNCESTON
N
0
400 m
437 y
Lindsay St.
Victoria Bridge
Lawrence St.
Willis St.
Esk River
North
Charles St. Bridge
Esplanade
Shields
William St.
Tamar St.
City Park
St. John
Cimitiere St.
George St.
Cameron St.
Post Office
Yorktown Sq.
Brisbane St.
Charles St.
Royal Park
Civic Sq.
Tasmanian Travel Centre
Earl St.
Wellman
Cameron St.
Quadrant
Paterson St.
The Mall
Vincent St.
Kingsway
Park St.
George St.
Wellington St.
Kings Park
Brisbane St.
Bathurst St.
Bridge Rd.
Elizabeth St.
Princes Sq.
St. John
Margaret St.
Charles St.
Frederick St.
Canning St.
Bourke St.
Upper York
Stone St.
Brickfields Reserve
Bathurst St.
Wellington St.
Balfour St.
Post Office
Information
Cataract Gorge 8
City Park 2
Design Centre of Tasmania 3
National Automobile Museum 1
Penny Royal World 7
Queen Victoria Museum & Art Gallery 6
The Mall 5
Town Hall 4
Waverley Woollen Mills 1
Launceston
5766

crafted Rollses, Aston Martins, and MGs with their softly gleaming flanks and profiles as sharply characteristic as an artist's signature.

Admission: $A4 adults, $A2 children.

Open: Daily 9am–5pm.

LAUNCESTON CASINO, in the Country Club, Country Club Ave., Prospect Vale. Tel. 44-8855.

Launceston Casino is the smaller, younger, more country-clubbish sibling of the big edifice in Hobart. Situated on 210 acres of landscaped grounds with a golf course and an ornamental lake, the casino forms part of the ultraplush Country Club, about 3½ miles south of Launceston. The place has a distinct plantation-house air, with a foyer that Scarlett O'Hara could only have dreamed about. It houses a disco, a 24-hour coffee shop, a sumptuous dining room, a health spa, eight bars, a cabaret, and the gaming room. You can play American roulette, blackjack, minidice, and the great Australian game of two-up (about which I'll say more in the "Hobart" section of this chapter). Instead of zooming skyward, this establishment spreads along the grounds in stylish two-story structures containing some of the most velvety bedroom suites in Australia. Even if you don't gamble yourself, the action is exciting to watch and the setting a scenic delight.

Admission: Free.

Open: Daily 1pm–3am.

WHERE TO STAY

DOUBLES FOR LESS THAN $A60

ROYAL HOTEL, 90 George St., Launceston, TAS 7000. Tel. 003/31-2526. Fax 003/345-296. 17 rms.

$ Rates (including breakfast): $A22 single, $A40 double. AE, BC, MC, V.

Royal Hotel stands in the heart of the town's shopping district, runs a very lively bar trade, and serves good budget-priced meals. Inside this small maroon-and-green structure, the rooms have hot and cold running water and are as neat as pins. Furnishings are not modern but comfortable. You get a nice dressing table with mirrors, indirect bedside lamps, and wall-to-wall carpeting. The place has six impeccable public bathrooms and a downstairs guest lounge with TV. The included breakfast is *big*.

WINDMILL HILL TOURIST LODGE, 22 High St., Launceston, TAS 7249. Tel. 003/31-9337. 10 rms (7 with bath). TV TEL

$ Rates: $A30–$A45 single, $A57–$A60 double. BC, MC, V.

Windmill Hill Tourist Lodge is a special charmer deserving of a special mention. A converted two-story home built in 1880 (it was never a windmill, merely built on the site of one), the hotel still retains the style and ambience of its colonial origins. Modern additions include electric blankets in all rooms, a laundry, good public bathrooms, and a pleasant little dining room serving home-cooked meals.

DOUBLES FOR LESS THAN $A71

ADINA PLACE, 50 York St., Launceston, TAS 7250. Tel. 008/030-181. 34 units (all with bath). TV TEL

$ Rates: $A35–$A60 per person. AE, BC, MC, V.

This motel offers self-contained apartments in three sizes: studios, large doubles, and family units. Furnishings are strictly functional, but the establishment has spas, a guest laundry, and units with fully equipped kitchens.

ALICE'S PLACE, 17 York St., Launceston, TAS 7250. Tel. 003/34-2231. Fax 003/342-696. 8 cottages (all with bath). TV

$ Rates (including breakfast): $A115 per cottage. No credit cards.

Alice's is not one place but a collection of charmers, offering ideal accommodations providing that there are several of you. The cottages, although in the heart of the city, lie half-hidden behind trees and flower gardens. Beautifully furnished, they have a lounge with a log fire, a laundry, fully equipped kitchens (breakfast ingredients supplied), and eccentric little touches like clutters of well-thumbed books, games, and an old gramophone with records. The cottages sleep two to six persons—those upstairs occupying regal four-poster canopy beds, with wooden steps to mount them in style.

HILLVIEW HOUSE, 193 George St., Launceston, TAS 7250. Tel. 003/31-7388. 10 rms (all with bath). TV

$ Rates (including breakfast): $A55 single, $A70 double. AE, BC, MC, V.

This colonial-style town house dating from around 1840 is about five minutes' walk from the town center. The interior has all the quiet spaciousness of the period, but the fittings have luckily been updated. Rates here include a quite grandiose home-cooked breakfast, and the house has parking facilities.

MOTEL MALDON, 32 Brisbane St., Launceston, TAS 7250. Tel. 003/31-3211. Fax 003/34-4641. 12 rms (all with bath). TV TEL

$ Rates (including continental breakfast): $A50 single, $A60 double. AE, BC, MC, V.

Motel Maldon is a white colonial charmer with lacy wrought-iron grillwork, an upstairs balcony, and bay windows. It's also slightly beyond our price range for single accommodations but just right for doubles. The units are surprisingly modern, not in the plastic sense but beautifully so: pastel colored, bright and airy, with refrigerators, microwaves, and bedside lamps. Bathrooms come with showers, toilets, and marble-top sinks. The continental breakfast is the only meal offered on the premises.

HOSTELS

Tasmania has 22 youth hostels strategically placed at beauty spots all over the island. You can tour the entire island loop by hopping from one hostel to another. But many other folks have the same idea, and in summer accommodation availability gets pretty tight. If you're planning a hosteling tour in peak tourist season, December to February, it would be wise to work out your itinerary beforehand and book your lodgings. Contact the **Tasmanian YHA office,** 28 Criterion St., Hobart, TAS 7001 (tel. 002/34-9617).

LAUNCESTON CITY YOUTH HOSTEL, 36 Thistle St., Launceston, TAS 7249. Tel. 003/44-9779. Fax 003/44-9779. 100 beds.

$ Rates: $A11 per person (no membership needed). AE, BC, MC, V.

This hostel is an erstwhile woolen-mills canteen set in parklike grounds about one mile from the city center. The place is well equipped and comfortable. The hostel also rents mountain bikes (15- to 18-speed) and touring bikes (12-speed) for Tasmania's hilly roads, plus helmets and complete backpacking equipment. The hostel closes at midnight and does not issue late passes.

CAMPING

The **Treasure Island Caravan Parks** form a chain with links in Launceston, Burnie, Bicheno, Zeenan, and Hobart, all of which are uniformly first class and supply standardized facilities at standard rates. They all rent on-site vans and permit camping. Some offer self-contained units, and one (at Burnie) has a luxurious swimming pool. All of them also feature laundries. The vans come equipped with thermostatic heating, cooking facilities, eating utensils, TVs, refrigerators, double beds, and bunks. Linen is supplied for $A3 per person. The rates are from $A30 per night for two people, plus $A7 per extra person. In Launceston the Treasure Island Park is on Glen Dhu Street, at the corner of Melbourne Street and Glen Dhu (tel. 003/44-2600).

WHERE TO EAT

By and large the culinary scene in Tasmania ranks several notches below that of the mainland—chiefly because the island is less cosmopolitan and still cooks happily in the bland old Anglo-Aussie tradition. With the exception of a few splurge restaurants in the bigger towns, the hostelries dish out solid, wholesome, and very dull fare, unmarred by either imagination or skill. Tasmanians get the freshest and tastiest fish in the country, but all they do with it is fry it Cockney style, a process guaranteed to eliminate every trace of flavor. With it they usually serve "chips," fried potatoes limp and greasy enough to hang across a clothesline.

In this chapter I've tried to pick out eateries that combine economy prices with a degree of culinary finesse. I haven't always succeeded because that combination is somewhat rare in these parts, particularly in the small resort towns. It makes the joy all the greater when you find one.

MEALS FOR LESS THAN $A11

POSH NOSH, 127 St. John St. Tel. 31-9180.

Cuisine: DELI. **Reservations:** Not necessary.

$ **Prices:** Appetizers $A2.50–$A5, main courses $A7–$A10. No credit cards.

Open: Mon–Fri 7:30am–5:30pm.

A real surprise is to find an almost New York–style deli in this town. In some respects it is better than the Manhattan model, because the ingredients used are fresher. In other respects it is worse, because the hours are shorter. You get the classic deli fare of hearty chicken soup, pastrami, lox, and cheeses; but you also get gourmet platters, such as a plowman's lunch that no plowman has ever had the privilege to eat—it includes caviar among other goodies. Posh Nosh gets very busy at lunchtime, which is hardly astonishing.

ROYAL OAK HOTEL, corner of Tamar and Brisbane Sts. Tel. 31-5346.

Cuisine: INTERNATIONAL. **Reservations:** Accepted.

$ **Prices:** Appetizers $A3–$A6, main courses $A8.50–$A11.50. AE, BC, MC, V.

Open: Daily noon–12pm.

The Royal Oak Hotel is famed for its hearty meals. The dining room doubles as a nostalgia nook—all the walls carry portraits of bygone movie greats and antique film posters. There is a large dining-and-entertainment area at the rear of the hotel. You get excellent grilled flounder or roast lamb in impressive quantities for $A9.50 as well as a comprehensive Greek menu. Half portions are available for children.

MEALS FOR LESS THAN $A14

DICKY WHITE'S STEAK HOUSE, in the Launceston Hotel, 107 Brisbane St. Tel. 34-3418.

Cuisine: AUSTRALIAN. **Reservations:** Accepted.

$ **Prices:** Appetizers $A4–$A5, main courses $A9–$A15. AE, BC, MC, V.

Open: Mon–Fri lunch and 6–11pm, Sat dinner only.

This is reputedly the oldest operational pub in Australia. Dicky White, incidentally, was a notorious highwayman who served his time in Van Diemen's Land, reformed, and founded the hotel in 1814. The bistro is beautifully decorated à la rustic inn, with whitewashed walls, milky oil lamps, carved wooden chairs, and stained-glass windows overlooking the street. On the wall is a framed reward notice promising "Fifty Sovereigns and Unconditional Pardon" to anyone helping capture three escaped convicts. You get your own wine from a small bar. The food is brought to your table, always preceded by warm sesame rolls. The place is famous for steak—a small filet steak in mushroom sauce costs $A12—and you can help yourself copiously to the salad bar. But don't miss out on the Tasmanian deep-dish apple pie with cream for $A2.50—the best there is.

SNACKS

CLAYTONS COFFEE SHOP, in the Quadrant Mall.

Cuisine: SNACKS. **Reservations:** Not necessary.

$ **Prices:** $A2.50–$A6.50. No credit cards.

Open: Mon–Sat 9am–5:30pm.

This is a small, modern eatery featuring outside tables that give you a view of the mall fountains, within screeching distance of the parrots inhabiting the miniature aviary. The interior is bright and smart with light-wood furniture and contemporary prints. The quiche Lorraine costs $A6 and is worth it; don't forget the quite outstanding chocolate-marble tart to go with your coffee. Unfortunately the place closes at a fairly ludicrous hour for a café.

ORGANIZED TOURS

Tasmanian Expeditions, 110 George St., Launceston (tel. 003/34-3477), is a mildly adventurous, strongly ecological outfit specializing in bush walking, rafting, and cycling excursions. They use some of the most experienced guides in Tasmania and practice minimal impact on the environment—what they carry in they take out.

Backpacking walks last from 1½ to 8 days, the shortest jaunt (easy grades) costing $A215. Rafting starts with a 1½-day trip through the Huon and Picton valleys over rapids described as "exciting, yet not too wild." The cost is $A190. **Bicycle tours** range from half a day to 8 days and nights (bikes supplied). The half-day pedal, through the Tamar Valley, costs $A40; a full-day tour to historic Evandale is $A90. The company office is actually in the Paddy Pallin Adventure Equipment shop; a handy location since the shop rents out most of the outdoor equipment you need for the expeditions.

SHOPPING

Yorktown Square, in the heart of Launceston, is a period piece: built like a colonial village square, paved with cobblestones, lit by "gas lamps," and containing an array of specialty shops designed to blend with the scene. Every Sunday is market day from 9am to 2pm. Stalls sell homemade goods, edible and otherwise, artists display their handiwork, bands play, and entertainers entertain. It's great colorful fun, but—like most things Launcestrian—it doesn't go on long enough.

EXCURSION ALONG THE COAST

Traveling east (clockwise) from Launceston, you reach the coast at **St. Helens.** A pretty holiday center by the calm waters of George Bay, the township offers safe swimming, sailing, fishing, and bush walking for visitors.

If you drive (or are driven) south, you pass through some of the loveliest countryside on the island. The excellent road winds through dark-green mountain forests, rising high and skirting the seashore, the ring of distant breakers shimmering through the treetops. Lone farms and little villages dance by, and small flocks of sheep or cattle graze in the emerald-green pastures.

Bicheno (accent on the first syllable) was once a whaling station where lookouts, posted in the trees, scanned the Tasman Sea for the telltale spouts of whale pods and signaled to the waiting boats in the cove below. It's an old place by Australian standards and an enchanting one by any standards. Bicheno looks like a Swiss mountain village, except that the cottages are rustic-luxurious and the children's playground is equipped with a genuine fishing boat resting on blocks.

Sea Life Centre (tel. 75-1121) on the Tasman Highway is Bicheno's top tourist attraction—and quite possibly the only place that combines a fish zoo with a seafood restaurant. Some of the menu items are the same as those floating behind the plate-glass windows. Others are rare and found only in Tasmanian waters. You can see giant crabs and miniature crayfish, seahorses of every size, eels big and little, small schools of sharks, sea slugs, and dozens of other denizens of the deep. Open daily from 9am to 5pm. Admission is $A4 for adults, $A1.50 for children.

Farther south, but inland, lies the 130-year-old former stagecoach stop of **Buckland.** The village nestles in the green valley of the Prosser River and has a wonderfully weathered stone church with a magnificent window that supposedly dates from the 14th century.

Directly south of Buckland lies the **Tasman Peninsula,** which would be a separate island off the coast except for a narrow strip of connecting land called **Eaglehawk Neck.** This is the cradle of Tasmania's history. It was here that Abel Tasman landed in 1642 (the village of Dunalley marks the spot) and christened the island Van Diemen's Land, after the then governor of the Netherlands Indies.

The narrow neck of land was the reason why the peninsula served as top-security holding bag for the entire penal colony. A line of savage guard dogs was chained across the center from shore to shore, and the area was patrolled by mounted soldiers, which rendered escape from the Tasman virtually impossible. Further, the water is rough there and few of the prisoners could swim. Many tried that route, and all drowned.

PORT ARTHUR

The strongbox of the peninsula is near the southern tip—the penitentiary settlement of **Port Arthur.** This was Australia's Alcatraz, a stone-and-iron complex that housed some 12,500 of the 120,000 men and women deported from England between 1803 and 1854. A large town grew around the central prison, its inhabitants living on the business of imprisoning people. The settlement operated until 1877, when the penitentiary was closed and the last of its inmates were transferred to the new Hobart Gaol.

Today Port Arthur is a semi-ghost town, haunted by its past but simultaneously living on it. This is one of Australia's chief tourist draws, visited by hundreds of thousands of mainlanders for the same reasons that U.S. tourists flock to Alcatraz. They learn about the unspeakable "dumb cells," where difficult convicts were broken and frequently driven mad by confinement in total darkness and total silence; about the "model prison" whose inmates had to wear masks during chapel services so that their solitary confinement would continue even there; and about desperation that reached such a pitch that some convicts murdered their cell mates simply in order to be taken to Hobart and hanged "among real people."

The main building still in use today is the old **Lunatic Asylum** (tel. 50-2363), now housing an audiovisual theater, a museum, and a scale model of the original Port Arthur. You can also see the ruins of the penitentiary, the convict-designed-and-built church, the model prison (considered remarkably advanced and humane in its period), the commandant's residence (now a private home), the guardhouse, and the hospital. And no matter how warm the day, you'll feel a slight shiver as you walk among those stone reminders of man's inhumanity to man. Admission to the penal settlement is $A12 for adults, $A5 for children; this includes a cruise to the **Isle of the Dead,** Port Arthur's burial ground.

WHERE TO STAY Port Arthur is a national park, so you can't bring dogs, cats, or firearms into the area. The Park Service operates the **Garden Point Caravan & Camping Park,** located about a mile from the historic site, off the Arthur Highway (for bookings, phone 50-2340). The park has toilets and showers, laundry facilities, powered sites, a large camper kitchen, dormitories, and self-contained cabins. Shopping facilities are at Port Arthur. Charges for powered sites are $A12 per night for two persons; for tent sites it's $A10 for two persons; for dormitories it's $A13; and for cabins it's $A50 for doubles.

2. HOBART

123 miles S of Launceston

GETTING THERE By Plane Qantas and Ansett fly to Hobart from Melbourne. The flight takes a bit over an hour and costs $A216.

Hobart Airport is located about 14 miles east of the city, and offers few amenities: a snack bar, a newsstand, and plastic seats designed for minimum comfort. The bus to town costs $A5, a taxi ride about $A18.

By Bus Redline coaches arrive at the downtown terminal at 96 Harrington St.

By Car From Launceston, you'll be on Route 1 (Brooker Highway), which runs past the Queen's Domain park. Turn right at the circle onto Liverpool Street, which takes you into the city center.

HOBART

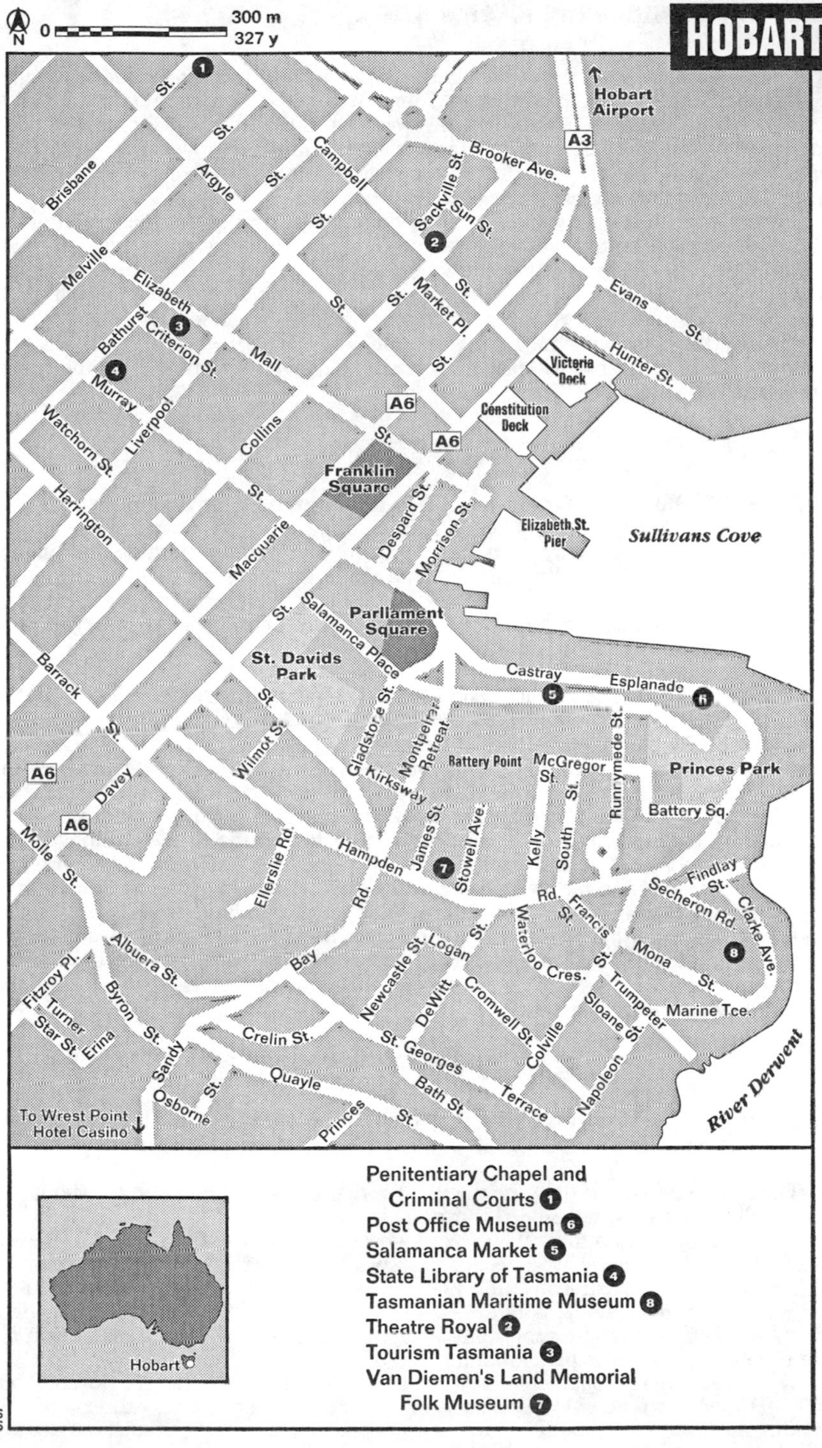

N
0
300 m
327 y
Hobart Airport
A3
Brooker Ave.
Brisbane St.
Argyle St.
Campbell St.
Sackville St.
Sun St.
Melville St.
Elizabeth St.
Market Pl.
Evans St.
Hunter St.
Victoria Dock
Constitution Dock
Bathurst St.
Criterion St.
Mall
Murray St.
Liverpool St.
Collins St.
Watchorn St.
Harrington St.
A6
Franklin Square
Despard St.
Morrison St.
Elizabeth St. Pier
Sullivans Cove
Macquarie St.
Salamanca Place
Parliament Square
St. Davids Park
Castray Esplanade
Barrack St.
Gladstone St.
Montpelier Retreat
Battery Point
McGregor St.
Runnymede St.
Princes Park
Battery Sq.
Wilmot St.
Kirksway
Davey St.
Molle St.
Ellerslie Rd.
Hampden Rd.
James St.
Stowell Ave.
Kelly St.
South St.
Findlay St.
Secheron Rd.
Clarke Ave.
Francis St.
Mona St.
Waterloo Cres.
Logan St.
Newcastle St.
Albuera St.
Bay Rd.
Fitzroy Pl.
Turner St.
Star St.
Erina
Byron St.
DeWitt St.
Cromwell St.
Colville St.
Sloane St.
Trumpeter St.
Marine Tce.
Crelin St.
St. Georges Terrace
Sandy Bay
Quayle St.
Osborne St.
Bath St.
Napoleon St.
Princes St.
River Derwent
To Wrest Point Hotel Casino
Penitentiary Chapel and Criminal Courts 1
Post Office Museum 6
Salamanca Market 5
State Library of Tasmania 4
Tasmanian Maritime Museum 8
Theatre Royal 2
Tourism Tasmania 3
Van Diemen's Land Memorial Folk Museum 7
Hobart
6767

Tasmania's capital is a city for which the term *picturesque* might have been specially invented. It lies between towering Mount Wellington and the serene Derwent River, about 15 miles upstream from the river mouth that forms one of the world's finest deep-water harbors. From the Tasman Peninsula it's 68 miles northwest. Few cities have been so blessed with their scenic setting—green wooded mountain ranges on one side, shimmering blue water on the other.

Hobart is small enough (about 185,000 people) not to blot out the surrounding landscape. And it is dotted with beautiful old Georgian buildings, constructed of solid freestone by convicts, that permeate it with old-world charm, particularly around the waterfront. Even the new steel-and-concrete monstrosities mushrooming all over haven't been able to destroy the town's colonial image—yet. The river estuary is still guarded by the 8-inch muzzle loaders mounted at Kangaroo Bluff Battery on the eastern shore of the Derwent—placed there after Russian warships showed the czar's flag in the Pacific in 1873.

ORIENTATION

INFORMATION The **Tasmanian Travel Centre,** centrally located at 80 Elizabeth St., Hobart, TAS 7000 (tel. 002/30-8222), is open Monday to Friday from 8:45am to 5pm, on Saturday from 9am to noon, and Sunday morning and public holidays from 9 to 11am. Bookings can be made for tours and accommodations anywhere in Tasmania. For information on current activities throughout Tasmania, consult *This Week in Tasmania,* free from the Travel Centre. The *Mercury* gives a good roundup of nighttime activities.

CITY LAYOUT The actual city lies on the west bank of the Derwent, linked to the suburbs on the eastern shore by the new **Tasman Bridge,** rebuilt since the old one was rammed by a runaway tanker. The downtown section adjoins the magically antique waterfront, a patch of colonial warehouses and colorful street markets, of small squares and tall masts irresistible to photographers. However, the patina that gives Old Hobart charm also makes it a devil of a place to drive or park in.

North of the city stretches the vast parkland called **Queen's Domain.** Across the river, linked by bridge and ferry, lie **Bellerive** and the other eastern suburbs, as well as the **airport.** To the south lies **Sandy Bay,** Hobart's main tourist area that houses **Wrest Point Casino,** the stubby white tower that has become the capital's landmark. This suburb is connected to the city by **Sandy Bay Road,** which crosses Davey Street and then becomes **Harrington Street,** one of the main commercial thoroughfares. Davey Street runs southwest and eventually takes you to the scenic slopes of **Mount Wellington.**

GETTING AROUND

Public transport in Hobart is supplied by the **MTT buses** (tel. 71-3223), which run by sections with fares ranging from $A1 to $A2.50, according to the number of sections.

The main **taxi** rank is opposite the GPO and also by main hotels in the shopping area. Call **City Cabs** (tel. 34-3633) if none is available.

For absolute rock-bottom rates on four wheels, try **Rent-A-Bug,** 105 Murray St. (tel. 002/31-0300). They have a fleet of Volkswagens, not exactly new but reasonably well maintained, that rent from $A19 per day, including unlimited kilometers but not insurance. For more modern transportation, try **Thrifty,** 156 Harrington St. (tel. 002/23-3577). Thrifty also rents fully equipped camper-vans, which enable you to use the excellent caravan parks that dot the island.

When **driving** in Hobart, keep in mind that traffic operates under the slogan "You can't get there from here." So don't try. Walk. There seem to be only three types of parking facilities—illegal, impossible, or someone else's.

FAST FACTS

The **American Express** office is at 60 Elizabeth St. (tel. 38-1200). The **Airlines of Tasmania** office is located at Hobart Airport (tel. 48-5030). The telephone **area code** is 002. The **Royal Automobile Club** is located at the corner of Murray and Patrick streets (tel. 38-2200). In case of **emergency,** dial **000. Royal Hobart Hospital** is on Liverpool Street (tel. 38-8308). The **post office** is at the corner of Elizabeth and Macquarie Streets (tel. 23-3074).

WHAT TO SEE & DO

ATTRACTIONS

TASMANIAN MUSEUM, 40 Macquarie St. Tel. 35-0777.

This museum was built in 1863 and is the second oldest in Australia. Inside you'll find the tragic and fascinating relics of the fate of Tasmania's Aborigines and whales. Both vanished into oblivion. The art gallery has a good collection of contemporary Australian paintings and colonial art.

Admission: Free (except for special exhibitions).

Open: Daily 10am–5pm.

THE ALLPORT LIBRARY, in the State Library, 91 Murray St. Tel. 33-7484.

The Allport Library contains a wonderful array of 18th-century books, prints, maps, antique furniture, glassware, ceramics, and silver—all once the property of the Allport family, who were among the cultural pioneers of the island.

Admission: Free.

Open: Mon–Fri 9:30am–5pm.

MODEL TUDOR VILLAGE, Tudor Court, 827 Sandy Bay Rd. Tel. 25-1194.

The Model Tudor Village is a faithful reproduction of an English 16th-century hamlet, authentic to the last detail, including the garb of the 2-inch-high populace. The scale model was constructed over 10 years by a polio victim. The village is electronically lit with colors that subtly change from dawn to dusk.

Admission: $A3.50 adults, $A1.50 children.

Open: Daily 9am–5pm. **Bus:** Stop 30.

SHOT TOWER, south of Hobart on Channel Hwy., Taroona. Tel. 27-8885.

The Shot Tower is a historic landmark built in 1870 and simultaneously one of the finest lookout spots in Hobart, offering magnificent views of the entire Derwent Estuary. The tower also contains a museum and a tearoom.

Admission: $A3 adults, $A1.50 children.

Open: Daily 9am–dusk.

VAN DIEMEN'S LAND FOLK MUSEUM, 103 Hampden Rd., Battery Point. Tel. 34-2791.

This museum is housed in one of Hobart's earliest colonial homes. The place, built by Captain Haig in 1836, is a carefully preserved example of how well and tastefully the gentry lived in this "hell on earth." The exhibits consist of period furniture, costumes, an entire nursery of the times, and a kitchen with all the gleaming utensils required to satisfy the Dickensian appetites of the age. On the grounds you'll find carriages, tools, and a complete smithy.

Admission: $A4 adults, $A1 children.

Open: Mon–Fri 10am–5pm, Sat–Sun 2–5pm.

ANGLESEA BARRACKS, Davey St. Tel. 21-2205.

Anglesea Barracks was built in 1811 for the original garrison of the island and is today the oldest military establishment in Australia still occupied by the army. It contains the restored officers' quarters and mess and the Georgian-colonial drill hall (and did they *drill* in those days).

Admission: Free.

Open: Tuesday only. Tours start at 11am.

TASMANIAN MARITIME MUSEUM, Secheron Rd., Battery Point. Tel. 23-5082.

The Tasmanian Maritime Museum has a splendid collection of material on the state's nautical history, including models, figureheads, and whaling implements.

Admission: $A2 adults, children free.

Open: Mon–Fri 1–4:30pm, Sat 10am–4:30pm, Sun 1–4:30pm.

RUNNYMEDE, 61 Bay Rd., New Town. Tel. 78-1269.

Runnymede is a late Georgian–style mansion built in 1844. The house illustrates the period furnishings of its three 19th-century owners: a lawyer, a bishop, and a sea captain.

Admission: $A5 adults, $A2.50 children.

Open: Daily 10am–4:30pm.

ROYAL TASMANIAN BOTANICAL GARDENS, Domain Rd.

Quite small by Australian standards but in a wonderful position overlooking the Derwent River, the gardens feature a floral clock, tropical greenhouses, a water garden with lily pond, and a conservatory with a magnificent display of begonias.

Admission: Free.

Open: Daily 8am–dusk.

PENITENTIARY CHAPEL AND CRIMINAL COURTS, corner of Brisbane and Campbell Sts. Tel. 31-0911.

One of Tasmania's earliest buildings, this is allegedly haunted by the ghosts of the legions of men sent to the gallows from these architecturally splendid premises.

Admission: $A5 adults, $A2.50 children.

Open: Daily tours 10am–2pm.

CASCADE BREWERY, Cascade Rd. Tel. 24-1144.

This is Australia's oldest brewery, and some say the best (though you can buy an argument over this). Looking like a Loire château from the outside, it still produces some of the hemisphere's finest beers. The tours here include a visit to the Cascade Museum and the adjoining Woodstock Gardens, famous in their own right. Tour bookings are essential, and the visits entail considerable climbing.

Admission: $A7 adults, $A2 children.

Open: Tours, Mon–Fri 9:30am and 1pm.

MT. NELSON SIGNAL STATION, Mount Nelson. Tel. 23-3407.

The old military signal station provides the most panoramic views of Hobart, the Derwent River, and the Tasman Peninsula. The station is now a teahouse.

Bus: No. 57, 58, or 59 to the door.

CADBURY SCHWEPPES CHOCOLATE FACTORY, Claremont. Tel. 71-3223.

This is the place where Australia's finest chocolate is concocted, some seven miles north of Hobart. Book tickets and transportation at the Tasmanian Travel Centre. Conducted tours show the entire chocolate-making process (with free samples), which is surprisingly engrossing.

Admission: $A8 adults, $A4 children.

Open: Tours, Mon–Fri 9 and 9:30am.

ORGANIZED TOURS

M.V. *Derwent Explorer*, a stubby yet comfortable little craft, takes you on sightseeing cruises around Hobart harbor. All cruises depart from Brooke Street Pier, Franklin Wharf (tel. 34-9294). Adults pay $A16, children $A8.

Hobart Sightseeing Tours, 199 Collins St. (tel. 31-3511), runs jaunts that take in city sights and then go on to Mount Wellington for a panoramic view of the entire area. The fare is $A15 for adults, $A7.50 for children.

Other excursions include a visit to **Richmond,** where you can see the bridge built by convicts in 1823 and the Old Gaol, built in 1825 for convicts considered too dangerous to run loose even in chains. Tickets cost $A15 for adults, $A7.50 for children, including admission fees.

SHOPPING

Hobart has two quite delightful shopping scenes standing in complete contrast to each other. The first is the **Cat and Fiddle Arcade,** which runs from Elizabeth to Murray streets. Highly contemporary in design, it is centered by a tree-shaded fountain plaza where an animated mural enacts the old nursery rhyme every hour on the hour. The second is **Salamanca Place,** at the waterfront. The warehouses along here, all built between 1835 and 1860, are probably the best-preserved colonial structures in Australia. One of them houses the famous **Ball and Chain Tavern,** a very classy restaurant decorated with grim memorabilia from the convict era. Every summer Saturday morning the place becomes the **Salamanca Market,** the most joyously colorful street market on the continent, where bands play; singers sing; and dozens of little stalls sell trash, treasure, and edibles.

WHERE TO STAY

Hobart is not well supplied with budget hostelries, miserably so compared to most mainland capitals. What there is belongs mainly to the pub variety, places that usually care more about the bar trade than houseguests. In the higher-rate brackets, however, the accommodation picture changes to middling rosy. The best territory for tourist lodgings is Sandy Bay.

DOUBLES FOR LESS THAN $A51

ALABAMA HOTEL, 72 Liverpool St., Hobart, TAS 7000. Tel. 002/34-3737. 10 rms (none with bath). TV

$ Rates: $A32.50 single, $A48 double. BC, MC, V.

A three-story establishment in a busy downtown street with a busy bar, the Alabama has guest rooms and public bathrooms. The bedroom fittings are pretty basic but include carpeting, bedside lamps, hot- and cold-water basins, and ample wardrobe space.

DR. SYNTAX, 139 Sandy Bay Rd., Hobart, TAS 7005. Tel. 002/23-6258. 7 rms (all with bath). TV TEL

$ Rates: $A36 single, $A50 double. AE, BC, MC, V.

This oddly named establishment dates back to colonial times—a little white-fronted hostelry on an elegant street, housing all of seven bedrooms. The furnishings are new; all rooms have coffee- and tea-making facilities, radios, TVs and excellent beds. The downstairs bar is very busy, indeed, and serves counter lunches and dinners.

GLOBE HOTEL, 178 Davey St., Hobart, TAS 7000. Tel. 002/23-5800. Fax 002/23-3868. 12 rms (none with bath).

$ Rates (including breakfast): $A30 single, $A45 double. BC, MC, V.

The downtown Globe Hotel is a red-brick corner pub with a splendid mural depicting a globe of the world as visualized in Shakespeare's time. The rooms are small but nicely furnished: with bedside lamps, good carpeting, ample wardrobes, modern hot- and cold-water basins, and electric blankets but no radios or TVs. The hotel, which is very well maintained, serves counter lunches and counter "teas" (meaning dinner) five days a week.

GOOD WOMAN INN, 186 Argyle St., Hobart, TAS 7000. Tel. 002/34-4796. 5 rms (none with bath).

$ Rates: $A19 single, $A34 double. AE, BC, MC, V.

The "good woman" in question here is a Tudor maiden carrying her head under one arm. The hotel exterior and guest rooms are appropriately decorated in Olde English style. The bedrooms have cheerfully patterned wallpaper, wall-to-wall carpeting, electric blankets, bedside lamps, and tea- and coffee-making equipment. The dining room has a great local reputation for its meals—no pub grub here.

TELEGRAPH HOTEL, 19 Morrison St., Hobart, TAS 7005. Tel. 002/346-254. 11 rms (1 with bath). TV

$ Rates (including breakfast): $A30 single, $A40 double, $A60 triple with bath. No credit cards.

A fairly modern, tile-fronted red-brick building overlooking the waterfront, the Telegraph has a proud and amiable owner and a breakfast room offering great views of the picturesque harbor. The bar is lively, and the hotel serves hearty counter lunches but no dinner. Bedrooms are rather small, the furnishings new; each room comes with a hot- and cold-water basin and a spacious wardrobe. There are two shared bathrooms and a very pleasant TV lounge for guests. Lighting arrangements, as in most Hobart pubs, are not the brightest, but the harbor views are great.

DOUBLES FOR LESS THAN $A66

ASTOR HOTEL, 157 Macquarie St., Hobart, TAS 7000. Tel. 002/34-6611. 25 rms (5 with shower; no toilet).

$ Rates (including breakfast): $A36 single, $A55 double. BC, MC, V.

The Astor Hotel has the advantage of being centrally located yet remarkably quiet. The hotel has a distinct 1930s look, with rather old-fashioned rooms. There's a very popular restaurant on the premises as well as a TV lounge. Some of the rooms come with private showers; all have hot and cold running water, small wardrobes, individual bedside lamps, and electric jugs for tea making. There are eight bathrooms for the benefit of the showerless guests.

CUSTOMS HOUSE HOTEL, 1 Murray St., Hobart, TAS 7000. Tel. 002/346-645. 12 rms (2 with bath).

$ Rates (including breakfast): $A35 single, $A60 double. AE, BC, MC, V.

The Customs House Hotel is a small, picturesque white waterfront structure in an ideal position: overlooking Hobart harbor as well as Tasmania's Parliament. The hotel is rather old-fashioned and a bit cramped but so atmospheric that you forget about lack of elbow space. It's a historic pub in a historic setting that conjures up the vision of windjammers anchored at the front door. The rooms, located up the pretty steep stairs, are smallish, with limited wardrobe space but plenty of drawers. There's wall-to-wall carpeting, bedside-and-ceiling lamps, and—from some windows—entrancing views of the busy waterfront.

RED CHAPEL HOUSE, 27 Red Chapel Ave., Hobart, TAS 7005. Tel. 002/25-2273. 9 rms (none with bath).

$ Rates (including breakfast): $A50 single, $A65 double. No credit cards.

The Red Chapel House is a pretty red-brick structure on a quiet street with a lovely garden and an air of old-fashioned coziness throughout the house—there's nothing cubistic about this place. The dining room looks like an ad from a 1920s home magazine. The house is proudly maintained, and the bedrooms are simple, well-groomed, and amply furnished with large wardrobes, wall-to-wall carpeting, bedside lamps, and electric blankets. There is no running water in the rooms, but four bathrooms are on the premises, as are a TV lounge, a refrigerator, a laundry, and a coffee bar. A large breakfast is included. Rates change with the season.

HOSTELS & BACKPACKER ACCOMMODATIONS

Backpackers lodgings are springing up all over Hobart. They're hard to keep track of because ordinary pubs and guest houses suddenly convert to this style, frequently unannounced, or switch *part* of their sleeping space for backpackers' use. This can be quite advantageous, since the establishment may be a multistar affair.

ADELPHI COURT, 17 Stoke St., New Town, TAS 7008. Tel. 002/28-4829. Fax 002/78-2047. 26 rms (two with bath). **Bus:** No. 15 or 16.

$ Rates: Dorms $A12 for members, $A15 nonmembers; $A40 single, $A45 double. BC, MC, V.

Located about two miles from downtown and operated by the Youth Hostel Association, this is a spacious place in quiet surroundings. It has a guest laundry, a fully equipped kitchen, a TV lounge, and a games room, but it charges extra for linens in the hostel rooms. Parking is available.

HOBART YOUTH HOSTEL, 52 King St., Bellerive, TAS 7018. Tel. 002/44-2552. 72 beds. **Bus:** No. 83, 84, 85 to Stop 19.

$ Rates: $A12–$A16 senior, $A6–$A12 junior. No credit cards.

The Hobart Youth Hostel is an atmospheric stone building across the river, erected as a school in 1859, with enough space to house a regiment. You take the ferry across from the city. The hostel has coin-operated showers, a refrigerator, and a washing machine.

WORTH THE EXTRA MONEY

ARGYLE MOTOR LODGE, corner of Argyle and Lewis Sts., Hobart, TAS 7008. Tel. 002/34-2488. Fax 002/34-2292. 36 rms (all with bath). TV TEL

$ Rates: Standard, $A62 single, $A67 double; deluxe, $A75 single, $A82 double. AE, BC, MC, V.

About 10 minutes by bus from downtown, the Argyle stands grouped around a large central parking area. It has a small reception lobby with an adjoining bar and dining nook. Breakfast, costing around $A5, is delivered to your room. Standard and deluxe rooms differ mainly in size. Both have refrigerators, bedside clock radios, toasters, and smallish wardrobes. Furnishings are new and comfortable, the light fixtures good; the deluxe honeymoon suites feature private spas. Although there is no restaurant on the premises, simple evening meals are prepared in the motel kitchen and served downstairs. The lodge also has a guest laundry. The stop for downtown buses is just across the road.

WHERE TO EAT

The capital has, logically, the best and most varied eating scene in Tasmania. Most of the food dispensaries are concentrated in three areas: downtown, Sandy Bay, and Battery Point, a romantic little spot near the waterfront between DeWitt and Colville streets. For some arcane reason, it's not marked on most city maps—perhaps they don't want the czar's fleet to know that there's no battery there. You reach it by the road winding up from Salamanca Place. It's a beautifully preserved complex of colonial residences, some of which have been converted into restaurants. They tend to be plushly intimate and rather expensive.

Early closing and a tendency to stay closed on Sunday is the bane of Tasmania's eating scene. The places listed below are chosen not only for their economy and quality but also for their reasonable dining hours.

The pubs are the best bets for lunches and snacks—some of the older and shabbier ones put on amazingly good counter lunches, possibly to compensate for their appearance.

MEALS FOR LESS THAN $A11

BANJO'S, 103 Elizabeth St. Tel. 34-1999.

Cuisine: SNACKS. **Reservations:** Not necessary.

$ Prices: $A1.60–$A5. No credit cards.

Open: Daily 5am–6:15pm.

Banjo's is conveniently placed opposite the Tasmanian Travel Centre. A bright and cheery coffee shop, redolent with the wonderful smell of baking bread, Banjo's has become a focal point for tourists of every age and monetary group. The frills are few and the lights downright merciless, but there are excellent coffee and tasty economy snacks like quiches for $A3.60 and large breakfasts for $A5.

CARLTON, corner of Liverpool and Argyle Sts. Tel. 34-4649.

Cuisine: AUSTRALIAN. **Reservations:** Accepted.
$ Prices: Appetizers $A2.50, main courses $A6.50–$A9. No credit cards.
Open: Daily 9am–9pm.

Located opposite Qantas, the functionality of the nuclear age reigns at the Carlton. Most of the premises are occupied by a milk bar with curved windows overlooking the busy street corner. At the rear there's a small, equally functional restaurant. A large wall mirror and scarlet curtains provide the ornaments. The roast chicken and bacon costs $A8.50, and I can recommend the apple pie dessert.

CHEQUERS, 53-A Murray St. Tel. 34-5850.
Cuisine: AUSTRALIAN. **Reservations:** Accepted.
$ Prices: Appetizers $A3–$A4, main courses $A8–$A10. AE, BC, MC, V.
Open: Mon–Sat 8am–8pm.

Chequers is another downtown quickie with a coffee lounge in front and a restaurant in the back. A pleasant modernistic eatery with plastic tabletops and swivel chairs, one wall lined with mirrors, the place is brightly lit and decorated with potted plants. The dessert shelves in front are tempting—and are meant to be. Chequers offers a large variety of economy meals, plus very fast, very cheerful service. Fried flounder costs $A7.50, the fisherman's platter $A9.50, and cappuccino $A1.

DOMINO, 55 Elizabeth Mall. Tel. 34-3783.
Cuisine: AUSTRALIAN. **Reservations:** Not necessary.
$ Prices: Appetizers $A2–$A3, main courses $A5–$A8. No credit cards.
Open: Mon–Sat 8am–6pm.

(S) Domino specializes in bargain lunches, possibly the best bargain in town, with a snack bar in front and a restaurant in the rear. Although it has tiled floors, narrow counters, bar stools, plastic everywhere, and no atmosphere to speak of, it dishes out surprisingly good fare at reasonable prices: lamb chops for $A7.50, top-grade apple strudel for $A2.50, and excellent espresso.

DON CAMILLO, in the Magnet Court shopping center, off Sandy Bay Rd. Tel. 34-1006.
Cuisine: ITALIAN. **Reservations:** Not required.
$ Prices: Appetizers $A2, main courses $A6–$A7. No credit cards.
Open: Mon–Sat 8:30am–11:30pm.

Don Camillo is a small, chic eatery in the small, fashionable Magnet Court shopping center—a bright little coffee bar out front and a more lavish (and expensive) restaurant in the rear. The food is very good in both sections, although understandably pricier in the licensed back quarters. In front, risotto costs $A6, lasagne $A6; the coffee is outstanding.

MEALS FOR LESS THAN $A17

ANTHONYS, in the Hobart Macquarie Hotel, 167 Macquarie St. Tel. 34-4422.
Cuisine: ENGLISH. **Reservations:** Accepted.
$ Prices: Appetizers $A4, main courses $A7–$A11. AE, BC, MC, V.
Open: Mon–Fri.

The decor and atmosphere here are that of a rather fashionable London West End club, a soft brown on brown with masterly marine sketches on the walls and an air of quiet enjoyment permeating the entire room. From Monday to Friday you get a really first-rate, low-cost single-course lunch here: grills for $A7 to $A10.

The hotel's Charcoal Grill, open daily, is considerably more pricey.

BLACK PRINCE, corner of Elizabeth and Melville Sts. Tel. 34-3501.
Cuisine: AUSTRALIAN. **Reservations:** Accepted.
$ Prices: Appetizers $A4, main courses $A6–$A15. AE, MC, V.
Open: Lunch Tues–Fri, dinner Mon–Thurs 5:30–9pm, Fri–Sat 5:30pm "until late."

This is a small modern hotel and dining room decked out as an automobile garage. Even the menu items have a horseless carriage theme. The staff wears overalls, there's a car hoist on the ceiling, the walls are hung with tools, and the floor decor includes entire car bodies. There are no oil leaks in the food, however, which is generally excellent, if oddly named. Every dish comes with an automotive blurb: steaks are described as "big, bold, and curvaceous, comes with full chassis"; and "we recommend the pink interior for all the above models"; the pork Biarritz is a "little beauty which has the grunt to impress"; and the description of the schnitzel Eldorado says "handling definitely a problem, very cumbersome." Patrons are encouraged to "help yourself to our salad car." On weekends there's live music to drive by.

BRANDY'S, Shop 77, Wellington Walk. Tel. 34-9450.
Cuisine: INTERNATIONAL. **Reservations:** Accepted.
$ Prices: Appetizers $A4.80, main courses $A8–$A9. AE, MC, V.
Open: Mon–Fri 8:15am–10pm, Sat until 2pm.

A smart and licensed little coffee-bar/restaurant, Brandy's is located just off the Mall. There should be more of this breed around town. Tables outside are in a glassed courtyard, and those inside are under discreet lighting in small dining booths. There is an unusually long and impressive wine list, and champagne breakfasts are served. Potables aside, you can get three versions of steak for $A8 to $A9, Hawaiian schnitzel for $A7.95, and excellent baked cheesecake in conclusion. The soups are homemade, as you can tell by the first spoonful.

CAFE RETRO, 33 Salamanca Place. Tel. 23-3073.
Cuisine: INTERNATIONAL. **Reservations:** Not necessary.
$ Prices: Appetizers $A4.50, main courses $A6–$A9. AE, BC, MC, V.
Open: Mon–Sat 8am–6pm, Fri until midnight.

A happily cluttered, relaxed, and faintly artsy eatery, Café Retro is packed with amiable vibes and student customers. The outdoor tables are shaded by colored umbrellas, and the interior walls are decked with travel-and-music posters. There are whirling fans on the ceiling, and a dinosaur's head peers through a window, contemplating the patrons—presumably for supper. The menu is chalked on no fewer than four blackboards, requiring some serious reading. Choices run from Retro burgers for $A7.50 to spinach crêpes. For an appetizer I can recommend the subtly flavored turkey pâté for $A4.50. The place serves excellent coffee.

MANDARIN, 177 Liverpool St. Tel. 34-5021.
Cuisine: CHINESE. **Reservations:** Accepted.
$ Prices: Appetizers $A3–$A4, main courses $A7–$A9. AE, BC, MC, V.
Open: Daily 5pm "until late."

The Mandarin is a nice and cozy Chinese restaurant, well carpeted and lit by Chinese lanterns in various inoffensive hues. Otherwise there's a minimum of pseudo-Asian knickknacks. The tables are bare and plastic, the chairs steel; the fare is a pleasant mixture of Cantonese, Mandarin, and Malaysian. Prawn crackers cost $A2.50; the sweet-and-sour chicken, pork, and pineapple is $A9. Unfortunately, a pot of mediocre Chinese tea sets you back A80¢.

SEOUL RESTAURANT, corner of Harrington and Collins Sts. Tel. 23-8397.
Cuisine: KOREAN. **Reservations:** Accepted.
$ Prices: Appetizers $A3–$A5, main courses $A10–$A12. AE, BC, MC, V.
Open: Mon–Sat noon–2pm, 6–10pm.

Seoul Restaurant is the pioneer of Korean cuisine on the Apple Isle. Most of the delicacies are suitably modified to avoid burning local palates. The kimchee, however, is fiery enough to please aficionados. Tastefully plain and very comfortable, with ample chopstick-wielding room, the Seoul charms you with soft, traditional Korean music in the background. Some of the best menu items are the *dak bool ko ki* (barbecued chicken in a richly spiced sauce) and a vegetarian dish called *jap chae,* consisting of vermicelli fried with fragrant mushrooms and mixed vegetables. Seoul Restaurant also serves special lunches: wonton, marinated beef, and steamed rice for $A8.90.

WORTH THE EXTRA MONEY

GUR PERTAB'S, 47 Hampden Rd., Battery Point. Tel. 23-7011.
Cuisine: INDIAN-MALAYSIAN. **Reservations:** Accepted.
$ Prices: Appetizers $A4.50–$A5, main courses $A12–$A15. AE, BC, MC, V.
Open: Tues–Sun 6pm "until late."

Housed in a historic 1850s building, this restaurant blends nicely with the colonial ambience of Battery Point. The exterior is unreservedly English—you have to step inside to catch a whiff of curried Orientalia. The fare, like the owners, is a cross of Indian and Malaysian, but with the accent on spiciness rather than bite. For good measure, the Gur also serves a large selection of Tasmanian wines. Meal prices depend largely on how many side dishes you order. *Chapatis,* for instance, cost $A1.20 each. The vegetarian *dhal,* a tangy lentil concoction, is $A5. As a main course, you should try the rich lamb curry, cooked in ginger, chiles, and coriander. Service is smooth and highly efficient, and a great many Tasmanians come here for their first-ever taste of North Indian culinary delights.

EVENING ENTERTAINMENT

WREST POINT HOTEL-CASINO, 410 Sandy Bay Rd. Tel. 25-0112.

Most of Hobart's nightlife is concentrated on the lavish premises of the Wrest Point Hotel-Casino, an ivory-colored tower complex soaring 21 stories above the Sandy Bay boat harbor. The place houses everything from the gambling casino to Tasmania's finest hotel, plushest show club, and swankiest restaurant. For good measure it also contains a swimming pool, a shopping arcade, and a revolving restaurant in the tower.

The interior is elegant but not overwhelming, more stylishly gemütlich than palatial—with cascading chandeliers, gloriously comfortable settees and armchairs, and noble woodwork polished to a splendid gloss. Above all, there's an atmosphere of relaxing quiet; no banging of slot machines assaults your eardrums. These vibes radiate from the staff as well, the coolest casino workers I've ever experienced. They have neither the chilling hauteur of their Monte Carlo counterparts nor the slightly sinister condescension of their Las Vegas ones. Here they're just amiably relaxed, very friendly, and remarkably knowledgeable. The only dress regulations state that gentlemen must wear jackets after 7pm and no one gets in wearing jeans, sneakers, or sandals.

The unique portion of the casino is the "two-up" room. That's where they play Australia's national game, outlawed everywhere except on such premises. Many mainland visitors come simply to gaze at those widely visible signs with an air of pleased incredulity, like first timers in a nudist colony.

The Aussies call two-up *swy* (from the German word *zwei,* meaning "two") and consider it as much a part of their military tradition as the famous Digger hat. You could allegedly spot Australian trenches and foxholes during both world wars by the two coins perpetually whirling in the air above them. And when a Sydney primary-school class was asked to name the greatest local celebrity, half the kids wrote "Tommo" (which happens to be the tag of Tommo's, the oldest floating swy game in town). To the best of anyone's knowledge, no such person ever existed.

Two-up is a fast and honest game. It's fast because all you do is bet whether two spun pennies will land heads or tails; it's honest because it's safer that way. One operator reputedly tried using a two-headed penny. He was last seen locked in his own car in the process of being rolled off Port Melbourne pier. There hasn't been a double-header around since.

The swy sanctum at the casino consists of a round pit and a surrounding circle for the gamblers. The walls are appropriately hung with huge photos depicting World War I and II Diggers playing guess what? You can learn the rules in about one minute flat, although it helps to know that the "spinner" is the coin tosser, the "kip" is the wooden board with which he tosses them, the "boxer" is the pit boss, and a "standoff" means all bets are frozen. The game is simple, but it hooks you: the speed of it, the breathless pace at which tension evaporates into triumph or loss, and the split-second acrobatics performed by those whirling coppers. The immemorial cry that some folks say should be elevated into a national motto is "Come in, spinner!"

Open: Sun–Thurs 1pm–3am, Fri–Sat until 4am.

EXCURSION TO THE HUON VALLEY

About 25 miles southwest of Hobart stretch the gently rolling hills of the Huon River Valley. Here you'll find the first of several exciting **Huon jet boat rides** at Esplanade, Huonville (tel. 64-1838). These high-speed river craft whiz you through the rapids at the gateway to Tasmania's wilderness region. They operate daily and cost $A25 for adults, $A15 for children.

Further south, at Cygnet on the road to Gordon, lies the **Talune Wildlife Park and Koala Gardens** in Gardners Bay (tel. 95-1775). This mainly free-range park harbors emus, parrots, koalas, wombats, wallabies, and—as top attraction—a large enclosure of Tasmanian devils. Here these normally ornery critters are surprisingly tame and friendly. You can even pick one up and pat him, a procedure not ordinarily advisable. Mainly you'll hear them feed; they're possibly the world's noisiest-eating carnivores, munching, chomping, and growling in a manner indicating that they never had to worry about another hunter snatching away their meal. The park is open daily from 9:30am to 5pm. Admission is $A5 for adults, $A2 for children.

At 183 Main Rd. in Huonville (behind the Shell service station) is the **Model Train World** (tel. 64-2116). This is a meticulously realistic layout of 20 scale-model trains, puffing and whirring through a miniature south German countryside. The setup includes working signals, turning windmills, loading cranes, and 200 twinkling lights. Open Tuesday to Sunday from 9:30am to 5pm. Admission is $A4 adults, $A2 children.

EN ROUTE TO DEVONPORT

The main road from Hobart heads inland to the northwest, cutting off a large slice of the island's rugged southwestern portion.

NEW NORFOLK Some 28 miles from Hobart, in the rich green Derwent Valley, nestles New Norfolk. A historic township with a striking resemblance to an English village, New Norfolk provides a sharp contrast to the backdrop of wild mountain ranges in the distance. To get a full taste of the local atmosphere, have afternoon tea at the **Old Colony Inn,** 21 Montagu St. (tel. 61-2731). A wonderfully mellow edifice built in 1835, it is now part museum, part refreshment parlor. Admission to the museum is $A1.50.

For a complete change of pace try the **Devil Jets,** which run daily every half hour from 9am to 4pm from beneath the Derwent River Bridge Bush Inn (book by phoning 61-3460). The jet boats zoom over the shallow river rapids at thrilling speeds, taking half an hour to complete their circuit back to the bridge. Adults pay $A30, children $A17.

For overnight stays there's **Rosie's Inn,** 5 Oast St., New Norfolk (tel. 61-1171). A bed-and-breakfast guest house with 13 large rooms (some with private bath), the inn dishes up grandiose country breakfasts (omelets with herbs from their own garden), plus incidental treats like homemade cookies with your tea and quilts on the beds. This is a nonsmoking house with award-winning gardens. Singles pay $A40 to $A60, doubles $A60 to $A75.

QUEENSTOWN Queenstown was once a rip-roaring mining town that has settled for less roaring in favor of tourism. First the mining here was gold and silver, then tin and copper, until the mountains were denuded of timber (used to stoke the smelters) and now glare naked with boulders glowing in multicolors when the sun hits them. The Mount Lyell mine still dominates this strange town. One of the highlights is a 2-hour tour of its innards, concluding with a visit to the **Mining Museum.**

Admission is $A6.50 adults, $A3.25 children. Inquire about touring times at the tourist information bureau on Orr Street.

STRAHAN At this point you should make a detour to the coast, to the quiet little town of **Strahan,** which has the distinction of being the only port on Tasmania's entire west coast. Some 80 years ago this was another mining boomtown, but today it caters to tamer tastes. Strahan is home base for the enthralling **Gordon River Cruises,** at Strahan Wharf (tel. 004/71-7187). The half-day jaunts, on sleek modern vessels that are fully licensed, view some of the continent's most haunting and dramatic sights. The trip goes to Hells Gates and Sarah Island, the infamous "Isle of the Dead." These tags weren't mere figures of speech—the island was the most dreaded penal hellhole in all Australia, worse even than Port Arthur. On Sarah Island death from natural causes was an envied rarity. Nearly all convict casualties resulted from prolonged floggings or slow starvation. The cruise costs $A44 for adults, $A24 for children; bookings are essential.

THE WILD WEST Heading due north, the road stays inland, skirting the west coast region. This is Tasmania's Wild West, the zone where the smiling Apple Island turns into something mean, moody, and magnificent. Patchily forested and sparsely populated, this is the refuge of the Tasmanian devils, those small but astonishingly fierce marsupial carnivores that attack and kill prey three times their size. The scenery is awesomely beautiful yet strangely forbidding: tangles of dense scrub and deep, cold blue rivers flanked by sand dunes up to 25 feet high, and in between towering hills, the barren moon landscapes where mining has stripped the earth bare.

BURNIE Located on the north coast, Burnie is an industrial port with a superb scenic hinterland and good, comfortable pubs and restaurants.

The town's top attraction is the **Pioneer Village Museum** (tel. 30-5746), a fragment of the past located in the brand-new Civic Centre Plaza on High Street. It shows an entire mid-Victorian village street under one roof, authentic down to the smallest boot buttoner. Gaslit storefronts illuminate the saddler, cobbler, journey shop, and grocery. There are an inn, a general store, a post office, a printing office, and a butter factory—all overflowing with the tools and wares of the period. Only the lockup is missing. Open Monday to Friday from 9am to 5pm, Saturday and Sunday from 1:30 to 5pm. Admission is $A3 for adults, A50¢ for children.

In the middle of Burnie Park stands the **Burnie Inn,** the city's oldest building. Originally licensed as a pub in 1847, the shingle-roofed structure with a broad and inviting porch is now operated by the National Trust. Alas, it's no longer a pub and now serves up only very genteel Devonshire teas and what goes with them.

ORGANIZED TOURS

Visitours, P.O. Box 214, Burnie, TAS 7320 (tel. 004/31-7206), is a highly individualized minibus outfit run by Gary Philips. Each tour is different because it's tailormade according to the wishes of the passengers. There's a half-day trip around Burnie and environs costing $A46. Day tours, starting at $A80, may take in the West Coast Wilderness and include panning for gold in the Gordon River, or may go through the Tamar Valley and stop at a vineyard for a round of wine tasting. Tours leave Burnie daily around 8am, but return times vary because Gary's passengers can take their own sweet time to explore places that arouse their interest.

3. DEVONPORT

124 miles NW of Hobart

GETTING THERE By Boat The ***Spirit of Tasmania*** operates three times a week between Melbourne and Devonport, a handsome vessel with a bar, shop, restaurant, and cafeteria on board. You leave Melbourne at 6pm and land at Devonport at 8:30 the next morning. A low-season bunk in a four-berth cabin costs $A115, dorm accommodations cost $A85. For further details contact the **T.T. Line Station Pier,** Port Melbourne (tel. toll free 008/030-344).

ESSENTIALS Getting Around Bicycles can be rented at the **Backpacker's Barn,** 10 Edward St. (tel. 24-3626).

Fast Facts The telephone **area code** is 004.

Now we turn east along the coastline and reach Devonport, the conclusion of our island circuit. With 25,000 people, Devonport is Tasmania's third-largest city. It lies at the mouth of the Mersey River and at the center of one of Australia's richest and lushest farming areas.

WHAT TO SEE & DO

MARITIME MUSEUM, 47 Victoria Parade.

The Maritime Museum has an outstanding collection of ships' models, starting with windjammers and finishing with today's oceangoing passenger ferries.

Admission: $A1 adults, A40¢ children.

Open: Tues–Sun 2–4pm.

GALLERY AND ARTS CENTRE, 45 Stewart St. Tel. 24-8296.

The Gallery and Arts Centre is housed in a converted church and offers a constantly changing and extremely varied array of paintings, prints, ceramics, woodcraft, sculptures, and photographs by Tasmanian artists and craftspeople.

Admission: Free.

Open: Mon–Fri 10am–5pm, Sun 2–5pm.

DON RIVER RAILWAY, Forth Main Rd., Don. Tel. 24-6335.

The Don River Railway (about 10 minutes from the city center) displays a large, nostalgic parade of steam engines, coaches, and railroad equipment—all functioning. You can ride a vintage steam train from there along the banks of the Don River.

Admission: $A6 adults, $A3 children.

Open: Daily 11am–4pm.

TIAGARRA ABORIGINAL CULTURAL CENTRE, Mersey Bluff. Tel. 24-0559.

The center, built to resemble a bark hut, is set on 10 acres of beautifully landscaped parkland overlooking the Bass Strait. It looks tranquil but houses the mementos of one of the grimmest tragedies of the hemisphere. Inside are 26 displays showing the life-style of a "late" people—the original Tasmanians. The Tasmanian Aborigines were a unique race, physically different from their mainland cousins, peaceful hunter-gatherers with a highly developed artistic sense. There were about 7,000 of them when the first Europeans arrived in the Derwent in 1803. By 1876, just 73 years later, not a single survivor was left. They had been systematically wiped out—slaughtered in a horribly one-sided "war" or deported from the island. Their story is told in huge murals inside the center, and you can see some of their artwork in the rock carvings in the surrounding park. Some of these carvings depict the stumpy Tasmanian emu, which is also extinct.

Admission: $A2.50 adults, $A1 children.

Open: Daily 9am–4:30pm.

WHERE TO STAY

DOUBLES FOR LESS THAN $A61

RIVER VIEW LODGE, 18 Victoria Parade, Devonport, TAS 7310. Tel. 004/24-7357. Fax 004/24-7357. 10 rms (4 with bath). TV TEL

$ Rates (including breakfast): $A50–$A60 single, $A60–$A70 double. AE, BC, MC, V.

Located a few minutes' walk from the city center, the lodge stands on a handsome street overlooking the Mersey River. The building dates from 1877 and has retained its period charm, but it is fitted with all modern conveniences, including a communal laundry.

WENVOE HEIGHTS, 44 McFie St., Devonport, TAS 7310. Tel. 004/24-1719. Fax 004/24-8766. 9 rms (6 with bath). TV TEL

$ Rates (including breakfast): $A47 single, $A60 double. BC, MC, V.

Wenvoe Heights is a large, rambling, colonial-style structure with a pleasant dining room in which to enjoy the hot breakfast included in the rates. There are ample parking space and panoramic views.

YOUTH HOSTEL

MACWRIGHT HOUSE YHA, 115 Middle Rd., Devonport, TAS 7310. Tel. 004/24-5696. 42 beds.

$ Rates: $A9 adults, $A5 guests 16 and under. No credit cards.

MacWright House, the local Youth Hostel, is a spacious former home equipped with four bathrooms, two lounges, laundry facilites, electric hot plates, and refrigerators. It is located about two miles from downtown.

INDEX

Aboriginal art and artifacts, 19, 20–22, 174, 197, 227, 306, 339, 342–43, 352. *See also* Namatjira, Albert
- Aboriginal Arts (Perth), 299
- Centre for Aboriginal Artists (Alice Springs), 343
- shopping for, 125, 168, 197, 226, 234, 299, 343
- Queensland Aboriginal Creations (Brisbane), 226

Aborigines, 20–22, 329
- cuisine of, 29, 223
- Dreamtime, 8–9, 328
- history of, 2, 10, 20–21, 328, 353–54, 367
- mythology of, 20, 174, 340, 346
- Tandanya Aboriginal Cultural Institute (Adelaide), 197
- Tiagarra Aboriginal Cultural Centre (Tasmania), 377
- Tjapukai Aboriginal Dance Theater (Kuranda), 270

Accommodations, 62–66. *See also* Backpackers' lodgings; Bed and Breakfasts; Camping and R.V. (caravan) parks

ADELAIDE, 179–201
- accommodations, 184–89
- Adelaide Festival Centre, 19, 196, 199
- Adelaide Zoo, 197
- arriving in, 181
- Botanic Gardens, 197
- Dazzleland, 197
- evening entertainment, 199–201
- Fast facts, 183–84
- Festival of the Arts, 179, 180, 193
- festivals, 41, 179, 180, 193
- Frommer's favorite experiences, 199
- gambling, 200–201
- historic sites
  - Ayers House, 196
  - Old Parliament House, 196
- itineraries, 194
- layout of, 181
- museums
  - Art Gallery of South Australia, 196
  - The Investigator, 198
  - Maritime Museum, 197
  - Migration Museum, 196
  - Port Dock Station Railway Museum, 197
  - Postal Museum, 197
  - South Australian Museum, 196
  - Tandanya Aboriginal Cultural Institute, 197
- neighborhoods, 181–82
- performing arts, 199–200
- restaurants, 189–93
- sightseeing, 193–98
- sports, 27, 198–99
- tourist information, 181
- tours of, 198
- transportation, 182–83

Adelaide Festival Centre, 19, 196, 199

Adelaide Festival of Arts, 40, 179, 180, 193

Adelaide River Queen (Darwin), 351

AIRLIE BEACH, 275

Air travel
- to Australia, 47–49
- within Australia, 49–52

ALDGATE, 189

ALICE SPRINGS, 328–44
- accommodations, 331–35
- arriving in, 330–31
- Camel Farm, 340
- Diorama Village, 340–41
- evening entertainment, 343–44
- festivals, 40, 41
- Ghan Preservation Society, 341
- historic sites
  - Adelaide House, 339
  - Chateau Hornsby, 341
  - Old Stuart Gaol, 341
  - Old Telegraph Station, 340
- John Flynn Memorial, 339
- layout of, 331
- Mecca Date Gardens, 342
- museums
  - Aviation Museum, 341
  - Stuart Auto Museum, 341
- Panorama "Guth," 340
- Pitchi Richi Aboriginal Cultural Experience, 339–40
- restaurants, 335–38
- Royal Flying Doctor Service (RFDS), 338
- School of the Air, 339
- shopping, 342–43
- sightseeing, 338–42
- tourist information, 331
- tours of, 342
- transportation, 331

Alternative and adventure travel, 43–46

America's Cup, 27, 295

Amusement and theme parks, 114, 164, 197, 198, 234–35, 236, 248, 294–95, 298

ANGASTON, 205

Animals. *See* Aquariums and marine life; Wildlife parks and sanctuaries; Zoos

Annual events, festivals and fairs, 39–42, 138, 180, 208, 253, 281, 308, 329, 351, 354. *See also specific events*

Apartments, serviced, 65

Aquariums and marine life
- Great Barrier Reef Wonderland (Townsville), 277
- Marineland Melanesia (Green Island), 274
- Oceanworld (Sydney), 114
- Sea Life Centre (Tasmania), 363
- Sea World (Surfers Paradise), 234
- Sydney Aquarium, 107
- Underwater Coral Observatory (Green Island), 274
- Underwater World (Mooloolaba), 247
- Underwater World (Perth), 294
- Vic Hislop's Shark Show (Cairns), 264

Architecture, 19

ARMADALE, 295
- Elizabethan Village, 295
- Pioneer World, 295

ARMIDALE, 134–35

Art, 18–19. *See also* Aboriginal art and artifacts

Art Gallery of New South Wales (Sydney), 112, 120

Art Gallery of South Australia (Adelaide), 196

Art museums and galleries, 106, 112, 113, 120, 135, 161, 174, 196, 225, 293, 320 21, 358, 377

Arts and crafts. *See also* Aboriginal art and artifacts
- festivals, 40, 41
- shopping for, 67, 168–69, 234

Atherton Tableland, 270

Australian Museum (Sydney), 113

Australian National Gallery (Canberra), 320–21

Australian National University (Canberra), 318

Australian War Memorial (Canberra), 320

Australian Woolshed (Brisbane), 226–27

Aviation museums, 294, 320, 341

AYERS ROCK, 2, 3, 9, 22, 346–48

Backpackers' lodgings, 46, 64, 92, 148–49, 219, 240, 249, 287–88, 348, 363, 370–71

BALLARAT, 177

BAROSSA VALLEY, 201–5

Batman, John, 9, 17

Beaches, 26, 28
- Adelaide and vicinity, 199, 201
- Cairns, 265
- Gold Coast, 232
- Great Barrier Reef, 275
- Melbourne, 138
- Perth, 295
- Sunshine Coast, 246
- Sydney, 114, 123–24

Bed & breakfasts, 65, 90–91, 148, 177, 187–88, 215, 218

Beer, 29–30, 351, 368

BENDIGO, 178

Beverages, 29–31. *See also* Beer; Rum; Wine and wineries

BICHENO (TASMANIA), 363

Bicycling, 46, 80, 142, 183, 211, 232, 257, 282, 363
- Bicycle Museum (Canberra), 321

Birds and birdwatching, 7–8. *See also* Wildlife parks and sanctuaries
- watching, 133, 236, 256, 277, 293, 298, 339

Blamey, Thomas, 17

BLI BLI, 247–48

Bligh, Capt. William, 10, 107, 353

BLUE DANDENONGS, 174, 176

Blue Mountains National Park, 133–34

Boating, 122–23, 300, 325. *See also* Canoeing; Yachting

Boat travel and cruises, 58
- Adelaide, 198
- Brisbane, 228–29
- Cairns, 266–67
- Great Barrier Reef, 274
- Melbourne, 163, 165–66
- Murray River, 206
- Perth, 298
- Sydney, 121–22
- Tasmania, 376

Bondi Beach, 76, 88, 90, 123

Bonner, Neville Thomas, 17

Books about Australia, 31–32

Boomerangs, 21, 125, 235

Botanical gardens, 120, 164, 197, 264, 321, 368

Botanic Gardens (Adelaide), 197

Botany Bay, 9, 10
Brabham, John, 17
Bradman, Donald, 17
BRAMPTON ISLAND, 275
BRAODBEACH, 234, 240
BRISBANE, 2, 207-31
accommodations, 214-20
arriving in, 209
Australian Woolshed, 226-27
Brisbane Forest Park, 227
Bunya Park, 228
evening entertainment, 229-31
Fast facts, 211, 214
festivals, 40-41
Frommer's favorite experiences, 227
historic sites
Newstead House, 226
Observatory (Old Windmill), 226
layout of, 210
Lone Pine Sanctuary, 227
museums
Maritime Museum, 225-26
Sciencentre, 226
neighborhoods, 210-11
Pioneer Valley Park, 228
Queensland Aboriginal Creations, 226
Queensland Cultural Centre, 224-25, 229
restaurants, 220-24
sightseeing, 224-28
Sir Thomas Brisbane Planetarium, 227
South Bank Parklands, 225
sports, 27, 229
tourist information, 210
tours of, 228-29
transportation, 211
Brisbane Forest Park, 227
BROADBEACH, 245
BROOME, 40
BUCKLAND (TASMANIA), 363
BUNBURY, 303-4
Bungee jumping, 235
Burke, Robert, 11, 17
BURLEIGH HEADS, 235-36
BURNIE (TASMANIA), 376
Pioneer Village Museum, 376
Bushrangers, 12-13, 162, 296, 297
Bush tucker cuisine, 29, 223, 336
Bus travel, 54-55
Butterflies, 162, 266, 267, 270
Bywong Town (Canberra), 322

CAIRNS, 252-69
accommodations, 258-61
beaches, 265
Cairns Historical Museum, 264
Edward River Crocodile Farm, 264-65
evening entertainment, 268-69
Fast facts, 257-58
festivals, 41
Flecker Botanic Gardens, 264
Hartley's Creek Crocodile Farm, 263-64
House of 10,000 Shells, 263
recreational activities, 267-68
restaurants, 261-63
Royal Flying Doctor Service (RFDS), 264
shopping, 267
sightseeing, 263-65
tourist information, 256
tours of, 266-67
transportation, 256-57
traveling to, 252-53
Vic Hislop's Shark Show, 264
Wild World, 263
CALOUNDRA, 248, 249
Camels, in Alice Springs
Camel Cup (race), 40
Camel Farm, 340, 342
tours by, 342
Camping and R.V. (caravan) parks, 64-65, 150, 176-77, 189, 204, 220, 240-241, 288-89, 334-35, 347, 361
CANBERRA, 2, 14, 137, 307-26
accommodations, 311-15
arriving in, 309-10
Australian National Botanic Gardens, 321
Australian War Memorial, 320
Bywong Town, 322
Canberra Carillon, 320
Canberra Maze, 322
Captain Cook Memorial, 322
Cockington Green, 323-24
evening entertainment, 325-26
festivals, 40
historic sites
Blundell's Cottage, 321
Lanyon, 323
layout of, 310
Mount Stromlo Observatory, 322
museums
Australian National Gallery, 320-21
Bicycle Museum, 321
Canberra Space Centre, 323
National Film and Sound Archive, 321
National Science and Technology Centre, 322
Poker Machine Museum, 321
National Library of Australia, 322
Parliament House, 319-20
public artworks, 319
recreational activities, 324-25
Rehwinkel's Animal Park, 323
restaurants, 315-18
Royal Australian Mint, 321
Royal Military College, 321
shopping, 324
sightseeing, 318-24
Telecommunications Tower, 323
Tidbinbilla Nature Reserve, 323
tourist information, 310
tours of, 324
transportation, 310
Canoeing, 46, 166. *See also* Boating
Caravan parks. *See* Camping and R.V. (caravan) parks
CARLISLE ISLAND, 275
Car museums, 341, 358, 360
Car racing, 41, 193
Cars and driving, 55-58
automobile clubs, 57-58
rentals, 56-57
Casinos. *See* Gambling
Cataract Gorge (Tasmania), 358
Caverns, 134, 278, 297, 306
Cawley, Evonne Fay, 17
Centre for Aboriginal Artists (Alice Springs), 343
CESSNOCK, 134
Château Yaldara (Lyndoch), 202
Chifley, Joseph, 17
Climate, 38-39
Cockington Green (Canberra), 323-24
Coffee, 31
Convicts, history of, 9-10, 17-18, 24, 111, 120, 121, 208, 226, 353, 354, 364, 376
exhibitions, 113, 118, 162, 293, 296, 369
gaols, 162, 295, 296, 341, 364, 369
COOBER PEDY, 193, 205
Cook, Capt. James, 2, 9, 162, 246, 266, 272, 322, 353
COOKTOWN, 270, 272
COOLANGATTA, 232, 237-40
COOLGARDIE, 304
COOMA, 327
CORAL COAST, 275-76
Cricket, 26, 122, 229
Crocodile Dundee (film), 3, 32, 107
Crocodiles, 7, 263-65, 266, 350-51. *See also* Wildlife parks and sanctuaries
Cuisine. *See* Food
CURRUMBIN, 236
Currumbin Bird Sanctuary, 236
Curtin, John, 17
Customs, 35

Daintree Connection in Cairns, 266
DANDENONGS, 174, 176
Darling Harbour (Sydney), 106-7, 110
Darling Range, 297
DARWIN, 330, 350-52
accommodations, 351-52
Adelaide River Queen, 351
Crocodile Farm, 350-51
East End Reserve, 350
festivals, 40, 351
safari tours, 351
Territory Wildlife Park, 351
DAYDREAM ISLAND, 275
DEVONPORT (TASMANIA), 376-78
Don River Railway, 377
Gallery and Arts Centre, 377
Maritime Museum, 377
Tiagarra Aboriginal Cultural Centre, 377
Diggers, 11-12, 14, 18, 169, 177, 178, 226, 272, 294, 304, 322
Diorama Village (Alice Springs), 340-41
Disabled travelers, tips for, 44
Dobell, William, 17
Documents for entry, 35
Dolphins, in Bunbury, 304
DORRIEN, 204
Doyle, Arthur Conan, 158
Dreamtime, 8-9, 328
Drinks, 29-31. *See also* Beer; Rum; Wine and wineries
Drysdale, Russell, 17
DUNK ISLAND, 274-75

Elizabeth Bay House (Sydney), 111-12
Ellis Beach, 265
Embassies and consulates, 35-36, 69, 318-19
Endeavor, H.M.S., 9, 234, 246, 272
Entry into the U.S., requirements for, 35
Eucalyptus gum trees, 6, 133
Eureka Stockade (1854), 12, 177
Evening entertainment, 25-26, 66

Families, tips for, 44-45
Famous and historical figures. *See specific people*
FAR WEST. *See* **WESTERN AUSTRALIA**
Fast facts, 68-71
Fauna, 6-8
Festival Centre (Adelaide), 19, 196, 199
Festival of Sydney, 41
Festivals, 39-42, 138, 180, 208, 253, 281, 308, 329, 351, 354. *See also specific festivals*
Films, 32-33
festivals, 40, 42
Fishing, 178, 254, 256, 327
Fleay's Fauna Centre (Burleigh), 235-36

Flinders Chase National Park, 205
Flinders, Matthew, 11
Flinders Ranges, 206
Flora, 6, 280, 304, 341
  tour of wildflowers around Perth, 304
Flynn, John, 17, 338, 339
Food, 28-29
Football, Australian rules, 26, 122, 166, 198, 229
Fraser, Dawn, 17
FRASER ISLAND, 246
FREMANTLE, 279, 295-97, 298-99
  Energy Museum, 297
  Fremantle Gaol, 296
  Fremantle Markets, 297
  Fremantle Museum, 296
  Sails of the Century, 296
  Western Australia Maritime Museum, 296-97
Fremantle Museum, 296

Gallery of Sport and Olympic Museum (Melbourne), 167
Gambling, 25-26, 132, 173-74, 200-201, 277, 302, 343-44, 350, 360
  Poker Machine Museum (Canberra), 321
Geography, 2-3, 6, 31
George Gill Ranges, 344, 346
Ghan Preservation Society (Alice Springs), 341
Gibson, Mel, 24
Gilmore, Dame Mary, 17
Ginger factory, in Yandina, 247
GIPPSLAND LAKES, 178
Glass House Mountains, 246
GLENELG, 201
GLENROWAN, 13
Gold, 9-10, 11-12, 177, 178, 272, 279, 304, 322, 375
GOLD COAST, 231-45
  accommodations, 237-41
  Boomerang Farm, 235
  Currumbin Bird Sanctuary, 236
  Dreamworld, 234
  evening entertainment, 243-45
  Fleay's Fauna Centre, 235-36
  gambling, 244-45
  Grundy's, 236
  The Hinterland, 236
  Land of Legend, 234
  Movie World, 234-35
  Rap Jumping, 235
  restaurants, 241-43
  Ripley's Believe It or Not, 235
  Sea World, 234
  shopping, 237
  sightseeing, 234-36
  tours of, 236-37
  transportation, 232
  traveling to, 231
  Tribal Arts, 234
  War Museum, 235
  Wet 'n' Wild, 235
Golf
  Adelaide, 198
  Brisbane, 229
  Canberra, 325
  Melbourne, 166-67
  Perth, 299-300
  Sydney, 122, 123
Gosse, William, 10
Government, 16-17
GREAT BARRIER REEF, 27, 254, 269, 272-78
GREAT KEPPEL ISLAND, 275
GREEN ISLAND, 274

Greenway, Francis, 17-18, 19, 107, 121
Greer, Germaine, 18
Griffin, Walter Burley, 10, 14, 308
Guth, Henk, 340

Halletts Valley (Tanunda), 204
Hartley's Creek Crocodile Farm (Cairns), 263-64
HAYMAN ISLAND, 275
HEALESVILLE, 176
Health concerns and precautions, 42-43
Helpmann, Robert, 18
HEPBURN SPRINGS, 174
HERMANNSBURG, 346
HERON ISLAND, 275
Historic Rambles in Melbourne, 166
History, 8-16, 31. *See also* Convicts, history of
Hitchhiking, 58-59
HOBART (TASMANIA), 41, 353, 364-75
  accommodations, 369-71
  The Allport Library, 367
  Anglesea Barracks, 367-68
  Cadbury Schweppes Chocolate Factory, 368
  Cascade Brewery, 368
  evening entertainment, 374-75
  Fast facts, 367
  gambling, 374-75
  Model Tudor Village, 367
  Mt. Nelson Signal Station, 368
  Penitentiary Chapel and Criminal Courts, 368
  restaurants, 371-74
  Royal Tasmanian Botanical Gardens, 368
  Runnymede, 368
  shopping, 369
  Shot Tower, 367
  sightseeing, 367-68
  Tasmanian Maritime Museum, 368
  Tasmanian Museum, 367
  tourist information, 366
  tours of, 368-69
  transportation, 366
  Van Diemen's Land Folk Museum, 367
Hogan, Paul, 24, 107
Holidays, 39
Horseracing, 26, 122, 167
  events, 41, 42, 158, 167
HUNTER VALLEY, 134
Huon River Valley (Tasmania), 375

Information sources. *See* Tourist information
Insurance, 42-43
Itineraries, 59-61

Jewish museums, 113, 164

Kaiser Stuhl (Nuriootpa), 204
Kakadu National Park, 3, 352
KALAMUNDA, 297
KALGOORLIE, 304
Kangaroo Island, 193, 205
Kangaroos, 6, 176, 205, 323. *See also* Wildlife parks and sanctuaries
Katherine Gorge National Park, 352
KATOOMBA, 133
Kelly, Ned, 10, 13, 20, 162, 223
Keneally, Thomas, 18
Kidman, Sidney, 2
Kimberley Plateau, 304, 306
Kings Canyon, 344, 346
Kings Park (Perth), 294

Koalas, 6, 113-14, 115, 176, 227-28, 375. *See also* Wildlife parks and sanctuaries; Zoos
Kondalilla National Park, 247
Kosciusko National Park, 135
KURANDA, 270
Ku-ring-gai Chase National Park, 122

Lalor, Peter, 12, 18
Language and slang, 23-24, 63
LAUNCESTON (TASMANIA), 357-64
  accommodations, 360-61
  Cataract Gorge, 358
  Design Centre of Tasmania, 358
  Franklin House, 358
  Launceston Casino, 360
  National Automobile Museum, 358, 360
  Penny Royal World, 358
  Queen Victoria Museum and Art Gallery, 358
  restaurants, 361-63
  shopping, 363
  sightseeing, 357-60
  tourist information, 357
  tours of, 363
  Waverly Woollen Mills, 358
Lawson, Henry, 18
LEURA, 133
Lifesavers, 26-27, 111, 123, 124
LIGHTNING RIDGE, 135-36
LINDEMAN ISLAND, 275-76
Lindsay, Norman, 133
Liquor laws, 30, 69
Literature, 19-20, 31-32
Lone Pine Sanctuary (Brisbane), 227-28
LONG ISLAND, 275
LOW ISLES, 275
LYNDOCH, 202

MacPherson Ranges, 232, 236
MAGNETIC ISLAND, 277
MANDURAH, 297-98
MANLY, 77, 114
Marapana Wildlife World (outside Perth), 297-98
Maritime Museum (Adelaide), 197
Maritime museums, 107, 162, 197, 225-26, 296-97, 368, 377
MAROOCHYDORE, 248-50
Melba, Nellie, 18, 24-25
MELBOURNE, 2, 137-74
  accommodations, 144-50
  festivals, 40, 41
  arriving in, 139-40
  clubs, 171-73
  evening entertainment, 170-74
  Fast facts, 143-44
  Frommer's favorite experiences, 163
  gambling, 173-74
  historic sites
    Captain Cook's cottage, 162
    Como, 163-64
    La Trobe cottage, 162
    Lippon Lea, 164
  itineraries, 160-61
  La Mama, 24
  layout of, 140-41
  Luna Park, 164
  movies, 173
  museums
    Gallery of Sport and Olympic Museum, 167
    Jewish Museum of Australia, 164
    Maritime Museum, 162
    Museum of Victoria, 161
    National Gallery, 161
    Old Melbourne Gaol & Penal Museum, 162

MELBOURNE *(cont'd)*
Performing Arts Museum, 158, 164
Worm Museum, 158
music, 171–73
performing arts, 170–71
restaurants, 150–58
Royal Botanic Gardens, 164
Royal Melbourne Zoo, 162
shopping, 167–69
Shrine of Remembrance, 162
sightseeing, 158–65
Southgate, 162–63
sports, 27, 166–67
tourist information, 140
tours of, 165–66
transportation, 141–42
Victorian Arts Centre, 161
Melbourne Cup, 41, 158, 163, 167
Menzies, Robert Gordon, 18
Migration Museum (Adelaide), 196
Military museums, 111, 235
Mineral springs, 174
Mints, 112, 294, 321
Model Train World (Tasmania), 375
Money, 36–37, 68
MOOLOOLABA, 247
MORETON ISLAND, 275
MOSSMAN, 265
Mount Dandenong Lookout, 174
MOUNT ISA, 278
Mount Kosciusko, 135
Mount Stromlo Observatory (Canberra), 322
MUDGEERABA, 235
Murdoch, Rupert, 193
Murray River Queen, 206
Mythology, 20, 174, 340, 346

Namatjira, Albert, 18, 19, 21, 342
National Film and Sound Archive (Canberra), 321
National Gallery (Melbourne), 161
National Library of Australia (Canberra), 322
National parks. *See specific parks*
National Science and Technology Centre (Canberra), 322
Natural history museums, 113, 161, 225
NEW ENGLAND, 134–35
NEW NORCIA, 303
NEW NORFOLK (TASMANIA), 375
NEW SOUTH WALES, 72–136
NEWSTEAD, 211
Nicholls, Douglas, 21
Nolan, Sidney, 18, 161, 323
NOOSA, 246, 248, 249, 250–51
NORTHERN TERRITORY, 8, 328–52
NURIOOTPA, 204

Old Melbourne Gaol & Penal Museum, 162
Old Parliament House (Adelaide), 196
Old Sydney Town, 115
Olgas, 347
Opals
prospecting for, 135, 205
shopping for, 67, 126, 169, 204, 299
Outback, 3, 135–36, 338, 342
OXENFORD, 234–35

Packing for your trip, 43–44
PALM COVE, 265
Palm Valley, 346
PALMVIEW, 248
Parks. *See specific parks*
Parliament House (Canberra), 319–20
PARRAMATTA, 77
Penal history. *See* Convicts, history of
Penguins, on Phillip Island, 176
Penny Royal World (Tasmania), 358
Peoples, 20–24
Performing arts, 24–25
Performing Arts Center (Melbourne), 19
Performing Arts Museum (Melbourne), 158, 164
PERTH, 279–302
accommodations, 283–89
Adventure World, 294–95
arriving in, 281
Caversham Wildlife Park, 294
evening entertainment, 300–302
Fast facts, 283
festivals, 40
Hay Street Pedestrian Mall, 292, 298
Kings Park, 294
layout of, 281–82
museums
Art Gallery of Western Australia, 293
Aviation Museum, 294
It's A Small World, 293
Perth Mint, 294
Scitech Discovery Centre, 294
Western Australian Museum, 293
recreational activities, 299–300
restaurants, 289–92
St. George's Terrace, 279, 281, 292
shopping, 298–99
sightseeing, 292–98
sports, 27
tourist information, 281
tours of, 298
transportation, 282
Underwater World, 294
zoo, 293
Phar Lap (racehorse), 20, 161
Phillip, Arthur, 9, 10, 120
PHILLIP ISLAND, 176–77
Pioneer Settlement (Swan Hill), 177
Pitchi Richi Aboriginal Cultural Experience (Alice Springs), 339–40
Planetariums, 161, 227
Planning and preparing for your trip, 34–71
Poker Machine Museum (Canberra), 321
PORT ARTHUR (TASMANIA), 364
PORT DOUGLAS, 270
Powerhouse Museum (Sydney), 107
Pubstays, 65–66

QUEENSLAND, 8, 207–78
Queensland Cultural Centre (Brisbane), 224–25, 229
QUEENSTOWN (TASMANIA), 375–76
Mining Museum, 375–76
Queen Victoria Building (Sydney), 110

Rainfall, average monthly, 38–39
Rappelling, 268
Recreational activities, 26–28. *See also specific activities*
Red Centre, 330, 344–48
Regions, 3, 6
Restaurants, 66
Ricketts, William, 174
ROCKHAMPTON, 278
ROCKINGHAM, 297–98
Rodeos, 40
ROTTNEST ISLAND, 297
Royal Australian Mint (Canberra), 321
Royal Botanic Gardens (Melbourne), 164
Royal Easter Agricultural Show (Sydney), 41–42
Royal Flying Doctor Service (RFDS)
Alice Springs, 338
Cairns, 264
Royal Melbourne Zoo, 162
Rum, 10
R.V. parks. *See* Camping and R.V. (caravan) parks

Safety, 26, 70
Sailing. *See* Boat travel and cruises; Yachting
ST. HELENS (TASMANIA), 363
St. James's Church (Sydney), 121
School of the Air (Alice Springs), 1–2, 339
Science and technology museums, 107, 198, 226, 294, 297, 322
Scuba diving/snorkeling, Great Barrier Reef, 267–68, 274
Seals, 193, 205
Seashells, 272, 275
museums of, 201, 263
Sea turtles, 275
Sea World (Surfers Paradise), 234
Senior citizens, tips for, 44
Seppeltsfield (Dorrien), 204
Shakespeare, William, 295
Sharks, 264
Shell Land (Glenelg), 201
Sherbrooke Forest, 174, 176
Shopping, money-saving tips, 67. *See also specific items*
SHUTE HARBOUR, 275
Single travelers, tips for, 45
Sir Colin Mackenzie Sanctuary (Healesville), 176
Skiing, 135, 198
Smith, Charles Kingsford, 18
Snowy Mountains Hydroelectric Scheme, 326–27
Social life, 20–24
SOUTH AUSTRALIA, 179–206
South Australian Museum (Adelaide), 196
South Bank Parklands (Brisbane), 225
SOUTHPORT, 243–45
Sovereign Hill (Ballarat), 177
Special events. *See* annual events, festivals and fairs
Sports, 26–28. *See also specific sports*
museum, 167
Standley Chasm, 346
State Library of New South Wales (Sydney), 112–13
Stations, 21, 45–46
STRADBROKE ISLAND, 236
STRAHAN (TASMANIA), 376
Stuart Highway, 348
Student travelers, tips for, 45
Sugarcane, 253, 254
SUNSHINE COAST, 245–51
accommodations, 248–50
Aussie World, 248
Fairytale Castle, 247–48
Forest Glen Deer Sanctuary, 247
Gingertown, Pioneer Rd., 247
Glass House Mountains, 246
Kondalilla National Park, 247
Nostalgia Town, 247
restaurants, 250–51
sightseeing, 246–48
Sunshine Plantation, 247
Superbee Honey Factory, 246–47
tours of, 248
Underwater World, 247
Surf Carnivals, 27, 111, 124
SURFERS PARADISE, 232, 234–44

Surfing, 26, 27, 123–24
Sutherland, Joan, 18, 25
SWAN HILL, 177–78
Swimming. *See* Beaches; Water sports
Sydney Harbour Bridge, 112, 120
Sydney-Hobart Yacht Race, 27, 42, 111
Sydney Opera House, 19, 105–6, 128
Sydney Tower, 19, 110
SYDNEY, 2, 72–136
accommodations, 84–94
bed and breakfasts, 90–91
Bondi Beach, 88, 90
campus accommodations, 93–94
for children, 91
downtown, 85–86, 88, 89
Glebe and suburban Sydney, 92–93
Haymarket and Darling Harbour, 89–90
hostels, 91–93
Kings Cross and vicinity, 85, 88–89, 92
money-saving tips, 89
motel apartments, 94
Argyle Tavern, 129
arriving in, 74–75
Cenotaph, 118, 120
Circular Quay, 120
cost of everday items, 37
Darling Harbour, 106–7
distances from, 49
evening entertainment, 126–32
Fast facts, 82–84
Featherdale Wildlife Park, 115
festivals and events, 41–42
Frommer's favorite experiences, 111
gambling, 132
harbor cruises, 121–22
Harbourside, 107, 110
historic sites
Cadman's Cottage, 118
Campbells Storehouse, 116
Elizabeth Bay House, 111–12
Fort Denison, 111
Hyde Park Barracks, 121
Nurses Walk, 118
Police Station, 118
Queens Square, 121
Sailors Home, 118
St. James's Church, 121
Suez Canal, 118
Susannah Place, 118
Victoria Barracks, 111
itineraries, 104–5
layout of, 74–75
Manley Beach, 114
movies, 131–32
museums
Art Gallery of New South Wales, 112, 120
Australian Museum, 113
Earth Exchange, 116
Holdsworth Galleries, 113
Mint, The, 112
Museum of Contemporary Art, 106
National Maritime Museum, 107
Powerhouse Museum, 107
State Library of New South Wales, 112–13
Sydney Jewish Museum, 113
Westpac Banking Museum, 116
music, 129, 130–31
neighborhoods, 76–77
nightclubs, 129–31
Nimrod Theatre, 24
Old Sydney Town, 115
parks and gardens
Chinese Garden, 110
Dawes Point Park, 116
The Domain, 120
Royal Botanic Gardens, 120
Tumbalong Park, 110
performing arts, 127–28
Queen Victoria Building, 110
recreational activities, 122–24
restaurants, 94–104
for children, 103
Darlinghurst, 99–101, 101–2
downtown, 98–99
Kings Cross and vicinity, 95, 98, 101
money-saving tips, 100
specialty dining, 102–4
shopping, 124–26
sightseeing, 104–21
sports, 27–28, 122
Sydney Aquarium, 107
Sydney Entertainment Centre, 110
Sydney Harbour Bridge, 112, 120
Sydney Opera House, 19, 105–6, 128
Sydney Tower, 19, 110
Taronga Zoo, 113–14
theaters, 128–29
tourist information, 74
tours of, 121
transportation, 77–81
walking tours, 115–21
downtown, 118–21
The Rocks, 115–18
Waratah Park, 115

Talune Wildlife Park and Koala Gardens (Tasmania), 375
Tamborine Mountain, 236
TANAWHAR, 246–47
TANUNDA, 202, 204
Taronga Zoo (Sydney), 113–14
TASMANIA, 3, 6, 353–78
sports, 28
tours of, 356–57
transportation, 356
Tasmanian devils, 7, 354, 375, 376
Temperatures, average monthly, 38–39
Tennis, 26
Adelaide, 199
Brisbane, 229
Canberra, 325
Melbourne, 167
Sydney, 122, 124
Theme parks. *See* Amusement and theme parks
THREDBO, 135
Tiagarra Aboriginal Cultural Centre (Tasmania), 377
TIDBINBILLA, 323
Tidbinbilla Nature Reserve, 323
Tipping, 67–68
Tjapukai Aboriginal Dance Theater (Kuranda), 270
Toad racing, 268
Top End (Northern Territory), 329–30, 348–52
Tourist information, 34–35
Tours
Adelaide, 198
Alice Springs, 342
Ayers Rock, 347–48
Blue Mountains, 134
Brisbane, 228–29
by bus, 55
Cairns, 266–67
Canberra, 324
Darwin, 351
Flinders Ranges, 206
Gold Coast, 236–37
to the Hinterland, 236
Hunter Valley, 134
Melbourne, 165–66
Perth, 298
of Snowy Mountains Hydroelectric Scheme, 327
Sunshine Coast, 248
Tasmania, 356–57, 376
by train, 54
of wildflowers around Perth, 304
TOWNSVILLE, 277
Train travel, 52–54
museums, 197
Puffing Billy, Victoria, 174
Transportation, 49–59
by bus, 54–55
by car, 55–58
by ferry, 58
by hitchhiking, 58–59
by plane, 49–52
by train, 52–54
Traveling to Australia, 46–49
TRINITY WATERS, 265
TUGUN, 234
TWEED HEADS, 238, 245

Uluru National Park, 346–47. *See also* Ayers Rock
Underwater World (Perth), 294
University of New England (Armidale), 134–35
Utzon, Joern, 19, 106

VICTORIA, 11–12, 137–78
Victorian Arts Centre (Melbourne), 161, 170
Vineyards. *See* Wine and wineries

Walker, Kath, 22
Waratah Park (Sydney), 115
Water parks. *See* Amusement and theme parks
Water sports, 26–27
Adelaide, 199
Cairns, 267–68
Great Barrier Reef, 275
Perth, 300
Sydney, 123–24
Wave Rock, 298
Weather, 38–39
Wentworth Falls Deer Park, 133–34
WESTERN AUSTRALIA, 279–306
Western Australian Museum (Perth), 293
Wet 'n' Wild (Oxenford), 235
White, Patrick, 18, 19
WHITSUNDAY COAST, 275–76
Wildflowers. *See* Flora
Wildlife, 6–8, 348
Wildlife parks and sanctuaries. *See also* Aquariums and marine life; Zoos
Bunya Park (Brisbane), 228
Butterfly farm (Kuranda), 270
Caversham Wildlife Park (Perth), 294
Currumbin Bird Sanctuary, 236
East End Reserve (Darwin), 350
Featherdale Wildlife Park (Sydney), 115
Fleay's Fauna Centre (Burleigh), 235–36
Forest Glen Deer Sanctuary (Forest Glen), 247
Fraser Island, 246
Hartley's Creek Crocodile Farm (Cairns), 263–64
Kakadu National Park, 352
Kangaroo Island, 193, 205
Lone Pine Sanctuary (Brisbane), 227–28
Marapana Wildlife World (outside Perth), 297–98

Queensland Reptile Park (Sunshine Coast), 246
Rehwinkel's Animal Park (Canberra), 323
Sherbrooke Forest, 174, 176
Sir Colin Mackenzie Sanctuary, 176
South Bank Parklands (Brisbane), 225
Talune Wildlife Park and Koala Gardens (Tasmania), 375
Territory Wildlife Park (Darwin), 351
Town Common (Townsville), 277
Waratah Park (Sydney), 115
Wentworth Falls Deer Park, 133–34
Wild World (Cairns), 263

Wild World (Cairns), 263
William Ricketts Sanctuary, 174
Wine and wineries, 2, 30, 280
  Alice Springs, 341
  Barossa Valley, 201–5
  festivals, 40
  Hunter Valley, 134
  Vintage Festival (Barossa Valley), 202
WODEN, 322
Wool products, 13–14
  shopping for, 67, 358
WOOMBYE, 247
World War I, 14–15, 30, 320
World War II, 15, 279, 320, 321, 348, 350

Wright, Judith, 18

Yachting, 27, 42, 295
Yanchep Park, 297
YANDINA, 247
YORKEY'S KNOB, 265

Zoos. *See also* Aquariums and marine life; Wildlife parks and sanctuaries
  Adelaide Zoo, 197
  Perth Zoo, 293
  Royal Melbourne Zoo, 162
  Taronga Zoo, 113–14

Now Save Money on All Your Travels by Joining FROMMER'S ™ TRAVEL BOOK CLUB

The World's Best Travel Guides at Membership Prices

FROMMER'S TRAVEL BOOK CLUB is your ticket to successful travel! Open up a world of travel information and simplify your travel planning when you join ranks with thousands of value-conscious travelers who are members of the FROMMER'S TRAVEL BOOK CLUB. Join today and you'll be entitled to all the privileges that come from belonging to the club that offers you travel guides for less to more than 100 destinations worldwide. Annual membership is only $25 (U.S.) or $35 (Canada and foreign).

The Advantages of Membership

1. Your choice of *three* free FROMMER'S TRAVEL GUIDES (any *two* FROMMER'S COMPREHENSIVE GUIDES, FROMMER'S $-A-DAY GUIDES, FROMMER'S WALKING TOURS *or* FROMMER'S FAMILY GUIDES—plus *one* FROMMER'S CITY GUIDE, FROMMER'S CITY $-A-DAY GUIDE *or* FROMMER'S TOURING GUIDE).
2. Your own subscription to **TRIPS AND TRAVEL** quarterly newsletter.
3. You're entitled to a **30% discount** on your order of any additional books offered by FROMMER'S TRAVEL BOOK CLUB.
4. You're offered (at a small additional fee) our **Domestic Trip-Routing Kits.**

Our quarterly newsletter **TRIPS AND TRAVEL** offers practical information on the best buys in travel, the "hottest" vacation spots, the latest travel trends, world-class events and much, much more.

Our **Domestic Trip-Routing Kits** are available for any North American destination. We'll send you a detailed map highlighting the best route to take to your destination—you can request direct or scenic routes.

Here's all you have to do to join:
Send in your membership fee of $25 ($35 Canada and foreign) with your name and address on the form below along with your selections as part of your membership package to **FROMMER'S TRAVEL BOOK CLUB, P.O. Box 473, Mt. Morris, IL 61054-0473.** Remember to check off your *three* free books.

If you would like to order additional books, please select the books you would like and send a check for the total amount (please add sales tax in the states noted below), plus $2 per book for shipping and handling ($3 per book for foreign orders) to:

FROMMER'S TRAVEL BOOK CLUB
P.O. Box 473
Mt. Morris, IL 61054-0473
(815) 734-1104

[ ] **YES.** I want to take advantage of this opportunity to join FROMMER'S TRAVEL BOOK CLUB.
[ ] **My check is enclosed.** Dollar amount enclosed________________*
(all payments in U.S. funds only)

Name____
Address______________________________________
City____________________ State__________ Zip__________
All orders must be prepaid.

To ensure that all orders are processed efficiently, please apply sales tax in the following areas: CA, CT, FL, IL, NJ, NY, TN, WA and CANADA.

*With membership, shipping and handling will be paid by FROMMER'S TRAVEL BOOK CLUB for the three free books you select as part of your membership. Please add $2 per book for shipping and handling for any additional books purchased ($3 per book for foreign orders).

Allow 4–6 weeks for delivery. Prices of books, membership fee, and publication dates are subject to change without notice. Prices are subject to acceptance and availability.

Please Send Me the Books Checked Below:

FROMMER'S COMPREHENSIVE GUIDES

(Guides listing facilities from budget to deluxe, with emphasis on the medium-priced)

	Retail Price	Code
☐ Acapulco/Ixtapa/Taxco 1993–94	$15.00	C120
☐ Alaska 1994–95	$17.00	C131
☐ Arizona 1993–94	$18.00	C101
☐ Australia 1992–93	$18.00	C002
☐ Austria 1993–94	$19.00	C119
☐ Bahamas 1994–95	$17.00	C121
☐ Belgium/Holland/ Luxembourg 1993–94	$18.00	C106
☐ Bermuda 1994–95	$15.00	C122
☐ Brazil 1993–94	$20.00	C111
☐ California 1994	$15.00	C134
☐ Canada 1994–95 (Avail. 4/94)	$19.00	C145
☐ Caribbean 1994	$18.00	C123
☐ Carolinas/Georgia 1994–95	$17.00	C128
☐ Colorado 1994–95 (Avail. 3/94)	$16.00	C143
☐ Cruises 1993–94	$19.00	C107
☐ Delaware/Maryland 1994–95 (Avail. 1/94)	$15.00	C136
☐ England 1994	$18.00	C129
☐ Florida 1994	$18.00	C124
☐ France 1994–95	$20.00	C132
☐ Germany 1994	$19.00	C125
☐ Italy 1994	$19.00	C130
☐ Jamaica/Barbados 1993–94	$15.00	C105
☐ Japan 1994–95 (Avail. 3/94)	$19.00	C144
☐ Morocco 1992–93	$18.00	C021
☐ Nepal 1994–95	$18.00	C126
☐ New England 1994 (Avail. 1/94)	$16.00	C137
☐ New Mexico 1993–94	$15.00	C117
☐ New York State 1994–95	$19.00	C133
☐ Northwest 1994–95 (Avail. 2/94)	$17.00	C140
☐ Portugal 1994–95 (Avail. 2/94)	$17.00	C141
☐ Puerto Rico 1993–94	$15.00	C103
☐ Puerto Vallarta/Manzanillo/ Guadalajara 1994–95 (Avail. 1/94)	$14.00	C028
☐ Scandinavia 1993–94	$19.00	C135
☐ Scotland 1994–95 (Avail. 4/94)	$17.00	C146
☐ South Pacific 1994–95 (Avail. 1/94)	$20.00	C138
☐ Spain 1993–94	$19.00	C115
☐ Switzerland/Liechtenstein 1994–95 (Avail. 1/94)	$19.00	C139
☐ Thailand 1992–93	$20.00	C033
☐ U.S.A. 1993–94	$19.00	C116
☐ Virgin Islands 1994–95	$13.00	C127
☐ Virginia 1994–95 (Avail. 2/94)	$14.00	C142
☐ Yucatán 1993–94	$18.00	C110

FROMMER'S $-A-DAY GUIDES

(Guides to low-cost tourist accommodations and facilities)

	Retail Price	Code
☐ Australia on $45 1993–94	$18.00	D102
☐ Costa Rica/Guatemala/ Belize on $35 1993–94	$17.00	D108
☐ Eastern Europe on $30 1993–94	$18.00	D110
☐ England on $60 1994	$18.00	D112
☐ Europe on $50 1994	$19.00	D115
☐ Greece on $45 1993–94	$19.00	D100
☐ Hawaii on $75 1994	$19.00	D113
☐ India on $40 1992–93	$20.00	D010
☐ Ireland on $45 1994–95 (Avail. 1/94)	$17.00	D117
☐ Israel on $45 1993–94	$18.00	D101
☐ Mexico on $45 1994	$19.00	D116
☐ New York on $70 1994–95 (Avail. 4/94)	$16.00	D120
☐ New Zealand on $45 1993–94	$18.00	D103
☐ Scotland/Wales on $50 1992–93	$18.00	D019
☐ South America on $40 1993–94	$19.00	D109
☐ Turkey on $40 1992–93	$22.00	D023
☐ Washington, D.C. on $40 1994–95 (Avail. 2/94)	$17.00	D119

FROMMER'S CITY $-A-DAY GUIDES

(Pocket-size guides to low-cost tourist accommodations and facilities)

	Retail Price	Code
☐ Berlin on $40 1994–95	$12.00	D111
☐ Copenhagen on $50 1992–93	$12.00	D003
☐ London on $45 1994–95	$12.00	D114
☐ Madrid on $50 1994–95 (Avail. 1/94)	$13.00	D118
☐ Paris on $50 1994–95	$12.00	D117
☐ Stockholm on $50 1992–93	$13.00	D022

FROMMER'S WALKING TOURS

(With routes and detailed maps, these companion guides point out the places and pleasures that make a city unique)

	Retail Price	Code		Retail Price	Code
☐ Berlin	$12.00	W100	☐ Paris	$12.00	W103
☐ London	$12.00	W101	☐ San Francisco	$12.00	W104
☐ New York	$12.00	W102	☐ Washington, D.C.	$12.00	W105

FROMMER'S TOURING GUIDES

(Color-illustrated guides that include walking tours, cultural and historic sights, and practical information)

	Retail Price	Code		Retail Price	Code
☐ Amsterdam	$11.00	T001	☐ New York	$11.00	T008
☐ Barcelona	$14.00	T015	☐ Rome	$11.00	T010
☐ Brazil	$11.00	T003	☐ Scotland	$10.00	T011
☐ Florence	$ 9.00	T005	☐ Sicily	$15.00	T017
☐ Hong Kong/Singapore/ Macau	$11.00	T006	☐ Tokyo	$15.00	T016
☐ Kenya	$14.00	T018	☐ Turkey	$11.00	T013
☐ London	$13.00	T007	☐ Venice	$ 9.00	T014

FROMMER'S FAMILY GUIDES

	Retail Price	Code		Retail Price	Code
☐ California with Kids	$18.00	F100	☐ San Francisco with Kids (Avail. 4/94)	$17.00	F104
☐ Los Angeles with Kids (Avail. 4/94)	$17.00	F103	☐ Washington, D.C. with Kids (Avail. 2/94)	$17.00	F102
☐ New York City with Kids (Avail. 2/94)	$18.00	F101			

FROMMER'S CITY GUIDES

(Pocket-size guides to sightseeing and tourist accommodations and facilities in all price ranges)

	Retail Price	Code		Retail Price	Code
☐ Amsterdam 1993–94	$13.00	S110	☐ Montréal/Québec City 1993–94	$13.00	S125
☐ Athens 1993–94	$13.00	S114	☐ Nashville/Memphis 1994–95 (Avail. 4/94)	$13.00	S141
☐ Atlanta 1993–94	$13.00	S112	☐ New Orleans 1993–94	$13.00	S103
☐ Atlantic City/Cape May 1993–94	$13.00	S130	☐ New York 1994 (Avail. 1/94)	$13.00	S138
☐ Bangkok 1992–93	$13.00	S005	☐ Orlando 1994	$13.00	S135
☐ Barcelona/Majorca/Minorca/ Ibiza 1993–94	$13.00	S115	☐ Paris 1993–94	$13.00	S109
☐ Berlin 1993–94	$13.00	S116	☐ Philadelphia 1993–94	$13.00	S113
☐ Boston 1993–94	$13.00	S117	☐ San Diego 1993–94	$13.00	S107
☐ Budapest 1994–95 (Avail. 2/94)	$13.00	S139	☐ San Francisco 1994	$13.00	S133
☐ Chicago 1993–94	$13.00	S122	☐ Santa Fe/Taos/ Albuquerque 1993–94	$13.00	S108
☐ Denver/Boulder/Colorado Springs 1993–94	$13.00	S131	☐ Seattle/Portland 1994–95	$13.00	S137
☐ Dublin 1993–94	$13.00	S128	☐ St. Louis/Kansas City 1993–94	$13.00	S127
☐ Hong Kong 1994–95 (Avail. 4/94)	$13.00	S140	☐ Sydney 1993–94	$13.00	S129
☐ Honolulu/Oahu 1994	$13.00	S134	☐ Tampa/St. Petersburg 1993–94	$13.00	S105
☐ Las Vegas 1993–94	$13.00	S121	☐ Tokyo 1992–93	$13.00	S039
☐ London 1994	$13.00	S132	☐ Toronto 1993–94	$13.00	S126
☐ Los Angeles 1993–94	$13.00	S123	☐ Vancouver/Victoria 1994–95 (Avail. 1/94)	$13.00	S142
☐ Madrid/Costa del Sol 1993–94	$13.00	S124	☐ Washington, D.C. 1994 (Avail. 1/94)	$13.00	S136
☐ Miami 1993–94	$13.00	S118			
☐ Minneapolis/St. Paul 1993–94	$13.00	S119			

SPECIAL EDITIONS

	Retail Price	Code
☐ Bed & Breakfast Southwest	$16.00	P100
☐ Bed & Breakfast Great American Cities (Avail. 1/94)	$16.00	P104
☐ Caribbean Hideaways	$16.00	P103
☐ National Park Guide 1994 (avail. 3/94)	$16.00	P105
☐ Where to Stay U.S.A.	$15.00	P102

Please note: if the availability of a book is several months away, we may have back issues of guides to that particular destination. Call customer service at (815) 734-1104.